CW00497492

STREE...

South Essex

Chelmsford, Harlow, Romford, Southend-on-Sea

w.philips-maps.co.uk
published in 1999 by
is, a division of
us Publishing Group Ltd
octopusbooks.co.uk
eron Quays, London E14 4JP
chette UK Company
hachette.co.uk

edition 2008
d impression 2009

84907-046-1 (pocket)
p's 2008

Ordnance Survey®

oduct includes mapping data
d from Ordnance Survey®
e permission of the Controller of
esty's Stationery Office.
n copyright 2008. All rights
d. Licence number 100011710.

mera data provided by
PSWorld.com Ltd

Toppan, China

Contents

II Mobile safety cameras
III **Key to map symbols**
IV **Key to map pages**
VI **Route planning**
VIII Major administrative and Postcode boundaries

1 **Street maps** at 2⅔ inches to 1 mile

183 **Index** of towns, villages, streets, hospitals, industrial estates, railway stations, schools, shopping centres, universities and places of interest

Digital Data

The exceptionally high-quality mapping found in this atlas is available as digital data in TIFF format, which is easily convertible to other bitmapped (raster) image formats.

The index is also available in digital form as a standard database table. It contains all the details found in the printed index together with the National Grid reference for the map square in which each entry is named.

For further information and to discuss your requirements, please contact
victoria.dawbarn@philips-maps.co.uk

Mobile speed cameras

The vast majority of speed cameras used on Britain's roads are operated by safety camera partnerships. These comprise local authorities, the police, Her Majesty's Court Service (HMCS) and the Highways Agency.

This table lists the sites where each safety camera partnership may enforce speed limits through the use of mobile cameras or detectors. These are usually set up on the roadside or a bridge spanning the road and operated by a police or civilian enforcement officer. The speed limit at each site (if available) is shown in red type, followed by the approximate location in black type.

A12
Braintree, Overbridge nr Kelvedon Interchange

A13
30 Castle Point, High St (Hadleigh twds London)
30 Leigh on Sea, London Rd
Southend, Bournes Green Chase
Southend, North Shoebury
Southend, Southchurch Boulevard

A1016
30 Chelmsford, Waterhouse Lane

A1017
30 Sible Hedingham, Swan St
30 Witham / Braintree, Rickstone Rd

A1023
30 Brentwood, Chelmsford Rd
30 Brentwood, London Rd
30 Brentwood, Shenfield Rd

A1025
40 Harlow, Second Avenue
40 Harlow, Third Avenue

A1060
Little Hallingbury, Lower Rd

A1090
30 Purfleet, London Rd
30 Purfleet, Tank Hill Rd

A1124
30 Colchester, Lexden Rd

A113
30 Epping, High Rd

A1158
30 Westcliff on Sea, Southbourne Grove

A1168
30 Loughton, Rectory Lane

A1169
40 Harlow, Southern Way

A120
Little Bentley, Pellens Corner
Wix, Harwich Rd nr Colchester Rd

A1205
40 Harlow, Second Avenue

A121
30 Epping, High Rd
30 Loughton, Goldings Hill (j/w Monkchester Close)
Loughton, High Rd

Waltham Abbey, Farm Hill Rd
Waltham Abbey, Sewardstine Rd

A126
30 Grays, London Rd
30 Tilbury, Montreal Rd

A128
Chipping Ongar, High St
30 Ingrave/Herongate, Brentwood Rd
40 Kelvedon Hatch, Ongar Rd

A129
30 Basildon, Crays Hill
Billericay, Southend Rd
Rayleigh, London Rd
30 Wickford, London Rd
Wickford, Southend Rd

A130
30 Canvey Island, Long Rd
South Benfleet, Canvey Way

A133
30 Elmstead Market, Clacton Rd
Little Bentley, Colchester Rd

A134
40 Great Horkesley, Nayland Rd

A137
30 Lawford, Wignall St

B170
Chigwell, Chigwell Rise
Loughton, Roding Lane

B172
Theydon Bois, Coppice Row

B173
Chigwell, Lambourne Rd

B184
40 Great Easton, Snow Hill

B186
30 South Ockendon, South Rd

B1002
30 Ingatestone, High St

B1007
30 Billericay, Laindon Rd
30 Billericay, Stock Rd
40 Chelmsford, Stock Rd

B1008
30 Chelmsford, Broomfield Rd

B1013
30 Hawkwell, High Rd
30 Hawkwell, Main Rd
30 Hockley/Hawkwell, Southend Rd
Rayleigh, High Rd

B1014
30 South Benfleet, Benfleet Rd

B1018
30 Latchingdon, The St
30 Maldon, The Causeway

B1019
30 Hatfield Peveral, Maldon Rd
30 Witham, Powers Hall End

B1021
Burnham on Crouch, Church Rd

B1022
30 Colchester, Maldon Rd
30 Heckfordbridge, Maldon Rd
30 Maldon, Colchester Rd
30 Tiptree Heath, Maldon Rd

B1027
30 Clacton-on-Sea, Valley Rd/Old Rd
30 St Osyth, Pump Hill
40 Wivenhoe, Brightlingsea Rd

B1028
30 Wivenhoe, Colchester Rd
30 Wivenhoe, The Avenue

B1033
30 Kirby Cross, Frinton Rd

B1335
40 South Ockendon, Stifford Rd

B1352
Harwich, Main Rd

B1383
30 Newport, London Rd
Stansted Mountfitchet, Cambridge Rd

B1389
30 Witham, Colchester Rd
30 Witham, Hatfield Rd

B1393
30 Epping, Palmers Hill

B1441
30 Clacton-on-Sea, London Rd
Tendring, Clacton Rd

B1442
30 Clacton-on-Sea, Thorpe Rd

B1464
30 Bowers Gifford, London Rd

UNCLASSIFIED
40 Alresford, St Osyth Rd
30 Aveley, Purfleet Rd
Aveley, Romford Rd
30 Barstable, Sandon Rd
30 Basildon, Ashlyns
Basildon, Clay Hill Rd
40 Basildon, Cranes Farm Rd (j/w Honywood Rd)
30 Basildon, Felmores
Basildon, London Rd, Wickford
30 Basildon, Vange Hill Drive
30 Basildon, Whitmore Way
30 Basildon, Wickford Avenue
30 Billericay, Mountnessing Rd
30 Bowers Gifford, London Rd
30 Braintree, Coldnailhurst Avenue
30 Brentwood, Eagle Way (nr j/w Clive Rd twds Warley Rd)

30 Brentwood, Eagle Way
30 Buckhurst Hill, Buckhurst Way/Albert Rd
30 Canvey Island, Dovercourt Rd
30 Canvey Island, Link Rd
30 Canvey Island, Thorney Bay Rd
Chadwell St Mary, Brentwood Rd
30 Chadwell St Mary, Linford Rd
30 Chadwell St Mary, Riverview
30 Chelmsford, Baddow Rd
30 Chelmsford, Chignall Rd
30 Chelmsford, Copperfield Rd
Chelmsford, Galleywood Rd
30 Chelmsford, Longstomps Avenue
30 Clacton-on-Sea, St Johns Rd
30 Clacton, Kings Parade
30 Clacton, Marine Parade East
30 Colchester, Abbots Rd
30 Colchester, Avon Way
30 Colchester, Bromley Rd
Colchester, Ipswich Rd
30 Colchester, Old Heath Rd
30 Colchester, Shrub End Rd
30 Corringham, Southend Rd
30 Corringham, Springhouse Rd
Danbury, Maldon Rd
30 Daws Heath, Daws Heath Rd
30 Eastwood, Green Lane j/w Kendal Way
30 Eastwood, Western Approaches j/w Rockall
30 Grays, Blackshots Lane
30 Grays, Lodge Lane
Grays, London Rd (nr Angel Rd)
Grays, London Rd (nr Bransons Way)
30 Hainault, Fencepiece Rd
40 Harlow, Abercrombie Way, twds Southern Way
40 Harlow, Howard Way
30 Hawkwell, Rectory Rd
30 Hockley, High Rd
30 Hullbridge, Coventry Hill
30 Laindon, Durham Rd
30 Laindon, High Rd
30 Laindon, Nightingales
30 Laindon, Wash Rd
Langdon Hills, High Rd
30 Leigh on Sea, Belton Way East
30 Leigh on Sea, Belton Way West
30 Leigh on Sea, Blenheim Chase
30 Leigh on Sea, Grand Parade/Cliff Parade
30 Leigh on Sea, Hadleigh Rd
30 Leigh on Sea, Highlands Boulevard
30 Leigh on Sea, Manchester Drive
30 Leigh on Sea, Mountdale Gardens
30 Leigh on Sea, Western Rd
30 Loughton, Alderton Hill
30 Loughton, Loughton Way
Loughton, Valley Hill
30 Maldon, Fambridge Rd
30 Maldon, Holloway Rd
30 Maldon, Mundon Rd
30 Pitsea, Rectory Rd

30 Prittlewell, Kenilworth Gardens
30 Prittlewell, Prittlewell Chase
30 Rayleigh, Bull Lane
Rayleigh, Downhall Rd
30 Rayleigh, Trinity Rd, nr Church Rd
30 Rochford, Ashingdon R
30 Rochford, Rectory Rd
Rush Green, St Osyth R
30 Shoeburyness, Ness Rc
30 South Woodham Ferre
Hullbridge Rd
30 South Woodham Ferre
Inchbonnie Rd
30 Southend on Sea, Lifst
Way
Southend, Bournemou
Park Rd
30 Southend, Hamstel Rd
Southend on Sea,
Bournemouth Park Rd
Southend, Western
Esplanade/Westcliff
Sea
30 Springfield, New Bow
Way
30 Stanford le Hope, Lor
Rd
30 Tendring, Burrs Rd,
Clacton
30 Tendring, Frinton Rd
Frinton
Tendring, Harwich R
Arch Cottages to Car
Lane
30 Tendring, Osyth Rd,
Green
Theydon Bois, Pierci
Hill
30 Thorpe Bay, Barnsta
30 Thorpe Bay, Thorpe
Avenue
Waltham Abbey,
Paternoster Hill
Weeley Heath, Clac
Weeley Heath, Clac
30 West Thurrock, Lor
Rd
30 Westcliff on Sea,
Chalkwell Avenue
30 Westcliff on Sea, Ki
30 Wickford, London F
30 Wickford, Radwinte
Avenue
30 Witham, Powers Ha
30 Witham, Rickstone

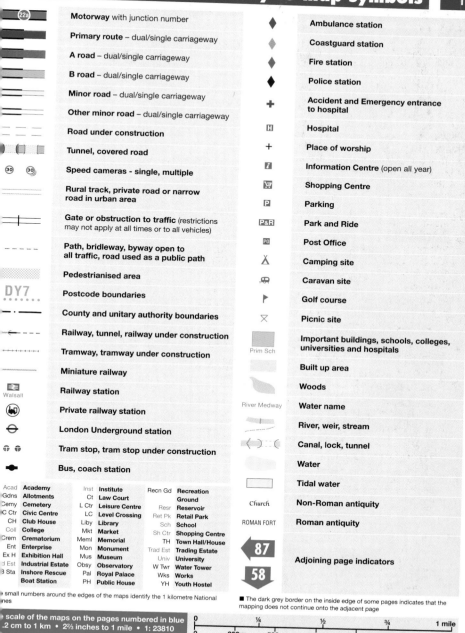

(22a)	
	Motorway with junction number
	Primary route – dual/single carriageway
	A road – dual/single carriageway
	B road – dual/single carriageway
	Minor road – dual/single carriageway
	Other minor road – dual/single carriageway
	Road under construction
	Tunnel, covered road
(30) (30)	Speed cameras - single, multiple
	Rural track, private road or narrow road in urban area
	Gate or obstruction to traffic (restrictions may not apply at all times or to all vehicles)
	Path, bridleway, byway open to all traffic, road used as a public path
	Pedestrianised area
DY7	Postcode boundaries
	County and unitary authority boundaries
	Railway, tunnel, railway under construction
	Tramway, tramway under construction
	Miniature railway
Walsall	Railway station
	Private railway station
	London Underground station
	Tram stop, tram stop under construction
	Bus, coach station

◆	Ambulance station
◆	Coastguard station
◆	Fire station
◆	Police station
✚	Accident and Emergency entrance to hospital
H	Hospital
+	Place of worship
i	Information Centre (open all year)
🛒	Shopping Centre
P	Parking
P&R	Park and Ride
PO	Post Office
Å	Camping site
🚐	Caravan site
►	Golf course
✕	Picnic site
Prim Sch	Important buildings, schools, colleges, universities and hospitals
	Built up area
	Woods
River Medway	Water name
	River, weir, stream
	Canal, lock, tunnel
	Water
	Tidal water
Church	Non-Roman antiquity
ROMAN FORT	Roman antiquity
87 58	Adjoining page indicators

Acad	Academy	Inst	Institute	Recn Gd	Recreation Ground
Gdns	Allotments	Ct	Law Court		
Cemy	Cemetery	L Ctr	Leisure Centre	Resr	Reservoir
C Ctr	Civic Centre	LC	Level Crossing	Ret Pk	Retail Park
CH	Club House	Liby	Library	Sch	School
Coll	College	Mkt	Market	Sh Ctr	Shopping Centre
Crem	Crematorium	Meml	Memorial	TH	Town Hall/House
Ent	Enterprise	Mon	Monument	Trad Est	Trading Estate
Ex H	Exhibition Hall	Mus	Museum	Univ	University
d Est	Industrial Estate	Obsy	Observatory	W Twr	Water Tower
3 Sta	Inshore Rescue Boat Station	Pal	Royal Palace	Wks	Works
		PH	Public House	YH	Youth Hostel

small numbers around the edges of the maps identify the 1 kilometre National nes

■ The dark grey border on the inside edge of some pages indicates that the mapping does not continue onto the adjacent page

scale of the maps on the pages numbered in blue
.2 cm to 1 km • 2⅔ inches to 1 mile • 1: 23810

0	¼	½	¾	1 mile
0	250 m 500 m	750 m 1 kilometre		

IV

Key to map pages

| 122 | Map pages at 2⅔ inches to 1 mile |

Buntingford

Stansted Mountfitchet

Stansted Airport

Great Dunmow

Bishop's Stortford

Ware

Hertford

Spellbrook · 1
Sawbridgeworth

Little Hallingbury
Hatfield Broad Oak · 2
Hatfield Heath · 3

Taverners Green
4   5
Aythorpe Roding

6   7
Pleshey
High Easter

Hunsdonbury ·
8   9 A414
Stanstead Abbotts
Roydon

Gilston
10 11
Eastwick

Sheering
12 13
Matching
Matching Green

White
Roding
14 15
Abbess Roding

Leaden Roding

Good Easter
16 17
Mashbury

Grea
Waltha
1

Harlow

Hoddesdon
21
Lower
Nazeing

Tye Green
22 23
Roydon Hamlet

Tilegate Green
24 25
Hastingwood

High Laver
26 27
Fyfield
Moreton

28 29
Willingale

Cooksmill
Green

Roxwell
30
31
Writ

Cheshunt

Aimes Green

Epping
Green
Bumble's
Green
43   44 45
Epping   Toot Hill

North Weald Bassett
46 47

Bobbingworth
48 49
High Ongar
Chipping Ongar

50 51 A414
Norton Heath

Edney Common
Loves Green
52 53

Cuffley

Waltham
Abbey
65
Holdbrook

Ivy Chimneys
Upshire
66 67
Theydon Bois

Fiddlers Hamlet
68 69
Stapleford Tawney

Stanford Rivers
70 71
Kelvedon Hatch

Blackmore
Mill
Green
72 73
Doddinghurst

Margarettin
74 75
Stoc
Ingatestone

Forty Hill

Enfield

Sewardstonebury
87

High Beach
88 89
Loughton

Abridge
90 91
Stapleford Abbotts

Navestock Heath
Bentley
92 93

Mountnessing
94 95
Pilgrims Hatch
Shenfield

96 97
Havering's Gr
Biller
South Green
Little Burstead
118

East
Barnet

Southgate

Friern
Barnet

Edmonton

Chingford

Chingford
Hatch
109

Buckhurst
Hill
110 111
Woodford

Chigwell

Chigwell Row
112 113
Havering-
atte-Bower

South Weald
114 115
Harold Hill

Brentwood
116 117
Ingrave
Great Warley

Dunton Wayle

Wood Green

Muswell Hill
Hornsey

Walthamstow

Barkingside
132 133
Wanstead
Ilford

A12
Romford
134 135
Goodmayes A124
Upminster

136 137
Cranham
Hornchurch

West Horndon
138 139

Laindon
140

Langdon Hills

Stoke
Newington

Camden
Town   Islington
Marylebone

Hackney
Bethnal
Green
Shoreditch
Finsbury
Bow
Poplar

Stratford
West
Ham

Becontree
Barking
152 153
Dagenham

Elm Park
154 155
Rainham

Corbets Tey
North Ockendon
156 157
Horndon on the Hill

Bulphan
158 159

Orsett
174
Linford

Sta
le

City of
London

Bermondsey

Westminster

Chelsea

Battersea
Clapham

Camberwell

Brixton

London City

Plumstead

Woolwich

Greenwich

Deptford

Lewisham

Wennington
169
Belvedere
Erith

Aveley
170 171
Purfleet

South Ockendon
172 173
Little Thurrock

176 177

Grays
178 179
Northfleet

Tilbury
East

Chadwell St

Streatham

Penge

Beckenham
Bromley

London
STREET ATLAS

Catford

Eltham

Crayford

Bexley

Sidcup

Chislehurst

Dartford

Swanscombe

Gravesend

Swanley

Kent
STREET ATLAS

Hartley

Mitcham

Hertfordshire
STREET ATLAS

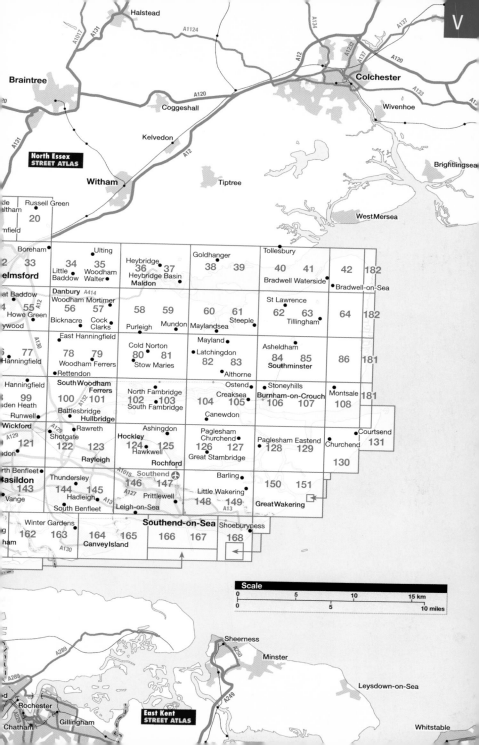

V

Halstead

Braintree

Colchester

Wivenhoe

Coggeshall

Kelvedon

Brightlingsea

North Essex
STREET ATLAS

Witham

Tiptree

WestMersea

Russell Green
Boreham

20

Chelmsford

Ulting

34 Little Baddow 35 Woodham Walter

Heybridge 36 37 Heybridge Basin Maldon

Goldhanger 38 39

Tollesbury 40 41 Bradwell Waterside

42 182 Bradwell-on-Sea

Great Baddow 55 Howe Green
Danbury A414 Woodham Mortimer 56 57 Bicknacre Cock Clarks

58 59 Purleigh Mundon Maylandsea

60 61 Steeple

St Lawrence 62 63 Tillingham

64 182

Hanningfield 77
East Hanningfield 78 79 Woodham Ferrers Rettendon

Cold Norton 80 81 Stow Maries

Mayland Latchingdon 82 83 Althorne

Asheldham 84 85 Southminster

86 181

Hanningfield
99 South Woodham Ferrers 100 101 Battlesbridge Hullbridge

North Fambridge 102 103 South Fambridge

Ostend 104 Creaksea 105 Canewdon

Stoneyhills Burnham-on-Crouch 106 107

Montsale 108 181

Wickford
121 Runwell
A129 Rawreth Shotgate 122 123 Rayleigh

Ashingdon Hockley 124 125 Hawkwell Rochford

Paglesham Churchend 126 127 Great Stambridge

Paglesham Eastend 128 129

Courtsend 131 Churchend 130

North Benfleet Basildon 143 Vange

Thundersley 144 145 Hadleigh A13 South Benfleet

Southend 146 147 Prittlewell Leigh-on-Sea

Barling 150 151 Little Wakering 148 149 Great Wakering

Winter Gardens 162 163

164 165 Canvey Island

166 167

168

Southend-on-Sea Shoeburyness

Scale
0   5   10   15 km
0   5   10 miles

Sheerness
Minster

Leysdown-on-Sea

Rochester
Chatham Gillingham

East Kent
STREET ATLAS

Whitstable

Route planning

Scale

0		5		10 km
0	1 2 3 4 5		6 miles	

Major administrative and Postcode boundaries

- County and unitary authority boundaries
- District boundaries
- Postcode boundaries
- Area covered by this atlas

Scale
0   5   10   15 km

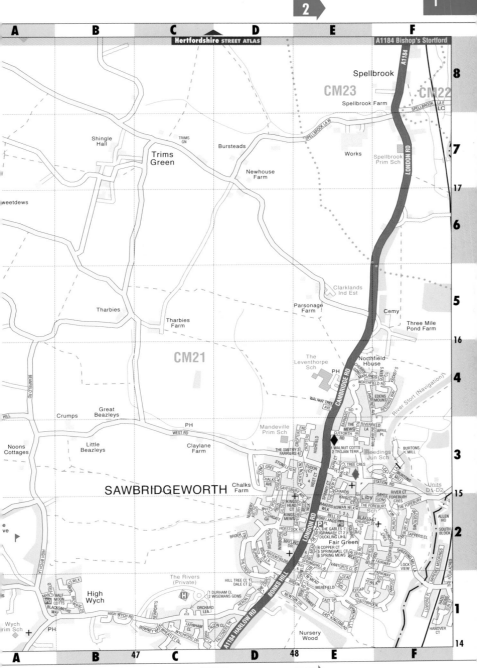

8

Wallbury

STADDLES

BARKERS MEAD 1
GEORGE GREEN VILLAS 2
REDBRICK ROW 3

Beadle
Common

POST
OFFICE
COTTS

Little
Hallingbury
CE Prim
Sch

Monksbury
Farm

Little
Hallingbury

Lock
Farm

Sewage
Works

Nursery

GOOSE LA

Millhide
Common

SUTTON ACRES

7

Gaston
House

PO

Gaston
Common

Wright's
Green

17

River Stort (Navigation)

Gaston
Green

OLD MILL LA

CM23

Tednambury
Farm

Mill
(dis)

Mott's
Green

6

Little
Bursteads

CM22

Little
Hallingbury
Park

5

South
House
Farm

Harcamlow Way

Little
Hallingbury
Hall

PH

16

Broadcroft

Spill
Timbers
Wood

Stone
Hall

STORTFORD RD

4

Kecksy's
Bridge

HALLINGBURY RD

WESTWICK

3

Sawbridgeworth

THE
STABLES

THE
GARDEN
HOS

GREAT
HYDE
HALL

Oak
Spring

Round
Spring

Little
Hyde
Hall

Eighteenacre
Spring

Wren's
Spring

15

LOWER
SHEERING

STATION RD

1 PRIORS CT
2 WATERSIDE PL

Cowick

SAWBRIDGEWORTH RD

2

THE MEADOWS

THE SUN GROVES

CM21

Quickbury
Farm

Stort Valley Way

Gladwyns

MEADOW

SHEERING MILL LA

1

Lower
Sheering

LADY'S
PROP

B183 THE STREET

Shrubs

MOORLANDS REACH

BACK LA

CROWN
CL

PRIMROSE LA

PLASHETS

Sheering
CE Prim
Sch

PO

14

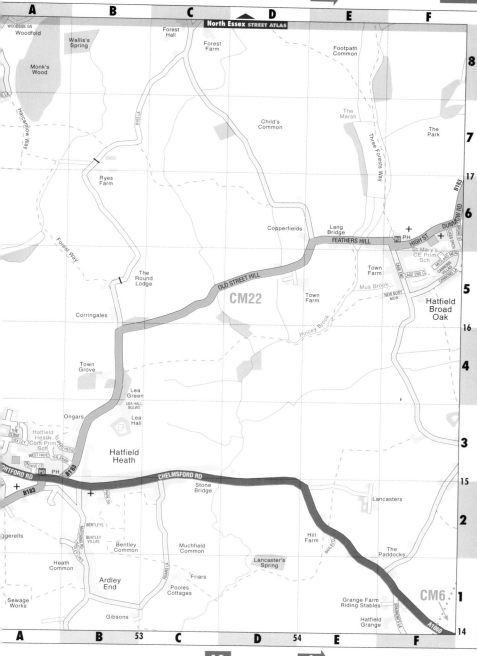

North Essex STREET ATLAS

North Essex STREET ATLAS

A B C D E F

8

Cannons

Taverners Green

Aldburys Farm

BOXLEY LA

Benningtons

Change Common

Barrington Hall

B183

Great Common

7

Braintris

Woolard's Ash

17

B183

6

Crabbs Green Farm

Broomshawbury

Broad Street Green

WATERS VILLAS

Waters Farm

HAMMONDS RD

CM22

5

Stanways

Broomshawbury Wood

Poplars Shaw

16

Anthonys

Anthonys

4

Sparrow Hall Farm

Poplars Wood

Needham Green

Philpotts

Poplars Farm

Pierce Williams

3

Cammasshall Wood

Cammas Hall

Row Wood

15

2

Three Forests Way

Prows Farm

Walkers Farm

CM6

1

Norrington

Pages Cottages

Marks Hall

14

55 A B 56 C D 57 E F

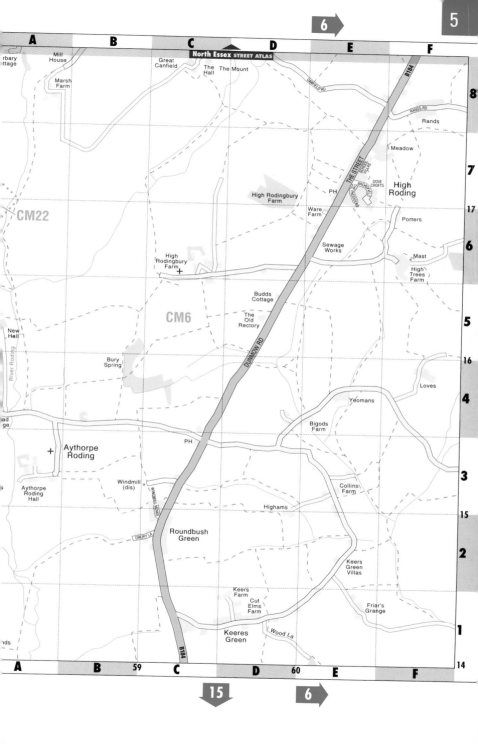

North Essex STREET ATLAS

A **B** **C** **D** **E** **F**

8

7

17

6

5

16

4

3

15

2

1

14

rbary ottage

Mill House

Great Canfield

Marsh Farm

The Hall

The Mount

CANFIELD RD

B184

RANDS RD

Rands

Meadow

THE STREET

BROOK STREET

DOVE CROFTS

High Roding

High Rodingbury Farm

PH

Ware Farm

Porters

Mast

High Trees Farm

CM22

High Rodingbury Farm

CM6

Sewage Works

Budds Cottage

The Old Rectory

New Hall

Bury Spring

River Roding

DUNMOW RD

Loves

Yeomans

Bigods Farm

ad ge

Aythorpe Roding

PH

Windmill (dis)

WINDHILL MEWS

Collins Farm

Aythorpe Roding Hall

DRURY LA

Roundbush Green

Highams

Keers Green Villas

Keers Farm

Cut Elms Farm

Friar's Grange

Keeres Green

Wood La

rds

B184

A **B** 59 **C** **D** 60 **E** **F**

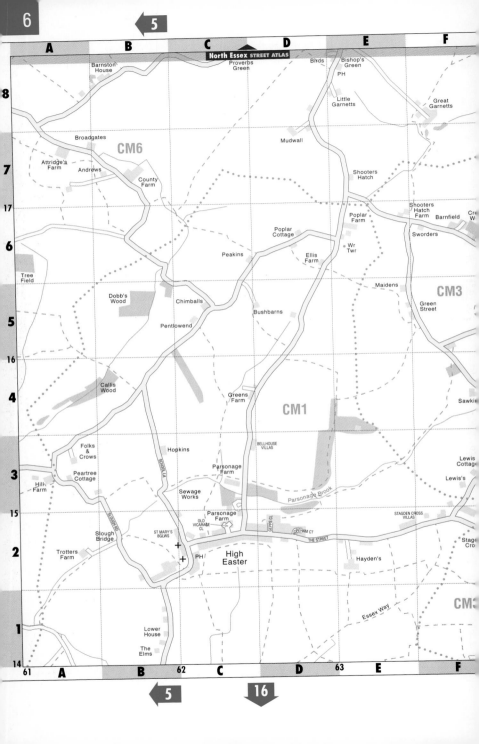

Widburyhill Farm
Widbury Wood
Mead Wood
The Dairy Farm
Easneye Wood
The Bournes
Harcamlow

River Ash

Easneye

SG12

Easneye Cottage

Sheepcote Farm

Ballard's Wood

Thirsty Spring

Amwell

Stansted Mill Stream

Little Briggens

Newlands

HUNSDON RD

St John the Baptist CE Prim Sch
Limes Farm

Hill House

HUNSDON ROAD COTTS

Hillside Farm

Swing Bridge

St Andrew's CE Prim Sch

WOODHAM WAY

St Margarets

ABBOTTS

HIGH ST

Stanstead Abbotts

St Margarets

STATION RD

The Maltings Ind Est

Cat's Hill

Coldha Woo

Amwell View Sch

Marina

ROYDON RD

Coldharbour Farm

HODDESDON

SG13

The Wilderness

Kingfisher Ct

NETHERFIELD CT

Netherfield House

The Granary

Netherfield Works

Nursery

Terbets Hill

Ryegate Farm

ST MARGARET'S RD

CHELSEA FIELDS

CHESTNUT GR

Lea Valley WIk
River Lee Navigation

EN11

Rye Meads

BEECHFIELD

HAILEY AVE

The John Warner Sch

CRANBOURNE HO

Toll

SHAKESPEARE

Toll House Stream

CHAUCER RD

Sewage Works

Nursery Rd

WALLERS WAY

Works

River Stort

Harcamlow

ROSELANDS AVE

Sch

A1
1 BOREHAM MEWS
2 PLOMER AVE
3 CATHROW MEWS
4 BEYERS RIDE
5 BRIDLE WAY
6 BEYERS GDNS

B1
1 WESTERN TERR
2 SOUTHERN TERR
3 PARKLAND CL
4 ESTFELD CL
5 CHITTENDEN CL

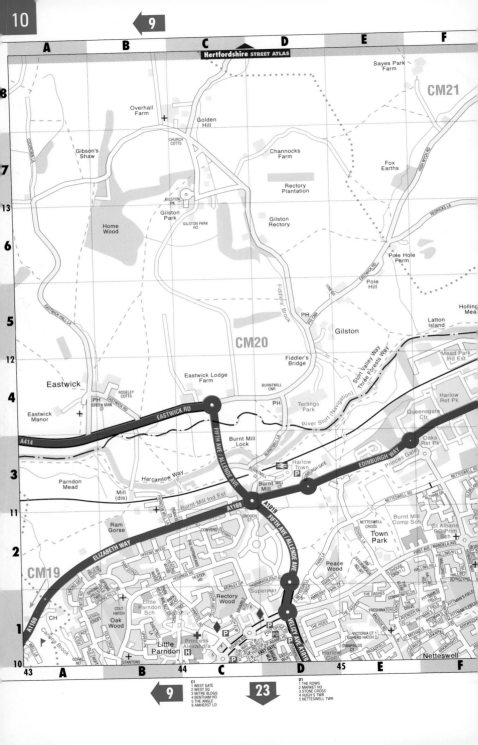

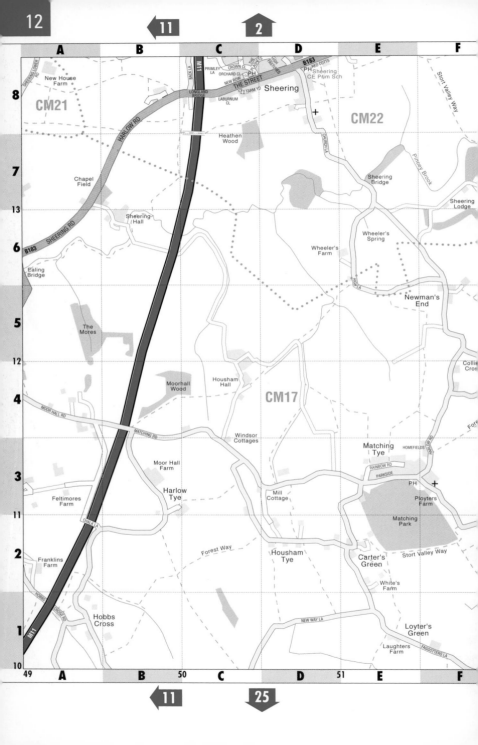

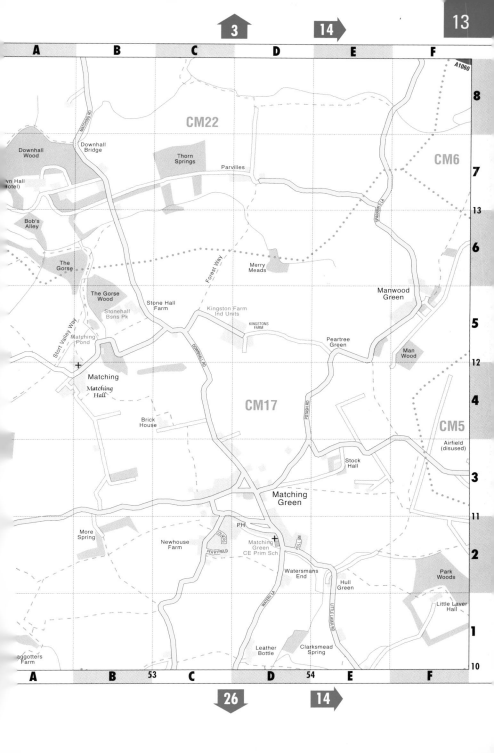

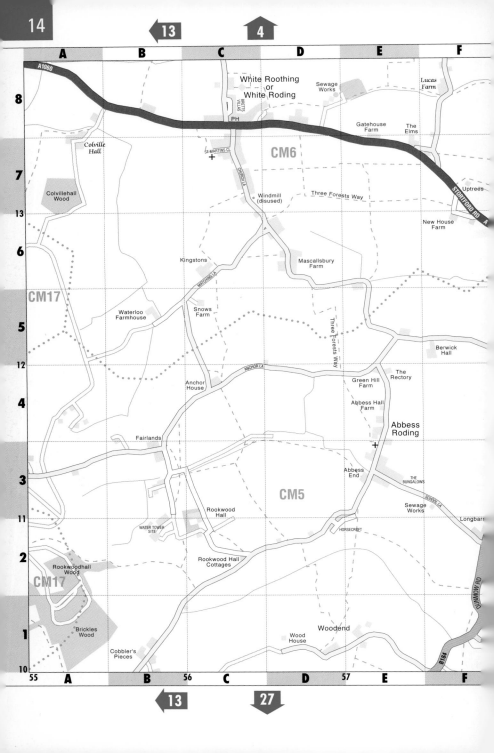

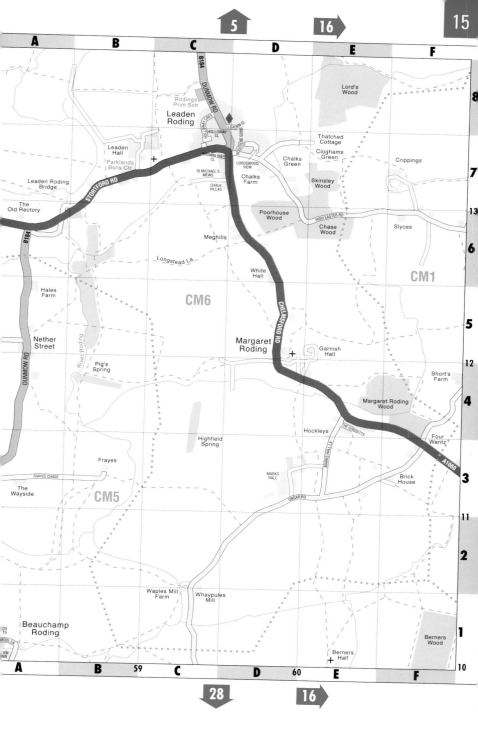

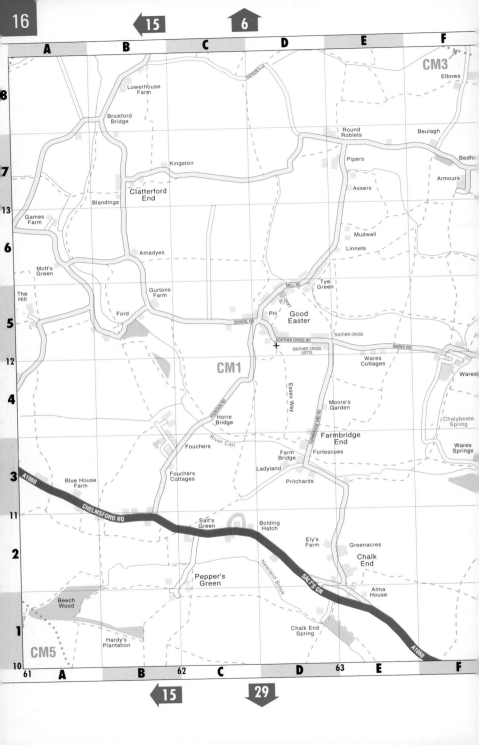

A   B   C   D   E   F

8

7

13

6

5

12

4

3

11

2

1

10

Bury
Hall

Ford

Waltham Brook

Essex Way

Five
Chequers

Langleys

Bury
Lodge

Deer
Park

BARRACK LA

Fitzjohn's
Farm

High
Houses

PH

1 BANBURY SQ
2 CHURCH HOUSE

CHELMSFORD RD

Great
Waltham

Great Waltham
CE Prim Sch

PO

BAKERS
MEAD

RAY
MEAD

Garnett's
Farm

MASHBURY RD

CHERRY MDW

GLEBE RD

CLEETHILL CT

SOUTH ST

HATCHFIELD

WOLMERS HEY

LUCY MOORS

Israel's
Farm

Queens
Orchard

Humphrey's
Farm

Breed's
Farm

Breeds

South House
Farm

Ba
Fa

Blatche's
Wood

CM3

Mansion
Cottage

PH

HELL'S LA

LARK'S LA

Fanner's
Green

Margaret Woods
Farm

WALNUT TREE
COTTS

Broad's
Green

Fanner's
Farm

FANNER'S GREEN
COTTS

Border
Wood

Beadle's
Hall

Walnut Tree
Farm

Partridge Green
Farm

Sports
Ground

WOODHOUSE LA

WOODLANDS W

Dyer's
Hall

CM1

The
Linden Ctr

EL

Maple
View

PH

Woodhall
Farm

WOODHALL HILL

Gray's
Farm

Woodside

Bushy
Wood

Stacey's
Farm

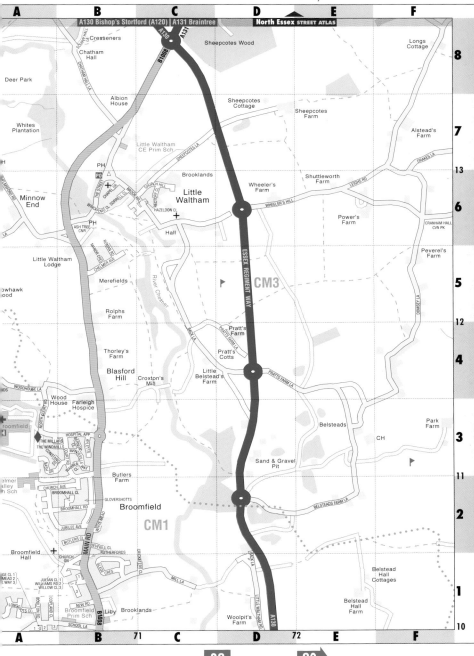

Cresseners
Chatham Hall
Sheepcotes Wood
Longs Cottage

8

Deer Park

Albion House
Sheepcotes Cottage
Sheepcotes Farm
Alstead's Farm

7

Whites Plantation

Little Waltham CE Prim Sch

SHEEPCOTES LA

PH
PO
THE STREET
CHAPEL DR
WINDKFORD DR SORRELL CL
BROAD LA
CHURCH HILL
CHELMER RD

Brooklands
Little Waltham

Wheeler's Farm

Shuttleworth Farm

LEIGHS RD

DRAKES LA

13

Minnow End

HAZELDON CL

PH
ASH TREE CNR

Half

WHEELER'S HILL

Power's Farm

6

CRANHAM HALL CVN PK

MAKIN RD
CHELMER AVE
ROMAN LA

Little Waltham Lodge

River Chelmer

Merefields

ESSEX REGIMENT WAY

CM3

Peverel's Farm

DENSEY LA

5

wowhawk ood

Rolphs Farm

BACK LA

PRATTS FARM LA

Pratt's Farm

12

Thorley's Farm

Blasford Hill
Croxton's Mill

Pratt's Cotts

Little Belstead's Farm

PRATTS FARM LA

4

WOODHOUSE LA

Wood House
Farleigh Hospice

oomfield
Belsteads

CH

Park Farm

3

NORTH COURT RD

HOSPITAL APP

THE MILLARS
THE WINDMILLS
THE CONSTABLE

Sand & Gravel Pit

11

elmer alley h Sch

CHURCH AVE
BROOMHALL CL
GLOVERSHOTTS
BROOMHALL RD

Butlers Farm

BELSTEADS FARM LA

Broomfield

CM1

JUBILEE AVE

Belstead Hall Cottages

2

Broomfield Hall

BUTLERS CL
DEVERILL CL
RUTHERFORDS

MAIN RD
WHITE MEAD
CRICKETERS CL

CHURCH GN

MILL LA

Belstead Hall Farm

1

GE CL 1
MEAD 2
WAY 3
WILLIAMS RD 2
WILLOW CL 3
JULIAN CL 1

LONG OTS CL
COLTON RD
COPLAND CL

NEW RD
B1008

Broomfield Prim Sch
Liby
Brooklands

LITTLE WALTHAM RD
A130
JACK LA

Woolpit's Farm

SCHOOL LA

10

A   B   71   C   D   72   E   F

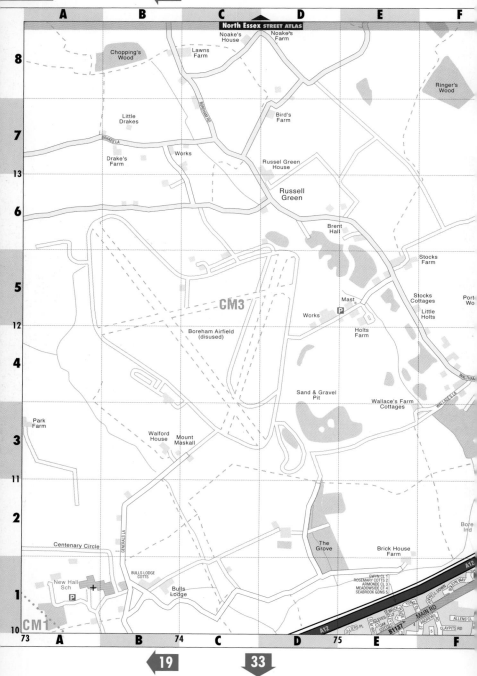

North Essex STREET ATLAS

	A	B	C	D	E	F

8

Roydon Prim Sch

Lightfoots

Worlds End

Harlow Bsns Pk

Roydonbury Ind Est

Greenway Bsns Ctr

New Horizon Bsns Ctr

Works

PARK DR

B181

ROYDON RD

ELIZABETH WAY A1169

CAWLEY HATCH

HANSELLS MEAD

Roydon Park

Nursery

Kingsmead

Kingsmead

PARK FIELDS

KINGSMEAD CL

KINGSMEAD HILL 1
WOODCREDON CL 2

Mast

HAROLDS RD

ASCROFT

Spire Green Ctr

Moat Ho

Westside Bsns Ctr

MERRING WAY

7

09

Downe Hall

Didgemere Hall

Didgemere Common

New Barns Farm

CM19

Harold's Grove

The Nurseries

WHITEHALL EST

ASH Ind

FLEX MDW

New Fro Science

Caravan Site

LOW HILL RD

6

Netherhall Common

Nurseries

Halls Green Farm

MATHEWS VILLAS

Nurseries

KYLE STREET

BYNG

SHEPPARDS

Totwellhill Bushes

GLEN HOUSE LA

Katherines

BROOKSIDE

5

Nursery

Nurseries

Halls Green

Nurseries

EPPING RD

Lower Wood

REEVES LA

RED PK

MOTT

Stort Valley Way

Three Forests Way

08

Nurseries

Merryweathers Farm

Barnfield Nurseries

Nursery

Parndon Brook

WATER LA

Gladwyns Farm

Paradise Farm

BARN HILL

Clay Hill

Thorndon Common

Nurseries

HAMLET HILL

Hill Farm

Roydon Hamlet

PH

Borne Farm

Ada Cole Memorial Stables Horse Sanctuary

Tylerscross

B1133

LIT

4

3

Stoneshot Common

Stoneshot Farm

TYLERS RD

Nurseries

PH

SLUDENWOOD CL

Nursery

07

Longfield Spring

Broadley Common

Nursery

Birchwood Ind Est

Nurseries

Oldfield Spring

Church Farm

EN9

SIBLEY MDW

PH

Nurseries

Harknett's Gate

POLE LA

BETTS LA

BACK LA

NAZEING COMM

BROADLEY LA

COMMON RD

2

GREENLEAVES CVN PK

Millbrook Bsns Pk

Nurseries

Rookswood

Nazeing

Nazeing Brook

BACK LA

1

06

| 40 | A | 41 | B | C | 41 | D | 42 | E | F |

CN

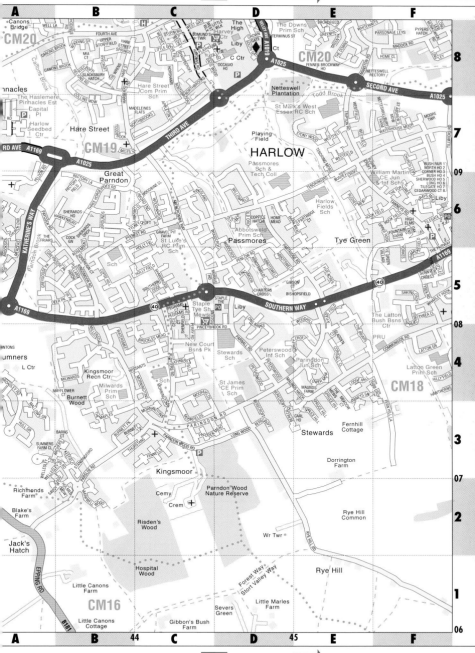

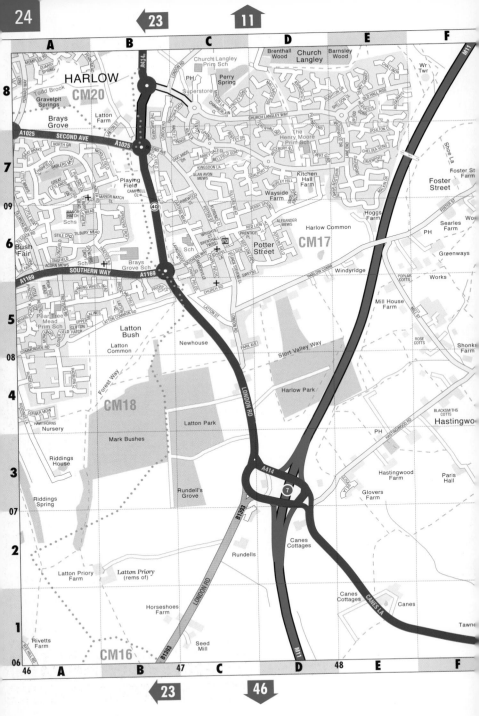

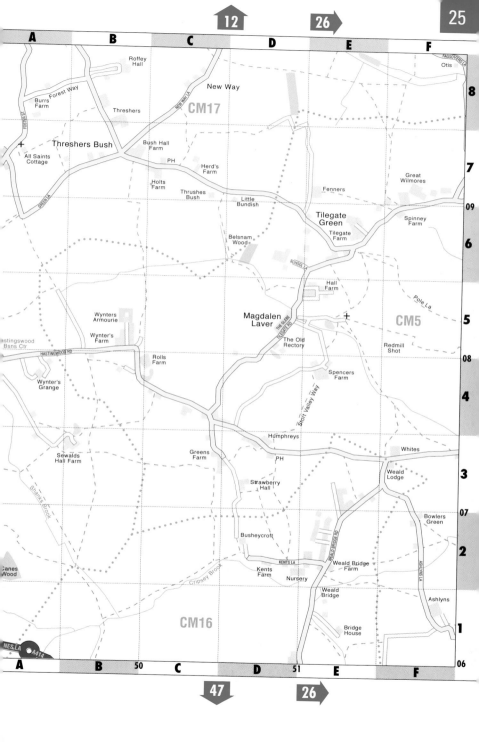

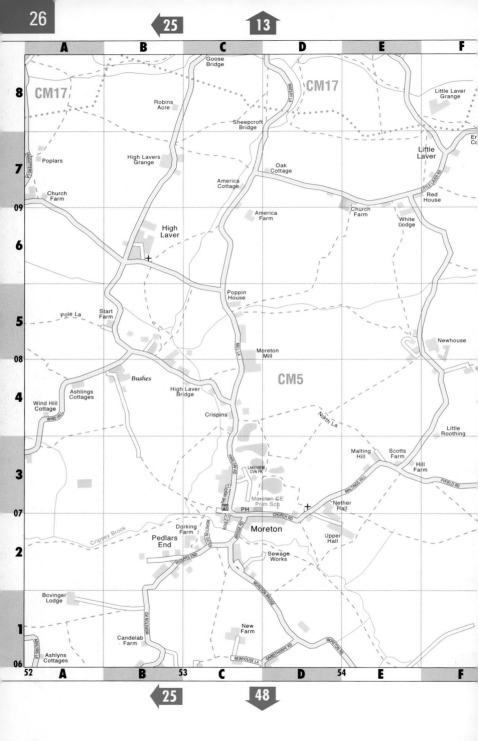

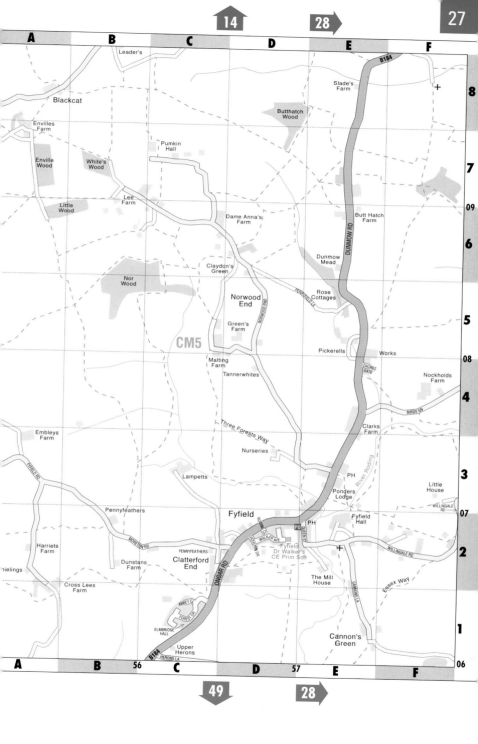

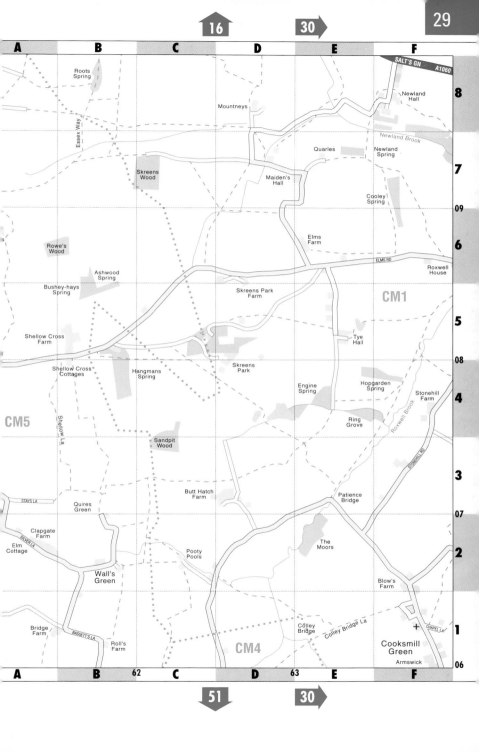

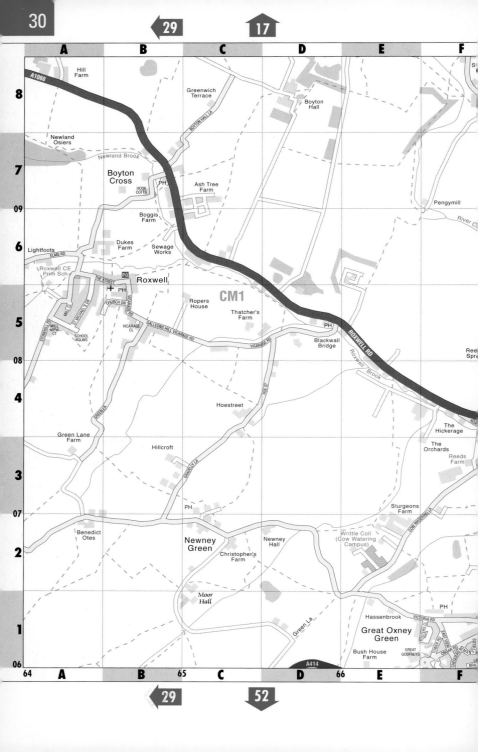

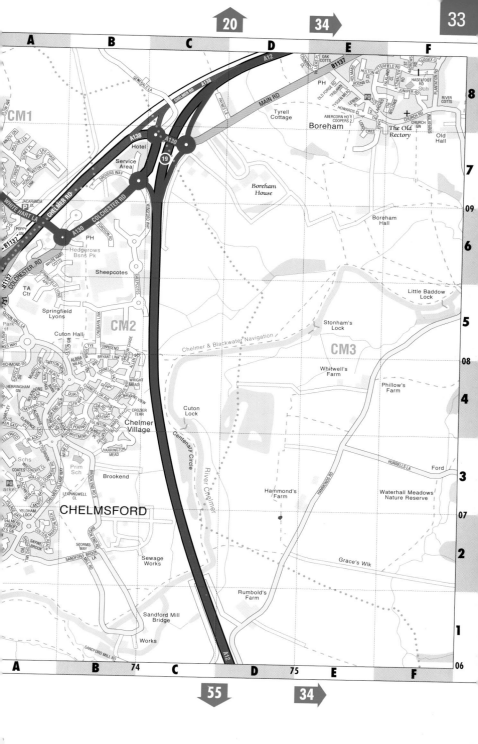

A B C D E F

8

Culverts Cottages

Brakey Wood

Rickstones

MOWDEN LA

Gardener Farm

Botter's Farm

Mulberries

Culvert's Farm

Belstead Cottages

World's End Cottage

Multum in Parvo

Chelmer & Blackwater Navigation

7

09

Weir

Paper Mill Lock

Paper Mill Bridge

Bassett's Farm

6

River Chelmer

New Wood

Brickwell Wood

LOFTS CHASE

Coleraines

VICA COTTS

SPRING CL

Tofts

5

CH RD

Holybreds Wood

WICKHAY COTTS

JARVIS CL

NORTH RD

RYES LA

Walters Cottage

Bassett's Wood

08

Little Baddow Hall

Holybreds Farm

HOLYBREAD LA

PH

Warren Wood

Scrub Wood

4

The Hoppet

Cuckoos

CM3

Little Baddow

MOUNT PLEASANT

The Warren

Gib

COLAM LA

Burghfields Farm

PO

HIGH PASTURES

Duke's Orchard

3

HURRELLS LA

Waterhall

CHAPEL LA

Belle Vue Farm

Elm Green Prep Sch

PARSONAGE LA

THE RYE FIELD

PH

MILL LA

SPRINGFIELD LA

POTTSFIELD LA

OAKLANDS WAY

Bir

07

NEW LODGE CHASE

New Lodge

Blake's Wood

Old Riffhams

RIFFHAMS CHASE

THE RIDGE

Long Wood

COMMON LA

Pheasanthouse Wood

2

Long Spring Wood

Nature Reserve

Po Pie Natur

1

Great Graces

GRACES LA

Great Graces Farm

RIFFHAMS LA

Riffhams

The White House

Ling Wood

RIDGE

FIR TREE LA

VOSSIDGE

CHESTNUT WALK

06

Hall Wood

76 A 77 B C 78 D E F

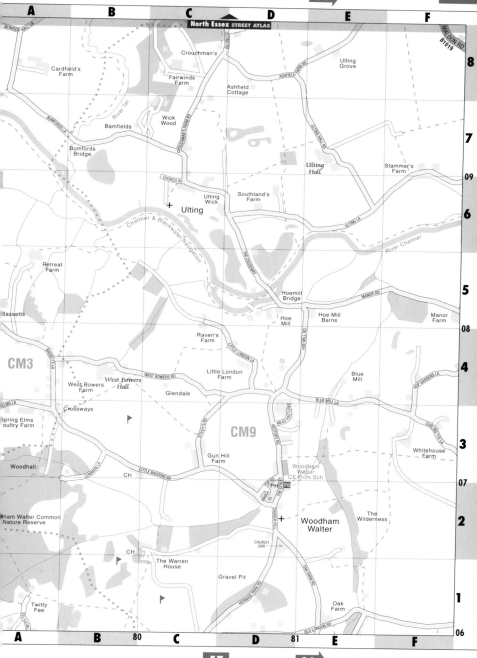

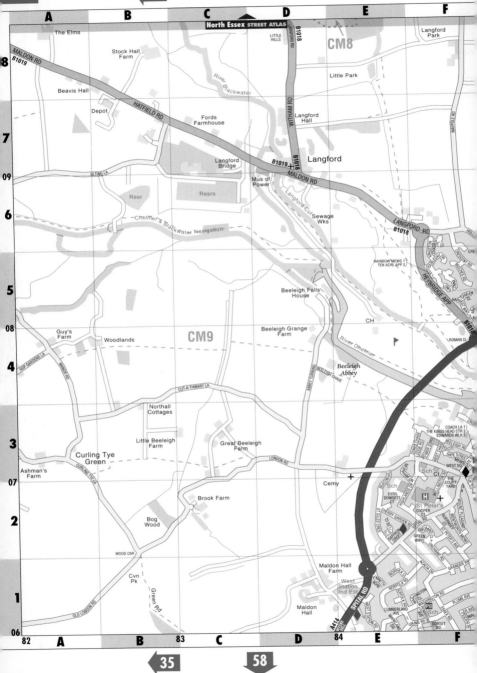

North Essex STREET ATLAS

A   B   C   D   E   F

The Elms

MALDON RD
B1019

8

Stock Hall
Farm

LITTLE
HILLS

CM8

Langford
Park

Little Park

River Backwater

Beavis Hall

HATFIELD RD

Depot

Fords
Farmhouse

Langford
Hall

WITHAM RD

B1018

LANGFORD RD

7

ULTING LA

Langford
Bridge

B1019

MALDON RD

Langford

09

Mus of
Power

Resr

Resrs

LANGFORD RD
B1018

6

Chelmer & Blackwater Navigation

Langford Cut

Sewage
Wks

HOLL

HEYBRIDGE APP

RAINBOW MEWS 1
TEN ACRE APP 2

GRE

Beeleigh Falls
House

5

CH

B1018

Guy's
Farm

Woodlands

CM9

Beeleigh Grange
Farm

River Chelmer

ROMAN CL

08

HOP GARDENS LA

MAYES RD

4

CUT-A-THWART LA

ABBEY TURNING

BEELEIGH CHASE

Beeleigh
Abbey

Northall
Cottages

COACH LA 1
THE KINGS HEAD CTR 2
EDWARDS WLK 3

3

Curling Tye
Green

CURLING TYE LA

Little Beeleigh
Farm

Great Beeleigh
Farm

LONDON RD

Sch

WEST SQ

THE
COURT
YARD

07

Ashman's
Farm

Cemy

Sch

CYRIL
DOWSETT

H

St Peter's

COOPER

2

Brook Farm

Bog
Wood

CHERRY GARDEN RD

GREEN
WAYS

WOOD CNR

Maldon Hall
Farm

1

OLD LONDON RD

Cvn
Pk

Green Rd

West
Station
Ind Est

SPITAL RD

A414

Maldon
Hall

CUMBERLAND
AVE

DORSET RD

06

82   A   83   B   C   83   D   84   E   F

North Essex STREET ATLAS

North Essex STREET ATLAS

Goldhanger

CM9

River Blackwater

Osea Island
CM9

North Essex STREET ATLAS

Lower
Grove

New
Barn

8

Wycke
Farm

Highams
Farm

Longwick
Farm

Bowstead Brook

7

09

Lauriston
Farm

Joyce's
Farm

LAURISTON
BGLWS

6

CM9

Gore
Saltings

5

08

4

River Blackwater

3

07

2

Osea
Island

Works

Osea
Farm

East
Point

1

Wr
Twr

06

39

North Essex STREET ATLAS

A   B   C   D   E   F

8

Boreham & Profits
Farm

Thisty Rd

Bohuns
Hall

MONKS WLK

WYCKE LA

MELL RD

Tollesbury

Mell
Farm

Wick
Farm

7

CM9

09

Decoy
Farm

Mill Cr

6

Rolls
Farm

Mill Farm
Marshes

Left Decoy
Marshes

Mill
Point

5

08

4

River Blackwater

3

07

2

1

St Lawrence

CM0

The
Stone

06

MOUNTVIEW PH
CRES

SEA VIEW PROM

RIVERTON DR

TINNOCKS LA

ST LAWRENCE DR

OYSTER
COTTS

MAIN RD

SEA VIEW
PAR

P

94   A   B   95   C   D   96   E   F

39
62

42

A | B | C | D | E | F

North Essex STREET ATLAS

8

CM9

7

09

Jetty

6

5

River Blackwater

Pewet
Island

08

Cvn
Pk
PARKER
CT

PO

Bradwell
Waterside

SHOEMENDERS
LA

B1021

OLD
COASTGUARD
COTTS

PH

Mast

4

Marina

TRUSSES RD

Bradwell Creek

Westwick
Farm

3

WATERSIDE RD

WOODYARDS

07

Down
Westwick

CM0

2

ORPLANDS
COTTS

Orplands

1

Kennel
Barn

MALDON RD

MALDON RD

B1021

06

A | B | C | D | E | F

98

99

63

42

	A	B	C	D	E	F

Sewage Works

GREEN LA

BLACK ADDER COTTS

ELIZABETH CL

B194

MAYFLOWER CL

HYDE MEAD

HYDE MEAD

CLINTON

WARD B

OVEY CL

MIDDLE ST

BERECROFT

Clayton Hill Country Park

Nazeing Prim Sch

Mulberries

Lower Nazeing

Mansion House Farm

8

Nazeing Marsh

Payne's Farm

Tatsfield Ave

Hyde Mead

Ninnings

Perry Hill Farm

PERRY HILL

EN10

Nurseries

Clayton Hill

PAYNE'S LA

7

King's Weir

Langridge

St Leonards

Snows

ST LEONARDS RD

LAUNDS LA

Netherkidders Farm

CEMETERY LA

05

6

Felsteads

Sailing Club

COLEMAN'S LA

Coleman's Shaw

WALTHAM RD

EN9

5

PH

04

Holyfield Marsh

Holyfield Hall Farm

Marsh Hill House

MARSH HILL

Denver Lodge Farm

Galley Hill

4

River Lea or Lea

Navigation

Galleyhill Wood

Broadgate Springs

Nature Reserve

Hayes Hill Farm

Visitor Ctr

Hayes Hill

HOLYFIELD RD

Holyfield

3

EN8

Nursery

Holyfield

Puck La

Aimes Green

Seventy Acres

CLAY HAMBURY RD

GALLEYHILL RD

Nightingales

Aimesgreen Farm

03

2

Fishers Green

MONKHAMS HALL

Homefield Wood

CLAYGATE LA

River Lee Country Park

Holyfield Farm

Kennel Wood

Hooks Marsh

CROOKED MILE

LONG WLK

Eagle Lodge

B194

Breaches Farm

BREACH BARNS LA

Dallance House

1

02

	A	B	38	C	D	39	E	F

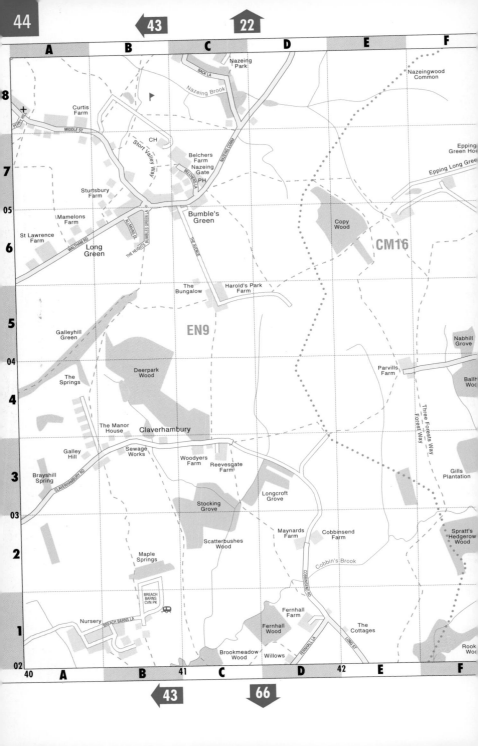

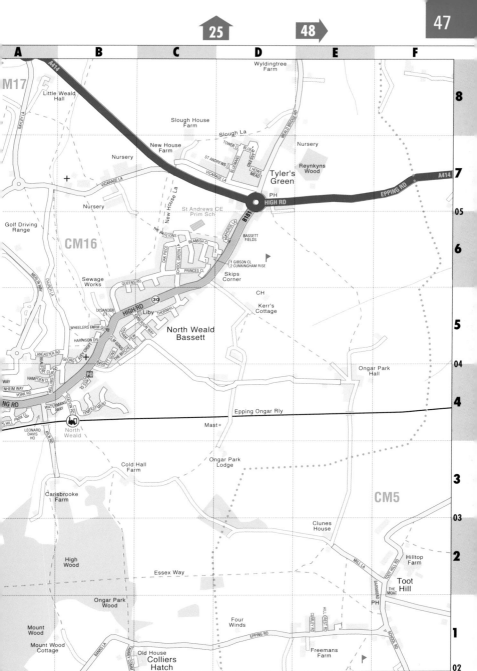

25
48
69
48

M17

A414

Little Weald Hall

Wyldingtree Farm

Slough House Farm

Slough La

New House Farm

Nursery

Nursery

TOWER LA

BLUEBELL CL

ST ANDREWS CL

VICARAGE LA

DEWS MEAD

Nursery

Reynkyns Wood

Tyler's Green

VICARAGE LA

+

St Andrews CE Prim Sch

New House La

PH

HIGH RD

A414

EPPING RD

05

Golf Driving Range

CM16

THE PAVILIONS

BEAMISH CL

OAK PIECE

SCHOOL GREEN LA

PRINCES CL

MADDELLS LA

BASSETT FIELDS

6

Sewage Works

QUEENS RD

1 GIBSON CL
2 CUNNINGHAM RISE

Skips Corner

CH

LYSANDER

HIGH RD

Liby

THORNHILL

39

CHEQUERS RD

Kerr's Cottage

North Weald Bassett

5

WHEELERS FARM GDNS

HARRISON DR

THE ELMS

THE BIRCHES

LANCASTER RD

GEORG

BASSETT GDNS

BASSETT GDNS

+

Ongar Park Hall

04

WAY

BLENHEIM WAY

YORK RD

HAMPDEN CL

PO

WATERMANS WALK

TEMPEST MEAD

Epping Ongar Rly

4

NG RD

'S HILL

PARK CL

OLD RD

Mast

Ongar Park Lodge

North Weald

LEONARD DAVIS HO

Cold Hall Farm

Carisbrooke Farm

Ongar Park Lodge

CM5

3

03

Clunes House

MILL LA

Hilltop Farm

2

High Wood

Essex Way

FOOT HILL

BARNARD RD

Toot Hill

THE MOAT

Ongar Park Wood

PH

Mount Wood

Four Winds

CURLEY RD

HILL CREST RD

EPPING RD

SCHOOL RD

1

Mount Wood Cottage

BANKS LA

Old House

Colliers Hatch

Freemans Farm

02

50

51

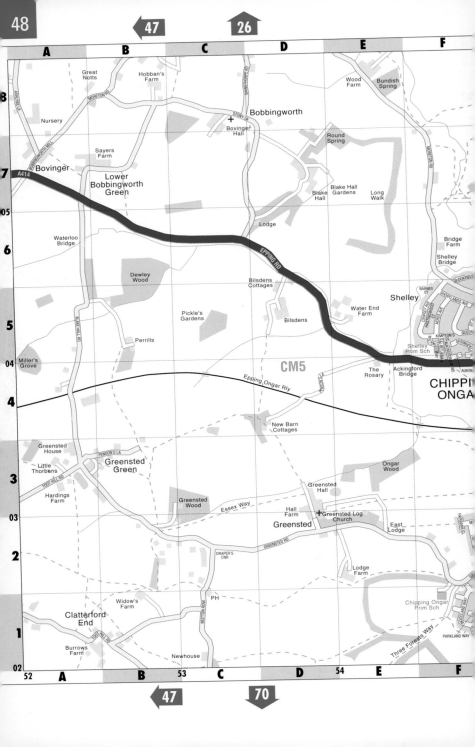

47
26

A   B   C   D   E   F

8

Great
Notts

Hobban's
Farm

Wood
Farm

Bundish
Spring

Nursery

MORETON RD

STONY LA

RD NORTH WEALD

Bobbingworth

Bovinger
Hall

Round
Spring

MORETON RD

7   A414   Bovinger

Sayers
Farm

Lower
Bobbingworth
Green

Blake
Hall

Blake Hall
Gardens

Long
Walk

Bridge
Farm

05

BOBBINGWORTH HILL

Lodge

Shelley
Bridge

6   Waterloo
Bridge

EPPING RD

BARNES
OF

BROOKFIELD

SHORTLANDS AVE

Dewley
Wood

Bilsdens
Cottages

Shelley

CHIPSTEAD
HASTINGWOOD
ACRES AVE

5   BLAKE HALL RD

Pickle's
Gardens

Bilsdens

Water End
Farm

KIMPTON'S
SPRING CL

QUEEN

Perrills

Shelley
Prim Sch

04   Miller's
Grove

CM5

The
Rosary

Ackingford
Bridge

AUKIN

CHIPPI
ONGA

Epping Ongar Rly

RISING LA

4

Greensted
House

New Barn
Cottages

Little
Thorbens

PENSON'S LA

Ongar
Wood

3   TOOT HILL RD

Greensted
Green

Greensted
Hall

Hardings
Farm

Greensted
Wood

Essex Way

Hall
Farm

Greensted Log
Church

East
Lodge

FAIRBANK RD

03   Greensted

Greensted Rd

DRAPER'S
CNR

2

Lodge
Farm

Chipping Ongar
Prim Sch

Widow's
Farm

PH

MAIN RD WILLIAM

Clatterford
End

TOOT HILL RD

PARKLAND WAY

1

Burrows
Farm

Newhouse

Three Forests Way

02
52   A   53   B   C   53   D   54   E   F

47
70

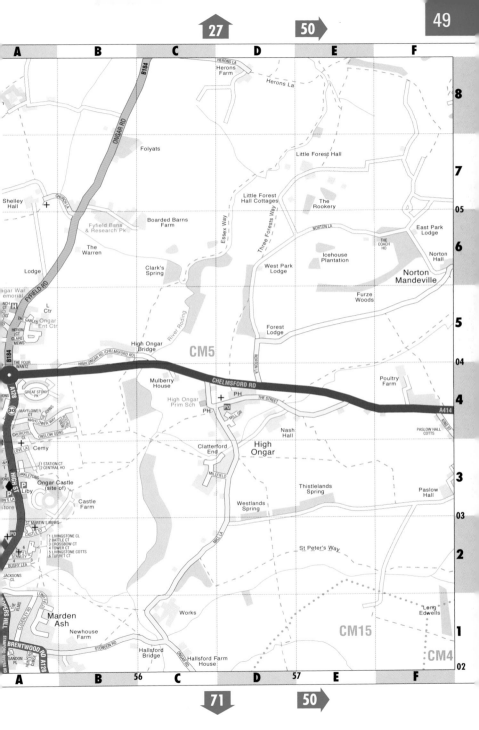

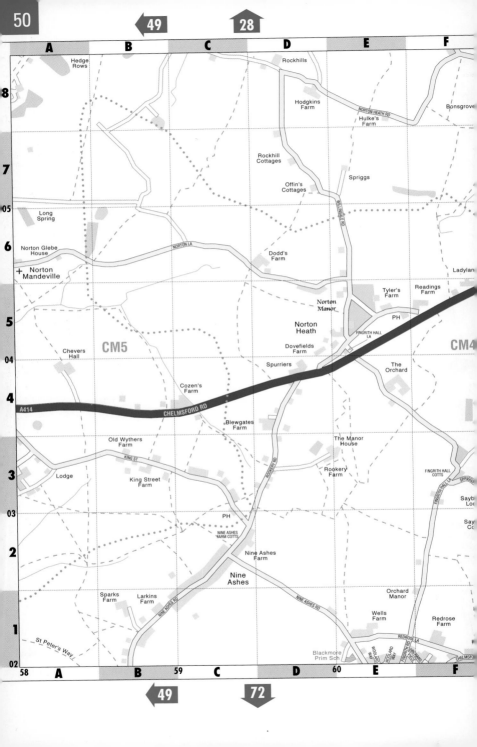

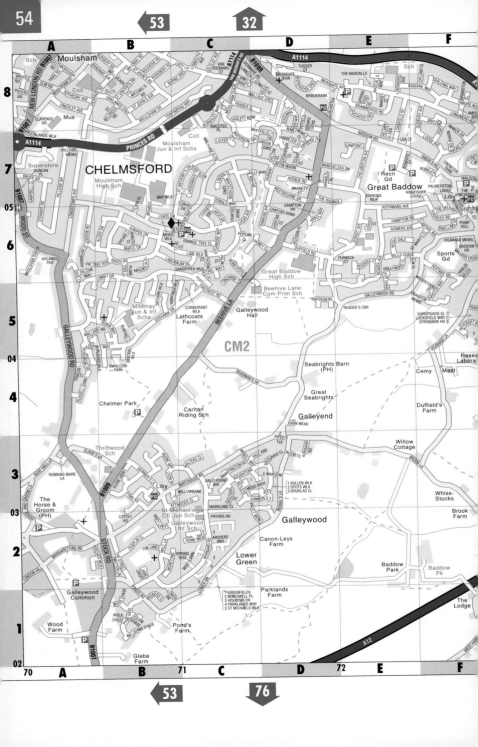

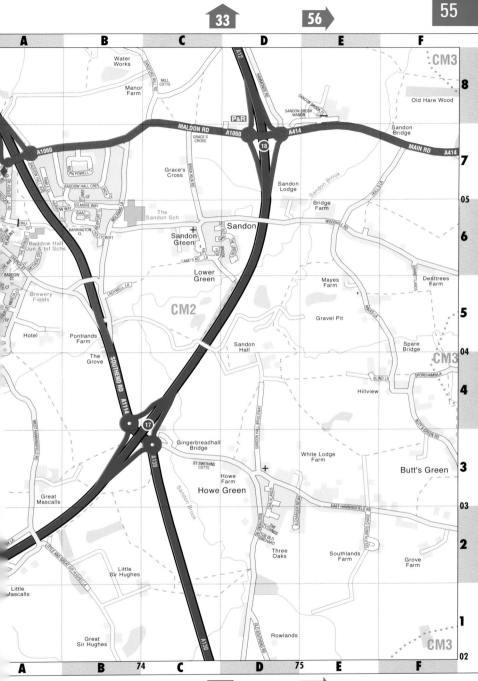

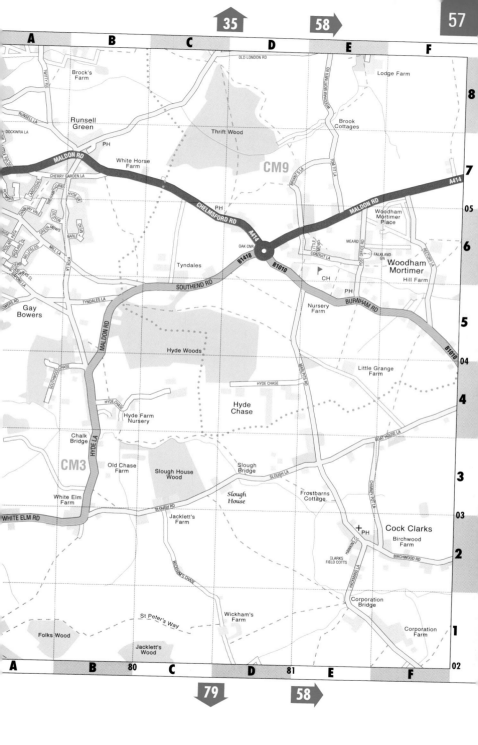

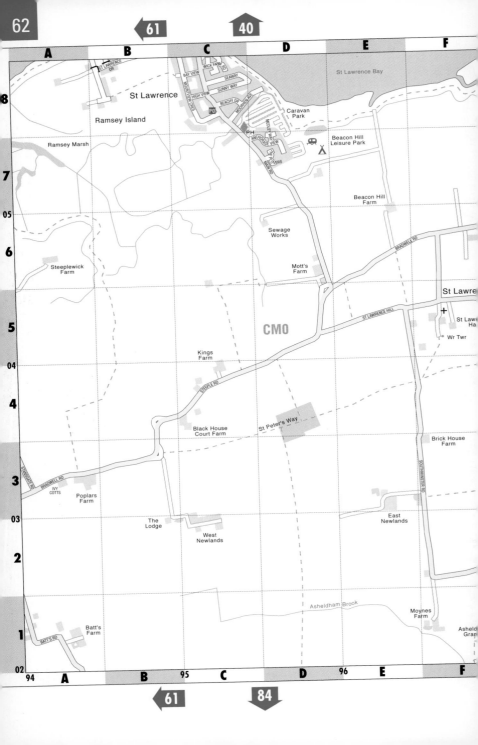

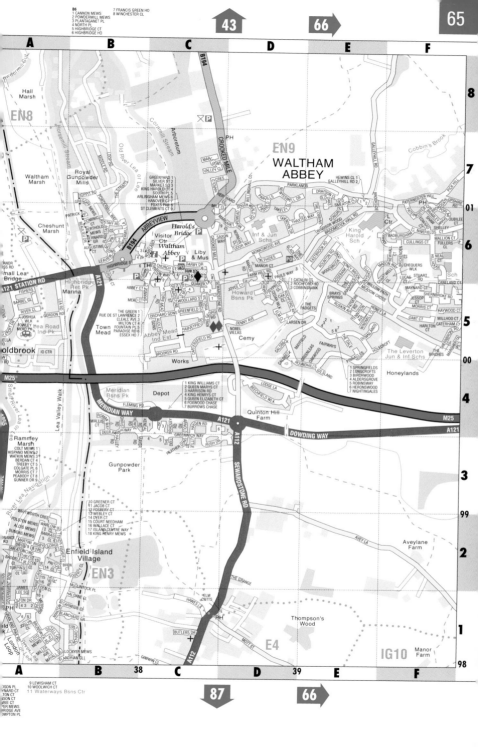

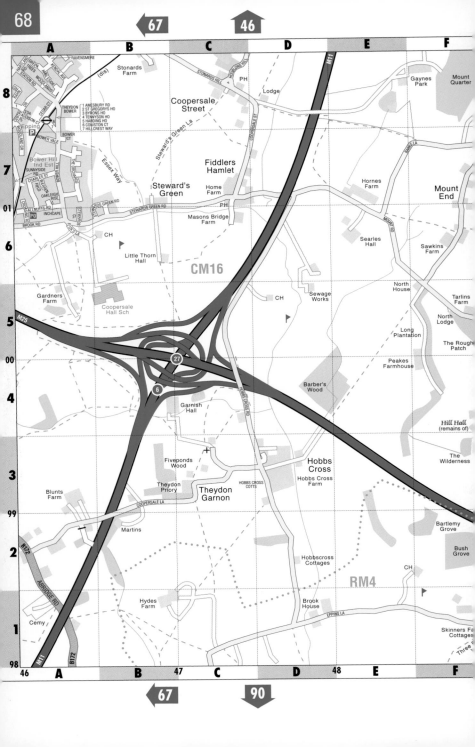

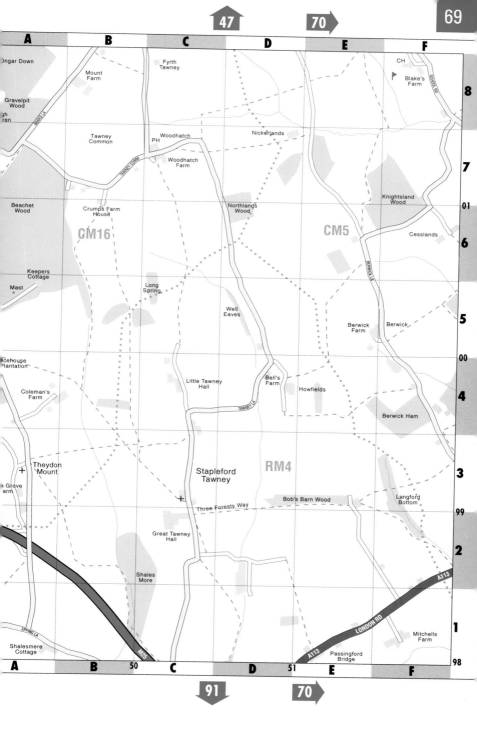

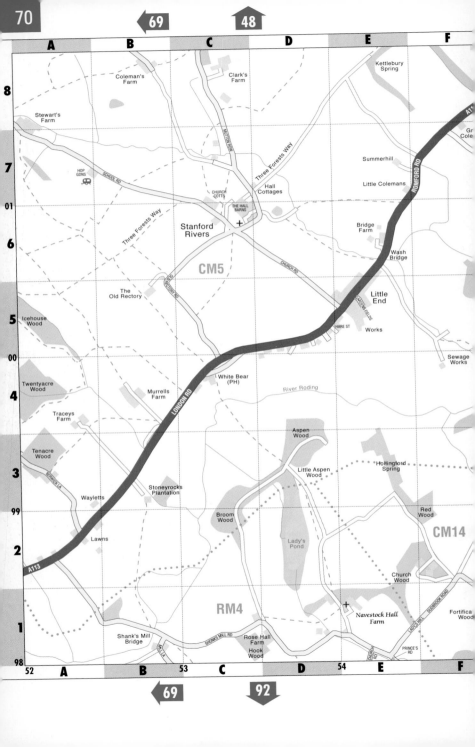

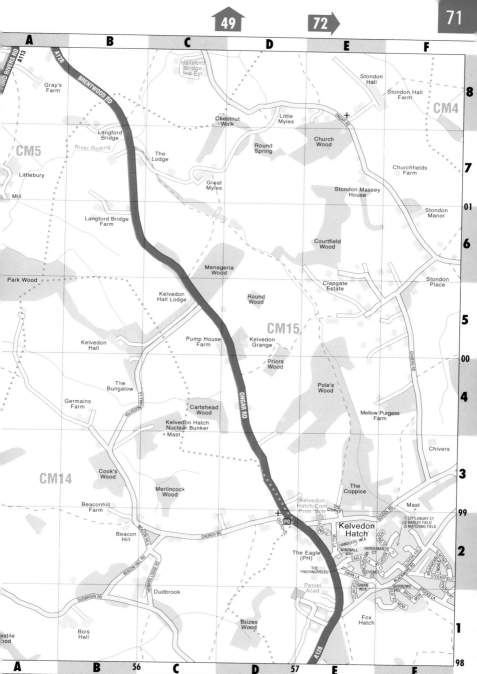

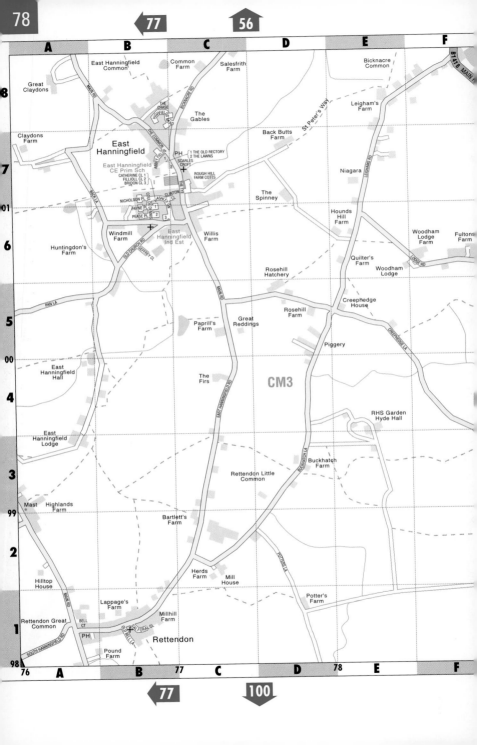

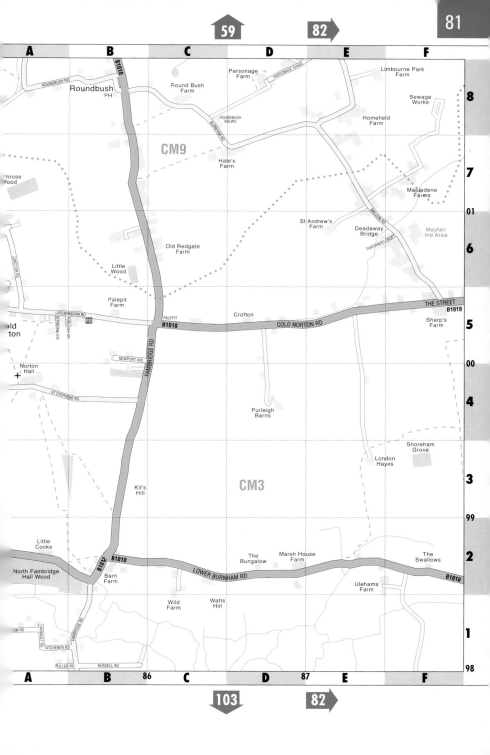

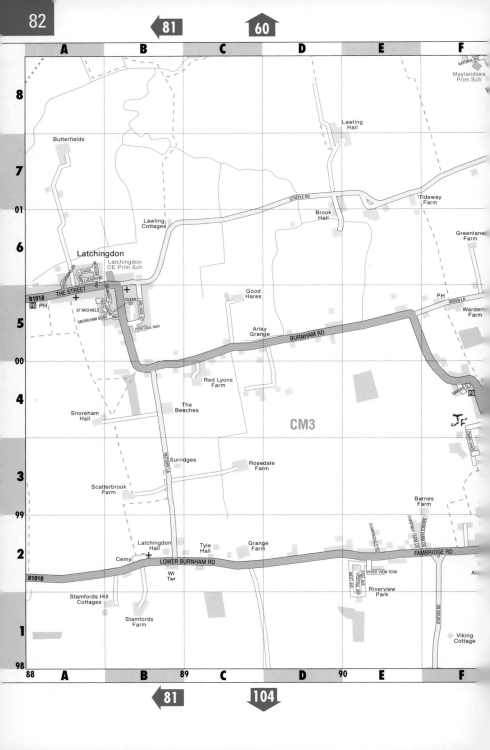

A B C D E F

8

Maylandsea Prim Sch
KATONIA AVE

Butterfields

Lawling Hall

7

01

STEEPLE RD

Tideway Farm

Lawling Cottages

Brook Hall

6

Greenlane Farm

Latchingdon

Latchingdon CE Prim Sch

Good Hares

PH

GREEN LA

Warden Farm

THE STREET
B1018

CHASE
LUDGROVE

CLEAR CT

5

PO PH

ST MICHAELS CL

SNOREHAM GDNS

HERITAGE WAY

Arley Grange

BURNHAM RD

00

GARDEN CT
PO

4

Red Lyons Farm

Snoreham Hall

The Beeches

CM3

JF

LOWER CHASE

RECTORY LA

Surridges

3

Rosedale Farm

Scatterbrook Farm

Barnes Farm

99

CHESTNUT FARM DR

GEORGES FARM CL

2

Latchingdon Hall

Tyle Hall

Grange Farm

SUNNINGDALE RD

FAMBRIDGE RD

Cemy

LOWER BURNHAM RD

RIVER VIEW TERR

Ala

B1010

Wr Twr

EAST AVE
WEST AVE
CENTRAL AVE

Riverview Park

Stamfords Hill Cottages

1

Stamfords Farm

STATION RD

Viking Cottage

98

88
A B
89
C D
90
E F

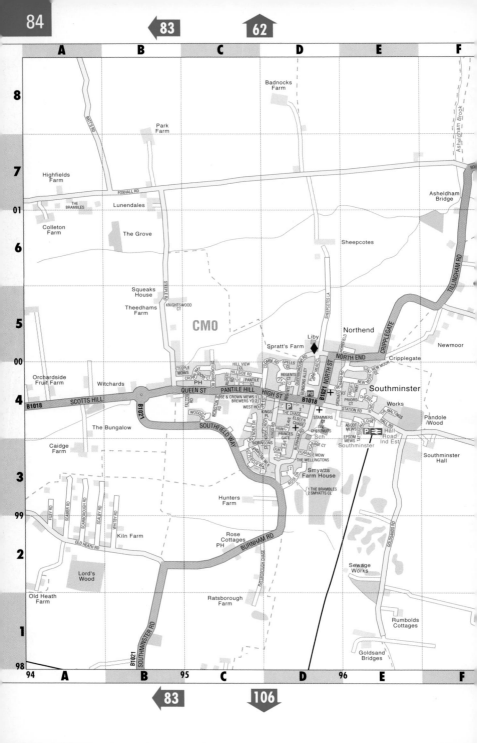

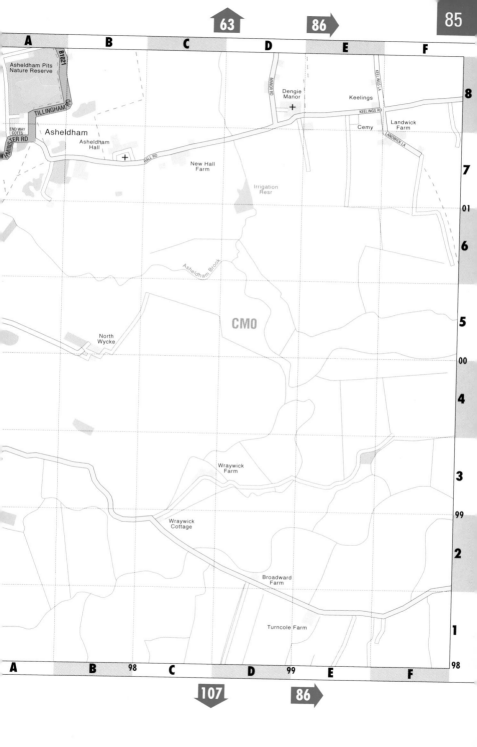

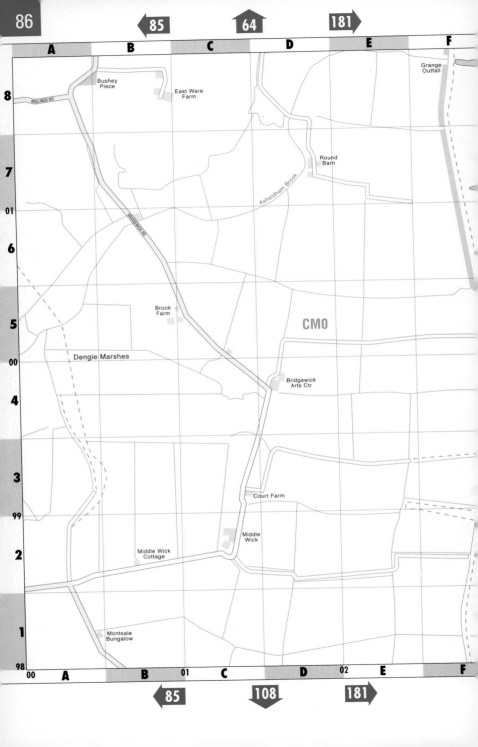

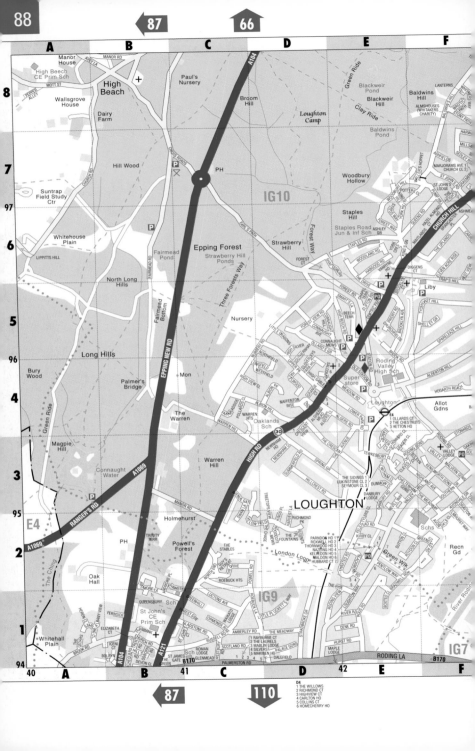

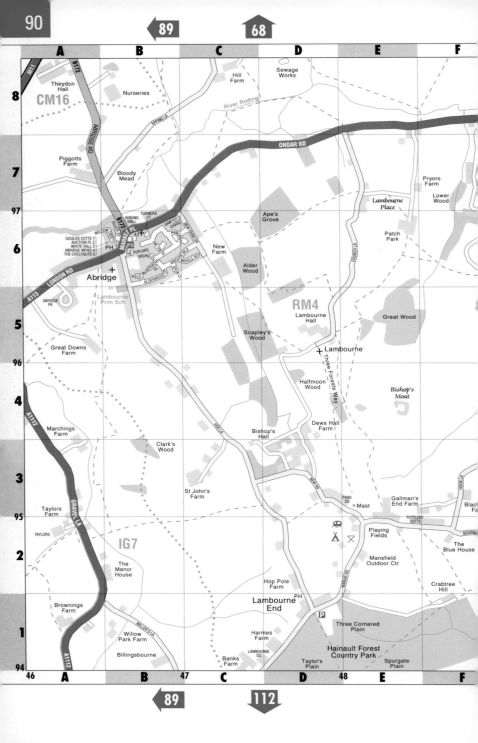

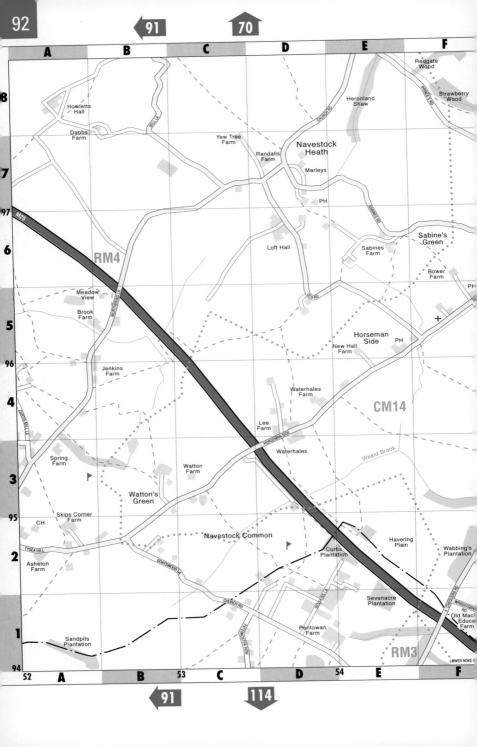

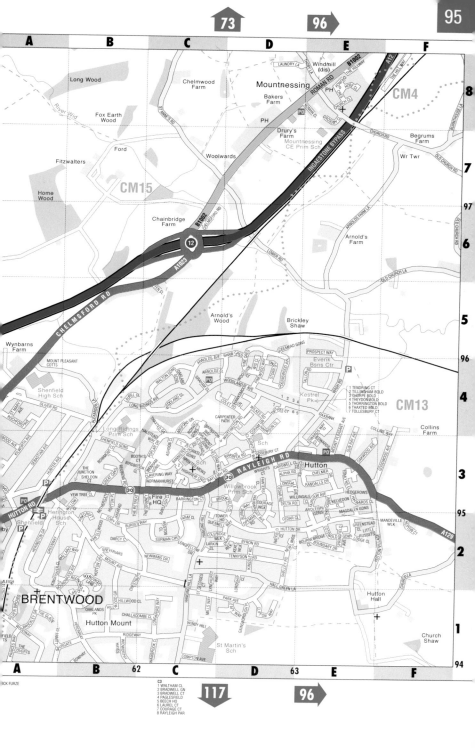

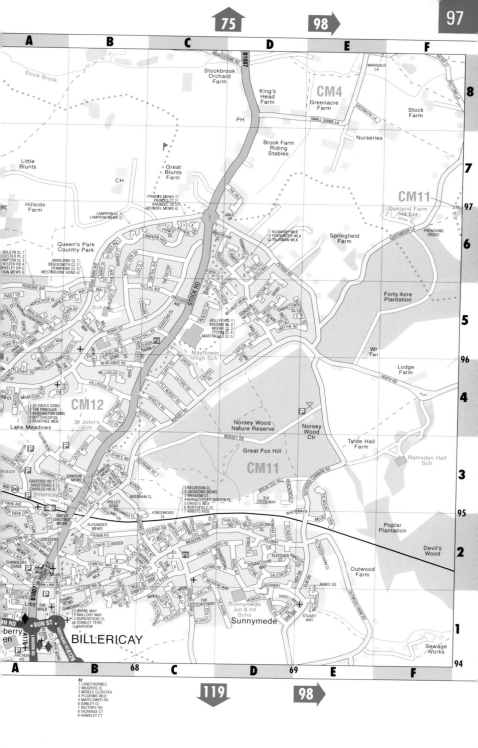

A B C D E F

WHITE'S HILL
Bishop's Farm

8

Kiln Common

Whitelillies Farm

BRITTONS LA
Great Bishop's Wood

CM4

Broom Wood

Hanningfield Resr

7

DOWNHAM RD
Fremnells

97

Crowsheath Farm

Visitor Ctr
P
HAWKSWOOD RD

Common Farm

Hilltop Nursery

Little Abbott's

6

Cock Wood

CROWSHEATH LA

Thriff Wood

Ramsden Back Common

MILL LA

DENGAYES LA

Nursery

PH

5

TIPLERS BRIDGE
NORMANS RD
STONEY HILLS
BIRDS CL
ACACIA DOWN WK

WILLOWMEADE

DOWNHAM RD

OAK RD

SCHOOL LA

Downham

96

PH
ST JOHN'S PL

HEATH RD

DOWNHAM RD

1 BAKERS CT
2 FARRIER SQ

WINDSOR RD

Windsor Trad Est

Greenacres Farm

Hunt's Farm

Chitham's Farm

Ramsden Heath

PH
LINDSAY CL
ST DR
CL
HOLMAN'S GR

CM11

Rectory Wood

4

BRABNER GDNS

SHORT CL
VICAR CL
BISHOP CL

Downham CE Prim Sch

Cox Green

The Orchard Farm

De Beauvoir House

3

Meepshole Wood

PARK LA

DE BEAUVOIR CHASE

95

CHURCH RD

ORCHARD WK

2

Crays Wood

Pump Hill

PH

Kent Hill

Barrenleys Wood

Claypitshills Wood

Ramsden Park Farm

RAMSDEN PARK RD

GLEBE RD

1

Ramsden Bellhouse

94

70 A B 71 C D 72 E F

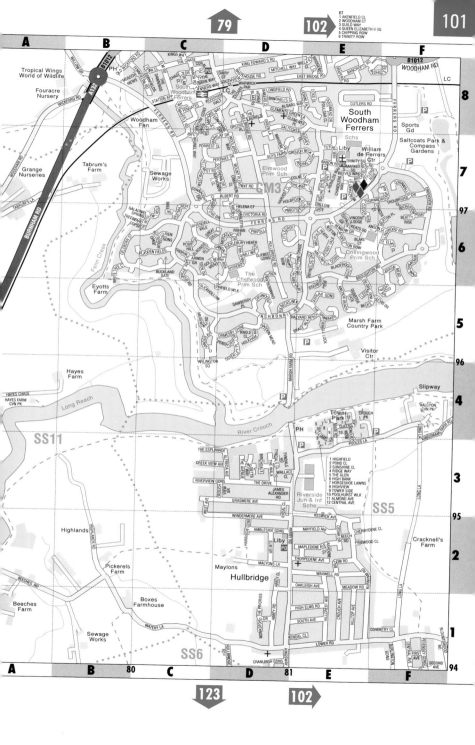

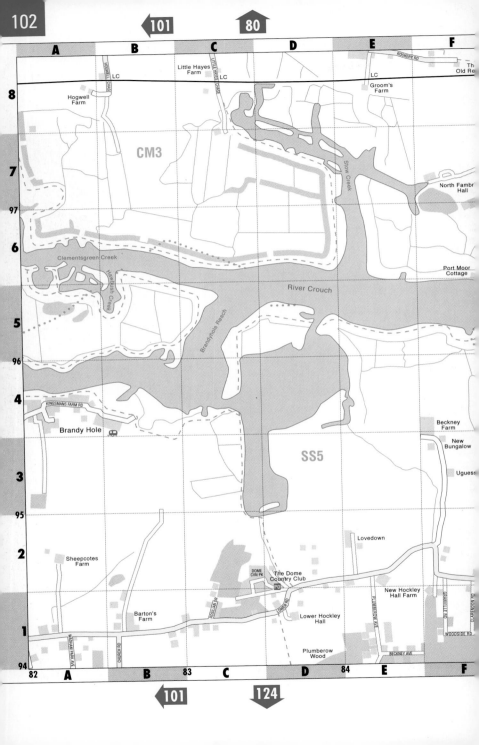

8

7

97

6

5

96

4

3

95

2

94

1

A B C D E F

Stoke's Hall Farm

Round Hill

Elm Farm

B1010

MALDON RD

PH

Little John's Farm

GREEN LA

CHERRY CL

Ostend

CM3

LC

CM0

Creeksea Hall

CH

The Cliff

Black Point

FERRY RD

CREEKSEA LA

B1010

Cliff Reach
River Crouch

Land's End

Creeksea Place

Creeksea Place Farm

Creeksea

White House

Slipway

Lower Raypits

Old Fleet

SS4

Ferry (F)

Jetty

Creeksea Ferry Inn (PH)

Hotel

Essex Yacht Marina

Wallasea Island

Lion Creek

CREEKSEA FERRY RD

Lion Wharf

Saltings Poultry Farm

Lion House

Lambourne Hall

LAMBOURNE HALL RD

LAMBOURNE MEAD COTTS

Paglesham Creek

A B 92 C D 93 E F 94

105
84

Mangapps
Rly Mus

GREEN LA

Cemy

Stoneyhills

Mill
Farm

Newman's
Farm

Panner's Brook

SOUTHMINSTER RD

B1021

BUCHAMPS

COBBINS CHASE

BADGERS
KEEP
BOLVIL

WOODCUTTERS

NO WAY

EVES
CNR

ASHWOOD
CL

ROMANS TRANS
CHASE

Pannel's
Bridge

Romans
Farm

Hall
Farm

St Peter's
High Sch

1 DEBDEN WAY
2 CHELMER WAY
3 EMBER WAY

St Mary's
CE Prim Sch

MARSH RD

DAMMERWICK
COTTS

DAMMER
WICK

Muscle
Bridge

ST PETERS RD

B1010

MALDON RD

COMPASS
GDNS

WELLAND RD

CHURCH RD

B1021

B1010

RAMBLE WAY

PLANE TREES

Burnham-
on-Crouch

THE LEAS

CMO

BURNHAM-ON-CROUCH

Burnham
Bsns Pk

Springfield
Nursery Est
Sand Island Ctr
Mayfield

Springfield
Ind Est

Station
Ind Est

Super
store

Allot
Gdns

Burnham-on-Crouch
Prim Sch

SHEERWATER CL
GALAHAD CL
HERMES DR
MILDMAY HO
Mildmay Ind Est

1
2
3
4
5

WINSTREE

PADS RD

STATION RD

ALPHA RD

BOOTH
PL

ARCADIA RD

LEY

NORMANDY
AVE

ARNHEM RD

WICK RD

Burnham
Wick

IRB
Sta

Country
Park

WARWICK
CT

MILLFIELD

Sports Gd
Dengie
Hundred
Sports
Ctr

Caravan
Site

MILL
LA

LIBY

QUEEN'S
RD

WESTERN RD

DILLIWAY

BROCKWALL

CROUCH RD

RAMBLERS
WAY

ARGYLE RD

Marina

KINGS RD

REGENTS

QUEENS

WITNEY RD

YORK RD

CHASE

ORCHARD RD

HIGH ST

B1021

THE
PROMENADE

THE BELVEDERE

PH

Sewage
Works

Burnham-on-Crouch
& District Mus

Slipways

C4
1 CURLEW HO
2 NELSON CT
3 HAMILTON CT
4 GRANVILLE TERR
5 STEBBINGS CT
6 ST MARY'S HO
7 ALIGERS
8 HARDINGS-REACH
9 CALMPATCH
10 SUNNYMEAD FLATS
11 BUCKINGHAM SQ

12 BELVEDERE CT
13 THE CROWSNEST
14 THE ANCHORAGE
15 PETTICROW QUAYS

SEA-END
CVN SITE

Gardenness
Point

Ferry (F)

River Crouch

Ringwood Bar

Overland
Point

Grassland
Point

Fleet
Point

Grapnells

Wallasea
Wetlands
Scheme

GRAPNELLS
FARM COTTS

WALLASEA ISLAND

SS4

CMO

105
128

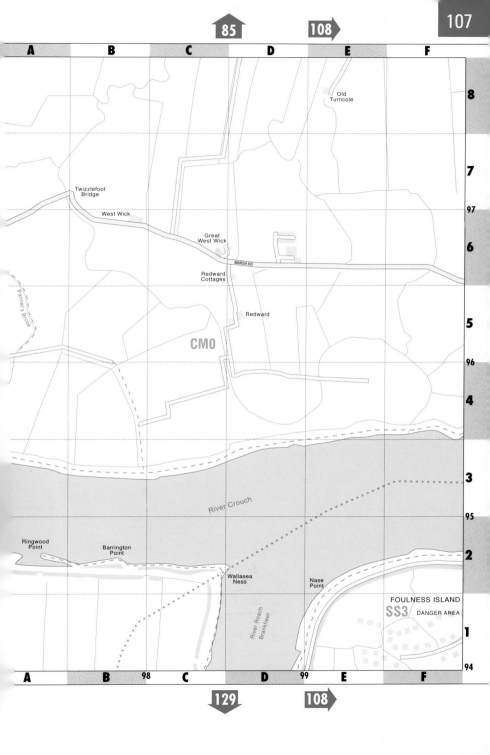

A B C D E F

8

7

97

6

5

96

4

3

95

2

1

94

Old
Turncole

Twizzlefoot
Bridge

West Wick

Great
West Wick

MARSH RD

Redward
Cottages

Redward

CM0

Pannel's Brook

River Crouch

Ringwood
Point

Barrington
Point

Wallasea
Ness

Nase
Point

River Roach
Brankfleet

FOULNESS ISLAND

SS3 DANGER AREA

A B 98 C D 99 E F

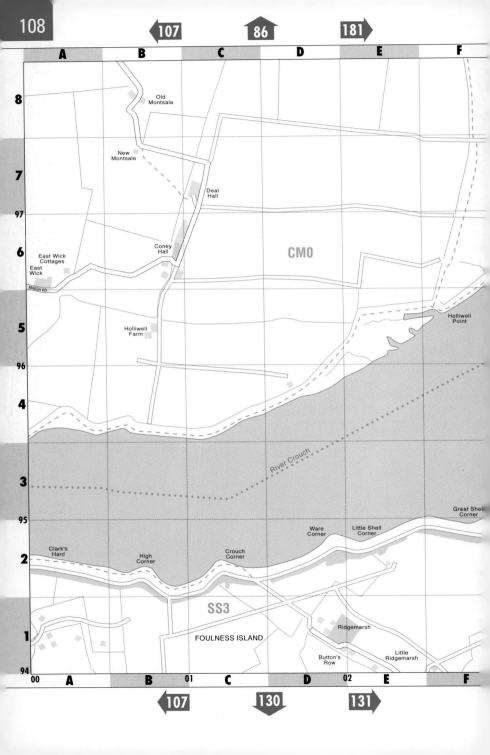

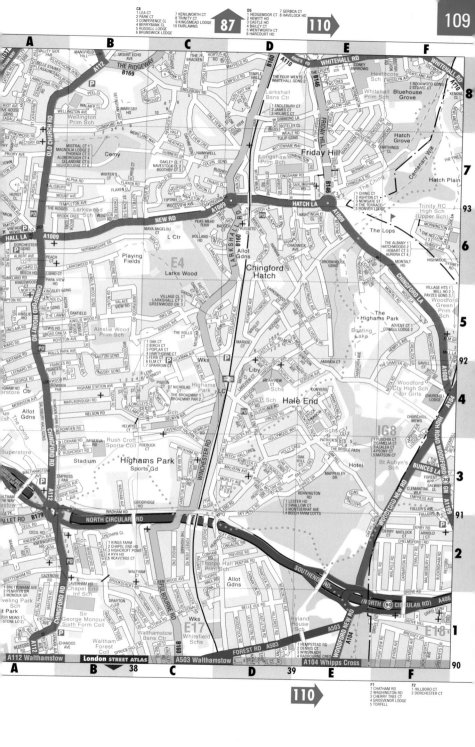

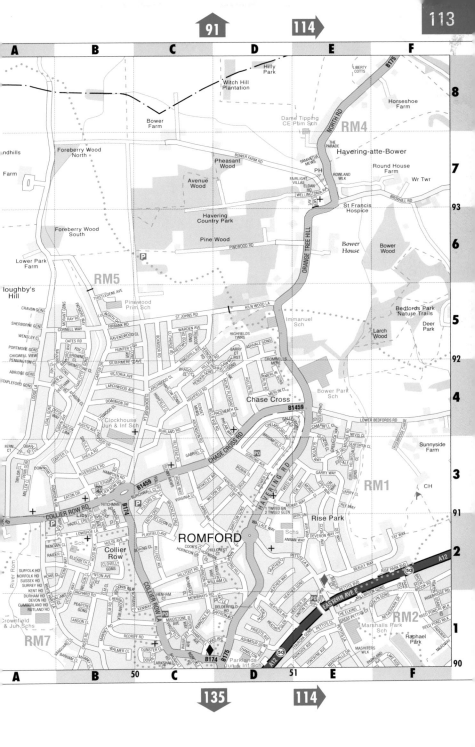

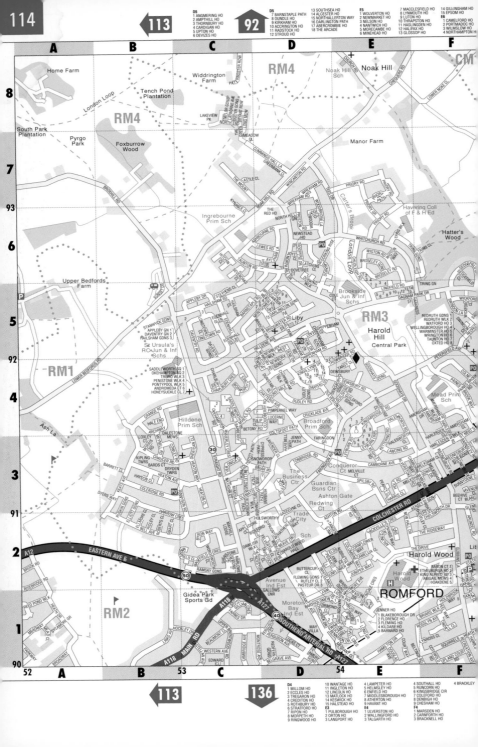

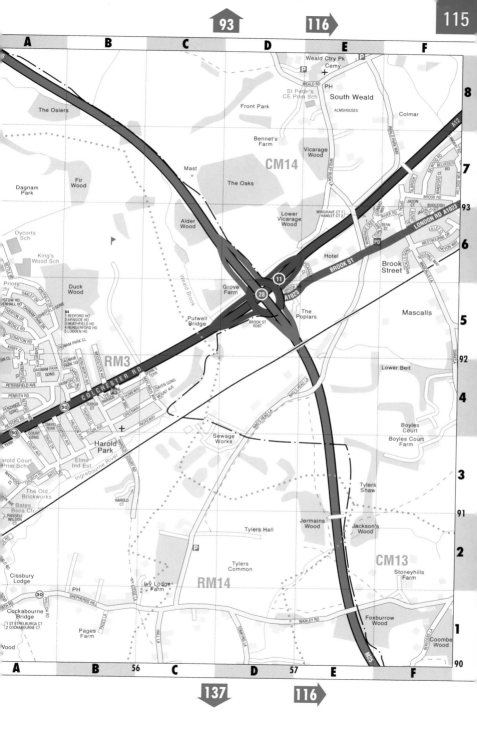

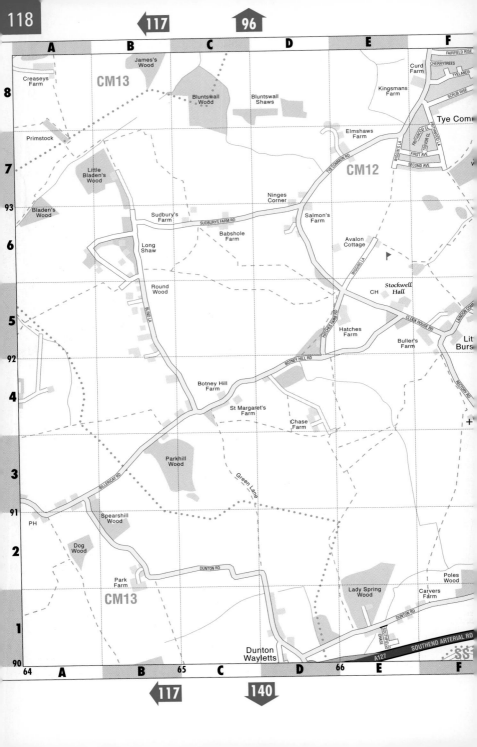

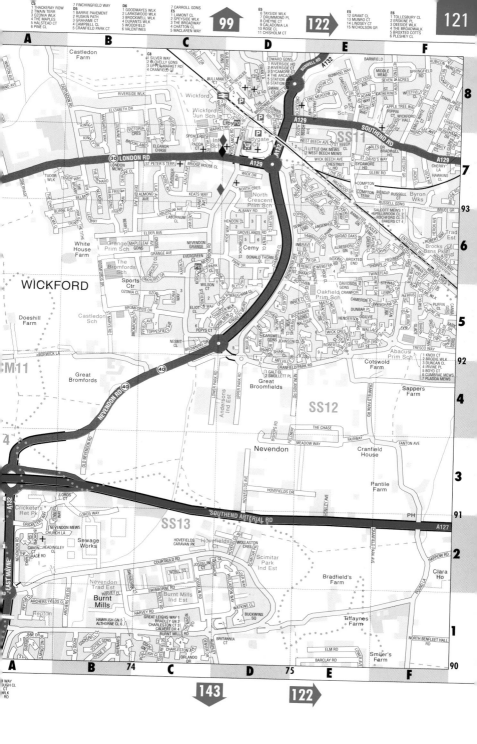

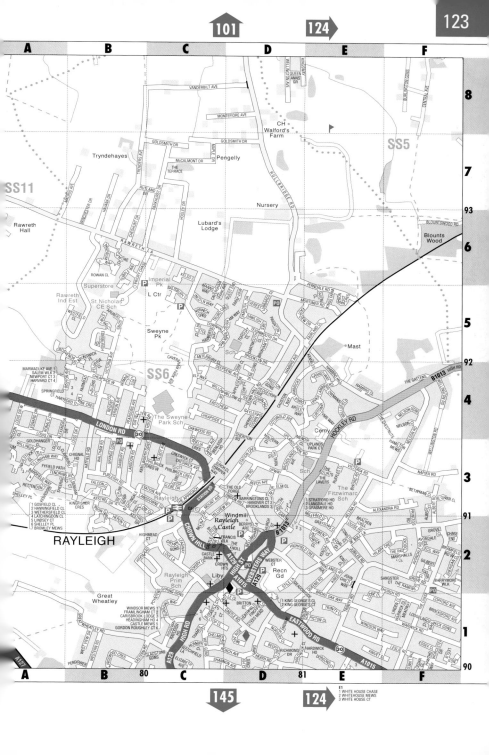

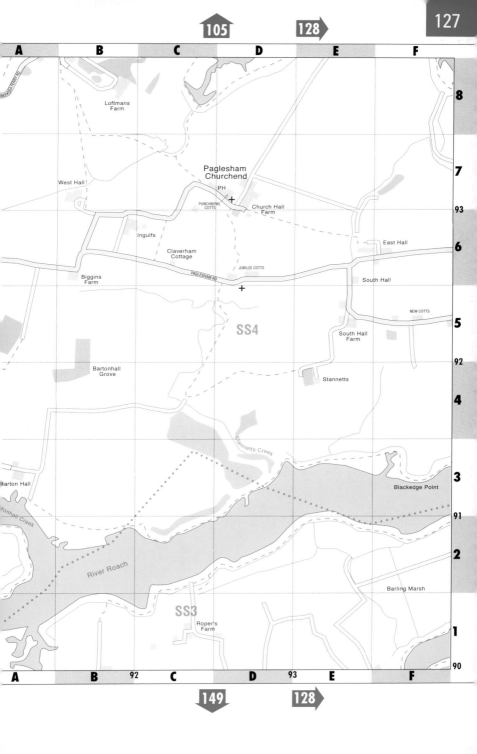

A B C D E F

8

7

93

6

92

5

4

91

3

2

1

90

Loftmans
Farm

West Hall

Paglesham
Churchend

PH

PUNCHBOWL
COTTS.

+

Church Hall
Farm

Ingulfs

Claverham
Cottage

JUBILEE COTTS

East Hall

Biggins
Farm

PAGLESHAM RD

South Hall

+

NEW COTTS

SS4

South Hall
Farm

Bartonhall
Grove

Stannetts

Stannetts Creek

Barton Hall

Blackedge Point

onhall Creek

River Roach

Barling Marsh

SS3

Roper's
Farm

A B 92 C D 93 E F

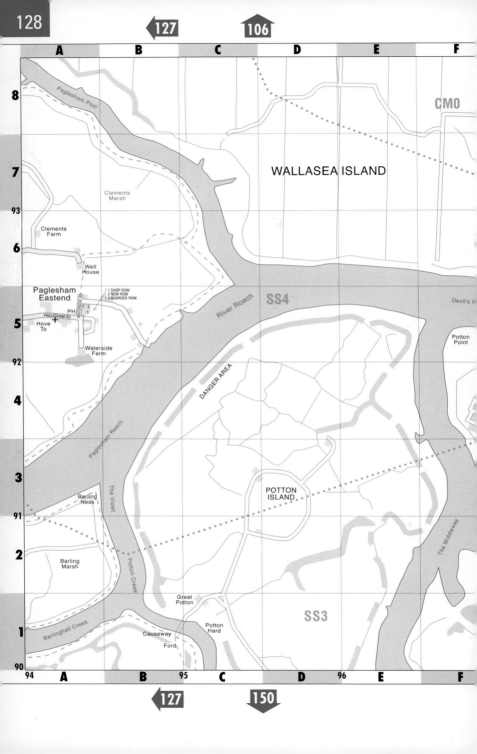

127
106

CM0

WALLASEA ISLAND

Paglesham Pool

Clements
Marsh

Clements
Farm

SS4

River Roach

Devil's P

Well
House

Paglesham
Eastend

1 SHOP ROW
2 NEW ROW
3 BOARDED ROW

PH
PAGLESHAM RD
Hove
To

Potton
Point

Waterside
Farm

DANGER AREA

Paglesham Reach

Barling
Ness

The Violet

POTTON
ISLAND

Barling
Marsh

Potton Creek

The Middleway

Great
Potton

SS3

Barlinghall Creek

Potton
Hard

Causeway
Ford

127
150

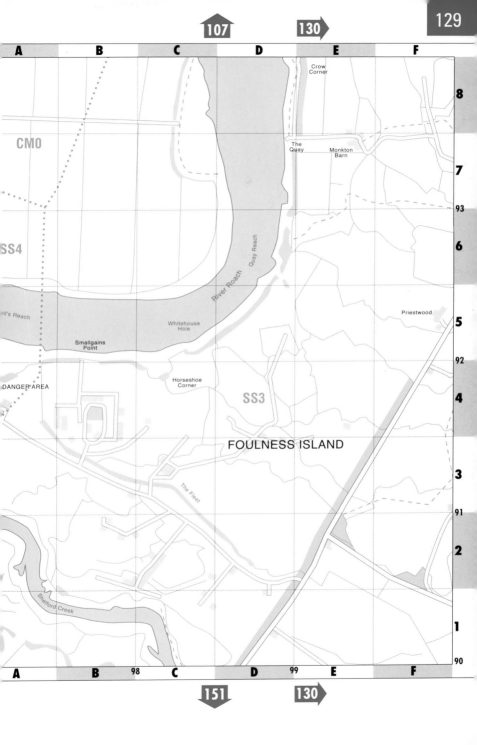

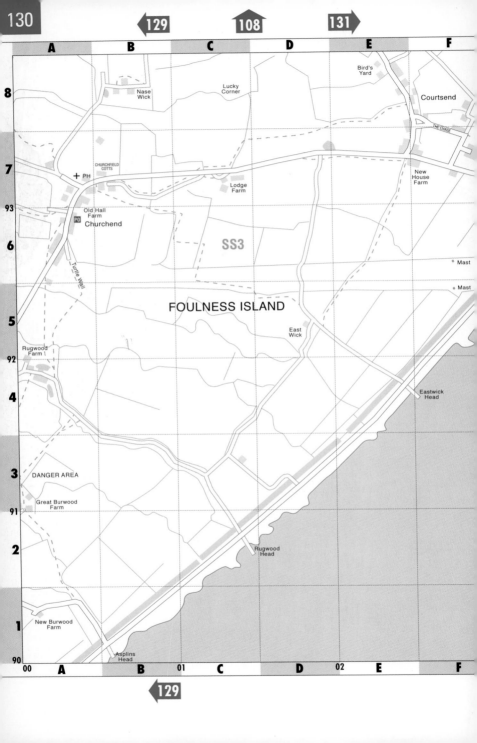

129
108
131

8

Bird's
Yard

Courtsend

THE CHASE

Nase
Wick

Lucky
Corner

7

CHURCHFIELD
COTTS

+ PH

Lodge
Farm

New
House
Farm

93

Old Hall
Farm

PO

Churchend

SS3

6

Turtle Well

Mast

Mast

FOULNESS ISLAND

5

East
Wick

Rugwood
Farm

92

Eastwick
Head

4

3

DANGER AREA

Great Burwood
Farm

91

2

Rugwood
Head

1

New Burwood
Farm

90

Asplins
Head

00   A   B   01   C   D   02   E   F

129

108

River Crouch

Foulness Point

East
Newlands

The Drift
(dis)

SS3

DANGER AREA

Masts

Mast

Northern
Corner

Fisherman's
Head

8

7

95

6

5

94

4

3

93

2

1

92

A   B   C   D   E   F

04   05

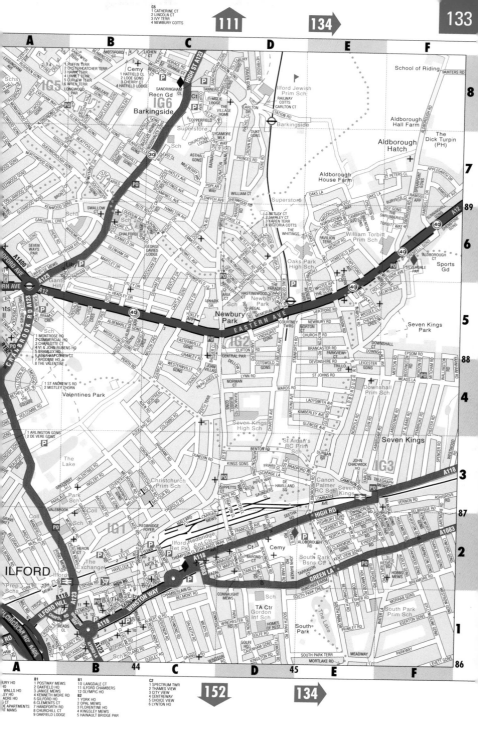

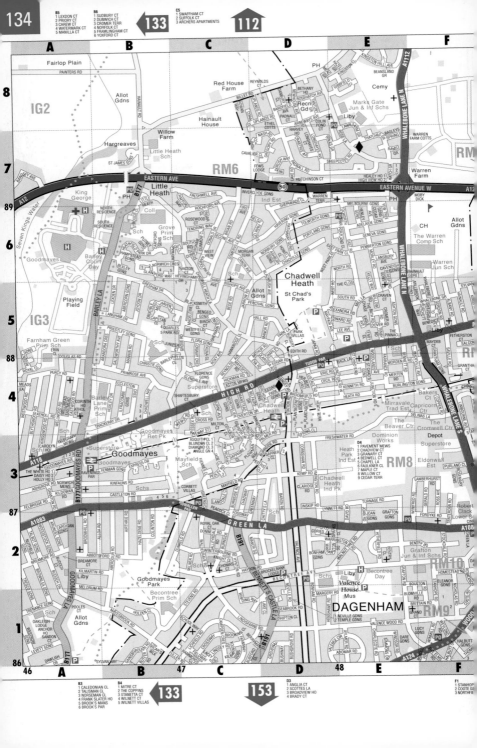

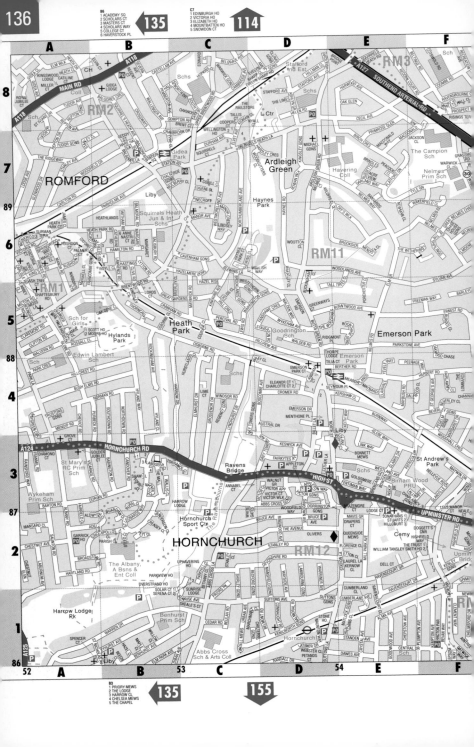

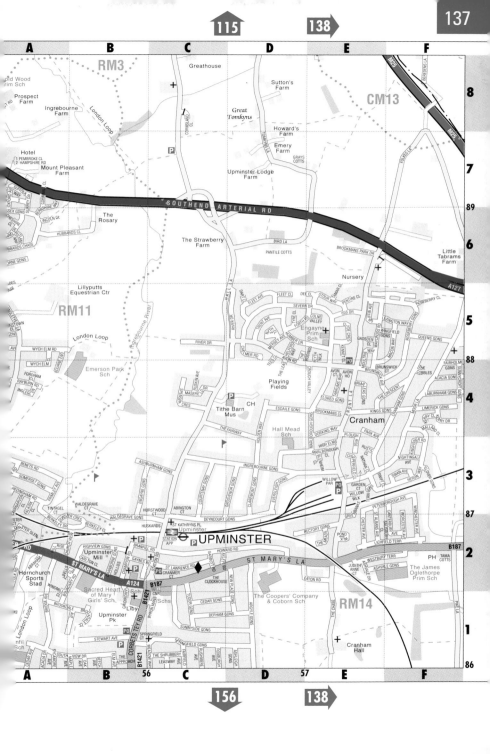

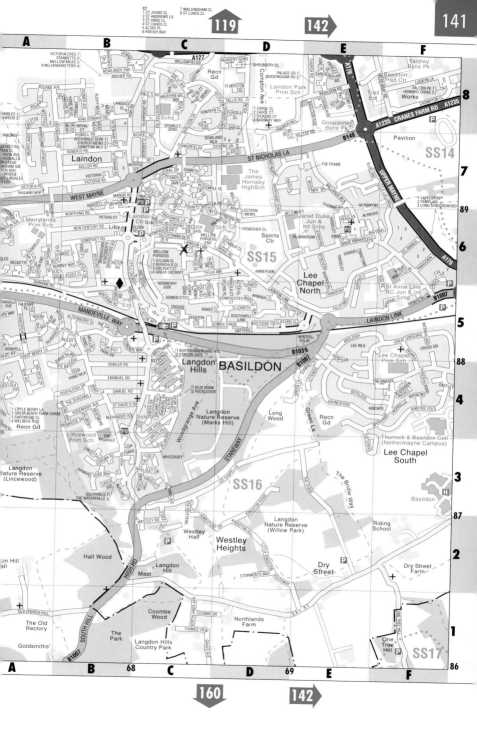

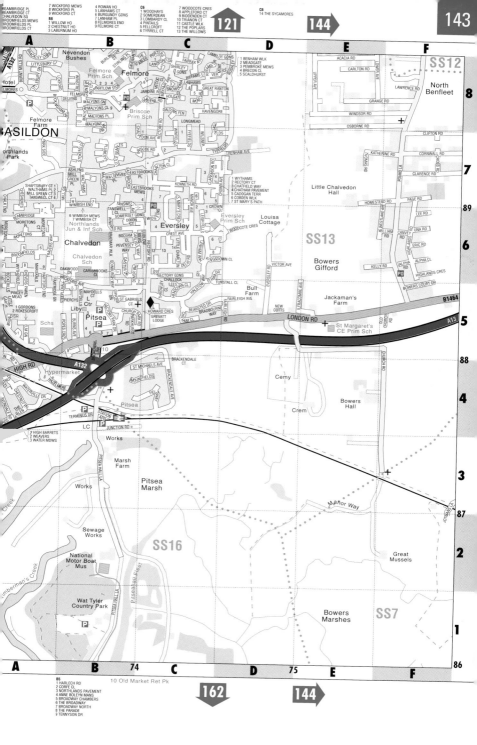

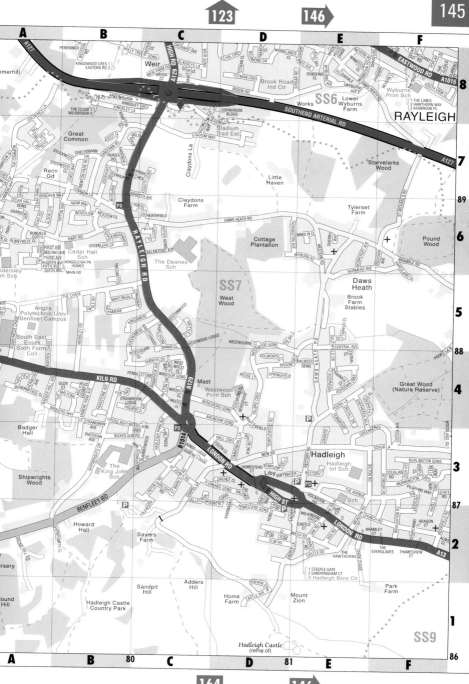

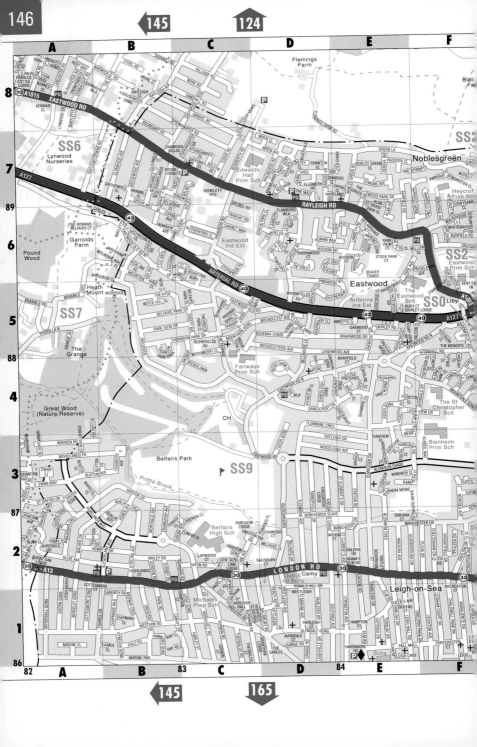

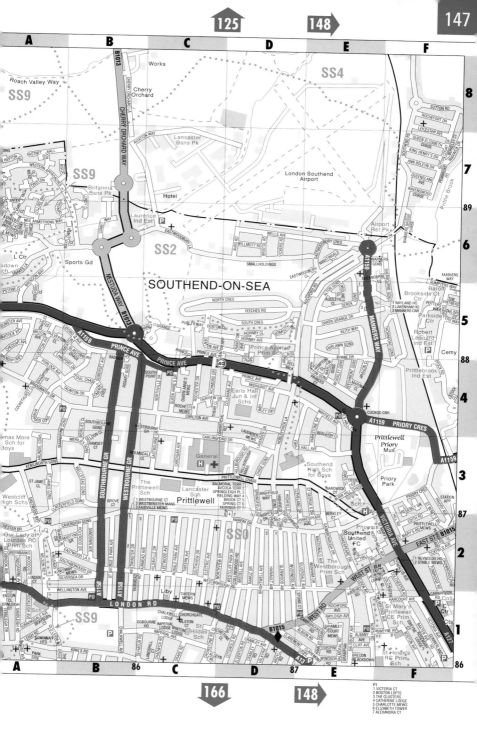

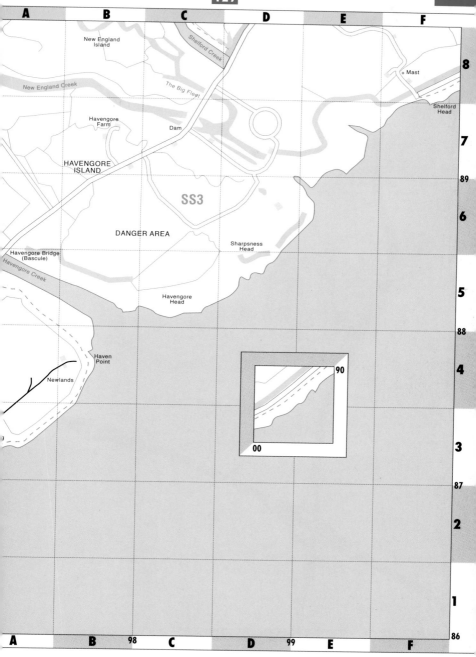

A B C D E F

New England
Island

Shelford Creek

8

New England Creek

The Big Fleet

Mast

Shelford
Head

Havengore
Farm

Dam

7

HAVENGORE
ISLAND

89

SS3

6

DANGER AREA

Sharpsness
Head

Havengore Bridge
(Bascule)

Havengore Creek

Havengore
Head

5

88

Haven
Point

4

90

Newlands

00

3

87

2

87

1

86

A B 98 C D 99 E F

157

139

A B C D E F

8

Bullens & Herds

Blankets Farm

Home Farm

Hatch Farm

Bulphan CE Prim Sch

Brandon Hall

Bulphan

Caylock's Farm

7

Corner Farm

FEN LA

Stone Hall

PH

RM14

The Elms Farm

85

Fen Farm

Bulphan Fen

Judds Farm

Greystead

6

The Downes

Stringcock Fen

5

PARKER'S FARM RD

84

Castle's Gorse

4

RM15

Fen Covert

Mar Dyke

3

Orsett Fen

83

Hobletts

RM16

2

The Decoy

FEN LA

1

Poplars Farm

GREEN LA

FEN LA

Works

82

61 A 62 B C 63 D E F

A B C D E F

8

GRAYS AVE
BLACKHEATH CHASE
Larkspur
Green Trees Farm
Old Hill
The Briars
Great Sutton Wood
Northlands Wood
Langdon Hills Country Park

Milo

7
Gary Owen Poultry Farm
Sutton Hall Farm
SS16

Tyelands Farm

85
B1007

6
The Chase

Wrens Park Farm

STRUAN AVE

5

84
Greenacres Farm

Arden Hall

4
B1007
NORTH HILL

EARNABY WAY 1
BYRD WAY 2
DOWLAND CL 3
DELIUS WAY 4
PURCELL WAY 5

St JOHNS MEWS
Liby
Park
Arthur Bugler Jun & Inf Schs

3
PH
SAFFRON CL
SOUTH HILL CRES
SS17
Balstonia

83
A1014
PLASHET CL
O'DONOGHUE HO
THE GLEN
THE MOUNT

2
The Gables
Horndon House
THE MANORWAY
Hassenbrook Sch
SANCTUARY GDN
BEVIN WLK

Saffron Garden Cottages
KINGS PAR 1
RUNNYMEDE CT 2
RECTORY TERR 3
St Joseph's RC Prim Sch
PARTRIDGE CT

1
OLD JENKINS CL 1
ROMSEY CL 2
Liby
Stanford-le-Hope
HASSENBROOK CT
Stanford-le-Hope Prim Sch
Ivy Wall House
Sports Gd
PH

St MARGARET'S AVE
1 THE PRECINCT
2 WENDOVER CT
3 THE GREEN
4 WALKERS SQ
Recn Gd
Stanford-le-Hope

82
67 A B 68 C D 69 E F

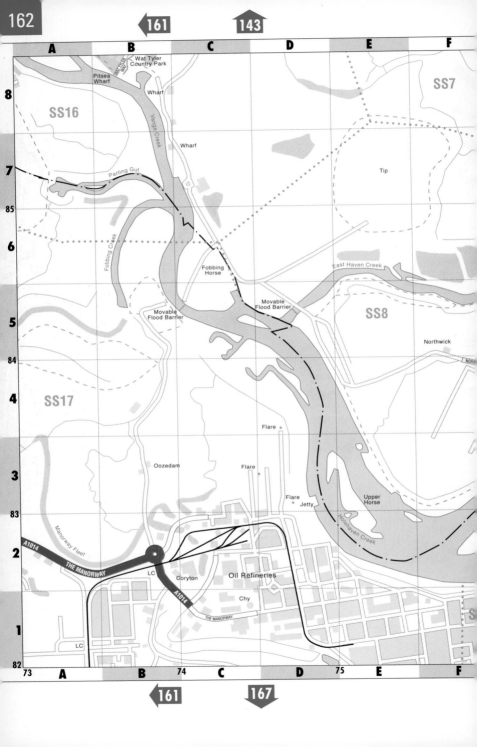

A B C D E F

8

SS16

SS7

Pitsea
Wharf

Wat Tyler
Country Park

Wharf

Vange Creek

Wharf

7

Parting Gut

Tip

85

Fobbing Creek

6

East Haven Creek

Fobbing
Horse

Movable
Flood Barrier

SS8

5

Movable
Flood Barrier

Northwick

84

NORT

4

SS17

3

Oozedam

Flare

Flare

Upper
Horse

83

Flare

Jetty

Holehaven Creek

Manorway Fleet

2

A1014

THE MANORWAY

LC

A1014

Coryton

Oil Refineries

Chy

THE MANORWAY

1

LC

82

73 A B 74 C D 75 E F

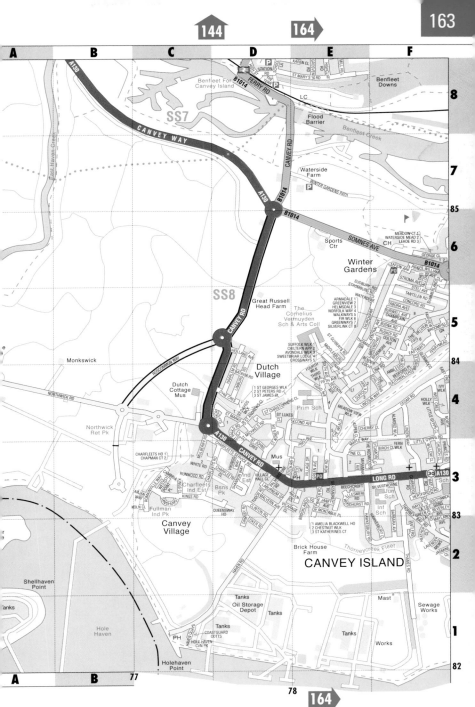

SS9

Belton Hills
Belton Gardens
MARINE PAR
RECTORY GR
PO
Belton Way E
SANS SOUCI
North St
Schs
Belton Way W
ST CLEMENT'S
Broadway W
Liby
Castle Dr
Belton Gdns
Leigh Park Ct
Broadway
Leigh
Playing
Field
Leigh-on-Sea
High St
Ho
Leigh
Cockle Sheds
The
Leigh Cliffs
Belton
Bridge
Alley Dock
New Rd
Gardens
Cliff Par
Leigh Creek
Leigh
Heritage
Ctr

1 BARYTA CT
2 THE TERRACE
3 PLEASANT TERR
4 NORMAN PL
5 NORMAN TERR
6 HILLSIDE RD

ESTUARY CT 1
RICHMOND CT 2
GRAND COURT W 3
SOUTHDOWN CT 4

MAPLE AVE
GRAND PAR
REGATTA
CT
UNDERCLIFF GDNS

Sewage
Works
Leigh Marsh

SOUTHEND-ON-SEA

Two Tree Island /
Nature Reserve

8

85

7

6

5

84

4

3

83

2

1

82

Oyster Creek

SS8

Canvey Point

Leighbeck
Point

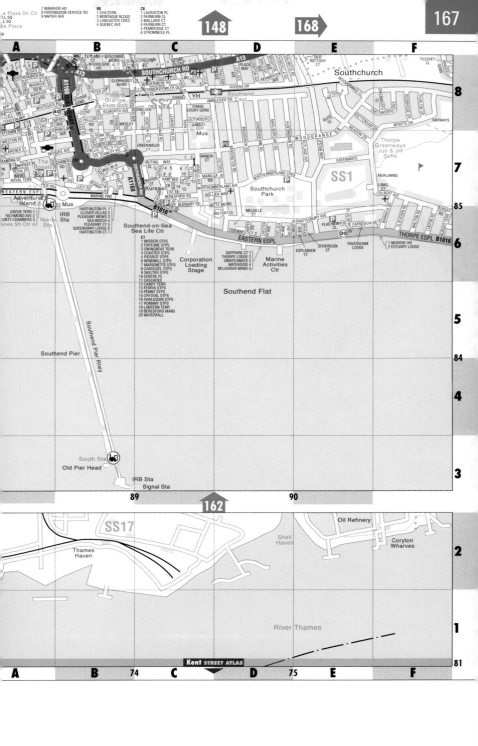

148

168

a Plaza Sh Ctr | 7 WARRIOR HO
LL SQ | 8 FARRINGDON SERVICE RD
L SQ | 9 NAPIER AVE
a Plaza

B8
1 CHILTERN
2 MONTAGUE BLDGS
3 LANCASTER CRES
4 QUEBEC AVE

C8
1 LAURISTON PL
2 FAIRBURN CL
3 MALLARD CT
4 FAIRBURN CT
5 PEMBRIDGE CT
6 STROMNESS PL

Southchurch

SS1

Southend-on-Sea
Sea Life Ctr

Southend Flat

Southend Pier

Southend Pier Rlwy

Old Pier Head

South Sta
IRB Sta
Signal Sta

SS17

Thames
Haven

Oil Refinery

Coryton
Wharves

Shell
Haven

River Thames

162

Kent STREET ATLAS

8
81
7
81
6
5
80
4
8
3
79
2
1
78

A B C D E F

RM9

Car Compounds

Jetty

Hornchurch Shoot

Halfway Reach

Jetty

Wharf

Jenningtree Point

Burts Wharf

Belvedere Ind Est

DA17

EASTERN WAY

PICARDY MANORWAY

HAILEY RD

Hailey Road Bsns Pk

B253

YARNTON WAY
WATERFIELD CL
SUTHERLAND PL
MAIDA RD
CALDY RD
Liby
STATION RD N
Railway Pl
DYLAN RD
MONARCH RD
PICARDY ST
NETHEWODE CT
THORNTON RD
AMBROOK RD
MORDEN RD
B253

Schs

Belvedere Nethewode Trad Est

Capital Ind Est

Elbourne Trad Est
KEATS RD
FISHER'S WAY
CANNINGTOWN
ANDERSON WAY
ST THOMAS RD
CLAYTONVILLE TERR
MIA FERRY WAY
CHURCH MANORWAY

Belvedere Link Bsns Pk

VIKING WAY

CABLES

Wharf

Wharf

Wharf

Mill

Pier

Pier

Pier

RM13

Rainham Marshes

River Thames

Erith Reach

Frog Island

Jetty

Jetty

Jetty

London Loop

P

LOWER RD
METHUEN RD
PARKSIDE RD
B213
BRONZE AGE WAY
50
PICARDY RD
B250
Liby
PICARDY ST
B253
Schs
HALT ROBIN LA
HALT ROBIN RD
REGENT CT
MITRE CT
EARDLEY RD
PROSPECT
DAVID COFFER CT
CLABBURNS
ROBERTS CT
CHAPMAN RD
WADEVILLE
LUMLEY CL
STILES

Green Chain Walk

Belvedere

Frank's Park

Bexley Coll

Trinity Sch

Pembroke Sch

Pembroke Par

Hillside

TOWER RD

David Coffer Ct

PARKSIDE LODGE

Parkside Lodge

ERITH RD

CH RD A206

A206

Belvedere Heath Prim & Sch

Bexley Coll

Lessness Heath

WADEVILLE
CHAPMAN RD
LUMLEY CL
STILES
SILVER SPRING CL
PILSTON RD
VICTORIA RD
FULL WAY
HILL WAY
ATHOL RD
DE LUCI RD
BLVDK
A206 FRASER RD
Madford

DA8

Jessett Cl
ST FRANCIS RD
CORINTHIAN MANORWAY
Wharf
Wharf

ERITH

Wharf

STONEWOOD

Coldharbour Point

Jetty

Wharf

Wharf

Pier

BOSWORTH HO
STONE
CT WATERS EDGE CT GARDEN WHARF

1 BLYTH HO
2 CUTTER HO
3 MACARTHUR CL
4 FRANCIS CT
5 WINDRISH CT
6 VICTORY LODGE
7 TRITON CT
8 SCHOONER HO
9 DRAKE POINT
10 CORRAL HTS
11 PLEASANT VIEW
12 WHARF HO
13 TRAMWAY HO

ST JOHNS CT
SYCAMORE MEWS
SYCAMORE CT
Europa Trad Est

Erith

P

Liby Mus

10 CAMDEN CT
11 NEWNHAM LODGE
12 COURT LODGE
13 FLAXMAN CT
14 HERTFORD WLK
15 RIVERVIEW CT
16 LESSNESS RD
1 BLETCHINGTON CT
2 BRUSHWOOD LODGE

3 UPPER SHERIDAN RD
4 WILLIAM CT
5 SAMSON CT
6 COWPER RD
7 VENMEAD CT
A3
1 CRESSINGHAM CT
2 TELFORD HO
3 KELVIN HO
4 FARADAY HO

5 JENNER HO
6 KEIR HARDIE HO
7 LENNOX HO
8 MARY MACARTHUR HO
9 ELIZABETH GARRETT ANDERSON HO
10 WILLIAM SMITH HO
11 BADEN POWELL HO
12 BAIRD HO
13 BOYLE HO
14 MARY SLESSOR HO

A13

A1306

NEW RD

B1335

WENNINGTON RD

LANDING LA

LC

P

LAMSON RD.

PLOVER HO 1
CURLEW HO 2
JACK SNIPE HO 3
RED SHANK HO 4

WANTZ LA
LAMBS LANE S

DERI AVE

The Chafford Sch

Brady Prim Sch

South Hall Farm

Southall Bridge

NEW COTTS

East Hall Farm

EAST HALL LA

CHURCH LANE

Channel Tunnel Rail Link

LAUNDRY COTTS
MARINE COTTS
KENT VIEW
THE GREEN

Wennington Hall Farm

B1335

PH

The Willows

RM

SAND

NEW RD

Rainham Marshes

RM13

Silt Lagoons

Nature Reserve

Wennington

Wennington Marshes

RM15

Thurrock Commercial Pk

Pur In

Thurrock Camm Cl

COLDHARBOUR LA

Aveley Marshes

Purfleet Rifle Ranges

RM19

P

Freightmaster Est

River Thames

RAPIER CL

TANK

LONDI PU

Erith Rands

Crayford Ness

Mast

Darent Valley Path

DA8

Darent Ind Pk

Kent STREET ATLAS

DAYTON DR

LANDAU WAY

BURNETT RD

8

81

7

6

5

80

4

3

79

2

78

1

A

B

C

D

E

F

52

53

54

A   B   C   D   E   F

8
81
7
6
81
5
80
4
3
79
2
78
1

Bretts Farm

PH

Moor Hall

Oak Wood

Long Pond

Ash Plantation

Kenningtons Prim Sch

PINFOLDS
WAYMANS
MERESMANS
HAYWARDS
FRANKLINS

GONS
STIFFEN RD
OAK RD
ROXFORD RD

P

SHANNON WAY
PERRY
GDNS
MONNOW GN
NETHAN DR

Belhus Park

CH

Dilkes Prim Sch

IRVING CLOSE
HUMBER AVE
LOMAN PATH
ERRIFF DR
HAMEL CL

LOMAN PATH
GATEHOPE DR
FRANCES GDNS
CARROLL CL
GROVES CL
FIELD CL
FULBROCK
B1335

The Aveley Sch

Aveley

ST PAUL
ST PAUL

SANDY LA

AVELEY BY-PASS

Sports Gd

RM15

Ponds Farm

PURFLEET RD

TOPLANDS AVE
BLENHEIM
LOWLANDS
THE ROWANS
ARNHEM AVE
MYRTLE DRI
CRESCENT RD
CENTRAL AVE
KENT VIEW
PEMBROKE DR
CLARE AVE
BEVIN HO 1
THE PARADE 2
LEEHOLM HO 3

ST MICHAELS
BUCHANAN
KELLY RD
MANOR RD
HANKY RD
MANOR CL
FIELD RD
HALL CRES
HALL RD
HALL TERR
TALL RD
CRESCENT WLK

MARTIN RD
DACRE CRES
ELM RD
HESTER CL
HIGH ST
CHURCH VIEW
DYKE

PARK VIEW
BROOME PL
STANFORD RD
LENNARD RD
LENNARD ROW
LENNARD HO

Liby
MANOR CL S
THE SYCAMORES
NEW MALTINGS

BROOME PL COMPLEX

STIFFORD RD

Hangman's Wood

30

A13

RM16

Oak Wood

Aveley Prim Sch

Fann's Farm

Sports Gd

PURFLEET INDUSTRIAL ACCESS RD

LC

THE CARAVAN SITE

Mar Dyke

SOUTH WAY
BACK LA

Causeway Bridge

Thurrock Service Area

A1306

A R T E R I A L R O A D P U R F L E E T

CARTEL CL
WATT'S WOOD
Broomhill

A1306

THURROCK

WEST THURROCK WAY
B186

TANK HILL RD
WATER LA
CORNWALL GATE
TANK LA

THE QUADRANT
WOOD AVE
NORTH RD
KATTS RD
BRAMBLE CL
GABION
BAILEY CL
MANOR RD

79

2

Purfleet

BOTANY
Beacon Hill Ind Est
Channel Tunnel Rail Link
PURFLEET BY-PASS

RM19

CON HILL
OAKHILL RD
LINNEL WAY
KENDAL
CONISTON AVE
JOSLIN RD
High House

STONEHOUSE LA

Neptune Bsns Pk
Dolphin Motorway Est

RM20

DOLPHIN WAY

Tunnel Est

CENTRAL AVE
WESTON AVE

A1090

A1090
Dolphin Point

M25

Freightways
The Glade Bsns Ctr

EASTERN AVE
BARCLAY WAY
JODRELL WAY

LC
Beacon Hill
Purfleet

A1090

78

A   B   56   C   D   57   E   F

B1
1 RIVERVIEW TERR
2 SUSSEX TERR
3 SOUTHLAND TERR
4 DUNCOMBE CT
5 HEBERDEN CT
6 WINGROVE DR
7 HOWBURGH CT
8 TRAYFORD CT
9 STORAS CT

10 SAWSTON CT
11 KYRKLY CT
12 BRADFIELD CT
13 RIVERVIEW FLATS
14 WROXALL CT
15 ROOKLEY CT
16 DUNNOSE CT
17 BRANSTONE CT
18 SHORWELL CT
19 BRIGHSTONE CT

20 BONCHURCH CT

A | B | C | D | E | F

8

The Ockendon Sch
ARCHERS
ARISDALE AVE
MOSS RD
30
B186
Bonnygate Prim Sch
Garden Ctr
Knowlton Cotts
Water Spo
Ctr

Beacon Hill Sch
ANNILEE AVE
Mardyke Country Park

Liby
DART GN
ASHDON
BUCKLES LA

7
DERWENT PAR
South Ockendon
RM15
30
Shaw Prim Sch
AVON GN
BINGHAM
Little Palmer's Shaw

Dilkes Park
JACK EVANS
FAYMORE GDNS
Great Palmer's Shaw

81
Holy Cross RC Prim Sch
KENNET
BROXBURN CT
COLNE
CHEL
CH
Hill Farm
Mushroom Farm

FULLARTON CRES
GARDON AVE
HELFORD CT
Ford Place
North Stifford
COPPID HALL
Hotel

6
STIFFORD RD
40
B1335
Stifford Bridge
Mar Dyke
HIGH RD
MERMAN CL

B1335
CARNACH GN
CHERWELL GDNS
Mast

Works
Millard's Garden
CORVE
CLAYBURN GDNS
CRANELL GN
CHANLOCK PATH 1
BROXBURN PAR 2
CANDER WAY 3
CULLEN
Stifford Bridge

5
Low Well Wood
Brannett's Wood
STIFD HILL
PILGRIMS LA
PH
BROWNS COTTS
Recn Gd

80
A13
Brickbarn Wood
Combe Wood
Davy Down
GUARDIAN AVE
COCKETHORPE CL
TREACLE RD

Oak Wood
RM19
B186
ARTERIAL RD NORTH STIFFORD

4
RM16
Motor Sport Complex
A126
Cvn Pk
WARREN TERR
DUDLEY CL
Tudor Co Prim Sch

3
A1306
ARTERIAL RD WEST THURROCK
P P
Superstore
GRIFON
TRELAWNEY PL
BURGHLEY RD
Visitor Ctr
Chafford Gorges Nature Park
DRAKE RD
MERLIN
Chafford Hundred

Hypermarket
NIGHTINGALE
GABRIEL CL
GILBERT CL
GIRONA CL

Lakeside Sh Ctr
Warren Prim Sch
HAYLEY
HAMPTON CL
RM16
SYLVAN CL
WARREN LA

79
Lakeside Ret Pk
BROMPTON WLK
FENNER RD
HATTON CL
HEPBURN CL
Outdoor Pursuits Ctr
BROADMAYNE
MOSS BANK

GREBE CREST
LAKE RISE
PO
KERSHAW CL
VICTORY CL
Depot

2
B186
Lake Rise Trad Est
B146
SAFFRON
FLOW CL
Chafford Hundred
LENDZ
SAN JUAN DR
Depot
RM
ADSTO
DE GREY
PRIOR

WEST THURROCK WAY
B186
Prim Sch
PLYMOUTH CL
HODGES CL
HOPE WELL CL
PORTSMOUTH CL
MOORE AVE
WINGLE
ASKERS FARM RD
Stifford Prim Sch

1
RM20
Frogmore Est
Chafford Hundred Bsns & Ent Coll
MAYFLOWER CL
PHILIP SYDNEY CL
PHILIP SYDNEY CL
HART CNR
PALMERSTON GDNS
South Stifford
Cliffside Ind Est
BELMONT RD

MOTHERWELL WAY
A125
Magnet Point
HAYTERR 1
HOPE TERR 2
HARE TERR 3
HIND TERR 4

78
Works

58 | A | 59 | B | C | 60 | D | E | F

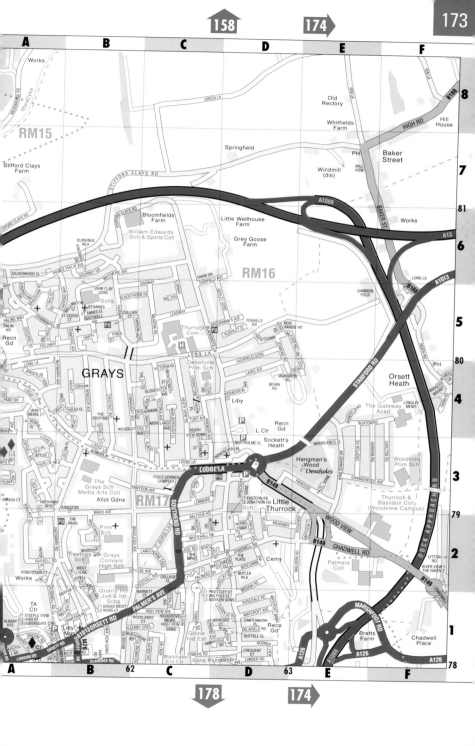

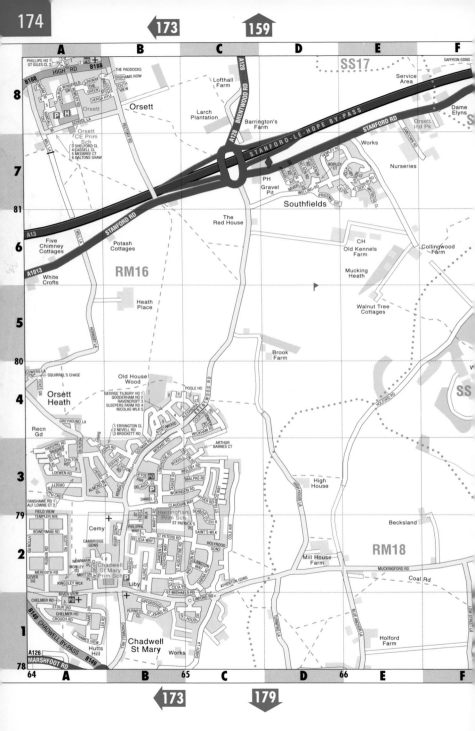

A B C D E F

8
7
81
6
5
80
4
3
79
2
1
78

Kent STREET ATLAS

A B 68 C D 69 E F

ANFORD RD A1013
Singlewell
Mayland
CH
St Cleres Hall
St Clere's Sch
PROSPECT AVE
WILSON RD
NITON CT
CHALE CT
BROADHOUSE RD
WHITWELL CT
FAIRVIEW GDNS
THE GROVE
CRES
KING EDWARD'S RD
Cemy
Sewage Works
Thames Haven Junction
LC
The Warren
WHARF RD
Ind Pk
Mucking
MUCKING WHARF RD
Stanford Marshes Nature Reserve
81
Bluehouse Farm
Sluice
Mucking Creek
SS17
Golden Cottages
WALTON'S HALL RD
Mucking Marshes
Travelling Crane
Jetty
Walton Hall Farm Mus
Walton's Hall
Turner's Farm
Sutton's Farm
Linford
HAMPSHIRE GDNS
DORSET GDNS
PO
PH
RM18
LC
East Tilbury
ALEXANDRA WAY
SEVERN
DERWENT
COLNE
COLNE CT
CORONATION
ROMAN
TORRIDGE
WELLAND
TYNE
CALDER
ORWELL
STRATH
ROACH
QUEEN MARY AVE
KENSINGTON GDNS
CORONATION
STANFORD RD
BATA AVE
GLOUCESTER AVE
Liby
Sewage Works
River Thames
East Tilbury Inf Sch
East Tilbury Jun Sch
Thames Ind Pk
East Tilbury
East Tilbury Marshes
Sand & Gravel Pit

A B C D E F

8

LONDON ROAD PURFLEET
A1090
CONISTON AVE
AMBLESIDE
ULVERSTON
KESWICK GDNS
LINDEN CL
HUTSON TERR
Stonehouse LA
London Road West Thurrock
STONEHOUSE CNR
A1090
A282
EASTERN
Tu
Waterglac
Ind Pk

Jetty
Mills LC
LC
Purfleet
LC
JARRAH COTTS
LC
Channel Tunnel Rail Link
Weston Ave
ST CLEMENT'S WAY
Thurrock Bsns Ctr
Bridge View Ind Est
OLIVER CL

RM19

7

Jetties
Purfleet Thames Terminal
Works
COSGROVE RD
OLIVER RD

RM20

77

Wharf
Jetties

6

Sewage Works
Long Reach
Jetty
River Thames
Jetties

5

Littlebrook Power Sta
Jetty
Dartford Tunnel
CANTERBURY WAY
Queen Elizabeth II Bridge
Dartford Crossing
Jetties

76

Kent STREET ATLAS

DA1

4

A206 Erith
Littlebrook Nature Reserve
MARSH ST
A206
BOB DUNN WAY
CORNWALL RD
Cemy
CHAUCER WAY
WODEHOUSE RD
WORDSWORTH WAY
HARDY AV
WORDSWORTH WAY
SHELL CRES
Edisons Pk
Crossways
CLIPPER BLVD
GALLION RD
CLIPPER RD
Hotel

3

WILKINSON CL
REESTON CT
ORFORD CT
BR
MACMILLAN GDNS
NIGHTINGALE
PEPYS CL
SHERIDAN CT
River View
COLERIDGE CT
SHAKESPEARE RD
P
Toll Booths
MARSHFOOT BLVD
MANOR BLVD
SKANOR RD
GALLEON BLVD
CROSSWAYS BLVD
NEWMAN RD
PO
Freightliner Terminal
CLARE CGR

DA2

75

ST EDMUNDS CT
ST GRIMES
PILGRIMS
FOXGLOVE HO
PATTERSON
Sch
SMITH
CL
BRIDGE
MANOR WAY
MAISEY CL
LITTLEBROOK MANOR WAY
1A
B2228
St Mary's Rd
Stone Crossing
ORCHARD TERR
ELIZABETH ST
LOWER CHURCH HILL
UPPER CHURCH HILL
RICH HILL
BELL CL
STAFFORD WLK
RICHARDSON
CHARLES ST
SUTHE

2

Temple Hill
KNIGHTS MANOR WAY
CADBURY CRES
DARTFORD
CHALICE
SWALLOW CL
CORN WLK
DA9
St
Sto

1

NORFOLK CL
BEECH ASPEN
REDWOOD CT
CHURCHILL
BOW ARROW LA
FULWICH RD
COLNEY RD
CARRINGTON RD
CARLISLE RD
EDENS CL
M25
HIGH TREES
BRENT CL
INVICTA RD
Bow Arrow
H
Little Brook
The Gateway Prim Sch
B2228
ALAMEIN GDNS
ROSE CT
A226
BEVIS CL
London Rd
30
Recn Gd
B2174
RIVERVIEW CT
Horns Cross
ST JAMES AV
CLIFF REACH
HEDGE PLACE R

74

55 A 56 B C D 57 E F

A2
1 LILAC HO
2 LAVENDER HO

B1
1 DONNINGTON CT
2 DENNY CT
3 BROUGHAM CT
4 BEESTON CT
5 ORFORD CT
6 ALNWICK CT
7 BRAMBER CT
8 KENILWORTH CT
9 WARDOUR CT
10 BERWICK CT
11 STOKESAY CT
12 CONISBOROUGH CT
13 PICKERING CT
14 MIDDLEHAM CT
15 PRUDHOE CT
16 NORHAM CT
17 BOWES CT
18 BARNARD CT
19 TATTERSHALL CT
20 CARISBROOKE CT
21 LONGTOWN CT
22 CLIFTON WLK
23 GALSHOT CT
24 DUNSTER CT
25 LYDFORD CT
26 PEVERIL CT
27 HARDWICK CRES
28 GRANGE CRES

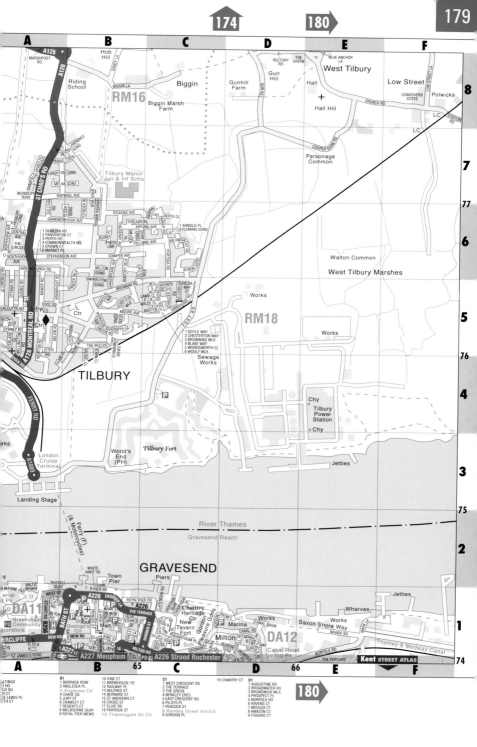

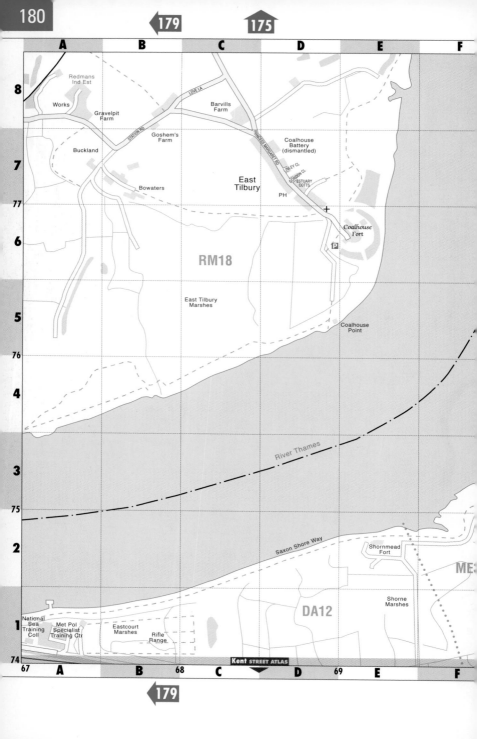

179
175
179

8

7

77

6

5

76

4

3

75

2

1

74

A B C D E F

Redmans
Ind Est

Works

Gravelpit
Farm

Buckland

Goshem's
Farm

Bowaters

LOVE LA

STATION RD

Barvills
Farm

PRINCESS MARGARET RD

East
Tilbury

PH

Coalhouse
Battery
(dismantled)

LINLEY CL

GORDON CL

ESTUARY
COTTS

Coalhouse
Fort

P

RM18

East Tilbury
Marshes

Coalhouse
Point

River Thames

Saxon Shore Way

Shornmead
Fort

DA12

ME

Shorne
Marshes

National
Sea
Training
Coll

Met Pol
Specialist
Training Ctr

Eastcourt
Marshes

Rifle
Range

Kent STREET ATLAS

67 A B 68 C D 69 E F

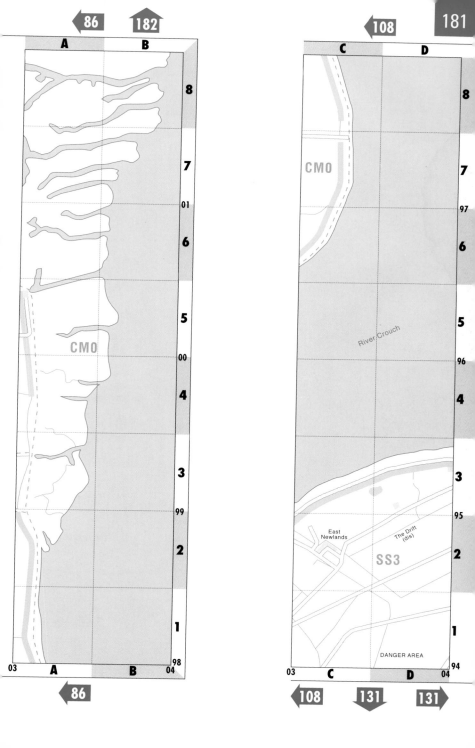

A B

C D

8

8

7

01

7

97

6

6

CMO

CMO

5

5

00

96

River Crouch

4

4

3

3

99

95

East
Newlands

The Drift
(dis)

2

2

SS3

1

1

98

94

03 A B 04

03 C D 04

DANGER AREA

42

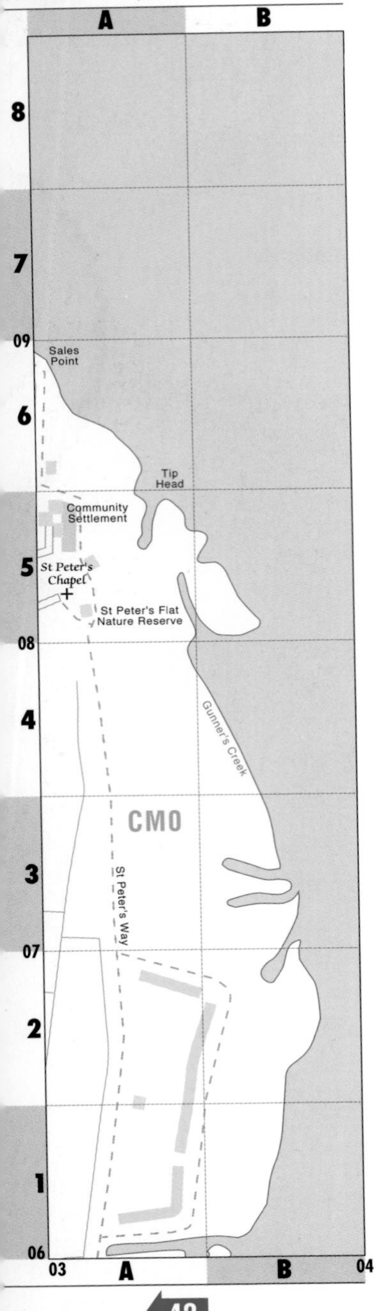

Left map (42)

A   B

8

7

09

Sales
Point

6

Tip
Head

Community
Settlement

St Peter's
Chapel

5

St Peter's Flat
Nature Reserve

08

Gunner's Creek

4

CMO

3

St Peter's Way

07

2

1

06

03   A   B   04

Right map (64)

64

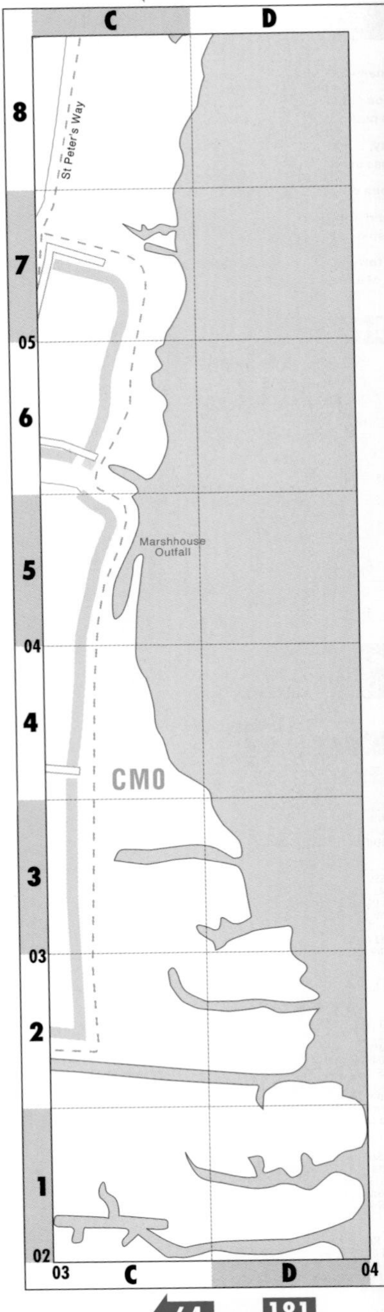

C   D

8

St Peter's Way

7

05

6

Marshhouse
Outfall

5

04

4

CMO

3

03

2

1

02

03   C   D   04

Index

e name May be abbreviated on the map → **Church Rd** **6** Beckenham BR2..........**53** C6

tion number Present when a number indicates the
's position in a crowded area of mapping

lity, town or village Shown when more than one
has the same name

code district District for the indexed place

and grid square Page number and grid reference
standard mapping

s, towns and villages are listed in CAPITAL LETTERS **Public and commercial buildings** are highlighted in magenta
es of interest are highlighted in blue with a star ★

breviations used in the index

Academy	Comm	Common	Gd	Ground	L	Leisure	Prom	Promenade
Approach	Cott	Cottage	Gdn	Garden	La	Lane	Rd	Road
Arcade	Cres	Crescent	Gn	Green	Liby	Library	Recn	Recreation
Avenue	Cswy	Causeway	Gr	Grove	Mdw	Meadow	Ret	Retail
Bungalow	Ct	Court	H	Hall	Meml	Memorial	Sh	Shopping
Building	Ctr	Centre	Ho	House	Mkt	Market	Sq	Square
Bus Business	Ctry	Country	Hospl	Hospital	Mus	Museum	St	Street
Boulevard	Cty	County	HQ	Headquarters	Orch	Orchard	Sta	Station
Cathedral	Dr	Drive	Hts	Heights	Pal	Palace	Terr	Terrace
Circus	Dro	Drove	Ind	Industrial	Par	Parade	TH	Town Hall
Close	Ed	Education	Inst	Institute	Pas	Passage	Univ	University
Corner	Emb	Embankment	Int	International	Pk	Park	Wk, Wlk	Walk
College	Est	Estate	Intc	Interchange	Pl	Place	Wr	Water
Community	Ex	Exhibition	Junc	Junction	Prec	Precinct	Yd	Yard

dex of towns, villages, streets, hospitals, industrial estates, railway stations, schools, pping centres, universities and places of interest

ve SS8 . . . . .164 F3
Prim Sch

. . . . .121 F5
 IG8 . . . . .110 C5
 Wlk RM13 . . . . . .154 F4
 CM1 . . . . .31 E2
RODING 14 E4

M5 . . . . .27 C1
 SS5 . . . . .101 D2
RM1 . . . . .136 A5
es DA17 . . . . . .169 A2
 EN9 . . . . .65 B5
e CI CM17 . . . . .24 C7
elds CM3 . . . . . . .78 B7
 EN9 . . . . .66 A5
ead Ind Est

. . . . .65 C5
rk Ind Est

. . . . .152 C4

G11 . . . . .152 B4
 SS1 . . . . .152 C3
CM12 . . . . .96 F1
9 Ave 177 C2
 SS5 . . . . .101 D1
. . . . .133 D6
ning CM9 . . . . . .36 D4
. . . . .65 C6
od La

. . . . .155 D3

d CM15 . . . . .95 A1
RM13 . . . . .155 C3
SS15 . . . . .119 E1
 Gdns IG8 . . . .110 A3
 Rd IG3 . . . . . . .134 B2
ll Prim Sch

. . . . .160 E3
k SS3 . . . . .168 C8
 SS7 . . . . .145 C5
d Gdns

. . . . .23 D6
h Rd CM3 . . . . .101 E7
d CM9 . . . . .36 F5
e CM11 . . . . .97 C2
d CM18 . . . . . . .23 D5
d Prim Sch

. . . . .23 D6
 SS7 . . . . .145 C5
d Gdns

. . . . .133 A7
G5 . . . . .132 F8

Abbotts CI
Romford RM7 . . . . . . .135 B8
Southend-on-S SS9 . . . .146 E5
Abbotts Cres E4 . . . . . .109 D6
Abbotts Ct
Romford RM3 . . . . . . .114 F2
Stanstead Abbotts SG12 . . .8 D4
Abbotts Dr
Stanford-le-H SS17 . . . .160 D2
Waltham Abbey EN9 . . . .66 A6
Abbotts Hall Chase
SS17 . . . . .160 E2
Abbotts Pl CM2 . . . . . . .32 D3
Abbotts Rise SG12 . . . . . .8 D4
Abbotts Way SG12 . . . . . .8 D4
Abbs Cross Gdns
RM12 . . . . .136 D3
Abbs Cross La RM12 . . .136 C2
Abbs Cross Sch & Arts
Coll RM12 . . . . .136 C1
Abell Way CM2 . . . . . . .33 B4
Abenberg Way CM13 . . .117 B8
Abensburg Rd SS8 . . . . .164 D5
Abercorn Gdns RM6 . . .134 B5
Abercorn Ho CM3 . . . . . .33 E8
Abercrombie Ho 17
RM3 . . . . .114 D5
Abercrombie Way CM18,
CM19 . . . . .23 C6
Aberdeen Gdns SS9 . . . .146 A2
Aberdour Rd IG3 . . . . . .134 B2
Abigail Ct SS14 . . . . . . .49 A5
Abigail Mews RM3 . . . .114 F1
Abingdon Ct **8** SS13 . . .121 A1
Abinger Cl IG11 . . . . . .153 A8
Abington Ct RM14 . . . .137 C3
Abraham Cohen Ct
IG1 . . . . .133 A5
Abraham Ct RM14 . . . .137 A2
Abraham Fisher Ho
E12 . . . . .152 A7
Abreys SS7 . . . . .145 A7
ABRIDGE 90 A6
Abridge Gdns RM5 . . . .113 A4
Abridge Mews RM4 . . . .90 B6
Abridge Pk RM4 . . . . . .90 A5
Abridge Rd
Chigwell IG7 . . . . .89 C4
Theydon Bois CM16 . . . . .68 A1
Abridge Way IG11 . . . .153 B3
Acacia Ave RM12 . . . . .135 F2
Acacia Ct EN9 . . . . .66 A5

Acacia Dr
Maldon CM9 . . . . .36 F1
Southend-on-S SS1 . . . .168 A8
Upminster RM14 . . . . . .156 A8
Acacia Gdns RM14 . . . .137 F4
Acacia Rd
Basildon SS13 . . . . . . .143 E8
Greenhithe DA9 . . . . . .176 E1
Acacias Ct **12** EN11 . . . .21 A6
Academy Fields Rd
RM2 . . . . .136 B6
Academy Sq **1** RM2 . . .136 B6
Accrington Ho 10
RM3 . . . . .114 D5
Acer Ave RM13 . . . . . .155 D2
Acer Gr CM1 . . . . .32 D4
Acle Cl IG6 . . . . .111 B3
Acorn Cl E4 . . . . .109 B5
Acorn Ct IG2 . . . . .133 E6
Acorn Ctr The IG6 . . . .112 B4
Acorn Mews CM18 . . . . .24 A6
Acorn Pl
Basildon SS16 . . . . . . .141 B5
Maldon CM9 . . . . .36 F5
Acorn St SG12 . . . . .9 D8
Acorns The
Chigwell IG7 . . . . .111 E6
Hockley SS5 . . . . .124 E7
Acorn Trad Ctr RM20 . . .177 E8
Acre Rd RM10 . . . . . . .154 B5
Acres Ave CM5 . . . . .48 F5
Acres End CM1 . . . . .31 E4
Acres Rd CM5 . . . . . . .125 D6
Acre View RM11 . . . . . .136 E7
Addison Ct CM16 . . . . . .68 A8
Addison Gdns RM17 . . .173 C2
Addison Rd
Redbridge IG6 . . . . . . .111 C2
Wanstead E11 . . . . . . .132 A5
Adelaide Gdns
Dagenham RM6 . . . . . .134 E6

Adelaide Gdns *continued*
South Benfleet SS7 . . . . .144 D1
Adelaide Rd
Ilford IG1 . . . . .133 B2
Tilbury RM18 . . . . .178 F6
Adeliza Cl IG11 . . . . . .152 C5
Adelphi Cres RM12 . . . .136 B2
Addington Rd SS8 . . . . .164 C4
Aden Rd IG1 . . . . .133 C4
Adingtons CM20 . . . . . . .10 F2
Admiral Ct IG11 . . . . . .153 C3
Admirals Cl E18 . . . . . .132 B7
Admirals Lo RM1 . . . . .135 F6
Admirals Pl SS0 . . . . . .166 C7
Admirals Way DA12 . . . .179 D1
Admirals Wlk
Chelmsford CM1 . . . . . . .31 F3
Greenhithe DA9 . . . . . .177 B2
Hoddesdon EN11 . . . . . . .21 B4
Southend-on-S SS3 . . . .168 D5
Adnams Wlk RM12 . . . .155 A7
Adomar Rd RM8 . . . . . .134 E1
Adstock Way RM17 . . . .172 F2
Adult Coll of Barking &
Dagenham RM9 . . . . .153 F7
Advent Ct IG8 . . . . . . .109 F5
Adventure Island ★
SS1 . . . . .167 A7
Advice Ave RM16 . . . . .173 A4
Afflets Ct SS14 . . . . . . .142 C8
Afton Dr RM15 . . . . . . .172 B7
Agister Rd IG7 . . . . . . .112 A5
Agnes Ave
Ilford IG1 . . . . .152 B8
Southend-on-S SS9 . . . .146 A3
Agnes Gdns RM8 . . . . . .153 D8
Agricultural/Domestic
Mus ★ CM9 . . . . .38 E7
Aidan Cl RM8 . . . . .153 E8
Ailsa Rd SS0 . . . . .166 C8
AIMES GREEN 43 F2
Ainsley Ave RM7 . . . . .135 C5
Ainslie Ho E4 . . . . .109 A5
Ainslie Wood Cres E4 . . .109 B5
Ainslie Wood Gdns
. . . . .109 B5
Ainslie Wood Prim Sch
E4 . . . . .109 B5
Ainslie Wood Rd E4 . . . .109 B5
Aintree Cres IG6 . . . . . .111 C1
Aintree Gr RM14 . . . . . .136 E3
Airborne Cl SS9 . . . . . .146 E5
Airborne Ind Est SS9 . . .146 E5

Aal-Alb 183

Aire Dr RM15 . . . . .157 B1
Airey Neave Ct RM16 . . .173 A4
Airfield Way RM12 . . . . .155 C6
Airlie Gdns IG1 . . . . . . .133 B3
Airport Ret Pk SS2 . . . .147 E6
Airthrie Rd IG3 . . . . . . .134 B2
Akenfield Cl **8** CM3 . . . .101 E7
Alamein Gdns DA2 . . . .176 D1
Alamein Rd
Burnham-on-C CM0 . . . .106 C4
Chelmsford CM1 . . . . . . .31 F6
Swanscombe DA10 . . . . .177 D1
Alan Cl SS9 . . . . .146 E6
Alan Dr RM7 . . . . .135 A4
Alan Gr SS9 . . . . .146 E6
Albany Ave SS0 . . . . . . .147 E1
Albany Cl CM1 . . . . .31 E5
Albany Ct
Chingford E4 . . . . .87 B3
Epping CM16 . . . . .45 F1
Albany Rd
Dagenham RM6 . . . . . .134 F5
Hornchurch RM12 . . . . .136 A2
Pilgrims Hatch CM15 . . . .94 B3
Rayleigh SS6 . . . . .124 A1
Tilbury RM18 . . . . .179 A6
Wickford SS12 . . . . . . .121 D6
Albany The IG8 . . . . . . .109 F6
Albany The, A Bsns & Ent
Coll RM12 . . . . .136 B2
Albany View IG9 . . . . . . .88 A1
Albert Ho CM17 . . . . . . .11 C1
Albemarle App IG1 . . . .133 B5
Albemarle Cl RM17 . . . .173 A4
Albemarle Gdns IG2 . . . .133 B5
Albemarle Link CM2 . . . .32 F8
Alber Ave E4 . . . . .109 A6
Albert Cl
Grays RM16 . . . . .173 C3
Rayleigh SS6 . . . . .123 F3
Albert Cres E4 . . . . . . .109 A6
Albert Gdns CM17 . . . . .24 D7
Albert Ho **5** E18 . . . . . .132 B8
Albert Mews
Romford RM1 . . . . .135 F5
Southend-on-S SS0 . . . .166 E8

Albert Rd
Buckhurst Hill IG9 . . . . . **110** D8
Bulphan RM14 . . . . **158** F8
Burnham-on-C CM0 . . . . . **106** C4
Dagenham RM8 . . . . **135** A3
Ilford IG1 . . . . **133** C1
Rayleigh SS6 . . . . **123** F3
Rochford SS4 . . . . **125** C7
Romford RM1 . . . . **135** F5
South Benfleet SS7 . . . . . **144** B6
Southend-on-S, Bournes
    Green SS1 . . . . **149** A1
South Woodham Ferrers
    CM3 . . . . **101** D7
Swanscombe DA10 . . . . . **177** F1
4 Wanstead E18 . . . . . **132** B8
Albert St CM14 . . . . **116** C5
Albert Terr IG9 . . . . **110** E8
Albion Cl RM7 . . . . **135** D5
Albion Ct
Billericay CM12 . . . . **97** A1
Chelmsford CM2 . . . . **32** B1
Albion Hill IG10 . . . . **88** D4
Albion Pk IG10 . . . . **88** D4
Albion Rd
Dagenham RM10 . . . . . . **153** F7
Gravesend DA12 . . . . . . **179** D1
South Benfleet SS7 . . . . . **144** D4
Southend-on-S SS0 . . . . . **147** E1
Albion Terr
Gravesend DA12 . . . . . . **179** D1
Sewardstone E4 . . . . **87** B5
Albra Mead CM2 . . . . **33** B4
Albright Ind Est RM13 . . **169** F8
Albury Mews E12 . . . . . . **132** C2
Albyns SS16 . . . . **141** C4
Albyns Cl RM13 . . . . **155** A5
Albyns La RM4 . . . . **91** D7
Alcester Ho **3** RM3 . . . **114** D5
Alcotes SS14 . . . . **142** F5
Aldborough Ct
Chingford E4 . . . . **109** B7
Ilford IG2 . . . . **133** F6
ALDBOROUGH HATCH
. . . . **133** F7
Aldborough Rd
Dagenham RM10 . . . . . . **154** C6
Ilford, Aldborough Hatch
    IG2 . . . . **133** F8
Ilford IG1 . . . . **133** C2
Upminster RM14 . . . . . . **137** A2
Aldborough Rd N IG2 . . . **133** F6
Aldborough Rd S IG3 . . . **133** E4
Aldeburgh Pl IG8 . . . . . . **110** A6
Aldeburgh Way CM1 . . . . **32** D5
Alder Ave RM14 . . . . **155** F8
Alderbury Lea CM3 . . . . . **56** F1
Alder Cl
Basildon SS15 . . . . **119** D1
Hoddesdon EN11 . . . . **21** B8
Alder Dr
Chelmsford CM2 . . . . **54** B6
South Ockendon RM15 . . . **157** C1
Aldergrove Wlk RM12 . . . **155** C6
Alderleys SS7 . . . . **145** A6
Alderman Ave IG11 . . . . . **153** A2
Aldermans Hill SS5 . . . . . **124** C5
Alderman Wlk SS17 . . . . **160** E5
Alderney Gdns SS11 . . . . . **99** C2
Alders Ave IG8 . . . . **109** E4
Aldersbrook Cl E12 . . . . . **132** C2
Aldersbrook La E12 . . . . **132** F1
Aldersbrook Prim Sch
E12 . . . . **132** C2
Alders Cl E11 . . . . **132** B2
Aldersey Gdns IG11 . . . . **152** D6
Aldersgrove EN9 . . . . **65** E5
Alders Wlk CM21 . . . . **1** E2
Alderton Cl
Loughton IG10 . . . . **89** A5
Pilgrims Hatch CM15 . . . . . **94** B4
Alderton Hall La IG10 . . . **89** A5
Alderton Hill IG10 . . . . . . **88** F4
Alderton Jun & Inf Schs
    The IG10 . . . . **89** A5
Alderton Mews IG10 . . . . **89** A5
Alderton Rd RM16 . . . . . **174** E7
Alderton Rise IG10 . . . . . **89** A5
Alderton Way IG10 . . . . . . **88** F4
Alder Wlk IG1 . . . . **152** D7
Alderwood Dr RM6 . . . . . **90** B6
Alderwood Way SS7 . . . . **145** C3
Aldham Dr RM15 . . . . . . **172** C8
Aldham Gdns SS6 . . . . . **122** F3
Aldham Hall **1** E11 . . . . **132** A5
Aldingham Ct RM12 . . . . **155** B7
Aldingham Gdns
RM12 . . . . **155** A7
Aldington Cl RM8 . . . . . . **134** C3
Aldis Mews EN3 . . . . **65** A2
Aldria Rd SS17 . . . . **160** E5
Aldriche Way E4 . . . . **109** C4
Aldridge Ave **7** EN3 . . . . **65** A1
Aldridge Cl CM2 . . . . **33** A4
Aldrin Cl SS17 . . . . **160** E2
Aldrin Way SS9 . . . . **147** A6
Aldwych Ave IG6 . . . . . . **133** C7
Aldwych Cl RM12 . . . . . . **136** B2
Alexander Ct
1 Chelmsford CM1 . . . . **32** F5
Epping CM16 . . . . **67** F8
Romford RM7 . . . . **135** D3

Alexander Hts SS1 . . . . . **168** B8
Alexander La CM15 . . . . . **95** B4
Alexander Mews
Billericay CM12 . . . . **97** B2
Harlow CM17 . . . . **24** D6
Howe Green CM2 . . . . **55** D2
Alexander Rd
Basildon SS16 . . . . **141** B4
Greenhithe DA9 . . . . **177** C2
Alexandra Cl RM16 . . . . **174** C4
Alexandra Ct
7 Southend-on-S SS1 . . **166** F7
7 Southend-on-S SS2 . . **147** F1
Alexandra Ho 1 IG8 . . . . **111** A3
Alexandra Pl 3 RM1 . . . . **135** F5
Alexandra Rd
Brentwood CM14 . . . . . . **116** C7
Burnham-on-C CM0 . . . . . **106** C5
Dagenham RM6 . . . . **134** E5
Great Wakering SS3 . . . . **150** A3
Rainham RM13 . . . . **154** F4
Rayleigh SS6 . . . . **123** F3
Rochford SS4 . . . . **125** C7
Romford RM1 . . . . **135** F5
South Benfleet SS7 . . . . . **144** D2
Southend-on-S, Clifftown
    SS1 . . . . **166** F7
Southend-on-S, Leigh Cliffs
    SS9 . . . . **165** E8
Tilbury RM18 . . . . **178** F5
Wallend E6 . . . . **152** A2
Wanstead E18 . . . . **132** B8
Alexandra St SS1 . . . . . . **167** A7
Alexandra Way RM18 . . . . **175** B3
Alexandria Dr SS6 . . . . . **123** A4
Alf Lowne Ct RM16 . . . . **174** A3
Alford Rd DA8 . . . . **169** C1
Alfreda Ave SS5 . . . . **101** D3
Alfred Gdns SS11 . . . . **99** D1
Alfred Prior Ho 7
E12 . . . . **152** A8
Alfred Rd
Aveley RM15 . . . . **171** C5
Brentwood CM14 . . . . . . **116** D8
Buckhurst Hill IG9 . . . . . **110** D8
Alfred's Gdns IG11 . . . . . **152** E3
Alfred St 5 RM17 . . . . . **178** C8
**Alfred's Way (East Ham &
    Barking By-Pass)**
IG11 . . . . **152** D3
Alfred's Way Ind Est
IG11 . . . . **153** A4
Algars Way CM3 . . . . . . **101** D8
Algers Cl IG10 . . . . **88** D4
Algers Rd IG10 . . . . **88** E4
Alghers Mead IG10 . . . . . . **88** D4
Alibon Gdns RM10 . . . . . **154** A7
Alibon Rd RM10 . . . . **154** A7
Alicia Ave SS11 . . . . **122** A7
Alicia Cl SS11 . . . . **122** A7
Alicia Way SS11 . . . . **122** A7
Alicia Wlk SS11 . . . . **122** A7
Alkerden La DA9,
    DA10 . . . . **177** C1
Allandale SS7 . . . . **145** A7
Allandale Rd RM11 . . . . . **135** F4
Allenby Cres RM17 . . . . . **173** C1
Allenby Dr RM11 . . . . . . **136** F3
Allender Ct 2 RM1 . . . . . **135** D7
Allen Ho CM21 . . . . **1** F2
Allen Rd RM13 . . . . **155** C2
Allens Cl CM3 . . . . **20** F1
Allens Rd CM11 . . . . **98** C5
Allensway SS17 . . . . **160** F3
Allen Way CM2 . . . . **33** B4
Allerton Cl SS4 . . . . **125** C6
Alley Dock SS9 . . . . **165** D8
Alleyn Court Prep Sch
SS3 . . . . **149** A3
Alleyn Court Sch SS0 . . . **147** C1
Alleyndale Rd RM8 . . . . . **134** B7
Alleyn Pl SS0 . . . . **147** C1
Allington Ct CM11 . . . . . **119** C7
Allis Mews 5 CM17 . . . . . **11** C1
Allison Cl CM9 . . . . **66** A7
Allistonway SS17 . . . . . . **160** F3
Allmains Cl EN9 . . . . **44** B6
Allnutts Rd CM16 . . . . **68** A6
Alloa Rd IG3 . . . . **134** A2
All Saints Church
DA10 . . . . **177** F2
All Saints Cl
Chelmsford CM1 . . . . **32** E4
Chigwell IG7 . . . . **112** A7
Doddinghurst CM15 . . . . . **72** B3
Swanscombe DA10 . . . . . **177** F2
**All Saints Maldon CE Prim
    Sch** CM9 . . . . **36** E2
**All Saints RC Sch & Tech
    Coll** RM8 . . . . **135** A3
Allsum Wlk CM12 . . . . **96** F5
Alma Ave
Chingford E4 . . . . **109** C3
Hornchurch RM12 . . . . . **136** E1
Alma Cl
South Benfleet SS7 . . . . . **146** A2
Wickford SS12 . . . . **121** A6
Alma Dr CM1 . . . . **32** A2
Alma Link CM12 . . . . **97** A1
Alma Rd
South Benfleet SS7 . . . . . **146** A2
Swanscombe DA10 . . . . . **177** F2
Almere SS7 . . . . **144** D4
Almond Ave
Hullbridge SS5 . . . . **101** E4
Wickford SS12 . . . . **121** C7
Almond Cl RM16 . . . . . . **174** A3

Almond Ho IG10 . . . . **88** F6
Almonds Ave IG9 . . . . . . **110** A8
Almshouses CM14 . . . . . **115** E8
Almshouses The 3
IG11 . . . . **152** C6
**Almshouses (Whitakers
    Charity)** RM10 . . . . . . **88** F8
Al-Noor Muslim Prim Sch
IG3 . . . . **134** B3
Alnwick Cl SS16 . . . . **140** F5
Alnwick Ct 6 DA2 . . . . . **176** B1
Alonso Ho 4 DA17 . . . . . **169** A1
Alp Ct SS13 . . . . **150** A3
Alpha Cl SS13 . . . . **143** F6
Alpha Rd
Basildon SS13 . . . . **143** F6
Brentwood CM13 . . . . **95** D3
Burnham-on-C CM0 . . . . . **106** C5
Chingford E4 . . . . **109** B7
Alracks SS15 . . . . **141** E6
Alresford Gn SS12 . . . . . **121** E6
Alston Cl SS0 . . . . **147** C1
Altar Pl 5 SS15 . . . . **141** C7
Altham Gr CM20 . . . . **10** F3
ALTHORNE **83** A3
Althorne St SS13 . . . . . . **121** B1
Althorne Sta CM3 . . . . . **104** F8
Althorne Way
Canewdon SS4 . . . . **104** E2
Dagenham RM10 . . . . . . **135** A2
Althorpe Cl SS5 . . . . **124** D6
Alton Gdns SS2 . . . . **147** E5
Aluric Cl RM16 . . . . **174** B2
Alverstoke Rd RM3 . . . . . **114** E3
Alverstone Rd E12 . . . . . **152** A8
Alveston Sq 12 E18 . . . . **110** A1
Alwen Gr RM15 . . . . **172** B8
Alwyne Ave CM15 . . . . . . **95** A3
Alyssum Cl CM1 . . . . **33** A6
Amanda Cl IG7 . . . . **111** D4
Amanda Ct E4 . . . . **109** E4
Amanda Mews RM7 . . . . **135** C6
Amazon Ct 8 DA12 . . . . **179** D1
Amber Ct 5 RM1 . . . . . . **135** E6
Amberden SS15 . . . . **141** D5
Amber La IG6 . . . . **111** D4
Amberley Rd IG9 . . . . **88** C1
Amberley Way RM7 . . . . **135** B7
Ambrey Ct CM20 . . . . **10** C1
Ambleside
Epping CM16 . . . . **68** A8
Purfleet RM19 . . . . **176** C8
Ambleside Ave RM12 . . . **155** B7
Ambleside Dr SS1 . . . . . **167** D8
Ambleside Gdns
Hullbridge SS5 . . . . **101** D2
Redbridge IG4 . . . . **132** E6
Ambleside Wlk SS6 . . . . **163** F5
Ambrook Rd DA17 . . . . . **169** A3
Amcotes Pl CM2 . . . . **54** C8
Ameland Rd SS8 . . . . . . **164** A6
Amelia Blackwell Ho
SS8 . . . . **163** E3
America St CM9 . . . . **37** A2
Amersham Ave SS16 . . . **140** F5
Amersham Ct RM3 . . . . . **114** F4
Amersham Dr RM3 . . . . . **114** F4
Amersham Gdns RM3 . . . **114** F4
Amersham Wlk RM3 . . . . **114** F4
Amery Gdns RM2 . . . . . . **136** D8
Amesbury EN9 . . . . **66** A7
Amesbury Cl CM16 . . . . . . **67** F8
Amesbury Dr E4 . . . . **87** B3
Amesbury Rd
Dagenham RM9 . . . . **153** D5
Epping CM16 . . . . **67** F8
Ames Rd DA10 . . . . **177** E1
Amherst Lo 6 CM20 . . . . **10** C1
Amidas Gdns RM8 . . . . . **153** B8
Amid Rd SS8 . . . . **164** C5
Amoss Rd CM7 . . . . **2** F1
Ampers End SS14 . . . . . **142** D6
Ampthill Rd 2 RM3 . . . . **114** D5
AMWELL **8** A6
Amwell Ct
Hoddesdon EN11 . . . . **21** A7
Waltham Abbey EN9 . . . . . **65** E6
Amwell La SS12 . . . . **121** B8
Amwell St EN11 . . . . **21** A7
Amwell View Sch SG12 . . . **8** B4
Anchorage Hill CM9 . . . . . **37** A3
Anchorage The
Burnham-on-C CM0 . . . . . **106** C3
Canvey Island SS8 . . . . . **164** B1
Great Wakering SS3 . . . . **150** A3
Anchorage View CM0 . . . . **62** D7
Anchor Bvd DA2 . . . . . . **176** D3
Anchor Cl IG11 . . . . **153** B2
Anchor Dr RM13 . . . . . . **155** B2
Anchor Ho IG3 . . . . **134** A1
Anchor La
Abbess Roding CM5 . . . . . **14** C4
Canewdon SS4 . . . . **104** E1
Heybridge CM9 . . . . **37** A5
Anchor Lane Cotts
SS4 . . . . **104** E1
Anchor Par SS4 . . . . **104** E1
Anchor Reach CM3 . . . . . **101** E5
Anchor St CM2 . . . . **32** B2
Anders Fall SS9 . . . . **147** A6
Anderson Ave CM1 . . . . . **31** F5
Anderson Ho 1 IG11 . . . . **152** D3
Anderson Rd IG8 . . . . . . **132** D8
Andersons SS7 . . . . **160** F3
Andersons Ind Est
SS12 . . . . **121** D4
Anderson Way DA17 . . . . **169** C4

Andrea Ave RM16 . . . . . **173** A4
Andrew Cl
Redbridge IG6 . . . . **111** D3
Stanford-le-H SS17 . . . . . **160** D4
Andrews Cl IG9 . . . . **110** C8
Andrews Pl CM1 . . . . **31** F3
Andromeda Ct RM3 . . . . **114** C4
Andy Hill Ho CM14 . . . . . **116** B6
Andyk Rd SS8 . . . . **164** E3
Anerley Rd SS0 . . . . **166** D8
Angel Cl SS16 . . . . **142** D3
Angel Terr SS3 . . . . **149** D1
Angel Way RM1 . . . . **135** E6
Angle Gn RM4 . . . . **134** C3
Angle Rd RM20 . . . . **177** D8
Anglesea Ctr 8 DA11 . . . **179** B1
Anglesea Pl 2 DA11 . . . . **179** B1
Anglesey Dr RM13 . . . . . **155** A1
Anglesey Gdns SS12 . . . **121** F5
Angle The 5 SS9 . . . . . . **10** C1
Anglia Cl 1 RM8 . . . . . . **134** D3
Anglia Ctr The RM13 . . . . **169** E8
Anglian Ind Est IG11 . . . **153** A1
**Anglia Polytechnic Univ
    Benfleet Campus**
SS7 . . . . **145** A5
Anglia Poly Univ
Chelmsford CM1 . . . . **32** B2
Chelmsford CM1 . . . . **32** B4
Anglia Wlk E6 . . . . **152** A4
Anglo-European Sch
CM4 . . . . **74** C4
Angmering Ho 1
RM3 . . . . **114** D5
Anjou Gn CM1 . . . . **33** A7
Annabel Cl RM12 . . . . . . **136** C3
Annabell Ave RM16 . . . . **174** D7
Annalee Gdns RM15 . . . . **172** B8
Annalee Rd RM15 . . . . . **172** B8
Annan Way RM1 . . . . **113** E2
Ann Boleyn Dr SS4 . . . . . **147** F7
Anne Boleyn Mans 4
SS13 . . . . **143** B5
Anne Heart Ct RM16 . . . **172** D2
Anne Nastri Ct RM2 . . . . **136** B6
Annett Ct 7 SS12 . . . . . **122** A5
Anne Way IG6 . . . . **111** C4
Anna Taylor Ho 2
E12 . . . . **152** A8
Annifer Way RM15 . . . . . **172** B8
Annonay Wlk 7 CM2 . . . . **32** C2
Annwood Lodge Bsns Pk
SS6 . . . . **122** D2
Anson Chase SS3 . . . . . **168** E8
Anson Cl
Romford RM7 . . . . **113** B1
South Woodham Ferrers
    CM3 . . . . **101** F6
Anstead Dr RM13 . . . . . **155** A3
Anstey Cl SS9 . . . . **146** D2
Antelope Ave RM16 . . . . **173** A3
Anthony Cl CM11 . . . . . . **119** D6
Anthony Dr SS17 . . . . . . **160** E4
Antlers SS8 . . . . **163** F2
Antlers Hill E4 . . . . **87** B4
Anton Rd RM15 . . . . **157** B1
Antony Cl SS8 . . . . **164** B5
Antrim Rd SS3 . . . . **168** D7
Anvil Way
Billericay CM12 . . . . **97** B5
Chelmsford CM1 . . . . **32** E8
Anworth Cl IG8 . . . . **110** B4
Apeldoorn SS7 . . . . **144** B7
Apex Cl SS12 . . . . **122** A7
Apollo Cl CM19 . . . . **23** C7
Apollo Way IG8 . . . . **136** D3
Appleby Cl E4 . . . . **109** C4
Appleby Dr
Basildon SS16 . . . . **140** F5
Romford RM3 . . . . **114** C5
Appleby Gn RM3 . . . . . . **114** C5
Appleton Way RM11 . . . . **136** D3
Appletree Cl SS2 . . . . . . **147** E3
Appletree Ct SS12 . . . . . **148** E3
Apple Tree Cl CM15 . . . . . **72** C1
Apple Tree Cres CM15 . . . **72** C1
Apple Tree Way SS11 . . . **121** F8
Appleyard Ave SS5 . . . . **124** E8
Approach Rd
Canvey Island SS8 . . . . . **164** F3
Crays Hill CM11 . . . . **120** D5
Approach The
Rayleigh SS6 . . . . **123** C3
Upminster RM14 . . . . . . **137** B1
April Pl CM21 . . . . **1** F3
Apton Hall Rd SS4 . . . . . **126** C6
Arabia Ct E4 . . . . **87** D2
Araglen Ave RM15 . . . . . **172** B8
Aragon Cl
Loughton IG10 . . . . **88** E3
Romford RM5 . . . . **113** A4
Southend-on-S SS2 . . . . . **147** C4
Aragon Ct
Hadleigh SS7 . . . . **145** F2

Aragon Ct continued
Redbridge IG6 . . . .
Aragon Dr IG6 . . . .
Arandora Cres RM6 . . . . .
Arbor Rd E4 . . . .
Arbour Cl CM14 . . . .
Arbour La CM1 . . . .
Arbour Way RM12 . . . . . .
Arbutus Cl CM2 . . . .
Arcade Pl 8 RM1 . . . . . .
Arcade The
18 Romford RM3 . . . . .
Wickford SS11 . . . .
Arcadian Gdns SS7 . . . . .
Arcadia Rd
Burnham-on-C CM0 . . . . .
Canvey Island SS8 . . . . . .
Arcany Rd RM15 . . . .
Archates Ave RM16 . . . . .
Archer Ave SS2 . . . .
Archer Cl SS2 . . . .
Archer Ho CM12 . . . .
Archer Rd SS13 . . . .
Archers CM19 . . . .
Archers Apartments 1
RM6 . . . .
Archers Cl CM21 . . . .
Archers Ct RM15 . . . .
Archers Fields SS13 . . . . .
Archers Fields Cl
SS13 . . . .
Archers Way CM2 . . . . . .
Archibald Rd RM3 . . . . . .
Archibald Terr SS15 . . . . .
Archway RM3 . . . .
Arden Cres RM9 . . . .
Ardleigh SS16 . . . .
Ardleigh Cl RM11 . . . . . .
Ardleigh Cl CM15 . . . . . .
Ardleigh Gdns CM15 . . . .
ARDLEIGH GREEN . . . . . .
Ardleigh Green Inf Sch
RM11 . . . .
Ardleigh Green Jun S
RM11 . . . .
Ardleigh Green Rd
RM11 . . . .
Ardleigh Ho 5 IG11 . . . . .
Ardley Cres CM22 . . . . . .
ARDLEY END . . . .
Ardley Way SS6 . . . .
Ardmore La IG9 . . . .
Ardmore Pl IG9 . . . .
Ardmore Rd RM15 . . . . . .
Ardwell Ave IG6 . . . .
Arethusa Pl DA9 . . . .
Argent Cl SS3 . . . .
Argent St RM17 . . . .
Argles Cl DA9 . . . .
Argus Cl RM7 . . . .
Argyle Gdns RM14 . . . . .
Argyle Rd
Burnham-on-C CM0 . . . . .
Ilford IG1 . . . .
Argyll Cl CM15 . . . .
Argyll Ho SS0 . . . .
Argyll Rd
Chelmsford CM2 . . . .
Grays RM17 . . . .
Southend-on-S SS0 . . . . .
Aria Ct IG2 . . . .
Ariel Ct 5 DA17 . . . .
Arisdale Ave RM15 . . . . .
Arjan Way SS8 . . . .
Ark Ave RM4 . . . .
Ark La SS4 . . . .
Arkwright Rd RM18 . . . . .
Arkwrights CM20 . . . . . .
Arlingham Mews EN9 . . . .
Arlington Gdns
Ilford IG1 . . . .
Romford RM3 . . . .
Arlington Ho 14 IG8 . . . .
Arlington Rd
Southend-on-S SS2 . . . . .
Woodford IG8 . . . .
Arlington Sq CM3 . . . . . .
Arlington Way CM12 . . . . .
Armada Cl SS15 . . . .
Armada Ct RM10 . . . .
Armadale SS8 . . . .
Armagh Rd SS3 . . . .
Armath Pl SS15 . . . .
Armitage Rd SS1 . . . .
Armonde Cl CM3 . . . .
Armor Rd RM19 . . . .
Armstead Wlk RM10 . . . .
Armstrong Ave IG8 . . . . .
Armstrong Cl
Dagenham RM8 . . . .
Danbury CM3 . . . .
Stanford-le-H SS17 . . . . .
Armstrong Rd SS7 . . . . . .
Arncroft Ct 8 IG11 . . . . .
Arne Ct SS17 . . . .
Arne Ct SS15 . . . .
Arne Mews SS15 . . . .
Arneways Ave RM6 . . . . .
Arnheim Rd CM0 . . . .
Arnhem Rd CM1 . . . .
Arnhem Rd CM1 . . . .
Arnold Ave
Basildon SS16 . . . .
Southend-on-S SS1 . . . . .
Arnold Ave E EN3 . . . . . .
Arnold Ct E18 . . . .
Arnold Ho CM2 . . . .
Arnold Pl RM18 . . . .

RM9 . . . . . 153 F5
RM10 . . . . . 154 A5
Abbey EN9 . . . . . 65 C4
ve CM13 . . . . . 95 C4
CM13 . . . . . 95 C4
rm La CM13 . . . . . 95 E6
ay SS4 . . . . . 125 D7
ay CM2 . . . . . 54 C3
o 2 RM3 . . . . . 115 A4
o IG2 . . . . . 133 A5
S12 . . . . . 121 F6
2 . . . . . 132 D2
h CI IG7 . . . . . 111 F5
h Path IG7 . . . . . 111 F5
h Rd IG7 . . . . . 111 F5
h La SS4 . . . . . 155 C1
on-S SS6,
ey SS6 . . . . . 145 B8
North Stifford 172 E4
West Thurrock 172 A3
ad Purfleet 171 C2
RM11 . . . . . 135 F4
nes Ct 174 C3
gler Inf Sch 160 E3
gler Jun Sch 160 E3
CM1 . . . . . 31 F5
RM17 . . . . . 178 C8
RM6 . . . . . 134 D5
RM17 . . . . . 178 C8
Ho RM17 . . . . . 178 B8
lls Ho 3 . . . . . 133 A1
IG2 . . . . . 133 D5
. . . . . 175 C2
l 32 C5
CM12 . . . . . 97 C6
ls SS17 . . . . . 161 A3
G8 . . . . . 110 A3
ns 134 A2
s S6 . . . . . 123 B5
n-S SS0 . . . . . 147 A3
ews CM12 . . . . . 97 C6
S4 . . . . . 103 C1
M3 . . . . . 114 F2
eet SS7 . . . . . 144 B7
S11 . . . . . 99 C1
ay CM12 . . . . . 97 C6
M3 . . . . . 101 C6
Bsns Pk 2 . . . . . 172 B3
RM5 . . . . . 113 C4
CM20 . . . . . 11 B5
E4 . . . . . 109 A3
G6 . . . . . 111 E4
y SS7 . . . . . 145 B7
s RM12 . . . . . 155 E8
S14 . . . . . 142 E6
s CM0 . . . . . 84 E4
CM13 . . . . . 116 C4
Ave E18 . . . . . 132 B7
Rd RM3 . . . . . 114 D6
SS6 . . . . . 145 F8
kd RM10 . . . . . 135 B1
m Gdns 137 C3
m Rd DA17 . . . . . 169 C2
n-S SS1 . . . . . 166 F8
Ave IG3 . . . . . 152 F8
ns RM6 . . . . . 134 D6
RM11 . . . . . 137 A3
6 . . . . . 174 E7
tch CM15 . . . . . 93 F4
s 113 B3
SS4 . . . . . 125 D4
CI SS9 . . . . . 146 B6
4 . . . . . 87 D2
M7 . . . . . 135 B5
n-S SS3 . . . . . 168 F7
18 . . . . . 110 C2
5 . . . . . 101 E2
CM13 . . . . . 95 C3
ndon RM15 . . . . . 172 C7
G8 . . . . . 110 B4
y SS16 . . . . . 142 A5
SS17 . . . . . 160 F5
res SS7 . . . . . 145 E4
t IG11 . . . . . 152 B6
o SS7 . . . . . 144 F6
Vlk RM7 . . . . . 113 B2
n 85 A7
Pits Nature 85 A8
S3 . . . . . 168 E6
5 . . . . . 122 F3
rm Rd CM9 . . . . . 35 D8
l 143 C8
10 . . . . . 88 F7

Ashford Ave CM14 . . . . . 116 B7
Ashford Ct RM17 . . . . . 173 D1
Ashford Rd
 Chelmsford CM1 . . . . . 31 C2
 Wallend E6 . . . . . 152 A5
 Woodford E18 . . . . . 110 B1
Ash Gn
 Billericay CM11 . . . . . 97 E2
 Canewdon SS4 . . . . . 104 D1
Ash Gr
 Burnham-on-C CM0 . . . . . 106 B6
 Dagenham RM9 . . . . . 54 D7
 Heybridge CM9 . . . . . 37 C6
Ashgrove Rd IG3 . . . . . 134 A3
Ash Groves CM21 . . . . . 2 A2
Ash Ind Est CM19 . . . . . 22 F7
Ashingdale CI SS8 . . . . . 164 C2
ASHINGDON 125 D7
Ashingdon CI E4 . . . . . 109 C7
Ashingdon Hts SS4 . . . . . 125 B7
Ashingdon Rd SS4 . . . . . 125 D6
Ashingdon Sch SS4 . . . . . 103 B1
Ashlands CM18 . . . . . 175 C2
Ashleigh CI SS8 . . . . . 164 A6
Ashleigh Ct
 Canvey Island SS8 . . . . . 164 A6
 Hoddesdon EN11 . . . . . 21 A5
 Ingatestone CM4 . . . . . 74 B3
 Waltham Abbey EN9 . . . . . 66 A5
Ashleigh Dr SS9 . . . . . 165 F8
Ashleigh Gdns RM14 . . . . . 137 D1
Ashley Ave IG6 . . . . . 111 B1
Ashley CI SS17 . . . . . 161 A3
Ashley Gn CM3 . . . . . 78 B7
Ashley Gr IG10 . . . . . 88 E6
Ashley Rd E4 . . . . . 109 A4
Ash Lo SS3 . . . . . 168 F8
Ashley Gr RM11 . . . . . 136 D8
Ashlyns SS13 . . . . . 143 B7
Ashlyns La CM5 . . . . . 25 F2
Ashlyns Rd CM16 . . . . . 45 F1
Ashmans Row CM3 . . . . . 101 D6
Ashmeads IG10 . . . . . 88 F6
Ashmour Gdns RM1 . . . . . 113 D1
Ash Rd
 Canvey Island SS8 . . . . . 164 C3
 Hadleigh SS7 . . . . . 145 E2
Ashton Ct E4 . . . . . 109 E7
Ashton Gate RM3 . . . . . 114 D3
Ashton Gdns RM6 . . . . . 134 E5
Ashton Pl
 Chelmsford CM2 . . . . . 33 A3
 Thundersley SS7 . . . . . 145 A6
Ashton Rd RM3 . . . . . 114 D2
Ash Tree CI CM1 . . . . . 31 F2
Ash Tree Cnr CM3 . . . . . 19 B6
Ash Tree Cres CM1 . . . . . 31 F2
Ashtree Ct EN9 . . . . . 66 A5
Ash Tree Ct
 Rochford SS4 . . . . . 126 D4
 Romford RM1 . . . . . 136 A6
Ash Tree Field CM20 . . . . . 10 A2
Ash Tree Wlk 1 SS14 . . . . . 142 F5
Ashurst Ave SS2 . . . . . 148 F2
Ashurst Dr
 Chelmsford CM1 . . . . . 32 D7
 Ilford IG6 . . . . . 133 C6
Ashvale Dr RM14 . . . . . 137 E2
Ashvale Gdns
 Romford RM5 . . . . . 113 D5
 Upminster RM14 . . . . . 137 F2
Ashway SS17 . . . . . 161 B4
Ash Way SS5 . . . . . 124 F8
Ashwells Rd CM16 . . . . . 93 E6
Ash Wlk
 Southend-on-S SS1 . . . . . 167 B7
 South Ockendon RM15 . . . . . 157 D2
Ashwood SS7 . . . . . 144 B7
Ashwood Ave RM13 . . . . . 155 B1
Ashwood CI CM0 . . . . . 106 B7
Ashwood Rd E4 . . . . . 109 D7
Ashworth PI CM17 . . . . . 24 D8
Ashworths
 Southend-on-S SS8 . . . . . 164 A6
 Rochford SS4 . . . . . 125 C6
Askews Farm Rd
 RM17 . . . . . 172 E1
Askwith Rd RM13 . . . . . 153 D3
Aspen CI
 Basildon SS15 . . . . . 119 C1
 Brentwood CM13 . . . . . 117 A7
 Chartford DA1 . . . . . 176 A1
 Redbridge IG3 . . . . . 132 E8
Aspen Gn SS4 . . . . . 125 C7
Aspen Gr RM14 . . . . . 156 A8
Aspens EN9 . . . . . 66 C4
Aspen Way RM15 . . . . . 157 D2
Asquith Ave SS7 . . . . . 145 B7
Asquith CI RM8 . . . . . 134 C3
Asquith Gdns SS7 . . . . . 145 C7
Assandune CI SS4 . . . . . 125 D7
Aster CI
 Basildon SS15 . . . . . 141 D5
 4 Chelmsford CM1 . . . . . 32 F6
Asthall Gdns IG6 . . . . . 133 C7
Astley RM17 . . . . . 177 F8
Aston CI 10 IG8 . . . . . 110 A4
Aston Mews RM6 . . . . . 134 C4
Astonplace IG6 . . . . . 133 A5
Astor Ave RM7 . . . . . 135 C5
Astra CI RM12 . . . . . 155 B6
Astra Ct E 3 RM12 . . . . . 155 B6
Astra Cnr CM20 . . . . . 10 F4
Astra Ct N 2 RM12 . . . . . 155 B6
Athelstan CI RM3 . . . . . 114 F1
Athelstan Ct E6 . . . . . 152 A3

Athelstan Gdns SS11 . . . . . 99 D1
Athelstan Rd RM3 . . . . . 114 F1
Athena Est CM20 . . . . . 11 B4
Atherstone CI SS8 . . . . . 164 C2
Atherstone Rd SS8 . . . . . 164 C2
Atherton End CM21 . . . . . 1 E3
Atherton Gdns RM16 . . . . . 174 C2
Atherton Ho
 8 Romford RM3 . . . . . 114 E3
 Woodford IG5 . . . . . 110 E1
Atherton Rd IG5 . . . . . 110 F1
Athol CI SS8 . . . . . 164 E2
Athol Ct IG3 . . . . . 134 A4
Atholl Rd
 Chelmsford CM2 . . . . . 32 F5
 Ilford IG3 . . . . . 134 A4
Athol Rd DA17 . . . . . 169 C1
Athos Rd SS4 . . . . . 164 C5
Atlanta Blvd RM1 . . . . . 135 E5
Atlantic CI DA10 . . . . . 177 E2
Atlantis CI IG11 . . . . . 153 B2
Atridge Chase CM12 . . . . . 97 A4
Atrium 9 IG9 . . . . . 110 D8
Attlee Ct RM17 . . . . . 173 A3
Attlee Dr DA1 . . . . . 176 A2
Attwoods CI CM2 . . . . . 54 C3
Aubrey CI CM1 . . . . . 32 B7
Aubrietia CI RM3 . . . . . 114 E2
Auckland Ave RM13 . . . . . 154 F2
Auckland CI
 Chelmsford CM1 . . . . . 31 C5
 Tilbury RM18 . . . . . 179 A5
Auckland Rd IG1 . . . . . 133 C4
Auction Pl RM4 . . . . . 90 B6
Audleigh Pl IG7 . . . . . 111 A4
Audley Gdns
 Ilford IG3 . . . . . 133 F2
 Loughton IG10 . . . . . 89 D7
 Waltham Abbey EN9 . . . . . 65 C5
Audleys CI SS7 . . . . . 147 E5
Audley Way SS14 . . . . . 142 B6
Audrey Rd IG1 . . . . . 133 B1
Augers 7 CM0 . . . . . 106 C4
Augustine Ct EN9 . . . . . 65 B6
Augustine Rd 1
 CM2 . . . . . 179 D1
Augustine Way SS4 . . . . . 56 F2
Aukingford Gdns CM5 . . . . . 48 F5
Aukingford Gn CM5 . . . . . 48 F4
Aundle Ho IG8 . . . . . 111 A4
Auriel Ave RM10 . . . . . 154 D6
Auriga CI E18 . . . . . 109 F6
Austen CI
 Greenhithe DA9 . . . . . 177 C1
 Loughton IG10 . . . . . 89 D6
Austen Dr CM4 . . . . . 75 D2
Austral Dr RM11 . . . . . 136 D4
Austral Way CM3 . . . . . 83 A3
Avocca Terr SS0 . . . . . 147 D2
Avebury Rd SS0 . . . . . 147 E2
AVELEY 171 C6
Aveley By-Pass RM15 . . . . . 171 D6
Aveley CI RM15 . . . . . 171 D5
Aveley Mans 1 IG11 . . . . . 152 B5
Aveley Prim Sch
 RM15 . . . . . 171 E5
Aveley Rd
 Romford RM1 . . . . . 135 E7
 Upminster RM14 . . . . . 156 C4
Aveley Sch The RM15 . . . . . 171 D6
Aveley Way CM9 . . . . . 58 F8
Aveling Park Rd E17 . . . . . 109 A1
Aveling Park Sch E17 . . . . . 109 A1
Avelon Rd
 Rainham RM13 . . . . . 155 A4
 Romford RM5 . . . . . 113 D4
Avenue CI RM13 . . . . . 114 F3
Avenue Ct IG5 . . . . . 132 C8
Avenue Ind Est
 Chingford E4 . . . . . 109 A4
 Romford RM3 . . . . . 114 D2
Avenue Rd
 Brentwood CM14 . . . . . 116 C6
 Chelmsford CM2 . . . . . 54 D7
 Hoddesdon EN11 . . . . . 21 D5
 Ilford RM6 . . . . . 134 B3
 Ingatestone CM4 . . . . . 74 B3
 Romford RM3 . . . . . 114 F3
 South Benfleet SS7 . . . . . 144 E3
 Southend-on-S, Clifftown
  SS0 . . . . . 166 F8
 Southend-on-S, Leigh Cliffs
  SS9 . . . . . 166 B6
 Theydon Bois CM16 . . . . . 67 D3
 Woodford IG8 . . . . . 110 C4
Avenue Terr
 Ilford IG2 . . . . . 133 E5
 Southend-on-S SS0 . . . . . 166 E8
Avenue The
 Billericay CM12 . . . . . 97 A2
 Brentwood CM13 . . . . . 116 F4
 11 Buckhurst Hill IG9 . . . . . 110 C8
 Canvey Island SS8 . . . . . 164 B2
 Chingford E4 . . . . . 109 D5
 Danbury CM3 . . . . . 56 F7
 Fobbing SS17 . . . . . 161 D4
 Greenhithe DA9 . . . . . 177 E2
 Hadleigh SS7 . . . . . 145 E3
 Hoddesdon EN11 . . . . . 21 A4
 Hornchurch RM12 . . . . . 136 D2
 Hullbridge SS5 . . . . . 101 D3
 Kelvedon Hatch CM15 . . . . . 93 E8
 Loughton IG10 . . . . . 88 E3
 Lower Nazeing EN9 . . . . . 44 F5
 North Fambridge CM3 . . . . . 103 A7
 Romford RM1 . . . . . 135 D7

Avenue The continued
 Wanstead E11 . . . . . 132 B6
Avery Gdns
 Ilford IG2 . . . . . 133 A6
 Redbridge IG2 . . . . . 132 F6
Avey La
 High Beach IG10 . . . . . 88 A8
 Waltham Abbey EN9 . . . . . 65 E2
Aviation Way SS2 . . . . . 147 B7
Avila Chase CM2 . . . . . 54 B1
Avington Wlk SS7 . . . . . 144 F6
Avocet Way CM9 . . . . . 37 C5
Avon CI SS4 . . . . . 125 C5
Avon Ct
 10 Chingford E4 . . . . . 87 C1
 Upminster RM14 . . . . . 137 E4
Avondale
 Loughton IG10 . . . . . 88 F2
 Rayleigh SS6 . . . . . 123 F2
Avondale Cres IG4 . . . . . 132 D6
Avondale CI
 Southend-on-S SS9 . . . . . 146 D1
 Woodford E18 . . . . . 110 B2
Avondale Dr
 Loughton IG10 . . . . . 88 F3
 Southend-on-S SS0 . . . . . 146 F4
Avondale Gdns SS17 . . . . . 160 E5
Avondale Rd
 Basildon SS14 . . . . . 143 A4
 Rayleigh SS6 . . . . . 123 F2
 South Benfleet SS7 . . . . . 144 D3
 Southend-on-S SS9 . . . . . 146 E8
Avon Gn RM15 . . . . . 172 B7
Avon Ho RM14 . . . . . 137 E4
Avon House Sch IG8 . . . . . 110 A6
Avon Rd
 Canvey Island SS8 . . . . . 164 A3
 Chelmsford CM2 . . . . . 54 B1
 Upminster RM14 . . . . . 137 D5
Avontar Rd RM15 . . . . . 157 B1
Avon Terr IG10 . . . . . 88 F3
Avon Way
 Wanstead E11 . . . . . 132 A8
Avril Way E4 . . . . . 109 C5
Avro Rd SS2 . . . . . 147 D6
Axe St IG11 . . . . . 152 C4
Axon PI IG1 . . . . . 133 C2
Aylesbeare SS16 . . . . . 138 D8
Aylesbury Dr SS16 . . . . . 141 F5
Aylesbury Mews SS15 . . . . . 119 F2
Aylets Field CM18 . . . . . 23 C2
Aylett CI SS8 . . . . . 164 C4
Aylett Rd RM14 . . . . . 137 C2
Ayletts
 Basildon SS14 . . . . . 142 F6
 Broomfield CM1 . . . . . 19 B3
Aylmer Rd RM8 . . . . . 153 F6
Ayloffe Rd RM9 . . . . . 153 F6
Ayloff Prim Sch RM12 . . . . . 155 B8
Ayloffs CI RM11 . . . . . 136 E6
Ayloff's Wlk RM11 . . . . . 136 E6
Aylsham La RM3 . . . . . 114 D6
Aylsham Rd EN11 . . . . . 21 C8
Aynsley Gdns CM17 . . . . . 24 C8
AYTHORPE RODING 5 B3
Azalea Ave SS12 . . . . . 121 C7
Azalea CI IG1 . . . . . 152 B7
Azalea Ct
 8 Chelmsford CM1 . . . . . 32 F6
 Chingford IG8 . . . . . 109 E3
Azalea Mews SS8 . . . . . 164 A2

B
Baardwyk Ave SS14 . . . . . 164 E3
Babbacombe Gdns
 IG4 . . . . . 132 E7
Babington Rd
 Dagenham RM8 . . . . . 153 C8
 Hornchurch RM12 . . . . . 136 B3
Back La
 Broomfield CM1 . . . . . 19 D1
 Buckhurst Hill IG9 . . . . . 110 D8
 Dagenham RM6 . . . . . 134 E4
 East Hanningfield CM3 . . . . . 78 B7
 Grays RM20 . . . . . 172 B4
 Ingatestone CM4 . . . . . 74 A6
 Little Hallingbury CM22 . . . . . 2 B7
 Little Waltham CM3 . . . . . 19 C4
 Lower Nazeing EN9 . . . . . 44 F5
 Pleshey CM3 . . . . . 18 A2
 Purfleet RM19 . . . . . 171 E3
 Rochford SS4 . . . . . 125 F1
 Sheering CM22 . . . . . 2 B1
 South Ockendon RM16 . . . . . 172 C5
 Stock CM4 . . . . . 75 D2
Backnang Sq 1 CM2 . . . . . 32 C8
Back Rd CM1 . . . . . 31 A1
Backwarden Nature
 Reserve* CM3 . . . . . 56 E5
Backwarders Nature
 Trail* CM3 . . . . . 56 E4
Bacon Link RM5 . . . . . 113 B4
Bacons Chase CM0 . . . . . 42 B2
Bacon Terr 3 RM8 . . . . . 153 B7
Badburgham CF EN9 . . . . . 65 F6
Baddeley CI EN3 . . . . . 65 A2
Baddow CI
 Dagenham RM10 . . . . . 154 A4
 Woodford IG8 . . . . . 110 D4
Baddow Hall Ave CM2 . . . . . 55 A7

Baddow Hall Cres CM2 . . . . . 55 B7
Baddow Hall Jun & Inf Sch
 CM2 . . . . . 55 A6
Baddow Place Ave
 . . . . . 55 A6
Baddow Rd
 Chelmsford CM2 . . . . . 32 C1
 Great Baddow CM2 . . . . . 54 E7
Baden Powell CI RM9 . . . . . 153 E4
Baden Powell Ho 11
 DA17 . . . . . 169 A3
Bader Rd IG1 . . . . . 152 B7
Bader Way RM13 . . . . . 155 B6
Badger CI IG2 . . . . . 133 C4
Badger CI E4 . . . . . 109 D6
Badger Hall Ave SS7 . . . . . 145 A4
Badgers CI
 Galleywood CM2 . . . . . 54 B1
 Southend-on-S SS0 . . . . . 147 B4
Badgers Keep CM0 . . . . . 106 B8
Badgers Mount
 Chadwell St M RM16 . . . . . 173 F4
 Hockley SS5 . . . . . 124 D5
Badgers Rise SS8 . . . . . 164 A6
Badgers The SS16 . . . . . 141 B4
Badgers Way SS7 . . . . . 145 B4
Badlis Rd E17 . . . . . 109 A1
Bag La CM4 . . . . . 73 E4
Bagleys Spring RM6 . . . . . 134 E2
Bailey CI
 Chingford E4 . . . . . 109 C6
 Purfleet RM19 . . . . . 171 D2
Bailey Ct 4 E4 . . . . . 109 D5
Bailey Rd SS9 . . . . . 146 B2
Bailey The SS6 . . . . . 123 C2
Bailie CI RM13 . . . . . 155 B1
Bainbridge Rd RM9 . . . . . 153 F8
Baird Ho 3 DA17 . . . . . 169 A3
Bairny Wood App IG8 . . . . . 110 B4
Baker CI SS15 . . . . . 141 C5
Baker Mews CM9 . . . . . 37 A2
Baker Rd RM3 . . . . . 101 D8
Bakers Cotts CM15 . . . . . 93 F8
Bakers Ct RM8 . . . . . 134 F4
Bakers Ct
 Ramsden Heath CM11 . . . . . 98 C4
 Wickford SS11 . . . . . 121 F6
Baker's Cross SS12 . . . . . 121 A2
Bakers Farm CI SS11 . . . . . 122 A7
Bakersfield CM3 . . . . . 82 F8
Bakers Field CM4 . . . . . 75 E2
Bakers La
 Danbury CM3 . . . . . 56 E7
 Epping CM16 . . . . . 45 F1
 Ingatestone CM4 . . . . . 74 B4
 West Hanningfield CM2 . . . . . 76 D2
Bakers Mdw CM15 . . . . . 72 C2
Bakers Mead CM3 . . . . . 18 F7
Bakers Mews CM4 . . . . . 74 B4
Baker St
 Chelmsford CM2 . . . . . 32 A1
 Orsett RM16 . . . . . 173 F6
BAKER STREET 173 F7
Bakers Villas The
 CM16 . . . . . 45 F1
Bakers Wlk CM21 . . . . . 1 E2
Bakery CI
 Roydon CM19 . . . . . 22 C8
 Tillingham CM0 . . . . . 63 E3
Baldocks Rd CM16 . . . . . 67 C4
Baldwin Ho E6 . . . . . 152 A5
Baldwin's Hill IG10 . . . . . 88 F8
Balfour CI SS12 . . . . . 121 E5
Balfour Rd
 Grays RM17 . . . . . 173 C2
 Ilford IG1 . . . . . 133 C3
Balgonie Rd E4 . . . . . 87 D1
Balgores Cres RM2 . . . . . 136 B8
Balgores La RM2 . . . . . 136 B7
Balgores Sq RM2 . . . . . 136 B7
Ballards CI RM10 . . . . . 154 B4
BALLARDS GORE 126 F6
Ballards Rd RM10 . . . . . 154 B3
Ballards Wlk SS15 . . . . . 141 E7
Balliol Ave E4 . . . . . 109 E6
Balmerino Ave SS7 . . . . . 145 C6
Balmoral Ave
 Corringham SS17 . . . . . 161 A3
 Stanford-le-H SS17 . . . . . 160 E3
Balmoral CI CM11 . . . . . 97 E1
Balmoral Ct CM2 . . . . . 32 C2
Balmoral Gdns
 Hockley SS5 . . . . . 124 C6
 Ilford IG3 . . . . . 133 F3
Balmoral Ho 3 SS0 . . . . . 166 E8
Balmoral Rd
 Hornchurch RM12 . . . . . 136 D1
 Mayland CM3 . . . . . 61 A2
 Pilgrims Hatch CM15 . . . . . 94 B6
 Romford RM2 . . . . . 136 B6
 Southend-on-S SS0 . . . . . 147 E1
Balmoral Terr SS0 . . . . . 147 D2
Balstonia Dr SS17 . . . . . 160 F5
Baltic Ave SS13 . . . . . 167 A8
Baltic Wharf DA11 . . . . . 179 B4
Bamber Ho 1 IG11 . . . . . 152 C4
Bamford CI SS15 . . . . . 152 C6
Bamford Rd IG11 . . . . . 152 A5
Bampton Rd RM3 . . . . . 114 C2
Banbury Ho 10 E4 . . . . . 110 A8
Bancroft Ave IG9 . . . . . 110 D8
Bancroft Chase RM12 . . . . . 135 F2
Bancrofts Rd RM4 . . . . . 101 E8
Bancroft's Sch IG8 . . . . . 110 D6
Bandhills CM3 . . . . . 101 D8
Banes Down EN9 . . . . . 21 E1

Bankart La CM2 . . . . .32 F4
Bank Chambers
CM15. . . . . 116 D8
Bank End Cotts CM4. . . . . .75 A8
Bankfoot RM17 . . . . 173 A1
Bank Pl 8 CM14. . . . . 116 C8
Bankside DA11 . . . . 178 C1
Bankside Cl CM3 . . . . .79 E1
Bankside Pk IG11 . . . . 153 A2
Bankside Rd IG11 . . . . 152 D7
Banks La
Epping CM16 . . . . .68 F7
Stapleford Tawney CM16. . .69 A8
Bank St DA11, DA12 . . . .179 B1
Banks Way E12. . . . . 152 A8
Bann Cl RM15. . . . . 172 B6
Banner Cl RM19 . . . . 171 D2
Bannister Dr CM13. . . . . . . .95 C3
Bannister Gn SS12. . . . . . 121 E6
Bannister Ho RM20 . . . . . 177 D8
Bansons Ct CM5. . . . . .49 A3
Banson's La CM5 . . . . .49 A3
Bansons Way CM5. . . . . . .49 A3
Bansons Yd CM5. . . . . .49 A3
Bantel Villas EN11 . . . . . . .21 C8
Banyards RM11 . . . . 136 E7
Banyard Way SS4. . . . . . . 125 C4
Barbara Ave SS8. . . . . . . 163 F2
Barbara Cl SS4 . . . . 125 E2
Barbara Ho CM2 . . . . .32 A2
Barbel Cl EN8. . . . . .65 A5
Barberry Cl RM3. . . . . . . 114 C3
Barbour Gn SS12 . . . . 121 D5
Barbrook Way CM3 . . . . . . .56 E1
Barclay Cl CM2. . . . . .55 A6
Barclay Cl EN11 . . . . .21 A5
Barclay Oval IG8 . . . . 110 A6
Barclay Rd SS13 . . . . 121 E1
Barclay Way RM20 . . . . . . 171 F1
Bardell Cl CM1. . . . . .31 F6
Bardenville Rd SS8 . . . . . 164 E3
Bardeswell Cl CM14. . . . . 116 C8
Bardfield SS16. . . . . 142 E5
Bardfield Ave RM6. . . . . . 134 D8
Bardfield Prim Sch
SS16. . . . . 142 E4
Bardfield Way SS6. . . . . . 123 A3
Bards Ct RM3. . . . . 114 B3
Barfields IG10. . . . . .89 A5
Barfields Gdns IG10 . . . . . .89 A5
Barfields Path IG10. . . . . . .89 A5
Barge Ct DA9. . . . . 177 C3
Barge Pier Rd SS3. . . . . . 168 E5
Barham Cl RM7. . . . . 113 B1
Bark Burr Rd RM16 . . . . . 172 F4
Barkers Mead CM22 . . . . . .2 B8
BARKING 152 D5
Barking Abbey Comp Sch
(Lower Sch) IG11 . . . . . 152 E7
Barking Abbey Sch
IG11. . . . . 152 F6
Barking Bsns Ctr
IG11. . . . . 153 A2
Barking Coll RM7. . . . . . . 135 D2
Barking Hospl IG11. . . . . . 152 F5
Barking Ind Pk IG11 . . . . . 153 A4
Barking Rd E6. . . . . 152 A4
BARKINGSIDE 133 C8
Barkingside Sta IG6. . . . . 133 D8
Barking Sta IG11 . . . . 152 C5
Barkis Cl CM1. . . . . .31 D7
Barkwood Cl RM7 . . . . . . 135 C6
Barle Gdns IG11 . . . . 172 B7
Barley Cl
Basildon SS15 . . . . 141 A3
Hatfield Heath CM22. . . . . .3 E2
Barleycorn Way RM11. . . 136 F5
Barley Court Day Hospl
IG3. . . . . 134 B6
Barley Croft CM18 . . . . . . .23 E4
Barley Field CM15 . . . . . . .71 F2
Barleyfields Cl RM6. . . . . 134 C4
Barley La IG3, RM6. . . . . . 134 C4
Barleylands Farm Mus*
CM11. . . . . 119 F5
Barleylands Rd CM11,
SS15. . . . . 119 F4
Barley Lane Prim Sch
RM6. . . . . 134 B4
Barley Mead CM3 . . . . . . 134 E7
BARLING 149 E7
Barling Magna Com Prim
Sch SS3 . . . . 149 D7
Barling Rd SS3 . . . . 149 B6
Barlow's Reach CM2. . . . . .33 A4
Barlow Way RM13 . . . . . . 169 E8
Barnaby Rudge CM1. . . . . .31 F7
Barnaby Way
Basildon SS15 . . . . 141 D7
Chigwell IG7 . . . . 111 B7
Barnard Acres EN9 . . . . . . .43 E8
Barnard Ct SS16. . . . . 142 E2
Barnard Ct 18 DA2. . . . . 176 B1
Barnard Ho RM4. . . . . 114 C1
Barnards Dr IG6 . . . . 133 C7
Barnard Rd
Galleywood CM2 . . . . .54 C2
Sawbridgeworth CM21 . . . . .1 E4
Southend-on-S SS9 . . . . . 146 C2
Barnards Ave SS8. . . . . . . 164 D4
Barncombe Cl SS7. . . . . . 144 D6
Barncroft Cl IG10. . . . . . . .89 A4
Barncroft Gn IG10. . . . . . . .89 A4
Barncroft Rd IG10. . . . . . . .89 A4

Barn Ct RM12 . . . . .1 E3
Barnes Ct
Chipping Ongar CM5 . . . . .48 F5
Woodford IG8 . . . . 110 D5
Barnes Farm Dr CM3 . . . . .82 F2
Barnes Farm Jun & Inf
Schs CM2. . . . . .33 A3
Barnes Ho 8 IG11. . . . . . 152 D4
Barnes Mill Rd CM2 . . . . . .32 F2
Barnes Rd IG1 . . . . 152 C7
Barnet Park Rd SS11. . . . . .99 F2
Barnett Ct RM17. . . . . . . 173 C1
Barneveld Ave SS8. . . . . . 164 E3
Barnfield
Epping CM16 . . . . .46 A3
Hatfield Broad Oak CM22. . .4 A5
Wickford SS11. . . . . 121 E8
Barnfield Cl
Greenhithe DA9. . . . . 176 F1
Hoddesdon EN11 . . . . .21 A8
Lower Nazeing EN9 . . . . . .21 F1
Barnfield Cotts CM9 . . . . . .37 B5
Barnfield Mews CM1. . . . . .32 A6
Barn Gn CM1. . . . . .32 E8
Barn Hill CM19 . . . . .22 B4
Barn Mead CM3 . . . . .47 F2
Barn Mead
Doddinghurst CM15. . . . . .72 C3
Harlow CM18. . . . . .23 E6
Theydon Bois CM16. . . . . .67 E3
Barnmead Ct RM9 . . . . . . 153 F7
Barnmead Gdns RM9 . . . . 153 F7
Barnmead Rd RM9. . . . . . 153 F7
Barnmead Way CM0. . . . . 106 B8
Barns Ct CM19. . . . . .23 B3
Barnsley Rd RM3. . . . . . . 114 F3
Barnstaple Cl SS1 . . . . . . 168 A8
Barnstaple Path 7
RM3 . . . . 114 D5
Barnstaple Rd
Romford RM3 . . . . 114 C5
Southend-on-S SS1 . . . . . 168 B8
Barnston Way CM13 . . . . . .95 C4
Barn The RM17 . . . . 173 B2
Barnwell Dr SS5. . . . . 124 D6
Barnyard The SS16. . . . . . 141 A4
Baron Ct RM3 . . . . 114 F2
Baron Gdns IG6 . . . . 133 C8
Baron Rd
Dagenham RM8. . . . . 134 D3
South Woodham Ferrers
SS0. . . . . 166 F8
Barons Ct IG1. . . . . 133 D2
Baron's La CM3, CM9 . . . . .58 E1
Barons Way SS16. . . . . . . 141 B4
Barrack Cl RM3. . . . . .18 E8
Barrack Rd CM1. . . . . .37 B5
Barrack Row 1 DA11. . . . 179 B1
Barrack Sq 16 CM2 . . . . . .32 B2
Barra Glade SS12. . . . . . . 121 F5
Barrass Cl EN3 . . . . .65 A2
Barrett Cl RM3 . . . . 114 B3
Barrie Pavement 1
SS12. . . . . 121 D5
Barrington Cl
1 Basildon SS14 . . . . . . 142 F8
Great Baddow CM2. . . . . . .55 A6
Loughton IG10. . . . . .89 C5
Southend-on-S SS3 . . . . . 149 E1
Woodford IG5 . . . . 110 F2
Barrington Ct CM13. . . . . . .95 C3
Barrington Gdns
SS14. . . . . 142 F8
Barrington Gn IG10. . . . . . .89 C5
Barrington Pl CM4 . . . . . . .74 B3
Barrington Rd
Little Ilford E12 . . . . 152 A6
Loughton IG10. . . . . .89 C5
Barringtons Cl SS6 . . . . . 123 D3
Barron's Cl CM5. . . . . .48 F4
Barrow Chase CM2. . . . . . .33 B4
Barrow Hall Rd SS3. . . . . 149 C5
Barrow Marsh SS9. . . . . . .38 A4
Barrowsand SS1. . . . . 168 B6
Barrows Rd CM19. . . . . . . .22 E8
Barry Cl RM16. . . . . 174 A3
Barry Ct RM5. . . . . 113 D5
Barrymore Wlk SS6. . . . . 124 A2
BARSTABLE 142 D6
Barstable Rd SS17. . . . . . 160 D1
Barstable Sch SS14 . . . . . 142 F6
Bartholomew Dr RM3 . . . 114 D1
Bartholomew Ho 16
IG8. . . . . 111 A3
Bartlett Cl CM3. . . . . .60 F1
Bartletts SS6. . . . . 146 A8
Bartletts Ho 15 RM10. . . 154 B6
Bartley Rd SS7 . . . . 144 B6
Bartlow End SS13. . . . . . . 143 B8
Bartlow Gdns RM5. . . . . . 113 D2
Bartlow Side SS13. . . . . . 143 B8
Barton Ave RM7 . . . . 135 B3
Barton Cl
Chigwell IG7 . . . . 111 C8
South Woodham Ferrers
CM3 . . . . .79 D3
Barton Ct 8 CM14 . . . . . . 116 C6
Barton Friars IG7. . . . . . . 111 C8
Barton Mdws IG6. . . . . . . 133 B7
Barton Rd RM12. . . . . 136 A3
Bartram Ct RM8 . . . . 153 B6
Baryta Ct SS17. . . . . 160 C1
Baryta Ct SS9 . . . . 165 E8
Basedale Rd RM9. . . . . . . 153 B5

BASILDON 142 C4
Basildon Ave IG5. . . . . . . 111 A2
Basildon Bsns Ctr
SS14. . . . . 142 A8
Basildon Dr SS15. . . . . . . 141 C8
Basildon Hospl SS16. . . . . 142 A3
Basildon Rd SS15. . . . . . . 141 E8
Basildon Rise SS15 . . . . . 141 E8
Basildon Sta SS14 . . . . . . 142 A5
Basildon Trad Ctr
SS14. . . . . 141 F8
Basildon Zoo* SS16 . . . . . 152 B2
Basilica Ho IG11 . . . . 122 B7
Basil Mews 1 CM17. . . . . .11 C1
Basing Ho 7 IG11. . . . . . . 152 D4
Basin Cl CM9. . . . . .37 E3
Bassenthwaite Rd
SS7. . . . . 144 E7
Bassett Bsns Units
CM16 . . . . .46 F4
Bassett Fields CM16 . . . . . .47 D6
Bassett Gdns CM16 . . . . . .47 B5
Bassett Ho RM9 . . . . 153 B4
Bassetts La CM3, CM9 . . . .35 A4
Bassett's La CM5 . . . . .51 B8
Bastable Ave IG11 . . . . . . 153 A3
Bata Ave RM18 . . . . 175 B1
Batavia Rd SS8 . . . . 163 D4
Bate-Dudley Dr CM0. . . . . .42 B3
Bateman Cl 2 IG11. . . . . . 152 C6
Bateman Rd E4. . . . . 109 A4
Batemans Mews
CM14 . . . . 116 B6
Bates Bsns Ctr RM3. . . . . 115 A3
Bates Rd
Maldon CM9. . . . . .37 B4
Romford RM3 . . . . 115 A3
Bath Rd RM6. . . . . 134 E5
Bath St DA11 . . . . 179 B2
Bathurst Rd IG1 . . . . 133 B3
Baton Cl RM19 . . . . 171 D2
Battis The 1 RM1 . . . . . . 135 E5
Battle Ct CM5. . . . . .49 A2
Battle Rd DA17 . . . . 169 C2
BATTLESBRIDGE 100 D1
Battlesbridge Antiques
Ctr* SS11 . . . . 100 C2
Battles Bridge Motorcycle
Mus* SS11. . . . . 100 D2
Battlesbridge Sta
SS11. . . . . 100 D2
Battleswick SS14 . . . . 120 C1
Batt's Rd CM0. . . . . .84 A8
Bawden Way CM2 . . . . .54 D8
Bawdsey Ave IG2. . . . . . . 133 F7
Baxter Ave SS2. . . . . 147 F1
Baxter Gdns RM3 . . . . . . 114 C8
Baxters CM3. . . . . .57 A7
Bay Cl SS8 . . . . 164 B2
Bayleys Mead CM13. . . . . 117 C8
Bayly Rd DA1. . . . . 176 A1
Bay Manor La RM20. . . . . 176 F8
Baymans Woods
CM15 . . . . 116 F8
Bay Tree Cl IG6. . . . . 111 B3
Baytree Ctr 18 CM14 . . . . 116 C8
Baytree Ho E4. . . . . .87 B2
Bay View CM0 . . . . .62 C8
Baywood Sq IG7. . . . . 112 B6
Beach Ave SS9 . . . . 166 A8
Beach Ct
Great Wakering SS3 . . . . . 150 C3
Southend-on-S SS1 . . . . . 166 C7
Beaches Cl SS5. . . . . 125 A6
Beach House Gdns
SS8. . . . . 164 C2
Beach Rd
Canvey Island SS8. . . . . . 164 D4
Southend-on-S, Shoeburyness
SS1. . . . . 168 B5
Beach's Dr CM1 . . . . .31 D3
Beachway SS8. . . . . 164 B2
Beacon Cl CM0 . . . . .62 C8
Beaconfield Ave CM16 . . . .46 A2
Beaconfield Way CM16. . . .46 A2
Beacon Hill
Kelvedon Hatch CM14. . . . .71 C2
Maldon CM9. . . . . .36 E2
Purfleet RM19 . . . . 171 B1
Beacon Hill Ind Est
RM19 . . . . 171 B1
Beacon Hill Rd CM14 . . . . .71 B2
Beacon Hill Sch
RM15 . . . . 172 A8
Beacons IG10 . . . . .67 A1
Beacontree Ave E17 . . . . . 109 D1
Beadle's Par RM10. . . . . . 154 C6
Beadles The CM22 . . . . .2 B8
Beads Hall La CM15 . . . . . .94 B4
Beal High Sch IG4 . . . . . . 132 F7
Beal Rd IG1 . . . . 133 A2
Beam Ave RM10 . . . . 154 B4
Beambridge SS13. . . . . . . 143 A6
Beambridge Ct 2
SS13. . . . . 143 A6
Beambridge Mews
SS13. . . . . 143 A6
Beambridge Pl 1
SS13. . . . . 143 A6
Beaminster Gdns
Ilford IG10 . . . . 133 B8
Redbridge IG6. . . . . 111 B1
Beamish Cl CM16. . . . . . . .47 C6
Beam Prim Sch RM10 . . . 154 C3
Beams CM11 . . . . 119 C8

Beams Way CM11. . . . . . . 119 C8
Beamway RM10. . . . . 154 D5
Beanfield Rd CM21 . . . . . . .1 A4
Beansland Gr RM6. . . . . . 134 E8
Bearblock Cotts
RM14 . . . . 156 C6
Bear Cl RM17. . . . . 135 B5
Beardsley Dr CM1 . . . . .32 F7
Beardsley Terr 2
RM8 . . . . 153 B7
Bearing Cl IG7 . . . . 112 A6
Bearing Way IG7 . . . . 112 A6
Bearmans CM3. . . . . .99 C8
Bearsted Dr SS13. . . . . . . 143 C5
Beaton Cl DA9. . . . . 177 B2
Beatrice Ave SS8 . . . . 164 B4
Beatrice Cl SS5. . . . . 124 D6
Beatrice Ct IG9 . . . . 110 D8
Beatty La SS14 . . . . 142 E6
Beatty Rise CM3. . . . . 101 F6
Beattyville Gdns IG6. . . . . 133 B7
BEAUCHAMP RODING
. . . . .15 A1
Beauchamps CM0 . . . . . . 106 B8
Beauchamps Dr SS11 . . . . .32 F8
Beauchamps Dr SS11 . . . . 122 A8
Beauchamps Sch
SS11. . . . . 122 A8
Beaufort Cl
Chingford E4 . . . . 109 B4
Grays RM16. . . . . 172 F3
North Weald Bassett
CM16 . . . . .47 A4
Beaufort Gdns IG1 . . . . . . 133 A3
Beaufort Rd
Billericay CM12 . . . . .96 F2
Chelmsford CM2 . . . . .33 A4
Beaufort St SS2 . . . . 148 D1
Beaulieu Bvd CM1. . . . . . . .33 A7
Beaulieu Dr EN9. . . . . .65 B6
Beauly Ct RM1. . . . . 113 E2
Beauly Way RM1. . . . . . . 113 E2
Beaumaris Dr IG8 . . . . . . 110 D3
Beaumont Cl RM2 . . . . . . 113 E3
Beaumont Cres RM13. . . . 155 A6
Beaumont Gdns CM3. . . . . .95 C3
Beaumont Park Dr
CM19 . . . . .22 B8
Beaumont Pk CM3 . . . . . . .56 C6
Beaumont Way CM9 . . . . . .36 F8
Beaumont Wlk CM1. . . . . . .31 D5
Beaver Ctr The RM8 . . . . . 134 E4
Beaver Rd IG6. . . . . 112 C5
Beaver Twr SS9. . . . . 146 E6
Beazley End SS12. . . . . . . 121 E6
Bebington Cl CM12 . . . . . . .97 A3
Beccles Ct SS11 . . . . 121 D8
Beccles Dr IG11 . . . . 152 F6
Becket Ave E6. . . . . 152 A2
Becket Cl
Brentwood CM13. . . . . . . 116 C4
Rochford SS4. . . . . 125 D5
Becket Ho 18 CM14 . . . . . 116 C8
Becket Rd SS17 . . . . 160 D4
Becketts SS15 . . . . 141 A6
Becketts Ct
Brentwood CM13. . . . . . . 116 C4
Chelmsford CM1 . . . . .33 A3
Becket Way CM3. . . . . 101 E5
Beckney Ave SS5 . . . . 102 E1
Beckon Rd SS8 . . . . 164 F3
Beckton Alps Ski Ctr*
E6. . . . . 152 A1
Beckton Triangle Ret Pk
E6. . . . . 152 B1
BECONTREE 153 E8
Becontree Ave RM8. . . . . 134 D2
Becontree Day Hospl
RM8 . . . . 134 E2
Becontree Prim Sch
RM8 . . . . 134 B1
Becontree Sta RM9 . . . . . 153 D6
Bedale Rd RM3. . . . . 115 A5
Beddington Rd IG3 . . . . . 133 F4
Bede Rd RM6. . . . . 134 C5
Bedford Cl SS16 . . . . 123 D1
Bedford Gdns RM12 . . . . . 136 C2
Bedford Ho 1 RM3 . . . . . 115 A4
Bedford Pl SS8 . . . . 163 F4
Bedford Rd
Basildon SS16. . . . . 141 B6
Chingford E17 . . . . 109 A1
Grays RM17. . . . . 173 B1
Ilford IG1 . . . . 133 B1
Wallend E6. . . . . 152 A4
Woodford E18 . . . . 110 A1
Bedfords Pk Nature
Trails* RM4. . . . . 113 F5
Bedloes Ave SS11. . . . . . . 122 E7
Bedloes Ct SS11 . . . . 122 F7
Bedwell Ct 4 RM6. . . . . . 134 D4
Bedwell Rd RM3 . . . . 169 A1
Beecham Ct SS15 . . . . 141 C8
Beech Ave
Brentwood CM13. . . . . . . 116 F7
Rayleigh SS6 . . . . 123 D3
Upminster RM14 . . . . 156 B8
Woodford IG9 . . . . 110 B8
Beech Cl
Burnham-on-C CM0 . . . . . 106 B6
Hornchurch RM12 . . . . . . 136 B1
Loughton IG10. . . . . .89 B6
Beechcombe SS17. . . . . . . 161 B4
Beechcroft Ave SS17. . . . . 175 A2

Beechcroft Rd
Canvey Island SS8. . . . . .
Woodford E18 . . . .
Beech Ct
Basildon SS14 . . . .
8 Buckhurst Hill IG9. . . . .
Dartford DA1. . . . .
Ilford IG2 . . . .
Beech Dr CM21. . . . .
Beeches EN9 . . . .
Beeches Cl CM1. . . . .
Beeches Rd
Chelmsford CM1 . . . .
Heybridge CM9 . . . .
Rawreth SS11 . . . .
Beeches The
Brentwood CM14. . . . . . .
Tilbury RM18 . . . .
Beech Farm Cotts
IG8. . . . .
Beechfield
Hoddesdon EN11. . . . . . .
Sawbridgeworth CM21. . .
Beechfield Gdns RM7. . . .
Beechfield Wlk EN9 . . . . .
Beechfield Rd RM10 . . . . .
Beech Gr
Aveley RM15. . . . .
Redbridge IG6. . . . .
Beech Hall Cres E4. . . . . .
Beech Hall Rd E4. . . . . . .
Beech Hill Gdns EN9. . . . .
Beech Ho
15 Brentwood CM13. . . .
Chingford E4 . . . .
Beech La IG9 . . . .
Beech Lo SS3 . . . .
Beechmont Gdns SS2. . . .
Beech Pl CM16 . . . .
Beech Rd
Basildon SS14 . . . .
Hadleigh SS7. . . . .
Hullbridge SS5. . . . .
Willingale CM5. . . . .
Beech Spinney CM14 . . . .
Beech St RM7 . . . .
Beech Terr RM10 . . . . . .
Beech Tree Glade E4. . . . .
Beechwood Dr IG8 . . . . .
Beechwood Gdns
Ilford IG5 . . . .
Rainham RM13 . . . .
Redbridge IG5. . . . .
Beechwood Pk E18 . . . . .
Beecroft Cres SS8 . . . . . .
Beedell Ave
Southend-on-S SS0 . . . . .
Wickford SS11. . . . .
Beehive Cl
Hatfield Heath CM22. . . .
Redbridge IG1 . . . .
Beehive La
Basildon SS14 . . . .
Chelmsford CM2 . . . .
Ilford IG1 . . . .
Redbridge IG1 . . . .
Beehive Lane Prim Sc
CM2. . . . .
Beehive Prep Sch
IG4. . . . .
Beeleigh Ave SS16. . . . . .
Beeleigh Chase CM9. . . . .
Beeleigh Cl SS2 . . . .
Beeleigh Cross SS14. . . . .
Beeleigh E SS14 . . . .
Beeleigh Link CM9 . . . . . .
Beeleigh Rd CM9 . . . .
Beeston Ct 1 DA2. . . . . .
Beeston Sts SS15 . . . .
Beggarhill CM4 . . . .
Begonia Cl CM1 . . . .
Beke Hall Chase N
SS6. . . . .
Beke Hall Chase S
SS6. . . . .
Bekeswell La CM2 . . . . . .
Bekeswell Pl CM2 . . . . . .
Belchamps Rd SS7 . . . . .
Belchamps Way SS5. . . . .
Belcher Rd 6 EN11. . . . .
Belchers La CM9 . . . .
Belcon Ind Est EN11 . . . .
Beldowes SS15 . . . .
Belfairs Cl SS9 . . . .
Belfairs Dr
Dagenham RM6. . . . .
Southend-on-S SS9 . . . . .
Belfairs High Sch
SS9. . . . .
Belfairs Park Cl SS9 . . . . .
Belfairs Park Dr SS9. . . . .
Belfry Rd E12 . . . .
Belgrave Ave RM2 . . . . . .
Belgrave Cl
Chelmsford CM2 . . . .
Rayleigh SS6 . . . .
Southend-on-S SS9 . . . . .
Belgrave Hts E11 . . . .
Belgrave Market IG1 . . . .
Belgrave Rd
Billericay CM12 . . . .
Ilford IG1 . . . .
Redbridge IG1 . . . .

Rd *continued*
d-on-S SS9 146 B7
d E11 132 A3
Terr IG8 110 A7
a Mans SS1 167 D6
Voods Ctry Pk*
156 D2
Rd E4 109 B4
RM3 114 B2
SS15 141 D7
he DA9 176 F2
RM14 137 C2
m CM16 67 E7
MMON 67 C7
M3 78 A1
ines Pleasaunce
109 A8
CM2 32 A1
Ave SS1 167 C8
Mews SS2 148 C1
Pl SS1 167 C8
Rd
CM12 96 F2
rch RM11 136 F3
d-on-S SS2 148 C1
Rd
d E17 109 D1
RM5 113 C4
n Ave RM10 135 C1
n Gn CM12 119 B8
SS16 142 E3
Gdns CM17 24 C7
er Path RM3 114 C3
CM3 56 C7
Cl CM12 119 B8
nham RM10 154 B6
RM17 177 F8
akering SS3 150 A3
e Cres SS9 146 D5
e La
Hatch CM14 93 E4
d-on-S SS9 146 D5
e Rd SS9 146 D6
se Rd RM7 135 C3
e Villas CM1 6 D3
am Ct 7
153 B2
am La SS6 123 D2
N11 21 A6
e Ave SS17 160 F4
Ho 3 IG7 112 A5
CM1 32 B2
d
one CM4 74 B3
geworth CM21 1 E2
ves Cl SS17 160 C2
ase CM2 54 E6
ner Par
142 B1
Rd SS16 142 B2
ddow CM2 54 F6
geworth CM21 1 E2
CM21 1 E2
SS2 147 D4
e Dr CM1 32 E7
Ave
er RM14 136 F2
SS12 121 B7
Cl
ord CM1 32 E7
d E4 109 D5
SS12 121 B7
d IG8 110 B6
Rd
M17 177 F8
rch RM12 136 D1
1 133 C1
s Farm La
19 E2
s SS15 141 D6
Rd RM3 136 F8
ridge SS9 165 D8
dns SS9 165 C8
ay E SS9 165 C8
ay W SS9 165 B8
Rd DA17 169 C2
ey Cl CM1 31 E6
RE 169 B2
e Ave
SS5 124 C6
e IG5 111 B1
e Cl CM3 56 F7
e Ct
-on-C CM0 106 C3
ord CM2 53 F8
on EN11 21 A5
CM9 58 F8
e Ind Est
169 C5
e Inf Sch
169 B3
e Jun Sch
169 B3
e Link Bsns Pk
169 C3
e Pl CM9 58 F8
e Rd
od CM14 115 F7
-on-C CM0 106 C3
CM3 56 F7
e Sta DA17 169 B3
e The CM0 106 C4
he CM4 74 A3
Dr CM3 101 E6
ch SS8 163 E4

Bendigo Wharf DA9 177 B3
Benedict Ct RM6 134 F5
Benedict Dr CM1 31 E2
Benets Rd RM11 137 A3
Benfleet For Canvey Island Sta SS7 163 D8
Benfleet Park Rd SS7 144 B2
Benfleet Rd SS7 145 B2
Bengal Rd IG1 133 B1
Bengeo Gdns RM6 134 C5
Benham Wlk SS13 143 C8
Benhurst Ave RM12 136 B1
Benhurst Prim Sch RM12 136 B1
Benjamin Cl RM11 136 A5
Benjamin Ct RM13 154 E2
Benleigh Ho SS6 123 C3
Bennett Rd RM6 134 E4
Bennett's Ave CM3 77 F3
Bennett's Castle La RM8 134 D1
Bennington Rd IG8 109 E3
Bennions Cl RM12 155 D6
Bennison Dr RM3 114 E1
Benrek Cl IG6 111 C2
Benskins La RM4 92 D1
Benson Ct 4 EN3 65 A1
Benson Rd RM17 178 C8
Benstede Ct 9 EN11 21 A6
Bentalls SS14 120 A1
Bentalls Bsns Pk SS14 120 A1
Bentalls Cl SS2 148 A4
Bentalls Complex The CM9 37 B5
Bentham Ho 4 CM20 10 C1
Ben Tillet Cl IG11 153 A5
BENTLEY 93 D6
Bentley Dr
Harlow CM17 24 C7
Ilford IG2 133 C5
Bentleys CM22 3 B2
Bentley St Paul's CE Prim Sch CM15 93 D6
Bentley St DA12 179 C1
Bentleys The SS2 147 A7
Bentley Street Ind Est 8 DA12 179 C1
Bentley Villas CM22 3 B2
Bentley Way IG8 110 A7
Benton Gdns SS17 160 F5
Benton Rd IG1 133 D3
Bentonwood SS7 145 C5
Bentry Cl RM8 134 E2
Bentry Rd RM8 134 F2
Benvenue Ave SS9 146 F6
Benyon Ct RM15 157 C3
Benyon Path RM15 157 C3
Benyon Prim Sch RM15 157 C3
Berberis Cl SS16 140 F4
Berberis Ct 2 IG11 152 B6
Berdan Ct EN3 65 A2
Berdens SS16 142 D5
Bere Cl DA9 177 C2
Berecroft CM18 23 D3
Beredens La CM13 115 F1
Berengers Pl RM9 153 B6
Berens Cl SS11 99 F1
Beresford Cl SS7 145 D4
Beresford Ct
Billericay CM12 96 F5
Hadleigh SS7 145 D4
Beresford Dr IG8 110 C6
Beresford Gdns
Dagenham RM6 134 E6
Hadleigh SS7 145 D4
Beresford Mans 19 SS1 167 C7
Beresford Rd
Chingford, Chingford Green E4 87 E1
Chingford, Highams Park E17 109 B2
Gravesend DA11 178 E1
Southend-on-S SS1 167 C7
Berg Ave SS8 164 D5
Bergen Ct CM9 58 E8
Bergholt Ave IG4 132 E6
Berica Ct IG6 133 C8
Berkeley Ave
Redbridge IG5 111 B1
Romford RM5 113 C3
Berkeley Cl RM11 137 B2
Berkeley Ct SS4 147 F7
Berkeley Dr
Billericay CM12 97 A5
Hornchurch RM11 137 A2
Berkeley Gdns SS9 146 A1
Berkeley La SS8 164 A3
Berkeley Terr RM18 179 A7
Berkely Dr CM2 32 F2
Berkhampstead Rd DA17 169 A1
Berkley Cres 4 DA12 179 C1
Berkley Ct SS0 147 E2
Berkley Hill SS17 160 E4
Berkley Rd DA12 179 B1
Berkshire Cl SS9 146 C5
Berkshire Way RM11 137 A7
Berman's Cl CM13 117 B8
Bermuda Rd RM18 179 A5
Bernard Gr EN9 65 B6
Bernard Rd RM7 135 C4
Bernards Cl IG6 111 D3
Bernard St 14 DA12 179 B1
BERNERS RODING 28 E8
Berners Wlk SS14 142 D8

Bernice Cl RM13 155 C1
Bernwell Rd E4 109 E7
Berrybank Cl 4 E4 109 C8
Berry Cl
Basildon SS16 141 B5
Dagenham RM10 154 A7
Hornchurch RM12 155 D7
Wickford SS12 121 B6
Berry La SS16 141 B4
Berryman Cl RM8 134 C1
Berrymore Wlk SS6 123 F2
Berrys Arc SS6 123 D2
Berry Vale CM3 101 E6
Bersham La RM17 172 F2
Berther Rd RM11 136 E4
Berthold Mews EN9 65 B6
Berwick Ave CM1 32 B7
Berwick Cl EN8 65 A5
Berwick Ct 10 DA2 176 B1
Berwick La CM5 69 E6
Berwick Pond Cl RM13 155 D3
Berwick Pond Rd RM13 155 F5
Berwick Rd RM13 155 D3
Berwood Rd SS17 160 F3
Betchworth Rd IG3 133 E1
Bethany Cl RM12 136 C2
Bethany Ho RM6 134 D8
Bethell Ave IG1 133 A4
Betjeman Cl SS6 123 F3
Betjeman Mews SS2 148 A2
Betjeman Way CM5 48 F5
Betony Cres CM12 96 F5
Betony Rd RM3 114 D4
Betoyne Ave E4 109 E6
Betoyne Cl CM11 97 D2
Betterton Rd RM13 154 E3
Betts La EN9 22 C2
Bett's La SS5 124 D6
Betula Wlk RM13 155 D2
Beulah Rd
Epping CM16 46 A2
Hornchurch RM12 136 C1
Bevan Ave IG11 153 A5
Bevan Ho
Barking IG11 153 B5
Grays RM16 173 D4
Bevans Cl DA9 177 C1
Bevan Way RM12 136 F1
Beveland Rd SS8 165 A3
Beverley Ave SS8 164 A3
Beverley Cl
Hornchurch RM11 136 F4
Orsett RM16 174 D7
Beverley Cres IG8 110 B3
Beverley Gdns
Hornchurch RM11 136 F4
Southend-on-S SS2 147 E4
Beverley Rd
Chingford E4 109 D4
Dagenham RM9 153 E8
Beverley Rise CM11 97 C1
Bevil Ct EN11 8 A1
Bevile Ho RM17 178 B7
Bevin Ho RM15 171 C4
Bevin Wlk SS17 160 D2
Bevis Cl DA2 176 C1
Bewley Ct SS2 148 E2
Bexhill Dr RM17 177 F8
Bexley Coll DA17 169 C2
Bexley Coll (Erith Rd Campus) DA17 169 B1
Bexley Gdns RM6 134 B6
Bexley Rd DA8 169 F1
Beyers Gdns 6 EN11 8 A1
Beyers Prospect EN11 8 A1
Beyers Ride 4 EN11 8 A1
Bibby Cl SS17 161 A2
Bickenhall SS3 168 D8
Bickerton Point CM3 101 F6
BICKNACRE 56 F2
Bicknacre Rd
Danbury CM3 56 F4
East Hanningfield CM3 78 C8
Biddenden Ct 9 SS13 143 C6
Bideford Cl
Romford RM3 114 C2
Southend-on-S SS0 147 A5
BIGGIN 179 C8
Biggin La RM16 179 B8
Bight The CM3 101 F5
BILLERICAY 97 B1
Billericay Com Hospl CM12 96 F1
Billericay Rd
Ingrave CM13 117 F3
Little Burstead CM12, CM13 118 B3
Billericay Sch The CM12 119 B8
Billericay Sta CM12 97 A3
Billers Chase CM1 33 A7
Billet La
Hornchurch RM11 136 D4
Stanford-le-H SS17 160 E1
Billet Rd
Chingford E17 109 A2
Ilford RM6 134 C8
Billings Cl RM9 153 C5
Bilton Rd
Chelmsford CM1 31 F1
Hadleigh SS7 145 E3
Bingham Cl RM15 172 B7
Bingley Rd EN11 21 C6
Binley Rd CM2 32 F2
Bircham Rd SS2 148 A2

Birch Cl
Buckhurst Hill IG9 110 D7
Canewdon SS4 104 E1
Canvey Island SS8 163 F3
Rayleigh SS6 123 C3
Romford RM7 135 B8
South Benfleet SS7 144 B7
South Ockendon RM15 157 D1
Birch Cres
Hornchurch RM11 136 E7
South Ockendon RM15 157 D2
Birch Ct
Chingford E4 109 B4
Dagenham RM6 134 C5
Birchdale SS5 101 D3
Birchdale Gdns RM6 134 D4
Birche Cl SS9 146 E4
Birches The
Brentwood CM13 116 E7
North Weald Bassett CM16 47 B5
South Benfleet SS7 144 C8
Waltham Abbey EN9 65 F5
Birches Wlk CM2 54 A2
Birchfield RM16 172 D5
Birch Gdns
Dagenham RM10 135 C1
Tillingham CM0 63 E4
Birch Gn SS12 121 D7
Birch La CM4 75 F3
Birchmores SS15 141 A7
Birch Pl DA9 176 E1
Birch Rd
Romford RM7 135 B8
Tillingham CM0 63 E4
Birch View CM16 46 B2
Birchwood
South Benfleet SS7 144 B7
Waltham Abbey EN9 65 E5
Birchwood Cl CM13 116 C4
Birchwood Dr SS9 147 A2
Birchwood Ind Est EN9 22 A2
Birchwood Rd
Cock Clarks CM3 57 F2
Corringham SS17 161 B4
Birdbrook Cl
Brentwood CM13 95 B3
Dagenham RM10 154 C5
Bird La
Great Warley CM13 138 D8
Little Warley CM13 116 C1
Upminster RM14 137 D6
Birds Cl CM11 98 C5
Birds Farm Ave RM5 113 B2
Birds Gn CM5 28 A5
BIRDS GREEN 28 B6
Birk Beck CM1 32 C5
Birkbeck Gdns IG8 110 A8
Birkbeck Rd
Brentwood CM13 95 D3
Ilford IG2 133 D6
Romford RM7 135 D3
Birkdale Ave RM3 115 A3
Birnam Wood Pru RM11 136 E3
Birs Cl SS11 99 D1
Biscay SS2 147 A7
Bishop Hall La CM1 32 B4
Bishop Rd CM1 32 B3
Bishops Ave RM6 134 C5
Bishops' CE & RC Prim Sch The CM1 32 F6
Bishops Cl SS13 121 A2
Bishops Court Gdns CM2 32 E4
Bishops Ct
Greenhithe DA9 176 E2
Romford RM7 135 B7
Bishop's Ct SS8 164 D3
Bishopsfield CM18 23 E5
Bishops Gate 9 CM14 116 C8
Bishop's Hall Rd CM15 94 B3
Bishops Rd
Stanford-le-H SS17 160 F3
Wickford SS12 121 D3
Bishopsteignton SS3 149 D1
Bishops Wlk CM15 116 F8
Bittern Ct E4 87 D2
Blackacre Rd CM16 67 E2
Black Adder Cotts EN9 43 D8
Blackall Ind Est CM3 79 E1
Blackberry Gr CM0 42 B3
Blackborne Rd RM10 154 B6
Blackbush Ave RM6 134 D6
Black Bush La SS17 159 D3
Blackbush Spring CM20 11 A1
BLACKCAT 27 A8
Black Chapel La CM6 7 E8
Blackdown SS0 147 E1
Blackgate Rd SS3 168 G7
Blackheath Chase SS16 160 D8
Blackhorse La CM16 47 D6
Black Lion Ct CM17 11 C4
Blacklock CM2 33 A3
BLACKMORE 72 F8
Blackmore Ave SS8 164 B2
Blackmore Ct EN9 66 A6
Blackmore Mead CM4 72 F8
Blackmore Prim Sch CM4 50 E1
Blackmore Rd
Blackmore CM1 51 D3
Buckhurst Hill IG9 88 E2
Grays RM17 173 C1

Blackmore Rd *continued*
Hook End CM15 72 C5
Ingatestone CM4 73 D6
Kelvedon Hatch CM15 71 F2
Blackmores SS15 140 F6
Blackmore Wlk SS6 124 A2
Blackshots La RM16 173 C5
Blacksmith Cl
Billericay CM12 97 B5
Chelmsford CM1 32 E8
Dagenham RM6 134 C5
Blacksmiths Alley CM4 72 E8
Black Smiths Cl SG12 8 A7
Blacksmiths Cotts CM17 24 F4
Blacksmith's La RM13 154 F4
Blacksmiths Way CM21 1 B1
Blackthorn Cl CM1 31 A1
Blackthorn Ct SS16 141 A4
Blackthorne Dr E4 109 D6
Blackthorne Rd SS8 164 C3
Blackthorn Rd
Barking IG1 152 D7
Grays RM16 173 B5
Hockley SS5 124 F8
Blackthorn Way CM14 116 D5
Blackwater SS7 144 F4
Black Water CM14 94 B1
Blackwater Cl
Burnham-on-C CM0 106 C5
Chelmsford CM1 32 C6
Heybridge Basin CM9 37 E3
Rainham RM13 169 E8
Southend-on-S SS3 149 E1
Blackwater Mews CM0 61 E2
Blackwood Chine CM3 101 E6
Blake Ave IG11 152 F4
Blakeborough Dr RM3 114 E1
Blake Cl RM13 154 F4
Blake Ct CM3 101 E6
Blake Hall Cres E11 132 A3
Blake Hall Dr SS11 122 A6
Blake Hall Gdns* CM5 48 E7
Blake Hall Rd
Chipping Ongar CM5 48 A5
Wanstead E11 132 A4
Blakes Ct CM21 1 E2
Blakesley Ho 4 E12 133 A1
Blake Way RM18 179 C5
Blanchard Gr EN3 65 B1
Blanchard Mews RM3 114 F3
Blandford Cl RM7 135 B7
Blandford Cres E4 87 C2
Blaney Cres E6 152 B2
Blatches Chase
Rayleigh SS2 146 F7
Southend-on-S SS2 147 A8
Blatchford Ho 8 RM10 135 A1
Blenheim Ave IG2 133 A5
Blenheim Chase SS9 146 E3
Blenheim Cl
Bicknacre CM3 56 F2
Hockley SS5 124 E8
Romford RM7 135 C7
Sawbridgeworth CM21 11 C8
Upminster RM14 137 E3
Blenheim Cres SS9 146 E2
Blenheim Ct
Hornchurch RM12 155 C7
4 Wickford SS11 122 A5
Woodford IG8 110 B3
Woodford IG8 110 C2
Blenheim Gdns
Aveley RM15 171 B5
Mayland CM3 61 A1
Blenheim Mews SS9 146 E3
Blenheim Park Cl SS9 146 F4
Blenheim Prim Sch SS9 146 F3
Blenheim Rd CM15 94 A3
Blenheim Way CM16 47 A4
Blessing Way IG11 153 C3
Bletchington Ct 1 DA17 169 A2
Blewetts Cotts RM13 154 F2
Bligh Rd DA11 179 A1
Blind La
Goldhanger CM9 38 C7
Howe Green CM2 55 F4
Little Burstead CM12 118 B5
Mundon CM9 59 C2
West Hanningfield CM2 76 F5
Blithbury Rd RM9 153 B6
Blockhouse Rd RM17 178 C8
Blomville Rd RM8 134 E1
Bloomfield Cres IG2 133 B5
Bloomsbury Ho IG8 110 E4
Bloomsbury Mews IG8 110 E4
Blossom Cl RM9 153 F4
Blountswood Rd
Hockley SS5 124 A8
Hullbridge SS5 123 F6
Blower Cl SS6 123 F3
Blows Cotts RM15 171 D5
Blue Anchor La RM18 174 E1
Bluebell Cl RM7 135 E2
Bluebell Gn 5 CM1 32 E7
Bluebell Way IG1 152 B6
Bluebell Wood CM12 96 E4

Blueberry Cl IG8 .... 110 A4
Bluebird La RM10....... 154 A5
Bluegate Pk CM14......116 B7
Blue House Farm Chase
CM3 ....103 B7
Bluehouse Rd E4 ....109 E7
Bluemans CM16 ....47 D7
Bluemans End CM16 ....47 D7
Blue Mill La CM9.......35 E4
Blunden Cl RM8 ....134 C3
Blunts Wall Rd CM12....96 E1
Blyth Ave SS3 ....168 C7
Blythe Rd
Hoddesdon EN11........21 D5
Stanford-le-H SS17 .....160 E4
Blythe Way
Maldon CM9..........59 A8
South Benfleet SS7 .....144 C7
Blyth Ho DA8..........169 E1
Blythswood Rd IG3 .....134 A4
Blyth Wlk RM14 ....137 E5
Blyton Cl SS12.........121 D5
Boar Cl IG7 ....112 A5
Boarded Row SS4.......128 A5
Boardman Ave E4 ....87 B4
Bobbing Cl SS4.........125 F2
BOBBINGWORTH 48 D8
Bobbingworth Mill
CM5...................48 A7
Bod Dunn Way DA1.....176 A4
Bockingham Gn SS13...143 A8
Bodell Cl RM16 ....173 B3
Bodiam Cl SS13 ....143 B6
Bodle Ave DA10 ....177 E1
Bodley Cl CM16........45 F1
Bodmin Rd CM1 ....32 D5
Bohemia Chase SS9 ....146 D5
Boiler Ho The SS4 ......125 E2
Boleyn Cl
Billericay CM12 ....97 A5
Grays RM16...........172 F3
Loughton IG10.........88 E3
Southend-on-S SS9 ....146 C7
Boleyn Ct IG9 ....88 B1
Boleyn Gdns
Brentwood CM13........117 A7
Dagenham RM10 ....154 C5
Boleyn Ho **1** SS4....125 F2
Boleyn Way
Boreham CM3 ....20 F1
Redbridge IG6 ....111 C4
Bolney Dr SS9.........146 C7
Boltons The IG8 ....110 A6
Bommel Ave SS8 ......165 A3
Bonchurch Ave SS9....146 D2
Bonchurch Ct **20**
RM19 ....171 B1
Bonds Cotts CM5.......15 A1
Bond St
Chelmsford CM2 ....32 C2
Grays RM17...........178 C8
Bonham Dr RM16.......174 A8
Bonham Gdns RM8 .....134 D2
Bonham Rd RM8........134 D1
Bonington Chase CM1 ..32 E6
Bonington Rd RM12....155 D7
Bonks Hill CM21.........1 D1
Bonner Wlk RM16 .....172 C7
Bonnet Mews RM16....136 E3
Bonningtons CM13......117 B7
Bonnygate SS14 ....142 D7
Bonnygate Prim Sch
RM15 ....172 B8
Boomes Ind Est RM13...154 F1
Boons Cl CM3 ....33 E8
Bootham Cl CM12 ......96 F1
Bootham Rd CM12 .....96 F1
Boothby Ct E4 ....109 C7
Booth Pl CM0 ....106 C5
Booth's Ct CM13........95 B3
Borda Cl CM1 ....32 A5
Border Edge Ho **6**
CM14 ....116 C6
Border's La IG10 ....89 B5
BOREHAM 33 E8
Boreham Cl SS11.......122 B5
Boreham Ct CM1 ....6 D2
Boreham Ind Est CM3...20 F2
Boreham Mews **1** EN11 ..8 A1
Boreham Prim Sch
CM3 ....33 F8
Borland Cl CM2 ....177 A2
Borley Ct RM16 ....174 D7
Borman Cl SS9 ....147 A6
Borrett Ave SS8 ....164 A4
Borrowdale Cl
Redbridge IG4.........132 E7
Thundersley SS7 ....144 F6
Borrowdale Rd
Thundersley SS7 ....144 F6
Thundersley SS7 ....144 F7
Borwick La
Crays Hill CM11........120 F4
Wickford CM11, SS12 ...121 A4
Bosanquet Rd EN11.....21 C8
Boscombe Ave
Grays RM17...........173 D2
Hornchurch RM11 .....136 D4
Wickford SS12.........120 F8
Boscombe Mews SS2 ..167 B8
Boscombe Rd SS2 .....148 B1
Bosgrove E4 ....109 C8
Bostocke Cl SS15 ......141 D5
Boston Ave
Rayleigh SS6 ....123 B4

Boston Ave continued
Southend-on-S SS2 ....147 F1
Boston Lofts **2** SS2 ...147 F1
Boswell Ave SS4.......125 D5
Bosworth Cl CM2 ......32 C2
Bosworths Sch The CM1 ...32 D6
Bosworth Cl SS5.......124 F4
Bosworth Cres RM3....114 C4
Bosworth Ho DA8......169 E1
Bosworth Rd
Dagenham RM10 ....135 A1
Southend-on-S SS9 ....146 C7
Botany Cotts RM19 ....171 A1
Botany Terr RM19......171 A1
Botany Way RM19......171 B1
Botelers SS16 ....141 E4
Boteley Cl E4..........146 C2
Botney Hill Rd CM12...118 D4
Botchers Mead CM1....32 F7
Boucher Wlk **2**
RM13 ....155 A6
Boudicca Mews **5**
CM2 ....32 B1
Bouldrewood Rd SS7 ..144 B5
Boulevard The
Greenhithe DA9.......177 C3
3 Redbridge IG8 .....111 A3
Rochford SS4..........125 F3
Boulter Gdns RM13 ....155 A7
Boulton Cotts CM9......37 B5
Boult Ho DA8..........134 F2
Boult Rd SS15.........141 C8
Boundary Cl IG3.......152 E8
Boundary Ct CM16......67 D7
Boundary Dr CM13......95 E2
Boundary Rd
Barking IG11 ....152 C3
Barking IG11 ....152 D4
Romford RM1 ....136 A5
Southend-on-S SS9 ....146 B8
Upminster RM14 ....137 B2
Boundary Way SS3 ....168 E6
Bounderby Gr CM1 .....31 E7
Bourne Ave SS15 ......141 A8
Bournebridge Cl CM13 ..95 E2
Bournebridge La RM4...91 B2
Bourne Ct SS15........141 A8
Bourne Ct
Wanstead E11 ....132 A6
Woodford IG8 ....110 D1
Bourne End RM11 .....137 A4
Bourne Gdns E4 ....100 D6
Bourne Ho IG9 ....110 D7
Bournemouth Prim
Sch SS2 ....148 B2
Bournemouth Park Rd
SS2 ....148 B2
BOURNES GREEN 149 B1
Bournes Green Chase
SS3 ....149 B1
Bournes Green Inf Sch
SS1 ....168 B8
Bournes Green Jun Sch
SS1 ....168 B8
Bouvel Dr CM0 ....106 B8
Bouverie Rd CM2 ......54 B8
Bovey Way RM15 ......172 B8
BOVINGER 48 A7
Bovinger Way SS1 .....148 F1
BOW ARROW 176 B1
Bow Arrow La
Dartford DA1..........176 A1
Dartford DA2..........176 B1
Bowbank Cl SS3.......149 F1
Bowden Dr RM11......136 E3
Bower Cl RM5.........113 D3
Bower Ct CM16........68 A7
Bower Farm Rd RM4...113 D7
Bower Gdns CM0 ....36 F3
Bower Hall Ind Est
CM16 ....68 A7
Bower La SS14 ....142 E8
Bowerman Rd RM16 ...174 A2
Bower Park Sch RM1...113 E4
Bowers Court Dr
SS13..................143 F5
BOWERS GIFFORD 143 E6
Bowers Ho **5** IG11 ...152 B5
Bowers Rd SS7........144 D5
Bower Vale CM16 ......68 A7
Bowery Ct **4** RM10 ..154 B6
Bowes Ct **8** DA2.....176 B1
Bowes Dr CM5 ....49 A4
Bowes Ho CM5 ....49 A4
Bowes Rd RM8 ....153 C8
Bowfell Cl SS16 ....141 A5
Bowfell Dr SS16.......141 A5
Bowhay CM13..........117 B8
Bowland Rd IG8 ....110 C4
Bowlers Croft SS14 ....120 F2
Bowls The IG7.........111 F7
Bowman Ave SS9 .....146 B6
Bowmont CM13.........95 B3
Bown Cl RM18.........179 B5
Bowness Way RM12...155 A7
Bowyer Ct **4** 87 C1
Box Cl SS15...........119 D1
Boxford Cl SS6 ....122 F3
Box La IG11 ....153 C3
Boxley La CM22.........4 D8
Boxmoor Rd RM5......113 C5
Boxoll Rd RM9........134 F1
Boxted Cl IG9 ....88 E1
Boyce Gn SS7.........144 D2
Boyce Hill Cl SS9......146 B5
Boyce Rd
Southend-on-S SS3 ....168 H8

Boyce Rd continued
Stanford-le-H SS17 ....160 C3
Boyce View Dr SS7....144 C2
Boyd Ct SS12..........121 F5
Boyden Cl SS2.........148 F2
Boyle Ho **21** DA17.....169 A3
Boyles Court Cotts
CM14 ....116 A3
Boyne Dr CM1 ....32 D6
Boyne Rd RM10........135 A1
Boyton Cl SS7.........145 A5
BOYTON CROSS 30 B7
Boyton Hall La CM1....30 C8
Boytons SS15..........141 E6
Brabant Rd CM3 ....143 A8
Brabner Gdns CM11 ....98 C4
Bracelet Cl SS17.......160 F5
Brace Wlk CM3 ....101 E5
Bracken Cl RM3 ....109 B8
Bracken Ct **1** DA4....111 F4
Brackendale CM11......97 D3
Brackendale Ave
SS13..................143 C4
Brackendale Cl SS15 ..124 E7
Brackendale Ct SS13 ..143 C4
Brackendale Gdns
RM14 ....143 C4
Bracken Dell SS6.......123 E2
Brackenden Dr CM1 ...32 D7
Bracken Dr IG7.........32 D7
Bracken Ind Est IG6 ...111 F2
Bracken Mews
Chingford E4 ....87 C1
Romford RM7 ....135 B5
Brackens Dr CM14 .....116 D5
Bracken The E4 ....109 C8
Bracken Way SS7 .....145 A6
Brackley Cres SS13 ....143 A8
Brackley Ho **41** RM3 ..114 F4
Brackley Sq IG8 ....110 D3
Bracknell Ho **3** RM1 ..54 A7
Bradbourne Rd RM17..178 B8
Bradbourne Way
SS13..................143 C5
Bradd Cl RM15 ....157 C2
Braddock Cl RM5......113 C4
Bradfield Cl **12** RM19 ..171 B1
Bradfield Dr IG11......153 A7
Bradfield Ho IG8 ......111 A4
Bradford Bury SS9 ....146 C6
Bradford Cl IG8 ......111 A4
Bradford St CM2 ....32 A1
Brading Cres E11 ......132 B2
Bradleigh Ave RM17 ..173 C2
Bradley Ave SS7 ......144 F5
Bradley Cl
Canvey Island SS8.....164 A5
Thundersley SS7 ....144 A5
Bradley Gn SS13 ......121 C1
Bradley Ho IG8 ....110 A3
Bradley Link SS7 ......144 F5
Bradley Rd EN8 ....65 C4
Bradley Way SS4 ......125 F1
Bradshaw Rd RM16 ...173 A5
Bradwall Ave RM10 ...135 A2
Bradwell Cl RM12......155 B6
Bradwell Ct **3** CM13 ..95 C3
Bradwell Gn **2** CM13 ..95 C3
Bradwell Ho SS11 .....121 F7
BRADWELL-ON-SEA ...42 B2
Bradwell Power Sta
Visitor Ctr* CM0 ......42 A6
Bradwell Rd
Buckhurst Hill IG9 .....88 E2
Steeple CM0 ....62 A3
St Lawrence CM0 ......62 E6
Tillingham CM0 ....63 E6
BRADWELL WATERSIDE
...................41 F4
Brady Ave IG10........89 C7
Brady Ct **4** RM8 .....134 D3
Brady Prim Sch RM13..170 C8
Braemar Ave CM2 .....54 B8
Braemar Cres SS9 ....146 A2
Braemar Gdns RM11 ..137 A5
Braemar Wlk SS13 ....143 B6
Braemore SS8 ....163 F5
Braeside Sch
Buckhurst Hill IG9 .....88 B1
Buckhurst Hill IG9.....110 C8
Bragg Cl RM8 ....153 B6
Braintree Ave IG4 .....132 E7
Braintree Rd RM10 ....135 A1
Brainwood Cl SS9 .....146 A5
Braiswick Pl SS15 .....141 B8
Braithwaite Ave RM7 ..135 A4
Bramber Ct **7** DA2...176 B1
Bramble Cl
Chigwell IG7 ....89 C1
Southend-on-S SS7 ....146 B7
Bramble Cres SS7 .....146 B7
Bramble Croft DA8 ....169 C2
Bramble Ct **2** IG6.....111 F4
Bramble La RM14......156 D4
Bramble Rd
Canvey Island SS8.....164 C3
Hadleigh SS7 ....145 F6
Southend-on-S SS9 ....146 B7
Brent Way DA2.........176 B1
Bramble Rise CM20 ....10 C1
Brambles The
Basildon SS15 ....141 A8
Chigwell IG7 ....111 C4
Southminster CM0 .....84 A7
Steeple CM0 ....84 A7
Brambles Way The SS15 ..119 F1
Bramblings The E4 ....109 D6
Bramerton Rd SS5.....124 D6
Bramfield Rd E SS6....124 A2

Bramfield Rd W SS6 ...123 F2
Bramley Cl IG8 ....110 C3
Bramley Cres IG2......133 A5
Bramley Ct
7 Chingford E4 .....87 C1
Hadleigh SS7 ....145 E2
Bramley Gdns SS15 ...141 C8
Bramley Ho IG2 ....133 A5
Bramley Pl CM2 ....54 D7
Bramleys SS17 ....160 D3
Bramley Shaw EN9 ....65 F6
Bramleys The SS4 .....125 D5
Bramley Way CM2 .....61 A1
Brampstead **5** SS15 ..141 A6
Brampton Cl
Corringham SS17......161 A4
Southend-on-S SS0 ...147 A4
Bramshill Cl IG7........111 E5
Bramston Cl
Great Baddow CM2 .....54 F8
Redbridge IG6.........111 F4
Bramston Link SS15 ...140 E6
Bramston Way SS15 ...140 E6
Bramwoods Rd CM2 ...54 E8
Brancaster Pl IG10 ....88 F6
Brancaster Rd IG2 ....133 E5
Brancepeth Gdns IG9...110 A8
Branch Rd
Hadleigh SS7 ....145 E2
Redbridge IG6.........112 B5
Brandenburg Rd IG9 ..110 D4
Brandesbury Sq **4**
IG8...................111 A3
Brandon Cl
Billericay CM12 ....97 A5
Grays RM16...........172 F3
Brandon Groves Ave
RM15 ....157 D2
Brandville Gdns IG6 ...133 B8
BRANDY HOLE 102 A4
Branfil Inf Sch RM14 ...137 A1
Branfil Jun Sch RM14...156 A8
Branfill Rd RM14 ......137 B2
Branksome Ave
Hockley SS5 ....124 E8
Stanford-le-H SS17 ....160 E4
Wickford SS12 ....120 F7
Branksome Ct SS17 ...160 D3
Branksome Rd SS2 ....148 C1
Branscombe Gdns
SS1...................149 B1
Branscombe Sq SS3 ..149 B1
Branscombe Wlk SS1 ..149 B1
Branstone Ct **17**
RM19 ....171 B1
Brant Ct **3** RM1 ......135 D7
Branton Rd DA9 ....176 F1
Brantwood Gdns IG4 ..132 E7
Brathertons Ct CM12...96 F3
Braxted Cl SS4 ....125 C4
Braxteds **10** SS15 ....141 A6
Braybrooke SS14 ......142 B6
Brayburn Ct SS0.......147 A1
Bray Ct SS3 ....149 E2
Brayers Mews SS4 ....125 F1
Brayfield Ct SS9 ......146 E4
BRAYS GROVE 24 A8
Brays La SS4 ....125 E5
Brays Mead RM18 .....23 F6
Brays Springs EN9 .....65 F5
Brazencroft Rd RM12 ..136 D3
Braziers Cl CM2 ....54 C7
Breach Barns Cvn Pk
EN9 ....44 B1
Breach Barns La EN9 ..43 F1
Breach La RM9 ....154 A2
Breach Rd RM20 ......176 F8
Bread & Cheese Hill
SS7...................144 E5
Break Egg Hill CM11 ...97 D3
Breakneck Hill **1**
DA9 ....177 B2
Bream Gdns E6........152 A2
Breamore Ct IG3 ......134 A2
Breamore Rd IG3......133 F2
Brean Wlk IG6 ....133 C8
Brecon Cl SS13 ....143 C8
Brede Cl E6 ....152 A2
Bredo Ho **6** IG11.....153 B2
Bree Hill CM3 ....101 C6
Brempsons SS14 ......142 A7
Brendon Cl EN11 ......21 A4
Brendon Gdns IG2 ....133 E6
Brendon Pl CM1 ....31 E1
Brendon Rd RM8 .....135 A4
Brendon Way SS0 .....147 A5
Brennan Cl CM3 ....80 F6
Brennans Field SS16 ..141 C4
Brent Ave CM3 ....79 D1
Brent Cl DA2 ....176 B1
Brent Ct RM2 ....136 C8
Brentfield Rd DA1 .....176 A1
Brenthall Twrs CM17 ...24 C6
Brentleigh Ct CM14 ...116 A7
Brent Way DA2.........176 B1
BRENTWOOD 116 E8
Brentwood Cathedral*
CM14 ....116 D8
Brentwood Ctr The*
CM15 ....94 C3
Brentwood Cty High Sch
CM15 ....94 D1
Brentwood Pl CM15...94 D1
Brentwood Rd
Bulphan CM14 ....139 F3

Brentwood Rd continued
Chipping Ongar CM5,
CM15 ....
Grays RM16...........
Ingrave CM13 ....
Orsett RM16, RM14 ....
Romford RM1, RM2 ....
West Horndon CM13 ...
Brentwood Sch
Brentwood CM15......
Shenfield CM15 ....
Brentwood Sta CM14 ..
Brentwood Ursuline
Convent High Sch
CM14 ....
Bressey Gr E18........
Bressingham Gdns
CM3 ....
Bretons SS15 ....
Bretons Cotts RM13...
Brettenham Ave E17...
Brettenham Dr SS1....
Brettenham Rd E17....
Brett Gdns RM9 ....
Bretts Villas CM6 .....
Brevet Ct RM19 ....
Brewers Yd CM0 ......
Brewery Fields CM2 ...
Brewery Rd EN11 .....
Brewery The RM1......
Brewery Wlk **7** RM1..
Brewhouse Yd **11**
DA1 ....
Brewood Rd RM8 .....
Brewster Cl SS8 ......
Brian Cl
Chelmsford CM2 ......
Hornchurch RM12 .....
Brian Rd RM6 ....
Briar Cl
Billericay CM11 ....
Buckhurst Hill IG9 .....
Hockley SS5...........
Briarleas Gdns RM14...
Briar Lo E18...........
Briar Mead SS15......
Briar Rd RM3 ....
Briars The
Harlow CM18 ....
Kelvedon Hatch CM15 ..
Briars Wlk RM3.......
Briarswood
Canvey Island SS8.....
Chelmsford CM1 ......
Briar View CM11 ......
Briarview Ct E4 ....
Briarwood Cl CM3.....
Briarwood Dr SS9 ....
Briary The SS12.......
Briceway SS17.........
Brick Ct RM17 ....
Brickenden Ct EN9 ....
Brickendon Ct EN11 ...
Brickfield Cl SS16 .....
Brickfield Cotts
Brentwood CM15......
Epping CM16 ....
Brickfield Rd
Basildon SS16 ....
Coopersale CM16 .....
Brickfields Rd CM3 ....
Brickfields Way SS4 ...
Brick House La CM3 ...
Brick Kiln Rd CM21 ...
Brickstock Furze **1**
CM15 ....
Brickwall Cl CM0......
Bridge Ave RM14......
Bridge Cl
Brentwood CM13......
Dartford DA2..........
Romford RM7 ....
Southend-on-S SS3 ....
South Woodham Ferrers
CM3 ....
Bridge Ct
Grays RM17...........
Maldon CM9..........
Bridge End E17........
Bridge Hill CM16 .....
Bridge House Cl
SS12..................
Bridgemans Gn CM3...
Bridgemarsh La CM3 ..
Bridgend Cl CM3 .....
Bridge Par CM12 .....
Bridge Point RM11....
Bridges Dr DA1........
Bridge St
Basildon SS15 ....
Writtle CM1............
Bridge View CM11 ....
Bridgeview Ct IG6.....
Bridge View Ind Est
RM20 ....
Bridgeways EN11 .....
Bridgewater Rd CM0...
Bridgwater Cl RM3 ...

ter Dr SS0. . . . . 147 A4
er Rd RM3. . . . . 114 D5
er Wlk RM3. . . . . . 114 D5
EN11. . . . . .8 A2
ath The IG8 . . . . . . 109 E3
y CM11 . . . . .97 D6
ay
hwell SG12 . . . . .8 A6
wsdon EN11 . . . . .8 A1
ay (N) EN11. . . . . . . .8 B2
ay (S) EN11. . . . . . . .8 A1
l CM3. . . . . .78 B6
Ave RM7. . . . . 135 B5
Rd CM1 . . . . .32 D5
Cl RM11. . . . . 136 C5
s Way SS3. . . . . 168 F6
ne Cl **19**
. . . . .171 B1
Rd SU1. . . . . 166 F8
Ave SS1. . . . . 167 D8
Rd E6. . . . . 152 A2
ve RM13. . . . . 155 B1
e CM12 . . . . .96 E4
e Cl CM3. . . . . .96 F4
e Prim Sch
. . . . .96 F5
i Ave SS0 . . . . 147 D2
, Rd DA17. . . . . 169 B2
, Rd RM19. . . . . . . 171 D2
rn Apartments
. . . . 141 B6
wn Ave SS15 . . . . . 141 B6
sland SS8. . . . . 163 F5
RM11 . . . . 136 E7
Cl
d CM13. . . . . 117 C8
S17. . . . . 175 A2
d Rd E4. . . . . 109 A7
he CM2. . . . . .55 A6
ch Cl SS5. . . . . 124 F6
n Rd IG5 . . . . 132 E8
d Rd RM3 . . . . 115 A1
Ho RM18. . . . . 178 F6
rim Sch
. . . . 143 B8
d
S13. . . . . 143 B7
n EN11. . . . . .21 A8
RM13 . . . . 155 D3
SS6. . . . . 123 C5
e **1** IG11 . . . . 153 A5
SS2. . . . . 147 D6
Ave CM2. . . . . .55 A6
Dr RM16 . . . . 174 D7
Bsns Pk
. . . . 147 B7
Cl CM11 . . . . .97 B2
ct SS13. . . . . 121 D1
Gdns SS0 . . . . 166 C8
Lo SS0 . . . . 166 C8
Rd
d CM14. . . . . 116 C5
. . . . 133 B1
on-S SS0 . . . . 166 C8
t Cl SS13. . . . . 149 A1
t Gdns SS1 . . . . . . 149 A1
20. . . . . .10 E1
ng CM6. . . . . .5 E7
Cl RM1 . . . . 135 F6
. . . . .1 B1
s Prim Sch
. . . . .10 E1
Way IG9. . . . . 110 C7
Prim Sch
. . . . 114 D4
EN9 . . . . .65 F7
3 SS14. . . . . 142 C7
e Ave SS17. . . . . . 175 C8
. Cl SS2. . . . . 152 F8
t Gdns IG7 . . . . . . 111 C6
t Wlk **3**
. . . . 155 A6
s
. . . . .7 A3
y, ... 172 F1
y SS7 . . . . 145 A6
s Ave
5. . . . . 124 A6
6. . . . . 123 D3
s Rd SS5. . . . . 124 C6
s SS0 . . . . 146 C4
h COMMON 23 A4
td CM19 . . . . .23 A4
err EN9. . . . . .22 E3
ne SS14,
. . . . 142 C6
n CM5. . . . . .71 F1
d CM1. . . . . .99 C8
ct Cl **6** IG8. . . . 110 A4
d Rd
IG8. . . . . 110 B3
IG8. . . . . 110 D3
IG8. . . . . 110 B5
Cl E4. . . . . 109 A5

Broadoaks CM16. . . . . .67 F8
Broad Oaks SS12 . . . . . . 121 E6
Broad Oak Way SS6. . . . . 123 E1
Broad Par SS5. . . . . 124 F6
Broad Rd DA10 . . . . 177 E1
BROAD'S GREEN 18 E5
Broad St
Barking RM10 . . . . 154 A5
Hatfield Broad Oak CM22 . . .3 F6
Broadstone Rd RM12 . . . 136 A2
BROAD STREET GREEN
. . . . .37 C7
Broad Street Green Rd
CM9. . . . . .37 C7
Broadstrood IG10. . . . . . . .67 A1
Broadview Ave RM16. . . . 173 D4
Broadview Ho **3**
RM8. . . . . 134 D3
Broadwalk E18 . . . . 132 A8
Broadwalk The **4**
SS12. . . . . 121 E6
Broadwater Gn SS15. . . . 140 F6
Broadwater Ho **2**
DA12 . . . . 179 D1
Broadway
Barking IG11 . . . . 152 C4
Grays RM17. . . . . 178 C3
Rainham RM13 . . . . 155 A1
Romford RM2 . . . . 114 A1
Southend-on-S SS9 . . . . 165 E8
Tilbury RM18 . . . . 178 F5
Broad Way SS5. . . . . 124 F6
Broadway Ave CM17 . . . . .11 B4
Broadway Chambers **5**
SS13. . . . . 143 B5
Broadway Cl IG8 . . . . . . 110 B4
Broadway Gdns IG8 . . . . 110 B4
Broadway Link SS13 . . . . 143 B5
Broadway Mkt IG6. . . . . . 111 D1
Broadway N **7** SS13 . . 143 B5
Broadway Par
Chingford E4 . . . . 109 C4
Hornchurch RM12 . . . . . 155 B8
Broadway The
6 Basildon SS13 . . . . . 143 B5
Chingford E4 . . . . 109 D4
Dagenham RM8 . . . . 135 A2
Hornchurch RM12 . . . . . 155 B8
Loughton IG10 . . . . .89 C5
Southend-on-S SS1 . . . . 168 A7
3 Wickford, Nevendon
SS12. . . . . 121 E5
Wickford SS11 . . . . 121 D8
Woodford IG8 . . . . 110 B4
Broadway W SS9 . . . . . . 165 E8
Broad Wlk N The
CM13 . . . . 117 A7
Broad Wlk S The
CM13 . . . . 117 A6
Broad Wlk
Harlow CM20. . . . . .10 D1
Southend-on-S SS9 . . . . 124 F6
Wickford SS12. . . . . 121 F5
Brockdish Ave IG11. . . . . 152 F7
Brockelbank Lo RM8. . . . 134 D2
Brockenhurst Dr
SS17. . . . . 175 C8
Brockenhurst Gdns
IG1. . . . . 152 C7
Brockenhurst Way
CM3 . . . . .56 F1
Brocket Ct **15** EN11 . . . .21 A6
Brocket Rd EN11. . . . . . . .21 A6
Brockett Rd RM16 . . . . . . 174 B3
Brocket Way IG7 . . . . 111 F5
Brock Gr RM15 . . . . 172 B7
Brockham Dr IG2. . . . . . . 133 C6
BROCK HILL. 99 B5
Brock Hill SS11. . . . . .99 C4
Brock Hill Rd SS11. . . . . . .99 C3
Brockles Mead CM19 . . . . .23 C4
Brockley Cres RM5 . . . . . 113 C3
Brockley Gr CM13 . . . . . . .95 A1
Bromley Cl CM20 . . . . .11 B4
Bromley Mews SS6 . . . . . 123 A3
Brompton Cl CM12. . . . . . .97 A5
Brompton Gdns SS9. . . . . .58 E8
Brompton Wlk RM20. . . . 172 B2
Bronte Cl
Ilford IG2. . . . . 133 B7
Southend-on-S SS3 . . . . 170 C6
Bronte Mews SS2. . . . . . . 148 A2
Bronze Age Way
DA17 . . . . 169 C2
Brook Ave RM10 . . . . 154 B5
Brookbank CM2 . . . . .54 E8

Brook Cl
Rochford SS4. . . . . 148 A8
Romford RM2 . . . . 113 F2
Woodham Walter CM9. . . .35 D2
Brook Cres E4. . . . . 109 B6
Brook Ct
6 Barking IG11 . . . . . . 152 C3
Barking IG11. . . . . 152 F4
Rayleigh SS6 . . . . 145 C8
Southend-on-S SS0 . . . . 147 D2
Brookdale Ave RM14. . . . 137 B1
Brookdale Cl RM14 . . . . . 137 B1
Brook Dr
Basildon SS12 . . . . 142 C1
Wickford SS12 . . . . 121 C6
Brook End CM21. . . . . .1 D2
Brook End Rd N CM2. . . . .33 A4
Brook End Rd S CM2. . . . .33 B3
Brooke Rd RM17. . . . . 173 A1
Brooker Rd EN9 . . . . .65 C5
Brooke Sq CM9 . . . . .37 A1
Brooke Trad Est RM1. . . . 135 F4
Brookfield CM16. . . . . .46 C6
Brookfield Cl CM13 . . . . . .95 D3
Brookfield House Sch
IG8. . . . . 109 E4
Brookfield Path IG8 . . . . . 109 E4
Brookfields
Chipping Ongar CM5. . . . .48 F6
Sawbridgeworth CM21 . . . .1 D2
Southend-on-S SS9 . . . . 146 D5
Brookfields Cl SS9 . . . . . 146 D5
Brook Gdns E4 . . . . 109 B6
Brook Hill CM3 . . . . .19 B6
Brookhouse Gdns E4 . . . . 109 E6
Brookhurst Cl CM2 . . . . . .32 J3
Brooking Cl RM8 . . . . 134 C1
Brook La
Chelmsford CM2 . . . . .33 B2
Doddinghurst CM15. . . . . .72 D2
Doddinghurst CM15. . . . . .72 E2
Galleywood CM2 . . . . .54 E3
Sawbridgeworth CM21 . . . .1 D2
Brooklands
Rayleigh SS6 . . . . 123 D3
Wickford SS12. . . . . 121 B7
Brooklands App **7**
RM1. . . . . 135 D7
Brooklands Ave SS9 . . . . 146 F6
Brooklands Cl **5**
RM7. . . . . 135 D7
Brooklands Gdns
RM11 . . . . 136 C5
Brooklands La RM7. . . . . 135 D7
Brooklands Pk SS15 . . . . 140 F6
Brooklands Rd RM7 . . . . 135 D7
Brooklands Sq SS8 . . . . . 163 E3
Brooklands Wlk CM2. . . . .54 A7
Brook Lo
Romford RM7 . . . . 135 D7
Wickford SS12. . . . . 146 B7
Brooklyn Ave IG10. . . . . . .88 E5
Brooklyn Cl SS6. . . . . 123 D5
Brookman's Ave
RM16 . . . . 173 D5
Brookmans Rd RM14 . . . . 137 E4
Brookmans Rd CM4 . . . . . .75 D2
Brook Mead
Basildon SS13 . . . . 141 B7
Great Waltham CM3 . . . . .18 E8
Brook Meadow Cl
IG8. . . . . 109 E4
Brook Par IG7. . . . . 111 B7
Brook Rd
Brentwood, Brook Street
CM14 . . . . 115 F7
Brentwood CM14. . . . . . 115 D5
Buckhurst Hill IG9 . . . . . .88 A1
Epping CM16 . . . . .68 A6
Ilford IG2 . . . . 133 E5
Loughton IG10 . . . . .89 A8
Rayleigh SS6 . . . . 145 D8
Romford RM2 . . . . 113 F2
Sawbridgeworth CM21 . . . .1 E1
South Benfleet SS7 . . . . 144 C2
St Lawrence CM0 . . . . . . .63 B5
Tillingham CM0 . . . . .63 E5
Brook Rise IG7 . . . . 111 A7
Brook Road Ind Ctr
SS6. . . . . 145 D8
Brook St Rdbt CM14 . . . . 115 D5
Brookscroft Rd E17. . . . . 109 B2
Brookside
Billericay CM11 . . . . .97 C6
Canvey Island SS8. . . . . 164 A5
Harlow CM19. . . . . .23 A5
Hockley SS5. . . . . 124 F4
Hoddesdon EN11 . . . . . . .21 A6
Hornchurch RM11 . . . . . 136 E6
Margaretting CM4. . . . . . .74 F7
Redbridge IG6 . . . . 111 C4
Waltham Abbey EN9 . . . . .65 C6
Brookside Ave SS3. . . . . . .50 C2
Brookside Cl CM11 . . . . . . .97 C6
Brookside Ctr SS2. . . . . . 147 F5
Brookside Jun & Inf Schs
RM3. . . . . 114 C5
Brook's Mans **5** IG3. . . 134 B3
Brook's Par **6** IG3 . . . . 134 B3
Brook St
Belvedere DA17 . . . . 169 B1
Brentwood CM14. . . . . . 115 E6
Chelmsford CM1. . . . . . . .32 B3
BROOK STREET. 115 F6
Brook View CM9 . . . . .55 C6
Brookway RM13 . . . . 170 B8

Brook Way IG7 . . . . .111 B7
Broome Cl CM11. . . . . .97 D5
Broome Pl RM15. . . . . . . 171 D5
Broome Pl Complex
RM15 . . . . 171 D5
Broome Rd CM11. . . . . . . .97 D5
BROOMFIELD 19 B2
Broomfield
Hadleigh SS7 . . . . 145 D4
Harlow CM20. . . . . .11 B3
Broomfield Ave
Loughton IG10. . . . . .88 F3
Rayleigh SS6 . . . . 123 A3
Southend-on-S SS9 . . . . 146 F5
Broomfield Ct RM5 . . . . . 113 D3
Broomfield Gn SS8 . . . . . 163 F5
Broomfield Hospl CM1. . . .19 A3
Broomfield Prim Sch
CM1. . . . . .19 B1
Broomfield Rd
Chelmsford CM1 . . . . .32 A5
Dagenham RM6 . . . . 134 D4
Southend-on-S SS0 . . . . 177 E2
Broomfields
Basildon SS13 . . . . 143 A6
Hatfield Heath CM22. . . . . .3 A3
Broomfields Ct **6**
SS13. . . . . 143 A6
Broomfields Mews **4**
SS13. . . . . 143 A6
Broomfields Pl **5**
SS13. . . . . 143 A6
Broomhall Cl CM1. . . . . . . .19 B2
Broomhall Rd CM1. . . . . . .19 B2
Broomhill Ct **2** IG8 . . . . 110 A4
Broomhill Rd
Ilford IG3 . . . . 134 A2
Woodford IG8 . . . . 110 A4
Broomhills Chase
CM12 . . . . 119 A5
Broomhill Wlk IG8. . . . . . 109 F3
Broomstick Hall Rd
EN9 . . . . .65 E6
Broomways SS3 . . . . 150 C3
Broomwood Gdns
RM1. . . . . .94 A3
Broseley Gdns RM3 . . . . . 114 E6
Broseley Rd RM3 . . . . 114 C6
Brougham Cl SS3 DA2.. 176 B1
Broughton Rd
Hadleigh SS7 . . . . 145 F2
South Woodham Ferrers
CM3. . . . . 101 C6
Browne Cl
Brentwood CM14. . . . . . . .94 B1
Romford RM5 . . . . 113 B5
Browning Cl SS2 . . . . 148 B2
Browning Cl RM5 . . . . 112 F3
Browning Dr SS12 . . . . . . 121 C5
Browning Rd
Dartford DA1. . . . . 176 A3
Maldon CM9. . . . . .59 A8
Brownings Ave CM1. . . . . .32 A5
Browning Wlk RM18 . . . . 179 C5
Brownlea Gdns IG3. . . . . . 134 A2
Brownlow Bend CM3 . . . . 142 D6
Brownow Cross
SS14. . . . . 142 D6
Brownlow Cl SS14. . . . . . 142 D6
Browns Ave SS11 . . . . .99 F2
Browns Cotts RM16 . . . . . 172 E5
Brownsea Dr CM13 . . . . . .95 C3
Brownstone Ave E18 . . . . 132 A7
Brummell Pl CM17. . . . . . .11 C3
Brundish SS13 . . . . 143 A5
Brunel Cl
Romford RM1 . . . . 135 C7
Tilbury RM18 . . . . 179 B5
Brunel Rd
Hadleigh SS7 . . . . .110 F5
South Benfleet SS7 . . . . 144 D7
Southend-on-S SS9 . . . . 146 C7
Brunel Way CM1. . . . . .31 C7
Brunswick Ave RM14. . . . 137 C4
Brunswick
Hoddesdon EN11 . . . . . . .21 A6
Upminster RM14 . . . . . . 137 E4
Brunswick Ct IG6. . . . . . . 111 C3
Brunswick Lo **6** E4. . . . 109 C8
Brunswick Pl SS6. . . . . . . 123 B5
Brunswick Rd
Holdbrook EN3. . . . . .65 A1
Southend-on-S SS1 . . . . 167 D7

Brunswick Wlk **8**
DA12 . . . . 179 D1
Brunwins Cl SS11. . . . . . . 121 F8
Brushwood Lo **2**
DA17. . . . . 169 A2
Brussum Rd SS8. . . . . 164 D2
Bruton Ave SS0. . . . . 147 A5
Bryanston Rd RM18 . . . . 179 C5
Bryant Ave
Romford RM3 . . . . 114 C1
Southend-on-S SS1 . . . . 167 E6
Bryant Link CM2. . . . . .33 B4
Bryant Row RM3. . . . . . . 114 C8
Bryant's La CM9 . . . . .57 D7
Bryce Rd RM8 . . . . 153 C8
Bryn Farm Cl SS14. . . . . 142 C8
Bryony Cl IG10 . . . . .89 B5
Buchanan Cl RM15. . . . . 171 C5
Buchanan Gdns CM2. . . . 121 E5
Buchanan Way CM3 . . . . .82 B5
Buckbean Path RM3 . . . . 114 C3
Buckeridge Way CM0 . . . . .42 B3
Buckerills SS13 . . . . 143 A6
Buckhatch La CM3. . . . . . .78 D3
Buckhurst Ct **2** IG9 . . . 110 D8
BUCKHURST HILL. 110 C8
Buckhurst Hill Com Prim
Sch IG9 . . . . .110 E8
Buckhurst Hill Ho
IG9. . . . . .110 B8
Buckhurst Sta
IG9. . . . . 110 D8
Buckhurst Way IG9. . . . . . 110 D7
Buckingham Cl RM11 . . . 136 C6
Buckingham Ct
2 Chelmsford CM2. . . . .32 F4
Loughton IG10. . . . . .89 A7
3 Romford RM1. . . . . 135 F6
Buckingham Rd Rd
Linford SS17, RM18 . . . . 174 F5
Stanford-le-H SS17 . . . . 175 A7
Buckingham Lo **6**
EN11 . . . . .21 A6
Buckingham Rd
Basildon SS15 . . . . 141 E8
Hockley SS5. . . . . 124 D6
Ilford IG1. . . . . 133 D2
Wanstead E11 . . . . 132 C6
Woodford IG8 . . . . 109 F2
Buckinghamshire Sq
SS11. . . . . 122 A5
Buckingham Sq **11**
CM0 . . . . 106 C4
Buckland SS3 . . . . 149 C1
Buckland Gate CM3. . . . . 101 C6
Bucklebury Heath
CM3. . . . . 101 D6
Bucklers Ct CM14. . . . . . . 116 C5
Buckles La RM15 . . . . . . 172 D8
Buckley Cl SS17 . . . . 162 F5
Bucknall's Mead CM1. . . . .52 A4
Bucknells Mead CM1 . . . . .52 A4
Buckthorne Ho **4**
IG7. . . . . .112 B6
Buckwins Sq SS13. . . . . . 121 D1
Buckwyns Chase CM12. . . .96 F6
Buckwyns Ct CM12 . . . . . .96 F4
Budleigh Cl CM14 . . . . . . 115 F6
Budna Rd SS8 . . . . 163 F5
Budoch Ct IG3. . . . . 134 A2
Budoch Dr IG3 . . . . 134 A2
Buglers Rise CM1. . . . . . . .53 B8
Bulbanks Rd DA17 . . . . . 169 C2
Bull Cl
Basildon SS16 . . . . 142 E5
Grays RM16 . . . . 172 F4
Bullen Ct IG6 . . . . 111 E4
Bullen Wlk CM2 . . . . .54 C3
Buller Rd
Barking IG11 . . . . 152 E5
Basildon SS13 . . . . 141 B7
North Fambridge CM3. . . .81 A1
Bullfields CM21. . . . . .1 E3
Bullivant Cl DA9 . . . . 177 A2
Bull La
Dagenham RM10 . . . . . . 135 B1
Hockley SS5. . . . . 124 C6
Maldon CM9. . . . . .37 A3
Rayleigh SS6 . . . . 123 E2
Bulls Lodge Cotts CM3. . . .20 B1
Bullwood Ave SS5 . . . . . . 124 B5
Bullwood Hall La SS5 . . . 124 A4
Bullwood Rd SS5. . . . . . . 124 B4
Bulmers Wlk CM3. . . . . . 155 C3
Bulow Ave SS8 . . . . 164 B3
BULPHAN 158 F8
Bulphan By-Pass
RM14 . . . . 140 A1
Bulphan CE Prim Sch
CM14. . . . . 158 F8
Bulphan Cl SS12. . . . . . . 121 E6
Bulphan View CM13. . . . . 140 E5
Bulwark Rd SS3 . . . . 168 E8
Bumble's Green 44 C6
Bumbles Green La EN9 . . .44 B6
Bumfords La CM3, CM9 . . .35 A4
Bunce Dr SS14 . . . . 142 B6
Bundick's Hill CM1. . . . . . .31 F3
Bungalows The
Abbess Roding CM5. . . . . .14 E3
Grays RM20. . . . . 177 A8
Redbridge IG6 . . . . 111 E2
Bunker's Hill DA17. . . . . . 169 A2

Bunters Ave SS3 . . . . 168 C6
Buntingbridge Rd
  IG2 . . . . 133 D6
Bunting CI CM2 . . . . .54 B5
Bunting La CM11 . . . . .97 C1
Burches SS14 . . . . 119 E1
Burches Mead SS7 . . . . . . 145 A7
Burches Rd SS7 . . . . 144 F8
Burchett Way RM6 . . . . . . 134 F5
Burch Rd DA11 . . . . 178 F1
Burchwall CI RM5 . . . . 113 C3
Burden Way E11 . . . . 132 B2
Burdett Ave SS0 . . . . 166 E8
Burdett Rd SS1 . . . . 167 C7
Burdetts Rd RM9 . . . . 153 F4
Bure RM18 . . . . 175 C3
Buren Ave SS8 . . . . 164 E3
Burfield CI SS9 . . . . 146 F6
Burfield Rd SS9 . . . . 146 F6
Burford CI
  Dagenham RM8 . . . . 134 C1
  Ilford IG6 . . . . 133 C7
Burford Gdns EN11 . . . . . . .21 B7
Burford Ho EN11 . . . . .21 B7
Burford Mews 9 EN11 . . . .21 A7
Burford PI 11 EN11 . . . . . . .21 A7
Burford St EN11 . . . . .21 A7
Burges CI
  Hornchurch RM11 . . . . . . 136 F5
  Southend-on-S SS1 . . . . . 168 C6
Burges Rd
  Southend-on-S SS1 . . . . . 168 B6
  Wallend E6 . . . . 152 A5
Burgess Ave SS17 . . . . . . 160 E1
Burgess Ct
  Brentwood CM15 . . . . .94 D1
  Wallend E12 . . . . 152 A5
Burgess Field CM2 . . . . . . .32 F4
Burgess Terr SS1 . . . . 167 F6
Burghley Rd RM16 . . . . . . 172 C3
Burghley Way CM2 . . . . . . .54 C8
Burghstead CI CM22 . . . . . .97 A1
Burgoyne Hatch CM20 . . . . .11 A1
Burgundy Ct CM2 . . . . .32 C2
Burgundy Gdns 8
  SS13 . . . . 143 B8
Burland Rd
  Brentwood CM15 . . . . .94 D1
  Romford RM5 . . . . 113 C4
Burleigh CI
  Billericay CM12 . . . . .97 B5
  Romford RM7 . . . . 135 B7
Burleigh Ct
  Southend-on-S SS0 . . . . . 166 C8
  Southend-on-S, Thorpe Bay
    SS1 . . . . 168 B8
Burleigh Sq SS1 . . . . 168 B8
Burlescoombe CI SS1 . . . . 168 A8
Burlescoombe Leas
  SS1 . . . . 149 B1
Burlescoombe Rd
  SS1 . . . . 149 A1
Burley CI E4 . . . . 109 A5
Burley Hill CM17 . . . . .24 D7
Burlington Ave RM7 . . . . . 135 B5
Burlington Ct SS13 . . . . . . 143 B8
Burlington Gdns
  Dagenham RM6 . . . . 134 E4
  Hadleigh SS7 . . . . 145 F3
  Hullbridge SS5 . . . . 101 F1
Burlington PI IG8 . . . . 110 A7
Burnaby Rd
  Gravesend DA11 . . . . 178 E1
  Southend-on-S SS1 . . . . . 167 C7
Burne Ave SS12 . . . . 121 A6
Burnell Gate CM1 . . . . .33 A7
Burnell Wlk CM13 . . . . 116 C4
Burnels Ave E6 . . . . 152 A2
Burnet PK CM19 . . . . .23 B3
Burnett Rd
  Erith DA8 . . . . 170 D1
  Redbridge IG6 . . . . 111 B3
Burney Ct IG7 . . . . 111 C5
Burney Dr IG10 . . . . .89 C6
Burnham Ave CM3 . . . . .81 A5
Burnham Bsns Pk
  CM0 . . . . 106 A6
Burnham Cres E11 . . . . . . 132 C2
BURNHAM-ON-CROUCH
  . . . . 106 B6
Burnham-on-Crouch &
  District Mus★ CM0 . . . . 106 A4
Burnham-on-Crouch Prim
  Sch CM0 . . . . 106 D5
Burnham-on-Crouch Sta
  CM0 . . . . 106 B6
Burnham Rd
  Althorne CM3 . . . . .83 B1
  Battlesbridge SS11 . . . . . 100 E3
  Chelmsford CM1 . . . . .32 D5
  Dagenham RM9 . . . . 153 B4
  Hullbridge SS5 . . . . 101 E2
  Latchingdon CM3 . . . . . . .82 D5
  Mundon CM9 . . . . .81 C8
  Romford RM7 . . . . 135 D8
  Southend-on-S SS9 . . . . . 146 C1
  Southminster CM0 . . . . . .84 C2
  Southminster CM0 . . . . . .84 D3
  South Woodham Ferrers
    CM3 . . . . .79 D1
  Woodham Mortimer CM9,
    CM3 . . . . .57 E5
Burnley Rd RM20 . . . . 177 A6
Burns Ave
  Basildon SS13 . . . . 143 B5

Burns Ave continued
  Dagenham RM6 . . . . 134 C4
Burns CI
  Billericay CM11 . . . . .97 B3
  Maldon CM9 . . . . .37 A1
Burns Cres CM2 . . . . .54 C8
Burnside
  Canvey Island SS8 . . . . . 164 A5
  Dagenham RM8 . . . . 134 C2
  Sawbridgeworth CM21 . . . . .1 D2
Burnside Ave E4 . . . . 109 A4
Burnside Cres CM1 . . . . . . .54 A1
Burnside Ct 6 RM1 . . . . . . 135 F5
Burnside Ind Est IG6 . . . . . 112 B5
Burnside Rd RM8 . . . . 134 C3
Burnside Terr CM17 . . . . . . .11 F3
Burns PI RM18 . . . . 179 B6
Burns Way CM13 . . . . .95 D3
Burnt Ho IG7 . . . . .89 F1
Burnthouse La
  Ingatestone CM4 . . . . .73 F1
  Mountnessing CM4 . . . .
  CM13 . . . . .96 A8
Burntmill CI CM20 . . . . .10 C3
Burntmill Cnr CM20 . . . . . . .10 D4
Burnt Mill Comp Sch
  CM20 . . . . .10 E2
Burnt Mill Ind Est
  CM20 . . . . .10 C3
Burntmill La CM20 . . . . .10 D3
BURNT MILLS 121 B1
Burnt Mills Ind Est
  SS13 . . . . 121 C1
Burnt Mills Rd SS13 . . . . . 121 C1
Burnt Oak Lo SS9 . . . . 146 A2
Burntwood CM14 . . . . 116 C7
Burntwood Ave RM11 . . . . 136 E5
Burntwood Ct
  Billericay CM12 . . . . .96 F2
  West Horndon CM13 . . . . 139 D5
Burnway RM11 . . . . 136 E4
Burr CI SS16 . . . . 140 E5
Burr Hill Chase SS2 . . . . . 147 E3
Burrow CI IG7 . . . . 111 F5
Burrow Gn IG7 . . . . 111 F5
Burrow Rd IG7 . . . . 112 A5
Burrows Chase EN9 . . . . . . .65 D4
Burrows Ho CM15 . . . . .71 F1
Burrows Way SS6 . . . . 123 C1
Burr's Way CM11 . . . . 161 B3
Burrswood PI CM9 . . . . .37 E3
Burses Way CM13 . . . . .95 C2
Burslem Ave IG6 . . . . 112 A4
Burstead Dr CM11 . . . . 119 D7
Burstead Grange
  CM11 . . . . 119 D6
Burton CI SS17 . . . . 160 F5
Burton Dr EN3 . . . . .65 A2
Burton PI CM2 . . . . .32 F4
Burton Rd
  Loughton IG10 . . . . .89 C5
  Wanstead E18 . . . . 132 B8
Burts Wharf DA17 . . . . 169 C5
Burwell Ave SS8 . . . . 163 F5
Burwood Ct CM2 . . . . .32 C1
Burwood Gdns RM13 . . . . 154 F2
Bury Farm Cotts
  RM14 . . . . 138 E2
Bury Farm La CM11 . . . . . . 120 D3
Bury La
  Epping CM16 . . . . .45 D2
  Great Waltham CM3 . . . . . .18 D8
Bury Rd
  Chingford E4 . . . . .87 E4
  Dagenham RM10 . . . . 154 C7
  Epping CM16 . . . . .67 E8
  Harlow CM17 . . . . .11 D4
Buryside CI IG3 . . . . 133 F7
Bush CI IG2 . . . . 133 D6
Bush Elms Rd RM11 . . . . . 136 A4
Bushey CI
  Chingford E4 . . . . 109 C7
  South Woodham Ferrers
    CM3 . . . . 101 E7
Bushey Croft CM18 . . . . . . .23 E7
Bushey Rd E13 . . . . 152 A4
BUSH FAIR 24 A6
Bush Fair CM18 . . . . .23 F6
Bushfields IG10 . . . . .89 A4
Bushgrove Rd RM8 . . . . . . 134 D1
Bush Hall Rd CM12 . . . . . . .97 C5
Bush Ho CM18 . . . . .23 F6
Bush Rd
  Wanstead E11 . . . . 132 A4
  Woodford IG9 . . . . 110 D6
Bushway RM8 . . . . 134 D1
Bushwood E11 . . . . 132 A3
Bushy Lea CM9 . . . . .49 A2
Bushy Mead SS15 . . . . 141 B8
Business Ctr The
  RM3 . . . . 114 D3
Bute Rd IG6 . . . . 133 B6
Butler Ct 2 RM8 . . . . 135 A2
Butler Ho RM17 . . . . 178 B8
Butler Rd RM8 . . . . 153 B8
Butlers CI CM1 . . . . .19 B2
Butlers Dr E4 . . . . .65 C1
Butlers Gr SS16 . . . . 141 B3
Butler Wlk RM17 . . . . 173 D2
Butneys SS14 . . . . 142 B7
Buttell CI RM17 . . . . 173 D1
Butterbur Chase CM36 . . . 101 C6
Buttercross La CM16 . . . . . .46 A1
Buttercup CI
  Billericay CM12 . . . . .97 A4
  Romford RM3 . . . . 114 D2
Buttercup Way CM0 . . . . . . .84 C3
Butterfield Rd CM3 . . . . . . .33 E8

Butteridges CI RM9 . . . . . . 153 F4
Butterwest Rise CM21 . . . . . .1 E1
Butterworth Gdns
  IG8 . . . . 110 A5
Butterys SS1 . . . . 167 E8
Buttfield CI RM10 . . . . 154 B6
Butt La CM9 . . . . .37 A3
Buttondene Cres EN10 . . . . .21 B1
Button Rd RM17 . . . . 172 F2
Button's Hill CM3 . . . . .83 B4
Buttsbury CM4 . . . . .74 E1
Buttsbury Inf Sch
  CM12 . . . . .97 B5
Buttsbury Jun Sch The
  CM12 . . . . .97 B5
Buttsbury Rd IG1 . . . . 152 C7
Buttsbury Terr CM4 . . . . . . .75 E2
Butts Green Rd RM11 . . . . 136 D5
Butt's Green Rd CM2 . . . . . .55 F3
Butts La
  Danbury CM3 . . . . .56 F7
  Stanford-le-H SS17 . . . . . 175 C8
Butts Paddock SS4 . . . . . . 104 D2
Butts Rd SS17 . . . . 160 C1
Butts Way CM2 . . . . .53 E3
Buxton Ave SS9 . . . . 146 A3
Buxton CI
  Southend-on-S SS9 . . . . . 146 A3
  Woodford IG8 . . . . 110 D4
Buxton Link SS15 . . . . 140 E6
Buxton Lo E11 . . . . 132 B2
Buxton Rd
  Chingford E4 . . . . .87 D2
  Grays RM16 . . . . 173 E4
  Ilford IG2 . . . . 133 E5
  Theydon Bois CM16 . . . . . .67 E3
  Waltham Abbey EN9 . . . . . .66 A6
Buxton Sq SS9 . . . . 146 A3
Buyl Ave SS8 . . . . 164 B5
Byfield CI SS9 . . . . 146 F7
Byfield Ct CM13 . . . . 139 C5
Byfletts SS16 . . . . 142 F4
Byford Rd SS6 . . . . 123 E3
Bynghams CM19 . . . . .22 F6
By-Pass Rd SS17 . . . . 160 A2
Byrd Ct SS15 . . . . 141 C8
Byrd Mead SS15 . . . . .72 A6
Byrne Dr SS2 . . . . 160 C3
Byron Ave
  Southend-on-S SS2 . . . . . 148 B2
  Woodford E18 . . . . 109 F1
Byron CI SS8 . . . . 164 C4
Byron Ct
  Basildon SS15 . . . . 141 B6
  1 Wanstead E11 . . . . 132 A7
  Woodford E18 . . . . 110 B2
Byron Gdns RM18 . . . . 179 C6
Byron Mans RM14 . . . . 137 C1
Byron Rd
  Brentwood CM13 . . . . .95 D2
  Chelmsford CM2 . . . . .32 D2
  Dartford DA1 . . . . 176 B3
Byrons Ho CM16 . . . . .68 A8
Byron Way RM3 . . . . 114 C2
Byron Wks SS11 . . . . 121 F7
Bysouth CI IG5 . . . . 111 B2
Bywater Rd CM3 . . . . 101 C6

C

Cabborns Cres SS17 . . . . . 175 D8
Cabinet Way SS9 . . . . 146 C6
Cables CI DA8 . . . . 169 C3
Cadiz Ct RM10 . . . . 154 C5
Cadiz Rd RM10 . . . . 154 C6
Cadmore La EN8 . . . . .43 A2
Cadogan Ave CM13 . . . . . 139 D5
Cadogan Gdns E18 . . . . . . 132 B8
Cadogan Ho 17 IG8 . . . . . 111 A3
Cadogan Terr SS13 . . . . . . 143 C7
Caernarvon CI
  Hockley SS5 . . . . 124 D6
  Hornchurch RM11 . . . . . . 137 A3
Caernarvon Dr IG5 . . . . . . 111 A2
Cage End CM22 . . . . .3 F5
Cage End CI CM22 . . . . .3 F5
Cage Field Cotts SS4 . . . . 126 D4
Cagefield Rd SS4 . . . . 126 E4
Caidge Row CM0 . . . . .42 A2
Cairns Ave IG8 . . . . 110 F4
Caister Dr SS13 . . . . 143 B6
Caladonia La 9 SS12 . . . . 121 E5
Calbourne Ave RM12 . . . . 155 B7
Calcott CI CM14 . . . . .94 B1
Calcroft Ave DA9 . . . . 177 B2
Calcutta Rd RM18 . . . . 179 B5
Caldbeck EN9 . . . . .65 D5
Calder RM18 . . . . 175 C2
Calder Ct 1 RM1 . . . . 135 D7
Caldwell Rd SS17 . . . . 160 B1
Caldy Rd DA17 . . . . 169 B3
Caledonia Ct SS13 . . . . . . 153 C3
Caledonian CI 1 IG3 . . . . . 134 B3
Caledon Rd E6 . . . . 152 A5
Calgary Ct RM7 . . . . 135 B7
Callan Gr SS4 . . . . 172 B6
Callow Ho RM13 . . . . 154 D2
Callowood Croft CM3 . . . . . .58 D1
Calmore CI RM12 . . . . 155 C7
Calmore Rd CM3 . . . . .58 C6
Caine Ave IG5 . . . . 111 B2
Calshot Ave CM16 . . . . .46 F4
Calshot Ct 2 DA2 . . . . 176 B1
Calverley Cres RM10 . . . . 135 A2
Calvert CI DA17 . . . . 169 B2
Calvert Rd CM2 . . . . 121 C1

Calverton Rd E6 . . . . 152 A4
Calvina CI SS16 . . . . 139 F2
Cambell Jun & Inf Schs
  RM9 . . . . 153 D5
Cambeys Rd RM10 . . . . . . 154 C7
Camborne Ave RM3 . . . . . 114 C3
Camborne CI CM1 . . . . .32 E5
Camborne Way RM3 . . . . . 114 C3
Cambria CI SS8 . . . . 163 C3
Cambrian Ave IG2 . . . . 133 E6
Cambridge Ave RM2 . . . . . 136 C8
Cambridge CI
  Basildon SS16 . . . . 140 F5
  Stock CM4 . . . . .75 D2
Cambridge Ct SS1 . . . . . . 166 F7
Cambridge Gdns
  Grays RM16 . . . . 174 B2
  Rochford SS4 . . . . 125 C5
Cambridge Ho
  Barking IG11 . . . . 152 C5
  Harlow CM17 . . . . .11 C5
Cambridge Park Rd
  E11 . . . . 132 A4
Cambridge Pk E11 . . . . . . 132 A5
Cambridge Rd
  Barking IG11 . . . . 152 C5
  Canvey Island SS8 . . . . . 163 F3
  3 Chingford E4 . . . . .87 D1
  Uppminster RM14 . . . .
Canterbury CI
  5 Basildon SS14 . . . .
  Chigwell IG7 . . . .
  Rayleigh SS6 . . . .
Canterbury Ct CM15 . . . .
Canterbury Ho 2
  IG11 . . . .
Canterbury Par RM15 . . . .
Canterbury PI RM17 . . . .
Canterbury Way
  Brentwood CM13 . . . .
  Chelmsford CM1 . . . .
  Dartford DA2 . . . .
Canters The SS7 . . . .
Cantley Rd IG3 . . . .
Canute CI SS4 . . . .
Canvey Heights Ctry Pk
  SS8 . . . .
Canvey Inf Sch SS8 . . . .
CANVEY ISLAND . . . .
Canvey Jun Sch SS8 . . . .
Canvey Rd
  Basildon SS13 . . . .
  Canvey Island SS8 . . . .
  Southend-on-S SS9 . . . .
CANVEY VILLAGE . . . .
Canvey Way SS7 . . . .
Canvey Wlk CM1 . . . .
Capability Way DA9 . . . .
Capadocia St SS1 . . . .
Cape CI IG11 . . . .
Capel CI
  Chelmsford CM1 . . . .
  Stanford-le-H SS17 . . . .
Capel Gdns IG3 . . . .
Capelston SS15 . . . .
Capel Terr SS1 . . . .
Capital Ind Est DA17 . . . .
Capital PI CM19 . . . .
Capital Trad Est IG11 . . . .
Capitol Ind Ctr 5
  SS11 . . . .
Capon CI CM14 . . . .
Capons La CM3 . . . .
Cappell La SG12 . . . .
Capricorn Ctr
  Basildon SS14 . . . .
Capstan CI RM6 . . . .
Capstan Ct DA2 . . . .
Capstan Dr RM18 . . . .
Capstan Dr 9 RM13 . . . .
Caravan Site The
  RM15 . . . .
Caravel CI RM15 . . . .
Carbis CI E4 . . . .
Carbury Ct RM12 . . . .
Cardamom Ct 1 E12 . . . .
Cardigan Ave RM3 . . . .
Cardigan Gdns IG3 . . . .
Cardigan Ho 4 RM3 . . . .
Cardinal Dr IG6 . . . .
Cardinal Rd RM16 . . . .
Cardinal Way RM13 . . . .
Card's Rd CM2 . . . .
Carew CI RM16 . . . .
Carew Ct 3 RM6 . . . .
Carey Ho SS0 . . . .
Carey Rd RM9 . . . .
Carfax Rd RM12 . . . .
Carisbrooke CI
  Basildon SS13 . . . .
  Hornchurch RM11 . . . .
Carisbrooke Ct 20
  DA2 . . . .
Carisbrooke Dr
  Corringham SS17 . . . .
  South Woodham Ferrers
    CM3 . . . .
Carisbrooke Rd SS0 . . . .
Carisbrook Lo SS6 . . . .
Carisbrook Rd CM15 . . . .
Carina Gdns IG8 . . . .
Carlingford Dr SS0 . . . .
Carlisle Gdns IG1 . . . .
Carlisle Ho IG1 . . . .
Carlisle Rd
  Dartford DA1 . . . .

d *continued*
M1 136 A6
'ay SS13 143 B6
/e
e DA9 176 E1
on-S SS0 147 C4
RM14 137 B2
133 D8
on-S SS2 148 A1
SS7 145 C4
133 D8
on-S SS9 146 F1
) 4 IG10 88 D4
d
S13 143 E8
16 173 F3
M2 136 A7
SS13 99 C2
rr E11 132 B6
las SS2 148 A1
ns
CM12 96 F5
SS12 121 E5
Cl SS3 149 F1
Way CM9 36 F2
n RM15 172 B6
Rd E17 109 D2
Rd
on-S SS2 147 F1
E18 109 F2
Cl
d CM1 32 F5
M7 135 E2
Cl EN3 65 B1
ch Ct 2
142 F5
Gdns RM12 155 A7
Ho 2 RM3 114 F4
SS14 120 B1
dns SS9 146 D4
15 141 D7
15 141 D7
Cl SS2 147 E5
IG3 134 A3
8 164 C3
tps 8 SS1 167 C7
Cl CM12 96 F3
Path CM13 95 D4
s Arms La
46 C6
s Cl SS3 149 E6
s Ct 10
154 B6
DA8 169 E1
r CM1 32 E7
lews IG1 133 C2
IG6 111 C2
Rd DA1 176 A1
ns 7 SS12 121 D6
IG10 88 F6
ad CM3 101 F6
RM9 153 B5
7 109 A1
Cl SS11 99 D1
Dr SS11 99 D1
CM11 98 C4
CM11 97 D5
l CM1 31 F2
l
CM13 95 D3
IG4 132 D7
dns SS12 121 D5
M19 171 D2
16 141 A5
M5 113 B3
M5 113 B4
d Rd EN9 65 C5
GREEN 12 E2
CM16 45 B7
ead CM17 24 C6
a Est EN9 21 C3
E4 87 E1
7 173 B1
Ave SS11 121 E8
Rd
RM9 153 F5
leet SS7 144 D7
Wlk CM2 32 F2
ood CM11 119 C7
IG9 110 D8
d IG9 110 D8
1 SS1 167 C7
M0 63 E4
Terr SS1 166 F7
Way SS16 142 D2
RM19 171 A1
ay
M19 171 A1
be DA10 177 E2
SS8 164 C5
RM16 174 A8
CM1 31 E6
G10 89 C5
Ave RM2 136 B8
IG10 89 C8
E4 109 D5
7 145 D1
M13 154 E5
k SS6 123 C2
EN11 8 C1
6 123 D2
M3 114 C7
n-S SS3 168 G8

Castle Cotts RM14 157 C6
Castle Ct
Dagenham RM9 153 E4
Hadleigh SS7 145 E2
Rayleigh SS8 123 C1
Castledon Rd CM11,
SS12 99 A2
Castledon Sch SS12 121 B5
Castle Dr
Rayleigh SS6 123 C3
Redbridge IG4 132 E5
Southend-on-S SS9 165 B8
CASTLE GREEN 153 C4
Castle Ho 3 E4 109 D5
Castle Hts RM9 153 B4
Castle La SS7 145 D1
Castle Mews SS6 123 C1
Castle Point Transport Mus* SS8 164 E3
Castle Rd
Dagenham RM9 153 B4
Grays RM17 177 F8
Hadleigh SS7 145 E2
Hoddesdon EN11 8 C1
Rayleigh SS6 123 D1
Swanscombe DA10 177 F1
Castle St
Chipping Ongar CM5 49 A2
Greenhithe DA9 177 A2
Swanscombe DA10 177 F1
Castle Terr SS6 123 C2
Castleton Rd
Chingford E17 109 D1
Ilford IG3 134 B3
Southend-on-S SS2 148 E1
Castleview Gdns IG1 132 F5
Castle View Rd SS8 164 A6
Castle View Sch SS8 164 B6
Castle Wlk
11 Basildon SS13 143 C6
Canvey Island SS8 164 A5
Caswell Cl SS17 161 A3
Caswell Mews CM2 32 F2
Catalina Ave RM16 172 F4
Catalin Ct EN9 65 D6
Catcher Ct CM4 74 A2
Caterham Ave IG5 111 A1
Caterham Ct EN9 65 F5
Caterham High Sch IG5 110 F1
Cater Mus The* CM12 97 A2
Cater Wood CM12 97 B3
Catharine Cl RM16 172 F4
Cathedral CE Prim Sch The CM1 32 C3
Cathedral Dr SS15 141 C7
Cathedral Pl CM14, CM15 116 D8
Cathedral Wlk CM1 32 B3
Catherine Cl
East Hanningfield CM3 78 B7
Pilgrims Hatch CM15 94 A4
Catherine Ct 1 IG2 133 C5
Catherine Godfrey Ho RM9 153 F4
Catherine Lo
4 Southend-on-S SS2 147 F1
Woodford E18 110 C2
Catherine Rd
Romford RM2 136 B6
South Benfleet SS7 144 E4
Cathrow Mews 3 EN11 8 A1
Catiline Ct RM2 136 A8
Cattawade End SS14 142 D7
Cattawade Link SS14 142 D7
Caulfield Rd
Southend-on-S SS3 168 D7
Wallend E6 152 A5
Causeway Cotts CM1 52 E8
Causeway The
Edney Common CM1 52 D7
Great Baddow CM2 54 F7
Maldon CM9 37 A4
Ulting CM9 35 D5
Causton Sq RM10 154 A5
Causton Way SS6 123 D4
Cautherly La SG12 8 A5
Cavalier Cl RM6 134 D7
Cavell Cres
Dartford DA1 176 B3
Romford RM3 114 E1
Cavell Rd CM11 97 C1
Cavendish Ave
Hornchurch RM12 155 B6
Woodford IG8 110 B3
Cavendish Cres RM12 155 B6
Cavendish Ct E4 87 E2
Cavendish Gdns
Aveley RM15 171 C4
Barking IG11 152 F7
Chelmsford CM2 32 E3
Dagenham RM6 134 E6
Ilford IG1 133 A3
Southend-on-S SS0 147 B2
Cavendish Rd
Chingford E4 109 C4
Hockley SS5 103 A1
Rochford SS5 103 A1
Cavendish Way SS15 119 D1
Cavenham Gdns
Hornchurch RM11 136 C6
Ilford IG1 133 D1
Caversham Ave SS3 149 E2
Caversham Park Ave SS6 123 C4
Cawdor Ave RM15 172 B6
Cawdor Ho CM14 116 D6

Cawkwell Cl CM2 33 A4
Cawley Hatch CM19 22 F8
Caxton Rd EN11 8 B2
Caxton Way RM1 135 E7
Cazenove Rd E17 109 A2
Cecil Ave
Barking IG11 152 D5
Grays RM16 172 F4
Hornchurch RM11 136 E8
Cecil Ct
Harlow CM18 23 C5
Southend-on-S SS2 147 E3
Cecil Ho E17 109 A2
Cecil Jones Coll (Lower Sch) SS2 148 B3
Cecil Jones Coll (Upper Sch) SS2 148 D3
Cecil Rd
Chingford E17 109 A2
Dagenham RM6 134 D4
Hoddesdon EN11 21 C8
Ilford IG1 152 B8
Cecil Way SS6 123 F2
Cedar Ave
Chelmsford CM1 32 A3
Dagenham RM6 134 E6
Upminster RM14 156 A8
Wickford SS12 121 D5
Cedar Ave W CM1 32 A3
Cedar Chase CM9 37 C5
Cedar Cl
Brentwood CM13 95 D2
Buckhurst Hill IG9 110 D8
Rayleigh SS6 123 F1
Romford RM7 135 C7
Sawbridgeworth CM21 1 E1
Southend-on-S SS2 148 A2
Cedar Ct
Epping CM16 68 A8
Southend-on-S SS3 168 E7
6 Wanstead E11 132 B6
5 Woodford E18 110 A2
Cedar Dr
Hullbridge SS5 101 E2
Loughton IG10 89 B7
Cedar Gdns RM14 137 C1
Cedar Gn EN11 21 A5
Cedar Gr CM0 106 B6
Cedar Hall Gdns SS7 145 A6
Cedar Hall Sch SS7 145 B6
Cedar Mews SS5 124 C6
Cedar Park Cl SS7 145 A6
Cedar Park Gdns RM6 134 D4
Cedar Pk IG7 111 A5
Cedar Rd
Brentwood CM13 95 D3
Canvey Island SS8 163 F4
Grays RM16 174 B3
Hornchurch RM12 136 C1
Romford RM7 135 C7
Thundersley SS7 145 A6
Cedar Rise RM15 157 D1
Cedars
Stanford-le-H SS17 160 E2
Waltham Abbey EN9 66 C4
Cedars The
Buckhurst Hill IG9 88 A1
Great Wakering SS3 150 B4
South Woodham Ferrers CM3 101 D8
Cedar Terr 9 RM8 134 D4
Cedar Wlk
Canewdon SS4 104 D1
Waltham Abbey EN9 65 D5
Cedarwood Ct CM18 23 F6
Cedric Ave RM1 135 E8
Celandine Cl
Billericay CM12 96 F4
South Ockendon RM15 157 C1
Celandine Ct E4 109 B7
Celeborn St CM3 101 B6
Celedon Cl RM16 172 E4
Cement Block Cotts 10 RM17 178 C8
Centaur Way CM9 59 A8
Central Ave
Althorne CM3 82 E2
Aveley RM15 171 C4
Basildon SS16 140 E4
Billericay CM12 97 C6
Canvey Island SS8 163 F5
Corringham SS17 161 A3
Grays RM20 171 F1
Hadleigh SS7 145 E5
Hullbridge SS5 101 F1
Hullbridge, Tower Park SS5 101 E4
Rochford SS4 125 D5
Southend-on-S SS2 148 C1
Stanford-le-H SS17 160 E4
Tilbury RM18 179 A6
Central Cl SS7 145 E4
Central Ct 11 IG7 111 E5
Central Dr RM12 136 E1
Central Ho CM5 49 A3
Central Par IG2 133 D5
Central Park Ave RM10 135 C1
Central Rd
Harlow CM20 11 A4
Stanford-le-H SS17 160 D1
Central Sq 7 CM1 32 B2
Central Wall SS8 164 A6
Central Wall Cotts SS8 164 B5
Central Wall Rd SS8 164 B5
Centre Ave CM16 67 F7

Centre Dr CM16 67 F7
Centre Gn CM16 67 F7
Centre Pl 10 SS1 167 C7
Centre Rd
Dagenham RM10 154 B3
Wanstead E11 132 A2
Centre Reach SS2 148 A1
Centreway 4 IG1 133 C2
Centric Par IG10 88 E5
Centurion Cl SS3 168 F8
Centurion Ct RM1 135 D8
Centurion Lo 7 RM10 154 B6
Centurion Way
Belvedere DA18 169 A3
Purfleet RM19 170 F2
Centurion Works RM13 154 E2
Century Rd EN11 21 A7
Ceylon Rd SS0 166 D8
Chadacre Ave
Redbridge IG5 132 F8
Woodford IG5 110 F1
Chadacre Rd SS1 149 B1
Chadfields RM18 179 A7
Chadview Ct 2 RM6 134 D4
Chadville Gdns RM6 134 D6
Chadway RM8 134 C3
Chadwell Ave RM6 134 B4
Chadwell By-Pass RM16 174 A1
CHADWELL HEATH 134 D5
Chadwell Heath Foundation Sch The RM6 134 B5
Chadwell Heath Ind Pk RM8 134 D3
Chadwell Heath La RM6 134 C5
Chadwell Heath Sta RM6 134 D4
Chadwell Hill RM16 174 B1
Chadwell Prim Sch RM6 134 C4
Chadwell Rd RM16, RM17 173 D2
CHADWELL ST MARY 174 B1
Chadwell St Mary Prim Sch RM16 174 B2
Chadwick Ave E4 109 D6
Chadwick Dr RM3 114 D1
Chadwick Rd
Ilford IG1 133 B1
Southend-on-S SS0 166 C8
South Woodham Ferrers CM3 79 E1
Chaffinch Cl SS3 168 E8
Chaffinch Cres CM11 97 C1
Chafford CM14 94 B1
Chafford Gdns CM13 139 D5
Chafford Gorges Nature Pk* RM15 172 D3
CHAFFORD HUNDRED 172 E3
Chafford Hundred Bsns & Ent Coll RM16 172 C1
Chafford Hundred Prim Sch RM16 172 C1
Chafford Hundred Sta RM16 172 B2
Chafford Sch The RM13 170 C8
Chafford Way
Grays RM16 173 B5
Ilford RM6 134 C7
Chafford Wlk RM13 155 C3
Chaingate Ave SS2 148 E2
Chale Ct SS17 175 C8
Chalfont Cl SS9 146 D4
Chalfont Ct 3 DA17 169 A1
Chalford Ct IG2 133 B6
Chalforde Gdns RM2 136 B7
Chalford Wlk IG8 110 D3
Chalgrove Cres IG5 110 E1
Chalice Cl SS14 142 E6
Chalice Way DA9 176 F2
Chalk Ct RM17 178 A8
CHALK END 16 E2
Chalk End SS13 143 A7
Chalk La CM17 12 A2
Chalklands CM2 55 D3
Chalk Rd SS8 164 A6
Chalks Ave CM21 1 D3
Chalk St CM3 99 F7
Chalk Villas CM6 15 C7
CHALKWELL 166 B8
Chalkwell Ave SS0 166 B8
Chalkwell Bay Flats SS9 166 A8
Chalkwell Espl SS0 166 B7
Chalkwell Hall Jun & Inf Schs SS0 147 A1
Chalkwell Lo SS0 147 C1
Chalkwell Park Dr SS9 146 F1
Chalkwell Sta SS9 166 A8
Challacombe SS1 149 C1
Challacombe Cl CM13 95 C1
Challinor CM17 24 E8
Challock Lees SS13 143 C5
CHALVEDON 143 B6
Chalvedon Ave SS13 143 B7
Chalvedon Sch SS13 143 B6
Chalvedon Sq 3 SS13 143 A6
Chamberlain Ave
Canvey Island SS8 164 C4

Chamberlain Ave *continued*
Corringham SS17 161 A4
Chamberlain Cl
Harlow CM17 24 C8
Ilford IG1 133 C1
Chamberlains Ride CM3 101 D6
Chambers Cl DA9 177 A2
Champion Cl
Stanford-le-H SS17 160 E3
Wickford SS12 121 D6
Champion Rd RM14 137 B2
Champions Gn EN11 8 A1
Champions Way
Hoddesdon EN11 8 A1
South Woodham Ferrers CM3 101 C8
Champlain Ave SS8 163 F5
Champness Rd IG11 152 F5
Chance Cl RM16 172 F3
Chancel Cl
Basildon SS15 141 C7
South Benfleet SS7 144 C6
Tillingham CM0 63 E4
Chancellor Ave CM2 33 B4
Chancellor Rd SS1 167 B7
Chancery Pl CM1 31 B1
Chandler Rd IG10 89 B8
Chandlers CM0 106 A6
Chandlers Chase CM12 97 A2
Chandlers Cnr RM13 155 C1
Chandlers Dr DA8 169 E2
Chandlers Mews DA9 177 C3
Chandlers Quay CM9 37 A3
Chandlers Way
Romford RM1 135 E6
Southend-on-S SS2 148 A5
South Woodham Ferrers CM3 101 E7
Chandlers Wlk CM15 71 E2
Chandos Ave E17 109 A1
Chandos Cl IG9 110 B8
Chandos Par SS7 146 A3
Chanlock Path RM15 172 B6
Channing Cl RM11 136 F4
Chanton Cl SS9 146 D7
Chantress Cl RM10 154 C4
Chantreywood CM13 117 B7
Chantry Cres SS17 160 C1
Chantry Ct 10 DA12 179 C1
Chantry Dr CM4 74 B3
Chantry Heritage Ctr* DA12 179 C1
Chantry Ho RM13 154 D3
Chantry La SS15 141 C7
Chantry Prim Sch DA12 179 C1
Chantry The
3 Chingford E4 87 C1
Harlow CM20 11 A2
Chantry Way
Billericay CM11 97 B2
Rainham RM13 154 D3
Chapel Ave E12 132 D1
Chapel Cl RM20 177 B8
Chapel Croft CM4 74 B4
Chapel Ct
Billericay CM12 97 B2
Swanscombe DA10 177 E1
Chapel Dr CM3 19 B6
Chapel End EN11 21 A5
Chapel End Ho E17 109 B2
Chapel End Inf Sch E17 109 B1
Chapel End Jun Sch E17 109 B2
Chapelfields SG12 8 D4
Chapel Fields CM17 24 C6
Chapel High CM14 116 C8
Chapel La
Chigwell IG7 111 F7
5 Dagenham RM6 134 D4
Great Wakering SS3 150 B4
Hadleigh SS7 145 C3
Harlow CM17 24 C6
Heybridge Basin CM9 37 E2
Little Baddow CM3 34 B3
Purleigh CM3 80 D8
Roxwell CM1 29 F1
Tillingham CM0 63 E4
Chapel Lo RM13 155 A1
Chapel Mews
Billericay CM12 97 B1
Chigwell IG8 111 A4
Chapel Pl SS3 168 F6
Chapel Rd
Burnham-on-C CM0 106 C4
Epping CM16 45 F1
Ilford IG1 133 B1
Southend-on-S SS3 168 F6
Chapel Row CM3 79 B5
Chapel St CM12 97 A2
Chapel Terr IG10 88 E5
Chapel The 5 RM11 136 B3
Chaplaincy Gdns RM11 136 E3
Chaplemount Rd IG8 110 F4
Chaplin Cl
Basildon SS15 119 E1
Galleywood CM2 54 B2
Chaplin Rd RM9 153 E5
Chapman Ct SS8 163 C3
Chapman Rd
Belvedere DA17 169 B1
Canvey Island SS8 165 A3

Chapmans Cl SS9.........146 B1
Chapmans Wlk SS9.......146 B1
Charfleets Cl SS8.........163 D3
Charfleets Farm Ind Est
SS8..................163 D3
Charfleets Ho SS8........163 C3
Charfleets Ind Est
SS8..................163 C3
Charfleets Rd SS8........163 C3
Charfleets Service Rd
SS8..................163 D3
Charity Farm Chase
CM12..................96 F3
Charlbury Cl RM3........114 C4
Charlbury Cres RM3......114 C4
Charlbury Gdns IG3......133 F2
Charlbury Ho
  1 Ilford IG12.........133 A1
  8 Little Ilford E12....152 A8
Charlecote Rd RM8.......134 E1
Charlemont Rd E6........152 A2
Charles Church Wlk
IG1..................132 F5
Charles Cl SS0.........147 A5
Charles Ho
  Billericay CM11.........97 B3
  8 Hoddesdon EN11.....21 D8
Charles Rd
  Dagenham RM10........154 D6
  Ilford RM6............134 D5
Charles St
  Epping CM16...........68 A7
  Grays RM17...........178 C8
  Greenhithe DA9.......177 A3
  Greenhithe, Stone DA9..176 F2
Charleston Ave SS13.....121 C1
Charleston Ct SS13......121 C1
Charlotte Ave SS12......121 C7
Charlotte Cl IG6.......111 C2
Charlotte Ct
  Hornchurch RM11......136 C4
  Ilford IG2............133 A5
  South Woodham Ferrers
  CM3.................101 C6
Charlotte Gdns RM5.....113 B4
Charlotte Mews **5**
SS2..................147 F1
Charlotte Pl RM20.......177 B8
Charlotte Rd RM10.......154 B6
Charlton Cl
  Basildon SS13.........143 C7
  Hoddesdon EN11........21 A6
Charlton Cres IG11......152 F3
Charlton Mead La
EN11..................21 D5
Charlton St RM20........177 D8
Charlton Way EN11.......21 B6
Charnwood Ave CM1......31 E1
Charnwood Dr E18.......132 B7
Charter Ave IG2.........133 D4
Charter Ho CM9..........37 A2
Charterhouse SS16......142 C5
Charterhouse Cotts
CM3...................80 F5
Charteris Rd IG8........110 B4
Charter Rd The IG8......109 F4
Charters Cross CM18.....23 D5
Charters Ct SS11........121 F8
Chartwell Cl EN9........65 E6
Chartwell Ct **8** IG8....110 A3
Chartwell Pl RM1.......135 F7
Chartwell Sq **2** SS1....167 A8
Chase Cl SS7..........144 F5
Chase Court Gdns
SS1..................167 C8
CHASE CROSS..........113 D4
Chase Cross Rd RM5.....113 D3
Chase Ct SS1..........167 C8
Chase Dr CM3..........101 C8
Chase End
  Basildon SS16.........142 F3
  Rayleigh SS6..........123 F2
Chase Gdns
  Chingford E4..........109 A6
  Southend-on-S SS0.....147 D3
Chase High Sch SS0......147 C3
Chase House Gdns
RM11.................136 F6
Chase La
  Chigwell IG7..........112 A7
  Ilford IG6............133 D6
Chase Nature Reserve
The* RM7..............135 E1
Chase Rd
  Brentwood CM14.......116 C7
  Corringham SS17......161 A2
  Southend-on-S SS1.....167 C8
Chaseside SS6.........145 E8
Chaseside Cl RM1.......113 E4
Chase Sq **4** DA1......179 B1
Chase The
  Basildon, Langdon Hills
  SS16................141 E3
  Basildon, Steeple View SS15,
  CM12................119 B2
  Billericay CM11........97 C8
  Boreham CM3..........33 E8
  Brentwood CM14.......116 D7
  Brentwood, Warley
  CM14................116 B6
  Chigwell IG7.........111 C6
  Dagenham RM6.........134 E5
  Dagenham RM7.........135 D1

Chase The continued
  East Hanningfield CM3...78 B8
  Foulness Island SS3.....130 F7
  Grays RM20...........177 D8
  Great Amwell SG12.......8 A6
  Great Baddow CM2.......54 F6
  Hadleigh SS7..........145 B5
  Harlow CM17...........11 C1
  Hornchurch RM7, RM12...135 F1
  Ingrave CM13..........117 C5
  Loughton IG10..........88 D2
  Osea Island CM9........39 A1
  Rayleigh SS6..........123 F1
  Rochford SS4..........125 C8
  Romford RM1..........135 E8
  Southminster CM0.......84 D4
  South Woodham Ferrers
  CM3.................101 C8
  Upminster RM14........137 E1
  Wickford, Nevendon
  SS12................121 E4
  Wickford, Runwell
  SS12................121 A6
Chaseway SS16.........142 F4
Chaseways CM21.........11 C8
Chatfield Way SS13......143 C7
Chatham Hall La CM3.....19 B8
Chatham Pavement
SS13.................143 C7
Chatham Rd **1** E18....109 F1
Chatham Way CM14......116 C8
Chatsworth SS7........144 F6
Chatsworth Gdns
SS5..................124 D6
Chatterford End SS14....142 B7
Chatteris Ave RM3.......114 D4
Chatton Cl **4** SS12....121 E5
Chaucer Cl
  Maldon CM9...........59 A8
  Tilbury RM18..........179 C5
Chaucer Ct EN11........8 A1
Chaucer Rd
  Chelmsford CM2........32 D1
  Chingford E17.........109 C1
  Romford RM3..........114 B3
  Great Amwell E11......132 A5
Chaucer Way
  Dartford DA1..........176 A3
  Hoddesdon EN11........8 A2
Chaucer Wlk SS12.......121 D5
Cheapside E SS6........123 C4
Cheapside W SS6........123 B4
Cheddar Ave SS0........147 A1
Chedington Ct CM11.....149 C1
Cheelson Rd RM15.......157 C3
Cheethams Rd E12.......132 E1
Cheldon Barton SS1.....168 C8
Chelmer Ave
  Little Waltham CM3.....19 B5
  Rayleigh SS6..........123 C1
Chelmer Cres IG11......153 B3
Chelmer Ct E18.........110 B2
Chelmer Dr
  Brentwood CM13........95 E3
  South Ockendon RM15...172 C6
Chelmer Ho RM16.......174 A1
Chelmer Lea CM2........54 E7
Chelmer Pl CM2.........32 D3
Chelmer Rd
  Chelmsford CM2........32 E2
  Grays RM16...........174 A1
  Upminster RM14.......137 D5
Chelmer Terr CM9.......37 B2
Chelmerton Ave CM2.....54 E7
Chelmer Valley High Sch
CM1...................19 A2
Chelmer Valley Rd
CM1...................32 B5
CHELMER VILLAGE......33 B4
Chelmer Village Ret Pk
CM2..................32 E2
Chelmer Way
  Burnham-on-C CM0.....106 A6
  Southend-on-S SS3.....168 D7
CHELMSFORD..........32 C4
Chelmsford Ave
  Romford RM5..........113 D4
  Southend-on-S SS2.....147 F1
Chelmsford Coll
  Chelmsford CM2........54 A8
  Chelmsford CM2........54 C7
Chelmsford Cty High Sch
for Girls CM1..........32 A4
Chelmsford Ct RM14.....136 F1
Chelmsford & Essex
  Regiment Mus* CM2....54 A8
Chelmsford Gdns IG1....132 F4
Chelmsford Rd
  Battlesbridge SS11....100 E1
  Brentwood CM15........95 B5
  Great Waltham CM3.....19 A6
  Hatfield Heath CM22.....3 C3
  High Ongar CM4, CM5....49 D4
  Margaret Roding CM6,
  CM5.................15 E4
  Mountnessing CM15.....95 C6
  Purleigh CM3..........58 D3
  Rawreth SS11.........122 E6
  Woodford E18.........109 F2
  Woodham Mortimer
  CM9.................57 C6
  Writtle CM1...........31 C1
Chelmsford Sta CM1.....32 B3
Chelsea Ave SS1.......167 D6

Chelsea Ct
  6 Chingford E4.....87 C1
  Rochford SS4..........125 E2
  Southend-on-S SS1.....167 C8
Chelsea Fields EN11.....8 B2
Chelsea Gdns CM17......24 E7
Chelsea Mews **4**
RM11.................136 B3
Chelston Ct **2** E11....132 B6
Chelsworth Cl
  Romford RM3..........114 F2
  Southend-on-S SS1.....167 F8
Chelsworth Cres SS1....167 F8
Chelsworth Dr RM14.....114 F2
Cheltenham Dr
  Southend-on-S SS9.....146 F2
  Thundersley SS7.......145 B7
Cheltenham Gdns
IG10..................88 E3
Cheltenham Ho IG8......111 A4
Cheltenham Rd
  Hockley SS5..........124 E4
  Southend-on-S SS1.....167 C8
Chelwater CM2.........54 D8
Chelwood Cl E4........87 B3
Chenies Dr SS15.......119 B1
Chepstow Ave RM12......136 E1
Chepstow Cl CM11.......97 D5
Chepstow Cres IG3......133 E5
Chepstow Ho RM3.......115 A5
Chequers
  Buckhurst Hill IG9.....88 B1
  Ingatestone CM4.......74 B4
Chequers La
  Dagenham RM9........154 A2
  Maldon CM9...........37 A2
Chequers Par RM9.......154 A4
Chequers Rd
  Brentwood CM14, RM3...92 F1
  Loughton SS10.........88 E2
  Writtle CM1...........30 F1
Chequers Wlk EN9.......65 F6
Cheriton Ave IG5.......111 A1
Cherries The SS8.......164 B1
Cherry Ave CM13........116 F7
Cherry Blossom Cl **3**
CM17.................11 C4
Cherry Blossom La
CM3...................80 F6
Cherrybrook SS1.......149 C1
Cherry Cl
  Canvey Island SS8.....163 F4
  Hockley SS5..........124 C7
Cherry Ct
  Canvey Island SS8.....164 B1
  Ilford IG6............133 B8
Cherrydene Cl SS5......101 C4
Cherrydown
  Grays RM16...........173 D5
  Rayleigh SS6..........123 D4
Cherrydown Ave E4......109 A7
Cherrydown Cl E4.......109 A7
Cherrydown E SS14......142 A5
Cherrydown W SS16......142 A5
Cherrydown Wlk RM7.....113 B1
Cherrygarden La **1**
SS2...................54 A8
Cherry Garden La CM3...57 B7
Cherry Garden Rd
  Great Waltham CM3.....18 E7
  Maldon CM9...........36 E2
Cherry Gdns
  Billericay CM12........96 E4
  Dagenham RM9........153 F7
  Epping Green CM16.....65 B7
  Little Baddow CM3......34 E1
  Woodford IG8.........110 A5
Cherry La SS11........122 A7
Cherrymeade SS7.......145 A4
Cherry Orch CM0.......84 C4
Cherry Orchard La
SS4..................147 B8
Cherry Orchard Way
  Rochford SS4..........125 B1
  Southend-on-S SS2.....147 B8
Cherry St RM7.........135 D6
Cherrytree Chase
SS3..................150 C1
Cherry Tree Cl
  Grays RM17...........178 D3
  Rainham RM13.........155 A3
Cherry Tree Ct **3**
E18..................109 F1
Cherry Tree La
  Harlow CM20..........10 B1
  Rainham RM13.........154 F2
Cherry Tree Prim Sch
SS16.................142 D5
Cherry Tree Rd CM11....21 A7
Cherry Tree Rise IG9...110 D6
Cherrytrees CM12......118 F8
Cherry Trees CM4......74 B4
Cherry Wlk
  Grays RM16...........174 A3
  Rainham RM13.........154 F3
Cherston Gdns IG10.....89 A5
Cherston Rd IG10......89 A5
Chertsey Cl SS3.......149 D1
Chertsey Rd IG1.......152 D8
Cherwell Dr CM1.......31 C8
Cherwell Gr RM15......172 B6
Chesham Cl RM7........135 D7
Chesham Dr SS15......119 B1
Chesham Ho **9** RM3....114 E4
Cheshire Cl
  Chingford E17.........109 B2
  Hornchurch RM11......137 A6
Cheshunt Dr SS6.......123 B6

Cheshunt Rd DA17.......169 A1
Cheshunts SS13........143 A7
Chester Ave
  Southend-on-S SS1.....167 D6
  Upminster RM14.......137 E2
Chester Cl
  Grays RM16...........172 E3
  Loughton IG10.........89 C8
Chesterfield Ave SS7....144 D6
Chesterfield Cres
SS9..................146 D6
Chesterfield Gdns **3**
SS14.................142 F8
Chesterford Gn SS14....142 F8
Chesterford Rd E12.....152 A7
Chester Gn IG10.......89 C8
Chester Hall La SS14....142 A8
Chesterman Rd SS3......168 F6
Chester Mews E17......109 A1
Chester Path SS10......89 C8
Chester Pl CM1........32 A5
Chester Rd
  Chigwell IG7.........111 A7
  Ilford IG3............133 F4
  Loughton IG10.........89 C8
  Wanstead E11.........132 B5
Chester Way SS14......142 F8
Chestnut Ave
  Billericay CM12........97 A2
  Buckhurst Hill IG9.....110 D7
  Grays RM16...........173 B4
  Heybridge CM9........37 C6
  Hornchurch RM12......136 A2
Chestnut Cl
  Buckhurst Hill IG9.....110 D8
  Burnham-on-C CM0.....106 A5
  Gravesend DA11.......178 F1
  Hornchurch RM12......155 C8
Chestnut Cotts CM16....67 E2
Chestnut Ct
  Basildon SS13.........143 A4
  Ingatestone CM4.......74 A2
  Southend-on-S SS2.....168 F7
Chestnut Dr
  Hatfield Heath CM22.....2 F3
  Wanstead E11.........132 A5
Chestnut Farm Dr CM3...82 E2
Chestnut Glen RM12.....136 A2
Chestnut Gr
  Brentwood CM14.......116 C8
  Hoddesdon EN11........8 C2
  Redbridge IG6.........111 E4
  South Benfleet SS7....144 B4
  Southend-on-S SS2.....148 B2
Chestnut Ho
  2 Basildon SS13....143 B8
  Wickford SS11.........121 E7
Chestnut La CM20......10 B1
Chestnut Path SS4.....104 D1
Chestnut Rd SS16......143 A4
Chestnuts CM13........95 B2
Chestnuts The
  Abridge RM4..........90 B6
  2 Loughton IG10...88 E4
  Rayleigh SS6.........123 E4
  Southminster CM0......84 D4
  Willingale CM5........28 D4
Chestnut Wlk
  Canvey Island SS8.....163 E3
  Chelmsford CM1.......32 A5
  Epping Green CM16.....65 B7
  Little Baddow CM3.....34 E1
  Woodford IG8.........110 A5
Chestwood Cl CM12......97 B5
Chetwood Prim Sch The
CM3..................101 D6
Cheveley Cl RM14.......114 F2
Chevely Cl SS16.......46 D2
Chevening Gdns SS5....126 C6
Chevers Pawen SS13.....143 A4
Chevington Pl RM12.....155 D7
Chevington Way
RM12.................155 D8
Cheviot Dr CM1........31 D6
Cheviot Ho DA11.......178 D1
Cheviot Rd RM11.......136 A4
Cheviot Way IG2.......133 E7
Chevron Ho RM17.......178 B7
Cheyne Ct **8** SS12....121 E5
Chichester Cl
  Aveley RM15..........171 C5
  Basildon SS14.........142 F8
  Canvey Island SS8.....164 A2
  Grays RM16...........172 D2
Chichester Dr CM1......32 C4
Chichester Gdns IG1....132 F4
Chichester Ho **1**
CM14.................116 C8
Chichester Wharf
DA8..................169 E1
Chieftan Dr RM19......171 A2
Chigborough Rd CM9.....37 F6
Chignal Ho SS6........123 C5
Chignal Rd CM1........31 D5
CHIGNALL ST JAMES....31 A8
CHIGNALL SMEALY.......17 F4
Chignalls The **4**
SS15.................141 A6
CHIGWELL............111 B8
Chigwell Cty Prim Sch
IG7..................111 C8

Chigwell La IG10
Chigwell Park Dr IG7
Chigwell Pk IG7
Chigwell Rd
  Wanstead E18
  Woodford IG8
Chigwell Rise IG7
CHIGWELL ROW
Chigwell Row Inf Sch
IG7
Chigwell Sch IG7
Chigwell Sta IG7
Chigwell View RM5
Childerditch Hall Dr
CM13
Childerditch Ind Pk
CM13
Childerditch La
  Little Warley CM13
  West Horndon CM13
Childerditch St CM13
Childers The IG8
Childs Cl RM11
Childs Cres DA10
Chilham Cl SS13
Chiltern **1** SS1
Chiltern App SS8
Chiltern Cl SS6
Chiltern Gdns RM12
Chiltern Ho IG2
Chilterns The SS8
Chiltern Way IG8
Chilton Cl CM2
Chilton Rd RM16
Chiltons The **4** E18
Chimes The SS7
Chimney Pot La CM3
China La CM14
Chinchilla Rd SS1
Chindits La CM14
Chingate Rd EN11
Ching Ct E4
Chingdale Rd E4
CHINGFORD
Chingford Ave E4
Chingford CE Inf Sch
E4
Chingford CE Jun Sch
E4
Chingford Foundation
E4
CHINGFORD GREEN
CHINGFORD HATCH
Chingford La IG8
Chingford Mount Rd
E4
Chingford Rd
  2 Basildon SS13
  Chingford E17
Chingford Sta E4
Chippenham Cl RM3
Chippenham Gdns
RM3
Chippenham Rd RM3
Chippenham Wlk
RM3
Chipperfield Cl RM14
Chippingfield CM17
Chipping Lo RM1
CHIPPING ONGAR
Chipping Ongar Prim S
CM5
Chipping Row **5**
Chisholm Ct **11** SS12
Chislett Row CM2
Chittenden Cl **8** EN11
Chittock Gate SS14
Chittock Mead SS14
Chitty's La RM8
Chivers Rd
  Grays RM16
  Stondon Massey CM15
Choats Manor Way
RM9
Choats Rd IG11
Choice View **5** IG1
Chorley Cl SS16
Christchurch Ave
  Rainham RM13
  Wickford SS12
Christchurch Prim Sch
IG1
Christchurch Rd
  Ilford IG1
  Southend-on-S SS2
  Tilbury RM18
Christian Cl EN11
Christie Ct **12** CM14
Christie Gdns RM6
Christie Rd EN9
Christies Ct **5** EN11
Christopher Cl RM12
Christopher Gdns
RM9
Christopher Martin Pl
CM11
Christopher Martin Rd
CM11
Christy Ave CM11
Christy Cl SS15
Christy Ct SS15
Christy Way SS15
Chudleigh Cres IG3
Chudleigh Rd RM3
Chulmleigh Ct CM16
Churchall Terr IG6.....111 C8

ve
d CM1 . . . . . 19 A2
E4 . . . . . 109 D4
E12 . . . . . 132 D1
hase CM3 . . . . 100 C5
..
sland SS8 . . . 163 F3
on t H SS17 . . 159 F3
Hatch RM14 . . . 71 D2
IG10 . . . . . 88 F7
ssing CM15 . . . 95 E8
-on-S SS3 . . . 168 D6
otts
nfleet SS7 . . . 144 D1
l Walter CM9 . . 35 D2
otts
RM20 . . . . . 10 C7
Rivers CM5 . . . 70 C7
res
sing CM15 . . . 95 E8
eworth CM21 . . . 1 F2
endon RM15 . . . 157 C2
E N10 . . . . . 21 A3
m La RM10 . . . 154 A4
ND 130 B6
ham CM3 . . . . 23 A6
nd Ave SS11 . . 99 E2
d La SS11 . . . 99 E2
eld CM16 . . . 46 A2
d Cotts
. . . . . 130 B7
.
te En10 . . . . 21 A3
IG10 . . . . . 88 E5
-on-S SS3 . . . 149 E2
E18 . . . . . 110 A2
ds Inf Sch
. . . . . 110 A2
ds Jun Sch
. . . . . 110 A2
ds La EN10 . . . 21 A3
te SS0 . . . . 147 C1
te CE Prim Sch
. . . . . 11 F3
e St CM17 . . . 11 E4
ATE STREET
. . . . . 11 F3
M4 . . . . . 90 E6
Burnt Mills
. . . . . 121 A2
CM13 . . . . . 95 F2
M14 . . . . . 158 F7
ford, Moulsham
. . . . . 32 B2
l, Springfield
. . . . . 32 D4
ngar CM5 . . . 49 B7
CM11 . . . . . 120 B6
RM10 . . . . . 154 C5
est CM15 . . . 72 B2
ey CM13 . . . 138 D5
IG10 . . . . . 88 F6
me CM4 . . . . 74 E6
endon RM14 . . 157 B7
ld Bassett
. . . . . 47 A6
M19 . . . . . 171 A1
M1 . . . . . 135 E7
M22 . . . . . 12 D7
ningfield CM3 . 138 D4
Abbotts RM4 . . 91 C5
es CM3 . . . . 80 D3
n RM13 . . . . 170 D7
ningfield CM7 . 2 E4
hing or White
M6 . . . . . 14 C7
1 . . . . . 31 B1
he Cotts
SS17 . . . . . 72 B2
SS17 . . . . . 170 C7
ANGLEY 24 D8
ngley Com Prim
. . . . . 24 D8
ngley Way
. . . . . 24 D8
ys CM18 . . . 23 F7

Church Manorway
  DA8 . . . . . 169 D3
Church Mead CM19 . . . 9 B1
Church Mews SS15 . . . 141 B7
Church Mill Grange
  CM17 . . . . . 11 E4
Church Par SS8 . . . 163 E5
Church Park Rd SS13 . . 143 B5
Church Path
  Greenhithe DA9 . . . 176 F2
  Northfleet DA11 . . . 178 C1
  Wanstead E11 . . . 132 A6
Church Rd
  Barking IG2 . . . 152 C6
  Barking SS3 . . . 149 E8
  Basildon, Barstable SS14,
    SS16 . . . . . 142 C6
  Basildon, Bowers Gifford
    SS13 . . . . . 143 F6
  Basildon, Great Berry
    RM14 . . . . . 140 D5
  Basildon, Noak Bridge
    SS15 . . . . . 119 E1
  Basildon, Pipps Hill
    SS15 . . . . . 141 E8
  Buckhurst Hill IG9 . . . 88 B1
  Bulphan RM14 . . . 158 F8
  Burnham-on-C CM0 . . . 106 B6
  Corringham SS17 . . . 161 B2
  Erith DA8 . . . 169 D1
  Greenhithe DA9 . . . 176 F2
  Hadleigh SS7 . . . 145 F2
  Harlow CM17 . . . 24 C5
  High Beach IG10 . . . 88 A7
  Hockley SS5 . . . 124 B7
  Ilford IG2 . . . 133 E5
  Kelvedon Hatch CM14 . . . 71 C2
  Little Baddow CM3 . . . 34 A6
  Little Ilford E12 . . . 152 A7
  Moreton CM5 . . . 26 D2
  Mountnessing CM15 . . . 95 F7
  Navestock Heath RM4 . . . 92 D8
  North Fambridge CM3 . . . 103 A7
  Ramsden Heath CM11, SS14,
    SS16, SS13 . . . 98 D2
  Rawreth SS11 . . . 122 D7
  Rayleigh SS6 . . . 123 F2
  Rochford SS4 . . . 125 C7
  Romford, Harold Park
    RM3 . . . . . 115 A3
  Romford RM4 . . . 92 C1
  South Benfleet, New
    Thundersley SS7 . . . 144 D6
  Southend-on-S, Cambridge
    Town SS3 . . . 168 D7
  Southend-on-S SS1 . . . 167 A7
  Stanford Rivers CM5 . . . 70 D6
  Swanscombe DA10 . . . 177 F1
  Tilbury RM18 . . . 178 F6
  Ulting CM9 . . . 35 C6
  West Hanningfield CM2 . . . 77 A4
  West Tilbury RM18 . . . 179 E8
Church Row RM16 . . . 159 A1
Church St
  Billericay CM11 . . . 119 C6
  Blackmore CM4 . . . 72 E8
  Chelmsford CM1 . . . 32 B2
  Dagenham RM10 . . . 154 B6
  Goldhanger CM9 . . . 38 E7
  Gravesend DA11 . . . 179 B1
  Grays RM17 . . . 178 C8
  Great Baddow CM2 . . . 55 A6
  Maldon CM9 . . . 37 B2
  Rayleigh SS6 . . . 123 D2
  Sawbridgeworth CM21 . . . 1 E2
  Waltham Abbey EN9 . . . 65 C6
Church Terr RM4 . . . 91 C5
Church View
  Aveley RM15 . . . 171 D4
  Steeple CM0 . . . 61 E2
  Upminster RM14 . . . 137 B2
Church View Cl SS2 . . . 148 B2
Church View Rd SS7 . . . 144 E6
Churchway SS7 . . . 145 F2
Church Wlk
  [2] Basildon SS14 . . . 142 A6
  Brentwood CM15 . . . 94 B2
  Maldon CM9 . . . 36 F3
Churchwood Gdns
  IG8 . . . . . 110 A6
Chuzzlewit Dr CM1 . . . 31 E7
Cillocks Cl EN11 . . . 21 A7
Cimarron Cl CM3 . . . 101 D7
Cinema Par RM8 . . . 134 F2
Circle The RM18 . . . 179 A6
City View [3] IG1 . . . 133 C2
Civic Sq RM18 . . . 179 A5
Civic Way IG6 . . . 133 C7
Clachar Cl CM2 . . . 33 A3
Claire Cl CM13 . . . 116 F6
Claire Ho
  Ilford IG1 . . . 152 B8
  Woodford IG5 . . . 110 F2
Clairvale RM11 . . . 136 E4
Clandon Rd IG3 . . . 133 E2
Claps Gate La E6 . . . 152 B1
Clare Ave SS11 . . . 99 D2
Clare Cswy DA2 . . . 176 F3
Clare Ct RM15 . . . 171 C4
Clare Gdns IG11 . . . 153 A5
Clare James Cotts [4]
  SS8 . . . . . 164 A3
Clare Mews CM5 . . . 49 A5
Claremont Cl
  Grays RM16 . . . 173 C3
  Southend-on-S SS0 . . . 147 E1
Claremont Dr SS16 . . . 143 A4

Claremont Gdns
  Ilford IG3 . . . 133 E2
  Upminster RM14 . . . 137 D3
Claremont Gr IG8 . . . 110 C4
Claremont Pl IG7 . . . 111 B7
Claremont Rd
  Basildon SS15 . . . 141 C8
  Hornchurch RM11 . . . 136 A5
  Southend-on-S SS0 . . . 147 D1
Clarence Ave
  Ilford IG2 . . . 133 A5
  Redbridge IG1 . . . 132 F5
  Upminster RM14 . . . 137 A2
Clarence Cl
  Chelmsford CM2 . . . 33 A4
  South Benfleet SS7 . . . 144 D4
Clarence Gate IG8 . . . 111 A4
Clarence Lo [8] EN11 . . . 21 A6
Clarence Rd
  Basildon SS13 . . . 143 F7
  Corringham SS17 . . . 161 C3
  Grays RM17 . . . 73 B1
  Pilgrims Hatch CM15 . . . 94 B3
  Rayleigh SS6 . . . 124 A1
  South Benfleet SS7 . . . 144 D3
  Southend-on-S SS1 . . . 167 A7
Clarence Rd N SS7 . . . 144 E4
Clarence St SS1 . . . 167 A7
Clarendon Gdns
  Ilford IG1 . . . 133 A4
  Redbridge IG1 . . . 132 F4
Clarendon Rd
  Basildon SS13 . . . 143 C7
  Canvey Island SS8 . . . 164 C4
  Gravesend DA12 . . . 179 C1
  Hockley SS5 . . . 102 F1
  Wanstead E18 . . . 132 A8
Clare Rd SS7 . . . 144 A6
Claridge Rd RM8 . . . 134 D3
Clarissa Rd RM6 . . . 134 D4
Clarkbourne Dr RM17 . . . 178 D8
Clarke Rd SS3 . . . 152 F5
Clarke Rise CM3 . . . 80 F5
Clarklands Ind Est CM21 . . . 1 E5
Clarks Cotts SS11 . . . 122 F7
Clarks Farm Rd CM3 . . . 56 F8
Clarks Field Cotts CM3 . . . 57 E2
Clarks La CM16 . . . 67 F8
Clarksons The IG11 . . . 152 C3
Clarks Prep Schs E12 . . . 133 A1
Clark's Rd IG1 . . . 133 D2
Clark Way CM1 . . . 19 A1
Claters Cl SS2 . . . 148 F2
Clatterfield Gdns SS0 . . . 147 B3
CLATTERFORD END
  Fyfield 27 C2
  Leaden Roding . . . 16 B7
  Toot Hill 48 A1
Claudian Way RM16 . . . 174 B3
Claughton Way CM13 . . . 95 D3
CLAVERHAMBURY . . . 44 B4
Claverhambury Rd
  EN9 . . . . . 44 A3
Clavering SS16 . . . 142 F4
Clavering Ct SS6 . . . 123 B3
Clavering Gdns CM13 . . . 139 D5
Clavering Rd E12 . . . 132 D2
Claverton CM3 . . . 95 C3
Claybrick Ave SS15 . . . 124 D5
Clayburn Circ SS14 . . . 142 D6
Clayburn End SS14 . . . 142 D6
Clayburn Gdns RM15 . . . 172 B6
Clayburn Side SS14 . . . 142 D6
Claybury Broadway
  IG5 . . . . . 132 E8
Claybury Rd IG8 . . . 110 E3
Claydon Cres SS14 . . . 142 C7
Claydon Ct RM12 . . . 154 F8
Claydons La SS6 . . . 145 C7
Claygate Cl RM12 . . . 155 A8
CLAYHALL . . . 110 F1
Clayhall Ave
  Redbridge IG5 . . . 111 A1
  Woodford IG5 . . . 110 E1
Clay Hill Rd SS16 . . . 142 C4
Claypit Hill EN9 . . . 66 C2
Claypits Rd CM3 . . . 20 F1
Clayside IG7 . . . 111 C5
Clay's La IG10 . . . 89 A8
Clayspring Ct SS5 . . . 124 D5
Clayswell Ct SS5 . . . 124 E6
Clayton Ave RM14 . . . 156 B7
Clayton Hill Ctry Pk*
  EN9 . . . . . 43 D8
Clayton Rd RM7 . . . 135 C3
Claytonville Terr
  DA17 . . . . . 169 C4
Clayton Way CM9 . . . 59 A8
Clay Tye Rd
  North Ockendon
    RM14 . . . . . 157 C8
  Upminster RM14 . . . 138 C1
Cleall Ave EN9 . . . 65 C5
Clear Ct CM3 . . . 101 D8
Cleland Path IG10 . . . 89 B8
Clementine Wlk CM15 . . . 109 F3
Clematis Cl RM3 . . . 114 C3
Clematis Gdns IG8 . . . 110 A5
Clematis Tye [3] CM1 . . . 32 E7
Clemence Rd RM10 . . . 154 C4
Clementhorpe Rd
  RM9 . . . . . 153 C6
Clementine Wlk [4]
  IG8 . . . . . 110 A3
Clements Cl CM2 . . . 33 B3
Clements Ct [6] IG1 . . . 133 B1
Clements Gdns SS5 . . . 125 A5

Clements Green La
  CM3 . . . . . 101 D8
Clements Hall La SS5 . . . 125 A5
Clements Hall Way
  SS5 . . . . . 125 A4
Clements La IG1 . . . 133 B1
Clements Pl CM3 . . . 101 D8
Clements Rd
  Ilford IG1 . . . 133 B1
  Wallend E6 . . . 152 A5
Clement Way RM14 . . . 136 F1
Clerks Piece IG10 . . . 88 F6
Cleveden Ho SS7 . . . 144 F6
Cleveland Ct SS7 . . . 147 E3
Cleveland Ho DA11 . . . 178 D1
Cleveland Jun & Inf Sch
  IG1 . . . . . 133 B1
Cleveland Rd
  Basildon SS14 . . . 142 C6
  Canvey Island SS8 . . . 164 B2
  Ilford IG1 . . . 133 B1
  Wanstead E18 . . . 132 A8
  [10] Woodford E18 . . . 110 A1
Cleves Ave CM14 . . . 94 B1
Cleves Cl IG10 . . . 88 E3
Cleves Ct CM3 . . . 20 E1
Cleves Wlk IG10 . . . 111 C3
Clevis Dr CM3 . . . 101 E5
Clickett End SS14 . . . 142 C6
Clickett Hill SS14 . . . 142 C6
Clickett Side SS14 . . . 142 C6
Clieveden Rd SS1 . . . 167 F6
Cliff Ave
  Southend-on-S, Chalkwell
    SS9 . . . . . 166 A3
  Southend-on-S SS1 . . . 147 E1
Cliff Gdns SS9 . . . 166 A8
Clifford Ave IG5 . . . 111 B1
Clifford Cl SS15 . . . 141 D5
Clifford Rd
  Chingford E17 . . . 109 C1
  Grays RM16 . . . 172 F3
Cliff Par SS9 . . . 165 E8
Cliff Pl RM15 . . . 157 C2
Cliff Rd SS9 . . . 166 A8
Cliff Reach DA9 . . . 176 F1
Cliffsea Gr SS9 . . . 146 F1
Cliffside Ind Est
  RM17 . . . . . 172 E1
CLIFFTOWN . . . 166 F7
Clifftown Par SS1 . . . 166 F7
Clifftown Rd SS1 . . . 167 A7
Clifton Ave SS7 . . . 144 C4
Clifton Cl CM3 . . . 101 D8
Clifton Ct [8] IG8 . . . 110 A4
Clifton Dr SS0 . . . 166 D7
Clifton Hatch CM18 . . . 24 A5
Clifton Marine Par
  DA11 . . . . . 178 F1
Clifton Mews SS1 . . . 167 A7
Clifton Rd
  Basildon SS13 . . . 143 F7
  Canvey Island SS8 . . . 164 B3
  Gravesend DA11 . . . 179 A1
  Hornchurch RM11 . . . 136 A5
  Ilford IG2 . . . 133 D5
  Loughton IG10 . . . 88 E5
  Rochford SS4 . . . 125 C7
Clifton Terr
  [4] Ingatestone CM4 . . . 74 C4
  Southend-on-S SS1 . . . 167 A7
Clifton Way
  Brentwood CM13 . . . 95 D1
  South Benfleet SS7 . . . 144 C4
Clifton Wlk
  [22] Dartford DA2 . . . 176 B1
  South Benfleet SS7 . . . 144 D4
Climmen Rd SS8 . . . 164 B5
Clinton Cl CM3 . . . 78 B7
Clinton Cres IG6 . . . 111 E4
Clinton Rd SS8 . . . 163 D3
Clipped Hedge CM22 . . . 3 B3
Clipper Bvd E16 . . . 176 E3
Clipper Bvd W DA2 . . . 176 D4
Clitheroe Rd RM5 . . . 113 C5
Cliveden Cl
  Chelmsford CM1 . . . 31 E3
  Shenfield CM15 . . . 94 F2
Clivedon Rd E4 . . . 109 E5
Clive Rd
  Belvedere DA17 . . . 169 A2
  Brentwood CM13 . . . 116 C3
  [17] Gravesend DA11 . . . 179 B1
  Romford RM2 . . . 136 B6
Clobbs Yd CM1 . . . 32 B8
Clock Ct [2] E11 . . . 132 B7
Clock Ho SS15 . . . 141 B6
Clockhouse Ave IG11 . . . 152 C4
Clockhouse Jun & Inf Sch
  RM5 . . . . . 113 B4
Clockhouse La
  Grays RM16 . . . 172 E3
  Romford RM5 . . . 113 C4
  South Ockendon RM15 . . . 172 E5
Clock House Par [1]
  E11 . . . . . 132 B5
Clock House Rd CM12 . . . 118 F5
Clockhouse The
  RM14 . . . . . 137 C2
Cloister Cl RM13 . . . 155 B1
Cloisters
  [1] Hornchurch RM13 . . . 155 A6
  Stanford-le-H SS17 . . . 160 E2
Cloisters The SS15 . . . 141 C6
Clopton Gn SS14 . . . 142 B7
Clore Tikva Sch IG6 . . . 111 C1
Close The
  Brentwood CM14 . . . 116 D7

Close The continued
  Chingford E4 . . . 109 C3
  Dagenham RM6 . . . 134 E5
  Grays RM16 . . . 173 C4
  Hatfield Heath CM22 . . . 3 A3
  Ilford IG2 . . . 133 C5
  South Benfleet, Hope's Green
    SS7 . . . . . 144 D1
  Thundersley SS7 . . . 145 B8
Cloudberry Rd RM3 . . . 114 D4
Clova Rd SS9 . . . 146 F2
Clovelly Ct RM11 . . . 136 F2
Clovelly Gdns
  Romford RM7 . . . 113 B2
  [2] Wickford SS11 . . . 121 C8
Clover Cl SS16 . . . 142 E3
Clover Ct RM17 . . . 178 D8
Clover Field CM18 . . . 24 A5
Clover Leas CM16 . . . 45 F2
Cloverley Rd CM5 . . . 49 A1
Cloverleys IG10 . . . 88 D4
Clover Villas SS16 . . . 167 B3
Clover Way SS16 . . . 142 E3
Cluff Ct CM14 . . . 116 C6
Clunas Gdns RM2 . . . 136 D8
Clune Ct CM15 . . . 95 A2
Clunford Pl CM1 . . . 32 F7
Cluny Sq SS2 . . . 148 C3
Clusters The [3] SS2 . . . 147 F1
Clyde RM18 . . . 175 C2
Clyde Cres
  Chelmsford CM1 . . . 31 D4
  Rayleigh SS6 . . . 145 D8
  Upminster RM14 . . . 137 E5
Clyde Rd EN11 . . . 21 D5
Clydesdale Rd RM11 . . . 135 F4
Clyde Way RM11 . . . 113 E2
Clynes Ho [9] RM10 . . . 135 A1
Coach Ho The CM5 . . . 49 F6
Coach La CM9 . . . 36 F3
Coach Mews CM11 . . . 97 D5
Coal Ct RM17 . . . 178 A8
COALHILL . . . 99 E7
Coalhouse Fort*
  RM18 . . . . . 180 E6
Coalport Cl CM17 . . . 24 D7
Coaster Steps [4] SS1 . . . 167 C7
Coastguard Cotts
  Bradwell on S CM0 . . . 63 B8
  Canvey Island SS8 . . . 163 C1
Coates Cl CM9 . . . 37 B4
Coates Quay CM2 . . . 32 C2
Cobbetts Ave IG4 . . . 132 D6
Cobbinsbank Ho EN9 . . . 65 D6
Cobbins Chase CM0 . . . 106 B8
Cobbins Cl CM0 . . . 106 B8
Cobbinsend Rd EN9 . . . 44 D2
Cobbins Gr CM0 . . . 106 B8
Cobbins The
  Burnham-on-C CM0 . . . 106 B8
  Waltham Abbey EN9 . . . 65 E6
Cobbins Way CM17 . . . 11 E4
Cobbles The
  Brentwood CM15 . . . 116 B8
  Hornchurch RM14 . . . 137 F4
Cobbs Pl CM1 . . . 32 D3
Cobdens IG7 . . . 111 D4
Cobden Wlk SS13 . . . 143 C7
Cobham RM16 . . . 173 B4
Cobham Cl DA9 . . . 177 B1
Cobham Ho IG11 . . . 152 C4
Cobham Rd
  Chingford E17 . . . 109 C2
  Ilford IG3 . . . 133 E1
  Southend-on-S SS0 . . . 166 C7
Cobham Terr [1] DA9 . . . 177 B1
Cobill Cl RM11 . . . 136 C7
Coburg Gdns
  Woodford IG5 . . . 110 E1
  Woodford IG5 . . . 110 E1
Coburg La SS13 . . . 140 F4
Coburg Pl CM12 . . . 101 D6
Cockabourne Ct RM3 . . . 115 A1
COCK CLARKS . . . 57 F2
Cockerell Cl SS13 . . . 121 B1
Cockethurst Cl SS0 . . . 147 A4
Cock Gn CM19 . . . 23 B6
Cock La
  Blackmore CM11 . . . 51 F2
  Edney Common CM1 . . . 52 A3
  Hoddesdon EN11 . . . 21 A5
Cockle Sheds SS9 . . . 165 D8
Cockridden Farm Ind Est
  CM13 . . . . . 139 F8
Cockrobin La CM20 . . . 10 F4
Codenham La SS16 . . . 142 B5
Codenham Straight
  SS16 . . . . . 142 B4
Codham Hall La
  CM13 . . . . . 138 C7
Cokefield Ave SS2 . . . 148 D3
Colam La SS3 . . . 34 C3
Colbert Ave SS2 . . . 167 F7
Colbourne Ct SS17 . . . 160 F3
Colchester Ave E12 . . . 132 F1
Colchester Cl SS2 . . . 147 F2
Colchester Rd
  Chelmsford CM2 . . . 33 A6
  Heybridge CM9 . . . 37 B5
  Romford RM3 . . . 114 E2
  Southend-on-S SS2 . . . 147 F2
Coldharbour La RM13 . . . 170 A4
Coldharbour Rd CM19 . . . 23 A7
COLD NORTON . . . 80 E6

Cold Norton Prim Sch
CM3 . . . . .80 F5
Cold Norton Rd CM3. . . . .81 D5
Cole Ave RM16 . . . . .174 C2
Colebrooke Dr E11 . . . . .132 C4
Colebrook Gdns IG10. . . . .89 B7
Colebrook La IG10. . . . . . .89 B7
Colebrook Path IG10 . . . . .89 B7
Cole Ct RM3. . . . . .114 D5
Coleford Ho **7** RM3 . . .114 E4
Coleman Rd
Belvedere DA17. . . . . .169 A2
Dagenham RM9. . . . . . . .153 E6
Colemans Ave SS0. . . . . .147 D4
Colemans La CM3 . . . . . . .56 D7
Coleman's La EN9 . . . . . . .43 E5
Coleman St SS2 . . . . .148 A1
Colenso Rd IG2 . . . . .133 E4
Coleridge Rd
Dartford DA1. . . . . .176 B3
Maldon CM9. . . . . .37 A1
Romford RM3 . . . . .114 B3
Tilbury RM18 . . . . .179 C5
Coleridge Wlk CM13 . . . . .95 D2
Coles Cl CM5. . . . . .49 A5
Coles Gn IG10. . . . . .89 A8
Colet Rd CM13 . . . . .95 D4
Coley Ct SS7 . . . . .144 B4
Colgate Pl EN3 . . . . .65 A2
Colin Cl IG12 . . . . .126 B1
Colin Pond Ct RM6 . . . . .134 D8
Colinton Rd IG3. . . . . . . .134 B2
Collard Ave IG10 . . . . .89 C7
Collard Gn IG10 . . . . .89 C7
College Ave RM17 . . . . . .173 C2
College Cl E17. . . . . .173 C2
College Ct **8** RM2 . . . .136 B6
College Gdns
Chingford E4 . . . . .87 B2
Redbridge IG4 . . . . .132 E6
College Pl DA9 . . . . .177 C3
College Rd
Grays RM17 . . . . .173 C2
Northfleet DA11. . . . . . . .178 B2
College Sq CM20 . . . . .23 D8
College Way SS1 . . . . . . .167 A8
Colley Rd CM2. . . . . .55 A6
Collier Ct RM16. . . . . . . .173 B5
COLLIER ROW 113 B2
Collier Row La RM5. . . . .113 C1
Collier Row Rd
Dagenham RM5 . . . . .112 F2
Romford RM5 . . . . .113 B3
COLLIERS HATCH 47 C1
Colliers The CM9 . . . . .37 E3
Collier Way SS1 . . . . .167 B7
Collindale Cl SS8. . . . . . .164 D4
Collingwood St SS7. . . . .144 E4
Collingwood Ho
Greenhithe DA9. . . . . . . .177 D2
Southend-on-S SS9 . . . . .147 D2
Collingwood Prim Sch
CM3. . . . . .101 E6
Collingwood Rd
Basildon SS16 . . . . .142 D4
Rainham RM13 . . . . .155 A3
South Woodham Ferrers
CM3. . . . . .101 F6
Collingwood Terr
SS16. . . . . .142 D5
Collingwood Way
SS3. . . . . .149 E1
Collingwood Wlk
SS16. . . . . .142 D5
Collins Cl SS17 . . . . .160 E2
Collins Ct **5** IG10 . . . . .88 D4
Collins Ho **3** IG11. . . . .152 B5
Collins Mdw CM19 . . . . . .23 B7
Collins Way
Brentwood CM13. . . . . . . .95 F4
Southend-on-S SS9 . . . . .147 A6
Collinwood Gdns
Ilford IG5 . . . . .133 A7
Redbridge IG5 . . . . .132 F6
Colman Cl SS17 . . . . .160 D3
Colne Rd RM18 . . . . .175 C3
Colne Cl
South Ockendon
RM15 . . . . .172 C6
South Woodham Ferrers
CM3. . . . . .101 E7
Colne Ct RM18 . . . . .175 C2
Colne Dr
Romford RM3 . . . . .114 F4
Southend-on-S SS3 . . . . .149 E1
Colne Ho **5** IG11. . . . . .152 B6
Colne Valley RM14 . . . . . .137 E5
Colney Rd DA1. . . . . .176 A1
Colombo Rd IG1. . . . . . . .133 C4
Colson Gdns IG10 . . . . . . .89 B5
Colson Path IG10. . . . . . . .89 A5
Colson Rd IG10. . . . . .89 B5
Colt Hatch CM20. . . . . . . .10 B1
Colthurst Gdns EN11. . . . .21 D8
Coltishall Cl SS11. . . . . . .122 B6
Coltishall Rd RM12 . . . . .155 C6
Colt Mews EN3 . . . . .65 A2
Coltsfoot Ct RM17 . . . . . .178 D8
Coltsfoot Path RM3 . . . . .114 D4
Columbia Wharf Rd
RM17 . . . . .178 A8
Columbine Way RM3. . . . .114 E2
Colvers CM17. . . . . .13 C2

Colville Cl SS17 . . . . .160 F5
Colville Mews CM12 . . . . .96 F5
Colvin Chase CM2 . . . . . . .54 B1
Colvin Gdns
Chingford E4 . . . . .109 C7
Redbridge IG6. . . . . .111 C3
Wanstead E11 . . . . .132 B7
Colwall Gdns IG8 . . . . . . .110 A5
Colworth Cl SS7 . . . . .145 D4
Colyers Reach CM2 . . . . . .33 A2
Combes Rd RM9. . . . . . . .153 F5
Comet Cl RM19 . . . . .171 A2
Comet Way SS2 . . . . .147 B6
Comfrey Ct RM17 . . . . . . .178 D8
Commerce Est E18 . . . . . .110 C1
Commercial Ho IG2 . . . . .133 A5
Commercial Pl DA12 . . . .179 C1
Commercial Rd SS0 . . . . .147 D4
Commercial Way
SS15. . . . . .140 E7
Commodore Ho SS14 . . . .142 E6
Common App SS7 . . . . . . .145 A7
Commonfields CM20. . . . . .10 C1
Commonhall La SS7. . . . .145 D3
Common La
Little Baddow CM3 . . . . . . .34 C2
Stock CM4 . . . . .75 C2
Thundersley SS7 . . . . . . .145 B7
Woodham Walter CM9. . . . .35 B3
Common Rd
Great Wakering SS3 . . . . .150 B4
Harlow EN9 . . . . .22 C2
Ingrave CM13 . . . . .117 C5
Stock CM4 . . . . .75 E3
Commonside Rd CM18 . . .23 F4
Common The
Danbury CM3. . . . . .56 E6
East Hanningfield CM3 . . . .78 B7
Thundersley SS7 . . . . . . .145 A7
Commonwealth Ho
RM18 . . . . .179 A5
Como St RM7 . . . . .135 D7
Compass Ct DA11. . . . . . .178 E1
Compass Gdns CM0. . . . .106 A6
Compton Ave
Brentwood CM13 . . . . .95 C1
Romford RM7 . . . . .136 C8
Compton Cl
Canvey Island SS8 . . . . . .164 D2
Southend-on-S SS9 . . . . .146 B1
Wickford SS11. . . . . .121 E7
Compton Terr SS11 . . . . .141 B7
Comrosten **13** EN11. . . .21 A6
Comyns Pl CM1. . . . . .31 B1
Comyns Rd RM9 . . . . .154 A5
Concorde Ho **1**
RM12 . . . . .155 B6
Concord Rd SS8 . . . . .163 F5
Condor Wlk RM12 . . . . . .155 B5
Condovers Cotts
RM18 . . . . .179 F8
Conduit La
Hoddesdon EN11. . . . . . . .21 A6
Woodham Mortimer CM9 . . .57 E6
Conduit La E EN11 . . . . . . .21 B6
Coney Burrows E4. . . . . .109 E8
Coney Gree CM21. . . . . . . .1 D3
Conference Ct **3** E4 . . .109 C8
Congreve Rd EN9 . . . . . . .65 E6
Conifer Ave RM5. . . . . . . .113 B5
Conifer Ct IG1. . . . . .152 B6
Conifer Dr CM14. . . . . . . .116 C6
Conifers SS7 . . . . .145 E3
Coningsby Gdns E4 . . . . .109 B4
Conisborough Ct **12**
DA2 . . . . .176 B1
Coniston SS2. . . . . .147 A7
Coniston Ave
Barking IG11 . . . . .152 E5
Purfleet RM19. . . . . .171 C1
Upminster RM14 . . . . . . .156 C8
Coniston Cl
Barking IG11 . . . . .152 E5
Rayleigh SS6 . . . . .123 E2
Coniston Ct CM16 . . . . . . .68 A8
Coniston Gdns IG4 . . . . . .132 E7
Coniston Rd
Canvey Island SS8 . . . . . .164 A3
South Benfleet SS7 . . . . .144 E8
Coniston Way RM12. . . . .155 A7
Connaught Ave
Chingford E4 . . . . .87 D2
Grays RM16. . . . . .173 C3
Loughton IG10. . . . . .88 D5
Connaught Ct E4 . . . . .87 E2
Connaught Dr CM3 . . . . .101 C7
Connaught Gdns SS3 . . . .168 C6
Connaught Hill IG10. . . . . .88 D5
Connaught La IG11 . . . . . .133 D2
Connaught Mews
Ilford IG1 . . . . .133 D2
Loughton IG10. . . . . .88 E5
Connaught Rd
Chingford E4 . . . . .87 E1
Hornchurch RM12 . . . . . .136 D1
Ilford IG1 . . . . .133 D2
Rayleigh SS6 . . . . .146 A8
Connaught Wlk SS6 . . . . .146 A8
Connect La IG6. . . . . .111 C1
Connington Cres E4 . . . . .109 D7
Connor Cl IG6. . . . . .111 C2
Connor Rd RM9 . . . . .153 F8
Conrad Ct SS7. . . . . .144 D3
Conrad Cl CM16. . . . . . . .173 B4
Conrad Gdns RM16 . . . . .173 B4
Conrad Rd SS17 . . . . .160 E1

Consort Cl CM14. . . . . . . .116 C5
Constable Mews **3**
RM8 . . . . .153 B8
Constable View CM1. . . . . .32 F6
Constable Way SS3 . . . . .168 G8
Constance Cl CM1 . . . . . . .19 A3
Constitution Hill SS7 . . . .144 D3
Consul Ave RM13 . . . . . . .154 D2
Convent Cl SS17 . . . . .141 C6
Convent Rd SS8 . . . . .164 B3
Con Way SS7 . . . . .144 D3
Conway Cres RM6 . . . . . .134 C5
Conway Gdns RM17. . . . .178 B7
Conway Cl RM13 . . . . . . .155 A5
Conway Rd RM16 . . . . . . .159 A3
Conybury Cl EN7 . . . . .66 A7
Conybury Ct EN9 . . . . .66 A7
Conyer Cl CM9 . . . . .58 F8
Conyers CM20 . . . . .10 C2
Conyers Cl IG8 . . . . .109 E4
Conyers Way IG10. . . . . . .89 B6
Cooke Ct RM16. . . . . .172 E3
Cooke St **3** IG11 . . . . .152 C4
Cookham Ct SS3 . . . . . . .149 E2
Cook Pl CM2 . . . . .32 F3
Cook's Cl RM5. . . . . .113 C2
Cooks Gn SS13 . . . . .121 C1
COOKSMILL GREEN 29 F1
Cooks Spinney CM20. . . . .11 A2
Coolgardie Ave
Chigwell IG7 . . . . .111 A7
Chingford E4 . . . . .109 D5
Coombe Dr SS16 . . . . . . .141 C1
Coombe Rd
Romford RM3 . . . . .136 F8
Southminster CM0. . . . . . .84 D5
Coombe Rise
Chelmsford CM1 . . . . .32 B7
Shenfield CM15. . . . . .94 F1
Stanford-le-H SS17 . . . . .160 E2
Coombes Cl CM12 . . . . . . .96 F4
Coombes Gr SS4 . . . . .146 B3
Coombes Rd RM9. . . . . . .153 F4
Coombewood Dr
Dagenham RM6 . . . . .134 F5
Thundersley SS7 . . . . . . .144 F5
Cooper Cl DA9 . . . . .176 F2
Coopers CM3. . . . . .33 E8
COOPERSALE 46 C2
Coopersale Cl **3** IG8 . . .110 C3
Coopersale Comm
CM16 . . . . .46 D3
Coopersale Hall Sch
CM16 . . . . .68 B5
Coopersale La CM16. . . . . .68 B3
Coopersales SS15 . . . . . .141 A6
Coopersale St CM16 . . . . .68 D7
COOPERSALE STREET
. . . . .68 C8
Coopersale & Theydon
Garnon CE Prim Sch
CM16 . . . . .46 D2
Coopers Ave CM9. . . . . . . .37 D5
Coopers Cl
Chigwell IG7 . . . . .112 B8
Dagenham RM10 . . . . . . .154 B6
Coopers' Company &
Coborn Sch The
RM14 . . . . .137 D2
Coopers Ct RM2 . . . . .136 C8
Coopers Dr CM11 . . . . . . .119 C6
Cooper Shaw Rd
RM18 . . . . .179 E7
Coopers Hill CM5. . . . . . . .49 A1
Coopers Mews CM5. . . . . .49 A2
Cooper's Row CM1 . . . . . .32 A5
Coopers Way SS2. . . . . . .148 A5
Coote Gdns **2** RM8. . . .134 F1
Copatol Cl CM8. . . . . .134 F1
Copdock SS14 . . . . .142 C7
Copeland Ho **7**
CM14 . . . . .116 C6
Copelands SS4 . . . . .125 D6
Copeman Rd CM13 . . . . . .95 D2
Copford Ave SS6 . . . . .123 F1
Copford Cl
Billericay CM11 . . . . .97 C2
Woodford IG8 . . . . .110 E4
Copford Rd CM11. . . . . . . .97 C3
Copland Cl
Broomfield CM1. . . . . .19 A1
Great Baddow CM2 . . . . . .54 F8
Copland Rd SS17 . . . . . . .160 D1
Coppen Rd RM8 . . . . .134 F4
Copping Gn SS12. . . . . . .121 E6
Copper Beech Cl IG5. . . .111 A2
Copper Beech Ct IG10 . . . .89 A8
Copper Beeches
Brentwood CM14 . . . . . . .116 C6
Thundersley SS7 . . . . . . .145 B7
Copper Beech Rd
RM15 . . . . .157 C2
Copper Ct CM21. . . . . .1 E2
Copperfield
Billericay CM11 . . . . .119 D6
Chigwell IG7 . . . . .111 D4
Copperfield Ct IG6 . . . . . .133 C8
Copperfield Gdns
CM14 . . . . .94 C1
Copperfield Rd CM1 . . . . . .31 E7
Copperfields SS15 . . . . . .141 C7
Copperfields Way
RM3 . . . . .114 D2
Coppergate Dr EN9 . . . . . .66 A5
Coppice Hatch CM18. . . . .23 D6
Coppice La
Basildon SS15 . . . . .119 F1

Coppice La continued
Pleshey CM6 . . . . .7 E8
Coppice Path IG7 . . . . . . .112 B6
Coppice Prim Sch
IG7. . . . . .112 A5
Coppice Row CM16 . . . . . .67 D3
Coppice The CM15. . . . . . .71 E2
Coppid Hall RM16 . . . . . .172 F5
Coppings The EN11. . . . . . .8 A1
Coppins Cl CM2 . . . . .32 E4
Coppins The **2** RM6 . . .134 B4
Copse Hill CM19 . . . . .23 B5
Copse The
Billericay CM12 . . . . .97 B4
Chingford E4 . . . . .87 F1
Copsfield Ct E18. . . . . . . .132 A8
Copshall Cl CM18. . . . . . . .23 E4
Coptfold Cl SS1 . . . . .148 F1
Coptfold Rd CM14 . . . . . .116 D8
COPTHALL GREEN 66 E6
Copt Hill CM3 . . . . .56 E6
Copthorne Ave IG6 . . . . . .111 B4
Copthorne Gdns
RM11. . . . . .137 A6
Coral Cl
Ilford RM6. . . . . .134 D8
March South Ferrers
CM3 . . . . .101 C8
Coral Ho CM20 . . . . .10 A1
Coram Gn CM13 . . . . .95 D4
Corasway SS7 . . . . .145 C5
Corbets Ave RM14 . . . . . .156 B7
CORBETS TEY 156 B7
Corbets Tey Rd RM14 . . .156 B8
Corbets Tey Sch
RM14 . . . . .156 C7
Corbett Rd E11. . . . . .132 C5
Corbett Villas RM8. . . . . .134 C2
Corbridge Mews **6**
RM1. . . . . .135 F6
Corcorans CM15 . . . . .94 C3
Cordelia Cres SS6 . . . . . .123 C3
Cordwainers The SS22 . . .148 A5
Corfe Cl **2** SS13. . . . . .143 B5
Cories Cl RM8 . . . . .134 D2
Corinth Ho IG3. . . . . .134 A4
Corinthian Manorway
DA8 . . . . .169 D2
Corinthian Rd DA8. . . . . .169 D2
Cormorant Wlk
Chelmsford CM2 . . . . .54 C5
8 Hornchurch RM12 . . .155 B6
Cornec Ave SS9 . . . . .146 B6
Cornec Chase SS9 . . . . . .146 C6
Cornelius Vale CM2 . . . . . .33 B4
Cornelius Vermuyden Sch
& Arts Coll The SS8 . . . .163 E5
Cornell Way RM5 . . . . . . .113 B5
Cornel Ho CM18 . . . . .23 F6
Corner Mdw CM18 . . . . . .24 A4
Corner Rd CM11 . . . . .120 D6
Cornfields IG3 . . . . .101 C8
Cornflower Dr CM1 . . . . . .32 F6
Cornflower Gdns CM2 . . . .96 F4
Cornflower Way RM3 . . . .114 E2
Cornhill **4** CM1 . . . . . . .32 A7
Cornhill Ave SS5 . . . . . . .124 E7
Cornhouse Bldgs SS6 . . .145 C8
Cornish Gr CM3 . . . . .101 E6
Cornmill 65 B6
Cornshaw Rd RM8 . . . . . .134 D3
Cornsland CM14 . . . . .116 D7
Cornsland Cl RM14 . . . . . .137 C8
Cornsland Ct
CM14 . . . . .116 C7
Cornwall Cl
Barking IG11 . . . . .152 F6
Hornchurch RM11 . . . . . .137 A2
Cornwall Cres CM1 . . . . . .32 A7
Cornwall Gate RM19 . . . .171 A2
Cornwall Gdns SS4 . . . . .125 C5
Cornwallis Dr CM3. . . . . .101 F7
Cornwallis Ho SS14 . . . . .142 A8
Cornwallis Rd RM9 . . . . .153 E8
Cornwall Rd
Basildon SS13 . . . . .143 F7
Dartford DA1. . . . . .176 B3
Pilgrims Hatch CM15. . . . .94 B4
Cornwell Cres SS17 . . . . .160 E3
Cornworthy SS3 . . . . .168 C8
Cornworthy Rd RM8 . . . . .153 C7
Corona Rd
Basildon SS16 . . . . .141 B3
Canvey Island SS8 . . . . . .164 D5
Coronation Ave RM18 . . .175 C2
Coronation Cl
Great Wakering SS3 . . . . .149 F4
Ilford IG6 . . . . .133 C7
Coronation Cotts
CM15 . . . . .116 E8
Coronation Ct RM18 . . . .175 C2
Coronation Dr RM12 . . . .155 B7
Coronation Hill CM16 . . . .45 F2
Coronation Rd CM0 . . . . .106 B4
Corporation Rd CM1 . . . . .32 A4
Corral Hts CM8 . . . . .169 E1
Corran Way RM15 . . . . . .172 B6
CORRINGHAM 161 C2
Corringham Prim Sch
SS17. . . . . .161 C3
Corringham Rd
Corringham SS17. . . . . . .161 A2
Stanford-le-H, Balstonia
SS17 . . . . .160 F2
Stanford-le-H SS17 . . . . .160 F3
Corsel Rd SS8 . . . . .164 E3
Cortina Dr RM13. . . . . . . .154 C3
Corton Trad Est SS7 . . . .144 D7

Corve La RM15 . . . .
Cory Dr CM13 . . . .
Cosgrove Ave SS9 . . . . . .
Cosgrove Rd RM20. . . . . .
Cossington Ct SS0. . . . . .
Cossington Rd SS0 . . . . .
Costead Manor Rd
CM14. . . . .
Coteford Cl IG10 . . . .
Cotelands SS16. . . . .
Cotesmore Gdns RM8. . .
Cotleigh Rd RM7 . . . .
Cotman Ave CM1 . . . .
Cotman Mews RM8 . . . . .
Cotswold Ave SS6 . . . . . .
Cotswold Cres CM1 . . . . .
Cotswold Gdns
Brentwood CM13. . . . .
Ilford IG2 . . . .
Cotswold Rd
Romford RM3 . . . .
Southend-on-S SS0 . . . . .
Cottage Pl CM1. . . . .
Cottages The SS2 . . . . . .
Cottesmore Ave IG5 . . . .
Cottesmore Cl SS8 . . . . .
Cottesmore Ct SS8 . . . . .
Cottesmore Gdns
SS9. . . . .
Cottey Ho CM2 . . . .
Cottis Cl SS16 . . . .
Cotton Cl RM9. . . . .
Cotton La CM2, DA9 . . . .
Cottons App RM7 . . . .
Cottons Ct **3** RM7 . . . .
Couchmore Ave IG5 . . . . .
Coulde Dennis CM3. . . . .
Coulson Cl RM8 . . . .
Coulter Ho DA9. . . . .
Coulter Mews CM11 . . . . .
Council Ave DA11. . . . . . .
Council Bglws SS17. . . . .
Council Hos
Bicknacre CM3. . . . .
Bradwell on S CM0 . . . . .
Corringham SS17. . . . . . .
County Chambers
SS1. . . . .
County Pl CM2 . . . .
Courage Cl CM11 . . . .
Courage Ct **7** CM13 . . .
Courage Wlk CM13 . . . . .
Courland Rd Ad SS13. . . .
Court Ave RM3 . . . .
Courtenay Dr RM16. . . . .
Courtenay Gdns
RM14 . . . .
Courtfield SS7. . . . .
Courtfield Cl EN10 . . . . . .
Court Gdns RM3 . . . .
Court Ind Est CM2 . . . . . .
Courtland Ave
Chingford E4 . . . .
Ilford IG1 . . . .
Redbridge IG1 . . . .
Courtland Dr IG7 . . . .
Courtland Mews CM9. . . .
Courtland Pl CM9. . . . . . .
Courtlands
Billericay CM12 . . . .
Chelmsford CM1 . . . .
Southend-on-S SS9 . . . . .
Court Lo **12** RM12 . . . .
Court Mews CM11 . . . . . .
Cotter Needham EN3 . . . .
Courtney Park Rd
SS16. . . . .
Courtney Rd RM16 . . . . . .
Courtney Twrs IG2. . . . . .
Court Rd CM1 . . . .
COURTSEND
Courts The SS6 . . . .
Court View CM1 . . . .
Courtway IG8 . . . .
Court Way
Ilford IG6 . . . .
Romford RM3 . . . .
Courtway Cotts SS17. . . .
Courtyard Mews **1**
DA9 . . . .
Courtyard The
Basildon SS14 . . . .
Billericay CM11 . . . .
Brentwood CM15. . . . .
Harlow CM17. . . . .
Maldon CM9. . . . .
Mayland CM3. . . . .
Coval Ave CM1 . . . .
Coval La CM1 . . . .
Coval Wells CM1. . . . .
Covenbrook CM13 . . . . . .
Coventry Cl RM3 . . . .
Coverdales The IG11. . . .
Coverley Cl CM13. . . . . . .
Covert Rd IG6. . . . .
Coverts The
Wrttle CM1. . . . .
Cowan Lo **1** IG8 . . . . . .
Cowbridge La CM1 . . . . .
Cowdray Way RM12. . . . .
Cowdrie Way CM2 . . . . . .
Cowell Ave CM1 . . . .
Cowell Lo IG8 . . . .
COW GREEN
Cowley Ave CM3 . . . .
Cowley Cl **3** E18 . . . . . .

...133 A4
IG1...132 F4
M3...114 B3
E11...132 B6
17...11 D4
re RM18...179 B6

RM13...155 A1
ead SS14...142 B6
E18...110 B1
ing La CM1...30 E2
Ct CM12...97 A2
17...160 D3
n Rd CM1...119 C7
22...3 A3
M16...172 E3
...101 E8
EEN...93 C4
n Rd
atch CM14...93 C5
d CM14...93 A2
ve RM6...134 D7
lanorway N

...169 C5
lanorway S

...169 C3
s Sq SS2...148 A5
Rd RM11...135 F4
E18...109 F1
ay CM2...54 F5
I St RM16...173 A1
lle Wlk **2**

...155 B1
n Wlk CM1...31 F3
Gdns

...137 B2
Rd
1...152 D4
EN11...21 C7
e Ave E11...132 B7
e Ct E18...132 B7
e Dr EN11...8 C2
e Gdns

...133 C8
e Ho EN11...8 C2
e Prim Sch The

...8 B2
Ave SS7...145 C4
Coll (Boys)

...133 A2
Dr RM2...136 C7
Lo SS7...145 C4
Rd IG1,

...133 A5
Rise

...133 A4
IG1...132 F5
M10...154 A6
RM15...172 B5
e Gdns
G1...120 F1
SS13...120 D7
m Rd SS14...120 D1
SS14...142 C8
t
d SS12...121 C8
rd IG8...110 A6
re Ave

...121 F2
Park Ct **5**

...121 D5
Park Rd

...121 D4
...137 C4
dns RM14...137 F4
RM14...157 A7
td RM11...136 B5
Dr SS9...146 E1
Gdns

...152 D6
SS5...101 D1
10...88 D3
e SS0...147 D1
IG2...133 C4
ins SS3...168 C6

...133 C4
Ave SS0...147 D1
I CM12...97 B6
RM14...137 C2
dns RM10...154 C8
o CM2...53 F7
ve SS0...147 D5
ane E4...109 B4
Park Ave

...156 C8
Cres **7** E4...87 F4
e SS8...164 A3
SS4...125 D5
RM6...134 C5
ns

...152 E3
...133 D8
IG6...111 D1
larold Park

...133 C7
Villoughby's Hill

...113 A5
ve RM16...173 B5
Chase SS12...121 E5
I CM12...97 C5
Compton Cl

...155 C6
SS17...161 A4
6 DA11...179 B1
CM9...58 E8

Craylands SS14...142 F7
Craylands La DA10...177 D2
Craylands Sch The
DA10...177 D2
Craylands Sq DA10...177 D2
CRAYS HILL...120 D5
Crays Hill CM11...120 C5
Crayshill Pk CM11...120 C5
Crays Hill Prim Sch
CM11...120 D6
Crays Hill Rd CM11...120 D4
Crays View CM12...119 B8
Crealock Gr IG8...109 F5
Creance Ct CM2...32 A2
Creasen Butt Cl CM9...37 A4
Creasey Cl RM11...136 B2
Creasy Ct SS14...142 E6
Crediton Ho **4** RM3...114 D4
Credo Way RM20...177 B8
Creeds Cotts CM16...67 C7
Creeds Farm Ho CM16...67 C7
Creekmouth Ind Pk
IG11...152 F1
Creek Rd
Barking IG11...152 F2
Canvey Island SS8...164 D4
CREEKSEA...105 F5
Creeksea Ferry Rd
SS4...105 C2
Creeksea La CM0...105 F6
Creekside RM13...154 F1
Creek The DA11...178 B2
Creek View SS16...142 E3
Creek View Ave SS5...101 D3
Creekview Rd CM3...101 F7
Creek Way RM13...169 E8
Creephedge La CM3...78 E5
Cree Way RM1...113 E3
Crescent Ave
Grays RM17...178 D8
Hornchurch RM12...135 F2
Crescent Cl CM12...96 F4
Crescent Ct
Billericay CM12...97 A2
Grays RM17...173 D1
Heybridge CM9...36 F5
Crescent Dr CM15...94 E1
Crescent Gdns CM12...96 F4
Crescent Rd
Aveley RM15...171 C4
Billericay CM12...96 F4
Brentwood CM14...116 B6
Canvey Island SS8...164 D2
Chingford E4...87 A3
Dagenham RM10...135 B1
Great Baddow CM2...55 A7
Heybridge CM9...36 F5
South Benfleet SS7...144 F2
Southend-on-S SS9...146 B1
Woodford E18...110 C2
Crescent The
Epping CM16...67 F7
Greenhithe DA9...177 C2
Hadleigh SS7...145 F3
Harlow CM17...11 C4
Ilford IG2...133 A5
Loughton IG10...88 D3
Upminster RM14...137 F4
Crescent View
Loughton IG10...88 D3
Crescent View RM15...171 D5
Crescent Wlk RM15...171 C4
Cressells SS15...141 F6
Cresset Cl SG12...8 C3
Cressingham Ct **1**
DA17...169 A3
Crest Ave
Basildon SS13...143 C6
Grays RM17...178 B7
Cresthill Ave RM17...173 C2
Crest The
Sawbridgeworth CM21...1 D2
Southend-on-S SS9...146 D6
Crest View DA9...177 D2
Creswick Ave SS6...123 C3
Creswick Ct SS6...123 C3
Crete Hall Rd DA11...178 E1
Crick Ct **3** IG11...152 C3
Cricket Ct E4...152 A2
Cricketers Cl
Broomfield CM1...19 C1
Shenfield CM15...94 E6
Cricketers La CM13...117 D3
Cricketers Ret Pk
SS13...121 A2
Cricketers Row CM13...117 D3
Cricketers Way SS13...121 A2
Cricketfield Gr SS9...146 F2
Crickhollow CM1...19 C1
Crickside Ave RM14...114 D4
Cringle Lock CM3...101 E8
Cripplegate CM0...84 E5
Cripsey Ave CM5...48 F5
Crispe Ho **4** IG11...152 D3
Crispin Ct SS15...168 A8
Crispin Terr IG8...110 D4
Critchett Terr **1** CM1...32 A3
Crocus Way CM1...32 F7
Croft Cl
South Benfleet SS7...144 C5
Southend-on-S SS9...146 E4
Croft Ct CM1...32 A3
Crofters CM21...1 E3
Crofters End CM21...1 E3
Croft Lodge Cl IG8...110 B4
Crofton Ave SS17...160 F4
Crofton Gr E4...109 D6
Crofton Rd RM16...173 C3
Croft Rd SS7...144 C5

Crofts The SS3...149 E4
Croft The
Chingford E4...109 E8
Loughton IG10...89 A7
Rayleigh SS6...145 F8
Cromarty Ho CM14...116 D6
Cromar Way CM1...31 F1
Crombie Cl IG4...132 F6
Cromer Ave SS15...141 B8
Cromer Cl SS15...141 B8
Cromer Rd
Dagenham RM6...134 C5
Hornchurch RM11...136 D4
Romford RM7...135 C5
Southend-on-S SS1...167 B8
Woodford IG8...110 A6
Cromer Terr **3** RM6...134 B6
Crompton Cl SS14...141 F8
Crompton Pl **8** EN3...65 A1
Crompton St CM1...31 F1
Cromwell Ave CM12...97 A3
Cromwell Cl CM3...33 D8
Cromwell Ct
Brentwood CM14...116 B6
Maldon CM9...37 A3
Cromwell Ctr
Barking IG11...153 A2
Redbridge IG6...112 B5
Cromwell Ctr The
RM8...134 F4
Cromwell Hill CM9...36 F3
Cromwell Ho CM9...36 F3
Cromwell Lo IG11...152 F7
Cromwell Rd
Brentwood CM14...116 B6
Grays RM17...173 A1
Hockley SS5...124 E6
Southend-on-S SS2...148 B3
Cromwells Mere RM5...113 D4
Cromwell Trad Ctr
IG11...152 F8
Crondon Park La CM4...75 E4
Crooked La DA11,
DA12...179 B1
Crooked Mile
Waltham Abbey EN9...65 C6
Waltham Abbey EN9...65 C7
Crooked Way EN9...21 E1
Cropenburg Wlk SS8...164 B5
Croppath Rd RM10...154 A8
Crosby Ct IG7...112 A7
Crosby Rd
Dagenham RM10...154 A4
Southend-on-S SS0...166 C8
Cross Ave SS12...121 C6
Crossbow Cl CM5...49 A2
Crossbow Rd IG7...111 F5
Crossby Cl CM15...95 B8
Crosse Cts SS15...141 C5
Crossfell Rd SS15...141 F7
Crossfield Rd
Hoddesdon EN11...21 B8
Southend-on-S SS2...148 D2
Crossfields IG10...89 A4
Cross Gdns SS16...141 F5
Crossing Rd CM16...68 A6
Crossness Rd IG11...152 F2
Cross Rd
Basildon SS13...143 F7
Chingford E4...87 E1
Dagenham RM6...134 C4
Gravesend DA11...178 F1
Hadleigh SS7...145 B4
Maldon CM9...37 A1
Romford RM7...135 B8
Woodford IG8...110 C3
Cross Roads IG10...88 C7
Cross St **10** DA11...179 B1
Crossway
Dagenham RM8...134 C1
6 Stanford-le-H SS17...160 F3
Woodford IG8...110 C6
Cross Way **3** CM17...11 D1
CROSSWAYS...176 D4
Crossways
Canvey Island SS8...163 E4
Chelmsford CM2...54 C7
Loughton IG10...89 A4
Romford RM2...136 B8
Shenfield CM15...95 A3
Crossways Byd DA2...176 C3
Crossways The SS0...166 A8
Crossway The CM11...97 D3
Crouch Ave
Barking IG11...153 B3
Hullbridge SS5...101 E1
Crouch Beck CM3...101 E7
Crouch Cl CM20...110 E7
Crouch Dr SS11...121 D8
Crouchman Ct RM16...173 C4
Crouchmans Ave SS4...75 C4
Crouchman's Farm Rd
CM9...35 C7
Crouch Mdw SS16...101 E4
Crouch Pk SS16...101 E4
Crouch Rd
Burnham-on-C CM0...106 C5
Grays RM16...174 A1
Crouch St SS15...119 C2
Crouch Valley RM14...137 E4
Crouchview Cl SS11...122 B7
Crouch View Cotts
CM3...100 C5
Crouch View Cres
SS5...125 A8
Crouch View Gr SS5...101 D3
Crouch View Villas
SS4...104 E2

Crouch Way SS3...168 E7
Crough Rd CM3...103 A7
Crowborough Rd SS2...148 A2
Crow Gn CM15...94 A5
Crow Green La CM15...94 A4
Crow Green Rd CM15...94 A5
Crow La RM7...135 B5
Crowlands Ave RM7...135 B5
Crowlands Jun & Inf Schs
RM7...135 C5
Crown Ave SS13...143 C7
Crown Bldgs **4** E4...87 D1
Crown Cl
Basildon SS13...143 C6
Sheering CM22...12 C8
Crown Ct RM18...179 A5
Crownfield IG10...21 A2
Crownfield Ave IG2...133 C6
Crownfield Jun & Inf Schs
RM7...113 A1
Crown Gate CM20...23 D8
Crown Gdns SS6...123 C2
Crown Hill
Loughton IG16...67 A5
Rayleigh SS6...123 C2
Waltham Abbey EN9,
CM20...66 F6
Crownhill Rd IG8...110 C3
Crown Hts SS6...123 D2
Crownmead Way
RM7...135 B7
Crown Par RM13...155 B1
Crown Rd
Billericay CM11...97 B2
Cold Norton CM3...80 F6
Grays RM17...178 A8
Hockley SS5...124 B5
Ilford IG6...133 D7
Kelvedon Hatch CM14...93 D8
Crown St
Brentwood CM14...116 C8
Dagenham RM10...154 C6
Crown Way CM0...84 C4
Crowsfield Cotts CM2...76 F4
Crowsheath La CM11...98 E6
Crows La CM3...79 D5
Crowsnest The CM0...106 C3
Crows Rd
Barking IG11...152 B6
Epping CM16...45 F1
Crowstone Ave SS0...166 C8
Crowstone Cl SS0...147 D1
Crowstone Prep Sch
SS0...166 C8
Crowstone Rd
Grays RM17...173 C4
Southend-on-S SS0...166 C8
Crowstone (Sutton) Prep
Sch SS4...148 B8
Croxford Way RM7...135 D3
Croxon Way CM0...106 B7
Crozier Terr CM2...33 B4
Crucible Cl RM6...134 B5
Cruick Ave RM15...172 C6
Crusader Cl RM19...171 A2
Crushes Cl CM13...95 E3
Crushton Pl CM1...31 F6
Crusoe Rd DA8...169 D2
Crystal Ave CM12...136 E1
Crystal Cl **1** RM13...155 A1
Crystal Stps **19** SS1...167 C7
Crystal Way E4...134 C3
Cuckoo Cnr SS2...147 E4
Cuckoo La RM16...172 F5
Culford Rd RM16...172 E8
Cullen Sq RM15...172 C5
Cullings Ct EN9...65 C6
Culpeper Cl IG6...111 B4
Culverdown SS14...142 A6
Culver Rise SS14...101 E6
Cumberland Ave
Hornchurch RM12...136 E1
Maldon CM9...36 E1
South Benfleet SS7...144 C3
Southend-on-S SS3...148 D2
Cumberland Cl
Hornchurch RM12...136 E1
Redbridge IG6...111 C2
Cumberland Cres SS14...32 A7
Cumberland Ct
8 Hoddesdon EN11...21 A7
Woodford IG8...110 B3
Cumberland Dr SS15...141 A6
Cumberland Ho
Romford RM7...113 A1
Southend-on-S SS3...147 F1
Cumberland Rd RM16...172 E3
Cumberland Mews SS12...121 F5
Cumley Rd CM5...47 E1
Cumming Rd CM11...99 A2
Cummings Hall La
RM3...114 D7
Cunningham Cl
Ilford RM6...134 C6
Southend-on-S SS3...168 F8
Cunningham Dr SS12...121 F5
Cunningham Rise
CM16...47 D6
Cupids Chase SS3...150 C2
Cupid's Cnr SS3...150 C2
Curlew Ave SS3...83 A8
Curlew Cl CM9...37 C5
Curlew Cres SS16...142 B3
Curlew Dr SS7...144 C2
Curlew Ho
1 Burnham-on-C
CM0...106 C4
Rainham RM13...170 A8

Curlew Terr IG5...133 A8
Curling La RM17...172 F1
Curling Tye SS14...142 D7
CURLING TYE GREEN...36 A3
Curling Tye La
Maldon CM9...36 A3
Woodham Walter CM9...35 F3
Curling Wlk SS14...142 D7
Curteys CM17...11 D5
Curtis Mill La RM4...91 F4
Curtis Rd RM11...136 F4
Curtisway SS6...123 E4
Curzon Cres IG11...152 F2
Curzon Dr RM17...178 C2
Curzon Way CM2...33 A2
Cusak Rd CM2...32 F3
Cut-A-Thwart La CM9...36 C4
Cutforth Rd CM21...1 E3
Cuthberga Cl **2** IG11...152 C5
Cutlers Rd CM3...101 E8
Cutmore PI CM2...53 F8
Cuton Hall La CM2...33 A5
Cutter Ho DA8...169 E1
Cutty Sark Ct DA9...177 A2
Cygnet Ct
Kelvedon Hatch CM15...71 E2
Wickford SS12...121 D8
Cygnet View RM20...171 F2
Cygnet Way CM0...9 A1
Cyna Ct **3** E11...132 A5
Cypress Cl
Basildon SS15...119 C1
Waltham Abbey EN9...65 D5
Cypress Dr CM2...54 C6
Cypress Gr IG6...111 E4
Cypress Path RM3...114 D3
Cyril Dowsett Ct CM9...36 E2
Cyril Hall Ct DA11...178 F1
Czar St SS15...141 E8

D

Daarle Ave SS8...164 A4
Dacre Ave
Aveley RM15...171 D5
Redbridge IG5...111 A1
Dacre Cl IG7...111 C6
Dacre Cres RM15...171 D5
Dacre Gdns IG7...111 C6
Dacres Gate CM15...27 E4
Dads Wood CM20...23 C8
Daen Ingas CM3...56 D7
Daffodil Ave CM15...94 B4
Daffodil Gdns IG1...152 B2
Daffodil Way CM1...32 E7
DAGENHAM...154 C4
Dagenham Ave RM9...153 E4
Dagenham Dock Sta
RM9...153 F3
Dagenham East Sta
RM10...154 C7
Dagenham Heathway Sta
RM9...153 F3
Dagenham Park Com Sch
RM10...154 B4
Dagenham Rd
RM7, RM10,
RM7...135 D2
Rainham RM13...154 C5
Dagmar Rd CM1...115 A5
Dagnam Pk Cl CM3...115 A5
Dagnam Park Dr RM3...114 A5
Dagnam Park Gdns
RM3...115 A4
Dagnam Park Sq RM3...115 B4
Dagwood La CM15...72 B1
Dahlia Cl **2** IG1...152 B6
Dahlia Gdns IG1...152 B6
Daiglen Dr RM15...172 B7
Daiglen Sch The IG9...110 C8
Daines Cl
Little Ilford E12...132 F1
Southend-on-S SS1...168 B8
South Ockendon RM15...172 C2
Daines Rd CM11...97 C2
Daines Way SS1...168 B8
Dairy Cl CM3...101 C8
Dairy Farm Rd CM3...83 D3
Dairy Rd CM2...32 F4
Daisy Ct CM1...33 A6
Daisy Ho IG3...134 A3
Dakin Cl E4...110 B1
Dakyn Dr CM4...75 D3
Dale Cl RM17...172 A7
Dale Cl
Sawbridgeworth CM21...1 D4
Woodford E18...110 A1
Dalefield IG9...88 D1
Dale Gdns IG8...110 B6
Dalen Ave SS8...164 A3
Dale Rd SS9...146 B1
Daleside Gdns IG7...111 C7
Dales The SS4...125 D5
Dalestone Mews RM3...114 B4
Dale The
Thundersley SS7...145 A4
Waltham Abbey EN9...65 E5
Dale View Ave E4...109 C8
Dale View Cres E4...109 C7
Dale View Gdns E4...109 D7
Dalewood Dr RM11...136 E4
Dalkeith Rd IG1...133 C1
Dalmatia Rd SS1...167 D8
Dalmeney SS16...141 B4

Dalroy Cl RM15 . . . . 172 A7
Dalrymple Cl CM1 . . . . 32 D3
Dalton Holme IG8 . . . . 110 F4
Daltons Fen SS13 . . . . 143 C8
Daltons Shaw RM16 . . . . . 174 A8
Dalwood SS3 . . . . 149 D1
Dalwood Gdns SS7 . . . . . . 145 E4
Dalys Rd SS4 . . . . 125 E2
Dame Elizabeth Ct
CM1 . . . . 18 F3
Dames Rd E7 . . . . 132 A1
Dame Tipping CE Prim
Sch RM4 . . . . 113 C7
Dammer Wick CM0 . . . . . 106 E6
Dammerwick Cotts
CM0 . . . . 106 D6
Danan Pl **16** CM14 . . . . . 116 C7
Danacre SS15 . . . . 141 C7
DANBURY 56 D7
Danbury Cl
Ilford RM6 . . . . 134 D8
Pilgrims Hatch CM15 . . . . 93 F4
Southend-on-S SS9 . . . . 146 F4
Danbury Cres RM15 . . . . . 172 B7
Danbury Ctry Pk*
CM3 . . . . 56 B7
Danbury Down SS14 . . . . . 142 E8
Danbury Lo IG10 . . . . 88 E3
Danbury Mans **3**
IG11 . . . . 152 B5
Danbury Park Com Prim
Sch CM3 . . . . 56 C7
Danbury Rd
Loughton IG10 . . . . 88 E3
Rainham RM13 . . . . 154 F4
Rayleigh SS6 . . . . 123 B3
Danbury Vale CM3 . . . . 57 A6
Danbury Way IG8 . . . . 110 C4
Dandelion Cl RM7 . . . . . . 135 E2
Dandies Chase SS9 . . . . . 146 E7
Dandies Cl SS9 . . . . 146 D7
Dandies Dr SS9 . . . . 146 D7
Danehurst Gdns IG4 . . . . . 132 F6
Danemead EN11 . . . . 8 A1
Dane Rd
Chelmsford CM1 . . . . 31 E2
Ilford IG1 . . . . 152 C7
Dane's Ave SS3 . . . . 168 F5
Danescroft Cl SS9 . . . . . . 146 E4
Danescroft Dr SS9 . . . . . . 146 D4
Danesfield SS7 . . . . 146 C2
Danesleigh Gdns SS9 . . . 146 D4
Dane Rd RM7 . . . . 135 C4
Dane St SS3 . . . . 168 G6
Danes Way CM15 . . . . 94 A4
Danette Gdns RM8 . . . . . . 134 F2
Dangan Rd E11 . . . . 132 A5
Daniel Cl
Grays, Chafford Hundred
RM16 . . . . 172 E4
Grays, Orsett Heath
RM16 . . . . 174 B3
Danyon Cl RM13 . . . . 155 C3
Daphne Gdns E4 . . . . 109 C7
Darby Dr EN9 . . . . 65 C6
D'arcy Ave CM9 . . . . 37 B1
Darcy Cl CM13 . . . . 95 B2
D'arcy Cl CM0 . . . . 106 C6
D'arcy Gdns RM9 . . . . 153 F4
Darcy Rise CM3 . . . . 34 E1
Dare Gdns RM8 . . . . 134 E1
Darell Way CM1 . . . . 97 D1
Darenth La RM15 . . . . 172 A7
Darenth Rd SS9 . . . . 146 B1
Darent Ind Pk DA8 . . . . . . 170 D1
Dark La
Brentwood CM14 . . . . . . 115 F5
Great Warley CM14 . . . . 116 A3
Thundersley SS7 . . . . . . 145 A6
Darlinghurst Gr SS7 . . . . . 147 A2
Darlinghurst Prim Sch
SS9 . . . . 146 F2
Darlington Ct
6 Harlow CM17 . . . . 11 C4
Pilgrims Hatch CM15 . . . . 94 A3
Darlington Gdns RM3 . . . 114 D5
Darlington Path **10**
RM3 . . . . 114 D5
Darnay Rise CM1 . . . . 31 D6
Darnley Rd
Gravesend DA11 . . . . . . 179 B1
Grays RM17 . . . . 178 B8
Woodford IG8 . . . . 110 B2
Darrell Cl CM1 . . . . 32 B6
Dart Cl RM14 . . . . 137 D5
Dartfields RM3 . . . . 114 D4
DARTFORD 176 B2
Dartford Gdns RM6 . . . . . 134 B6
Dart Gn RM15 . . . . 172 B7
Dartmouth Cl SS0 . . . . . . 123 D5
Dartmouth Rd CM1 . . . . . . 32 E6
Dartview Cl RM17 . . . . . . 173 E2
Darwell Cl E6 . . . . 152 A3
Darwin Rd RM18 . . . . 178 F6
Dashes The CM20 . . . . 10 E1
Datchet Dr SS3 . . . . 149 E2
Davall Ho RM17 . . . . 178 C8
Davenant Foundation Sch
Loughton IG10 . . . . 67 C1
Loughton IG10 . . . . 89 C8
Davenants SS13 . . . . 143 B8
Davenport CM17 . . . . 24 E7
Davenport Ctr IG11 . . . . . 153 B3
Daventry Gdns RM3 . . . . 114 C5
Daventry Gn RM3 . . . . . . 114 C5

Daventry Rd RM3 . . . . . . 114 C5
David Ave SS11 . . . . 99 D2
David Coffer Ct DA17 . . . 169 B2
David Dr RM3 . . . . 115 A3
David Rd RM8 . . . . 134 E2
Davidson Gdns SS12 . . . . 121 E5
Davidson Ho DA9 . . . . . . 177 C2
Davidson Way RM7 . . . . . 135 E5
Davids Way IG6 . . . . 111 E3
David's Wlk CM11 . . . . 97 C2
David Terr RM3 . . . . 115 A4
Davies Cl RM13 . . . . 155 C2
Davington Gdns RM8 . . . . 153 B7
Davington Rd RM8 . . . . . . 153 B7
Davinia Cl IG8 . . . . 110 F4
Davis Rd
Aveley RM15 . . . . 171 D5
Grays RM16 . . . . 172 F3
Dawberry Pl CM3 . . . . . . 101 D5
Dawes Ave RM12 . . . . . . 136 E1
Dawes Cl CM9 . . . . 176 F2
Dawley Gn RM15 . . . . 172 A7
Dawlish Cres SS6 . . . . . . 123 D5
Dawlish Dr
Ilford IG3 . . . . 152 F8
Southend-on-S SS9 . . . . 146 E1
Dawlish Wlk RM3 . . . . . . 114 C2
Dawn Cl CM9 . . . . 59 B8
Dawnings The CM3 . . . . . 101 C8
Daws Cl CM9 . . . . 30 F1
DAWS HEATH 145 E5
Daws Heath Rd
Hadleigh SS7 . . . . 145 E4
Rayleigh SS6 . . . . 145 E8
Thundersley SS7 . . . . . . 145 D6
Daws Hill E4 . . . . 87 C6
Dawson Ave IG11 . . . . . . 152 F5
Dawson Dr RM13 . . . . . . 155 B5
Dawson Gdns **10** IG11 . 152 F5
Dawson Mews CM11 . . . . . 97 B3
Daylop Dr IG7 . . . . 112 B7
Days Cl CM1 . . . . 32 B8
Days La
Doddinghurst CM15 . . . . . 72 C1
Pilgrims Hatch CM15 . . . . 94 B7
Dayton Dr DA8 . . . . 170 D1
Deacon Dr SS13 . . . . 141 C7
Deacon Way IG8 . . . . 110 F4
Deadman's La CM2 . . . . . . 54 C4
Dealtree Cl CM15 . . . . 72 B4
Dean Ct RM7 . . . . 135 D5
Deanes Sch The SS7 . . . . 145 C6
Deans Cl CM14 . . . . 116 B6
Deans Ind Est RM13 . . . . 155 D1
Deans Rd CM14 . . . . 116 B6
Dean Way CM1 . . . . 31 E1
Dearsley Ho RM13 . . . . . 154 D3
DEBDEN 89 C7
Debden Cl IG8 . . . . 110 D3
Debden Gn SS16 . . . . 141 C7
DEBDEN GREEN 67 B1
Debden La IG10 . . . . 67 C1
Debden Park High Sch
IG10 . . . . 89 D7
Debden Rd IG10 . . . . 67 B1
Debden Sta IG10 . . . . 89 C5
Debden Wlk CM0 . . . . . . 106 A6
Debden Wlk **4** RM12 . . 155 B6
De Beauvoir Chase
CM11 . . . . 98 E3
Deben RM18 . . . . 175 C3
Deborah Ct **7** E18 . . . . 132 B8
Dedham Ct CM11 . . . . 97 C2
Dedham Rd CM11 . . . . 97 C2
Dee Ct RM14 . . . . 137 E5
Deepdale SS7 . . . . 144 F6
Deepdene
Basildon SS16 . . . . 142 B5
Ingatestone CM4 . . . . . . 74 B3
Deepdene Ave SS6 . . . . . 123 D4
Deepdene Cl E11 . . . . 132 A7
Deepdene Path IG10 . . . . . 89 B5
Deepdene Rd IG10 . . . . . . 89 A5
Deeping **5** SS1 . . . . . . 167 A8
Deepwater Rd SS8 . . . . . 163 E3
Deerbank Rd CM11 . . . . . . 97 C3
Deere Ave RM13 . . . . 155 A6
Deerhurst SS7 . . . . 145 B7
Deerhurst Chase CM3 . . . . 56 F1
Deerhurst Cl SS7 . . . . . . 145 B7
Deerleap Gr E4 . . . . 87 B4
Deer Mead Ct **1** RM2 . 135 F6
Deer Park Way EN9 . . . . . . 65 B4
Deer Pk CM19 . . . . 23 B5
Deeside Wlk **3** SS12 . . 121 E6
Dee Way RM1 . . . . 113 E2
Defoe Par RM10 . . . . 174 B3
Defoe Way RM5 . . . . 113 B4
De Havilland Sq IG1 . . . . 133 D3
Deidre Chapman Ho
DA10 . . . . 177 E1
Deirdre Ave SS12 . . . . . . 121 E7
Deirdre Cl SS12 . . . . 121 E7
Delafield Rd RM17 . . . . . 173 D1
Delamere Rd CM1 . . . . 31 E1
Delargy Cl RM16 . . . . 174 B3
De La Salle Sch SS14 . . . 142 C8
Delaware Cres SS3 . . . . . 168 D7
Delaware Rd SS3 . . . . . . 168 D7
Delder Ave SS8 . . . . 164 A3
Delderfield Ho RM1 . . . . 113 D1
Delft Rd SS8 . . . . 164 A4
Delfzul Rd SS8 . . . . 164 A4
Delgada Rd SS8 . . . . 164 D3
Delhi Rd SS13 . . . . 143 C6
Delimands SS15 . . . . 141 F6
Delius Way SS17 . . . . . . 160 C3
Dell Cl IG8 . . . . 110 B7

Dell Ct
Grays RM17 . . . . 173 B1
Hornchurch RM12 . . . . . 136 E2
Dellfield Ct **4** CM17 . . . . 11 C4
Dell La CM22 . . . . 2 A8
Dellow Cl IG2 . . . . 133 D4
Dell Rd RM17 . . . . 173 B2
Dells Cl E4 . . . . 87 B2
Dell The
Basildon SS16 . . . . 142 B3
Brentwood CM13 . . . . . . 116 B4
Great Baddow CM2 . . . . . 54 F6
5 Greenhithe DA9 . . . 177 B2
Waltham Abbey EN9 . . . . 65 C3
Wickford SS11 . . . . 121 E7
Woodford IG8 . . . . 110 B7
Dellwood Gdns IG5 . . . . . 133 A8
Delmar Gdns SS11 . . . . . . 99 C2
Delmores SS16 . . . . 141 C3
Delta Rd CM13 . . . . 95 D3
De Luci Rd RM9 . . . . 169 C1
Delvers Mead RM10 . . . . 154 C8
Delview SS8 . . . . 163 F5
Delvins SS13 . . . . 143 B8
Denbar Par RM7 . . . . 135 C2
Denbigh Cl RM11 . . . . . . 137 A7
Denbigh Ho **8** RM3 . . . 114 E4
Denbigh Rd SS15 . . . . . . 141 B5
Denby Grange CM17 . . . . . 24 E8
Dencourt Cres SS14 . . . . 142 F5
Dene Cl SS6 . . . . 123 D4
Denecroft Gdns
RM17 . . . . 173 D3
Dene Ct CM1 . . . . 31 D5
Dene Gdns SS6 . . . . 123 D4
Deneholm Prim Sch
RM16 . . . . 173 C4
Denehurst Gdns
Basildon SS16 . . . . 140 E4
Woodford IG8 . . . . 110 B6
Dene Path SS15 . . . . 172 A7
Dene Rd IG9 . . . . 88 E1
Denesmere SS7 . . . . 144 C4
Deneway SS16 . . . . 142 D2
Dengayne SS14 . . . . 142 D6
DENGIE 63 D1
Dengie Hundred Sports
Ctr CM0 . . . . 106 B4
Denham Dr IG2 . . . . 133 C5
Denham Rd SS8 . . . . 164 A4
Denham Vale SS6 . . . . . . 123 A3
Denham Way IG11 . . . . . 152 F4
Denholme Wlk RM13 . . . . 154 F6
Denmark Ho CM2 . . . . 54 D8
Denner Rd E4 . . . . 109 A8
Dennis Ct E17 . . . . 109 D1
Dennises La RM14 . . . . . 156 E5
Dennis Rd RM15 . . . . 157 A4
Denny Ave EN9 . . . . 65 D5
Denny Ct **8** DA2 . . . . . 176 B1
Denny Gdns RM9 . . . . . . 153 B5
Dent Cl RM15 . . . . 172 A7
Denton App SS0 . . . . 147 C5
Denton Cl SS0 . . . . 147 C5
Denver Dr SS13 . . . . 121 C1
Denver Ind Est RM13 . . . 169 F8
Denys Dr SS14 . . . . 120 F1
Derby Ave
Romford RM7 . . . . 135 C5
Upminster RM14 . . . . . . 137 A1
Derby Cl
Basildon SS16 . . . . 140 F4
Billericay CM11 . . . . 97 D5
Mayland CM3 . . . . 61 A1
Derby Ct E18 . . . . 109 F2
Derbydale SS4 . . . . 125 C6
Derby Rd
Grays RM17, RM18 . . . . 178 C7
Mayland CM3 . . . . 61 B1
Tilbury RM18 . . . . 178 F5
Dockwra La CM3 . . . . 57 A7
DODDINGHURST 72 C2
Doddinghurst CE Jun Sch
CM15 . . . . 72 B2
Doddinghurst CM15 . . . . . 94 C2
Doddinghurst Inf Sch
CM15 . . . . 72 B2
Doddinghurst Rd
Brentwood CM15 . . . . . . 94 D5
Doddinghurst CM15 . . . . . 72 C1
Doesgate La RM14 . . . . . 140 C1
Doeshill Dr SS12 . . . . . . 121 E7
Doggetts Chase SS4 . . . . 126 A4
Doggett's Cnr RM11 . . . . 136 F2
Doggetts Prim Sch
SS4 . . . . 125 F3
Dog Kennel La CM4 . . . . . 74 C7
Dolby Rise CM2 . . . . 32 F2
Dollant Ave SS8 . . . . 164 A3
Dolphin App RM1 . . . . . . 135 F7
Dolphin Ct IG7 . . . . 111 B7
Dolphin Gdns CM12 . . . . . 96 F5
Dolphin Motorway Est
RM19 . . . . 171 E1
Dolphin Point RM19 . . . . 171 E1
Dolphins SS0 . . . . 147 D4
Dolphin Way RM19 . . . . . 171 E1
Dombey Cl CM1 . . . . 31 F7
Dome Cvn Pk SS5 . . . . . . 102 C2
Dominic Ct EN9 . . . . 65 B6
Dominion Dr RM5 . . . . . . 113 B4
Dominion Way RM13 . . . . 155 A2
Dominion Wks RM8 . . . . 134 E3
Domsey La CM3 . . . . 19 F5
Donald Dr RM6 . . . . 134 C6
Donald Thorn Cl
SS12 . . . . 121 D6
Donald Way CM2 . . . . 54 C7

Devon Ho
Romford RM7 . . . . 113 A1
6 Wanstead E11 . . . . 132 A6
Devonport Gdns IG1 . . . . 132 F5
Devon Rd IG11 . . . . 152 E4
Devonshire Cl SS15 . . . . 141 A8
Devonshire Gdns
SS17 . . . . 175 A3
Devonshire Ho RM10 . . . 111 B3
Devonshire Rd
Basildon SS15 . . . . 141 A7
Burnham-on-C CM0 . . . . 106 C5
Grays RM16 . . . . 172 E2
Hornchurch RM12 . . . . . 136 D3
Ilford IG2 . . . . 133 E4
Southminster CM0 . . . . . 84 C4
Devon Way SS8 . . . . 164 B5
De Warren Ho DA11 . . . . 178 D1
Dewey Path RM12 . . . . . 155 C6
Dewey Rd RM10 . . . . 154 C6
Dewlands SS14 . . . . 142 A7
Dewsbury Cl RM3 . . . . . . 114 E4
Dewsbury Gdns RM3 . . . 114 E4
Dewsbury Rd RM3 . . . . . 114 E4
Dewsgreen SS16 . . . . . . 142 E4
Dewyk Rd SS8 . . . . 164 C5
Dexter Cl RM17 . . . . 173 A3
Deyncourt Gdns E11 . . . . 132 C7
Deyncourt Rd RM11 . . . . 136 A3
Dial Cl DA9 . . . . 177 D2
Diamond Cl
Dagenham RM8 . . . . . . 134 C3
Grays RM16 . . . . 172 F3
Romford RM1 . . . . 135 E5
Diamond Ct RM11 . . . . . . 136 A3
Diana Cl
Grays RM16 . . . . 172 F3
Woodford E18 . . . . 110 B2
Diban Ave RM12 . . . . 155 B8
Diban Ct RM12 . . . . 155 B8
Dickens Ave
Dartford DA1 . . . . 176 A3
Tilbury RM18 . . . . 179 B6
Dickens Cl SS2 . . . . 148 B2
Dickens Ct
Basildon SS15 . . . . 141 D7
10 Wanstead E11 . . . 132 A7
Dickens Dr SS15 . . . . 141 D7
Dickens Pl CM1 . . . . 31 D7
Dickens Rise IG7 . . . . . . 111 B7
Dickens Way RM1 . . . . . . 135 E2
Dicky Moors CM3 . . . . 18 F7
Digby Gdns RM10 . . . . . . 154 A4
Digby Rd
Barking IG11 . . . . 152 F5
Corringham SS17 . . . . . 161 C4
Digby Wlk **1** RM12 . . . 155 C2
Diggens Ct IG10 . . . . 88 E6
Dilkes Prim Sch
RM15 . . . . 171 F7
Dilliway Ct CM0 . . . . 106 B4
Dilston CM3 . . . . 57 A6
Dinant Ave SS8 . . . . 163 E4
Dinant Link Rd EN11 . . . . 21 B7
Disney Cl CM4 . . . . 74 B4
Disraeli Rd SS6, SS9 . . . 146 B8
District Ctr SS3 . . . . 149 D1
Ditchfield Rd CM12 . . . . . . 8 A1
Ditton Court Rd SS0 . . . . 166 D8
Dixon Ave CM1 . . . . 31 F4
Dixon Ct SS13 . . . . 143 B6
Dobb's Weir Rd EN11 . . . . 21 D5
Dobsons Cl SS6 . . . . 123 E1
Dock Approach Rd RM16,
RM17 . . . . 173 E2
Docklands Ave CM4 . . . . . 74 C4
Dock Rd
Grays RM17, RM18 . . . . 178 C7
Mayland CM3 . . . . 61 B1
Tilbury RM18 . . . . 178 F5

Doncaster Way RM14 . . .
Doncel Ct E4 . . . .
Doncella Cl RM16 . . . . . .
Donington Ave IG6 . . . . .
Donne Rd RM8 . . . .
Donnington Ct **1**
DA2 . . . .
Donovan's Ct CM13 . . . .
Don Way RM1 . . . .
Dorchester Ave EN11 . . .
Dorchester Ct **2** E18 . .
Dorchester Gdns E4 . . . .
Dorchester Rd CM12 . . . .
Dordells SS15 . . . .
Dore Ave E12 . . . .
Dorian Rd RM12 . . . .
Doric Ave SS4 . . . .
Doric Lo SS0 . . . .
Dorking Rd RM3 . . . .
Dorking Rise RM3 . . . . . .
Dorking Wlk
Great Baddow CM2 . . . .
Romford RM3 . . . .
Dorkins Way RM14 . . . . .
Dorothy Barley Jun &
Sch RM8 . . . .
Dorothy Farm Rd SS6 . . .
Dorothy Gdns
Dagenham RM8 . . . . . .
Thundersley SS7 . . . . . .
Dorrington Gdns
RM12 . . . .
Dorset Ave
Great Baddow CM2 . . . .
Romford RM1 . . . .
Dorset Cl CM2 . . . .
Dorset Gdns
Linford SS17 . . . .
Rochford SS4 . . . .
Dorset Rd
Burnham-on-C CM0 . . . .
Maldon CM9 . . . .
Dorset Way
Billericay CM12 . . . . . .
Canvey Island SS8 . . . .
Doubleday Dr CM9 . . . . .
Doubleday Rd IG10 . . . . .
Doublegate La SS11 . . . .
Doublet Mews CM11 . . . .
Douglas Ave
Chingford E17 . . . .
Romford RM3 . . . .
Douglas Cl
Galleywood CM2 . . . . . .
Grays RM16 . . . .
Redbridge IG6 . . . .
Douglas Dr SS12 . . . . . .
Douglas Matthew Ho
CM14 . . . .
Douglas Rd
Chingford E4 . . . .
Hadleigh SS7 . . . .
Ilford IG3 . . . .
Romford RM11 . . . .
Douglas Wlk **3** CM2 . .
Doug Siddons Ct
RM17 . . . .
Doulton Cl CM17 . . . .
Doulton Way SS4 . . . . . .
Dounsell Ct CM15 . . . . . .
Dove Cl RM16 . . . .
Dove Crofts CM6 . . . .
Dovecote SS3 . . . .
Dovedale Cl
Basildon SS16 . . . .
Ramsden Heath CM11 . .
Dove Dr SS7 . . . .
Dovehouse Croft CM20 .
Dove House Gdns E4 . . .
Dovehouse Mead
IG11 . . . .
Dove La CM2 . . . .
Dover Cl RM5 . . . .
Dovercliff Rd SS8 . . . . . .
Dover Rd
Dagenham RM6 . . . . . .
Northfleet DA11 . . . .
Wanstead E12 . . . .
Dovers Corner Ind Pk
RM13 . . . .
Dovervelt Rd SS8 . . . . . .
Dover Way SS13 . . . .
Dovesgate SS7 . . . .
Doves Mews SS15 . . . . . .
Dovetree Cr RM3 . . . .
Dove Wlk **7** RM12 . . . .
Dow Ct CM0 . . . .
Dowding Way
Hornchurch RM12 . . . . .
Waltham Abbey EN9 . . .
Dowland Cl SS17 . . . . . .
Dowland Wlk SS15 . . . . .
Downer Rd SS7 . . . .
Downer Rd N SS7 . . . . . .
Downesway SS7 . . . .
Downey Cl SS14 . . . .
Downhall Cl SS6 . . . .
Downhall Park Way
SS6 . . . .
Down Hall Prim Sch
SS6 . . . .
Downhall Rd CM17,
CM22 . . . .
Down Hall Rd SS6 . . . . . .
DOWNHAM . . . .

CE Prim Sch
..........................98 C4
CI RM5 ....113 A3
Rd
nd SS8...............164 A3
leath CM11..........98 D5
..........................76 B1
CM11 ....98 D7
S11.......................99 C3
d RM9 ....153 F5
e 65 E5
CM3 ....101 E8
S16 ....142 E3
Ave IG3 ....133 F5
Ct IG3.................133 E5
Prim Sch
..........................133 E4
Dr CM14 ....116 C7
n Sch The
..............................23 E8
CM9 ....37 B3
CM20 ....23 E8
CM1.......................32 D6
sa CM14...............98 C6
RM18.................179 C5
CM0 ....106 A5
3.............................83 A8

CM14...................116 D5
7 ....145 C5
SS14 ....142 F5
s RM12 ....155 A6
t DA8..................169 E1

15 ....141 D6
.............................172 D3
.............................172 E4
-S SS0 ....147 C1

M3 ....20 B7
am CM3 ....19 F7
v CM17 ....11 E4
SS3....................168 E8
ase CM9 ....37 D4
or CM5 ....48 C2
RM12 ....136 E2
CM3 ....101 E8
E11......................132 B4
EN9......................65 E7
e IG10.................88 F3

..........................133 D3
M9..........................37 A1
E17......................109 B1
ton SS3 ....168 D8
RM8..................153 B6
16 ....142 F4

.............................152 F5
CM13.................116 C4
oil IG9.................88 C2
CM1......................32 A6
...............................87 D2
......................10 E1
CM11..................21 A8
5........................101 D3
3...........................133 A3
10.........................88 E5
3...........................82 F8
8.........................146 B8
18......................132 F4
..........................125 F3
lier Row
..........................113 D3
rold wood
..........................114 F2
CM21.....................1 E2
-S SS0 ....166 B8
8.........................132 A8
se SS8 ....164 B3
ye SS2 ....148 D1
Ins RM8 ....153 C7
1...........................31 F7
ad CM14 ....116 B6
10.........................89 B7
Ave RM7 ....135 D7
Ct CM15 ....94 C2
PI 7
..........................121 E5
Rd
.............................135 D7
1.........................132 C5
The
ll IG9.................110 B8
..............................46 A1
............................5 C2
SS2 ....148 B2

..............................59 A8
16.......................111 F4
e18 ....179 B6
RM3 ....114 B3
e E4....................87 B3
..........................141 E1
13.......................101 D5
16.......................172 F3
S7 ....149 C6
CM1 ....110 B8
CM1 ....17 C7
ad
4.........................104 D2
.............................9 B1
ol Ct
.............................135 E7
.............................46 C6
CM21 ....1 E2
CM14 ....71 B1

Dudley CI
Boreham CM3 ....20 E1
Grays RM16...........172 E4
Dudley Ct 14 E11 ....132 A6
Dudley Gdns RM3....114 D4
Dudley Rd
Chingford E17 ......109 A1
Ilford IG2 ....152 B8
Romford RM3 ......114 D4
Duffield CI RM16 ...172 F3
Duffield Rd CM2.......54 D6
Duffries CI CM3 .....18 E7
Duke Gdns IG6......133 D7
Duke PI SS15.......141 E8
Dukes Ave
Grays RM17..........173 A4
Southminster CM0......7 C6
Theydon Bois CM16.....67 E4
Dukes CI CM16........47 B4
Dukes Ct E6..........152 A4
Dukes Farm CI CM12....97 C5
Dukes Farm Rd CM12 ....97 B5
Dukes La
3 Chelmsford CM2 ....32 F4
Willingale CM5 ....28 C5
Dukes Orch
Hatfield Broad Oak
CM22 ....3 F6
Writtle CM1 ....31 B1
Dukes Park Ind Est
CM2......................32 F4
Dukes PI CM14 ....94 C1
Dukes Priory Hospl The
CM1.......................32 D4
Dukes Rd
Billericay CM11........97 C4
Wallend E6...........152 A4
Duke St
Chelmsford CM1 ......32 B2
Hoddesdon EN11.......21 A7
Dulverton Ave SS0....147 A5
Dulverton CI SS0 .....147 A5
Dulverton Rd RM3...114 D4
Dunbar Ave RM10...135 A1
Dunbar Gdns RM10 ....154 B7
Dunbar PI SS12.......121 E5
Duncan CI SS12.....121 F5
Duncannon PI DA9 ...177 C3
Dunchurch Ho RM10....154 A5
Duncombe Ct 4
RM19 ....171 B1
Dundas Mews EN3....65 A2
Dundee Ave SS9.....146 B2
Dundee CI SS9 ....146 C2
Dundee Ct SS14.....142 F8
Dundonald Dr SS9...146 F1
Dunedin Ho RM18 ...179 A5
Dunedin Rd
Ilford IG1 ....133 C3
Rainham RM13 .....154 F2
Dunfane CM11.........97 C5
Dungannon Chase
SS1.....................168 B6
Dungannon Dr SS1 ...168 B6
Dunkeld Rd RM8.....134 C2
Dunkellin Gr RM15....172 A7
Dunkellin Way RM15....172 A7
Dunkin Rd DA1 ......176 A3
Dunkirk Rd CM0......106 C5
Dunlin CI
Heybridge CM9 ....37 C5
South Woodham Ferrers
CM3 ....79 D1
Dunlop CI RM18......178 F5
Dunlop Rd RM18......178 F6
Dunmore Rd CM2......33 A3
Dunmow CI
Ilford RM6...........134 C6
Loughton IG10........88 E3
Dunmow Dr RM13...154 F4
Dunmow Gdns CM13....139 D5
Dunmow Ho RM9....153 B4
Dunmow Rd
Fyfield CM5 ....27 E6
Hatfield Broad Oak CM22 ...3 F6
High Roding CM6.......5 D5
Leaden Roding CM6....15 A4
Dunning CI RM15....172 A7
Dunningford CI CM2 ....154 F7
Dunningford Prim Sch
RM12 ....154 F7
Dunnings La CM13...139 B2
Dunnose Ct 16 RM19...171 B1
Dunspring La SS13...111 B1
Dunstable CI RM3 ...114 D4
Dunstable Rd
Romford RM3 ......114 D4
Stanford-le-H SS17...160 D3
Dunstalls CM19........23 A4
Dunster Ave SS0.....147 A1
Dunster CI RM5 .....113 C1
Dunster Cres RM11...137 B2
Dunster Ho 24 DA2...176 B1
Dunster Ho SS7 .....144 F6
Dunton Park Cvn Pk
CM13...................140 E5
Dunton Rd
Basildon CM12, SS15...119 B1
Romford RM1 ....135 C7
Dunton View CM13...140 E5
DUNTON WAYLETTS
..........................118 C1
Dunwich Dr 2 RM6...134 B6
Dupre CI RM16........172 B2
Durants Wlk 4 SS13...121 D6
Durban Gdns RM10 ....154 C5
Durban La SS15......119 F2

Durban Rd IG2, IG3 ...133 E3
Durdans The SS16 ...141 B4
Durell Rd RM9 ....153 D7
Durell Rd RM9.......153 D7
Durham Ave
Romford RM2 ......136 C7
Woodford SS8 .....110 D5
Durham CI
Sawbridgeworth CM21.....1 C1
Stanstead Abbotts SG12...8 B5
Durham Ho
3 Barking IG11 ......153 A5
Romford RM7 ......113 A1
Durham PI IG1 ......152 C8
Durham Rd
Basildon SS15 ......140 E6
Dagenham RM10 ...154 C7
Rochford SS4..........125 B6
Southend-on-S SS2....148 B1
Durham Way SS6...123 D5
Durley Ave SS12....120 F8
Durley CI SS7 ....144 E4
Durnell Way IG10......89 A6
Durninge Wlk RM16 ...173 B6
Durrants CI SS13.....155 C3
Durrington CI SS14....142 C5
Dury Falls CI RM11 ....137 A3
Dutch Cottage Mus*
SS8.....................163 C4
DUTCH VILLAGE ...163 D4
Duxford SS11.........122 A6
Duxford Ct RM12 ...155 C6
Dycorts Sch RM3....115 A6
Dyer Ct EN3.............65 A2
Dyer's Rd CM9..........37 A2
Dyers Way RM3......114 B3
Dyke Cres SS8.......163 D4
Dykes Chase CM9......36 F3
Dylan Rd DA17 ......169 A3
Dymchurch CI IG5...111 A1
Dymoke Rd RM11....135 F4
Dymokes Way EN11.....8 A1
Dynevor Gdns SS9...146 B1
Dytchleys La CM14....93 A5
Dytchleys Rd CM14 ...92 F5

E

Eagle Ave RM6.......134 E5
Eagle CI
Hornchurch RM12 ...155 B6
Waltham Abbey EN9....66 A5
Eagle Ct 6 E11 ......132 A7
Eagle Ho RM17......177 F8
Eagle La
Kelvedon Hatch CM15...71 E2
Wanstead E11 ......132 A7
Eagle Rd SS8 ....163 D4
Eagle Terr IG8......110 B3
Eagle Way
Great Warley CM13....116 D4
Northfleet DA11......178 A2
Southend-on-S SS3...168 F8
Eardley Rd DA17.....169 A1
Earl Mountbatten Dr
CM12.......................96 F4
Earlsdown Ho 6
IG11....................152 D3
Earlsfield Dr CM2......32 F3
Earls Hall Ave SS2...147 E3
Earls Hall Inf Sch
SS0.....................147 D4
Earls Hall Jun Sch
SS0.....................147 E4
Earls Hall Par SS2...147 E4
Earl's Path IG10........88 C6
Earls Wlk RM8.......153 B8
Earlswood SS7 .....144 D4
Earlswood Gdns IG5...133 A8
Easebourne Rd RM8....153 C7
Easedale Dr RM12 ...155 B7
Easington Way RM15...172 A8
East Ave CM3............82 E2
Eastbourne Gr SS0...147 C3
Eastbourne Rd E6 ...152 A2
East Bridge Rd CM0...101 E8
Eastbrook Ave RM10 ...154 C8
Eastbrook Comp Sch
RM10 ....154 C8
Eastbrookend Ctry Pk*
Rainham RM7 ......154 E8
Romford RM7 ......135 D1
Eastbrook Rd EN9 ....65 E6
Eastbrooks SS13......143 B7
Eastbrooks Mews
SS13.....................143 B7
Eastbrooks PI SS13...143 B7
Eastbury Ave
Barking IG11 ....152 E4
Rochford SS4.........125 D4
Eastbury Comp Sch
Barking IG11 ....152 E6
Barking IG11 ....152 F5
Eastbury CI IG11 ...152 E4
Eastbury Inf Sch IG11...152 F5
Eastbury Rd
Romford RM7 ......136 C7
Wallend E6...........152 A1
Eastbury Sq IG11...152 F4
East Canney Cotts CM3...80 F5
Eastcheap SS6 ....123 D7
East CI RM13........155 B1
Eastcote Gr SS2 ...147 E4
Eastcourt Ind Sch
IG3......................134 A3
East Cres SS8.........163 F4

East Crescent Rd 5
DA12....................179 C1
East Dene Dr RM3 ...114 D5
East Dr CM21.............1 E1
EASTEND 9 E1
Eastend Cotts CM19....9 D1
East End Rd CM0 ......42 C3
East Entrance RM10...154 B3
Eastern App IG11....153 A3
Eastern App CM2.......32 F5
Eastern Ave
Aveley RM15 ....171 C4
Grays RM20..........176 F8
Ilford IG2 ....152 B8
South Benfleet SS7...144 C5
Southend-on-S SS2...148 B3
Wanstead E11 .....132 C5
Eastern Ave E RM1, RM2,
RM3...................113 C1
Eastern Avenue Ret Pk
RM7 ....135 C7
Eastern Avenue W
RM7 ....135 B7
Eastern CI SS2 .....148 A3
Eastern Cres CM1....31 F5
Eastern Espl
Canvey Island SS8...164 D2
Southend-on-S SS1...167 D6
Eastern Rd
Burnham-on-C CM0 ...106 C5
Grays RM17 ....173 D2
Rayleigh SS6 ....123 B1
Romford RM1 ......135 F6
Easternville Gdns
IG2.....................133 C5
Eastern Way
Belvedere DA18......169 A4
Grays RM17 ....173 A1
Eastfield Gdns RM10...154 A8
Eastfield Rd
Basildon SS15 ......119 F2
Brentwood CM14....116 D8
Canvey Island SS8...164 D5
Dagenham RM9 ....153 F8
Dagenham, Rush Grn
RM10 ....154 A8
Eastgate SS14 ....142 B5
Eastgate Bsns Ctr 2
SS14....................142 B6
East Hall La RM13 ...170 D7
Eastham Cres CM13...117 A7
EAST HANNINGFIELD ...78 B7
East Hanningfield CE Prim
Sch CM3 ....78 B7
East Hanningfield Ind Est
CM3........................78 C6
East Hanningfield Rd
Howe Green CM2 ....55 E2
Rettendon CM3........78 C4
EAST HORNDON 113 B4
Eastleigh Rd SS7 ...144 E1
Eastley SS15 ....141 F4
East Mayne SS13 ...121 A2
Eastmead IG3 ....134 A4
East Mill SS11 ....179 A1
East Mill Sch SS15...141 A6
East Park CI RM6....134 E6
East Pk
Harlow CM17 ....11 C3
Sawbridgeworth CM21...1 E1
East Rd
Dagenham, Chadwell Heath
RM6 ....134 C6
Harlow CM20 ....11 B4
Romford RM7 ......135 D4
East Row E11 ....132 A5
East Sq SS14 ....142 B6
East St
Barking IG11 ....153 A7
Grays RM17 ....178 C8
West Thurrock
RM20 ....177 E8
Rochford SS4.........125 F2
Southend-on-S, Leigh Cliffs
SS9.....................165 E8
Southend-on-S SS2...147 F2
East Terr DA12......179 C1
East Thorpe SS14 ...142 C6
East Thurrock Rd
RM17...................178 C8
EAST TILBURY 175 C1
East Tilbury Inf Sch
RM18...................175 C1
East Tilbury Jun Sch
RM18...................175 C1
East Tilbury Rd SS17...175 A4
East Tilbury Sta
RM18...................175 B2
East View
Chingford E4 ......109 F1
Writtle CM1...........30 F1
East Walk SS6.......123 C5
Eastway SS11.......132 B6
Eastways CM9 ......163 F5
EASTWICK 10 A4
Eastwick Hall La CM20...10 A5
Eastwick Rd
Eastwick CM20 ......10 B4
Harlow CM20.........10 B4
EASTWOOD 146 E5
Eastwood CI SS9...146 D5
Eastwoodbury Cres
SS2.....................147 A6
Eastwoodbury La SS2...147 C6

Eastwood Bvd SS0 ...147 A2
Eastwood CI E18 ...110 A1
Eastwood Dr RM13 ...170 B7
Eastwood Ind Est SS9...146 C6
Eastwood La S SS0...147 B2
Eastwood Old Rd SS9...146 B6
Eastwood Park CI
SS9.....................146 E6
Eastwood Park Dr
SS9.....................146 E7
Eastwood Prim Sch
SS9.....................146 F6
Eastwood Rd
Ilford IG3 ....134 A4
Rayleigh SS6 ....123 E1
Southend-on-S SS9...146 D3
Woodford E18 .....110 A1
Eastwood Rd N SS9...146 D4
Eastwood Rise
Rayleigh SS6 ....124 C1
Southend-on-S SS9...146 C8
Eastwood Sch The
SS9.....................146 F5
Eaton CI SS11 ....97 A5
Eaton Ct RM10 .....154 C6
Eaton Dr RM5 ....113 B3
Eaton Gdns RM9 ...153 E5
Eaton Rd
Southend-on-S SS9...146 C2
Uppminster RM14 ...137 E2
Eaton Rise E11 .....132 C6
Eatons Mead E4 ...109 A8
Ebbsfleet Ind Est
DA11...................178 A2
Ebbsfleet Int Sta
DA10......................178 A1
Ebbsfleet Wlk DA11...178 B1
Ebenezer Terr CM2...54 F7
Eccles Ho 2 RM3 ...114 D4
Eccleston Cres RM6...134 B4
Eccleston Gdns RM12...97 A5
Echo Hts E4 ....87 B1
Eckersley Rd CM1....32 A2
Eckford CI RM7......135 B5
Eden CI RM3............65 A1
Eden Gn RM15.......172 B8
Edenhall CI RM3 ...114 C5
Edenhall Glen RM3...114 C5
Edenhall Rd RM3 ...114 C5
Edens Mount CM21......1 F4
Eden Way CM1........31 C5
Edgar Ho E11 ....132 A4
Edgar Rd RM6 ......134 D4
Edgecotts SS16 .....141 E4
Edgefield Ave IG11...152 F5
Edgefield Ct 3 IG11...152 F5
Edgehill Gdns RM10...154 A8
Edinburgh Ave
Corringham SS17...160 F4
Southend-on-S SS9...146 B2
Edinburgh CI SS6...123 B5
Edinburgh Gate CM20...10 D3
Edinburgh Ho 1
RM2 ....136 C7
Edinburgh Mews
RM18...................179 B5
Edinburgh PI CM20...11 A4
Edinburgh Way
Basildon SS13 ......143 B6
Harlow CM20.........10 E3
Edison Ave RM12...135 F3
Edison CI RM12.....135 F3
Edisons Pk DA2.....176 D4
Edith CI
Canvey Island SS8...163 D3
Dagenham RM6 ...134 D6
Southend-on-S SS17...161 A4
Edith Rd
Canvey Island SS8...163 D3
Dagenham RM6 ...134 D6
Southend-on-S SS17...161 A4
Edmund Rd
Grays RM16..........172 D4
Rainham RM13 .....154 E2
Edmunds Ho CM16....67 F8
Edmund's Twr CM19...23 C8
EDNEY COMMON ...52 D5
Edward Ave E4 .....109 B4
Edward Bright CI CM9...32 F2
Edward CI
Billericay CM12 ......96 F5
Grays RM16..........172 D4
Rochford SS4.........125 C6
Edward Ct E4 ....65 F6
Edward Ct CM2........54 C7
Edward Francis Jun Sch
SS6.....................123 E3
Edward CI RM13 ...154 F2
Edward Mans 6 IG11...152 F5
Edward St E4........131 A8
Edwards CI CM13......95 E3
Edwards Hall Prim Sch
SS9.....................146 C2
Edwards Rd DA17...169 A2
Edwards Way CM13...95 E3
Edwards Wlk CM9 ...36 F3
Edwin Ave E6.........152 A3
Edwin CI RM13......154 F2
Edwin Hall View CM3...79 C1
Edwin Lambert Sch
RM11...................137 B2
Edwin's Hall Rd CM3...79 D3
Edwin St DA12......179 B1
Egbert Gdns SS11...99 D1

Egerton Dr SS16 . . . . .140 E5
Egerton Gdns IG3 . . . . .133 F1
Egg Hall CM16 . . . . .46 A2
Eglington Rd E4 . . . . .87 C2
Eglinton Dr CM2 . . . . .33 B4
Eglinton Rd DA10 . . . . .177 F1
Eisenhower Rd SS15 . . . . .141 A6
Elan Rd RM15 . . . . .172 A8
Elbourne Trad Est
  DA17 . . . . .169 B3
Elbury Ct IG8 . . . . .110 E3
Eldan Ho RM4 . . . . .113 E7
Eldbert Cl SS2 . . . . .148 E2
Eldeland SS15 . . . . .141 E7
Elder Ave SS12 . . . . .121 C6
Elderberry Cl
  Basildon SS15 . . . . .141 B5
  Redbridge IG6 . . . . .111 B3
Elderfield CM17 . . . . .11 D3
Elderfield Wlk E11 . . . . . . .132 B6
Elderstep Ave SS8 . . . . . . .164 E3
Elderton Rd SS0 . . . . .147 D1
Elder Tree Rd SS4 . . . . . . .164 C4
Elder Way
  Rainham RM13 . . . . .155 D2
  Wickford SS12 . . . . .121 C6
Eldon Rd EN11 . . . . .21 D4
Eldonwall Est RM8 . . . . . . .134 F3
Eldon Way SS5 . . . . .124 E6
Eldon Way Ind Est
  SS5 . . . . .124 D6
Eldred Gdns RM14 . . . . . . .137 E4
Eldred Rd IG11 . . . . .152 E4
Eldridge Ct ▣ RM10 . . . . .154 B6
Eleanor Chase SS12 . . . . . .121 C7
Eleanor Cross Rd EN8 . . . . .65 A5
Eleanor Ct RM11 . . . . .136 D4
Eleanor Gdns RM8 . . . . . . .134 F2
Eleanor Way CM14 . . . . . . .116 E5
Eleanor Wlk ▣ DA9 . . . . . .177 C3
Electric Ave SS0 . . . . .147 C2
Electric Ho ▣ E4 . . . . .87 D1
Electric Par
  Ilford IG3 . . . . .133 F2
  Woodford IG8 . . . . .110 C3
Eleven Acre Rise IG10 . . . . .88 F6
Elgar Cl
  Basildon SS15 . . . . .141 D8
  Buckhurst Hill IG9 . . . . . . .110 D8
  South Benfleet SS7 . . . . . .144 B6
Elgar Gdns RM18 . . . . .179 B6
Elgin Ave
  Chelmsford CM1 . . . . .32 A2
  Romford RM3 . . . . .115 B4
Elgin Ho CM14 . . . . .116 D6
Elgin Rd IG3 . . . . .133 E4
Elham Dr SS13 . . . . .143 C6
Eliot Cl SS12 . . . . .121 C5
Eliot Mews SS2 . . . . .148 A2
Eliot Rd
  Dagenham RM9 . . . . .153 D8
  Dartford DA1 . . . . .176 B2
Eliot Way CM9 . . . . .37 A1
Elizabeth Ave
  Ilford IG3 . . . . .133 D2
  Rayleigh SS6 . . . . .123 C1
Elizabeth Cl
  Hockley SS5 . . . . .124 E4
  Lower Nazeing EN9 . . . . . . .43 D8
  Romford RM7 . . . . .113 B2
  Tilbury RM18 . . . . .179 B5
Elizabeth Ct
  Buckhurst Hill IG9 . . . . .88 B1
  ▣ Gravesend DA11 . . . . .179 A1
  ▣ Woodford E18 . . . . . . .110 A2
  ▣ Woodford IG8 . . . . . . .110 C3
Elizabeth Dr
  Theydon Bois CM16 . . . . . .67 E3
  Wickford SS12 . . . . .121 B8
Elizabeth Garrett
  Anderson Ho ▣
  DA17 . . . . .169 A3
Elizabeth Ho
  Pilgrims Hatch CM15 . . . . . .94 B3
  ▣ Romford RM2 . . . . . . .136 C7
  Southend-on-S SS9 . . . . . .146 D7
Elizabeth Rd
  Grays RM16 . . . . .172 F4
  Pilgrims Hatch CM15 . . . . . .94 B3
  Rainham RM13 . . . . .170 B8
  Southend-on-S SS1 . . . . . .167 D6
Elizabeth St DA9 . . . . .176 E2
Elizabeth Twr ▣ SS2 . . . . .167 A1
Elizabeth Way
  Basildon SS15 . . . . .141 D5
  Hadleigh SS7 . . . . .145 C4
  Harlow CM20 . . . . .10 B2
  Heybridge CM9 . . . . .37 A5
Eliza Cook Cl DA9 . . . . . . .177 B3
Elkins The RM1 . . . . .113 E1
Ellenbrook Cl SS9 . . . . . . .146 E3
Ellen Ct ▣ E4 . . . . .87 C1
Ellen Wilkinson Ho ▣
  RM10 . . . . .135 A1
Ellerman Rd RM18 . . . . . . .178 F5
Ellerton Gdns RM9 . . . . . . .153 C5
Ellesmere Ct SS9 . . . . .146 E5
Ellesmere Gdns IG4 . . . . . .132 E5
Ellesmere Rd
  Canvey Island SS8 . . . . . . .163 E3
  Rochford SS4 . . . . .103 C1
Ellie Cl SS17 . . . . .160 C2
Elliot Cl
  South Woodham Ferrers
  CM3 . . . . .101 F6

Elliot Cl continued
  Woodford IG8 . . . . .110 D4
Elliott Gdns RM3 . . . . .114 B3
Ellis Ave RM13 . . . . .170 A8
Ellis Cl RM16 . . . . .174 E7
Ellmore Cl RM3 . . . . .114 B2
Ellswood SS15 . . . . .119 D1
Elm Ave
  Heybridge CM9 . . . . .37 C5
  Upminster RM14 . . . . .156 B8
Elm Bank Pl SS17 . . . . .159 F4
Elmbourne Dr DA17 . . . . . .169 B2
Elmbridge CM17 . . . . .11 F3
Elmbridge Hall CM5 . . . . . . .27 C1
Elmbridge Rd IG6 . . . . .112 A4
Elmbrook ▣ E18 . . . . .132 A8
Elm Cl
  Buckhurst Hill IG9 . . . . . . .110 D8
  Chelmsford CM1 . . . . .32 A8
  Epping Green CM16 . . . . . . .45 B7
  Great Baddow CM2 . . . . . . .54 F6
  Rayleigh SS6 . . . . .123 D3
  Romford RM7 . . . . .113 B1
  Southend-on-S SS3 . . . . . .168 E7
  Waltham Abbey EN9 . . . . . .65 D5
  Wanstead E11 . . . . .132 B5
Elm Cotts
  Billericay CM11 . . . . .119 C7
  Southend-on-S SS2 . . . . . .147 F2
  Waltham Abbey EN9 . . . . . .65 D1
Elm Court Pk CM4 . . . . .50 F1
Elmcroft Ave E11 . . . . .132 B7
Elmcroft Cl E11 . . . . .132 B7
Elm Ct
  Chingford E4 . . . . .109 C4
  Theydon Bois CM16 . . . . . .67 E2
  Woodford IG8 . . . . .110 F4
Elmdene Ave RM11 . . . . . . .136 F6
Elmdon Rd RM15 . . . . .172 A8
Elm Dr SS6 . . . . .123 D3
Elmer App SS1 . . . . .167 A8
Elmer Ave
  Romford RM4 . . . . .113 E7
  Southend-on-S SS1 . . . . . .167 A8
Elmer Cl RM13 . . . . .155 A5
Elmer Gdns RM13 . . . . .155 A5
Elmfield Rd E4 . . . . .109 D8
Elm Gdns CM16 . . . . .47 B5
Elm Gn
  Basildon SS13 . . . . .143 A5
  Billericay CM11 . . . . .97 C2
Elm Gr
  Hornchurch RM11 . . . . .136 E5
  Hullbridge SS5 . . . . .101 D2
  Southend-on-S SS1 . . . . . .168 A8
  Woodford IG8 . . . . .109 F5
Elm Green La CM3 . . . . .56 C8
Elm Green Prep Sch
  CM3 . . . . .34 D3
Elm Hall Gdns E11 . . . . . . .132 B5
Elm Ho SS8 . . . . .164 B1
Elmhurst
  ▣ Greenhithe DA9 . . . . . .177 B1
  Hoddesdon EN10 . . . . .21 A4
Elmhurst Ave SS12 . . . . . . .144 B4
Elmhurst Dr
  Hornchurch RM11 . . . . .136 C4
  Woodford E18 . . . . .110 A1
Elmhurst Way IG10 . . . . .88 F2
Elmores IG10 . . . . .89 A6
Elm Par RM12 . . . . .155 B8
ELM PARK 155 B7
Elm Park Ave
  Hornchurch RM12 . . . . .155 A8
  Rainham RM12 . . . . .154 F8
Elm Park Sta RM12 . . . . . .155 A8
Elm Rd
  Aveley RM15 . . . . .171 D5
  Basildon SS13 . . . . .121 E1
  Canvey Island SS8 . . . . . . .164 C3
  Chelmsford CM2 . . . . .54 A8
  Grays RM17 . . . . .178 C8
  Greenhithe DA9 . . . . .176 E1
  Hadleigh SS7 . . . . .145 D2
  Romford RM7 . . . . .113 B1
  Southend-on-S, Leigh-on-S
  SS9 . . . . .146 E1
  Southend-on-S, Shoeburyness
  SS3 . . . . .168 E8
  South Woodham Ferrers
  CM3 . . . . .101 C8
  Wickford SS11 . . . . .121 D8
Elms EN9 . . . . .66 C4
Elms Dr CM1 . . . . .32 A4
Elms Farm Rd RM12 . . . . .155 C7
Elms Gdns RM9 . . . . .153 F8
Elms Ind Est RM3 . . . . .115 B3
Elmsleigh Dr SS9 . . . . .146 E3
Elmslie Cl IG8 . . . . .110 F4
Elmslie Lo IG6 . . . . .133 C8
Elms Rd CM1 . . . . .29 F6
Elmstead Cl SS17 . . . . .161 B4
Elmstead Rd IG3 . . . . .133 F2
Elms The CM5 . . . . .49 A1
Elmswood IG7 . . . . .111 D4
Elm Terr RM20 . . . . .177 B8
Elmtree Ave CM15 . . . . .71 F2
Elmtree Rd SS16 . . . . .143 A4
Elm View Rd SS7 . . . . .144 B3
Elmway RM16 . . . . .173 C5
Elm Way
  Boreham CM3 . . . . .20 E1
  Dagenham CM14 . . . . .116 A6
Elm Wlk RM2 . . . . .136 A8
Elmwood
  Sawbridgeworth CM21 . . . . .1 F1
  Woodford E18 . . . . .110 B2
Elmwood Ave SS5 . . . . . . .124 F4

Elmwood Ct SS5 . . . . .124 E6
Elmwood Prim Sch
  CM3 . . . . .101 D7
Elounda Ct SS7 . . . . .144 D4
Elrington Rd IG8 . . . . .110 A5
Elronds Rest CM3 . . . . .101 C6
Elsden Chase CM0 . . . . .84 D4
Elsenham Cres SS14 . . . . .142 F6
Elsenham Ct SS6 . . . . .123 B3
Elsenham Mews SS14 . . . . .142 F6
Elsenham Rd E12 . . . . .152 A7
Elstow Gdns RM9 . . . . .153 E4
Elstow Rd RM9 . . . . .153 E4
Elstree Cl RM12 . . . . .155 B5
Elstree Gdns IG1 . . . . .152 C7
Eltisley Rd IG1 . . . . .152 B8
Elverston Cl SS15 . . . . .141 D8
Elvet Ave RM2 . . . . .136 B5
Elvin Ct RM2 . . . . .136 B8
Elvin Dr RM16 . . . . .172 D5
Elwick Rd RM15 . . . . .172 C7
Elwood CM17 . . . . .24 E8
Ely Cl CM0 . . . . .84 D4
Ely Gdns
  Dagenham RM10 . . . . .135 C1
  Redbridge IG1 . . . . .132 E4
Ely Pl IG8 . . . . .111 A5
Ely Rd SS2 . . . . .148 C2
Ely Way
  Basildon SS14 . . . . .142 E7
  Rayleigh SS6 . . . . .123 C4
Emanuel Rd SS16 . . . . .141 B4
Embassy Ct
  Maldon CM9 . . . . .37 A2
  ▣ Wanstead E18 . . . . . . .132 A8
Emberson Ct CM2 . . . . .32 F4
Emberson Way CM16 . . . . . .47 C5
Ember Way CM0 . . . . .84 D4
Emerald Gdns RM8 . . . . . . .135 A3
Emerald Ho ▣ RM13 . . . . .155 A1
Emerson Dr RM11 . . . . .136 D4
Emerson Ho RM11 . . . . . . .136 D5
EMERSON PARK 136 E5
Emerson Park Ct
  RM11 . . . . .136 D4
Emerson Park Sch
  RM11 . . . . .137 B4
Emerson Park Sta
  RM11 . . . . .136 E4
Emerson Rd IG1 . . . . .133 A4
Emerson Terr IG8 . . . . .110 D4
Emily White Ct SS11 . . . . .121 F8
Emma's Cres SS12 . . . . .8 B4
Emmaus Way E4 . . . . .109 B5
Emmett Ave IG6 . . . . .133 C6
Empire Wlk
  ▣ Chelmsford CM2 . . . . . .32 C2
  Greenhithe DA9 . . . . .177 C3
Empress Ave
  Chingford E4 . . . . .109 B3
  Ilford IG1 . . . . .133 A2
  Redbridge IG1 . . . . .132 F2
  Wanstead E12 . . . . .132 D2
  Woodford IG8 . . . . .109 F3
Empress Par E4 . . . . .109 A4
Emsworth Rd IG6 . . . . .111 B1
Enborne Gn RM15 . . . . . . .172 A8
Endeavour Sch The
  SS14 . . . . .120 B1
Endeavour Way IG11 . . . . .153 A3
Endley Wood CM1 . . . . .52 E5
Endlebury Ct E4 . . . . .109 D8
Endlebury Rd E4 . . . . .109 C8
Endsleigh Gdns IG1 . . . . . .132 F3
Endway SS7 . . . . .145 E2
End Way Cotts CM0 . . . . . . .85 A7
Endways Ct CM15 . . . . .94 C1
Endway The CM3 . . . . .43 D3
Enfield Ho ▣ RM3 . . . . . . .114 C3
ENFIELD ISLAND VILLAGE
  . . . . .65 B2
Enfield Rd SS11 . . . . .122 C7
Engayne Gdns RM14 . . . . .137 B3
Engayne Prim Sch
  RM14 . . . . .137 E5
England's La IG10 . . . . .89 B7
Englefield Cl SS5 . . . . .125 A4
Englefields CM0 . . . . .63 E3
Ennerdale Ave RM12 . . . . .155 A7
Ennerdale Ct E11 . . . . .132 A4
Ennismore Gdns SS2 . . . . .148 A3
Ensign Cl SS9 . . . . .147 A1
Ensign Ct IG11 . . . . .178 E1
Ensign Ho RM17 . . . . .177 F8
Enterprise Ctr The
  SS14 . . . . .120 E2
Enterprise Ho RM11 . . . . . .152 F2
Enterprise Ho E4 . . . . .87 C2
Enterprise Way SS11 . . . . .121 F6
EPPING 46 A3
Epping Cl
  Chelmsford CM1 . . . . .31 E1
  Romford RM7 . . . . .135 B8
  Southend-on-S SS9 . . . . . .146 E7

Epping La
  Chipping Ongar RM4 . . . . . .69 A1
  Stapleford Abbotts RM4 . . . .91 B8
  Theydon Bois RM4 . . . . .68 D1
Epping New Rd
  Buckhurst Hill IG9,
  IG10 . . . . .88 B4
  Loughton IG10, CM16 . . . . . .66 E2
Epping Ongar Rly*
  CM16 . . . . .47 D4
Epping Rd
  Chipping Ongar CM5 . . . . . .48 D6
  Coopersale CM16 . . . . .46 D4
  Epping Green CM16 . . . . . . .23 A1
  Loughton CM16 . . . . .67 A4
  Roydon CM19 . . . . .22 D5
  Toot Hill CM5 . . . . .47 D1
  Tipping Sta CM16 . . . . .68 A8
EPPING UPLAND 45 C7
Epping Upland CE Prim
  Sch CM16 . . . . .45 B7
Epping Way E4 . . . . .87 B3
Epsom Cl CM11 . . . . .97 D5
Epsom Ho ▣ RM3 . . . . . . .114 C5
Epsom Mews CM0 . . . . .84 E4
Epsom Rd IG3 . . . . .133 F5
Epsom Way RM12 . . . . .155 F8
Equinox Ho ▣ IG11 . . . . . .152 C6
Eric Clarke La IG11 . . . . . . .152 C2
Erick Ave CM1 . . . . .32 B7
Eric Rd
  Basildon SS13 . . . . .143 F6
  Dagenham RM6 . . . . .134 D4
Eridge Cl CM1 . . . . .32 D7
Erin Cl IG3 . . . . .134 A5
ERITH 169 E2
Erith Cres RM5 . . . . .113 C2
Erith Ct RM19 . . . . .171 A2
Erith High St DA8 . . . . .169 E1
Erith Mus* DA8 . . . . .169 E1
Erith Rd DA17 . . . . .169 B1
Erith Sta DA8 . . . . .169 E1
Ernan Cl RM15 . . . . .172 A8
Ernan Rd RM15 . . . . .172 A8
Ernest Rd RM11 . . . . .136 F5
Erriff Dr RM15 . . . . .172 A8
Errington Cl RM16 . . . . .174 B3
Erroll Rd RM1 . . . . .135 F7
Erskine Pl ▣ SS12 . . . . . . .121 E6
Esdaile Gdns RM14 . . . . . .137 D4
Esdaile La EN11 . . . . .21 A5
Esgors Farm CM16 . . . . .46 B7
Esher Ave RM7 . . . . .135 C5
Esher Rd IG3 . . . . .133 E1
Eskley Gdns
  South Ockendon
  RM15 . . . . .157 B1
  South Ockendon RM15 . . . .172 B8
Esk Way RM1 . . . . .113 E3
Esmond Cl RM13 . . . . .155 B5
Esplanade CM3 . . . . .60 E1
Esplanade Ct SS1 . . . . .167 E6
Esplanade Gdns SS0 . . . . .166 B8
Esplanade Rd SS0 . . . . . . .166 B8
Esplanade The SS5 . . . . . . .101 D3
Essenden Rd DA17 . . . . . . .169 A1
Essex Ave CM1 . . . . .32 A7
Essex Cl
  Basildon SS15 . . . . .141 B6
  Canvey Island SS8 . . . . . . .164 A2
  Rayleigh SS6 . . . . .123 F2
  Romford RM7 . . . . .135 B7
Essex County Cricket
  Club* CM2 . . . . .32 B2
Essex Gdns
  Hornchurch RM11 . . . . .137 A6
  Linford SS17 . . . . .175 A4
  Southend-on-S SS9 . . . . . .146 E4
Essex Ho EN9 . . . . .65 C5
Essex Nuffield Hospl The
  CM15 . . . . .94 E1
Essex Rd
  Barking IG11 . . . . .152 D5
  Burnham-on-C CM0 . . . . . .106 C5
  Canvey Island SS8 . . . . . . .164 C4
  Chingford E4 . . . . .87 E1
  Dagenham, Goodmayes
  RM6 . . . . .134 C4
  Dagenham RM10 . . . . .154 C7
  Grays RM20 . . . . .177 A8
  Hoddesdon EN11 . . . . .21 C6
  Maldon CM9 . . . . .36 F1
  Romford RM7 . . . . .135 B7
  Woodford E18 . . . . .110 B1
Essex Regiment Way
  CM3 . . . . .19 D5
Essex St SS1 . . . . .167 A8
Essex Way
  Brentwood CM13 . . . . .116 C4
  South Benfleet SS7 . . . . . .144 F1
Estate Rd SS7 . . . . .145 F3
Estella Mead CM1 . . . . .31 E7
Estfeld Cl ▣ EN11 . . . . .8 B1
Eston Ct ▣ E18 . . . . .110 A1
Estuary Cl IG11 . . . . .153 B2
Estuary Cotts RM18 . . . . . .180 D7
Estuary Ct SS9 . . . . .165 F8
Estuary Gdns SS3 . . . . .150 C2
Estuary Lo SS1 . . . . .167 F8
Estuary Mews SS3 . . . . . . .168 E6
Ethelbert Gdns IG2 . . . . . . .133 A6
Ethelbert Rd SS4 . . . . .103 C1
Ethelburga Rd RM3 . . . . . .114 F2
Ethel Cotts RM6 . . . . .134 D8
Ethel Rd SS6 . . . . .124 E8
Ethelred Gdns SS11 . . . . . . .99 E1
Etheridge Gn IG10 . . . . .89 C6

Etheridge Rd IG10 . . . . .89 B6
Eton Cl SS8 . . . .
Eton Rd IG1 . . . .
Eton Wlk SS3 . . . .
Eugene Cl RM2 . . . .
Europa Pk RM20 . . . .
Europa Trad Est DA8 . . . .
Eustace Rd RM6 . . . .
Evans Cl DA9 . . . .
Evansdale RM13 . . . .
Evanston Ave E4 . . . .
Evanston Gdns IG4 . . . .
Eva Rd RM6 . . . .
Evelyn Pl CM1 . . . .
Evelyn Rd SS5 . . . .
Evelyn Sharp Cl RM2 . . . .
Evelyn Sharp Ho RM2 . . . .
Evelyn Wlk CM13 . . . .
Everard Rd SS14 . . . .
Everest SS0 . . . .
Everest Rise CM12 . . . .
Everest Way CM9 . . . .
Everglades The SS7 . . . .
Evergreen Ct SS12 . . . .
Evergreens The SS3 . . . .
Everik Bsns Ctr CM13 . . . .
Everslight Gdns
  RM14 . . . .
EVERSLEY . . . .
Eversley Cl IG10 . . . .
Eversley Ct SS7 . . . .
Eversley Lo ▣ EN11 . . . .
Eversley Prim Sch
  SS13 . . . .
Eversley Rd
  Basildon SS13 . . . .
  South Benfleet SS7 . . . .
Eves Cnr
  Burnham-on-C CM0 . . . .
  Danbury CM3 . . . .
Eves Cres CM1 . . . .
Evesham Ave E17 . . . .
Evesham Way IG5 . . . .
Ewan Cl SS13 . . . .
Ewan Rd RM3 . . . .
Ewanrigg Terr IG8 . . . .
Ewan Way SS9 . . . .
Ewellhurst Rd IG5 . . . .
Exchange St
  Romford RM1 . . . .
  Romford RM1, RM7 . . . .
Exchange The IG1 . . . .
Exchange Way ▣ CM
Exeter Cl
  Basildon SS14 . . . .
  Southend-on-S SS3 . . . .
Exeter Gdns IG1 . . . .
Exeter Ho
  ▣ Barking IG11 . . . .
  Southend-on-S SS3 . . . .
Exeter Rd
  Chelmsford CM1 . . . .
  Dagenham RM10 . . . .
Exford Ave SS0 . . . .
Exhibition La SS3 . . . .
Exley Cl CM4 . . . .
Exmoor Cl
  Chelmsford CM1 . . . .
  Redbridge IG6 . . . .
Exmouth Dr SS4 . . . .
Exmouth Rd RM17 . . . .
Express Dr IG3 . . . .
Exton Gdns RM8 . . . .
Eyhurst Ave RM12 . . . .
Eynesham Way ▣
  SS13 . . . .
Eynsford Rd
  Greenhithe DA9 . . . .
  Ilford IG3 . . . .
Eyre Cl RM2 . . . .

F

Factory Rd DA11. . . . .
Faggotters La CM17 . . . .
Fagus Ave RM13 . . . .
Failand Mews SS17 . . . .
Fairbank Cl CM5 . . . .
Fairburn Cl ▣ SS1. . . . .
Fairburn Ct ▣ SS1 . . . .
Faircroft CM17 . . . .
FAIR CROSS . . . .
Fair Cross SS11 . . . .
Faircross Ave
  Barking IG11 . . . .
  Romford RM5 . . . .
Faircross Par IG11. . . . .
Fairfax Ave SS4 . . . .
Fairfax Dr SS0 . . . .
Fairfax Mead CM2 . . . .
Fairfax Rd
  Grays RM17 . . . .
  Tilbury RM18 . . . .
Fairfield
  Great Wakering SS3 . . . .
  Ingatestone CM4 . . . .
Fairfield Ave RM12 . . . .
  Upminster RM14 . . . .
Fairfield Cl RM12 . . . .
Fairfield Cres SS9 . . . .
Fairfield Ct ▣ SS8 . . . .
Fairfield Rd
  Brentwood CM14 . . . .
  Chelmsford CM1 . . . .

Rd *continued*
Ongar CM5 . . . . . .48 F2
M16 . . . . .46 B2
on EN11 . . . . . .21 A8
1 . . . . .152 B6
on-S SS9 . . . . .146 E2
d IG8 . . . . . . .110 A4
Rise CM12 . . . .118 F8
s CM3 . . . . .58 D1
Sq [3] DA11 . . .179 A1
CI CM3 . . . . .115 B4
Way RM3 . . . .115 B4
Ave RM15 . . . .172 A6
e Ave RM2 . . .136 B7
e Gdns
. . . . .137 F4
e Rd
l 133 A4
e IG1 . . . . . . .132 F4
e Com Jun & Inf
4 . . . . .142 D6
Ct SS14 . . . . .142 D6
Ct SS0 . . . . .147 D2
Ave RM11 . . . .136 D3
CI SS6 . . . . . .123 E5
Ave IG9 . . . . .110 A8
Dr IG8 . . . . . .110 A3
Gdns SS2 . . . .147 E5
Ave
E4 . . . . .109 D8
IG8 . . . . . . .110 A4
CI E4 . . . . . .109 D8
Rd SS7 . . . . . .145 C3
Villas RM1 . . . .113 E7
. . . . .111 E2
re SS8 . . . . . .164 A4
RM12 . . . . . .155 B6
dns
SS14 . . . . . .142 D6
e IG6 . . . . . .111 C3
PLAIN 111 F1
rim Sch IG6 . .111 C2
d IG6 . . . . . .111 C1
a IG6 . . . . . .111 D1
aters Cntry Pk*
. . . . .111 E1
SS6 . . . . . . .123 B4
l SS14 . . . . .142 C8

Fairways The
Cold Norton CM3 . . . . . . .80 F5
South Benfleet ss7 . . . .144 D2
Fairway The
Harlow CM18 . . . . .24 A6
South Benfleet SS7 . . . .144 C7
Southend-on-S SS9 . . . .146 C5
Upminster RM14 . . . . . .137 D4
Falbro Cres SS7 . . . . . .145 D4
Falcon Ave RM17 . . . . . .178 C8
Falcon Cl
Rayleigh SS6 . . . . .123 B3
Sawbridgeworth CM21 . . . . .1 C1
Southend-on-S SS9 . . . .146 F5
Waltham Abbey EN9 . . . . .66 A5
Falcon Ct [6] E18 . . . . . .132 B8
Falconer Rd IG6 . . . . . .112 C5
Falconers Pk CM21 . . . . . .1 D1
Falcon Fields CM9 . . . . . .58 F8
Falcon Mews CM9 . . . . . .58 F8
Falcon Pk SS14 . . . . . . .141 F8
Falcon Rd CM0 . . . . .84 C4
Falcons Mead CM2 . . . . . .32 A1
Falcon Way
Basildon SS16 . . . . . . .142 C4
Chelmsford CM2 . . . . . . .54 A6
Rainham RM13 . . . . . . .155 A5
Southend-on-S SS3 . . . .149 E1
Wanstead E11 . . . . . . .132 A2
Falkenham End SS14 . . .142 C7
Falkenham Path [1]
SS14 . . . . .142 C7
Falkenham Rise SS14 . . .142 C7
Falkenham Row SS14 . . .142 C7
Falkirk CI RM11 . . . . . . .137 A3
Falkland Ct CM3 . . . . . . .33 E8
Falkland Gn CM9 . . . . . . .57 E6
Falklands Rd CM0 . . . . .106 B5
Falkland Way IG8 . . . . . .110 A4
Falkner Ct CM4 . . . . .75 F3
Fallaize Ave IG1 . . . . . . .152 B8
Fallow CI IG7 . . . . .111 F5
Fallowfield SS3 . . . . . . .149 D1
Fallow Fields IG10 . . . . . .88 C2
Fallows The SS8 . . . . . .163 F6
Falmouth Ave E4 . . . . . .109 C5
Falmouth Gdns IG4 . . . . .132 E6
Falmouth Rd CM1 . . . . . .32 E5
Falstaff PI SS16 . . . . . . .141 A5
Falstones SS15 . . . . . . .141 E5
Fambridge CI CM9 . . . . . .37 F4
Fambridge Dr [2] RM7 . . .135 D6
Fambridge Dr SS12 . . . .121 E6
Fambridge Rd
Althorne CM3 . . . . .82 F2
Cold Norton CM9, CM3 . . . .81 C5
Dagenham RM8 . . . . . . .135 A3
Maldon CM9 . . . . .36 F2
Rochford SS4, CM3 . . . . .103 C3
Farringdon Sta CM3 . . . .103 B8
Fane Rd SS7 . . . . .144 D8
FANNER'S GREEN 18 C5
Fanner's Green Cotts
CM3 . . . . .18 C5
Fanns Rise RM19 . . . . . .171 A2
Fanshawe Ave IG11 . . . . .152 C6
Fanshawe Cres
Dagenham RM9 . . . . . . .153 F7
Hornchurch RM11 . . . . . .136 D5
Fanshawe Rd RM16 . . . .174 A3
Fanshawe The RM9 . . . .153 D5
Fantasia Ct CM14 . . . . . .116 B5
Fanton Ave SS12 . . . . . .121 F3
Fanton Chase SS11 . . . .122 A6
Fanton Gdns SS11 . . . . .122 B6
Fanton Wlk SS11 . . . . . .122 B6
Faraday Ho [4] DA17 . . .169 A3
Faraday Rd SS9 . . . . . . .146 C6
Faringdon Ave RM3 . . . .114 D3
Faringdon Gr RM3 . . . . .114 D3
Farington Dr IG3 . . . . . .133 E3
FARMBRIDGE END 16 D3
Farmbridge End Rd
CM1 . . . . .16 D4
Farm CI
Brentwood CM13 . . . . . . .95 C2
Buckhurst Hill IG9 . . . . . .110 C7
Dagenham RM10 . . . . . .154 C5
Roydon CM19 . . . . .9 B1
Farm Cres SS11 . . . . . . .100 E4
Farm Dr RM16 . . . . .173 C6
Farm End E4 . . . . .87 E4
Farmer Ct EN9 . . . . .66 A6
Farm Hill Rd EN9 . . . . . . .65 D6
Farm La E11 . . . . .21 C8
Farm Rd
Canvey Island SS8 . . . . .164 B5
Chadwell St M RM16 . . . .173 F4
East Tilbury RM18 . . . . .175 C2
Rainham RM13 . . . . . . .155 C2
Wanstead E12 . . . . .132 E2
Farm View SS6 . . . . . . .123 D5
Farm Way
Buckhurst Hill IG9 . . . . . .110 C6
Hornchurch RM12 . . . . . .155 C8
Thundersley SS7 . . . . . .145 B6
Farnaby Way SS17 . . . . .160 C3
Farnborough Ave E17 . . .109 B1
Farne CI CM3 . . . . .10 E5
Farne Dr SS12 . . . . .121 F5
Farnes Ave SS9 . . . . . . .121 C7
Farnes Dr RM2 . . . . .114 C1
Farnham CI CM21 . . . . . . .1 C1
Farnham Green Prim Sch
IG3 . . . . .134 A5
Farnham Rd
Ilford IG3 . . . . .133 F4
Romford RM3 . . . . .114 D5
Farnley Rd E4 . . . . .87 E2

Farnol Rd DA1 . . . . .176 A3
Farrance Rd RM6 . . . . . .134 E4
Farr Ave IG11 . . . . .153 A3
Farriers
Great Amwell SG12 . . . . . .8 A6
Sawbridgeworth CM21 . . . . .1 E3
Farriers Dr CM12 . . . . . . .97 B5
Farrier Sq CM11 . . . . . . .98 C4
Farriers Way SS2 . . . . . .147 F5
Farringdon Service Rd [8]
SS1 . . . . .167 A8
Farrow Gdns RM16 . . . . .173 C5
Farrow Ho CM15 . . . . . . .94 C1
Farrow Rd CM1 . . . . .53 E7
FARTHER HOWEGREEN
. . . . .80 E7
Farthingale Ct EN9 . . . . . .66 A5
Farthingale La EN9 . . . . . .66 A5
Farthing Ct E4 . . . . .109 E7
Fastnet SS2 . . . . .147 A7
Faulkner Ct [8] RM8 . . . .134 D4
Fauna Cl RM6 . . . . .134 C5
Fauners SS16 . . . . .142 A5
Faversham Ave E4 . . . . . .87 F1
Faversham Cl IG7 . . . . . .112 B8
Faversham La EN9 . . . . . .66 A5
Fawbert & Barnards Prim
Sch CM17 . . . . .11 C3
Fawbert & Barnard Inf Sch
CM21 . . . . .1 E2
Fawcett Dr SS15 . . . . . .119 E1
Fawkner CM21 . . . . .32 F2
Fawkon Wlk EN11 . . . . . .21 A6
Fawn Rd IG7 . . . . .111 F5
Fawters Cl CM13 . . . . . . .95 D3
Faymore Gdns RM15 . . . .172 A2
Fazal Lag IG1 . . . . .133 C2
Fearns Mead CM14 . . . . .116 D5
Featherby Way SS4 . . . . .126 A1
Feathers Hill CM22 . . . . . .3 E6
Feeches Rd SS2 . . . . . . .147 D5
Feenan Highway
RM18 . . . . .179 B6
Feering Dr SS14 . . . . . . .142 F5
Feering Rd SS14 . . . . . . .142 F5
Feering Row [5] SS14 . . .142 F5
Felbridge Rd IG3 . . . . . .133 F3
Felhurst Cres RM10 . . . .154 C8
Felicia Way RM16 . . . . . .174 B2
Felipe Rd RM16 . . . . . . .172 C3
Fell Christy CM1 . . . . . . .32 B5
Fellcroft [5] SS13 . . . . . .143 C6
Felmongers CM20 . . . . . .11 B2
FELMORE 143 B8
Felmore CI [9] SS13 . . . .143 B8
Felmore Prim Sch
SS13 . . . . .143 B8
Felmores End [8]
SS13 . . . . .143 B8
Fels Cl RM10 . . . . .135 C1
Fels Farm Ave RM10 . . . .135 C1
Felstead Ave SS7 . . . . . .144 D4
Felstead Cl
Brentwood CM13 . . . . . . .95 C3
South Benfleet SS7 . . . .144 D4
Felstead Rd
Loughton IG10 . . . . .88 E2
Romford RM5 . . . . .113 C3
Wanstead E11 . . . . .132 A4
Fels Way CM3 . . . . .83 A8
Felton Gdns IG11 . . . . . .152 E3
Felton Rd IG11 . . . . .152 E3
Fencepiece Rd IG7 . . . . .111 C3
Fen Cl
Brentwood CM15 . . . . . . .95 C5
Wickford SS11 . . . . . . .122 A6
Fenchurch Ave RM18 . . .158 F8
Fengates CM3 . . . . .101 C8
Fen La
Bulphan RM14 . . . . .158 C7
North Ockendon RM14 . . .157 E7
Orsett RM16 . . . . .173 E8
Fenman Gdns IG3 . . . . . .134 B3
Fenmere Cl CM3 . . . . . . .10 C8
Fennells CM19 . . . . .23 C3
Fenner Brockway Ho
CM20 . . . . .23 E8
Fenner Rd IG3 . . . . .172 C3
Fenners Way SS11 . . . . .121 A2
Fennfields Rd CM3 . . . . .101 B8
Fennimore Gn CM17 . . . . .24 C7
Fenton Grange CM17 . . . .24 C7
Fenton Rd RM16 . . . . . . .172 E3
Fenton Way SS15 . . . . . .140 F7
Fenwick Way SS8 . . . . . .164 A6
Ferguson Ave RM2 . . . . .114 D1
Ferguson Dr RM2 . . . . . .114 D1
Fermoy Rd SS1 . . . . . . .168 B7
Fernbank
Billericay CM12 . . . . .96 F1
Fernbank Ave SS1 . . . . .168 D8
Fernbrook Ave SS1 . . . . .167 D8
Fern Cl CM3 . . . . .97 B4
Ferndale
Chingford E4 . . . . .109 C4
Romford RM5 . . . . .113 A3
Stanford-le-H SS17 . . . .168 F7
Ferndale Cres SS15 . . . . .141 B6
Ferndale Rd
Rayleigh SS6 . . . . .123 E5
Romford RM5 . . . . .113 C1
Southend-on-S SS2 . . . .148 C2

Ferndown Way RM7 . . . . .135 B5
Ferndown
Hornchurch RM11 . . . . . .136 F5
[7] Wanstead E18 . . . . .132 A8
Ferndown CI SS22 . . . . .167 C8
Fernhall Dr IG4 . . . . .132 D6
Fernhall La EN9 . . . . .66 D8
Fern Hill SS16 . . . . .141 C4
Fernhill Ct E17 . . . . .109 D1
Fernhill La CM18 . . . . . . .23 F3
Fernie Cl IG7 . . . . .112 A5
Fernlea Rd
Burnham-on-C CM0 . . . . .106 B5
South Benfleet SS7 . . . . .144 E3
Fernleigh Ct
Romford RM7 . . . . .135 C6
Southend-on-S SS0 . . . .147 A1
Fernleigh Dr SS9 . . . . . .147 A1
Fernside IG9 . . . . .88 B1
Fernside Cl SS17 . . . . . .161 B4
Fernways IG1 . . . . .152 B8
Fern Wlk
Basildon SS16 . . . . . . .140 E4
Canvey Island SS8 . . . . .163 F3
Fernwood SS7 . . . . .145 E4
Ferns The CM3 . . . . .101 D6
Ferris Ave E4 . . . . .80 F5
Ferris Stps [13] SS1 . . . .167 C7
Ferry La RM13 . . . . .169 E7
Ferrymead SS8 . . . . . . .163 F5
Ferry Rd
Burnham-on-C CM0 . . . . .105 C6
Hullbridge SS5 . . . . . . .101 D2
North Fambridge CM3 . . . .103 A6
South Benfleet SS7 . . . .163 D8
Tilbury RM18 . . . . .179 A4
Feryby Rd RM16 . . . . . . .174 B3
Feryngs Cl CM17 . . . . . . .11 D4
Fesants Croft CM20 . . . . .11 B3
Festival Way SS14 . . . . .120 B1
Fetherston Ct RM6 . . . . .134 F5
Fetherston Rd SS17 . . . .160 D1
Fetherston Ct [5] IG11 . .152 C3
Fews Lo RM6 . . . . .134 D7
Fiddlers CI DA9 . . . . . . .177 B3
Fiddlers Way EN11 . . . . .21 D8
FIDDLERS HAMLET 68 C7
Field CI
Abridge RM4 . . . . .90 B6
Buckhurst Hill IG9 . . . . . .110 C7
Chingford E4 . . . . .109 B4
Fielders CI [4] CM14 . . . .116 C8
Fielders The SS8 . . . . . .164 A2
Fieldhouse CI E18 . . . . . .110 B2
Fielding Ave RM18 . . . . .179 C6
Fielding Way
Brentwood CM13 . . . . . . .95 C3
Field Rd RM15 . . . . .171 C5
Fields Park Cres RM6 . . .134 E5
Field View RM16 . . . . . . .174 A3
Field View CI RM7 . . . . .135 A8
Fifth Ave
Canvey Island SS8 . . . . .163 E4
Chelmsford CM1 . . . . . . .32 B6
Grays RM20 . . . . .177 A8
Thundersley SS7 . . . . . .145 A6
Wickford SS11 . . . . . . .122 A6
Fifth Ave / Allende Ave
. . . . .20 F2
Filey Rd CM0 . . . . .84 A3
Fillebrook Ave SS9 . . . . .147 A2
Fillebrook Cl SS9 . . . . . .147 A2
Fillioll CI CM3 . . . . .78 B6
Filston Rd DA8 . . . . .169 C1
Finch Cl CM5 . . . . .49 A5
Finches Cl SS17 . . . . . . .161 F1
Finches The SS7 . . . . . . .145 A7
Finch Dr RM16 . . . . .173 D1
Finch Gdns E4 . . . . .109 A5
Finchingfield Ave
IG8 . . . . .110 C3
Finchingfield The
CM15 . . . . .71 C2
Finchingfield Way [7]
SS12 . . . . .121 C5
Finchland View CM3 . . . .101 D6
Finchley Ave CM3 . . . . . .141 B6
Finchley CI DA1 . . . . . . .176 A1
Finchley Rd
Grays RM17 . . . . .178 B8
Southend-on-S SS0 . . . .166 D8
Findon Gdns RM13 . . . . .170 B8
Fingrith Hall Cotts
CM4 . . . . .50 F3
Fingrith Hall La CM4 . . . . .50 F3
Finnymore Rd RM9 . . . . .153 E5
Finucane Gdns RM13 . . .155 A6
Firbank Rd RM5 . . . . . . .113 B5
Fir Ct SS15 . . . . .119 C1
Firecrest Rd CM2 . . . . . . .54 C6
Firfield Rd SS7 . . . . .145 C6
Firham Park Ave
RM3 . . . . .115 A3
Firle The SS16 . . . . .141 B3
Firmans SS16 . . . . .141 B3

Fir Pk CM19 . . . . .23 B5
Firs EN9 . . . . .66 C4
Firs Ct SS16 . . . . .142 F4
Firs Dr
Loughton IG10 . . . . .89 A8
Wrttle CM1 . . . . .31 B1
Firsgrove Cres CM14 . . . .116 B6
Firsgrove Rd CM14 . . . . .116 C6
First Ave
Basildon RM14, SS16 . . . .140 E4
Billericay CM12 . . . . . . .118 F7
Canvey Island SS8 . . . . .163 C4
Chelmsford CM1 . . . . . . .32 B5
Dagenham RM10 . . . . . .154 B3
Grays RM20 . . . . .177 A8
Hook End CM15 . . . . .72 C5
Hullbridge SS5 . . . . . . .101 F1
Newbury Park IG2 . . . . . .133 D6
Southend-on-S SS0 . . . .166 B8
Stanford-le-H SS17 . . . .160 D3
Wickford SS11 . . . . . . .122 A6
First Ave / Mandela Ave
. . . . .20 F2
Firs The
Canvey Island SS8 . . . . .163 F5
Grays RM16 . . . . .173 C5
Pilgrims Hatch CM15 . . . .94 A3
Woodford IG8 . . . . .110 C3
Firs Wlk IG8 . . . . .110 A5
Fir Tree La
Grays RM17 . . . . .178 D8
Romford RM1 . . . . .135 D8
Fir Tree La CM3 . . . . .34 E1
Fir Tree Rise CM2 . . . . . .54 B6
Fir Trees
Abridge RM4 . . . . .90 B6
Epping CM16 . . . . .46 B2
Fir Tree Wlk
Dagenham RM10 . . . . . .135 C1
Heybridge CM9 . . . . .37 C5
Fir Wlk SS16 . . . . .163 F5
Fisgard Ct [9] DA12 . . . .179 D1
Fisher Cl EN3 . . . . .65 B2
Fisher Dr CM3 . . . . .177 B3
Fishermans Way EN11 . . .21 D8
Fishermen's Hill
. . . . .178 B2
Fishers Cl EN8 . . . . .65 A5
Fishers Hatch CM20 . . . . .10 C1
Fisher's Way DA17 . . . . .169 C5
Fish St CM9 . . . . .38 E6
Fiske Cl IG11 . . . . .152 D3
Fitches Cres CM9 . . . . . . .37 B1
Fitches Mews CM9 . . . . . .37 B1
Fitzgerald Rd E11 . . . . . .132 A6
Fitzilian Ave RM3 . . . . . .114 F2
Fitzroy Cl CM12 . . . . .97 A4
Fitzstephen Rd RM8 . . . .153 E2
Fitzwalter La SS13 . . . . . .56 D6
Fitzwalter Pl CM1 . . . . . . .31 E3
Fitzwalter Rd CM3 . . . . . .33 F8
Fitzwarren SS3 . . . . .149 D1
Fitzwilliams Ct CM17 . . . .11 E4
Fitzwimarc Sch The
SS6 . . . . .123 C3
Five Acres
Bicknacre CM3 . . . . .56 F3
Harlow CM18 . . . . .23 E5
Five Elms Prim Sch
RM8 . . . . .134 F1
Five Elms Rd RM9 . . . . . .134 F1
Five Oaks SS7 . . . . .144 B7
Five Oaks La IG7 . . . . . . .112 E5
Flagstaff CI CM3 . . . . . . .65 B6
Flagstaff Rd EN9 . . . . . . .65 B6
Flambird's Chase
Purleigh CM3 . . . . .80 A7
Stow Maries CM3 . . . . . . .79 F6
Flamboro Cl SS9 . . . . . . .146 D6
Flamboro Wlk SS9 . . . . .146 D6
Flamingo Wlk [4]
RM13 . . . . .155 A6
Flamstead Gdns RM9 . . .153 C5
Flamstead Rd RM9 . . . . .153 C5
Flanders Rd E6 . . . . .152 A3
Flandrian CI EN3 . . . . . . .65 B1
Flats The
Grays RM17 . . . . .173 D2
Greenhithe DA9 . . . . . . .177 C2
Flaxen Cl E4 . . . . .109 B7
Flaxen Rd E4 . . . . .109 B7
Flaxman CI [8] DA17 . . . .169 A1
Fleece Rd CM3 . . . . .137 D5
Fleet Hall Cotts SS4 . . . .148 B8
Fleethall Gr SS4 . . . . . . .173 A5
Fleethall Rd SS4 . . . . . . .148 A8
Fleet Rd SS7 . . . . .144 D1
Fleetway SS16 . . . . .142 F4
Fleetwood SS8 . . . . .164 E2
Fleetwood Ave CM3 . . . .147 C2
Fleming Gdns
Romford RM3 . . . . .114 D1
Tilbury RM18 . . . . .179 C6
Fleming Ho RM18 . . . . . .114 E1
Fleming Rd
Chelmsford CM1 . . . . . . .32 B5
Southend-on-S SS9 . . . .146 D8
Flemings Cres SS9 . . . . .146 D3
Flemings Way SS9 . . . . .146 D4
Fletcher Cl CM11 . . . . . . .97 D2
Fletcher Dr SS12 . . . . . .121 E6

Fleming Cres SS9 . . . . . .146 D3
Flemings Farm Rd
SS9 . . . . .146 D8

Fletcher Rd IG7 . . . . 111 F5
Fletchers SS16 . . . . 141 E3
Fletchers Sq SS2 . . . . 148 A5
Flex Mdw CM19 . . . . 22 F7
Flint Cl SS16 . . . . 140 F5
Flint St RM20 . . . . 177 B8
Flintwich Manor CM1 . . . . . . 31 E7
Flora Gdns RM6 . . . . 134 C5
Florence Cl
Grays RM20 . . . . 177 E8
Hadleigh SS7 . . . . 145 D3
Harlow CM17 . . . . 24 C6
Hornchurch RM12 . . . . 136 E2
Florence Ct E11 . . . . 132 C7
Florence Gdns
Dagenham RM6 . . . . 134 C4
Hadleigh SS7 . . . . 145 D3
Florence Ho RM3 . . . . 114 E1
Florence Neale Ho **2**
SS8 . . . . 164 A3
Florence Rd SS8 . . . . 164 D3
Florence Root Ho **3**
E14 . . . . 132 F6
Florence Terr SS17 . . . . 159 F4
Florence Way SS16 . . . . 141 B5
Florentine Ho **3** IG1 . . . . . 133 B2
Flux's La CM16 . . . . 68 A6
FOBBING 161 D5
Fobbing Farm Cl
SS16 . . . . 142 A3
Fobbing Rd SS17 . . . . 161 C3
Fodderwick **1** SS14 . . . . . 142 A5
Fogerty Cl EN3 . . . . 65 B2
Foksville Rd SS8 . . . . 164 C4
Fold Croft CM20 . . . . 10 A1
Fold The SS14 . . . . 142 B6
Folkes La RM14, CM13 . . . . . 137 F7
Folkestone Rd E6 . . . . 152 A2
Folly Chase SS5 . . . . 124 B6
Folly La SS5 . . . . 124 C6
Folly View SG12 . . . . 8 B4
Fontayne Ave
Chigwell IG7 . . . . 111 C6
Rainham RM13 . . . . 154 E5
Romford RM1 . . . . 113 E1
Font Cl SS15 . . . . 141 C6
Fonteyn Cl SS15 . . . . 141 C8
Fonteyne Gdns IG8 . . . . 110 D1
Fontwell Park Gdns
RM12 . . . . 155 E8
Forbes Cl RM11 . . . . 136 B3
Ford Cl
Basildon SS15 . . . . 141 A6
Rainham RM13 . . . . 154 F5
Ford End IG8 . . . . 110 B4
Fordham Cl RM11 . . . . 137 A4
Fordhams Row RM16 . . . . . . 174 B8
Ford Ho SS3 . . . . 168 F6
Ford La RM13 . . . . 154 F5
Ford Rd
Dagenham RM10 . . . . 154 A5
Northfleet DA11 . . . . 178 B2
Fordson Rd CM2 . . . . 33 B6
Fordview Ind Est
RM13 . . . . 154 D2
Fordyce Cl RM11 . . . . 137 A4
Fordyke Rd RM8 . . . . 134 F2
Forebury Ave CM1 . . . . 1 F2
Forebury Cres CM2 . . . . 1 F2
Forebury The CM21 . . . . 1 F2
Forefield Gn CM1 . . . . 32 F7
Forelands Pl CM21 . . . . 1 E2
Foremans CM1 . . . . 31 E3
Foremark Cl IG6 . . . . 111 F4
Fore St
Basildon SS15 . . . . 119 E2
Harlow CM17 . . . . 11 C4
Forest App
Chingwell IG7 . . . . 111 A5
Chingford E4 . . . . 87 E2
Forest Ave
Chigwell IG7 . . . . 111 A5
Chingford E4 . . . . 87 E2
Forest Ct
Chingford E4 . . . . 87 F1
Loughton IG10 . . . . 88 D6
Forest Dr
Chelmsford CM1 . . . . 31 E1
Chingford IG8 . . . . 109 E3
Fyfield CM5 . . . . 27 C1
Theydon Bois CM16 . . . . 67 E3
Wanstead E12 . . . . 132 D1
Forest Edge IG9 . . . . 110 D7
Forester Ct CM12 . . . . 96 F3
Foresters Ct IG10 . . . . 89 A7
Forest Farm Cotts
IG6 . . . . 111 E2
Forest Glade
Basildon SS16 . . . . 140 F4
Chingford E4 . . . . 109 E5
Epping CM16 . . . . 46 E4
Forest Ho E4 . . . . 87 E2
Forest Hts IG9 . . . . 110 A8
Forest Ind Pk IG6 . . . . 111 E2
Forest La IG7 . . . . 111 A5
Forest Mount Rd IG8 . . . . . . 109 D3
Forest Rd
Chingford E17 . . . . 109 D1

Forest Rd continued
Loughton IG10 . . . . 88 E5
Redbridge IG6 . . . . 112 B4
Romford RM7 . . . . 135 B8
Woodford IG8 . . . . 110 A7
Forest Side
Buckhurst Hill IG9 . . . . 88 C1
Chingford E4 . . . . 87 F1
Epping CM16 . . . . 67 D6
Forest Terr IG7 . . . . 111 A5
Forest View E4 . . . . 87 D2
Forest View Dr SS9 . . . . 146 A3
Forest View Rd
Chingford E17 . . . . 109 C2
Loughton IG10 . . . . 88 D5
Forest Way
Loughton IG10 . . . . 88 E6
Woodford IG8 . . . . 110 B6
Forfar Cl SS9 . . . . 146 D2
Forge Cotts CM22 . . . . 2 F3
Forges Rd E12 . . . . 132 D2
Forres Cl EN11 . . . . 21 A8
Forres Ho CM14 . . . . 116 D6
Forres Prim Sch EN11 . . . . . . 8 B1
Forrest Cl CM3 . . . . 101 C7
Forster Cl E4 . . . . 109 D3
Forsters Cl RM6 . . . . 134 F5
Forsyth Ct **1** RM10 . . . . . 154 B6
Forsythia Cl
Chelmsford CM1 . . . . 32 E7
Ilford IG1 . . . . 152 B7
Forterie Gdns IG3 . . . . 153 A8
Fortescue Chase SS1 . . . . . . 168 F7
Forth Rd RM14 . . . . 137 D5
Fortinbras Way CM2 . . . . 54 B8
Fortin Cl RM15 . . . . 172 A6
Fortin Path RM15 . . . . 172 A6
Fortin Way RM15 . . . . 172 A6
Fort Rd RM18 . . . . 179 C5
Fortune Ct IG11 . . . . 153 C3
Fortunes The CM18 . . . . 23 F6
Fortune Stps **2** SS1 . . . . 167 C7
Fort William Rd SS16 . . . . . . 142 B2
Forum The SS2 . . . . 148 A5
Fosbery Ct EN3 . . . . 65 A2
Fossetts Way SS2 . . . . 148 C4
Fossway RM8 . . . . 134 C2
Fostal Cl SS9 . . . . 146 E3
Foster Rd E13 . . . . 164 C4
Fosters Cl
Woodford E18 . . . . 110 B2
Writtle CM1 . . . . 30 F1
Foster St CM17 . . . . 25 F7
FOSTER STREET 24 F7
Foulgar Cl CM3 . . . . 101 E8
FOULNESS ISLAND 130 C5
Founders Rd EN11 . . . . 8 B1
Foundry Cl RM15 . . . . 124 E6
Foundry Bsns Pk SS5 . . . . . . 124 E6
Foundry La CM0 . . . . 106 B5
Founes Dr RM16 . . . . 172 E3
Fountain Farm CM18 . . . . 23 F6
Fountain La SS5 . . . . 124 B6
Fountain Pl EN9 . . . . 65 C5
Fountain Rd CM1 . . . . 16 C4
Fountains The IG10 . . . . 88 D2
Fountain Wlk DA11 . . . . 178 F1
Four Acres The CM21 . . . . 2 A2
Four Sisters Cl SS9 . . . . 146 F5
Four Sisters Way SS9 . . . . . . 146 F5
Fourth Ave
Basildon SS16 . . . . 140 E3
Chelmsford CM1 . . . . 32 B5
Grays RM20 . . . . 177 B8
Harlow CM19 . . . . 23 B8
Romford RM7 . . . . 135 D3
Stanford-le-H SS17 . . . . 160 E5
Thundersley SS7 . . . . 145 A6
Wickford SS11 . . . . 122 A6
Fourth Wlk SS8 . . . . 163 E4
Four Wantz The CM5 . . . . 49 A4
Fourways Ct **1** EN11 . . . . 21 A7
Four Wents The E4 . . . . 109 D8
Fowey Ave IG4 . . . . 132 D6
Fowler Cl SS1 . . . . 167 C8
Fowler Ct CM2 . . . . 54 A4
Fowler Rd IG6 . . . . 112 C5
Fowley Mead Pk EN8 . . . . 65 A5
Foxborough Chase
CM4 . . . . 76 B5
Fox Burrow Rd IG7 . . . . 112 D6
Fox Burrows La CM1 . . . . 31 B2
Fox Cl
Romford RM5 . . . . 113 B5
Thundersley SS7 . . . . 144 F6
Fox Cres CM1 . . . . 31 F4
Foxes Gn RM16 . . . . 174 A4
Foxes Gr CM13 . . . . 96 C2
Foxes Par RM9 . . . . 65 C6
Foxfield Chase CM3 . . . . 83 A8
Foxfield Cl SS5 . . . . 125 A6
Foxfield Dr SS17 . . . . 160 E5
Foxglove Cl EN11 . . . . 21 C1
Foxglove Ct SS15 . . . . 141 C5
Foxglove Gdns E11 . . . . 132 C7
Foxglove Ho DA1 . . . . 176 A2
Foxglove Rd
Romford RM7 . . . . 135 E2
South Ockendon RM15 . . . . 172 C2
Foxgloves The CM12 . . . . 96 F4
Foxglove Way CM11 . . . . 32 F6
Foxhall Rd
Mayland CM0 . . . . 83 E7
Steeple CM0 . . . . 84 B7
Upminster RM14 . . . . 156 C7
Foxhatch SS12 . . . . 121 F6
Fox Hatch CM15 . . . . 71 E1
Foxhills Rd RM16 . . . . 173 D5

Foxholes Rd CM2 . . . . 54 F6
Fox House Rd DA17 . . . . 169 B1
Foxhunter Wlk CM11 . . . . 97 D6
Foxlands Cres RM10 . . . . 154 C7
Foxlands Rd RM10 . . . . 154 C7
Foxleigh CM12 . . . . 119 A8
Foxleigh Cl CM12 . . . . 119 A8
Foxley Cl SS16 . . . . 89 B7
Fox Manor Way RM20 . . . . . 177 B8
Foxmeadows SS7 . . . . 144 F6
Foxton Rd
Grays RM20 . . . . 177 D8
Hoddesdon EN11 . . . . 21 A6
Foxwood Chase EN9 . . . . 65 C4
Foxwood Ct SS9 . . . . 146 D2
Foxwood Pl SS9 . . . . 146 D2
Foyle Dr RM15 . . . . 172 A7
Foys Wlk CM11 . . . . 119 C7
Frame The SS15 . . . . 141 E7
Framlingham Ct
5 Ilford RM6 . . . . 134 B6
Rayleigh SS6 . . . . 123 C1
Frampton Rd
5 Basildon SS13 . . . . . . 121 A1
Epping CM16 . . . . 46 A3
Frances Ave RM16 . . . . 172 C2
Frances Bardsley Sch for
Girls The RM1 . . . . 136 A5
Frances Cottee Lo
SS6 . . . . 146 A8
Frances Ct E4 . . . . 109 A4
Frances Gdns RM15 . . . . 171 F7
Frances Rd CM1 . . . . 33 A7
Frances Rd E4 . . . . 109 A4
Francis Ave IG1 . . . . 133 D2
Francis Cl SS17 . . . . 159 F3
Francisco Cl RM16 . . . . 172 C3
Francis Ct
3 Basildon SS14 . . . . . . 142 F5
Erith DA8 . . . . 169 E1
Francis Ct CM20 . . . . 10 B2
Francis Green Ho **7**
EN9 . . . . 65 B6
Francis Mews CM9 . . . . 59 B8
Francis Rd IG1 . . . . 133 D2
Francis St IG1 . . . . 133 D2
Francis Wks EN11 . . . . 21 B6
Francis Wlk SS6 . . . . 123 D2
Francombe Gdns
RM1 . . . . 136 A5
Frank Bailey Wlk E12 . . . . . . 152 A6
Frank Bretton Ho CM5 . . . . . . 49 A3
Frankland Cl IG8 . . . . 110 C5
Frankland Rd E4 . . . . 109 A5
Franklin Rd
Hornchurch RM12 . . . . 155 C6
North Fambridge CM3 . . . . . 103 B8
Franklins RM15 . . . . 171 D7
Franklins Way SS11 . . . . 121 E8
Franklyn Gdns IG6 . . . . 111 D4
Franks Cotts RM14 . . . . 138 B3
Frank Slater Ho **4**
IG3 . . . . 134 B3
Franmil Rd RM14 . . . . 136 A3
Fraser Cl
Basildon SS15 . . . . 140 F6
Chelmsford CM2 . . . . 54 C8
Southend-on-S SS3 . . . . 168 F8
Fraser Rd DA8 . . . . 169 D1
Frating Cres IG8 . . . . 110 B4
Frayes Chase CM5 . . . . 15 A3
Frazer Rd RM1 . . . . 135 F4
Frederica Rd E4 . . . . 87 D2
Frederick Andrews Ct
RM17 . . . . 178 D8
Frederick Rd RM14 . . . . 154 E3
Fred Leach Ho **1**
SS8 . . . . 164 A3
Fredrick J French Meml
Homes CM1 . . . . 32 B6
Fred Tibble Ct RM9 . . . . 153 E8
Freebone Gdns
RM13 . . . . 155 A6
Freeman Cl SS17 . . . . 160 F3
Freemantle Ho RM18 . . . . . . 178 F6
Freeman Way RM11 . . . . 136 F5
Freightmaster Est
RM13 . . . . 170 A2
Freightways RM20 . . . . 177 F1
Fremantle Cl SS3 . . . . 168 D5
Fremantle Cl CM3 . . . . 79 D1
Fremantle Rd
Belvedere DA17 . . . . 169 A2
Ilford IG6 . . . . 111 C1
Redbridge IG6 . . . . 111 C1
Fremnells The SS14 . . . . 142 D7
French Rd CM3 . . . . 80 F1
French's Cl SG12 . . . . 8 B4
French's Wlk **4** CM2 . . . . 32 C2
Frerichs Cl SS12 . . . . 121 D5
Freshfields Ave RM14 . . . . . . 156 C7
Freshwater Cres CM9 . . . . . . 37 B4
Freshwater Dr SS16 . . . . 142 F4
Freshwater Rd RM8 . . . . 134 E3
Freshwaters CM20 . . . . 10 E1
Freshwell Ave RM6 . . . . 134 C7
Freshwell Gdns CM13 . . . . . 139 D5
Fresh Wharf Est IG11 . . . . . . 152 B4
Fresh Wharf Rd IG11 . . . . . . 152 B3
Frettons SS14 . . . . 142 E6
Friar's Ave CM15 . . . . 95 A2
Friars Cl
Basildon SS15 . . . . 141 C6
Chingford E4 . . . . 109 C7
Ilford IG1 . . . . 133 D3
Friar's Cl CM15 . . . . 95 A2
Friarscroft EN10 . . . . 21 A3
Friars Gate Cl IG8 . . . . 110 A4

Friars La
Hatfield Heath CM22 . . . . 3 C1
Maldon CM9 . . . . 36 F2
Friars Prim Sch SS3 . . . . . . 168 F8
Friars St SS3 . . . . 168 F7
Friars The
Chigwell IG7 . . . . 111 E6
Harlow CM19 . . . . 23 A6
Friars Wlk CM2 . . . . 32 B1
Friary Fields CM9 . . . . 37 A2
Friary La IG8 . . . . 110 A6
FRIDAY HILL 109 E7
Friday Hill E4 . . . . 109 E7
Friday Hill E E4 . . . . 109 E7
Friday Hill W E4 . . . . 109 E8
Friday Rd DA8 . . . . 169 D1
Friern Gdns SS12 . . . . 121 B7
Friern Pl SS12 . . . . 121 B6
Friern Rd SS12 . . . . 121 B7
Frimley Ave RM11 . . . . 137 A3
Frimley Rd IG3 . . . . 133 E1
Frinton Dr IG8 . . . . 109 D3
Frinton Mews CM2 . . . . 133 A5
Frinton Rd RM5 . . . . 113 A3
Friston Path **4** IG6 . . . . . 111 E5
Frithwood Cl CM12 . . . . 118 F7
Frithwood La CM12 . . . . 118 F7
Frizlands La RM10 . . . . 135 B1
Frobisher Cl
Basildon SS15 . . . . 141 D6
Maldon CM9 . . . . 59 A8
Frobisher Gdns RM16 . . . . . . 172 E3
Frobisher Way
Greenhithe DA9 . . . . 177 B3
Southend-on-S SS3 . . . . 149 E1
Froden Brook CM11 . . . . 119 C7
Froden Cl CM11 . . . . 119 C7
Froden Ct CM11 . . . . 119 C6
Froghall La IG7 . . . . 111 D6
Frog La RM13 . . . . 169 D8
Frogmore Est RM20 . . . . 172 A1
Frog St CM15 . . . . 93 E8
Frome RM18 . . . . 175 C2
Front La RM14 . . . . 137 E4
Fry Cl RM5 . . . . 113 A4
FRYERNING 74 A5
Fryerning La CM4 . . . . 74 B4
FRYERNS 142 E8
Fryerns Terr SS14 . . . . 142 F8
Fryth The SS14 . . . . 142 E8
Fuchsia Cl RM7 . . . . 135 E2
Fulbourne Rd E17 . . . . 109 C1
Fulbrook La RM15 . . . . 171 F6
Fulcher Ave CM2 . . . . 32 F3
Fulford Dr SS9 . . . . 147 A6
Fullarton Cres RM15 . . . . . . 171 F7
Fullbridge CM9 . . . . 37 A3
Fuller Rd RM8 . . . . 153 C8
Fuller's Ave IG8 . . . . 109 F3
Fullers Cl
Romford RM5 . . . . 113 C3
Waltham Abbey EN9 . . . . 66 A6
Fuller's La RM5 . . . . 113 C3
Fullers Mead CM17 . . . . 24 C7
Fuller's Rd E18 . . . . 109 F3
Fuller Terr IG1 . . . . 152 D7
Fullman Ind Pk SS8 . . . . 163 C3
Fullwell Ave IG5 . . . . 111 B2
FULLWELL CROSS 111 D2
Fullwell Cl IG5 . . . . 111 A2
Fullwell Par IG5 . . . . 111 A2
Fullwood Prim Sch
IG6 . . . . 133 C7
Fulmar Rd RM12 . . . . 155 B6
Fulmar Way SS11 . . . . 122 A5
Fulton Ct **3** EN3 . . . . 65 A1
Fulton Rd SS7 . . . . 144 D7
Fulwich Rd DA1 . . . . 176 A1
Furlongs SS16 . . . . 142 D4
Furlongs The CM4 . . . . 74 B3
Furlong Way SG12 . . . . 8 A7
Furness Cl RM16 . . . . 174 B1
Furness Way RM12 . . . . 155 A7
Furrowfelde SS16 . . . . 142 A4
Further Mdw CM1 . . . . 53 A8
Furtherwick Park Sch
SS8 . . . . 164 C3
Furtherwick Rd SS8 . . . . 164 C2
Furze Farm Ct RM6 . . . . 112 E1
Furze Glade SS16 . . . . 141 B4
Furze Inf Sch RM6 . . . . 134 E5
Furze La CM4 . . . . 76 A1
Fuschia Cl IG8 . . . . 109 E4
Fusedale Way RM15 . . . . 171 F6
Fyefields SS13 . . . . 143 C7
FYFIELD 27 D2
Fyfield Ave SS12 . . . . 121 C5
Fyfield Bsns & Research
Pk CM5 . . . . 49 B6
Fyfield Cl CM13 . . . . 139 D5
Fyfield Dr RM14 . . . . 171 F6
Fyfield Dr Walker's Ce
Prim Sch CM5 . . . . 27 D2
Fyfield Ho RM9 . . . . 153 B5
Fyfield Path SS6 . . . . 123 A3
Fyfield Rd
Chipping Ongar CM5 . . . . . . 49 A5
Moreton CM5 . . . . 26 F3
Rainham RM13 . . . . 154 F4
Willingale CM5 . . . . 28 C3
Woodford IG8 . . . . 110 C3

G

Gabion Ave RM19 . . . .
Gablefields CM2 . . . .
Gable Hall Sch SS17 . . . . . .
Gables The
Barking IG11 . . . .
Basildon SS13 . . . .
Brentwood CM13 . . . .
Chipping Ongar CM5 . . . . .
Sawbridgeworth CM21 . . . .
Southend-on-S, Eastwood
SS9 . . . .
Southend-on-S SS9 . . . . . .
Gabriel Cl
Grays RM16 . . . .
Romford RM5 . . . .
Gadsden Cl RM14 . . . .
Gafzelle Dr SS8 . . . .
Gaiger Cl CM1 . . . .
Gainsborough Ave
Canvey Island SS8 . . . .
Little Ilford E12 . . . .
Tilbury RM18 . . . .
Gainsborough Cl CM11
Gainsborough Cres
CM2 . . . .
Gainsborough Ct **4**
CM14 . . . .
Gainsborough Dr SS6 . . . . .
Gainsborough Ho
2 Barking RM8 . . . . . .
Redbridge IG8 . . . .
Gainsborough Pl
Brentwood CM13 . . . .
Chigwell IG7 . . . .
Gainsborough Rd
Dagenham RM8 . . . .
Rainham RM13 . . . .
Woodford IG8 . . . .
Gains Cl SS8 . . . .
Gainsthorpe Rd CM5 . . . . .
Gaitskell Ho RM16 . . . .
Galadriel Spring CM3 . . . . .
Galahad Cl CM0 . . . .
Galaxie Lo SS7 . . . .
Galeborough Ave
IG8 . . . .
Gale St RM9 . . . .
Gales Way IG8 . . . .
Galey Gn RM15 . . . .
Galleon Bvd DA2 . . . .
Galleon Cl DA8 . . . .
Galleon Rd RM16 . . . .
Galleons Dr IG11 . . . .
Galleydene SS7 . . . .
Galleydene Ave CM2 . . . . .
GALLEYEND . . . .
Galley Gn SG13 . . . .
Galleyhill Rd EN9 . . . .
Galley Hill Rd
Northfleet DA11 . . . .
Swanscombe DA10 . . . . . .
Galley Hill Trad Est
DA10 . . . .
GALLEYWOOD . . . .
Galleywood Cres
RM5 . . . .
Galleywood Inf Sch
CM2 . . . .
Galleywood Rd
Chelmsford CM2 . . . .
Great Baddow CM2 . . . . . .
Galliford Rd CM9 . . . .
Galliford Road Ind Est
CM9 . . . .
Gallions Cl IG11 . . . .
Gallops The SS16 . . . .
Gallows Cnr RM3 . . . .
Galsworthy Ave RM8 . . . . .
Galsworthy Rd RM18 . . . . .
Galt Cl SS12 . . . .
Galton Rd SS0 . . . .
Gambleside SS16 . . . .
Gammon Field RM16 . . . . .
Gandalf's Ride CM3 . . . . . .
Ganels Cl CM11 . . . .
Ganels Rd CM11 . . . .
Gangies Hill CM14 . . . .
Ganley Ct **6** CM11 . . . . .
Gant Ct EN9 . . . .
GANTS HILL . . . .
Gantshill Cres IG2 . . . .
Gants Hill Sta IG2 . . . .
Garbutt Rd RM14 . . . .
Garden Cl
Althorne CM3 . . . .
Chingford E4 . . . .
Steeple CM0 . . . .
Garden Ct RM14 . . . .
Garden End CM4 . . . .
Gardeners CM2 . . . .
Gardeners La SS4 . . . .
Garden Fields CM0 . . . . . .
Garden Hos The CM21 . . . .
Gardenia Way IG8 . . . .
Gardens Fields CM5 . . . . .
Gardens The
Doddinghurst CM15 . . . . .
Southend-on-S SS9 . . . . . .
Garden Terrace Rd **2**
CM17 . . . .
Garden Way IG10 . . . .
Garden Wharf DA8 . . . . . .
Gardiner Cl RM8 . . . .
Gardiners Cl SS14 . . . .
Gardiners La N CM11 . . . .

La S SS14 . . . . .120 E2
Link SS14 . . . . .120 D2
The CM17 . . . . . . .24 B8
Way SS14 . . . . .120 D2
t E11 . . . . .161 A3
Ct CM1 . . . . .132 B5
Ct RM7 . . . . .135 C6
t 8 E4 . . . . .87 C1
d E4 . . . . .87 D1
Vay RM11 . . . . . . .136 E7
Mah 134 D3
T IG7 . . . . .109 C2
The SS4 . . . . .125 F2
ead CM16 . . . . . . .46 D3
o CM2 . . . . .55 F6
o RM12 . . . . .136 A2
DA1 . . . . .179 B1
Par RM19 . . . . . .171 A2

endon

. . . . .171 F7
endon RM15 . . . . .112 E4
M1 . . . . .113 E3
r RM1 . . . . .113 E3
RM15 . . . . .157 C1
e Gdns IG8 . . . . . .109 E3
e Prim Sch

. . . . .152 C4
e Rd IG11 . . . . . . .152 C3
e Way CM11 . . . . .97 D2
Cl RM3 . . . . .114 D3
d E4 . . . . .177 E1
REEN 2 B7
Dr RM15 . . . . . . .171 F7
e Mews CM4 . . . . .74 B3
e The 4

. . . . .135 E6
e The 2

. . . . .74 B3
e Sq SS15 . . . . . . .119 F2
e Way SS15 . . . . . .119 F2
9. . . . . .36 F3
e Mews 36 F3
9. . . . . .34 E6
cad The

. . . . .173 F4
e 4 IG1 . . . . . . .152 C4
rim Sch The

. . . . .176 B1
et Pk E6 . . . . .152 B1
e Cl SS5 . . . . .124 D6
 ens SS6 . . . . .123 C4
ew CM12 . . . . . . .119 B8
Par RM2 . . . . . . .136 F1
ath RM15 . . . . . . .171 F2
ERS 57 A5
s

. . . . .142 D7
S 124 B6
's La CM3 . . . . .56 F6
s Rd CM3 . . . . .56 F6
d IG5 . . . . .132 F8
RM10 . . . . .154 C7
SS6 . . . . .123 D4
SS14 . . . . .142 D7
RM18 . . . . .178 F6
RM14 . . . . .156 B8
ns SS14 . . . . .141 E4
l Rd IG8 . . . . .110 E3
rk Rd

. . . . .156 B8
RM14 . . . . .137 B2
RM10 . . . . .154 C7
Ave IG2 . . . . .133 B6
Hall IG5 . . . . .133 B8
a 104 C2
SS2 . . . . .148 A2
SS15 . . . . .141 A7
l Sch IG2 . . . . . . .133 B6
n Sch IG2 . . . . . . .133 B6
e Gdns

. . . . .133 B7
M14 . . . . .94 C1
M14 . . . . .94 C1
Rd EN11 . . . . .21 B6
RM2 . . . . .136 B7
he SS17 . . . . .161 A2
SS8 . . . . .164 C5
CM3 . . . . .78 B6
Ct EN9 . . . . .66 A6
RM5 . . . . .113 B3
ospl SS0 . . . . .147 C3
a CM3 . . . . .20 B2
SS0 . . . . .166 D8
ns RM6 . . . . .134 E6
. . . . .109 A5
8. . . . . .164 B5
SS8 . . . . .164 B5
d SS8 . . . . .164 B5
ews 3

. . . . .155 C7
e RM3 . . . . .115 B3
ey Croft

. . . . .60 E1
rdnell Way

. . . . .60 E1
SS8 . . . . .163 F6
mberton Wlk 8

. . . . .152 A7
ooks Ho

. . . . .178 B8
rst Hill Way 110 D8
l CM2 . . . . .32 B1
vies Lo

. . . . .133 C6

George Green Villas
CM22 . . . . .2 B8
George La
Wanstead E18 . . . . . .132 B8
Woodford E18 . . . . . .110 A1
George Lovell Dr EN3 . .65 A2
George Rd E4 . . . . . . .109 A4
Georges Dr CM15 . . . . .93 F4
George St
Barking IG11 . . . . . .152 C5
Chelmsford CM2 . . . . .32 B1
Grays RM17 . . . . . . .178 A8
Romford RM1 . . . . . .135 F5
Southend-on-S SS3 . .168 G6
George Tilbury Ho
RM16 . . . . .174 B4
Georgeville Gdns IG6 . .133 B7
George Williams Ho
RM7 . . . . .135 F4
Gepp Pl CM2 . . . . .33 B4
Gepps Cl CM1 . . . . .6 C2
Gerald Rd RM8 . . . . . .134 F3
Gerard Gdns RM13 . . .154 E3
Gerboa Ct 7 E4 . . . . .109 D5
Gernon Cl
Broomfield CM1 . . . . . .19 B3
Rainham RM13 . . . . .155 D3
Gernons SS16 . . . . . . .141 F4
Gerpins La RM14 . . . . .156 A4
Gerrard Cres CM14 . . .116 C7
Gertrude Rd DA17 . . . .169 A2
Geylen Rd SS8 . . . . . .164 C4
GHYLLGROVE 142 B7
Ghyllgrove SS14 . . . . .142 B7
Ghyllgrove Cl SS14 . . .142 B8
Ghyllgrove Com Jun Sch
SS14 . . . . .142 A7
Gibbards Cott 1
IG11 . . . . .152 F5
Gibb Croft CM18 . . . . . .23 F4
Gibbfield Ct RM6 . . . . .134 E8
Gibcracks SS14 . . . . . .142 E6
Gibraltar Cl IG13 . . . . .116 C4
Gibraltar Ho CM13 . . . .116 C4
Gibson Cl CM16 . . . . . .47 C6
Gibson Ct
Harlow CM18 . . . . . . .23 E5
7 Romford RM1 . . .135 E5
Gibson Rd RM8 . . . . . .134 C3
Gibson Vale CM1 . . . . . .32 B8
Gidea Av RM2 . . . . . . .136 A8
Gidea Cl
Romford RM2 . . . . . .136 A8
South Ockendon RM15 .157 C2
Gidea Park Coll RM2 . .136 A8
Gidea Park Prim Sch
RM2 . . . . .136 A8
Gidea Park Sta RM2 . . .136 B7
Gideon Cl DA17 . . . . . .169 B2
Gideons Way SS17 . . . .160 E3
Giffards Prim Sch
SS17 . . . . .160 F4
Gifford Gn SS13 . . . . .143 B5
Gifford Pl CM14 . . . . . .116 D5
Gifford Rd SS17 . . . . . .144 D5
Giffords Cross Ave
SS17 . . . . .161 A3
Giffords Cross Rd
SS17 . . . . .161 B2
Gifhorn Rd SS8 . . . . . .164 E3
Gilbert Calvin Prim Sch
IG11 . . . . .111 A1
Gilbert Cl
Rayleigh SS6 . . . . . .123 F2
Swanscombe DA10 . . .177 D1
Gilbert Dr SS16 . . . . . .141 A5
Gilbert Rd
Belvedere DA17 . . . . .169 A3
Grays RM16 . . . . . . .172 C3
Romford RM1 . . . . . .135 F7
Gildborne Cl SS17 . . . .161 D4
Gilden Cl CM17 . . . . . . .11 E4
Gilden Way CM17 . . . . .11 D3
Gilders CM21 . . . . .1 D2
Gilean Cl CM13 . . . . . .155 D3
Gilford Ho 9 IG1 . . . .133 B3
Gillan Way RM13 . . . . .155 A6
Gilsland Ent 36 F6
Gilson Cl CM2 . . . . .32 E4
Gilstead Hall Mews Cotts
CM14 . . . . .93 A4
Gilstead Ho 1 IG11 . .153 B3
GILSTON 10 E5
Gilston Park Ho CM20 . .10 C6
Gilston Pk CM20 . . . . . .10 C7
Gilwell Ct E4 . . . . .87 D5
Gilwell La E4 . . . . .87 D5
Gimli Watch CM3 . . . . .101 D6
Gippeswyk SS14 . . . . .142 C7
Gipson Park Cl SS9 . . .146 D6
Gipsy La RM17 . . . . . . .178 D3
Girona Cl RM16 . . . . . .172 C3
Gisborne Gdns RM13 . .154 F2
Gladden Ct CM14 . . . . .23 E4
Gladden Fields CM3 . . .101 C6

Glade Bsns Ctr The
RM20 . . . . .171 F1
Glade Ct IG5 . . . . .110 F2
Glade Prim Sch IG5 . . .110 F1
Gladeswood Rd DA17 . .169 B2
Glade The
Basildon SS16 . . . . . .142 C4
Brentwood CM13 . . . . .95 A1
Upminster RM14 . . . .156 C7
Woodford, Clayhall IG5 .110 E3
Woodford, Woodford Wells
IG8 . . . . .110 B7
Gladeway The RM6 . . . .65 D6
Gladstone Ct CM2 . . . . .32 B1
Gladstone Gdns SS6 . . .123 C1
Gladstone Rd
Buckhurst Hill IG9 . . . .88 C1
Hockley SS5 . . . . . . .124 E6
Hoddesdon EN11 . . . . .21 B7
Gladwyns SS15 . . . . . .141 E7
Glamis Dr RM11 . . . . . .136 E3
Glamis Ho CM14 . . . . .116 C6
Glan Avon Mews CM1 . .24 C7
Glandford Way RM6 . . .134 B6
Glanmead SS16 . . . . . . .94 E1
Glanmire CM1 . . . . .97 D6
Glanthams Cl CM15 . . .116 F8
Glanthams Rd CM15 . . .116 F8
Glanville Dr RM11 . . . .136 F3
Glasseys La SS6 . . . . . .145 C8
Glastonbury Ave IG8 . .110 D4
Glastonbury Chase
SS0 . . . . .147 B5
Glebe Ave IG8 . . . . . . .110 A4
Glebe Cl
Great Wakering SS3 . .150 D3
Rayleigh SS6 . . . . . .123 C3
Southend-on-S SS1 . . .167 E8
Glebe Cres CM1 . . . . . . .19 B1
Glebe Dr SS6 . . . . .123 C3
Glebe Field SS14 . . . . .142 C8
Glebe Gdns CM13 . . . . .117 E3
Glebe Jun & Inf Sch
SS6 . . . . .123 C3
Glebe La CM0 . . . . .63 D1
Glebelands
Chigwell IG7 . . . . . . .112 B7
Harlow CM20 . . . . . . .10 F3
South Benfleet SS7 . . .144 B7
Glebelands Ave
Ilford IG2 . . . . .133 D5
Wanstead E11 . . . . . .132 A6
Glebe Mdw CM3 . . . . . .18 E7
Glebe Rd
Chelmsford CM1 . . . . . .32 B3
Chipping Ongar CM5 . . .48 F2
Dagenham RM10 . . . .154 B6
Heybridge CM9 . . . . . .37 C5
Rainham RM13 . . . . .155 C2
Ramsden Bellhouse
CM11 . . . . .98 F1
Wickford SS11 . . . . . .121 E7
Glebe The
Harlow CM20 . . . . . . .10 E1
Magdalen Laver CM5 . .25 D5
Purleigh CM3 . . . . . . .58 D1
Glebe View CM2 . . . . . .54 B3
Glebe Way
Burnham-on-C CM0 . . .106 C6
Hadleigh SS7 . . . . . .145 F3
Hornchurch RM11 . . . .136 E3
Woodford IG8 . . . . . .110 C5
Glenarm Coll IG1 . . . . .133 B2
Glenavon Lo 5 E18 . . .132 A8
Glenbervie Dr SS9 . . . .146 F2
Glencoe Ave IG2 . . . . . .133 E4
Glencoe Dr
Dagenham RM10 . . . .154 A8
Wickford SS11 . . . . . .122 A8
Glen Cres IG8 . . . . .110 B4
Glencrofts SS5 . . . . . . .124 F6
Glen Ct SS7 . . . . .145 B4
Glendale SS16 . . . . .79 E1
Glendale Ave RM6 . . . .134 C4
Glendale Cl
Burnham-on-C CM0 . . .106 C6
Shenfield CM15 . . . . . .94 E1
Glendale Gdns SS9 . . . .146 D1
Glendale Ho CM15 . . . . .94 E2
Glendale Rd
Burnham-on-C CM0 . . .106 C6
Erith DA8 . . . . .169 C2
Glendower Rd E4 . . . . . .87 D1
Gleneagles SS7 . . . . . .144 A8
Gleneagles Cl RM3 . . . .114 F3
Gleneagles Rd SS9 . . . .146 C5
Glenester Cl EN11 . . . . . .8 A1
Glen Faba CM19 . . . . . .21 F6
Glen Faba Rd CM19 . . . .21 F6
Glenfield Rd SS17 . . . . .161 B4
Glengall Rd IG8 . . . . . .110 A5
Glenham Dr IG2 . . . . . .133 B6
Glen Hazel CM5 . . . . . . .72 D4
Glenhurst Mans SS1 . . .167 B8
Glenhurst Rd SS2 . . . . .148 A2
Glenmead IG9 . . . . .88 C1
Glenmere SS16 . . . . . . .142 D2
Glenmere Pare Ave
SS7 . . . . .145 B4
Glenmere Terr SS12 . . .117 C3
Glenmore Ho SS4 . . . . .125 F2
Glenmore St SS2 . . . . .148 D1
Glenmore Way IG11 . . .153 A3
Glenny Rd IG11 . . . . . .152 C5
Glen Rd
South Benfleet SS7 . . .144 E5
Southend-on-S SS9 . . .166 A8

Glenridding SS7 . . . . . .144 D5
Glen Rise IG8 . . . . .110 B4
Glenside
Billericay CM11 . . . . . .97 D2
Chigwell IG7 . . . . . . .111 B4
Glen The
Basildon SS16 . . . . . .143 A4
Hullbridge SS5 . . . . . .101 E4
Rainham RM13 . . . . .155 C1
Rayleigh SS6 . . . . . .145 E8
Stanford-le-H SS17 . . .160 F3
Glenthorne Gdns IG6 . .133 B7
Glenton Cl RM1 . . . . . .113 C3
Glenton Way RM1 . . . .113 C3
Glenwood SS7 . . . . . . .163 F5
Glenwood Ave
Hockley SS5 . . . . . . .124 F5
Rainham RM13 . . . . .155 B1
Southend-on-S, Eastwood
SS0 . . . . .146 B7
Southend-on-S, Prittlewell
SS0 . . . . .147 D2
Glenwood Cl 6 E18 . . .132 A8
Glenwood Dr RM2 . . . .136 A7
Glenwood Gdns
Basildon SS16 . . . . . .140 E4
Ilford IG2 . . . . .133 A6
Glenwood Sch SS7 . . . .144 B7
Gleten Rd SS8 . . . . . . .164 D4
Globe Ind Est RM17 . . .173 C1
Globe Rd
Hornchurch RM11 . . . .136 A5
Woodford IG8 . . . . . .110 C4
Glossop Ho 13 RM3 . .114 C5
Gloucester Ave
Chelmsford CM2 . . . . . .54 C6
East Tilbury RM18 . . . .175 C1
Grays RM16 . . . . . . .173 C4
Maldon CM9 . . . . .36 F1
Rayleigh SS6 . . . . . .146 A8
Gloucester Bsns Pk
SS15 . . . . .141 E8
Gloucester Cres CM1 . . .32 A5
Gloucester Ct
Redbridge IG1 . . . . . .132 F4
Tilbury RM18 . . . . . .178 F5
Gloucester Pl CM12 . . . .97 A5
Gloucester Rd
Little Ilford E12 . . . . .132 F1
Pilgrims Hatch CM15 . . .94 B4
Wanstead E11 . . . . . .132 C6
Gloucester Terr SS1 . . .168 A6
Glovers Field CM15 . . . .71 A6
Glovers La CM17 . . . . . .24 E3
Glyders SS7 . . . . .144 E1
Glynde Way SS2 . . . . . .148 F1
Glynn Rd CM0 . . . . . . .106 B5
Goat Hall La
Chelmsford CM2 . . . . . .53 F3
Galleywood CM2 . . . . . .54 A3
Goat House La CM3 . . . .57 F4
Goatsmoor La
Billericay CM4, CM11 . . .97 F6
Stock CM4 . . . . .98 A8
Goatswood La RM4 . . . .92 B2
Gobions SS16 . . . . . . .142 A4
Gobions Ave RM5 . . . .113 D3
Goddard Rd RM13 . . . .173 A5
Goddards Way IG1 . . . .133 D3
Godfreys Mews CM2 . . .32 B1
Godman Rd RM13 . . . .174 B3
Godsafe CM17 . . . . .11 E4
Godwin Cl E4 . . . . .65 C1
Godwin Prim Sch
RM9 . . . . .153 E5
Goirle Ave SS8 . . . . . . .164 C4
Goldace RM17 . . . . . . .177 F8
Gold Berry Mead
CM3 . . . . .101 C6
Goldcrest Dr CM11 . . . . .97 C1
Goldenacres CM1 . . . . . .32 F8
Golden Cross SS4 . . . . .125 D4
Golden Cross Mews
SS4 . . . . .125 D5
Golden Cross Par
SS4 . . . . .125 D5
Golden Cross Rd SS4 . .125 D6
Golden Jubilee Ct
RM12 . . . . .136 A3
Golden Manor Dr SS7 . .144 F5
Goldfinch La SS7 . . . . .145 B8
GOLDHANGER 38 F7
Goldhanger Cl SS6 . . . .123 A3
Goldhanger Cross
SS14 . . . . .142 E7
Goldhanger Rd CM9 . . . .37 D4
Golding Cl SS17 . . . . . .160 E3
Golding Ct 8 IG1 . . . . .133 A1
Goldingham Ave IG10 . .89 C7
Goldings Cotts CM13 . .116 B1
Goldings Cres SS16 . . .142 E3
Goldings Hill IG10,
. . . . .66 F2
Goldings Rd IG10 . . . . . .89 A8
Goldings Rise IG10 . . . . .89 A8
Golding Thoroughfare
CM2 . . . . .32 F3
Goldington Cres CM2 . . .96 F5
Goldlay Ave CM2 . . . . . .54 C8
Goldlay Gdns CM2 . . . . .54 C8
Goldlay Rd CM2 . . . . . . .54 C8
Goldmer Cl SS8 . . . . . .168 C8
Goldsands Rd CM0 . . . . .84 C2

Goldsborough Cres
E4 . . . . .109 C8
Goldsmere Ct RM11 . . .136 E3
Goldsmith Ave E12 . . . .132 A2
Goldsmith Ave RM7 . . .135 A4
Goldsmith Dr SS6 . . . .123 D7
Goldsmith Ho IG8 . . . .111 B4
Goldsmiths Ave
Corringham SS17 . . . .161 A2
4 Stanford-le-H SS17 .160 F3
Goldsworthy Dr SS3 . . .150 C2
Golfe Ho IG1 . . . . .133 D1
Golfe Rd IG1 . . . . .133 D1
Golf Ride SS7 . . . . .144 D3
GOOD EASTER 16 D5
Gooderham Ho RM16 . .174 B4
Goodey Rd IG11 . . . . . .152 F5
Goodier Rd CM1 . . . . . . .31 F4
Goodman St SS3 . . . . . .150 B3
GOODMAYES 134 A3
Goodmayes Ave IG3 . . .134 A3
Goodmayes Hospl
IG3 . . . . .134 B3
Goodmayes La IG3 . . . .134 A1
Goodmayes La RM8 . . .153 A4
Goodmayes Prim Sch
IG3 . . . . .134 B3
Goodmayes Rd IG3 . . . .134 A3
Goodmayes Ret Pk
IG3 . . . . .134 B3
Goodmayes Sta IG3 . . .134 A3
Goodmayes Wlk 1
SS12 . . . . .121 D6
Goodridge Ho E17 . . . .109 C3
Goodrington Sch
RM1 . . . . .136 D5
Goodview Rd SS14 . . . .120 A2
Goodwin Cl CM2 . . . . . .54 D8
Goodwood Ave
Brentwood CM13 . . . . .95 F3
Hornchurch RM12 . . . .155 F3
Goodwood Cl
Hoddesdon EN9 . . . . . .21 A7
Thundersley SS7 . . . . .145 B7
GOOSEBERRY GREEN . . .97 A1
Goose Cotts SS13 . . . . .100 B5
Goose La CM22 . . . . .2 E7
Gooseley La E6 . . . . . . .152 A2
Gooshays Dr RM3 . . . . .114 E4
Gooshays Gdns RM3 . . .114 E4
Gordon Ave
Chingford E4 . . . . . . .109 E4
Hornchurch RM12 . . . .135 F2
Gordon Cl
Billericay CM12 . . . . . .96 F3
East Tilbury RM18 . . . .180 D7
Gordon Cotts RM4 . . . . .91 B5
Gordon Inf Sch IG11 . . .133 D1
Gordon Pl
9 Gravesend DA12 . .179 A1
Southend-on-S SS1 . . .166 F8
Gordon Prom E DA12 . .179 C1
Gordon Rd
Barking IG11 . . . . . . .152 E4
Basildon SS14 . . . . . .142 D5
Belvedere DA17 . . . . .169 C2
Brentwood CM15 . . . . .95 A1
Chelmsford CM2 . . . . . .54 A6
Chingford E4 . . . . .87 C2
Corringham SS17 . . . .160 F3
Dagenham RM6 . . . . .134 F5
Gravesend DA11 . . . . .178 E1
Grays RM16 . . . . . . .173 F3
Holbrook EN9 . . . . . . .65 A5
Horndon on t H SS17 . .159 F3
Ilford IG1 . . . . .133 D1
Southend-on-S, Westcliff-on-S
SS1 . . . . .166 F8
Wanstead E11 . . . . . .132 A5
Woodford E18 . . . . . .110 B2
Gordon Roughley Ct
SS6 . . . . .123 C1
Gordons SS13 . . . . . . .123 A1
Gore Rd SS4 . . . . .126 E6
Goresbrook Rd RM9 . . .153 D4
Gore The SS14 . . . . . . .142 A7
Goring Cl RM5 . . . . . . .113 C2
Goring Gdns RM8 . . . . .153 C8
Gorseway RM7 . . . . . . .135 E4
Gosfield Cl SS6 . . . . . . .123 A3
Gosfield Rd RM8 . . . . . .135 A3
Gosford Gdns IG4 . . . . .132 F6
Goshawk Dr CM2 . . . . . .54 B5
Goslings The SS3 . . . . .168 G7
Gosport Dr RM12 . . . . .155 C6
Gossets The CM6 . . . . . .15 C4
Gould Cl CM5 . . . . .26 C2
Goulds Cotts RM4 . . . . .90 B6
Goulton Rd CM 19 A1
Gourney Gr RM16 . . . . .173 B6
Government Row EN3 . . .65 A2
Gowan Brae SS7 . . . . . .144 B5
Gowan Ct SS7 . . . . . . .144 B5
Gowan Cl SS7 . . . . .144 B5
Gowan Lea 4 E18 . . . .132 A7
Gower Chase SS15 . . . .141 D5
Gower Ho 3 IG11 . . . .152 C5
Gower Pl 1 RM16 . . . .172 B3
Gowers Ave SS4 . . . . . .54 E6
Gowers La RM16 . . . . . .172 A3
Gowers The CM20 . . . . .11 B2
Goya Rise SS3 . . . . . . .168 G8
Grace Cl IG6 . . . . .111 F4

Grace Rd SS13 . . . . 121 A2
Grace's Cross CM2 . . . . .55 C7
Graces La CM1 . . . . .34 B1
Grafton Gdns RM8 . . . . . . 134 E2
Grafton Inf Sch RM8 . . . . . 134 F2
Grafton Jun Sch RM8 . . . . 134 F2
Grafton Pl CM2 . . . . .33 A4
Grafton Rd
  Canvey Island SS8 . . . . . . 164 C2
  Dagenham RM8 . . . . 134 E2
Graham Cl
  Billericay CM12 . . . . .97 C5
  Brentwood CM13 . . . . .95 C4
  Hockley SS5 . . . . 124 E7
  Stanford-le-H SS17 . . . . . 160 E4
Grahame Cl **3** SS12 . . . . 121 D5
Grahame Ho SS2 . . . . 148 C3
Graham James Prim Sch
  SS17 . . . . 160 F3
Graham Mans **11**
  IG11 . . . . 153 A5
Grainger Cl SS2 . . . . 148 A1
Grainger Rd SS2 . . . . 148 A1
Grainger Road Ind Est
  SS2 . . . . 148 A1
Grampian SS0 . . . . 147 E1
Grampian Gr CM1 . . . . .31 D6
Granaries The EN9 . . . . .65 E5
Granary Cl CM3 . . . . .82 B5
Granary Ct
  3 Dagenham RM8 . . . . 134 D4
  Sawbridgeworth CM21 . . . . .1 E2
Granary Mdw CM15 . . . . . . .72 E3
Granary The
  Roydon CM19 . . . . .9 B1
  Stanstead Abbotts SG12 . . . .8 C3
Granby Rd DA11 . . . . 178 D1
Grand Court W SS9 . . . . . . 165 F8
Grand Ct RM8 . . . . 134 E1
Grand Dr SS9 . . . . 165 F8
Grand Par SS9 . . . . 165 F8
Grandview Rd SS7 . . . . 144 F7
Grange Ave
  Mayland CM3 . . . . .83 C7
  South Benfleet SS7 . . . . . 146 A5
  Wickford SS12 . . . . 121 C6
  Woodford IG8 . . . . 110 A3
Grange Cl
  Ingrave CM13 . . . . 117 C5
  Southend-on-S SS9 . . . . . 146 E3
  Woodford IG8 . . . . 110 A3
Grange Cres
  Chigwell IG7 . . . . 111 D5
  26 Dartford DA2 . . . . . . 176 B1
Grange Ct
  Chelmsford CM2 . . . . .53 F7
  Ilford IG6 . . . . 133 C8
  Loughton IG10 . . . . .88 D4
  Waltham Abbey EN9 . . . . . .65 C5
Grange Gdns
  Rayleigh SS6 . . . . 123 B3
  Southend-on-S SS1 . . . . . 167 B8
GRANGE HILL 111 D5
Grange Hill Sta IG7 . . . . . . 111 D6
Grange Ho **6** IG11 . . . . . 152 D4
Grange La CM19 . . . . .22 C8
Grange Par CM11 . . . . 119 C7
Grange Park Dr SS9 . . . . . . 146 F2
Grange Prim Sch
  SS12 . . . . 121 B6
Granger Ave CM9 . . . . .36 F1
Grange Rd
  Aveley RM15 . . . . 171 C5
  Basildon SS13 . . . . 143 E8
  Billericay CM11 . . . . 119 D7
  Grays RM17 . . . . 178 C8
  Ilford IG1 . . . . 152 C8
  Pleshey CM3 . . . . .7 E2
  Romford RM3 . . . . 114 B4
  Southend-on-S SS9 . . . . . 146 D1
  Thundersley SS7 . . . . 144 F7
  Tillingham CM0 . . . . .64 A1
  Wickford SS11 . . . . .99 E2
Granger Row RM1 . . . . .31 F6
Granger Way RM1 . . . . 136 A5
Grange The
  Hoddesdon EN11 . . . . .21 A5
  Waltham Abbey EN9 . . . . . .65 D2
  4 Wanstead E18 . . . . . . 132 A8
Grangeway
  Thundersley SS7 . . . . 145 A6
  Woodford IG8 . . . . 110 C6
Grangeway Gdns IG4 . . . . . 132 E6
Grangewood SS7 . . . . 144 D5
Grangewood Ave
  Grays RM16 . . . . 173 E3
  Rainham RM13 . . . . 155 C1
Grangewood Cl CM13 . . . . 117 A7
Granites Chase CM11 . . . . . 119 F5
Grant Cl **12** SS12 . . . . . . 121 E5
Grant Ct **2** E4 . . . . .87 C1
Grantham Ct RM6 . . . . 134 F4
Grantham Gdns RM6 . . . . . 134 F4
Grantham Lo SS9 . . . . 146 D1
Grantham Rd
  Ilford IG12 . . . . 133 A1
  Little Ilford E12 . . . . 152 A8
Grantham Way RM16 . . . . . 173 A5
Grantock Rd E17 . . . . 109 D2
Granton Ave RM14 . . . . . . 136 F2
Granton Rd IG3 . . . . 134 A3
Granville Cl
  Billericay CM12 . . . . .96 F5
  South Benfleet SS7 . . . . . 144 E4
Granville Gdns EN11 . . . . . . .8 A2

Granville Rd
  Epping CM16 . . . . .46 B2
  Hockley SS5 . . . . 102 F1
  Ilford IG1 . . . . 133 E2
  Woodford IG8 . . . . 110 B1
Granville Terr **4**
  CM0 . . . . 106 C4
Grapnells SS15 . . . . 142 F4
Grapnells Farm Cotts
  SS4 . . . . 106 A2
Grasmead Ave SS9 . . . . 146 F2
Grasmere Ave SS9 . . . . 101 D3
Grasmere Cl IG10 . . . . .88 F7
Grasmere Gdns IG4 . . . . . . 132 F6
Grasmere Ho SS6 . . . . 123 D2
Grasmere Rd
  Canvey Island SS8 . . . . . . 163 E3
  Thundersley SS7 . . . . 144 E6
Grass Croft RM17 . . . . 173 B1
Grassmere Rd RM11 . . . . . 136 F7
Gratmore Gn SS16 . . . . 142 F3
Gravel Cl IG7 . . . . 112 A8
Gravel Hill IG10 . . . . .66 A1
Gravel La CM1 . . . . .90 A3
Gravel Pit Farm CM19 . . . . .23 C6
Gravel Rd SS9 . . . . 146 C8
GRAVESEND 179 C2
Gravesend Sta DA11 . . . . . 179 B1
Gravesham Com Hospl
  DA11 . . . . 179 A1
Gravesham Mus*
  DA11 . . . . 179 B1
Gray Ave RM8 . . . . 134 F3
Gray Gdns RM13 . . . . 155 A6
Graylands
  Grays RM17 . . . . 177 E8
  Theydon Bois CM16 . . . . . .67 D2
GRAYS 178 A7
Grays Ave SS16 . . . . 141 C1
Grays Convent High Sch
  RM17 . . . . 173 B2
Grays Cotts RM14 . . . . 137 D7
Grays Court Hospl
  RM10 . . . . 154 B5
Grays End Cl RM17 . . . . . . 173 A3
Graysons Cl SS6 . . . . 123 E2
Grays Sch Media Arts Coll
  The RM17 . . . . 173 B3
Grays Sh Ctr RM17 . . . . . . 178 A8
Grays Sh Ctr RM17 . . . . . . 178 A8
Grays Wlk CM13 . . . . .95 D2
Great Augur St **4**
  CM17 . . . . .11 D1
GREAT BADDOW 54 E7
Great Baddow High Sch
  CM2 . . . . .54 D6
GREAT BARN 140 F4
Great Berry Farm Chase
  SS16 . . . . 141 A4
Great Berry La SS16 . . . . . 141 A5
Great Berry Prim Sch
  SS16 . . . . 140 F4
Great Brays CM18 . . . . .24 A7
Great Burches Rd
  SS7 . . . . 145 A7
GREAT BURSTEAD 119 C5
Great Cob CM1 . . . . .32 E5
Great Cullings RM7 . . . . . . 135 E2
Great Eastern Ave
  SS2 . . . . 148 A1
Great Eastern Rd
  Brentwood CM14 . . . . 116 C6
  Hockley SS5 . . . . 124 E6
Greatfields Rd IG11 . . . . . . 152 D3
Great Fleete Way
  IG11 . . . . 153 C3
Great Fox Mdw CM15 . . . . .71 F1
Great Galley Cl IG11 . . . . . 153 C2
Great Gardens Rd
  RM11 . . . . 136 F6
Great Gibcracks Chase
  CM2 . . . . .56 A2
Great Godfreys CM1 . . . . . . .30 F1
Great Gregorie SS16 . . . . . 141 F5
Great Gregories La
  CM16 . . . . .67 E6
Great Hall The **1** E11 . . . 132 B7
Great Hays SS9 . . . . 146 C5
Greathouse Chase
  SS17 . . . . 161 C5
Great Hyde Hall CM21 . . . . .2 B3
Great Knightleys
  SS15 . . . . 141 E6
Great Lawn CM5 . . . . .49 A4
Great Leighs Way
  SS13 . . . . 121 C1
Great Leylands CM18 . . . . . .24 A7
Great Mdw EN10 . . . . .21 A1
Great Mead SS13 . . . . 149 E1
Great Mistley SS16 . . . . . . 142 C5
Great Nelmes Chase
  RM11 . . . . 136 F6
Great Oaks
  Basildon SS14 . . . . 142 A6
  Brentwood CM13 . . . . .95 B3
  Chigwell IG7 . . . . 111 C6
Great Owl Rd IG7 . . . . 111 A7
GREAT OXNEY GREEN 30 E1
GREAT PARNDON 23 B6
Great Pettits Ct RM11 . . . . 113 E1
Great Plumtree CM20 . . . . .10 F2
Great Ranton SS13 . . . . . . 143 C8
Great Ropers La
  CM13 . . . . 116 B4
Great Saling SS11 . . . . 122 A6

Great Smials CM3 . . . . 101 C6
Great Spenders SS14 . . . . . 142 D8
GREAT STAMBRIDGE
  . . . . 126 D4
Great Stony Pk CM5 . . . . . . .49 A4
GREAT WAKERING 150 A4
Great Wakering Prim Sch
  SS3 . . . . 150 A3
GREAT WALTHAM 18 E7
Great Waltham CE Prim
  CM3 . . . . .18 E7
GREAT WARLEY 116 A2
Great Warley St
  CM13 . . . . 116 B1
Great Wheatley Rd
  SS6 . . . . 123 B1
Greaves Cl IG11 . . . . 152 E5
Grebe Cl
  Billericay CM12 . . . . 153 A1
  Mayland CM3 . . . . .83 A8
Grebe Crest RM20 . . . . 172 A2
Greding Wlk CM13 . . . . . . 117 B8
Greenacre La CM44 . . . . .97 E8
Greenacre Mews SS9 . . . . . 146 E2
Greenacres
  Epping CM16 . . . . .45 F3
  Hadleigh SS7 . . . . 145 E3
Greenacres Cl RM13 . . . . . 155 E2
Green Ave SS8 . . . . 163 E3
Greenbank Cl
  Chingford E4 . . . . 109 C8
  Romford RM3 . . . . 114 D7
Greenbanks
  Southend-on-S SS9 . . . . . 147 A2
  Upminster RM14 . . . . 137 E2
Green Cl
  Chelmsford CM1 . . . . .32 D4
  Epping Green CM16 . . . . . .45 B7
  Writtle CM1 . . . . .31 B1
Greendyke SS8 . . . . 163 F5
Greener Ct SS10 . . . . .65 A2
Greenfield Gdns RM9 . . . . 153 C4
Greenfield Rd RM9 . . . . . . 153 C4
Greenfields
  Billericay CM12 . . . . 119 A8
  Galleywood CM2 . . . . .54 C2
  Loughton IG10 . . . . .89 A5
Greenfields Cl
  Billericay CM12 . . . . 119 A8
  Brentwood CM13 . . . . 116 C4
  Loughton IG10 . . . . .89 A5
Greenfield St EN9 . . . . .65 C5
Green Glade CM16 . . . . .67 E2
Green Glades RM11 . . . . . . 137 A5
Greenheys Dr E18 . . . . 109 F1
Greenhill
  IG9 . . . . .88 C1
Greenhills CM20 . . . . .23 E8
GREENHITHE 177 A3
Greenhithe for Bluewater
  Sta DA9 . . . . 177 A2
Green La
  Basildon, Lee Chapel South
    SS14 . . . . 141 E4
  Basildon, Steeple View
    CM12 . . . . 119 A2
  Brentwood CM14 . . . . .94 A1
  Burnham-on-C CM0 . . . . . 106 A7
  Canvey Island SS8 . . . . . . 163 F3
  Chigwell, Grange Hill
    IG7 . . . . 111 E7
  Chigwell IG7 . . . . .89 C1
  Dagenham IG3, RM8 . . . . 134 C2
  Great Warley CM13,
    CM14 . . . . 116 A3
  Hoddesdon EN10 . . . . .43 B8
  Ilford IG1, IG3 . . . . 133 E2
  Kelvedon Hatch CM14 . . . .93 D8
  Mayland CM3 . . . . .83 B6
  Orsett RM16 . . . . 173 C8
  Pilgrims Hatch CM15 . . . . .94 C3
  Roxwell CM1 . . . . .30 A4
  Southend-on-S SS9 . . . . . 146 E7
  South Woodham Ferrers
    CM3 . . . . 101 D8
  Threshers Bush CM17 . . . .25 A6
  Waltham Abbey EN9 . . . . . .66 D4
Greenlands SS4 . . . . 125 D4
Greenleafe Dr IG6 . . . . 133 B8
Greenleas
  Thundersley SS7 . . . . 145 B6
  Waltham Abbey EN9 . . . . . .65 E5
Greenleaves Cvn Pk
  EN9 . . . . .22 A2
Green Man Ct CM20 . . . . . .10 A4
Green Mdws CM3 . . . . .57 A6
Green Mead CM3 . . . . 101 C8
Greenoaks SS7 . . . . 144 E3
Greenock Way RM1 . . . . . . 113 C3
Green Pk CM20 . . . . .23 E8
Green Rd SS7 . . . . 144 D1
Greens Cl The IG10 . . . . . . .89 A7
Greens Farm La CM11 . . . . .97 C1
Greenshaw CM15 . . . . .94 B2
Greenside RM8 . . . . 134 C3
Greenslade Rd IG11 . . . . . . 152 D5
Greensleeves Dr
  CM14 . . . . 116 B5
Green St
  2 Harlow CM17 . . . . . . .11 D1
  Ingatestone CM4 . . . . .73 C4
Greenstead Ct 21 E1
Greenstead Ave IG8 . . . . . 110 C4
Greenstead Cl
  Brentwood CM13 . . . . .95 E2
  Woodford IG8 . . . . 110 C4
Greenstead Gdns IG8 . . . . 110 C4
Greenstead Jun & Inf Schs
  SS14 . . . . 142 F6

Greenstead Rd CM5 . . . . . . .48 F2
GREENSTED 48 D2
Greensted Cl SS14 . . . . 142 F5
GREENSTED GREEN 48 B3
Greensted Log Church*
  CM5 . . . . .48 D2
Greensted Rd
  Chipping Ongar CM5 . . . . . .48 D2
  Loughton IG10 . . . . .88 F2
Greensted The SS14 . . . . . 142 F5
Greenstone Mews
  E11 . . . . 132 A5
GREEN STREET 73 D4
Greensward Coll The
  SS5 . . . . 124 F7
Greensward La SS5 . . . . . . 124 F7
Green The
  Blackmore CM4 . . . . .72 E8
  Buckhurst Hill IG9 . . . . . . .88 B1
  Chelmsford CM1 . . . . .31 F4
  Chingford E4 . . . . .87 D1
  Orsett RM16 . . . . 174 A8
  Romford RM3 . . . . 114 C7
  Southend-on-S SS9 . . . . . 146 C7
  South Ockendon RM15 . . 157 D2
  Stanford-le-H SS17 . . . . . 160 D1
  Theydon Bois CM16 . . . . . .67 D3
  Theydon Bois CM16 . . . . . .67 E2
  Waltham Abbey EN9 . . . . . .65 C5
  Wanstead E11 . . . . 132 B5
  West Tilbury RM18 . . . . . 179 D8
  Woodford IG8 . . . . 110 A5
  Writtle CM1 . . . . .31 B1
Green Trees CM16 . . . . .68 A8
Green Trees Ave CM3 . . . . . .80 F5
Greenview SS8 . . . . 163 F5
Green View CM16 . . . . .67 E2
Greenway
  Billericay CM11 . . . . .97 D2
  Brentwood CM13 . . . . .95 A2
  Dagenham RM8 . . . . 134 C3
  Harlow CM19 . . . . .22 E8
  Romford RM3 . . . . 115 B4
  Woodford IG8 . . . . 110 C5
Greenway Bsns Ctr
  CM19 . . . . .22 E8
Greenway Ct IG1 . . . . 133 B3
Greenways
  Canvey Island SS8 . . . . . . 163 F5
  Chelmsford CM1 . . . . .32 B6
  Maldon CM9 . . . . .36 E4
  Rochford SS4 . . . . 125 F2
  South Benfleet SS7 . . . . . 144 C2
  Southend-on-S SS1 . . . . . 167 C7
Greenways Ct RM11 . . . . . . 136 F7
Greenway The SS11 . . . . . . .99 C3
Greenwich Way EN9 . . . . . .65 C3
Green Wlk
  Chipping Ongar CM5 . . . . . .49 A1
  Woodford IG8 . . . . 110 E4
Green Wlk The E4 . . . . .87 D1
GREENWOOD 110 A3
Greenwood Ave
  South Benfleet SS7 . . . . . 144 E1
Greenwood Dr E4 . . . . 109 D5
Greenwood Gdns IG6 . . . . 111 C3
Greenwood Ho RM17 . . . . 178 B8
Greenwood Mans **9**
  IG11 . . . . 153 A5
Greenwood Rd IG7 . . . . . . 112 B6
Greenyard EN9 . . . . .65 C6
Gregory Cl SS5 . . . . 124 F4
Gregory Mews EN9 . . . . . . .65 B7
Gregory Rd RM6 . . . . 134 D7
Grenfell Ave RM12 . . . . . . 135 F3
Grenfell Gdns IG2 . . . . 133 F6
Grennan Cl CM13 . . . . 117 A8
Grenville Gdns IG8 . . . . . . 110 C3
Grenville Rd RM16 . . . . . . 172 B1
Gresham Cl **6** CM14 . . . . 116 C7
Gresham Dr RM6 . . . . 134 B5
Gresham Rd CM14 . . . . 116 C7
Gretsit Ct SS4 . . . . 125 D2
Grevatt Lo SS13 . . . . 143 C5
Greyfriars CM13 . . . . .95 B2
Greygoose Pk CM19 . . . . . .23 A5
Greyhound La RM16 . . . . . 174 A4
Greyhound Pk SS2 . . . . 148 A1
Greyhound Way SS2 . . . . . 148 A1
Grey Lady Pl CM11 . . . . . . .97 B3
Grey Ladys CM2 . . . . .54 B2
Greystone Gdns IG6 . . . . . 111 C3
Grey Towers Ave
  RM11 . . . . 136 D3
Grey Towers Gdns
  RM11 . . . . 136 C3
Gridiron Pl RM14 . . . . 137 B2
Griffin Ave
  Canvey Island SS8 . . . . . . 164 C5
  Upminster RM14 . . . . 137 E5
Griffins The RM16 . . . . 173 B4
Griffin's Wood Cotts
  CM16 . . . . .67 D7
Griffin Wlk DA9 . . . . 176 F2
Griffin Cl CM8 . . . . 134 E2
Grifon Cl RM16 . . . . 172 C3
Grifon Rd RM16 . . . . 172 C3
Griggs App IG1 . . . . 133 C2
Griggs Gdns RM12 . . . . . . 155 C2
Grimshaw Way RM1 . . . . . 135 F6
Grimstone Cl RM5 . . . . 113 B4
Grimston Rd SS14 . . . . 142 F8
Grinstead La CM22 . . . . .2 C6
Grosvenor Cl
  Chelmsford CM2 . . . . .54 D7

Grosvenor Cl *continued*
  Loughton IG10 . . . .
Grosvenor Ct
  Southend-on-S SS0 . . . .
  8 Wanstead E11 . . . .
Grosvenor Dr
  Hornchurch RM11 . . . .
  Loughton IG10 . . . .
Grosvenor Gdns
  Billericay CM12 . . . .
  Upminster RM14 . . . .
  Woodford IG8 . . . .
Grosvenor Hts E4 . . . .
Grosvenor Lo **4** E18 . . . .
Grosvenor Mans SS0 . . . .
Grosvenor Mews SS0 . . . .
Grosvenor Path SS0 . . . .
Grosvenor Rd
  Dagenham RM8 . . . .
  Ilford IG1 . . . .
  Orsett RM16 . . . .
  Rayleigh SS6 . . . .
  Romford RM7 . . . .
  South Benfleet SS7 . . . .
  Southend-on-S SS0 . . . .
  Wanstead E11 . . . .
Grove Ave SS16 . . . .
Grove Cl SS6 . . . .
Grove Cotts IG7 . . . .
Grove Cres IG7 . . . .
Grove Ct
  Hornchurch RM11 . . . .
  Rayleigh SS6 . . . .
  Southend-on-S SS0 . . . .
  Upminster RM14 . . . .
Grove End E18 . . . .
Grove Gdns RM10 . . . .
Grove Hill
  Southend-on-S SS9 . . . .
  Woodford E18 . . . .
Grove Ho CM14 . . . .
Grove La
  Chigwell IG7 . . . .
  Epping CM16 . . . .
Grovelands SS12 . . . .
Grovelands Rd SS12 . . . .
Grovelands Way
  RM17 . . . .
Grove Lo SS3 . . . .
Grove Park Ave E4 . . . .
Grove Park Rd RM13 . . . .
Grove Pk E11 . . . .
Grove Prim Sch E4 . . . .
Grove Rd
  Billericay CM12 . . . .
  Canvey Island SS8 . . . .
  Chelmsford CM2 . . . .
  Chingford E4 . . . .
  Grays RM17 . . . .
  Ilford RM6 . . . .
  Northfleet RM17 . . . .
  Rayleigh SS6 . . . .
  South Benfleet SS7 . . . .
  Stanford-le-H SS17 . . . .
  Woodford E18 . . . .
Grover Wlk SS17 . . . .
Groves Cl RM15 . . . .
Groveside Rd E4 . . . .
Grove Terr SS1 . . . .
Grove The
  Bicknacre CM3 . . . .
  Billericay CM11 . . . .
  Brentwood CM14 . . . .
  3 Gravesend DA12 . . . .
  Southend-on-S SS2 . . . .
  Stanford-le-H SS17 . . . .
  Swanscombe DA10 . . . .
  Upminster RM14 . . . .
Groveway RM8 . . . .
Grove Wlk SS3 . . . .
Growewood Ave SS9 . . . .
Growewood Cl SS9 . . . .
Growewood Pl IG8 . . . .
Grove Wood Prim Sch
  SS6 . . . .
Guardian Bsns Ctr
  RM3 . . . .
Guardian Ct RM11 . . . .
Guardsman CM14 . . . .
Gubbins La RM3 . . . .
Guernsey Cl CM9 . . . .
Guernsey Gdns SS11 . . . .
Guildford Ct SS2 . . . .
Guildford Gdns RM3 . . . .
Guildford Rd
  Chingford E17 . . . .
  Ilford IG3 . . . .
  Romford RM3 . . . .
Guild Way **3** CM3 . . . .
Guilford Lo **5** CM14 . . . .
Guilfords CM17 . . . .
Gull Wlk RM12 . . . .
Gumley Rd RM20 . . . .
Gunfleet SS3 . . . .
Gun Hill Pl SS16 . . . .
Gunnels Ct & Hasting
  Ct **8** IG9 . . . .
Gunner Dr EN3 . . . .
Gunners Gr E4 . . . .
Gunners Rd SS3 . . . .
Gunners View SS3 . . . .
Gunn Rd DA10 . . . .
Gunpowder Pk* EN9 . . . .
Gunson Gate CM2 . . . .

I IG11 ....152 B6
ind Singh Khalsa 88 F1
ll La SS5 ....124 E3
e La RM4 ....91 C3
a CM1 ....32 C7
CM1 ....31 B1
n Rd CM3 ....101 D7
CI RM13 ....155 A4
RM3 ....155 A4
reat IG9 ....88 C2
en Ave SS8 ....164 E4
M3 ....20 E1
o E CI21 ....132 A6
Park Ave IG8 ....110 F4
ne Gdns 133 F1

Rd SS8 ....163 D4
SS8 ....164 D3
SS8 ....164 A6
Rd IG10 ....88 E6
ks CM3 ....57 E2
on CM3 ....80 B6
r RM12 ....155 D3
r RM14 ....155 F8
ar RM12 ....136 F1
rn Sch 155 E8
I SS6 ....123 A4
Mead CM3 ....101 D5
Rd SS17 ....160 D1
.........................145 E3
Bsns Ctr 145 E2
Castle* 145 B1
Castle Grn Pk* 145 B1
Ct CM14.............116 A7
Ed 87 E2
Hall Ct SS9 ......146 C1
nf Sch SS7 ....145 E3
Jun Sch 145 E3
Lo E IG8 ....110 A4
Park Ave 145 C3
rd
on-S SS9 ....146 C1
on-S, Westcliff-on- 166 E7
grange CM17.....24 C7
Way CM9 ....37 A4
CM3 ....80 D5
M2 ....32 A1
M16 ....174 A3
Gdns IG6 ....133 B7
e EN11 ....8 A2
SG13 ....8 A2
DA18 ....169 A4
d Bsns Pk
CI RM3 ....114 A5
Gdns RM3 ....114 C5
Rd RM3 ....114 C5
.........................111 F3
ave
SS4 ....125 D4
on-S SS0 ....147 D2
ridge Par E 133 B2
I SS7 ....145 E4
orest Ctry Pk* 112 C7
orest High Sch 112 B5
ore RM6 ....134 E6
r
d CM1 ....31 E1
G7 ....111 C6
d
G7 ....111 C6
RM6 ....134 F5
.........................134 B8
bridge CM3 ....81 A1
RM6 ....112 B2
M5 ....135 C8
t IG1 ....133 B2
e IG12 ....111 E3
Ins RM9 ....134 F1
RM9 ....153 F7
n Pk SS5 ....101 F4
Vay RM11 ....136 F3
I EN3 ....65 B1
e E4 ....109 C4
E IG7 ....111 E5
............................109 C7
DA9 ....177 C2
M3 ....109 D4
RM3 ....114 B4
Rd E17 ....109 D2
M11 ....136 A5
CI CM14 ....113 A3
n Rd RM3 ....114 E4
............................109 D3
E E18 ....132 A8

Half Moon La CM16......67 F8
Halfway Ct RM19 ......171 A2
Haidon Rise RM3 ......115 B4
Halifax Ho E RM3 ....114 C5
Hallam CI CM15 ....72 B3
Hallam Ct CM12 ....96 F4
Hall Ave RM15 ....171 C5
Hall Barns The CM5.....70 C6
Hall Bridge Rise CM9....37 C4
Hall CI
  Great Baddow CM2 ....55 A6
  Stanford-le-H SS17 .....160 E4
Hall Cotts CM3 ....100 B6
Hall Cres
  Aveley RM15 ....171 C4
  Hadleigh SS7 ....145 D3
Hall Est SS9 ....38 E7
Hallet Rd SS8 ....164 E3
Halley Rd RM9 ....65 B3
Hall Farm CI SS7 ......144 D1
Hall Farm Rd SS7 .....144 D1
Hall Green La CM13......95 D2
Hallingbury Rd CM21....2 A4
Halling Hill CM20 ....10 F2
Hall La
  Brentwood CM15 ....95 A4
  Chelmsford CM2 ....55 C6
  Ingatestone CM4 ....74 C1
  Romford RM14 ....115 C1
  Shenfield CM15 ....94 F4
  Shenfield CM15 ....94 F6
  South Ockendon RM15 ..137 D5
  Upminster RM14 ....137 D5
  West Hanningfield CM2..76 D6
Hall Mead Sch RM14....137 D3
Hallmores EN10 ....21 A4
Hallowell Down CM3....101 E6
Hall Park Ave SS0 ......166 B8
Hall Park Rd RM14 .....156 C7
Hall Rd
  Ashledham CM0...........85 C7
  Aveley RM15 ....171 C4
  Hockley SS5 ....125 A2
  Ilford RM6 ....134 D5
  Maldon CM0.................37 B4
  Rochford SS4 ....125 D1
  Romford RM2 ....136 B8
  Southminster CM0.........84 E4
Hall Road Ind Est CM0..84 E4
Hallsford Bridge Ind Est
  CM5 ....71 C8
HALLS GREEN 22 C5
Hall St CM2 ....32 B1
Hall Terr
  Aveley RM15 ....171 A4
  Romford RM3 ....115 A3
Hallwood Cres CM15.....94 E3
Halsham Cres CM11....152 F7
Halstead St E SS12 ....121 C5
Halstead Ho E RM3 ....114 D4
Halstead Rd RM11 .....132 B6
Halstead Way CM13....155 A1
Halston Ct SS17 ....161 B3
Halston PI CM9 ....58 F8
Halstow Way SS13 .....143 C5
Halt Dr SS17 ....175 B2
Halton Rd RM14 ....174 C3
Halt Robin La DA17 ....169 B2
Halt Robin Rd DA17 ....169 B2
Haltwhistle Rd CM3 ....101 C8
Halyard Reach CM3 ....101 C5
Hamberts Rd CM3 ....79 E1
Hamble La RM15 ....171 F8
Hamble Way CM0 ....106 A6
Hamboro Gdns SS9 ....146 B1
Hamboro Ave SS6 ......146 B1
Hambro CI SS6 ....123 E4
Hambro Hill SS6 ....123 E4
Hambro Rd RM10 ......135 B1
Hamerton Rd DA11 ....178 B2
Hameway E E4 ....152 A1
Hamilton Ave
  Hoddesdon EN11..........21 A8
  Ilford IG6 ....133 C6
  Romford RM1 ....113 D1
Hamilton Cres CM14 ...116 C6
Hamilton Ct
  Althorne CM3..............82 F4
  E Burnham-on-C CM0..106 C4
  Chelmsford CM1..........31 D6
Hamilton Dr RM3 ....114 E1
Hamilton Gdns SS5 ....124 E7
Hamilton Grange SS0..166 C7
Hamilton Mews SS6 ...123 F3
Hamilton Rd
  Ilford IG1 ....152 B8
  Romford RM2 ....136 B6
Hamlet CI RM5 ....113 A3
Hamlet Court Mews 147 E1
Hamlet Court Rd SS0..166 E8
Hamlet La CM14 ....115 C6
Hamlet Hill CM19 ....22 B4
Hamlet International Ind
  Est DA8..................169 D1
Hamleton Terr RM9 ....153 C5
Hamlet Rd
  Chelmsford CM2 ....32 B1
  Romford RM5 ....113 A3
  Southend-on-S SS1....166 F7
Hamley Ct SS7 ....144 B6
Hammarskjold Rd
  CM20 ....10 D2
Hammond Ct RM12 .....135 F3
Hammonds CI RM8 .....134 C1

Hammonds La
  Billericay CM11 ....119 C7
  Brentwood CM13 ....116 B4
Hammonds Rd
  Hatfield Broad Oak
    CM22 ....4 A6
  Little Baddow CM3 ....33 E3
Hampden CI CM16 ....47 A4
Hampden Cres CM14 ...116 C5
Hampden Rd
  Grays RM17 ....173 B1
  Romford RM5 ....113 B3
Hampshire Gdns
  SS17 ....175 A4
Hampshire Rd RM11 ...137 A7
Hampshire Villas SS2...158 F4
Hampstead Ave E
  IG8 ....111 A3
Hampstead Gdns
  Hockley SS5 ....124 F7
  Ilford RM6 ....134 B6
Hampton CI
  Grays RM17 ....172 C3
  Southend-on-S SS2 ....147 E4
Hampton Ct
  Hockley SS5 ....124 D6
  Southend-on-S, Chalkwell
    SS9 ....165 F8
  Southend-on-S SS9 ....146 E1
Hampton Gdns
  Sawbridgeworth CM21 ...11 C7
  Southend-on-S SS2 ....147 E4
Hampton Mead IG10.....89 B6
Hampton Rd
  Chingford E4 ....109 A5
  Great Baddow CM2 ....54 E6
  Ilford IG1 ....152 C8
Hamstel Inf Sch SS2 ...148 D2
Hamstel Jun Sch SS2...148 D2
Hamstel Mews SS2 .....148 D1
Hamstel Rd
  Harlow CM20................10 C1
  Southend-on-S SS2 ....148 D2
Hanbury Rd CM1 ....53 E8
Handel Cres RM18 ......179 B7
Handel Rd SS8 ....164 D2
Handforth Rd E IG1 ....133 B1
Hand La CM21...............1 C1
HANDLEY GREEN 74 D8
Handleys Chase SS15..119 F2
Handleys Ct SS15 ......119 F2
Handsworth Ave E4....109 D4
Handsworth Prim Sch
  E4 ....109 D4
Handtrough Way
  IG11 ....152 B3
Hanford Rd RM15 ......171 C5
Hanging Hill La CM13..117 B8
Hanging Hill La CM13..117 B8
Hanlee Brook CM3 ....54 F6
Hannah CI SS8 ....164 A6
Hannards Way IG6......112 B5
Hannett Rd SS8 ....164 E3
Hanningfield CI SS6 ...123 A3
Hanningfield Nature
  Reserve* CM11...........99 A7
Hanningfield Nature
  Trail* CM3.................99 B8
Hanningfield Reservoir
  Visitor Ctr* CM3.........98 F7
Hanover CI SS14.........142 E5
Hanover Ct
  Hoddesdon EN11..........21 A7
  Rayleigh SS6 ....123 D3
  Sawbridgeworth CM21 ....1 F1
  Waltham Abbey EN9 ......65 C6
Hanover Dr SS14 ....142 E6
Hanover Gdns IG6......111 C3
Hanover Mews SS5 ....124 D6
Hanover PI CM14 ....116 B5
Hansells Mead CM19....22 B8
Hanson CI IG10............89 C7
Hanson Dr IG10 ....89 C7
Hanson Gn IG10 ....89 C7
Harberts Rd RM9 ....23 B8
Harberts Way SS9 .....123 C5
Harbourer CI IG6 ....112 B5
Harbourer Rd IG6 ......112 B5
Harcourt Ave SS2 ......147 F1
Harcourt Ho E E4 ....109 D5
Harcourt Mews E
  RM2 ....135 F6
Hard Ct IG8 ....110 C4
Hardie Rd
  Dagenham RM10 ....135 C1
  Stanford-le-H SS17 ....160 D2
Harding Ho CM16..........68 A8
Harding Rd RM16.......174 A3
Harding's Elms Rd
  CM11 ....120 B4
Harding's La CM4..........74 A7
Hardings Reach E
  CM0 ....106 C4
Hardley Cres RM11 .....136 D7
Hardwick CI SS4.........123 D1
Hardwick Cres E
  DA2 ....176 B1
Hardwick Ct
  Southend-on-S SS2 ....147 E3
  E Wanstead E11 ....132 A5
Hardwick St IG11........152 C5
Hardwicke Rd SS6......123 E1
Hardy's SS3 ....168 D5
Hardy Ct E IG11 ....132 A7
Hardy Gr DA1 ....176 A3
Hardy Rd SS14 ....142 E4
Hardys Way SS8 ....164 A6
Harebell CI CM12 ....96 F4

Harebell Way RM3 .....114 D3
Hare Bridge Cres CM4...74 A2
Harefield CM20.............11 A1
Hare Hall La RM2.......136 B7
Hares Chase CM12 ....96 F3
Haresfield Rd RM10....154 A6
Haresland CI SS7 ....145 F6
Hare St
  Harlow CM19...............23 B8
  Stanford Rivers CM5 ....70 E5
HARE STREET 23 B7
Hare Street Com Prim Sch
  CM19 ....23 C8
Hare Street Springs
  CM19 ....23 B8
Hare Terr RM20 ....172 D1
Harewood Ave SS4 .....125 D5
Harewood Dr IG5.........110 F1
Harewood Rd CM16.......67 E4
Harewood Rd
  Chelmsford CM1 ....31 E1
  Pilgrims Hatch CM15.....94 B3
Harford CI E4 ....87 B2
Harford Rd E4 ....87 B2
Harfred Ave CM9 ....37 E3
Harkness CI RM3........114 F5
HARKNETT'S GATE 22 E2
Harlech Rd E SS13 .....143 B5
Harlequin Stps E
  SS1 ....167 C2
Harlesden CI RM3 ......114 F4
Harlesden Rd RM3 .....114 F4
Harlesden Wlk RM3....114 F3
Harley CI E11 ....132 A4
Harley St SS9 ....146 C1
Harlings Gr CM1 ....32 C3
HARLOW 11 C2
Harlow Bsns Pk CM19..22 E8
Harlowbury Prim Sch
  CM17 ....11 D4
Harlow Coll CM20 ....10 D1
Harlow Comm CM17 .....24 D6
Harlow Fields Sch
  CM18 ....23 E6
Harlow Gdns RM5 ......113 C4
Harlow Mans E RM1...152 B5
Harlow Mill Sta CM20...11 C5
Harlow Rd
  Moreton CM5..............26 C3
  Rainham RM13 ....154 F4
  Roydon CM19...............9 C1
  Sawbridgeworth CM21 ...11 C8
  Sheering CM22, CM17....12 B8
  Sheering, Matching Tye
    CM22 ....12 C7
Harlow Ret Pk CM20.....10 F4
Harlow Seedbed Ctr
  CM19 ....23 A7
Harlow Stad (Greyhounds)
  CM19 ....9 E1
Harlow Town Sta
  CM20 ....10 D3
HARLOW TYE 12 B3
Harlton Ct EN9.............65 F5
Harman Ave IG8.........109 F4
Harman CI E4 ....109 D6
Harmer Rd DA10........177 F1
Harmer Rd DA10........177 F1
Harmer St DA12 ....179 C1
Harness CI CM1 ....22 F7
Harold CI CM19 ....22 F7
Harold Court Prim Sch
  RM3 ....115 A3
Harold Court Rd RM3..115 B3
Harold Cres EN9...........65 C7
Harold Ct RM3 ....115 B3
Harold Gdns SS9 ....99 E1
HAROLD HILL 114 E5
HAROLD PARK 115 B3
Harold Rd
  Chingford E4 ....109 C7
  Woodford IG8 ....110 A2
Harold Rise CM9 ....36 F5
Harolds Rd CM19 ....22 F7
Harold View RM11 ......114 F1
HAROLD WOOD 114 F2
Harold Wood Hall
  RM3 ....114 D2
Harold Wood Hospl
  RM3 ....114 E2
Harold Wood Prim Sch
  RM3 ....137 A8
Harold Wood Sta
  RM3 ....114 F2
Haron CI SS8 ....164 B3
Harpenden Rd E12 .....132 C2
Harper CI RM16 ....172 C1
Harper La CM15 ....72 D2
Harper Way SS6 ....123 C3
Harpour Rd IG11 ....152 C6
Harrap Chase RM17....172 F1
Harridge CI SS9 ....146 E3
Harridge Rd SS9 ....146 E3
Harrier Ave E11 ....132 B5
Harrier CI
  Hornchurch RM12 ......155 B6
  Southend-on-S SS3 ....149 E1
Harrier Way EN9 ....66 A5
Harriescourt EN9 ....66 A7
Harrington Cres
  RM16 ....172 D5
Harris CI
  Corringham SS17.......161 B4
  Romford RM3 ....114 E3
  Wickford SS12...........121 F5
Harris Ct SS5 ....124 C5
Harrison CI CM13.........95 D4
Harrison Ct CM1..........31 F3

Harrison Dr CM16 ....47 B5
Harrison Gdns SS5 .....101 D2
Harrison Rd
  Dagenham RM10 ....154 B6
  Waltham Abbey EN9 .....65 C4
Harrisons Wharf
  RM19 ....171 A1
Harris Rd RM9...........153 F7
Harrods Ct RM11 ....97 E2
Harrogate Dr SS5 ......124 F8
Harrogate Rd SS5 .....124 F7
Harrold Rd RM8 ....153 B7
Harrowbond Rd E
  CM17 ....11 C1
Harrow CI
  Hockley SS5 ....125 A5
  E Hornchurch RM11...136 B3
Harrow Cres RM3 ....114 B2
Harrow Dr RM11.........136 C4
Harrow Gdns SS5 ......125 A5
Harrow La RM14 ....158 C6
Harrow Lo RM11 ....136 C3
Harrow Rd
  Barking IG11 ....152 E4
  Basildon SS12 ....122 A2
  Bulphan RM14 ....158 C7
  Canvey Island SS8 ......164 B5
  Ilford IG1 ....152 C8
  North Benfleet SS12 ...121 F2
Harrow Way CM2 ....55 A6
Harston Dr EN3............65 A1
Hart CI SS7 ....145 A6
Hart Cnr RM20 ....177 D1
Hart Cres E4 ....111 F5
Hart Ct E12 ....152 A5
Hartford CI SS6..........123 B4
Hartford End SS13 .....143 A5
Hartington Ct SS1 ......167 B7
Hartington PI SS1 ......167 B7
Hartington Rd SS1 .....167 B7
Hartland CI SS7 ....146 D7
Hartland Rd
  Epping CM16 ....46 A1
  Hornchurch RM12 ......136 A2
Hartley CI CM4 ....33 A4
Hart Rd
  Harlow CM17 ....11 C6
  Thundersley SS7 ....145 A3
Harts Gr IG8 ....110 A5
Hartshorn Gdns E6 ....152 A1
Harts La IG11 ....152 B6
Hart St
  Brentwood CM14 ....116 C8
  Chelmsford CM2 ....32 A1
Hartswood CI CM14 ...116 E6
Hartswood Rd CM14 ...116 C5
Hartwell Dr E4 ....109 C4
Harty CI RM16 ....172 B5
Harvard Ct SS6 ....123 B4
Harvard Wlk RM12 .....155 A8
Harvest CI CM3..........101 D7
Harvest Rd SS8 ....164 B5
Harvest Way CM9.........58 B8
Harvey RM12..............173 B4
Harvey CI SS13 ....121 B1
Harvey Ctr CM20..........23 D8
Harveyfields EN9 ....65 C5
Harvey Gdns IG10 ....89 B6
Harvey Ho
  E Barking IG11 ....152 C5
  Ilford RM6 ....134 D7
Harvey Rd
  Basildon SS13 ....121 C3
  Ilford IG1 ....152 B7
Harvey's La RM7.........135 C2
Harwater Dr IG10 ....88 F7
Harwood Ave RM11 ....136 E8
Harwood CI E RM17....178 C8
Harwood Hall La
  RM14 ....156 B6
Haselfoot Rd CM3 ....33 F8
Haskard Rd RM9 ....153 F7
Haskins SS17.............160 F2
Haslemere Est The
  EN11 ....21 D6
Haslemere Pinnacles Est
  The CM19................23 A7
Haslemere Rd
  Ilford IG1 ....133 C2
  Wickford SS12...........99 C2
Haslers Ct CM4..........74 C4
Haslewood Ave EN11....21 A6
Haslingden Ho E
  RM3 ....114 C5
Hassell Rd SS8 ....164 D3
Hassenbrook Ct SS17..160 E1
Hassenbrook Ho
  SS17.....................160 D1
Hassenbrook Rd
  SS17.....................160 E1
Hassenbrook Sch
  SS17.....................160 E2
Hasted CI DA9...........177 C1
Hastings Ave IG6 ....133 C7
Hastings CI RM17.......177 E8
Hastings Rd
  Romford RM2 ....136 B6
  Southend-on-S SS1 ....167 B8
Hastings The SS1 ....99 E1
Hastingswood Bsns Ctr
  CM17 ....25 A5
HASTINGWOOD 24 F4

Hastingwood Ct
 Chipping Ongar CM5 . . . . .48 F5
 Ilford IG2 . . . . .133 D5
Hastingwood Rd CM17 . . .24 E4
Hatches Farm Rd
 CM12 . . . . .118 D5
Hatchfields CM3 . . . . .18 F7
Hatch Gn CM22 . . . . .2 B8
Hatch Gr RM6 . . . . .134 E7
Hatch La E4 . . . . .109 E7
Hatch Rd CM15 . . . . .94 B4
Hatch Side IG7 . . . . .111 A5
Hatchwoods IG8 . . . . .109 F6
HATFIELD BROAD OAK . . .3 F5
Hatfield Cl
 Brentwood CM13 . . . . .95 D2
 Hornchurch RM12 . . . . .155 D7
 Ilford IG6 . . . . .133 B8
 Redbridge IG6 . . . . .111 B1
Hatfield Gr CM11 . . . . .97 D2
Hatfield Gr CM3 . . . . .31 D1
HATFIELD HEATH 3 B3
Hatfield Heath Com Prim
 Sch CM22 . . . . .3 A3
Hatfield Ho SS4 . . . . .125 F2
Hatfield Lo IG6 . . . . .133 B8
Hatfield Mews RM9 . . . . . .153 C5
Hatfield Rd
 Dagenham RM9 . . . . .153 E5
 Grays RM16 . . . . .172 D1
 Langford CM9 . . . . .36 D7
 Rayleigh SS6 . . . . .123 B3
Hatfields IG10 . . . . .89 B6
Hathaway Cl IG6 . . . . .111 B4
Hathaway Cres E12 . . . . . . .152 A6
Hathaway Gdns
 Grays RM17 . . . . .173 A3
 Ilford RM6 . . . . .134 D6
Hathaway Rd RM17 . . . . . . .173 A2
Hatherleigh Way
 RM3 .114 D2
Hatherley The SS14 . . . . . .142 D7
Hatley Ave IG6 . . . . .133 C7
Hatley Gdns SS7 . . . . .144 C5
Hatterill SS15 . . . . .141 D5
Hatton Cl RM16 . . . . .172 C3
Hatton Mews DA9 . . . . .177 C3
Hatton Sch IG8 . . . . .132 D8
Havalon Cl SS14 . . . . .142 D7
Havana Cl RM1 . . . . .135 E6
Havana Dr SS6 . . . . .123 B7
Havant Ho B RM1 . . . . .114 E3
Havelock Ho B E4 . . . . .109 D5
Havelock St IG1 . . . . .133 B2
Haven Cl
 Basildon SS16 . . . . .142 E3
 Canvey Island SS8 . . . . .163 E3
 Hadleigh SS7 . . . . .145 D3
Havencourt CM1 . . . . .32 B3
Havengore
 Basildon SS13 . . . . .143 C8
 Chelmsford CM1 . . . . .32 F5
Havengore Cl SS3 . . . . .150 C3
Havengore Ho SS9 . . . . . . .146 F5
Haven Pl RM16 . . . . .173 C4
Haven Quays SS8 . . . . .163 C1
Haven Rd SS8 . . . . .163 D2
Haven Rise CM11 . . . . .119 D6
Havenside SS3 . . . . .149 E5
Haven The RM6 . . . . .173 F2
Havenwood Cl CM13 . . . . .116 C4
Haverhill Rd E4 . . . . .87 C1
HAVERING-ATTE-BOWER
 . . . . .113 E7
Havering Cl SS13 . . . . .150 B4
Havering Coll, Ardleigh
 Green Campus
 RM11 . . . . .136 E7
Havering Coll of F & H Ed
 RM3 .114 E6
Havering Ctry Pk* . . . .
 RM4 .113 C6
Havering Dr RM1 . . . . .135 E8
Havering Gdns RM6 . . . . . .134 D6
Havering Music Sch . . . .
 RM11 . . . . .136 F2
Havering Rd RM1 . . . . .113 D3
HAVERING'S GROVE . .96 B2
Havering Sixth Form Coll . . . .
 RM11 . . . . .136 F3
Havering Way SS13 . . . . . .153 B2
Haverstock Pl B RM2 . .136 B6
Havis Rd SS17 . . . . .160 E4
Haward Rd E17 . . . . .21 C8
Hawbush Gn SS13 . . . . . . .121 B1
Hawes La E4 . . . . .65 C1
Hawfinch Wlk CM2 . . . . . . .54 B5
Hawk Cl EN9 . . . . .66 A5
Hawk Cnr RM20 . . . . .172 D1
Hawkdene E4 . . . . .87 C3
Hawkenbury CM19 . . . . .23 B6
Hawkesbury Bush La . . . .
 SS16 . . . . .142 B2
Hawkesbury Cl
 Canvey Island SS8 . . . . .163 F2
 Redbridge IG2 . . . . .133 B8
Hawkesbury Rd SS8 . . . . .163 E2
Hawkes Cl RM17 . . . . .178 B8
Hawk Hill SS11 . . . . .100 D2
Hawkhurst Cl CM1 . . . . .31 E2
Hawkhurst Rd SS5 . . . . . . .113 D4
Hawkinge Way RM12 . . . . .155 C6
Hawkins SS3 . . . . .168 D5

Hawkins Cl
 Cock Clarks CM3 . . . . .57 E2
 Wickford SS11 . . . . .121 F7
Hawkins Dr RM16 . . . . .172 D4
Hawk La SS11 . . . . .100 D2
Hawkley Ct B CM12 . . . . .97 B2
Hawkridge SS3 . . . . .168 C8
Hawkridge Cl RM6 . . . . . . .134 C5
Hawkridge Dr RM17 . . . . . .173 D1
Hawks Cl CM3 . . . . .57 A6
Hawks Hill CM3 . . . . .47 A4
Hawks La SS5 . . . . .124 E5
Hawksmoor Gn CM13 . . . . .95 D4
Hawksmouth E4 . . . . .87 C2
Hawksway SS16 . . . . .142 B4
Hawkswood Rd CM11, ...
 SS11 .99 A6
Hawk Terr IG5 . . . . .133 A8
HAWKWELL 125 A4
Hawkwell Chase SS5 . . . . .124 E4
Hawkwell Ct E4 . . . . .109 C7
Hawkwell Ho B RM8 . . . .135 A2
Hawkwell Park Dr
 SS5 .124 F5
Hawkwell Rd SS5 . . . . .124 F6
Hawkwood Cl CM3 . . . . . . .79 E1
Hawkwood Cres E4 . . . . . . .87 B3
Hawsted IG9 . . . . .88 B2
Hawthorn Ave
 Brentwood CM13 . . . . .116 F6
 Rainham RM13 . . . . .155 B1
Hawthorn Cl
 Chelmsford CM2 . . . . .54 C6
 Hockley SS5 . . . . .124 F5
Hawthorn Ct IG5 . . . . .132 F8
Hawthorne Ct E4 . . . . .109 B4
Hawthorne Gdns SS5 . . . .124 B6
Hawthorne Rd SS17 . . . . .160 F4
Hawthornes CM3 . . . . .58 D1
Hawthorn Pl DA8 . . . . .169 C1
Hawthorn Rd
 Canvey Island SS8 . . . . .164 C3
 Hoddesdon EN11 . . . . .21 B8
 Woodford IG9 . . . . .110 D6
Hawthorns
 Harlow CM18 . . . . .23 F4
 South Benfleet SS7 . . . . . . .144 C4
 Southend-on-S SS9 . . . . . .146 E4
 Woodford IG8 . . . . .110 A7
Hawthorns The
 Burnham-on-Cr CM0 . . . . . .106 A7
 Corringham SS17 . . . . .161 C3
 Danbury CM3 . . . . .57 A7
 Hadleigh SS7 . . . . .145 B2
 Loughton IG10 . . . . .89 A5
Hawthorn Way SS6 . . . . . .123 F1
Hawthorn Wlk CM3 . . . . . . .79 E1
Hawtree Cl SS1 . . . . .167 C2
Hayburn Way RM12 . . . . . .135 F3
Hayden Rd EN9 . . . . .65 C4
Hayden Rd CM20 . . . . .23 C8
Hayden Way RM5 . . . . .113 C1
Haydock Cl RM12 . . . . .155 F8
Haydon Rd RM8 . . . . .134 C2
Hayes Barton SS1 . . . . .168 C8
Hayes Chase SS11 . . . . . . .101 A4
Hayes Cl
 Chelmsford CM2 . . . . .32 B1
 Grays RM20 . . . . .177 C8
Hayes Dr RM13 . . . . .155 B5
Hayes Farm Cvn Pk . . . .
 SS11 . . . . .101 A4
Hayes Hill Farm* EN9 . . . . .43 C3
Hayes La SS8 . . . . .163 F3
Hayes Rd DA9 . . . . .176 E1
Hay Gn
 Danbury CM3 . . . . .56 F8
 Hornchurch RM11 . . . . .137 A5
Hay Green La CM15 . . . . . . .72 E4
Hayle RM18 . . . . .175 C3
Hayley Cl RM16 . . . . .172 D3
Hayling Gr SS12 . . . . .122 A5
Haynes Park Ct RM11 . . . .136 C6
Haynes Rd RM11 . . . . .136 D6
Hayrick Cl SS16 . . . . .141 A4
Hayron's La CM1 . . . . .16 D8
Haysoms Cl RM1 . . . . .135 E7
Hayter Ct E11 . . . . .132 B2
Hay Terr RM20 . . . . .172 D1
Haywards RM15 . . . . .171 D7
Hayward Sch The CM1 . . . .32 A4
Haywards Cl
 Brentwood CM13 . . . . .95 C3
 Ilford RM6 . . . . .134 C6
Haywards Rd B CM15 .95 C3
Haywood Cl EN9 . . . . .65 F5
Hazard Ho B DA11 . . . . . . .179 A1
Hazelbrouck Gdns . . . .
 IG6 .111 D3
Hazel Cl
 Basildon SS15 . . . . .119 F2
 Hadleigh SS7 . . . . .145 F3
 Hornchurch RM12 . . . . .136 B1
 Southend-on-S SS9 . . . . . .146 C2
Hazel Ct
 B Chigwell IG6 . . . . .111 E5
 Loughton IG10 . . . . .88 F6
Hazeldene Rd IG3 . . . . .134 B2
Hazeldon Cl CM3 . . . . .19 C6
Hazel Dr RM15 . . . . .157 D2
HAZELEIGH 58 A4
Hazeleigh CM13 . . . . .117 B7
Hazeleigh Gdns IG8 . . . . . .110 E5
Hazeleigh Hall La CM3 . . . .58 C4
Hazel Gdns
 Grays RM16 . . . . .173 E3
 Sawbridgeworth CM21 . . . . .1 F1

Hazel Gr RM6 . . . . .134 E8
Hazel La IG6 . . . . .111 B3
Hazell Cres RM5 . . . . .113 B2
Hazelmere SS13 . . . . .143 B4
Hazelmere Gdns . . . .
 RM11 . . . . .136 C6
Hazel Rise RM11 . . . . .136 C5
Hazelwood
 Hockley SS5 . . . . .124 F4
 Linford SS17 . . . . .175 A2
 Loughton IG10 . . . . .88 D4
 South Benfleet SS7 . . . . . . .144 B7
Hazelwood Ct CM9 . . . . . . .37 B6
Hazelwood Gdns CM15 . . .94 A3
Hazelwood Gr SS9 . . . . . . .146 E5
Hazelwood Ho E4 . . . . .87 D2
Hazelwood Park Cl B . . . .
 IG7 .111 E5
Hazlemere Rd SS7 . . . . . . .144 D6
Headcorn Cl SS13 . . . . . . .143 C5
Headingham Ho SS6 . . . . .123 C1
Headingley Cl . . . .
 Basildon SS13 . . . . .121 A2
 Redbridge IG6 . . . . .111 F4
Headley App IG2 . . . . .133 B6
Headley Chase CM14 . . . . .116 D6
Headley Comm CM12 . . . .116 B3
Headley Dr IG2 . . . . .133 B5
Headley Rd CM11 . . . . .97 C4
Head St CM9 . . . . .38 E6
Healey Ho RM6 . . . . .134 E7
Heard's La CM15 . . . . .94 F6
Hearn Rd RM11 . . . . .135 F5
Hearsall Ave
 Chelmsford CM1 . . . . .32 B7
 Stanford-le-H SS17 . . . . . . .160 E2
Heath Cl
 Billericay CM12 . . . . .96 F1
 Romford RM2 . . . . .136 A8
Heathcote Ave IG5 . . . . . . .110 F1
Heathcote Ct IG5 . . . . .110 F1
Heathcote Gdns CM17 . . . .24 E8
Heathcote Gr E4 . . . . .109 C8
Heathcote Sch . . . .
 Chingford E4 . . . . .109 E8
 Danbury CM3 . . . . .56 E7
Heathcroft Rd SS11 . . . . . .100 F3
Heathen Dr DA17 . . . . .169 B2
Heath Dr
 Chelmsford CM2 . . . . .54 B6
 Romford RM2 . . . . .114 A1
 Theydon Bois CM16 . . . . . . .67 E4
Heather Ave RM1 . . . . .113 D1
Heather Bank CM11 . . . . . .97 C2
Heather Cl
 Canvey Island SS8 . . . . .163 F2
 Pilgrims Hatch CM15 . . . . . .94 B4
 Romford RM1 . . . . .113 D2
Heather Dr
 Romford RM1 . . . . .113 E1
 South Benfleet SS7 . . . . . . .146 A2
Heather Gdns
 Romford RM1 . . . . .113 E2
 Waltham Abbey EN9 . . . . . . .65 C3
Heather Glen RM1 . . . . . . .113 F8
Heather Way RM1 . . . . .113 D2
Heatherwood Cl E12 . .132 C2
Heathfield
 Chingford E4 . . . . .109 C7
 Rayleigh SS6 . . . . .123 D1
 Thundersley SS7 . . . . .145 C6
Heathfield Ho . . . .
 B Romford RM4 . . . . .115 A4
 Southend-on-S SS1 . . . . . .166 F7
Heathfield Park Dr . . . .
 RM6 . . . . .134 B6
Heathfield Rd CM1 . . . . .32 B7
Heathlands RM2 . . . . .136 B6
Heathleigh Dr SS16 . . . . . .141 B4
HEATH PARK 136 C5
Heath Park Rd RM2 . . . . . .136 B6
Heath Park Ind Est . . . .
 RM8 . . . . .134 E3
Heath Park Rd RM2 . . . . . .136 B6
Heath Rd
 Billericay CM11 . . . . .97 F4
 Chadwell St M RM16 . . . . .173 F5
 Dagenham RM6 . . . . .134 E4
 Grays RM16 . . . . .174 A3
 Ramsden Heath CM11 . . . . .98 B4
Heathside Cl IG2 . . . . .133 D6
Heath Terr CM3 . . . . .34 D4
Heath View Gdns . . . .
 RM16 . . . . .173 C3
Heath View Rd RM16 . . . . .173 C4
Heathway . . . .
 Dagenham RM9, ...
 RM10 . . . . .150 A4
 Woodford IG8 . . . . .110 C5
Heaton Ave RM3 . . . . .114 B3
Heaton Grange Rd . . . .
 RM2 . . . . .113 F1
Heaton Way RM3 . . . . .114 C3
Heavitree Ct E17 . . . . .109 B2
Heberden Ct B RM19 . . .171 B1
Hedgehope Ave SS10 . . . .123 D4
Hedge La SS7 . . . . .145 D4
Hedgemans Rd RM9 . . . . .153 E5
Hedgemans Way RM9 . . . .153 E6
Hedgemoor Ct B E4 . . . .109 D5
Hedge Place Rd DA9 . . . . .176 F1

Hedgerow Ct SS15 . . . . . .119 F2
Hedgerows . . . .
 Brentwood CM13 . . . . .95 E3
 Sawbridgeworth CM21 . . . . .1 F2
Hedgerows Bsns Pk . . . .
 CM2 .33 A6
Hedgerow The SS16 . . . . .142 E4
Hedgers Cl IG10 . . . . .89 A6
Hedgewood Gdns IG2, ...
 IG5 .133 B6
Hedingham Dr SS12 . . . . .121 F6
Hedingham Pl SS4 . . . . . . .125 D4
Hedingham Rd . . . .
 Basildon SS13 . . . . .153 B7
 Grays RM16 . . . . .172 C1
 Hornchurch RM11 . . . . .137 A3
Hedley Ave RM20 . . . . .177 C8
Hedley Cl B RM1 . . . . . .135 E6
Heenan Cl B IG11 . . . . . .152 C6
Heeswyk Rd SS8 . . . . .164 D5
Heidberg Rd SS8 . . . . .164 D5
Heideck Gdns CM13 . . . . .117 B8
Heighams CM19 . . . . .22 F5
Heights The . . . .
 Danbury CM3 . . . . .56 D7
 Loughton IG10 . . . . .88 F7
 Lower Nazeing EN9 . . . . . . .44 F6
 Theydon Bois CM16 . . . . . . .67 E3
Heilsburg Rd SS8 . . . . .164 D5
Helden Ave SS8 . . . . .164 B5
Helena Cl SS5 . . . . .124 F5
Helena Ct CM3 . . . . .101 D6
Helena Rd SS6 . . . . .123 E3
Helen Ho B CM14 . . . . . . .116 C7
Helen Rd RM11 . . . . .136 D8
Helford Ct RM15 . . . . .172 B6
Helford Way RM14 . . . . . . .137 D5
Helions Rd RM19 . . . . .23 B8
Helleborine RM17 . . . . .172 F1
Hellendoorn Rd SS8 . . . . .164 D2
Helmons La CM2 . . . . .77 A4
Helmore Rd IG11 . . . . .152 F5
Helmores SS15 . . . . .140 F6
Helmsdale SS8 . . . . .163 F5
Helmsdale Cl RM1 . . . . . . .113 E3
Helmsdale Rd RM1 . . . . . .113 E3
Helmsley B IG18 . . . . .132 A8
Helmsley Ho B RM3 . . . .114 E3
Helpeston CM3 . . . . .142 D6
Helston Rd CM1 . . . . .32 E6
Helwys Ct E4 . . . . .109 C4
Hemley Rd RM16 . . . . .174 D7
Hemmells SS15 . . . . .141 B8
Hemmells Pk SS15 . . . . . .119 A1
Hemmings Ct CM9 . . . . . . .58 E8
Hemnal Ho CM16 . . . . .67 E7
Hemnall St CM16 . . . . .67 F8
Hemnal Mews CM16 . . . . . .46 A1
Hempstalls SS15 . . . . .141 F5
Hempstead Cl IG9 . . . . . . .110 A8
Hempstead Rd E17 . . . . . .109 D1
Henbane Path RM3 . . . . . .114 D3
Henderson Cl RM11 . . . . . .136 B2
Henderson Dr DA1 . . . . . . .176 A3
Henderson Gdns . . . .
 SS12 . . . . .121 E5
Henderson Ho B . . . .
 RM10 . . . . .135 A1
Hendon Cl SS12 . . . . .121 D6
Hendon Gdns RM5 . . . . . . .113 C4
Hengist Gdns SS11 . . . . . . .99 D1
Henham Cl CM11 . . . . .97 D2
Henham Ct RM5 . . . . .113 C1
Henley Cres SS0 . . . . .147 D4
Henley Cl IG1 . . . . .152 B8
Henley Gdns RM6 . . . . . . .134 E6
Henley Rd IG1 . . . . .152 D8
Henney Cl CM3 . . . . .80 F6
Henniker Gate CM2 . . . . . . .33 A4
Henry De Grey Cl . . . .
 RM17 . . . . .172 F2
Henry Green Prim Sch . . . .
 RM8 . . . . .134 D2
Henry Moore Prim Sch . . . .
 The CM17 . . . . .24 D7
Henry Rd CM1 . . . . .32 B4
Henry's Ave IG8 . . . . .109 F5
Henry's St B RM17 . . . . .178 D8
Henry's Wlk IG6 . . . . .111 D3
Henshawe Rd RM8 . . . . . .134 D1
Henson Ave SS8 . . . . .164 E3
Henwood Side IG8 . . . . . . .110 F4
Hepburn Cl RM16 . . . . .172 D2
Hepworth Ct IG11 . . . . . . .153 A7
Hepworth Gdns IG11 . . . . .153 A7
Hepworth Ho IG8 . . . . .110 A7
Heralds Way CM3 . . . . .101 E7
Herbage Park Rd CM9 . . . . .35 D1
Herbert Gdns RM6 . . . . . . .134 D4
Herbert Gr SS1 . . . . .167 B7
Herbert Rd
 Canvey Island SS8 . . . . .164 C4
 Hornchurch RM11 . . . . .136 F4
 Ilford IG3 . . . . .133 E2
 Southend-on-S SS3 . . . . . .168 C6
 Swanscombe DA10 . . . . . . .177 F1
Herd La SS17 . . . . .161 C3
Hereford Ct CM2 . . . . .55 A5
Hereford Rd E11 . . . . .132 B6
Hereford Wlk SS14 . . . . . .142 F7
Herent Dr IG5 . . . . .132 F8
Hereward Cl EN9 . . . . .65 C2
Hereward Gdns SS11 . . . . .99 D1
Hereward Gn IG10 . . . . .89 C8
Hereward Mount CM4 . . . . .75 C1

Hereward Prim Sch . . . .
 IG10 .89 C8
Herewood Lincoln Ho . . . .
 DA11 . . . .
Herga Hyll RM15 . . . .
Herington Gr CM13 . . . .
Herington House Sch . . . .
 CM13 . . . .
Heriot Ave E4 . . . .
Heritage Ctr Mus The* . . . .
 SS8 . . . .
Heritage Quay DA12 . . . .
Heritage Way . . . .
 Latchingdon CM3 . . . .
 Rochford SS4 . . . .
Hermes Dr CM0 . . . .
Hermes Way SS3 . . . .
Hermitage Ave SS7 . . . .
Hermitage Cl SS7 . . . .
Hermitage Ct B E18. . . . .
Hermitage Dr SS15 . . . .
Hermitage Rd SS0 . . . .
Hermitage Wlk E18 . . . .
Hermon Hill E11 . . . .
Hernen Rd SS8 . . . .
Hernshaw CM13 . . . .
Heron Ave SS11 . . . .
Heron Chase CM13 . . . .
Heron Cl . . . .
 Buckhurst Hill IG9 . . . .
 Rayleigh SS6 . . . .
 Sawbridgeworth CM21. . . . .
Heron Ct . . . .
 Chipping Ongar CM5 . . . .
 Ilford IG1 . . . .
Heron Dale SS14 . . . .
Heron Dr SG12 . . . .
Heron Flight Ave . . . .
 RM12 . . . .
HERONGATE . . . .
 Herongate . . . .
 South Benfleet SS7 . . . .
 Southend-on-S SS3 . . . .
Herongate Rd E12 . . . .
Heron Gdns SS6 . . . .
Heron Mead EN3 . . . .
Heron Mews CM13 . . . .
Herons Cl SS14 . . . .
Heronsgate Trad Est . . . .
 SS14 . . . .
Herons La CM5 . . . .
Heronswood EN9 . . . .
Herons Wood CM20 . . . .
Heronway . . . .
 Brentwood CM13 . . . .
 Woodford IG8 . . . .
Heron Way . . . .
 Grays RM20 . . . .
 Heybridge CM9 . . . .
 Mayland CM3 . . . .
 Roydon CM19 . . . .
 Upminster RM14 . . . .
Herringham Gn CM2 . . . .
Herringham Prim Sch . . . .
 RM16 . . . .
Herschell Rd SS9 . . . .
Hertford Dr SS17 . . . .
Hertford Rd . . . .
 Barking IG11 . . . .
 Canvey Island SS8 . . . .
 Hoddesdon EN11 . . . .
 Ilford IG2 . . . .
Hertford Wlk B DA17 . . . .
Hesketh Rd E7 . . . .
Hesselyn Dr RM13 . . . .
Hester Cl B RM10 . . . .
Hester Ho CM20 . . . .
Hester Pl CM0 . . . .
Hetton Ho B IG10 . . . .
Hetzand Rd SS8 . . . .
Hever Cl SS5 . . . .
Hevingham Dr RM6 . . . .
Hewett Rd RM8 . . . .
Hewetts Quay IG11 . . . .
Hewins Cl EN9 . . . .
Hewitt Ho B E4 . . . .
Hew Watt Cl RM16 . . . .
HEYBRIDGE . . . .
 Ingatestone . . . .
 Maldon . . . .
Heybridge App CM9 . . . .
HEYBRIDGE BASIN . . . .
Heybridge Dr . . . .
 Ilford IG6 . . . .
 Redbridge IG6 . . . .
 Wickford SS12 . . . .
Heybridge House Ind Est . . . .
 CM9 . . . .
Heybridge Prim Sch . . . .
 CM9 . . . .
Heybridge Rd CM4 . . . .
Heybridge St CM9 . . . .
Heycroft Prim Sch . . . .
 SS2 . . . .
Heycroft Rd . . . .
 Hockley SS5 . . . .
 Southend-on-S SS9 . . . .
Heycroft Way CM2 . . . .
Heygate Ave SS1 . . . .
Heymeads Ct CM9 . . . .
Heynes Rd RM8 . . . .
Heyrick Cl CM2 . . . .
Heythrop The . . . .
 Chelmsford CM2 . . . .
 Ingatestone CM4 . . . .
Heywood Ct CM9 . . . .
Heywood Way CM9 . . . .
Hibbard Ho CM14 . . . .

Holly Ct
Billericay CM12 . . . . .97 A2
Hockley SS5 . . . . .124 E5
Northfleet DA11 . . . . .178 B1
Holly Dr
Chingford E4 . . . . .87 B2
South Ockendon RM15 . . . .157 D1
Hollyfield CM19 . . . . .23 C5
Hollyford CM11 . . . . .97 C5
Holly Hill Rd DA17 . . . . .169 B1
Holly Ho
Brentwood CM15 . . . . .94 D1
Ilford IG3 . . . . .134 A3
Holly Ho Hospl IG9 . . . . . . .110 B8
Hollymead SS17 . . . . .160 E4
Holly Tree Gdns SS6 . . . . .145 B8
Holly Trees Prim Sch
CM14 . . . . .116 B6
Holly Way CM2 . . . . .54 D7
Holly Wlk SS8 . . . . .163 F4
Hollywood Cl CM2 . . . . .54 E6
Hollywood Way IG8 . . . . . .109 D4
Holmans CM3 . . . . .33 E8
Holme Rd RM11 . . . . .137 A3
Holmes Ct SS17 . . . . .159 F3
Holmes Ct
Canvey Island SS8 . . . . .164 C4
Chingford E4 . . . . .109 D8
Holmes Mdw CM19 . . . . . . .23 B2
Holme Rd DA17 . . . . .169 B1
Holmfurst Rd DA17 . . . . . . .169 B1
Holmsdale Cl SS0 . . . . .147 C3
Holmswood SS8 . . . . .164 E5
Holmwood Ave CM15 . . . . . .95 A3
Holmwood Rd IG3 . . . . .133 E2
Holst Ave SS15 . . . . .141 C8
Holst Cl SS17 . . . . .160 C3
Holstock Rd IG1 . . . . .133 C2
Holsworthy SS3 . . . . .168 D8
Holsworthy Ho RM3 . . . . . .114 D2
Holt Cl IG7 . . . . .111 F5
Holt Farm Inf Sch
SS4 .125 D3
Holt Farm Jun Sch
SS4 .125 D3
Holt Farm Way SS4 . . . . . .125 D4
Holton Rd
Canvey Island SS8 . . . . .164 F3
Rayleigh SS6 . . . . .124 A2
Holt Rd RM3 . . . . .114 E3
Holt The IG6 . . . . .111 C4
Holt Way IG7 . . . . .111 F5
Holtynge SS7 . . . . .144 C4
Holy Acre CM19 . . . . .9 A1
Holybread La CM3 . . . . .34 C4
Holy Cross RC Prim Sch
SS7 .144 D5
Holy Family RC Prim Sch
SS7 .144 D5
HOLYFIELD 43 C3
Holyfield Hall Farm*
EN9 . . . . .43 C3
Holyfield Rd EN9 . . . . .43 D2
Holyoak La SS15 . . . . .124 E4
Holyrood Dr SS0 . . . . .147 B2
Holyrood Gdns RM10 . . . . .174 C2
Homebush Ho E4 . . . . .87 B2
Homecherry Ho ▣
IG10 . . . . .88 D4
Home Cl CM20 . . . . .23 F8
Homecove Ho SS0 . . . . .166 D7
Homecroft Gdns IG10 . . . . . .89 B5
Home Farm Cl SS3 . . . . .150 B4
Home Farm Rd CM13 . . . . .116 C2
Homefield
Southminster CM0 . . . . .84 C5
Waltham Abbey EN9 . . . . .66 A7
Homefield Ave CM2 . . . . . .133 E6
Homefield Cl
Billericay CM11 . . . . .119 D6
Chelmsford CM1 . . . . .31 D5
Epping CM16 . . . . .46 A4
Homefields CM17 . . . . .12 F3
Homefields Ave SS7 . . . . . .144 B5
Home Gdns RM10 . . . . .135 C1
Homeheather Ho ▣
IG4 . . . . .132 F6
Homeholly Ho SS15 . . . . .99 D2
Homehurst Ho CM15 . . . . . . .94 D1
Homelands Gr CM11 . . . . . . .98 C4
Home Mdws CM12 . . . . .97 A2
Homemead ▣ DA9 . . . . . . .177 B1
Home Mead
Basildon SS15 . . . . .141 B8
Galleywood CM2 . . . . .54 C2
Harlow CM18 . . . . .23 D6
Writtle CM1 . . . . .31 A1
Homesdale Cl E11 . . . . .132 A6
Homes Of Rest IG1 . . . . . . .133 D1
Homestead CM1 . . . . .32 B7
Homestead Ct SS7 . . . . .145 D3
Homestead Dr SS16 . . . . . .141 C2
Homestead Gdns SS7 . . . . .145 D2
Homestead Rd
Basildon, Bowers Gifford
SS13 .143 E7
Dagenham RM8 . . . . .134 F2
Hadleigh SS7 . . . . .145 D2
Ramsden Heath CM11 . . . . . .120 D8
Homesteads The SG12 . . . . . .9 D8
Homestead Way SS7 . . . . . .145 D3
Homeway RM3 . . . . .115 B4

Honey Brook EN9 . . . . .65 E6
Honey Cl
Chelmsford CM2 . . . . .54 D6
Dagenham RM10 . . . . .154 B6
Wyatts Green CM15 . . . . .72 D4
Honeycombe Lo
DA11 . . . . .178 D1
Honeycroft IG10 . . . . .89 B5
Honey La EN9 . . . . .65 E5
Honeymeade CM21 . . . . .11 C7
Honeypot La
Basildon SS14 . . . . .142 B6
Brentwood CM14 . . . . .116 A8
Stock CM4 . . . . .75 C1
Waltham Abbey EN9 . . . . .66 C5
Honey Pot La CM3 . . . . .80 D3
Honeypots CM2 . . . . .54 C6
Honeysuckle Cl
Pilgrims Hatch CM15 . . . . . . .94 B4
Romford RM3 . . . . .114 C4
Honeysuckle Ct ▣
IG11 .152 B6
Honeysuckle Path ▣
CM1 . . . . .32 F6
Honey Tree Ct IG10 . . . . .89 B7
Honiley Ave SS12 . . . . .121 E3
Honington Cl SS11 . . . . .122 B6
Honiton Rd
Romford RM7 . . . . .135 D5
Southend-on-S SS1 . . . . .167 C8
Honor Link CM1 . . . . .33 A7
Honor St ▣ CM17 . . . . .11 D1
Honywood Bsns Pk
SS14. . . . . .120 F2
Honywood Rd SS14 . . . . . . .120 F2
Hood Cl SS12 . . . . .121 E6
Hood Lo E11 . . . . .132 B2
Hood Rd RM13 . . . . .154 F3
Hood Wlk RM7 . . . . .113 B2
Hook Cotts CM1 . . . . .30 B7
HOOK END 72 C4
Hook End La CM15 . . . . .72 C5
Hook End Rd CM15 . . . . .72 C4
Hook Field CM18 . . . . .23 F6
Hook La RM4 . . . . .91 A3
Hooks Hall Dr RM10 . . . . . .135 C1
Hookstone Way IG8 . . . . . . .110 D3
Hooley Dr SS6. . . . . .123 C6
Hoo The CM17 . . . . .11 C5
Hoover Dr SS15 . . . . .140 F6
Hope Ave SS17 . . . . .160 E5
Hope Cl
Ilford RM6 . . . . .134 D7
Mountnessing CM15 . . . . .95 E8
▣ Woodford IG8 . . . . .110 C4
Hope Rd
Canvey Island SS8 . . . . .164 D3
Crays Hill CM11 . . . . .120 C5
South Benfleet SS7 . . . . .144 D2
Swanscombe DA10 . . . . .177 F1
HOPE'S GREEN 144 D2
Hope Terr RM20 . . . . .172 D1
Hopewell Cl RM16 . . . . .172 D1
Hop Gardens La CM9 . . . . . .35 F4
Hop Gdns CM5 . . . . .70 A7
Hopkins Cl
Chelmsford CM2 . . . . .33 A3
Romford RM2 . . . . .113 E3
Hopkins Mead CM2 . . . . .33 A2
Hopkirk Cl CM3 . . . . .56 F8
Hoppet The CM4 . . . . .74 C4
Hoppett Rd E4 . . . . .109 E8
Hopping Jacks La CM3 . . . . .56 F7
Hoppit Rd EN9 . . . . .65 B7
Hoppitt The CM5 . . . . .26 C3
Hopps Ho ▣ EN11 . . . . .21 A6
Horace Ave RM7 . . . . .135 D3
Horace Rd
Billericay CM11 . . . . .97 C4
Ilford IG6 . . . . .133 C8
Southend-on-S SS1 . . . . .167 B7
Horkesley Way SS12 . . . . . .121 B8
Horksley Gdns CM13 . . . . . . .95 C3
Hornbeam Ave RM14. . . . . .156 A8
Hornbeam Chase
RM15 . . . . .157 D2
Hornbeam Cl
▣ Barking IG11 . . . . .153 B2
Brentwood CM13 . . . . .95 A3
Buckhurst Hill IG9 . . . . .110 D7
Chelmsford CM2 . . . . .54 A6
Ilford IG1 . . . . .152 D7
Theydon Bois CM16 . . . . .67 E2
Hornbeam Gr E4 . . . . .109 F7
Hornbeam Ho IG9 . . . . .110 D7
Hornbeam La E4 . . . . .87 E4
Hornbeam Rd
Buckhurst Hill IG9 . . . . .110 D7
Theydon Bois CM16 . . . . .67 D2
Hornbeams SS7 . . . . .144 B8
Hornbeams The CM20 . . . . . .10 C2
Hornbeam Way SS15 . . . . . .119 D1
Hornby Ave SS0 . . . . .147 D5
Hornby Cl SS0 . . . . .147 D5
HORNCHURCH 136 C2
Hornchurch Cl SS11 . . . . . .122 A6
Hornchurch Ctry Pk*
RM12 . . . . .155 D6
Hornchurch Rd RM11. . . . . .136 B3
Hornchurch Sports Stad
RM14 . . . . .137 A2
Hornchurch Sta
RM12 . . . . .136 D1
Horndon Cl RM5 . . . . .113 C2
Horndon Gn RM5 . . . . .113 C2
Horndon Ind Pk
CM13 . . . . .139 C5

HORNDON ON THE HILL
. . . . .159 E3
Horndon on the Hill CE
Prim Sch SS17 . . . . .159 F3
Horndon Rd
Horndon on t H SS17. . . . . . .160 A1
Romford RM5 . . . . .113 C2
HORNE ROW 56 D5
Horne Row CM3 . . . . .56 D5
Horner's Cnr SS3 . . . . .149 F4
Hornet Way CM0 . . . . .106 B5
Hornford Way RM7 . . . . .135 E4
Horn La IG8 . . . . .110 A3
Hornminster Glen
RM11 . . . . .137 A2
Hornsby La RM16. . . . . .174 A5
Hornsby Sq SS15 . . . . .140 F7
Hornsby Way SS15 . . . . .140 F7
Horns Croft IG11 . . . . .152 E5
Hornsland Rd SS8 . . . . .164 E3
Horns Rd IG2, IG6 . . . . .133 C6
Horsebridge Cl RM9 . . . . . .153 E4
Horsecroft CM5 . . . . .14 D2
Horsecroft Ho CM19 . . . . . . .22 E7
Horsecroft Rd CM19 . . . . . . .22 E7
Horse & Groom La
CM2 . . . . .54 A3
Horseman Ct CM15 . . . . .71 F2
HORSEMAN SIDE 92 E5
Horseman Side CM14 . . . . . .92 D3
Horseshoe Cl
Billericay CM12 . . . . .97 A5
Waltham Abbey EN9 . . . . .66 A5
Horseshoe Cres SS14 . . . . .168 F6
Horseshoe Ct SG12 . . . . .8 D4
Horseshoe Hill EN9 . . . . .66 C7
Horseshoe Lawns
SS5. .101 E4
Horshams CM19 . . . . .23 C8
Horsley Cross SS14 . . . . . . .142 B7
Horsley Rd E4 . . . . .109 C8
Hortus Rd E4 . . . . .109 C8
Hospital App CM1. . . . . .19 B3
Hospital Cotts CM14 . . . . . .116 B6
HOSPITAL HILL 111 B3
Hospital Rd SS3 . . . . .168 F6
Houblon Dr CM2 . . . . .54 C2
Houblons Hill
Coopersale CM16 . . . . .46 D1
Epping CM16 . . . . .68 C8
Houchin Dr CM5 . . . . .27 D2
HOUSHAM TYE 12 D2
Hove Cl
Brentwood CM13 . . . . .117 C8
Grays RM17 . . . . .178 A8
Hovefields Ave SS12 . . . . . .121 D3
Hovefields Cvn Pk
SS13 .121 D2
Hovefields Dr SS12 . . . . . . .121 D3
Hovenor Way IG6 . . . . .111 A8
Howard Bsns Pk EN9 . . . . . .65 D6
Howard Rd CM14 . . . . .142 A8
Howard Cl
Loughton IG10 . . . . .88 E3
Waltham Abbey EN9 . . . . .65 D5
Howard Cres SS13 . . . . .143 C5
Howard Ct ▣ SS11 . . . . .152 D4
Howard Dr CM2 . . . . .33 A2
Howard Lodge Rd
CM14 .71 C2
Howard Pl SS8 . . . . .164 B2
Howard Rd
Barking IG11 . . . . .152 D4
Dartford DA1. . . . . .176 A1
Grays RM16 . . . . .172 C3
Ilford IG1 . . . . .152 B8
Upminster RM14 . . . . .137 D2
Howards Chase SS0 . . . . . .147 F2
Howards Cl CM15 . . . . .33 E8
Howards Ct SS0 . . . . .166 E8
Howard Way CM20 . . . . .10 F2
Howburgh Ct ▣
RM19 . . . . .171 B1
Howe Cl RM7 . . . . .113 A2
HOWEGREEN 80 D8
HOWE GREEN 55 C3
Howe Green Rd CM3. . . . . . .80 E7
Howell Cl RM6. . . . . .134 D5
Howell Rd SS17 . . . . .160 F6
Howerd Ho ▣ CM14 . . . . . .116 C6
Howfield Gn EN11 . . . . .8 A1
Howlett Hts SS9 . . . . .146 C7
Howse Rd EN9 . . . . .65 B4
Hows Mead CM16. . . . . .47 D7
Hoylake Gdns RM3. . . . . . . .115 A3
Hoynors CM3. . . . . .57 A7
Hubbard Cl IG10 . . . . .88 E2
Hubbards Chase
RM11 . . . . .137 A6
Hubbards Cl RM11. . . . . .137 B6
Hubert Rd
Brentwood CM14 . . . . .116 B7
Rainham RM13 . . . . .154 F3
Hucknall Cl RM3. . . . . .114 F4
Hudson Cres SS13 . . . . .146 E6
Hudson Ct SS9 . . . . .146 E6
Hudson Rd SS9 . . . . .146 D6
Hudsons Cl SS17 . . . . .160 D3
Hudson Way SS8 . . . . .164 A6
Hugg's Coll
(Almshouses) DA11 . . . . . . .178 B2
Hughes Rd RM16 . . . . .174 A3
Hugh's Twr ▣ CM20 . . . . . . .10 D1
Hugo Gdns ▣ RM13 . . . . . .155 A6
HULLBRIDGE 101 D2
Hullbridge Rd
Rayleigh SS6 . . . . .123 D7

Hullbridge Rd continued
South Woodham Ferrers
CM3 .101 D6
Hullett's La CM15. . . . . .93 F4
Hull Gn CM17 . . . . .13 D2
Hull Gr CM19 . . . . .23 A3
Hull's La CM2 . . . . .55 E7
Hulse Ave
Barking IG11 . . . . .152 E6
Romford RM7 . . . . .113 B2
Hulton Cl CM3. . . . . .33 E8
Humber Ave RM15 . . . . .171 F7
Humber Cl SS6. . . . . .123 C1
Humber Rd CM14 . . . . .137 D5
Humber Rd CM1. . . . . .32 C5
Hume Ave RM18. . . . . .179 B5
Hume Cl RM18 . . . . .179 A4
Humphrey Cl IG5 . . . . .110 F2
Humphrey's Farm La
CM3 . . . . .18 C7
Humphries Cl RM9. . . . . .153 F8
Hungerdown E4 . . . . .87 C1
Hungerford Ho ▣
RM3 .115 A4
HUNSDONBURY 9 C7
Hunsdon Cl RM9. . . . . .153 E6
Hunsdon Rd SG12 . . . . .8 E5
Hunsdon Road Cotts
SG12. .8 E5
Hunt Ave CM9 . . . . .37 B5
Hunter Ave CM15 . . . . .95 A3
Hunter Cl ▣ E11 . . . . .132 A6
Hunter Dr
Hornchurch RM12 . . . . .155 C8
Wickford SS12 . . . . .121 E6
Hunters Ave CM12 . . . . .119 B7
Hunters Chase
Brentwood CM13 . . . . .96 C2
Chipping Ongar CM5 . . . . .49 A1
Hunter's Gr RM5 . . . . .113 B5
Hunters Hall Prim Sch
RM10. . . . . .154 B7
Hunters Hall Rd
RM10. . . . . .154 A7
Hunters Rd IG1. . . . . .152 B7
Hunters Sq RM10 . . . . .154 A8
Hunters Way CM1 . . . . .32 F7
Hunters Wlk ▣ CM14 . . . . .116 C8
Huntingdon Rd SS1. . . . . . . .167 D7
Huntings Farm IG1 . . . . .133 E2
Huntings Rd RM10 . . . . .154 A6
Huntland Cl RM13 . . . . .170 B8
Huntley Ave DA11. . . . . .178 C1
Hunt's Cl CM1 . . . . .53 B8
Hunt's Dr CM1. . . . . .53 B8
Hunts Hill Cotts
RM14. . . . . .156 C3
Huntsman Rd IG6 . . . . .112 B5
Huntsmans Dr RM14 . . . . . .156 C7
Hunts Mead CM12 . . . . .97 A1
Hurlock Rd CM3 . . . . .90 E8
Hurrell Down CM3. . . . . .20 F1
Hurrells La CM3 . . . . .33 F3
Hurricane Cl SS11 . . . . .122 B5
Hurricane Way
North Weald Bassett
CM16 .47 A4
Wickford SS11 . . . . .122 A5
Hursley Rd
Chigwell IG7 . . . . .111 F5
Redbridge IG7 . . . . .112 A5
Hurst Ave E4 . . . . .109 A7
Hurstbourne Gdns
IG11 .152 E6
Hurst Cl E4 . . . . .109 A7
Hurstcombe IG9 . . . . .110 A8
Hurst Ct IG8 . . . . .110 B4
Hurst Ho SS7 . . . . .145 B7
Hurstlands Cl RM11. . . . . . . .136 C5
Hurstleigh Gdns IG5 . . . . . .111 A2
Hurst Park Ave RM12 . . . . . .155 E8
Hurst Rd IG9. . . . . .88 D1
Hurst Way
Chelmsford CM2 . . . . .32 F2
Southend-on-S SS9 . . . . .146 F4
Hurstwood Ave
Pilgrims Hatch CM15. . . . . . . .94 B2
Wanstead E18 . . . . .132 B7
Hurstwood Ct RM14. . . . . . . .137 C2
Huskards
Ingatestone CM4 . . . . .74 A5
Upminster RM14 . . . . .137 C2
Hutchins Cl RM12. . . . . .136 E1
Hutchinson Ct RM6 . . . . .134 D7
Hutson Terr RM19 . . . . .176 D8
HUTTON 95 D3
Hutton All Saints' CE Prim
Sch CM13 . . . . .95 D3
Hutton Cl IG8 . . . . .110 B4
Hutton Dr CM13 . . . . .95 F2
Hutton Dr CM13 . . . . .95 D2
Hutton Gate CM13. . . . . .95 B2
HUTTON MOUNT 95 B1
Hutton Pl CM13. . . . . .95 B3
Hutton Rd
Brentwood CM15 . . . . .95 A2
Shenfield CM15 . . . . .94 F2
Hutton Village CM13 . . . . . . .95 F2
Huxley Dr RM6 . . . . .134 B4
Hyacinth Cl IG1 . . . . .152 A6
Hyacinth Ct ▣ CM1 . . . . .32 E7
Hyclife Gdns IG7 . . . . .111 C6
HYDE CHASE 57 D4
Hyde Chase
Danbury CM3 . . . . .57 D4
Woodham Mortimer
CM3 . . . . .57 D4
Hyde Cl RM16 . . . . .172 C3

Hyde Gn CM3 . . . . .57 C4
Hyde La CM3 . . . . .57 C4
Hyde Mead EN9 . . . . .65 E3
Hyde Mead Ho EN9 . . . . .65 E3
Hyder Rd RM16 . . . . .172 C3
Hyde The CM15 . . . . .116 C6
Hydeway SS7 . . . . .144 C6
Hyde Way SS12 . . . . .121 E5
Hyde Wood La SS4 . . . . .125 B5
Hyh Ho E17 . . . . .109 A1
Hyland Cl RM11 . . . . .137 A5
Hyland Gate SS11 . . . . .122 A5
Hyland House Sch
E17 . . . . .109 A1
Hylands Ho ▣ 53 B8
Hylands House Sixth Form
Coll SS9 . . . . .146 E7
Hylands Par CM2 . . . . .53 B8
Hylands Rd E17 . . . . .109 A1
Hylands Sch CM5 . . . . .53 B8
Hylands The SS5 . . . . .124 D6
Hylands Way CM15 . . . . .94 B4
Hyndford Cres DA9 . . . . .177 C1
Hyndman Ho ▣
RM10 . . . . .154 C7
Hynton Rd RM8. . . . . .134 D3
HYTHE 37 B5
Hythe The CM9 . . . . .37 B4

I

Ian Rd CM12. . . . . .97 A1
Ibbetson Path IG10. . . . . .89 B7
Ibrox Ct ▣ IG9 . . . . .89 B7
Ibscott Cl RM10 . . . . .154 C6
I Butts Rd SS3 . . . . .168 D8
Iceni Ct IG9 . . . . .89 C7
Icknield Dr IG2 . . . . .133 C6
Ilchester Rd RM8 . . . . .134 C4
ILFORD 133 C4
Ilford Chambers ▣
IG1. . . . . .133 E4
Ilford Cty High Sch
IG6. . . . . .133 E7
Ilford Hill IG1 . . . . .152 C8
Ilford Jewish Prim Sch
IG6. . . . . .133 E7
Ilford La IG1 . . . . .152 D7
Ilford Prep Sch IG3 . . . . . . .133 D3
Ilford Ret Pk IG1 . . . . .133 B4
Ilford Sta IG1 . . . . .133 D4
Ilford Trad Est SS14 . . . .
Ilford Ursuline High Sch
IG6. . . . . .133 C6
Ilfracombe Ave
Basildon SS13 . . . .
Southend-on-S SS1 . . . .
Ilfracombe Cres
RM12 . . . .
Ilfracombe Gdns RM6. . . . . .
Ilfracombe Rd SS2. . . . .
Ilgars Rd SS11 . . . .
Ilmington Dr SS13 . . . .
Immanuel Sch RM5 . . . .
Imperial Ave
Mayland CM3 . . . .
Southend-on-S SS0 . . . .
Imperial Bsns Pk
DA11 . . . .
Imperial Ho ▣ SS4 . . . .
Imperial Lo SS0 . . . .
Imperial Pk
Rayleigh SS6 . . . .
Southend-on-S SS3 . . . .
Imperial Ret Pk DA11. . . . . . .
Imperial Trad Est
RM13. . . . .
Impresa Pk EN11 . . . .
Inchbonnie Rd CM3. . . . .
Inchcape CM16 . . . .
Ingaraby Bypass
CM4 . . . .
INGATESTONE . . . .
Ingatestone By-Pass
CM4 . . . .
Ingatestone & Fryerning
CE Jun Sch CM4 . . . .
Ingatestone Hall*
CM4 . . . .
Ingatestone Inf Sch
CM4 . . . .
Ingatestone Rd
Blackmore CM4 . . . .
Edney Common CM4 . . . .
Roxwell CM1 . . . .
Stock CM4 . . . .
Wanstead E12 . . . .
Woodford IG8 . . . .
Ingatestone Sta CM4. . . . . . .
Ingaway SS16 . . . .
Ingels Mead CM16. . . . .
Ingleby Gdns IG7. . . . .
Ingleby Rd
Dagenham RM10 . . . .
Grays RM16 . . . .
Ilford IG1. . . . .
Inglefield Rd SS17 . . . .
Ingleglen RM11 . . . .
Inglehurst Gdns IG4 . . . .
Ingleton Ho
▣ Ingatestone CM4. . . . .
▣ Romford RM3 . . . .
Inglewood Cl
Hornchurch RM12 . . . .
Redbridge IG6 . . . .
Ingram Cotts CM1 . . . .
Ingram Rd RM17. . . . .
INGRAVE . . . .

...ve Cl SS12 ....121 E6
...ve Ho RM9 ....153 B4
...ve Johnstone CE
... Sch CM13.........117 C4
...ve Rd
...twood CM13,
...15 ....116 E7
...ord RM1 ....135 E2
...bourne Ct E4.......109 B8
...bourne Gdns
... .137 D3
...bourne Prim Sch
...SS5.........114 C6
...bourne Rd RM13...155 B1
...bourne Valley*
... .155 E7
...ss Gdns DA9.......177 B2
...ss Park Ave DA9...177 C3
...vay RM3 ....115 C4
...pole Pl CM2 ....32 F4
...ss Row SS8 ....110 A6
...CI SS12.........121 E5
...e Way EN3 ....65 A3
... Dr RM11 ....136 E3
...d RM8 ....134 D3
...t Rd CM16 ....46 D2
...ted Support Ctr,
...CM18 ....23 F4
...national Bsns Pk
... .163 D3
...yde Gdns RM6....134 D7
...ay Ct CM3 ....94 C1
...ess Ave SS6 ....147 D2
...ess Dr IG6 ....111 E4
... Ct CM12.........96 E3
...h Ctr The IG11 ...153 A4
...ld DA2 ....176 B1
...n Wlk SS11.......122 A8
...ill 152 F1
...CN9 ....69 A2
...ay SS12 ....121 F6
...s Mews SS16......140 F5
...J RM17 ....173 A2
...ford CM1 ....32 F5
...s Hatch CM15......94 B4
...G11 ....153 B5
...vss SS15 ....141 C5
...n RM3 ....114 C3
...ay RM5 ....113 C3
...t La 125 A3
...dns RM15 ....171 F7
...SS12 ....121 F5
...ay CM12 ....97 A1
...n Ct SS9 ....146 D4
...ll Rd SS12 ....121 C7
...i EN1 ....21 B8
...Ho EN8 ....65 A5
...ns RM1 ....113 B3
...M14.........137 E5
...entre Way EN3...65 A2
... Bldg The
... .11 C6
...CM15.........94 B3
...s RM1 ....135 F7
...k RM8 ....153 B7
...La 11 A8
...one CM4 ....74 A8
...tting CM4 ....52 C1
...r Cl **2** DA9 ...177 B2
... EN10 ....21 A4
...NEYS 67 E7
...CM16.........67 E7
...Prim Sch
... .67 F7
...d RM16 ....67 F7
...re 176 A3
...CM0 ....66 A3
...Cl SS11 ....121 E8
...d RM9 ....153 E6
...La RM3.........115 B1
... .144 A6

...n EN11 ....21 C8
...G12.........133 C5

...Cl CM1 ....33 A1
...k Ho **9**
...SS12 ....152 B5
...well St E12.......152 A8
...Cl
...on-S SS3 ....168 E8
...s Ct RM15 ....172 A7
...IG8 ....110 A6
...SS11 ....121 F7
...TCH 23 A2
...e Ho RM3.........170 A8

...n DA9 ....177 A2
...RM11 ....136 F7

...am RM10 ....154 A6
...RM11.........132 B3
...CM2 ....54 D6
...IG11 ....152 D4
...CM5 ....49 A2

Jacksons La CM11.........97 C2
Jacksons Mews CM11.....97 C2
Jack Stevens Cl CM17 ...24 C6
Jacob Ct RM3.........45 A2
Jacobs Ave RM3 ....114 E1
Jacobs Ct RM8 ....134 C3
Jacobs Rd RM10.......154 B8
Jacqueline Gdns CM12...97 B5
Jade Ct E4 ....134 C3
Jade Ho **2** RM13......155 A1
Jaffe Rd IG1 ....133 D3
James Alexander Ho
...SS5.........101 D3
James Ave RM8 ....134 F3
James Cl RM2 ....136 A6
James Croft CM2 ....54 B2
James Ct
...Chingford E4 ....109 D8
3 Woodford E18 ...110 B1
James Hornsby High Sch
...The SS15 ....141 D7
James Lee Sq EN3.........65 A1
James Oglethorpe Prim
...Sch The RM14.......137 F2
James Sq CM11 ....97 E2
James St
...Barking IG11 ....152 C5
...Epping CM16 ....46 A3
Jane Ct **7** RM1.......135 F6
Janet Duke Inf Sch
...SS15 ....141 D6
Janet Duke Jun Sch
...SS15.........141 D6
Janette Ave SS8 ....163 E3
Janice Mews **3** IG1 ...133 B1
Janmead CM13 ....95 B2
Japan Rd RM6.........134 D5
Jardine Rd SS13 ....143 C8
Jarndyce CM14 ....31 F6
Jarrah Cotts RM19......176 D8
Jarrow Rd RM6 ....134 C5
Jarvis Cl **1** IG11 ...152 D4
Jarvis Field CM3 ....34 D5
Jarvis Rd
...Canvey Island SS8......164 A6
...South Benfleet SS7 ...144 E4
...Grays RM3 ....114 E1
Jasmine Cl
...Basildon SS16 ....140 F4
...Canvey Island SS8...163 F2
2 Chelmsford CM1 ...32 E7
...Ilford IG1 ....152 B7
Jasmine Rd RM7 ....135 E2
Jason Cl
...Brentwood CM14......115 F6
...Canvey Island SS8......164 B5
...Orsett RM16 ....174 E7
Jason Ct CM14.........115 F6
J Ct CM20 ....10 F1
Jeffcut Rd CM2 ....32 E2
Jefferies Way **5**
...SS17.........160 F3
Jefferson Ave **3**
...SS5.........141 A4
Jefferson Cl IG2.........133 B6
Jeffery Rd CM2 ....55 A7
Jellicoe Ct E4 ....109 D4
Jena Cl SS3 ....168 E7
Jenkins La IG11 ....152 C2
Jenner Ho
5 Belvedere DA17...169 A3
...Romford RM3 ....114 E1
Jenner Mead CM2 ....33 A3
Jennington Dr RM16...173 D3
Jennings Pl CM2 ....75 A8
Jenningtree Way
...DA17.........169 C4
Jenny Path RM3 ....114 D3
Jericho Pl CM3 ....94 D3
Jermayns SS15 ....141 E6
Jerningham Ave IG5.....111 B1
Jerounds CM19 ....23 B6
Jerounds Com Jun & Inf
...Sch CM19.........23 B6
Jersey Gdns EN11 ....21 A7
Jersey Gdns SS11.......121 D8
Jersey Rd
...Ilford IG1 ....152 B8
...Maldon CM9 ....37 B1
...Rainham RM13 ....155 B1
Jervis Ct **14** RM1 ...110 A6
Jesmond Rd
...Canvey Island SS8...164 B2
...Grays RM16.........173 D5
Jessel Dr IG10 ....89 C7
Jessett Cl DA8.........169 D2
Jessop Ct EN9.........65 F5
Jetty Mews SS1 ....167 D7
Jetty Wlk RM17.........178 A8
Jim Desormeaux Bglws
...IG6.........112 A4
Joan Gdns RM8 ....134 E2
Joan Rd RM8 ....134 E2
Jocelyns CM17 ....11 C4
Jodrell Way RM20 .....171 F1
John Barker Ho IG11 ...133 E2
John Bramston Prim Sch
...IG6.........112 A4
John Burns Dr IG11 ...152 E5
John Chadwick Ho
...SS6.........123 C2
John Childs Way SS6...123 E2
John Clay Gdns RM16...73 E8
John Cornwell VC Ho **6**
...E12.........152 A8
John Ct EN11.........8 A1
John Eliot Cl EN9.........65 F5

John Henry Keene Meml
...Homes CM1.........32 A4
John Parker Cl RM10...154 B5
John Perry Prim Sch
...RM10 ....154 D6
Johnson Cl
...Rochford SS4 ....125 C4
...Wickford SS12.......121 D5
Johnson Ct SS4 ....125 F2
Johnson Rd CM2 ....55 A5
Johnson's Way DA9 ...177 C1
John St
...Grays RM17 ....178 C8
...Southend-on-S SS3 ...168 G6
...John's Terr RM3 ....115 C4
Johns The CM5 ....49 A4
Johnstone Rd SS1 ....168 A7
Johnston Rd IG8 ....110 A5
Johnston Way DA9.......59 A8
John Warner Sch The
...EN11.........8 B1
John William Cl
...RM16 ....172 D1
Jonathan Cl CM11 ....136 E3
Jonathan Ho RM17 ...173 E2
Jones Cl SS2 ....147 E3
Jones Cnr SS8 ....164 A3
Jordans Cl RM10 .....154 B8
Jordans The SS2 ....148 A2
Jordans Way RM13 ...155 D3
Jo Richardson Com Sch
...RM9 ....153 D4
Joseph Clarke Sch
...E4.........109 D4
Joseph Ct CM14 ....116 B5
Joseph Lister Lo E11 ...132 B3
Joshua Wlk EN8 ....65 A5
Josling Cl CM17.........177 F8
Joslin Rd RM3 ....171 D1
Joslyn Cl EN3 ....65 A1
Josselin Cl SS13 ....121 C2
Josselin Rd SS13 ....121 C2
Jotmans Hall Prim Sch
... .144 B4
Jotmans La
...South Benfleet SS7 ...143 F2
...South Benfleet SS7 ...144 A3
Journeymans Way
...SS2 ....148 A5
Joyce Ct EN9 ....65 D5
Joyce's Chase CM9 ....39 A8
Joydon Dr RM6 ....134 B5
Joyes Cl RM3 ....114 D6
Joyners Cl RM9.........153 F8
Joyners Field CM18 ....23 C4
Jubilee Ave
...Broomfield CM1.........19 B2
...Chingford E4 ....109 C8
...Romford RM7 ....135 C6
Jubilee Cl
...Greenhithe DA9.........177 C1
...Hockley SS5 ....124 E5
...Romford RM7 ....135 B6
Jubilee Cotts SS4 ....127 D6
Jubilee Ct CM9 ....65 F6
Jubilee Dr SS11 ....121 C8
Jubilee Par IG8 ....110 C4
Jubilee Rd
...Grays Hill CM11.........120 C4
...Grays RM20.........177 B8
...Rayleigh SS6 ....123 E2
Jubilee Rise SS7 ....57 A6
Jubilee Terr
...Chelmsford CM1 ....32 A4
...Woodham Ferrers CM3...79 B4
Jubilee Villas **8** E4......87 D1
Judge Rd CM2 ....33 B4
Judith Anne Ct RM14 ...137 E2
Judith Ave RM5.........113 B4
Julia Gdns IG11 ....153 D3
Julian Cl CM1 ....19 E1
Julie Ho EN11 ....21 C8
Juliers Cl SS8 ....164 D3
Juliers Rd SS8 ....164 D3
Juliette Way RM15.....170 F5
Junction Rd
...Basildon SS13 ....143 B4
...Brentwood CM14......116 C6
...Cold Norton CM3.........81 A6
...Romford RM1 ....135 B7
Junction Rd E RM6.....134 C4
Junction Rd W RM6.....134 C4
Junction The CM13 ....95 B3
Juniper Cl CM11.........97 C4
Juniper Ct
...Brentwood CM13.......116 F7
...Ilford RM6 ....134 C5
Juniper Dr
...Chelmsford CM2 ....54 B6
...South Ockendon RM15...157 C2
Juniper Rd
...Boreham CM3 ....33 F8
...Ilford IG1 ....152 B8
...Southend-on-S SS9 ...146 F4
Juniper Way RM3.........114 C2
Jury St **5** DA11 ....179 B1
Jutsums Ave RM7 ....135 B5
Jutsums Cl RM7 ....135 B5
Jutsums La RM7 ....135 B5

K

Kale Rd SS7.........144 C4
Kamerwyk Ave SS8 ...164 C4
Kandlewood CM13.........95 D4
Karen Cl
...Brentwood CM15.........94 C2

Karen Cl *continued*
...Rainham RM13 ....154 E3
...South Benfleet SS7 ...163 E8
...Stanford-le-H SS17 ...160 C1
...Wickford SS12.........121 C6
Karen Terr CM2 ....133 D6
Karina Cl DA2 ....111 E5
Katella Trad Est IG11 ...152 E2
Katemon Ct SG12.........32 D4
Katherine Cl SS6 ....124 A1
Katherine Gdns IG6.....111 C3
Katherine Rd SS13.....143 E7
KATHERINES 22 F5
Katherines Hatch
...CM19.........23 A6
Katherines Ho CM19.....23 A6
Katherines Prim Sch
...CM19.........23 A6
Katherine's Way CM19...23 A6
Kathleen Cl SS17 ....160 E4
Kathleen Dr SS9 ....146 F2
Kathleen Ferrier Cres
...SS15.........141 D8
Kathryn Ct SS3 ....168 E7
Katonia Ave CM3 ....60 F1
Kavanaghs CM14 ....116 B7
Kavanaghs Rd CM14 ...116 B7
Kavanaghs Terr CM14 ...116 B7
Keary Rd SS4 ....177 F1
Keats Ave RM3 ....114 B3
Keats Cl
...Chigwell IG7 ....111 C4
...Maldon CM9.........59 A8
...Wanstead E11 ....132 B6
Keats Gdns RM18 ....179 B5
Keats Rd DA17.........169 C3
Keats Sq SS13 ....101 E6
Keats Way SS12 ....121 C7
Keats Wlk
...Brentwood CM13.........95 D2
...Rayleigh SS6 ....124 A2
Kecksy's CM21.........1 F4
Keeble Pk CM9.........58 F8
Keefield CM19 ....23 B3
Keegan Pl SS8 ....164 C4
Keelan Ct IG1 ....133 B1
Keel Cl IG11 ....153 C3
Keelings La CM14 ....85 E8
Keelings Rd CM0 ....85 E8
Keene Way CM14 ....54 B3
Keer Ave SS8 ....164 C4
KEERES GREEN 5 D1
Keighley Mews CM19 ...149 D2
Keighley Rd RM3 ....114 E3
Keir Hardie Ho
6 Belvedere DA17......169 A3
...Grays RM16.........173 D5
Keir Hardie Way
...Basildon SS11 ....153 A5
...Romford RM7 ....99 C3
...Southend-on-S SS3 ...152 D3
Keith Ave SS11 ....99 C3
Keith Rd IG11 ....152 D3
Keith Way
...Hornchurch RM11 ....136 E4
...Southend-on-S SS2 ...147 E5
Kelburn Way RM13.....155 D1
Kellington Rd SS8 .....164 C5
Kelly Ho RM15.........171 C5
Kelly Rd SS13 ....143 E6
Kelly Way RM6 ....134 E5
Kelsie Way IG6 ....111 C4
Kelso Cl SS6 ....123 C6
Kelso Lo E18 ....110 B1
Kelston Rd IG6 ....111 B1
Kelvedon Cl
...Billericay CM11.........97 C2
...Brentwood CM13.........95 E3
...Chelmsford CM1 ....32 A6
...Rayleigh SS6 ....123 A3
Kelvedon Gn CM15 ....71 F2
Kelvedon Hall La CM14...71 E2
KELVEDON HATCH 71 E2
Kelvedon Hatch Com Prim
...Sch CM15.........71 D1
Kelvedon Hatch Nuclear
...Bunker* CM14.........71 C4
Kelvedon Rd IG9 ....88 C2
Kelvedon Rd CM1.........97 C2
Kelvedon Way IG8.........110 F4
Kelvin Ho **3** DA17 ...169 A3
Kelvin Rd
...South Benfleet SS7 ...144 D7
...Tilbury RM18 ....179 A5
Kelvinside SS17 ....160 E4
Kembles SS6 ....123 C4
Kemp Ho IG6 ....152 A6
Kempley Ct RM17 ....178 D8
Kemp Rd RM8 ....134 D3
Kempton Ave RM12 ...136 F1
Kempton Cl SS17 ....145 B7
Kempton Rd E6 ....152 A4
Kemsley Cl DA9 ....177 B1
Kendal CM12 ....171 C1
Kendal Ave
...Barking IG11 ....152 C1
...Epping CM16 ....68 A8
Kendal Cl
...Hullbridge SS5 ....101 E1
...Rayleigh SS6 ....123 E2
...Woodford IG8 ....109 F8
Kendal Croft RM12.....155 A7
Kendal Ct
9 Chingford E4 ....87 C1
...Wickford SS11.........122 A5
Kendale RM16 ....174 B3
Kendal Rd EN9 ....65 C4
Kendal Way SS9 ....146 E7
Kendon Ct E11 ....132 B6

Kenholme SS9 ....146 E4
Kenilworth Ave
...Chingford E17 ....109 A1
...Romford RM3 ....115 B4
Kenilworth Cl CM12.........96 E2
Kenilworth Ct
7 Chingford E4 ....109 C8
3 Dartford DA2 ....176 B1
Kenilworth Gdns
...Hornchurch RM12 ....136 D3
...Ilford IG3 ....133 F2
...Loughton IG10.........88 F3
...Rayleigh SS6 ....123 C3
...Southend-on-S SS9,
...SS9.........147 A3
Kenilworth Pl SS15 ...119 E1
Kenley Cl CM2.........122 B6
Kenley Gdns RM12.....136 F2
Kenmar Cl SS6 ....146 A8
Kenmore Cl SS8 ....164 E2
Kennedy Ave SS15 ...140 F6
Kennedy Cl
...Rayleigh SS6 ....146 A8
...South Benfleet SS7 ...144 B7
Kennel La CM12,
...CM11.........119 C7
Kennet Cl RM14 ....137 E5
Kennet Gn RM15.........172 B6
Kenneth Ave IG1 ....152 B8
Kenneth Chambers Ct
...IG8.........110 C4
Kenneth Gdns SS17...160 F5
Kenneth More Rd **4**
...IG1.........133 B1
Kenneth Rd
...Basildon SS13 ....143 C7
...Dagenham RM6.........134 E4
...Thundersley SS7 ....144 F5
Kennet Way CM1 ....31 D5
Kenning Rd EN11 ....21 B8
Kennington Ave SS7 ...144 C6
Kenningtons Prim Sch
...RM15.........171 C7
Kennylands Rd IG6.....112 A3
Kensington Ct **8**
...RM17.........178 C8
Kensington Dr IG8.......110 D1
Kensington Gdns
...Billericay CM12.........97 A4
...East Tilbury RM18 ...175 C2
...Redbridge IG1 ....132 F3
Kensington Ho **7**
...IG8.........111 A3
Kensington Rd
...Pilgrims Hatch CM15...94 A3
...Romford RM7 ....135 C5
...Southend-on-S SS1 ...167 D7
Kensington Way SS16...124 D7
Kent Ave
...Canvey Island SS8......164 B5
...Dagenham RM9 ....154 A1
...Southend-on-S SS9 ...146 F3
Kent Cl SS15 ....141 B6
Kent Dr RM12 ....155 D8
Kent Elms Cl SS2 ....146 E5
Kent Elms Cnr SS9......146 F5
Kent Green Cl SS5 .....124 F5
Kent Ho RM7 ....113 A2
Kentish Rd DA17.........169 A2
Kent Kraft Ind Est
...DA11.........178 A2
Kenton Way SS16.......140 F7
Kent Rd
...Dagenham RM10.......154 B7
...Grays RM17.........173 C1
Kents Farm La CM2.......76 D4
Kents Hill Inf Sch
...SS7.........144 D4
Kents Hill Jun Sch
...SS7.........144 D4
Kents Hill Rd SS7 .....144 D4
Kents Hill Rd N SS7...144 D6
Kents La CM16.........25 D2
Kent View
...Aveley RM15 ....171 C4
...Rainham RM13 ....170 D6
Kent View Ave SS9.....166 A8
Kent View Cl SS8 .....164 B1
Kent View Gdns IG3.....133 E2
Kent View Rd SS16.....142 F4
Kent Way SS6 ....146 A8
Kentwell Ct SS7 ....144 C3
Kenway
...Rainham RM13 ....155 D2
...Romford RM5 ....113 C1
...Southend-on-S SS2 ...148 A2
Kenway Cl RM13 ....155 C2
Kenway Wlk RM13 .....155 D2
Kenwood Gdns
...Ilford IG2 ....133 A6
1 Wanstead E18 ....132 B8
Kenwood Rd SS17 ....161 B4
Keppel Rd RM9.........153 E8
Kerby Rise CM2 ....32 F2
Kernow Cl RM12.........136 E2
Kerril Croft CM20 ....10 A1
Kerry Ave RM15.........170 F4
Kerry Cl RM14 ....137 F4
Kerry Ct RM13 ....155 C1
Kerry Dr RM14 ....137 F4
Kerry Rd RM16 ....173 D5
Kersbrooke Way
...SS17.........161 B4
Kersey Gdns RM3 ....114 F3

Kershaw Cl
Grays RM16 . . . . 172 C2
Hornchurch RM11 . . . . . . 136 E4
Kershaw Rd RM10 . . . . . 135 A1
Kershaws Cl SS12 . . . . . 121 C6
Kesteven Cl IG6 . . . . . . .111 F4
Kestrel Cl
Hornchurch RM12 . . . . . . 155 B5
Redbridge IG6 . . . . 112 C6
Kestrel Gr SS6 . . . . 123 B3
Kestrel Ho SS3 . . . . 149 F1
Kestrel Mews CM9 . . . . . 59 B8
Kestrel Pk CM13 . . . . .95 E4
Kestrel Rd EN9 . . . . 66 A5
Kestrel Wlk CM2 . . . . 54 B5
Keswick Ave
Hornchurch RM11 . . . . . . 136 D3
Hullbridge SS5 . . . . 101 E2
Keswick Cl SS6 . . . . 123 E2
Keswick Gdns
Purfleet RM19 . . . . 176 C8
Redbridge IG4 . . . . 132 E7
Keswick Ho 11 RM3 . . . . 114 D4
Keswick Rd SS7 . . . . 144 E7
Ketleys CM2 . . . . 54 C3
Kettering Rd RM3 . . . . . 114 C3
Kettlebury Way CM5 . . . . 48 F1
Kevin Cl CM11 . . . . 119 D7
Keyes Cl SS3 . . . . 149 E1
Keyes Rd DA1 . . . . 176 A3
Keynsham Ave IG8 . . . . . 109 C6
KEYSERS ESTATE 21 B1
Keysland SS7 EN10 . . . . . 21 B1
Keysland SS7 . . . . 145 B7
Keys The CM13 . . . . 116 C4
Khartoum Pl DA12 . . . . . 179 C1
Khartoum Rd IG1 . . . . . . 152 B7
Kibcaps SS16 . . . . 141 F4
Kidd Ho RM9 . . . . 153 F8
Kidman Cl RM2 . . . . 136 C8
Kielder Cl IG6 . . . . .111 F4
Kierbeck Bsns Pk
SS16 . . . . 142 F3
Kilbarry Wlk CM11 . . . . . .97 D6
Kildare Ho RM3 . . . . . . .114 E1
Kildare Rd IG3 . . . . 134 A3
Kildowan Rd IG3 . . . . . . 134 A3
Kilmarnock Gdns
RM8 . . . . 134 C1
Kilmartin Rd IG3 . . . . . . 134 A2
Kilmartin Way RM12 . . . . 155 B7
Kilmington Cl CM13 . . . . .117 B8
Kiln Cotts CM13 . . . . 56 C6
Kilnfield
Chipping Ongar CM5 . . . . . 48 F2
Wyatts Green CM15 . . . . . .72 D3
Kiln La CM17 . . . . .24 C7
Kiln Rd
Brentwood CM15 . . . . .95 A3
Southend-on-S SS1 . . . . . 167 B8
Kilnwood Ave SS3 . . . . . 167 B8
Kiln Shaw SS16 . . . . 141 C4
Kiln Way RM17 . . . . 172 F1
Kilnwood Ave SS3 . . . . . 124 D5
Kiln Wood La RM4 . . . . . 113 D5
Kilowan Cl SS16 . . . . . . 140 F4
Kilsby Wlk RM9 . . . . 153 B6
Kilworth Ave
Brentwood CM15 . . . . .95 A3
Southend-on-S SS1 . . . . . 167 B8
Kimberley Ave
Ilford IG2 . . . . 133 E4
Romford RM7 . . . . 135 C5
Kimberley Ct SS7 . . . . . 144 C3
Kimberley Rd
Chingford E4 . . . . 87 E1
Little Wakering SS3 . . . . . 149 E6
South Benfleet SS7 . . . . . 144 C3
Kimberley Way E4 . . . . . . 87 E1
Kimberly Dr SS15 . . . . . 119 F2
Kimpton Ave CM15 . . . . . 94 C2
Kimpton's Cl CM5 . . . . . . 48 F5
Kinfauns Ave RM11 . . . . 136 C5
Kinfauns Rd IG3 . . . . . . 134 B3
Kingaby Gdns RM13 . . . . 155 A5
King Alfred Rd RM3 . . . . .114 F1
King Edmund Sch The
SS4 . . . . 125 E5
King Edward Ave
Burnham-on-C CM0 . . . . . 106 B6
Rainham RM13 . . . . 155 D2
King Edward Ct CM1 . . . . . 32 A3
King Edward Dr
RM16 . . . . 173 E3
King Edward Rd
Basildon SS15 . . . . 141 B8
Brentwood CM14 . . . . . . .116 C7
Greenhithe DA9 . . . . 177 A2
Romford RM1 . . . . 135 F5
King Edward's Rd
Barking IG11 . . . . 152 D3
South Woodham Ferrers
CM3 . . . . 101 D8
Stanford-le-H SS17 . . . . . 175 D8
King Edward Terr
SS15 . . . . 141 B8
King Edward VI Gram Sch
CM1 . . . . 32 A3
Kingfisher Ave E11 . . . . 132 B5
Kingfisher Cl
Brentwood CM13 . . . . .95 A2
Heybridge CM9 . . . . 37 C5
Southend-on-S SS3 . . . . . 168 B5
Stanstead Abbotts SG12 . . . .8 C3
Kingfisher Cres SS6 . . . . 123 B3

Kingfisher Dr
Greenhithe DA9 . . . . 177 A1
South Benfleet SS7 . . . . . 144 C2
Kingfisher Hts RM17 . . . . 173 A1
Kingfisher Lo CM2 . . . . . . 54 F7
Kingfisher Rd RM14 . . . . 137 F3
Kingfishers
Basildon SS16 . . . . 142 C4
Ingatestone CM4 . . . . 74 C5
Kingfishers The 11
SS11 . . . . 122 A5
Kingfisher Way CM19 . . . . .9 A1
King George Ave IG2 . . . . 133 D5
King George Cl RM7 . . . . 135 C8
King George Hospl
IG3 . . . . 134 A6
King George Rd EN9 . . . . . 65 C5
King George's Cl SS6 . . . 123 D1
King George's Cl SS6 . . . 123 D1
King George's Pl CM9 . . . . 37 A2
King George's Rd
CM15 . . . . 94 B3
King George VI Ave
RM18 . . . . 175 B2
King Harold Ct EN9 . . . . . . 65 C6
King Harold Sch EN9 . . . . . 65 E6
King Henrys Ct EN9 . . . . . . 65 C3
King Henry's Dr SS4 . . . . 147 F7
King Henry's Mews
EN3 . . . . 65 A2
King John Sch The
SS7 . . . . 145 B3
Kingley Cl SS12 . . . . 121 B7
Kingley Dr SS12 . . . . 121 B7
Kings Ave RM6 . . . . 134 F5
King's Ave
Buckhurst Hill IG9 . . . . . . 110 D8
Woodford IG8 . . . . 110 C5
Kingsbridge Cir 6
RM3 . . . . 114 E4
Kingsbridge Cl RM3 . . . . 114 E4
Kingsbridge Ind Est
RM11 . . . . 152 E2
Kingsbridge Rd
Barking IG11 . . . . 152 D3
Romford RM3 . . . . 114 E4
King's Chase CM14 . . . . . 116 C7
Kings Cl
Canvey Island SS8 . . . . . 163 C3
Rayleigh SS6 . . . . 123 E2
Kings Cres SS15 . . . . . . 119 B1
Kingscroft SS2 . . . . 148 B1
Kings Croft CM0 . . . . 84 D4
Kings Ct
3 Buckhurst Hill IG9 . . . . 110 D8
Burnham-on-C CM0 . . . . . 106 B4
Kingsdale Ct
Swanscombe DA10 . . . . . 177 E1
Waltham Abbey EN9 . . . . . 66 A5
Kingsdale Ind Est The
CM1 . . . . 32 C3
Kingsdon La CM17 . . . . . . 24 C7
Kingsdown Cl SS13 . . . . . 143 C6
Kingsdown Sch SS2 . . . . 146 F6
Kingsdown Wlk SS8 . . . . 164 A5
Kings Eight CM14 . . . . . . 116 C7
Kings Farm
Chingford E17 . . . . 109 B2
Rayleigh SS6 . . . . 123 E5
Kings Farm Mdw CM0 . . . .63 E4
Kingsfield EN11 . . . . .21 A8
Kingsford Dr CM2 . . . . . . .33 B4
Kingsgate Ct SS0 . . . . . . 166 C8
Kings Gdns
Ilford IG1 . . . . 133 D3
Upminster RM14 . . . . . . 137 E4
King's Gn IG10 . . . . .88 E6
Kings Gr RM1 . . . . 136 A6
Kingshawes SS7 . . . . . . 145 B6
Kings Head Ct CM21 . . . . . .1 E2
Kings Head Hill E4 . . . . . . 87 B2
Kings Head Wlk 6
CM2 . . . . 32 C2
King's Hill IG10 . . . . 88 E7
Kingshill Ave RM5 . . . . . 113 C5
Kings Keep SS0 . . . . 166 C8
Kingsland CM18 . . . . .23 C6
Kingsleigh Pk Homes
SS7 . . . . 145 B6
Kingsley Ave DA1 . . . . . . 176 A2
Kingsley Ct RM10 . . . . . . 154 B8
Kingsley Cres SS7 . . . . . 145 C8
Kingsley Ct RM2 . . . . 136 B5
Kingsley Gdns
Chingford E4 . . . . 109 A5
Hornchurch RM11 . . . . . . 136 D7
Kingsley Grange 11
E11 . . . . 132 A6
Kingsley La SS7 . . . . 145 B8
Kingsley Mdws SS12 . . . . 121 D5
Kingsley Mews
Dagenham RM9 . . . . 153 D8
4 Ilford IG1 . . . . 133 B2
Kingsley Rd
Brentwood CM13 . . . . .95 D2
Chingford E17 . . . . 109 C1
Loughton IG10 . . . . 89 D6
Redbridge IG6 . . . . .111 C2
Kingsley Wlk RM16 . . . . . 174 A2
Kings Lo SS7 . . . . 145 C3
Kings Lynn Dr RM3 . . . . . 114 D4
Kingsman Dr RM16 . . . . . 173 B6
Kingsman Rd SS17 . . . . . 160 B1
Kingsmans Farm Rd
SS5 . . . . 102 A4
Kingsmead
Lower Nazeing EN9,
EN10 . . . . .21 C1

Kingsmead continued
Sawbridgeworth CM21 . . . . .1 E1
Kingsmead Ave RM1 . . . . 135 F5
Kingsmead Cl CM19 . . . . . 22 B7
Kingsmead Hill CM19 . . . . 22 B7
Kingsmead Lo 9 E4 . . . . 109 C8
Kingsmead Mans 4
RM1 . . . . 135 E5
Kings Meadow Ct EN9 . . . . 66 A5
Kingsmere SS7 . . . . 145 C5
Kings Mews
Chigwell IG7 . . . . 111 C8
Sawbridgeworth CM21 . . . . .1 E2
Kingsmill Gdns RM9 . . . . 153 F7
Kingsmill Rd RM9 . . . . . . 153 F7
KINGSMOOR 23 C3
Kingsmoor Prim Sch
CM18 . . . . .23 C4
Kingsmoor Rd CM19 . . . . . 23 B5
Kings Oak RM7 . . . . 135 A8
King Solomon High Sch
IG6 . . . . 111 D1
Kings Par SS17 . . . . 160 C1
Kings Park Chalet &
Mobile Home Pk
SS8 . . . . 164 E4
Kingspark Ct E18 . . . . . . 132 A8
Kings Pk SS7 . . . . 144 F5
Kings Rd
Buckhurst Hill IG9 . . . . . . 110 D8
Loughton IG10 . . . . 88 D2
Southminster CM0 . . . . . . 84 D4
Kings Rd
Basildon SS15 . . . . 119 B1
Burnham-on-C CM0 . . . . . 106 B4
Canvey Island SS8 . . . . . 163 C3
Chelmsford CM1 . . . . .31 F4
Rayleigh SS6 . . . . 123 E2
Southminster CM0 . . . . . . 84 D4
King's Rd
Barking IG11 . . . . 152 C5
Brentwood CM14 . . . . . . .116 C7
Chingford E4 . . . . 87 D1
Romford RM1 . . . . 136 A6
South Benfleet SS7 . . . . . 144 E2
Southend-on-S SS0 . . . . . 147 B1
Kings Road Prim Sch
CM1 . . . . 31 F4
King St
Gravesend DA12 . . . . 179 B1
High Ongar CM5 . . . . .50 B3
Maldon CM9 . . . . 37 A1
Stanford-le-H SS17 . . . . . 160 C1
Kingsteignton SS3 . . . . . 168 D8
Kingston Ave
Chelmsford CM2 . . . . .32 E3
Southend-on-S SS3 . . . . . 149 E2
Kingston Chase CM9 . . . . . 36 F5
Kingston Cl RM6 . . . . 134 E8
Kingston Cres CM2 . . . . . . 32 E3
Kingston Ct
Grays RM17 . . . . 173 B3
Northfleet DA11 . . . . 178 B2
Kingston Farm Ind Units
CM17 . . . . .13 C5
Kingston Hill SS16 . . . . . 141 D2
Kingston Hill Ave
RM6 . . . . 134 E8
Kingston Prim Sch
SS7 . . . . 144 E6
Kingston Rd
Ilford IG1 . . . . 152 C8
Romford RM1 . . . . 135 F7
Kingston Ridge SS16 . . . . 141 D3
Kingstons Farm CM17 . . . 13 D5
Kingston Way SS7 . . . . . 144 F6
Kingsview Ct SS0 . . . . . . 166 C8
Kingsview Cl SS11 . . . . . 121 F6
Kingsway
Hullbridge SS5 . . . . 123 D8
Southend-on-S SS0 . . . . . 147 A2
Woodford IG8 . . . . 110 C5
Kings Way
Billericay CM11 . . . . 119 D6
South Woodham Ferrers
CM3 . . . . .79 C1
Kingsway Mews SS0 . . . . 147 B2
Kingswear Cl SS6 . . . . . . 123 B1
KINGSWOOD 142 A4
Kingswood Chase
SS9 . . . . 146 D3
Kingswood Cl CM11 . . . . . .97 C2
Kingswood Cres SS6 . . . . 123 B1
Kingswood Ct
Basildon SS14 . . . . 142 E5
Bradwell on S CM0 . . . . . .42 B2
Chingford E4 . . . . 109 A5
Kingswood Inf Sch
SS16 . . . . 142 B5
Kingswood Lo
Romford RM2 . . . . 136 A8
Southend-on-S SS9 . . . . . 146 D3
Kingswood Rd
Basildon SS16 . . . . 142 C5
Ilford IG3 . . . . 134 A4
King's Wood Sch
RM3 . . . . 115 A6
King Williams Ct EN9 . . . . .65 C4
Kinnaird Way IG8 . . . . . . 110 F4
Kipling Ave RM18 . . . . . . 179 C6
Kipling Cl
Brentwood CM14 . . . . . . .116 B5
Chelmsford CM1 . . . . .32 A5
Kipling Mews SS2 . . . . . 148 A2
Kipling Rd DA1 . . . . 176 B2
Kipling Twrs RM3 . . . . . . 114 B3
Kirby Cl
Loughton IG10 . . . . 88 E2
Redbridge IG6 . . . . .111 E4

Kirby Cl continued
Romford RM3 . . . . 115 A5
Kirby Rd SS14 . . . . 142 F6
Kirkham Ave SS16 . . . . . 159 F7
Kirkham Ho 9 RM3 . . . . .110 E6
Kirkham Rd SS17 . . . . . . 159 F8
Kirkham Shaw SS17 . . . . 159 F8
Kirkland Ave IG5 . . . . . . .111 A1
Kirklees CM1 . . . . .31 F4
Kirklees Rd RM8 . . . . . . 153 C7
Kirkmans Rd CM2 . . . . . . 54 D3
Kirk Mews CM3 . . . . 83 B2
Kirk Pl CM2 . . . . 32 F3
Kirton Cl RM12 . . . . 155 C6
Kitchener Rd
Chingford E17 . . . . 109 B2
Dagenham RM10 . . . . . . 154 B6
North Fambridge CM3 . . . . 81 A1
Kitkatts Rd SS8 . . . . 164 A3
Kitson Way CM20 . . . . 10 C1
Kittiwake Dr CM9 . . . . 37 C5
Knapton Cl CM1 . . . . .32 D7
Knares The SS16 . . . . . . 141 F4
Knebworth Ave E17 . . . . 109 A2
Knebworth Ho E17 . . . . . 109 A2
Knightbridge Wlk
CM12 . . . . .97 A4
Knight Cl RM8 . . . . 134 C2
Knight Ct 1 E4 . . . . .87 C1
Knight Ho IG10 . . . . .89 D5
Knighton Cl
Romford RM7 . . . . 135 D5
Woodford IG8 . . . . 110 B6
Knighton Dr IG8 . . . . 110 B6
Knighton Gn IG9 . . . . 110 B8
Knighton La IG9 . . . . 110 B8
Knighton Rd
Romford RM7 . . . . 135 C5
Wanstead E7 . . . . 132 A1
Knighton Terr 17 E11 . . . 132 A6
Knightsbridge Gdns 5
RM7 . . . . 135 D6
Knight's Ct
4 Basildon SS14 . . . . . . 142 F8
Sawbridgeworth CM21 . . . . .1 E2
Knights Manor Way
DA1 . . . . 176 A2
Knights Properties
EN11 . . . . .21 B6
Knight St
Sawbridgeworth CM21 . . . . .1 E2
South Woodham Ferrers
CM3 . . . . 101 E2
Knight's Way IG6 . . . . . . .111 C4
Knight's Way CM13 . . . . . 117 A7
Knightswick Ctr SS8 . . . . 164 C4
Knightswick Rd SS8 . . . . 164 B4
Knights Wlk RM4 . . . . 90 B6
Knightswood Rd
RM3 . . . . 155 A3
Knivet Cl SS6 . . . . 123 E1
KNOCKHALL 177 C1
Knockhall Chase DA9 . . . 177 C2
Knockhall Com Prim Sch
DA9 . . . . 177 C2
Knockhall Rd DA9 . . . . . . 177 C2
Knole Cl CM3 . . . . 101 D5
Knollcroft SS3 . . . . 168 D6
Knoll The
Billericay CM12 . . . . 97 B4
Rayleigh SS6 . . . . 123 D2
Knowle Ho EN11 . . . . .21 A5
Knowle The
Basildon SS16 . . . . 142 C4
Hoddesdon EN11 . . . . . . .21 A5
Knowlton Cotts RM15 . . . 172 C8
Knox Cl CM9 . . . . 59 A8
Knox Ct SS12 . . . . 121 F5
Kolburg Rd SS8 . . . . 164 D2
Kollum Rd SS8 . . . . 164 F3
Koln Cl SS8 . . . . 164 A3
Komberg Cres SS8 . . . . . 164 C5
Konnybrook SS7 . . . . . . 145 A4
Korndyk Ave SS8 . . . . . . 164 C4
Kursaal Way SS1 . . . . . . 167 C2
Kyme Rd RM11 . . . . 135 F5
Kynance Cl RM3 . . . . 114 C6
Kynoch Ct SS17 . . . . 160 E1
Kyrkly Cl 11 RM19 . . . . . 171 B1

L

Laars Ave SS8 . . . . 164 C5
Laburnham Ct RM14 . . . . 138 A4
Laburnham Ct SS3 . . . . . 168 F8
Laburnum Gdns
RM14 . . . . 137 F4
Laburnum Ave
Hornchurch RM12 . . . . . . 136 A2
Wickford SS12 . . . . 121 C6
Laburnum Cl
Hockley SS5 . . . . 124 C6
Sheering CM22 . . . . .12 C8
Wickford SS12 . . . . 121 C6
Laburnum Dr
Chelmsford CM2 . . . . .54 C6
Corringham SS17 . . . . . . 161 B3
Laburnum Gr
Canvey Island SS8 . . . . . 163 D3
Hockley SS5 . . . . 124 B6
South Ockendon RM15 . . . 157 C1
Laburnum Ho
3 Basildon SS13 . . . . . . 143 B8
3 Dagenham RM10 . . . . 135 A2
Laburnum Rd
Coopersale CM16 . . . . 46 C2

Laburnum Rd continued
Hoddesdon EN11 . . . . . . .21 A5
Laburnum Way SS6 . . . . 124 C7
Laburnum Wlk RM12 . . . . . .
Labworth Rd SS8 . . . .
Lacey Dr RM8 . . . .
Ladram Cl SS1 . . . .
Ladram Rd SS1 . . . .
Ladram Way SS1 . . . .
Ladyfields Cl IG10 . . . . . .
Ladygate Ctr SS12 . . . . .
Lady Hamilton Ct SS1 . . .
Lady La CM2 . . . .
Lady's Hill CM4 . . . .
Ladyshot CM20 . . . .
Ladysmith Ave IG2 . . . . .
Ladysmith Way SS15 . . . .
Ladywell La CM2 . . . .
Ladywell Prospect
CM21 . . . .
Lagonda Ave IG6 . . . .
LAINDON . . . .
Laindon Common Rd
CM12 . . . .
Laindon Ctr SS15 . . . .
Laindon Link SS15,
SS16 . . . .
Laindon Park Prim Sc
SS15 . . . .
Laindon Rd CM12 . . . .
Laing Cl IG6 . . . .
Laird Ave RM16 . . . .
Lake Ave
Billericay CM12 . . . .
Rainham RM13 . . . .
Lake Cl RM8 . . . .
Lakedale Cl IG11 . . . .
Lake Dr SS7 . . . .
Lakefields Cl RM13 . . . . .
Lake Gdns RM10 . . . .
Lake House Rd E11 . . . . .
Lakeland Cl IG7 . . . .
Lake Meadows Office
Village CM12 . . . .
Lakenham Ho SS2 . . . . . .
Lake Rd
Ilford RM6 . . . .
Lower Nazeing EN9 . . . . .
Lake Rise
Grays RM20 . . . .
Romford RM1 . . . .
Lake Rise Trad Est
RM20 . . . .
Lakes Cl SS12 . . . .
Lakeside
Billericay CM12 . . . .
Rainham RM13 . . . .
Rayleigh SS6 . . . .
Lakeside Ave IG4 . . . .
Lakeside Cl IG2 . . . .
Lakeside Cres
Brentwood CM14 . . . .
Canvey Island SS8 . . . . . .
Lakeside Path SS8 . . . . .
Lakeside Ret Pk
RM20 . . . .
Lakeside Sh Ctr RM20 . . .
Lakeview Ho
Chingford E4 . . . .
Lake View SS16 . . . .
Lakeview Ct E4 . . . .
Lakeview Cvn Pk CM5 . . .
Lakeview Pk RM3 . . . . . .
Lakes Cl CM2 . . . .
Lamb Cl RM18 . . . .
Lamberhurst Rd RM8 . . . .
Lambert Ct RM7 . . . .
Lambeth Mews SS5 . . . . .
Lambeth Rd
South Benfleet SS7 . . . . .
Southend-on-S SS9 . . . . .
Lambley Rd RM9 . . . .
Lambourn Cl SS15 . . . . . .
LAMBOURNE . . . .
Lambourne
Canvey Island SS8 . . . . . .
East Tilbury RM18 . . . . . .
Lambourne Cl IG7 . . . . . .
Lambourne Cres
Basildon SS14 . . . .
Chigwell IG7 . . . .
Lambourne Ct 5 IG8 . . . .
LAMBOURNE END . . . . . .
Lambourne Gdns
6 Barking IG11 . . . .
Chingford E4 . . . .
Hornchurch RM11 . . . . . .
Lambourne Gr CM9 . . . . .
Lambourne Hall Rd
SS4 . . . .
Lambourne Mead Co
RM4 . . . .
Lambourne Prim Sch
RM4 . . . .
Lambourne Rd
Barking IG11 . . . .
Chigwell IG7 . . . .
Ilford IG3 . . . .
Lambourne Sq RM4 . . . . .
Lamb's La N RM13 . . . . .
Lamb's La S RM13 . . . . .
Lambs Mdw IG8 . . . .
Lamerton Rd IG6 . . . .
Lamont Cl 11 SS12 . . . . .
Lamorna Cl E17 . . . .

ᵃCl CM12. . . . . .97 B6
Cres CM12 . . . . . .97 C6
Mews CM12 . . . . . .97 B6
ᵃ Ho 4 RM3 . . . .114 E3
owne SS17. . . . .161 A4
N11. . . . . .21 B6
ᵃill SS17. . . . . . . .161 B4
ᵃill Ave
. . . . .161 A4
ᵃa SS17. . . . . . . .161 A4
ters Cl EN9. . . . . . . .66 A5
ᵃRd RM3. . . . . .154 F1
ᵃ Ave
. . . . .152 E4
ᵃ E18 . . . . .132 B7
ᵃ
ᵃ Cl CM15. . . . . . . .94 A4
ᵃ Cres 3
. . . . .167 B8
ᵃ Dr
ᵃSS16 . . . . .140 F5
ᵃch RM12 . . . . . .155 C8
IG10. . . . . .88 E3
ᵃ Gdns
ᵃSS6 . . . . .146 A8
ᵃon-S SS1 . . . . .167 B8
ᵃ Pl IG1 . . . . . . .152 C8
ᵃ Rd
ᵃ16. . . . . .172 D2
ald Bassett
. . . . .47 A5
ᵃSS6 . . . . .146 A8
ᵃ Sch SS0. . . . . . . .147 C3
ᵃRd IG6 . . . . . .111 E3
ᵃay CM12. . . . . .96 F3
ᵃRd
. . . . .133 D5
ᵃRM3 . . . . .114 E3
ᵃay DA8 . . . . . . .170 D1
ᵃre SS14. . . . . .142 B7
ᵃd RM17. . . . . . .173 D1
ᵃ Ct CM1 . . . . . .31 E5
ᵃe CM3 . . . . .57 A7
ᵃg Rd SS8 . . . . . .164 D5
ᵃe Rd IG8 . . . . . .110 B3
ᵃ Ave E12 . . . . . .152 A7
ᵃCl RM11. . . . . .136 B3
ᵃCt SS0. . . . . .147 C1
ᵃ Gdns CM5. . . . . .49 A1
ᵃCotts SS3. . . . . .150 D4
ᵃ La CM0. . . . . . . .85 F7
ᵃCM17. . . . . .177 C1
ᵃCM17. . . . . .24 E7
ᵃys E12. . . . . . . .132 F1
ᵃ Ave RM8 . . . . . .134 F4
ᵃCt RM8 . . . . . .134 C3
ᵃCt 10 IG1 . . . . . .133 B1
ᵃRd
ᵃrd CM2. . . . . . . .54 D8
ᵃch RM12 . . . . . .155 A7
ᵃ Ho SS6 . . . . . .123 D2
ᵃ Conservation
ᵃ6 . . . . .140 E3
ᵃCres E6 . . . . . .152 A3
ᵃ14 . . . . .134 C3
ᵃ HILLS 141 C4
ᵃ Hills Ctry Pk*
. . . . .160 F8
ᵃMews CM1 . . . . .97 B3
ᵃ Nature Reserve
ᵃood)* SS16 . . . .141 A3
ᵃ Nature Reserve
ᵃHill)* SS16 . . . .141 C4
ᵃ Nature Reserve
ᵃPark)*
. . . . .141 D2
ᵃRd
ᵃSS6 . . . . .123 B3
ᵃ6. . . . . .152 A4
ᵃSch SS6. . . . . .152 A4
ᵃ Way SS17 . . . .161 B4
ᵃre Way CM11 . . .97 B1
ᵃe SS12. . . . . . .121 E6
ᵃCl EN9. . . . . . .21 E1
ᵃD 36 D7
ᵃCres SS7. . . . . .144 F6
ᵃGn CM13. . . . . .95 C4
ᵃGr SS13. . . . . .143 C8
ᵃRd
ᵃ16. . . . . .134 B5
ᵃSS6 . . . . .123 A3
ᵃ Ho 3 E11 . . . . .132 B7
ᵃe Rd RM10 . . .154 A5
ᵃCl SS17. . . . . .161 A3
ᵃDr
ᵃRM3 . . . . .114 D3
ᵃon-S SS9 . . . . .146 B7
ᵃres
ᵃn RM9. . . . . . . .153 D5
ᵃd E11. . . . . . . .132 C4
ᵃDr
ᵃd CM14. . . . . . .116 A7
ᵃ14. . . . . .132 B4
ᵃdns RM9. . . . . .153 D5
ᵃ Pl CM12. . . . . .96 E3
ᵃSS16. . . . . .142 B4
ᵃe Dr SS0. . . . . .147 B4
ᵃ Ho 3 RM3. . . .114 E3
ᵃ Rd IG10 . . . . . .89 D5

Langthorne Cres
RM17. . . . . .173 C2
Langthornes 1 CM11 . . .97 B2
Langton Ave
Chelmsford CM1 . . . . . . .31 E5
Wallend E6. . . . . .152 A2
Langtons Jun & Inf Sch
RM1. . . . . .136 E3
Langton Way RM16. . . . .174 C2
Lanham Pl 7 SS13 . . . .143 B8
Lanhams SS13. . . . . .143 C8
Lanhams Ct 5 SS13 . . . .143 B8
Lansbury Ave
Barking IG11. . . . . .153 A5
Dagenham RM6. . . . . . . .134 E6
Lansbury Cres DA1 . . . .176 A2
Lansbury Gdns RM18. . . .69 A6
Lansdown Ave SS7. . . . .145 F6
Lansdown Ct SS9 . . . . . .147 A1
Lansdowne Ct
Hoddesdon EN10. . . . . . .21 A3
Redbridge IG3. . . . . . . .132 E8
Lansdowne Dr SS6 . . . .123 C3
Lansdowne Prim Sch
RM18. . . . . .178 F5
Lansdowne Rd
Chingford E4 . . . . .109 A8
Ilford IG3 . . . . .133 F4
Wanstead E18 . . . . .132 A8
Lansdowne Sq DA11. . . .178 F1
Lansdown Rd RM18. . . . .179 A5
Lanterns IG10 . . . . .88 F8
Lantern Terr 10 SS11 . . .167 C7
La Plata Gr CM14 . . . . . .116 B7
Lappmark Rd SS8 . . . . . .164 D3
Lapwater Cl SS9. . . . . . .146 C2
Lapwater SS9. . . . . .146 C2
Lapwing Dr CM9. . . . . . .37 C5
Lapwing Ho 6 RM13. . . .155 A1
Lapwing Rd SS11. . . . . . .99 C2
Larch Cl SS15 . . . . .119 C1
Larches The
Boreham CM3 . . . . .33 E8
South Benfleet SS7 . . . .144 C8
Larch Gr CM2. . . . . .54 C6
Larch Wlk CM9 . . . . .37 C6
Larchwood Ave SS16. . .113 B4
Larchwood Cl
Romford RM5 . . . . .113 C4
Southend-on-S SS6 . . . . .94 A3
Larchwood Gdns CM15. . .94 A3
Larchwood Ho 2 IG7. . . .112 B6
Larchwood Prim Sch
CM15. . . . . .94 A3
Lark Cl CM14. . . . . .116 B6
Larke Rise SS2 . . . . .147 D5
Larkfield SS17. . . . . .161 B4
Larkfield Cl SS4 . . . . . . .125 D4
Larkhill Ave SS4. . . . . . .104 A2
Lark Hill Rd SS4 . . . . . . .104 B1
Larkin Cl CM13 . . . . .95 C2
Larkrise Prim Sch CM2 . .54 E8
Larks Gr IG11. . . . . .152 E5
Larkshall Bsns Ctr E4. . . .109 D8
Larkshall Cres E4. . . . . .109 C6
Larkshall Ct
Chelmsford E4 . . . . .109 C5
Romford RM7 . . . . .113 C1
Larkshall Rd E4 . . . . . . .109 D6
Larkspur Cl CM19. . . . . . .19 A6
Great Waltham CM3 . . . . .18 F5
Larkspur Cl CM1. . . . . . .157 C2
Larkspur Ct 3 CM11. . . . .32 F6
Larkswood CM17 . . . . . . .24 C6
Larkswood Ct CM1 . . . . .109 D5
Larkswood Prim Sch
E4. . . . . .109 B6
Larkwood Rd
Chingford E4 . . . . .109 B6
Corringham SS17. . . . . . .161 B3
Larkswood Wlk 2
SS12. . . . . .121 D6
Larsen Dr EN9. . . . . .65 D5
Larup Ave SS8 . . . . .164 C4
Larup Gdns SS8 . . . . . . .164 C4
La Salette Rd CM18
RM13. . . . . .154 F2
Lascelles Cl CM15. . . . . . .94 F2
Lascelles Gdns SS4. . . . .125 D6
Latchett Rd E18. . . . . . . .110 B2
Latchetts Shaw SS16. . . .142 B4
Latchford Pl IG7. . . . . . .112 B6
Latching Cl RM3. . . . . . .114 D6
LATCHINGDON. 82 A6
Latchingdon CE Prim Sch
CM3 . . . . .82 B6
Latchingdon Cl SS13. . . .123 A3
Latchingdon Gdns
IG8. . . . . .110 E4
Latchingdon Rd CM3. . . .81 B5
Latchmore Bank CM22 . . .2 B8
Lathcoates Cres CM2 . . . .54 E8
Lathom Rd E6. . . . . .152 A5
Latimer Dr
Basildon SS15. . . . . . . .119 B1
Hornchurch RM12. . . . . .136 D1
LATTON BUSH. 24 B5
Latton Bush Bsns Ctr The
CM18. . . . . .24 B5
Latton Common Rd
CM18. . . . . .24 B5
Latton Gn CM18 . . . . .23 F4
Latton Green Prim Sch
CM18. . . . . .24 B5
Latton Hall Cl CM20. . . . .11 A1
Latton Ho CM18 . . . . .24 B5

Latton St
Harlow, Brays Grove CM18,
CM20. . . . . .24 B7
Harlow, Potter Street
CM17. . . . . .24 C5
Launceston Cl RM3 . . . .114 C2
Launder's La RM13. . . . .155 F1
Laundry Cotts RM13 . . . .170 D6
Laundry La
Lower Nazeing EN9. . . . . .43 E6
Mountnessing CM15 . . . . .95 D8
Laura Cl E11 . . . . .132 C6
Laura Ave SS12 . . . . . . .121 C7
Laurel Cl
Brentwood CM13. . . . . . . .95 B4
Redbridge IG6 . . . . .111 D4
Southend-on-S SS9 . . . .165 D8
Laurel Cres RM7. . . . . . .135 E3
Laurel Ct
6 Brentwood CM13 . . . . .95 C3
Rainham RM13 . . . . .155 C1
Laurel Dr RM15. . . . . . . .157 D1
Laurel Gdns E4. . . . . .87 B2
Laurel Gr 4 CM2 . . . . . . .54 A8
Laurel La 4 RM12. . . . . .136 E2
Laurel Mead Ct 8
E18. . . . . .110 A2
Laurels The
8 Belvedere DA17. . . . . .169 A1
Buckhurst Hill IG9. . . . . . .88 C1
Rayleigh SS6 . . . . .145 F8
South Woodham Ferrers
CM3 . . . . .101 D8
Laurence Croft CM1 . . . . .31 B1
Laurence Ind Est SS2 . . .147 B6
Laurie Wlk RM1 . . . . . . .135 E6
Lauriston Bglws CM9 . . . .39 C6
Lauriston Pl 1 SS1. . . . .167 C8
Lavender Ho E17 . . . . . .109 B2
Lavender Ave CM15. . . . . .94 B3
Lavender Cl
Harlow CM20. . . . . .10 E1
Romford RM3 . . . . .114 D7
South Ockendon RM15. . .157 E1
Lavender Ct 1 CM1 . . . . .32 F5
Lavender Gr SS0 . . . . . . .147 D3
Lavender Ho 2 DA1 . . . .176 A2
Laveham Ct CM15. . . . . . .94 D1
Lavers The SS6 . . . . .123 E3
Lawford Cl RM12 . . . . . .155 C8
Lawford La
Chelmsford CM1 . . . . . . .31 D3
Writtle CM1. . . . . .31 C3
Lawford Mead Inf Sch
CM1. . . . . .31 D5
Lawford Mead Jun Sch
CM1. . . . . .31 D5
Law Ho IG11 . . . . .153 A3
Lawling Ave CM9 . . . . . . .37 C5
Lawlinge Rd CM3 . . . . . . .82 B5
Lawn Ave SS2. . . . . .148 B2
Lawn Farm Gr RM6. . . . .134 E7
Lawn Hall Chase CM6. . . .7 D8
Lawn La CM1. . . . . .32 D6
Lawn Prim Sch DA11 . . . .178 C1
Lawn Rd DA11. . . . . .178 C1
Lawns Cres RM17. . . . . .178 D8
Lawns Ct SS2. . . . . .144 B7
Lawns Pl RM17 . . . . .178 D8
Lawns The
Brentwood CM14. . . . . . .116 E5
Chelmsford CM1 . . . . . . .32 D5
Chingford E4 . . . . .109 A5
East Hanningfield CM3 . . .78 C7
South Benfleet SS7 . . . .144 C7
Lawns Way RM5 . . . . . . .113 C3
Lawn The CM20. . . . . . . .11 B3
Lawrence Ave
Little Ilford E12. . . . . . . .152 A8
Sawbridgeworth CM21 . . .1 E4
Stanstead Abbotts SG12 . . .8 C4
Lawrence Cres RM10. . . .135 B1
Lawrence Ct 3 IG8. . . . . .110 C4
Lawrence Gdns RM18. . . .179 B7
Lawrence Hill E4 . . . . . . .109 A8
Lawrence Moorings
CM21. . . . . .1 F2
Lawrence Rd
Basildon SS13. . . . . . . .143 F8
Romford RM2. . . . . .136 B6
Lawrence Trad Est
RM17. . . . . .177 E8
Lawson Cl IG1. . . . . .152 D7
Lawton Rd IG10 . . . . .89 B6
Laxtons SS17. . . . . .161 D1
Laxtons The SS4 . . . . . . .125 D5
Layborne Ave RM3 . . . . .114 C8
Lea Cl 1 E4 . . . . .109 C8
Leadale Ave E4 . . . . .109 C8
Leaden Cl CM6. . . . . .15 C8
LEADEN RODING. 15 C8
Leader Ave E12. . . . . . . .152 A7
Leady Way CM13. . . . . . . .95 D1
Lea Hall Bglws CM22 . . . .3 B3
Leamington Cl RM3. . . . .115 A4
Leamington Gdns
IG3. . . . . .133 F2
Leamington Rd
Hockley SS5. . . . . .124 F7
Romford RM3 . . . . .115 A5
Southend-on-S SS1 . . . . .167 C8

Leapingwell Cl CM2 . . . . .33 A3
Lea Rd
Grays RM16. . . . . .174 A1
Hoddesdon EN11. . . . . . .21 C8
Holdbrook SS6. . . . . .65 A5
South Benfleet SS7 . . . .144 C5
Lea Road Ind Pk EN9 . . . .65 A5
Leas Cl SS0 . . . . .166 B8
Leas Ct CM0. . . . . .106 C6
Leas Gdns SS0 . . . . .166 B8
Leaside SS7 . . . . .144 B6
Leaside Bsns Ctr EN3. . . .87 A7
Leaside Lo 6 EN11. . . . . .21 D8
Leas Rd
Burnham-on-C CM0 . . . .106 C6
Ingatestone CM4. . . . . . .74 A2
Southend-on-S SS0 . . . .166 C7
Upminster RM14 . . . . . . .137 D4
Leasway
Brentwood CM14. . . . . . .116 D7
Grays RM16. . . . . .173 C5
Rayleigh SS6 . . . . .123 C2
Upminster RM14 . . . . . . .156 C8
Wickford SS12 . . . . .121 B6
Leasway The SS0. . . . . . .166 B8
Leat Cl CM21. . . . . .1 F3
Leatham Rd E17 . . . . . . .109 B2
Leathart Cl RM12 . . . . . .155 B5
Leatherbottle Hill CM4. . .76 A2
Leather La
Hornchurch RM11. . . . . .136 D3
Southend-on-S SS1 . . . .167 A8
Lea Valley Rd E4 . . . . . . .87 A6
Lea Valley Rd EN3 . . . . . .65 B6
Lea Way CM12. . . . . .119 B8
Lechmere App IG8 . . . . .110 D1
Lechmere Ave
Chigwell IG7. . . . . .111 C6
Woodford IG8 . . . . .110 D1
Leconfield Wlk RM12 . . .155 C6
Lectern Mews SS15. . . . .141 D6
Ledbury Rd RM16 . . . . . .174 C1
Lee Ave RM6. . . . . .134 C5
Lee Chapel La SS16. . . . .141 D3
Lee Chapel North SS16. . .141 E6
LEE CHAPEL NORTH. . . .141 E6
Lee Chapel Prim Sch
SS16. . . . . .141 F4
LEE CHAPEL SOUTH. . . .141 F3
Lee Cl SG12. . . . . .8 C4
Leecon Way SS4. . . . . . .125 E3
Lee Ct CM2. . . . . .54 E7
Leeds Rd IG1. . . . . .133 D3
Leefield CM1 . . . . .31 F6
Lee Gardens Ave
RM11. . . . . .137 A3
Lee Gr IG7. . . . . .111 B8
Leeholm Rd RM15 . . . . . .171 C4
Lee Lotts SS3 . . . . .150 A4
Lee Rd SS13. . . . . .143 F6
Lee Rd RM11. . . . . .136 F2
Lees The SS3 . . . . .164 A6
Lee Valley Ctry Pk*
. . . . .21 B3
Lee Valley Ho EN9. . . . . . .66 A5
Lee Valley Park Visitor
Ctr* EN9 . . . . .43 C3
Lee Valley Pk Vst Ctr*
EN9 . . . . .43 C3
Leeview Ct E4. . . . . .87 A8
Leeward Rd CM3 . . . . . . .101 C5
Leeway The CM3. . . . . . . .56 F7
Lee Wlk SS16. . . . . .141 E5
Lee Woottens La
SS16. . . . . .142 A4
Legon Ave RM7. . . . . . . .135 C3
Legra Ave EN11. . . . . . . .21 A6
Leicester Ave SS4 . . . . . .147 F8
Leicester Gdns IG3 . . . . .133 C4
Leicester Rd
Tilbury RM18. . . . . .178 F6
Wanstead E11. . . . . .132 B6
Leige Ave SS8 . . . . .164 C4
Leigham Court Dr
SS9. . . . . .146 F1
Leighams Rd CM3 . . . . . . .78 E7
Leigh Ave CM2. . . . . .132 D7
LEIGH BECK. 164 F2
Leigh Beck Jun & Inf Sch
SS8. . . . . .164 E2
Leigh Beck La SS8. . . . . .164 E2
Leigh Beck Rd SS8 . . . . .164 F2
Leighcliff Rd SS9. . . . . . .165 F8
Leighcroft Gdns SS9 . . . .146 D4
Leigh Ct 11 E18. . . . . . . .110 A1
Leigh Fells SS13. . . . . . .143 C6
Leighfields SS7. . . . . . . .145 B6
Leighfields Ave SS9 . . . .146 C6
Leighfields Rd SS9 . . . . .146 C6
Leigh Gdns SS9 . . . . . . .146 C6
Leigh Hall Rd SS9 . . . . . .146 A2
Leigh Heath Ct SS9 . . . . .146 A2
Leigh Heritage Ctr*
. . . . .165 D8
Leigh Hill Cl SS9. . . . . . .165 E8
Leighlands CM3. . . . . . . .101 C7
LEIGH-ON-SEA. 146 A1
Leigh-on-Sea Sta
SS9. . . . . .165 C8
Leigh Park Cl SS9. . . . . .165 D8
Leigh Park Ct SS9 . . . . . .165 D8
Leigh Park Rd SS9. . . . . .165 D8

Leigh Rd
Canvey Island SS8. . . . . .164 B2
Southend-on-S SS9 . . . .146 F1
Wallend E6. . . . . .152 A1
Leighs Rd CM3 . . . . .19 E6
Leighs Rifleman CM12 . . .96 F3
Leighton Ave
Little Ilford E12. . . . . . . .152 A7
Southend-on-S SS9 . . . .146 F1
Leighton Gdns RM18. . . .179 B7
Leighton Rd SS17 . . . . . .144 C7
Leigh View Dr SS9 . . . . . .146 F4
Leighville Gr SS9. . . . . . .146 D1
Leighwood Ave SS9. . . . .146 E5
Leinster Ct IG6. . . . . .112 A4
Leinster Rd SS15. . . . . . .141 D6
Leitrim Ave SS3 . . . . .168 C5
Lekoe Rd SS8 . . . . .163 F6
Lena Kennedy Cl E4 . . . .109 C4
Lenham Way SS13 . . . . . .143 C6
Lenmore Ave RM17 . . . . .173 C3
Lennard Ho RM15. . . . . .171 D5
Lennard Row RM15 . . . . .171 D5
Lennox Cl
Grays RM16. . . . . .172 C2
Romford RM1 . . . . .135 F5
Lennox Dr SS2 . . . . .121 F5
Lennox Gdns IG1 . . . . . . .132 F3
Lennox Ho
7 Belvedere DA17. . . . . .169 A3
15 Brentwood CM14 . . . .116 C7
Lennox Rd DA11 . . . . . . .178 F1
Lenthall Ave RM17. . . . . .173 A3
Lenthall Rd IG10 . . . . . . .89 D5
Len Wastel Inf Sch The
SS13. . . . . .143 A5
Leonard Ave RM7 . . . . . .135 D3
Leonard Davis Ho
CM16. . . . . .47 A4
Leonard Dr SS6 . . . . . . .123 A4
Leonard Rd
Basildon SS16. . . . . . . .142 B2
Chingford E4 . . . . .109 A4
Southend-on-S SS0 . . . .166 D7
Leonard Way CM14 . . . . .115 C6
Leon Dr SS16. . . . . .142 D3
Leslie Cl SS9 . . . . .146 D6
Leslie Dr SS9 . . . . .146 D6
Leslie Gdns SS6 . . . . . . .123 F1
Leslie Newnham Ct 1
CM9. . . . . .37 A1
Leslie Pk CM0 . . . . .106 C4
Leslie Rd SS6 . . . . .123 F1
Lesney Gdns SS4 . . . . . .125 D3
Lessingham Ave IG5 . . . .133 A8
Lessington Ave RM7 . . . .135 C5
LESSNESS HEATH 169 B1
Lessness Heath Prim Sch
DA17. . . . . .169 A1
Lessness Pk DA17 . . . . . .169 A1
Lessness Rd 16 DA17. . . .169 A1
Lester Ho IG1 . . . . .109 D3
Lettons Chase CM3 . . . . .101 E6
Letzen Rd CM3. . . . . . . .164 A4
Leveller Row CM12 . . . . . .96 F3
Leventhorpe Sch The
CM21. . . . . .1 E4
Lever La SS4 . . . . .125 F1
Leverton SS16. . . . . .174 A2
Leverton Inf Sch The
EN9 . . . . .65 F5
Leverton Jun Sch The
EN9 . . . . .65 F5
Leverton Way EN9 . . . . . .65 C6
Leveson Rd RM16. . . . . .174 B3
Levett Gdns IG3 . . . . . . .152 F8
Levett Rd
Barking IG11. . . . . .152 E6
Stanford-le-H SS17 . . . . .160 E2
Levine Gdns IG11 . . . . . .153 D3
Lewes Cl RM17 . . . . .178 A8
Lewes Ct SS2. . . . . .148 C3
Lewes Rd
Romford RM3 . . . . .114 C6
Southend-on-S SS2 . . . .148 C3
Lewes Way SS7. . . . . . . .145 B7
Lewin Pl CM3 . . . . .33 E8
Lewis Ave E17 . . . . .109 A2
Lewis Cl CM15. . . . . .94 F2
Lewis Dr CM2 . . . . .54 B6
Lewisham Ct 8 EN3. . . . . .65 A1
Lewis Ho E4. . . . . .109 A5
Lewis Rd
Hornchurch RM11. . . . . .136 C5
Swanscombe DA10 . . . . .177 E1
Lewis Way RM10 . . . . . . .154 B6
Lexden Cl SS6 . . . . .123 B5
Lexden Dr RM6. . . . . . . .134 B5
Lexham Ho 9 IG11. . . . . .152 D4
Lexington Way RM11. . . .137 C5
Leybourne Dr CM1. . . . . .32 E7
Leyburn Cres RM3. . . . . .114 E3
Leyburn Rd RM3. . . . . . .114 E3
Leycroft Cl IG10 . . . . .89 C5
Leyland Ct SS1. . . . . .167 B8
Leyland Gdns IG8 . . . . . .110 C5
Leys Cl RM10 . . . . .154 D5
Leysings SS16. . . . . .141 E4
Leys Prim Sch The
RM10. . . . . .154 C5
Ley St
Ilford IG1 . . . . .133 B2

Ley St continued
Ilford, Newbury Park IG1,
IG2 . . . . 133 D3
Leys The
Basildon SS16 . . . . . 142 C4
Chelmsford CM2 . . . . . 32 F5
Leyswood Dr IG2 . . . 133 E6
Liberty Cotts RM4 . . 113 E8
Liberty Ct IG11 . . . . 153 C3
Liberty II Ctr RM1 . . 135 E6
Liberty The RM1 . . . 135 E6
Library Hill CM4 . . . . 116 D8
Libro Ct E4 . . . . 109 A6
Lichen Ct IG6 . . . . . 133 B8
Lichfield Cl CM1 . . . . 31 E4
Lichfield Rd
Dagenham RM8 . . . . . 134 C1
Woodford IG8 . . . . . . 109 E6
Lichfields The SS14 . 142 F7
Lichfield Terr RM14 . 137 F2
Lifstan Way SS1 . . . . 167 E2
Lightermans Way
DA9 . . . . 177 C3
Lilac Ave
Canvey Island SS8 . . . 164 C4
Wickford SS12 . . . . . 121 C7
Lilac Cl
Chelmsford CM2 . . . . . 54 C6
Pilgrims Hatch CM15 . . 94 B4
Lilac Gdns RM7 . . . . 135 E3
Lilac Ho 11 E3 . . . . . 176 A2
Lilac Rd EN11 . . . . . . 21 B8
Lilford Rd CM11 . . . . 97 C4
Lilian Cres CM13 . . . 117 C8
Lilian Gdns IG8 . . . . 110 B2
Lilian Pl SS6 . . . . . . 146 A8
Lilian Rd CM0 . . . . . 106 C5
Lilechurch Rd RM8 . . 153 C6
Lilley Cl CM14 . . . . . 115 F6
Lilliard Cl EN11 . . . . . 8 B2
Lilliput Rd RM7 . . . . 135 D4
Lillyputts Equestrian Ctr
RM11 . . . . 137 A5
Lillyville Wlk SS6 . . . 124 A1
Lily Albon Ct RM9 . . 153 F8
Lily Cl CM1 . . . . 32 F6
Lilystone Cl CM4 . . . . 75 D1
Lilystone Hall CM4 . . . 75 D1
Limberg Rd SS8 . . . . 163 D4
Limbourne Ave RM8 . 134 F4
Limbourne Dr CM9 . . . 37 D5
Limburg Rd SS8 . . . . 163 D4
Lime Ave
Brentwood CM13 . . . . 116 F7
Southend-on-S SS9 . . 146 C2
Upminster RM14 . . . . 156 A8
Limebrook Way CM9 . . 58 E7
Lime Cl
Buckhurst Hill IG9 . . . 110 D8
Romford RM7 . . . . . . 135 C7
South Ockendon RM15 . 157 C2
Lime Ct
Hockley SS5 . . . . 124 E6
Hornchurch RM11 . . . 136 C4
Lime Gr
Doddinghurst CM15 . . . 72 C1
Redbridge IG6 . . . . . . 111 F4
Lime Lo SS9 . . . . 146 C2
Lime Pl SS15 . . . . . . 119 C1
Lime Rd SS2 . . . . . . 148 C4
Limerick Gdns RM14 . 137 F4
Limes Ave
Chigwell IG7 . . . . 111 C4
Little Ilford E12 . . . . . 132 F1
Wanstead E11 . . . . . . 132 B7
Limes Ct
Brentwood CM15 . . . . . 94 D1
17 Hoddesdon EN11 . . . 21 A6
Limes Farm Jun & Inf Sch
IG7 . . . . 111 D5
Limeslade Cl SS17 . . 161 A3
Limes The
Brentwood CM13 . . . . 116 F7
Galleywood CM2 . . . . . 54 B2
Ingatestone CM4 . . . . . 74 C4
Purfleet RM19 . . . . . . 171 A1
Rayleigh SS6 . . . . 123 F1
Romford RM11 . . . . . . 136 D8
Limetree Ave SS7 . . . 144 B4
Lime Tree Cl E11 . . . 132 C7
Limetree Rd SS8 . . . 164 E4
Lime Way CM0 . . . . . 106 A5
Lime Wlk CM2 . . . . . . 54 C6
Limewood Ct IG4 . . . 132 F6
Lincefield SS16 . . . . 141 B3
Lincewood Prim Sch
Basildon SS16 . . . . . . 141 B3
Basildon SS16 . . . . . . 141 C4
Lincoln Ave RM7 . . . . 135 E3
Lincoln Chase SS2 . . 148 E3
Lincoln Cl RM11 . . . . 137 A6
Lincoln Ct
2 Ilford IG2 . . . . 133 C5
Redbridge IG1 . . . . . . 132 F4
Lincoln Gdns IG1 . . . 132 E4
Lincoln Ho 12 RM3 . . 114 D4
Lincoln Rd
Basildon SS14 . . . . . . 142 F7
Rochford SS4 . . . . . . 125 C5
Woodford E18 . . . . . . 110 A2
Lincolns Field CM16 . . 45 F1
Lincolns La CM14 . . . . 93 C3
Linda Ave SS8 . . . . . 163 E8
Linda Gdns CM12 . . . . 96 E4
Lindal Ct 11 E18 . . . . 110 A2

Linden Cl
Chelmsford CM2 . . . . . 54 C7
Purfleet RM19 . . . . . . 176 C8
Rayleigh SS6 . . . . 123 F1
South Benfleet SS7 . . . 144 C6
Linden Cres IG8 . . . . 110 B4
Linden Ct
South Benfleet SS7 . . . 144 C6
Southend-on-S SS9 . . 147 A2
Linden Leas SS7 . . . . 144 C6
Linden Rd SS7 . . . . . 144 C6
Linden Rise CM14 . . . 116 D5
Lindens EN9 . . . . 66 C4
Lindens The
Basildon SS16 . . . . . . 141 A5
Loughton IG10 . . . . . . 88 F4
Stock CM4 . . . . 75 F2
Linden Way SS8 . . . . 163 F4
Linde Rd IG8 . . . . . . 110 B4
Lindfield Rd RM3 . . . 114 E5
Lindhurst Dr CM11 . . . 98 C4
Lindisfarne Ave SS9 . 147 A2
Lindisfarne Cl
Basildon SS12 . . . . . . 122 A5
Maldon CM9 . . . . 58 E8
Lindisfarne Rd RM8 . . 134 C1
Lindon Rd SS11 . . . . . 99 C3
Lindsell Gn SS14 . . . 142 E5
Lindsell La SS14 . . . . 142 E5
Lindsey Cl CM14 . . . . 116 A6
Lindsey Ct
Rayleigh SS6 . . . . 123 A3
10 Wickford SS12 . . . 121 E5
Lindsey Rd
Dagenham RM8 . . . . . 134 C1
Great Wakering SS3 . . 150 B4
Lindsey St CM16 . . . . 46 A2
Lindsey Way RM11 . . 136 C6
Lindum SS1 . . . . 168 A6
Linford Cl CM19 . . . . . 23 C6
Linford Dr SS14 . . . . 142 F6
Linford End CM19 . . . . 23 C6
Linford Mews CM9 . . . 58 E8
Linford Rd RM16 . . . . 174 C1
Lingcroft SS16 . . . . . 142 A4
Lingfield Ave RM14 . . 137 A1
Lingfield Dr SS4 . . . . 126 A3
Lingmere Cl IG7 . . . . 111 C8
Lingrove Gdns IG9 . . 110 B8
Lingwood Cl CM4 . . . . 56 E7
Linkdale CM12 . . . . . 119 B8
Link Rd
Canvey Island SS8 . . . 163 F4
Dagenham RM9 . . . . . 154 B3
Rayleigh SS6 . . . . 123 D3
Stanford-le-H SS17 . . 160 D3
Links Ave RM2 . . . . . 114 B1
Links Ct SS1 . . . . 167 F7
Links Dr CM2 . . . . 53 F7
Linkside IG7 . . . . 111 C5
Links Rd IG8 . . . . . . 110 A5
Links The CM12 . . . . . 96 E4
Linksway SS9 . . . . . . 146 C4
Links Way SS7 . . . . . 145 F3
Linkway
Basildon SS14 . . . . . . 142 B6
Dagenham RM8 . . . . . 153 C8
Link Way RM11 . . . . . 136 E3
Linkway Rd CM14 . . . 115 F7
Linley Rd RM18 . . . . 180 D7
Linley Cres RM7 . . . . 135 C8
Linne Rd SS8 . . . . . . 164 C5
Linnet Cl SS3 . . . . . . 168 E8
Linnet Dr
Chelmsford CM2 . . . . . 54 B6
South Benfleet SS7 . . . 144 C2
Linnet Ho DA9 . . . . . 177 A1
Linnets SS14 . . . . . . 142 A3
Linnett Cl E4 . . . . . . 109 C6
Linnet Terr IG5 . . . . . 133 A8
Linnet Way RM19 . . . 171 B1
Linroping Ave SS8 . . 164 F3
Linsdell Rd IG11 . . . . 152 C4
Linton Cl RM14 . . . . . 113 C1
Linton Rd
Barking IG11 . . . . 152 C5
Southend-on-S SS3 . . 168 E6
Lintons Cl EN11 . . . . . 21 B7
Lintons The
1 Barking IG11 . . . . . 152 C5
Chelmsford CM2 . . . . . 55 D6
Linwood CM21 . . . . 1 E2
Lionel Oxley Ho RM17 . 178 B8
Lionel Rd SS8 . . . . . . 164 B3
Lion Fields SS3 . . . . 150 B3
Lionfield Terr CM1 . . . . 32 D3
Lion Hill SS17 . . . . . . 161 D3
Lion La CM12 . . . . 97 A2
Lion & Lamb Ct 7
CM14 . . . . 116 C8
Liphook Cl RM12 . . . 154 F8
Lippitts Hill IG10 . . . 141 C3
Lippitts Hill IG10 . . . . 87 F7
Lisa Cl CM12 . . . . 97 B6
Lisle Pl RM17 . . . . . . 173 A3
Lister Ave RM3 . . . . . 114 E1
Lister Rd RM18 . . . . . 179 A5
Lister Tye CM2 . . . . . . 54 C7
Liston Way 11 IG8 . . 110 C3
Listowel Rd RM10 . . . 135 A1
Litchborough Pk CM3 . . 56 F8
Littell Tweed CM2 . . . . 33 A3
Little Aston Rd RM3 . . 115 A3
LITTLE BADDOW 34 D4
Little Baddow Rd
Danbury CM3 . . . . 56 E7

Little Baddow Rd continued
Woodham Walter CM9 . . 35 C3
Little Belhus Cl RM15 . 157 A1
Little Bentley SS14 . . 142 B7
Little Berry La SS16 . 141 A4
Little Brays CM18 . . . . 24 A6
Little Brook Hospl
DA2 . . . . 176 C1
Littlebrook Manor Way
DA1 . . . . 176 A2
Little Brook Rd CM19 . . 22 C8
LITTLE BURSTEAD . . 118 F5
Littlebury Ct
Basildon SS13 . . . . . . 143 A8
Kelvedon Hatch CM15 . . 71 F2
Littlebury Gn SS13 . . 143 A8
Little Cattins CM19 . . . 22 F4
Little Charlton SS13 . 143 C6
Little Chittock SS14 . 142 E6
Littlecroft CM1 . . . . . 101 D6
Little Dodden SS16 . . 141 F4
Little Dorrit CM1 . . . . . 31 E7
Little Dragons IG10 . . 88 D5
LITTLE END 70 C5
Little Fields CM3 . . . . 57 A7
Little Fretches SS9 . . 146 E4
Little Friday Rd E4 . . 109 E8
Little Garth SS13 . . . 143 A5
Little Gaynes Gdns
RM14 . . . . 156 B8
Little Gaynes La
RM14 . . . . 156 B8
Little Gearies IG6 . . . 133 B7
Little Gerpins Rd
RM14 . . . . 155 F4
Little & Great Sir Hughes
La CM2 . . . . 55 B2
Little Gregories La
CM16 . . . . 67 D5
Little Grove Field
CM19 . . . . 23 C8
Little Gypps Cl SS8 . 163 F4
Little Gypps Rd SS8 . 163 F3
LITTLE HALLINGBURY . 2 B8
Little Hallingbury CE Prim
Sch CM22 . . . . 2 C7
Little Hayes Chase
Hullbridge CM3 . . . . . 102 C8
South Woodham Ferrers
CM3 . . . . 80 C1
Little Hays SS9 . . . . . 146 B6
LITTLE HEATH 134 B7
Little Heath
Hatfield Heath CM22 . . . 3 A3
Ilford RM6 . . . . 134 B7
Little Heath Sch RM6 . 134 B7
Little Hills CM9 . . . . . . 58 A5
Little Holt 10 E11 . . . 132 A6
Little Hyde La CM4 . . 74 B6
LITTLE ILFORD 152 A7
Little Kingston SS16 . 141 D2
Little Laver CM5 . . . . . 26 F7
Little Laver Rd CM5 . . 26 F7
Little London La CM9 . 35 D4
Little Lullaway SS15 . 141 F7
Little Malgraves Ind Est
RM14 . . . . 140 F1
Little Mdw CM11 . . . . . 31 A1
Little Mdws CM9 . . . . . 57 E6
Littlemoor Rd IG1 . . . 133 D1
Little Nell CM1 . . . . . . 31 E7
Little Norsey Rd CM11 . 97 C4
Little Oak Mews SS11 . 121 D7
Little Oaks SS14 . . . . 142 A6
Little Oxcroft SS15 . . 141 B6
LITTLE OXNEY GREEN
. . . . 52 E8
LITTLE PARNDON 10 B1
Little Parndon Sch
CM20 . . . . 10 B1
Little Pluckett's Way
IG9 . . . . 88 D1
Little Pound CM15 . . . 72 C3
Little Pynchons CM18 . . 24 A5
Little Russets CM13 . . 95 E2
Little Searles SS14 . . 143 B7
Little Spenders SS14 . 142 D8
Little St EN9 . . . . 65 D3
Little Stambridge Hall Rd
SS4 . . . . 126 B3
Little Stile CM1 . . . . . 53 A8
Littlethorpe SS16 . . . 142 F4
Little Thorpe SS1 . . . 149 B1
LITTLE THURROCK . . 173 D3
Little Thurrock Prim Sch
RM17 . . . . 173 D3
Littleton Ave E4 . . . . . 87 F1
Little Totham Rd CM9 . . 38 D8
LITTLE WAKERING . . 149 D6
Little Wakering Hall La
SS3 . . . . 150 A4
Little Wakering Rd
SS3 . . . . 149 E6
LITTLE WALTHAM 19 C6
Little Waltham CE Prim
Sch CM3 . . . . 19 B7
Little Waltham Rd
CM1 . . . . 19 D1
LITTLE WARLEY 19 D1
Little Warley Hall La CM13,
RM14 . . . . 138 E6
Little Wheatley Chase
SS6 . . . . 123 A4
Little Wlk CM20 . . . . . 23 D8
Liverymen Wlk 5
DA9 . . . . 177 C3
Livingstone Cl CM5 . . . 49 A2

Livingstone Cotts CM5 . . 49 A2
Livingstone Lo E17 . . 109 A1
Livingstone Terr
RM13 . . . . 154 E4
Llewellyn Cl CM1 . . . . 32 D3
Lloyd Mews EN3 . . . . . 65 A1
Lloyd Rd RM9 . . . . . . 153 F5
Lloyd Wise Cl SS2 . . . 148 D3
Lobelia Cl CM1 . . . . . . 33 A6
Locarno Ave SS11 . . . . 99 E2
Locke Cl
Rainham RM13 . . . . . . 154 F6
Stanford-le-H SS17 . . 160 C3
Lockfield Ave E4 . . . . . 87 E2
Lock Hill CM9 . . . . 37 E2
Locks Hill SS4 . . . . . 125 F1
Lock View CM21 . . . . . 1 F2
Lockwell Rd RM10 . . . 135 A1
Lockwood Pl E4 . . . . 109 A4
Lockwood Wlk RM1 . . 135 E6
Lockyer Mews EN3 . . . 65 B1
Lockyer Rd RM17 . . . 178 A1
Lodden Ho 5 RM3 . . . 115 A4
Lodge Ave
Dagenham RM8, RM9 . . 153 B7
Great Baddow CM2 . . . 54 F7
Romford RM2 . . . . . . 136 A7
Lodge Cl
Brentwood CM13 . . . . . 95 E2
Chigwell IG7 . . . . 112 A7
Rayleigh SS6 . . . . 123 E1
Thundersley SS7 . . . . 145 A5
Lodge Cres CM3 . . . . . 33 E7
Lodge Ct RM12 . . . . . 136 E2
Lodge Farm Cl SS9 . . 146 D5
Lodge Hall CM18 . . . . 23 E4
Lodge Hill IG4 . . . . . 132 E7
Lodge La
Grays RM16, RM17 . . . 173 B3
Purleigh CM3 . . . . 58 C2
Romford RM5 . . . . 113 A4
Waltham Abbey EN9 . . . 65 D4
Lodgelands Cl SS6 . . 123 F1
Lodge Rd
Loughton CM16 . . . . . . 67 A5
Maldon CM9 . . . . 36 F3
Woodham Ferrers CM3 . 78 F6
Woodham Mortimer CM3,
CM9 . . . . 58 B5
Writtle CM1 . . . . 53 A8
Lodge The
Epping CM16 . . . . 46 A1
29 Hornchurch RM11 . . 136 B3
Redbridge IG6 . . . . . . 111 E3
Lodge Villas IG8 . . . . 109 F4
Lodwick SS3 . . . . 168 C5
Loewen Rd RM16 . . . . 174 A3
Loftin Way CM2 . . . . . 54 D7
Loftus Rd SS11 . . . . . 152 C6
Logan Ct 8 IG11 . . . . 135 E6
Logan Link SS12 . . . . 121 F5
Logan Mews 2 RM1 . . 135 E6
Loman Path RM15 . . . 171 F7
Lombard Ave IG3 . . . . 133 E3
Lombard Ct RM7 . . . . 135 C7
Lombards Chase
CM3 . . . . 139 D5
Lombards The RM11 . . 136 F4
Lombardy Cl
3 Basildon SS13 . . . . 143 C6
Redbridge IG6 . . . . . . 111 B3
Lombardy Pl CM1 . . . . 32 B3
London Cruise Terminal
RM18 . . . . 179 A3
London Hill
Chelmsford CM2 . . . . . 53 F2
Galleywood CM2 . . . . . 54 A2
Rayleigh SS6 . . . . 123 D3
London Mews SS12 . . 121 B7
London Rd
Abridge RM4 . . . . 90 A6
Aveley RM15 . . . . 171 A4
Barking IG11 . . . . 152 C5
Basildon SS13 . . . . . . 143 D5
Basildon, Vange SS16 . 142 D3
Billericay CM12 . . . . . . 96 E2
Brentwood CM14 . . . . 116 A7
Chelmsford CM2 . . . . . 53 E6
Crays Hill CM11, SS12 . 120 E6
Gravesend DA11 . . . . 178 E1
Grays RM17, RM20 . . . 177 D8
Greenhithe DA9, DA2 . . 177 C2
Hadleigh SS7 . . . . . . 145 D3
Harlow CM17 . . . . 11 C8
Harlow, Latton Bush
CM17 . . . . 24 C4
Maldon CM9 . . . . 36 D3
Romford RM7 . . . . 135 B5
Sawbridgeworth CM21 . . 1 E2
South Benfleet SS7 . . . 144 D5
Southend-on-S SS9 . . 146 D2
Southend-on-S, Westcliff-on-S
SS1 . . . . 166 F8
Spellbrook CM23 . . . . . 1 F7
Stanford-le-H SS17 . . 160 B1
Stanford Rivers CM5 . . 70 C4
Stapleford Tawney RM4 . 91 D8
Thorndon Heath 179 B5
Wickford SS11, SS6 . . 122 D5
London Road Purfleet
RM19 . . . . 176 C8
London Road Ret Pk
SS0 . . . . 166 F8
London Road West
Thurrock RM20 . . . . . 177 A8
Londons Cl RM14 . . . 156 C7

London Southend Airp
SS2 . . . .
Longacre CM1 . . . .
Long Acre
Basildon SS14 . . . .
Harlow CM17 . . . .
Longacre Rd E17 . . . .
Longaford Way CM13 . . . .
Long Banks CM18 . . . .
Longborough Cl 2
SS13 . . . .
Longbow SS2 . . . .
Long Brandocks CM1 . . . .
Longbridge Ho 1
RM8 . . . .
Longbridge Rd
Barking IG11 . . . .
Dagenham RM8 . . . .
Long Comm CM9 . . . .
Long Croft Dr EN8 . . . . . .
Longcroft Rise IG10 . . . . .
Longcrofts CM9 . . . .
Long Ct RM19 . . . .
Long Deacon Rd E4 . . . . .
Longdon Ct RM1 . . . .
Longfellow Dr CM13 . . . . .
Longfield
Harlow CM18 . . . .
Loughton IG10 . . . .
Longfield Ave RM11 . . . . .
Longfield Cl SS11 . . . .
Longfield Cotts IG10 . . . . .
Longfield Rd
Great Baddow CM2 . . . . .
South Woodham Ferrers
CM3 . . . .
Wickford SS11 . . . .
Long Fields CM5 . . . .
Long Gages SS14 . . . .
Long Gn IG7 . . . .
Long Gr RM3 . . . .
LONG GREEN . . . .
Longhams Dr CM3 . . . . . .
Longhayes Ave RM6 . . . . .
Longhayes Ct RM6 . . . . . .
Longhouse Rd RM16 . . . . .
Long La
Chadwell St M RM16 . . . .
Grays RM16 . . . .
Hullbridge SS5 . . . .
Longland Bridge CM22
Longleat Cl CM1 . . . .
Long Ley CM20 . . . .
Longley Mews CM9 . . . . . .
Long Leys E4 . . . .
Long Lynderswood
SS15 . . . .
Longmans SS3 . . . .
Long Mdw
Brentwood CM13 . . . .
Romford RM3 . . . .
Longmead SS13 . . . .
Longmead Ave CM2 . . . . .
Longmead Cl CM15 . . . . . .
Long Meadow Dr
SS11 . . . .
Longmeads Cl CM1 . . . . . .
Longmore Ave SS14 . . . . .
Longport Cl IG6 . . . .
Long Rd SS8 . . . .
Longreach Ct IG11 . . . . . .
Long Reach Rd IG11 . . . . .
Long Riding SS14 . . . .
Long Ridings Ave
CM13 . . . .
Long Ridings Prim Sch
CM13 . . . .
Longrise CM2 . . . .
Longsands SS3 . . . .
Longshaw Prim Sch
E4 . . . .
Longshaw Rd E4 . . . .
Longship Way CM9 . . . . . .
Longshots Cl CM1 . . . .
Long St EN9 . . . .
Longstomps Ave CM2 . . . .
Longtail CM11 . . . .
Longtown Cl RM3 . . . .
Longtown Ct 21 DA2 . . . . .
Longtown Rd RM3 . . . .
Longview Way RM5 . . . . . .
Longwick SS16 . . . .
Long Wlk EN8 . . . .
Long Wood CM18 . . . .
Longwood Cl RM14 . . . . . .
Longwood Ct RM14 . . . . . .
Longwood Gdns
Ilford IG5, IG6 . . . .
Redbridge IG5 . . . .
Longwood Par IG6 . . . . . .
Lonsdale Ave
Brentwood CM13 . . . .
Romford RM7 . . . .
Lonsdale Cres IG2 . . . . . .
Lonsdale Cl SS2 . . . .
Lonsdale Rd SS2 . . . .
Looe Gdns IG6 . . . .
Loop Rd EN9 . . . .
Lord Ave IG5 . . . .
Lord Gdns IG5 . . . .
Lord Roberts Ave SS9 . . .
Lords Ct
Basildon SS13 . . . .
Hornchurch RM11 . . . . . .
Lordship Cl CM1 . . . .
Lordship Rd CM1 . . . .

N11 . . . . .21 A6
y SS13 . . . . . . .121 B2
d View CM6 . . . . .15 D7
ins CM3 . . . . . .101 C6
ns E11 . . . . . . .132 C7
CM4 . . . . .116 C6
SS2 . . . . .148 D3
CI CM11 . . . . . .119 D6
Ct
hithe DA9 . . . . . .177 B1
rd RM1 . . . . . . .135 F6
e CI CM12 . . . . .96 F5
SS7 . . . . .144 B2
d SS8 . . . . .164 D2
Ave IG6 . . . . . .133 B6
N 88 D3
e SS7 . . . . .66 B6
La CM16 . . . . . .67 D2
Seedbed Ctr
. . . . .89 D5
Sta IG10 . . . . . .88 E4
Way IG6 . . . . . .88 E1
ie SS7 . . . . .144 B6
S6 . . . . .123 A3
3 RM10 . . . . . .134 B6
S56 . . . . .123 A4
W SS6 . . . . . . .123 A4
4 E11 . . . . .132 B6
ns RM13 . . . . . .154 E2
aham Ho 5
. . . . .152 D4
SS6 . . . . .123 E2
CI SG12 . . . . . . .8 A8
r CM1 . . . . .32 F7
Ave SS12 . . . . .121 B7

15 . . . . .171 C4
Gdn 110 F4
Ongar CM5 . . . . .49 A3
ry RM18 . . . . . .180 C8
S56 . . . . .123 C2
Ave SS1 . . . . . .167 D8
Gdns
ll 153 A8
on-S SS2 . . . . .148 D1
Villas SS2 . . . . .148 D1
Mans 7
. . . . .152 F5
e SS9 . . . . .147 A6
k RM12 . . . . . .155 A6
SS8 . . . . .164 C2
on DA9 . . . . . .177 D3
EEN 52 B5
CM1 . . . . .31 B1
CM19 . . . . .23 A7
PI 4 CM2 . . . . . .32 F4
Rd IG1 . . . . . . .152 B8
. . . . .177 A2
S57 . . . . .112 A5
RM13 . . . . . . .154 D3
erton Hall La
. . . . .89 A4
chor St CM2 . . . .32 A1
dfords Rd RM1
. . . . .114 A4
OBBINGWORTH
. . . . .48 B7
oad St RM10 . . .154 A4
rnham Rd
. . . . .81 C2
ry La CM16 . . . .67 E8
ase CM3 . . . . . .82 F4
urch Hill
. . . . .176 E2
urch Rd SS7 . . .144 B6
ister CM11 . . . . .97 B2
rs SS17 . . . . . .175 A3
nton Rd SS17,
. . . . .3 D3
CM2 . . . . .140 D4
CM2 . . . . .54 C2
REEN
d 54 C2
. . . . .55 C6
nbricks
. . . . .123 D4
rdyke Ave
. . . . .154 C3
w CM18 . . . . . . .23 E4
AZEING 21 F1
ke CI RM3,
. . . . .114 F8
rk Rd
DA17 . . . . .169 A2
IG10 . . . . .88 E4
SS12 . . . . .121 C4
een's Rd
. . . . .110 D8
DA17 . . . . .169 B3
well SG12 . . . . . .8 A6
S4 . . . . .102 D2
SS5 . . . . .101 E1
ngbury CM22 . . . .2 C7
IG10 . . . . .89 A8
sing CM15 . . . . .95 D6
DA11 . . . . .178 A3
ntering CM21 . . . .2 A3
uthend Rd
. . . . .121 D8
SS15 . . . . .119 E1
ck Rd CM4 . . . . .76 C4
aines CM16 . . . .45 F1
IG7 . . . . .112 A5
t Mus*
. . . . .21 A5
CM21 . . . . .1 E1

Lowfield Ct 14 EN11 . . . .21 A6
Lowfield La EN11 . . . . . .21 A6
Low Hall CI E4 . . . . .87 B2
Low Hill Rd CM19 . . . . . .22 A6
Lowland Gdns RM7 . . . .135 B5
Lowlands Rd RM15 . . . .171 C5
Lowry CI
  Erith SS8 . . . . .169 D2
  Southend-on-S SS3 . . .149 F1
Lowshoe La RM5 . . . . . .113 B2
LOW STREET 179 F8
Low Street La
  East Tilbury RM18 . . . . .179 F8
  West Tilbury RM18 . . . .174 F1
LOXFORD 152 C7
Loxford CI SS13 . . . . . .143 A8
Loxford La IG1 . . . . . . .152 D7
Loxford Rd IG11 . . . . . .152 B6
Loxford Sch of Science &
  Tech IG1 . . . . .152 D7
Loxham Rd E4 . . . . . . .109 B3
Loxley CI RM3 . . . . . . .114 B3
Loyola Prep Sch IG9 . . . .88 C1
LOYTER'S GREEN 12 E1
Lubbards CI SS6 . . . . . .123 D5
Lubbins Park Com Prim
  Sch SS8 . . . . .164 C2
Lucam Lo SS4 . . . . . . .125 F2
Lucas Ave CM2 . . . . . . .54 C6
Lucas Ct
  Doddinghurst CM15. . . . .72 C3
  Romford RM2 . . . . . . .114 D1
  Waltham Abbey EN9 . . . .65 F6
Lucas Rd RM17 . . . . . .173 A3
Lucerne Dr CM19 . . . . .122 A7
Lucerne Way
  Romford RM3 . . . . . . .114 D4
  Writtle CM1 . . . . .53 B8
Lucerne Wlk SS11 . . . . .122 A7
Lucksfield Way CM2 . . . .54 F5
Luckyn La SS14 . . . . . .141 F8
Lucton Mews IG10. . . . . .89 B5
Luctons Ave IG9 . . . . . . .88 C1
Lucy Gdns RM8 . . . . . .134 E1
Lucy Rd SS1 . . . . .167 B7
Ludgate Ho E4 . . . . . . .87 F5
Ludgores La CM3 . . . . . .56 D5
Ludgrove CM3 . . . . .82 A6
Ludham CI IG6 . . . . . . .111 C2
Ludlow Ct 8 RM10 . . . .154 A6
Ludlow Mews SS13 . . . .143 B6
Ludlow PI RM17 . . . . . .173 B3
Lugg App E12 . . . . . . .133 A1
Luker Rd SS1 . . . . .167 A8
Lukin Cres E4 . . . . . . .109 D7
Lukinstone CI IG10 . . . . .88 E3
Lullington Rd RM9 . . . . .153 E5
Lulworth CI SS17 . . . . .175 B8
Lulworth Dr RM5 . . . . . .113 B5
Lumley CI DA17 . . . . . .169 A1
Luncies Rd SS14 . . . . .142 F5
Lundy CI SS2 . . . . .147 B7
Lupin CI RM7 . . . . .135 D2
Lupin Cres 3 IG11 . . . .152 B6
Lupin Dr CM1 . . . . .32 F6
Lupin Mews 1 CM1 . . . .32 F6
Luppit CI CM13 . . . . . . .95 A1
Lushes Ct IG10 . . . . . . .89 B4
Lushes Rd IG10. . . . . . .89 B4
Lutea CI SS15 . . . . . . .119 D1
Luthers CI CM15 . . . . . .71 E2
Luton Ho 9 RM3 . . . . . .114 E5
LUXBOROUGH 110 F6
Luxborough La IG7 . . . . .110 F6
Luxford PI CM21. . . . . . . .1 F1
Lych Gate SS15 . . . . . .141 C6
Lychgate Ind Est SS6 . .122 E1
Lyford CI E2 DA2 . . . . .176 B1
Lydford Rd SS0 . . . . . .166 E7
Lylt Rd SS8 . . . . .164 A3
Lyme Rd SS2 . . . . .148 C1
Lymington Ave SS9 . . . .146 E1
Lymington Rd RM8 . . . .134 D3
Lympstone CI SS0 . . . . .147 A5
Lynbrook CI RM13 . . . . .154 D3
Lynceley Grange CM16. . . .66 A2
Lynch The EN11 . . . . . . .21 B6
Lyndale CI SS1 . . . . . . .71 F2
Lyndale Ave SS2 . . . . . .148 B3
Lyndale Est RM20. . . . . .177 B8
Lyndbourne Ct SS7 . . . .144 C3
Lyndene SS7 . . . . .144 B6
Lyndhurst St 11 E18 . . .110 A2
Lyndhurst Dr
  Bicknacre CM3. . . . . . . .56 F1
  Hornchurch RM11 . . . . .136 C4
Lyndhurst Gdns
  Barking IG11. . . . . .152 E6
  Ilford IG2 . . . . .133 D5
Lyndhurst Rd
  Chingford E4 . . . . .109 C3
  Corringham SS17. . . . . .160 F4
  Rochford SS4. . . . . . . .103 C1
Lyndhurst Rise SS12 . . .111 A6
Lyndhurst Way CM13. . . .95 C2
Lyndon Ho DA17 . . . . . .169 A2
Lynford Gdns IG3 . . . . .133 F2
Lynfords Ave SS11 . . . .100 A3
Lynfords Dr
  Wickford, Runwell
  SS11. . . . . .99 F2
  Wickford SS11 . . . . . .100 A3
Lynmouth Ave CM2 . . . . .32 C1
Lynmouth Gdns CM2 . . . .32 C1
Lynmouth Ho 6 RM3 . . .114 E5
Lynnett Rd RM8 . . . . . .134 D2

Lynn Rd IG2. . . . . .133 D4
Lynn View CI SS7 . . . . .144 C5
Lynross CI RM3. . . . . . .114 F1
Lynstede SS14 . . . . . . .143 A5
Lynton Ave RM7 . . . . . .113 B2
Lynton Cres IG2 . . . . . .133 B5
Lynton Dr CM1 . . . . . . .32 E5
Lynton Rd 6 IG1 . . . . . .133 C2
Lynton Rd
  Chingford E4 . . . . .109 B5
  Hadleigh SS7 . . . . . . .145 C3
  Southend-on-S SS1 . . .167 F6
Lynwood CI
  Romford RM5 . . . . . . .113 B4
  Woodford E18 . . . . . . .110 C2
Lynwood Dr RM5 . . . . . .113 B3
Lynwood Gn SS6 . . . . . .146 A8
Lyon Bsns Est IG11 . . . .152 E3
Lyon CI CM2 . . . . .54 B3
Lyon Rd RM1 . . . . .135 F4
Lysander Ct CM16 . . . . .47 B5
Lyster Ave CM2 . . . . . . .55 A7
Lytton CI IG10 . . . . .89 D6
Lytton Rd
  Chadwell St M RM16 . . .173 F2
  Grays RM16. . . . . .174 A2
  Romford RM2 . . . . . . .136 B6
Lyttons Way EN11 . . . . . .8 A1

M

Mabey's Wlk CM21. . . . . .1 B1
Mablin Lo IG9 . . . . .88 C1
McAdam CI EN11 . . . . . .21 A8
Macarthur CI DA8 . . . . .169 E1
Macarthur PI 20
  CM14 . . . . .116 C7
Macaulay Rd SS16 . . . .141 A5
McCalmont Dr SS6 . . . .123 C7
Macclesfield Ho 7
  RM3. . . . . .114 E5
McClintock PI EN3. . . . . .65 B2
McDivitt Wlk SS9 . . . . .147 A6
Macdonald Ave
  Dagenham RM10 . . . . .135 B1
  Hornchurch RM11 . . . . .136 F7
  Southend-on-S SS0 . . .147 E2
Macdonald Rd E17 . . . .109 C1
Macdonald Way
  RM11. . . . . .136 E7
Mace Ct RM17 . . . . . . .178 E8
Mace Wlk CM1 . . . . . . .31 F3
McGrail Ct SS8 . . . . . . .164 F2
Macgregor Dr SS12 . . . .121 E5
McIntosh CI RM1 . . . . .135 E8
McIntosh Rd RM1 . . . . .135 E8
Mackenzies Wlk SS4 . . .125 C6
Mackenzie CI SS12 . . . .121 E6
McKenzie Rd EN10 . . . . .21 A3
Mackley Dr SS17 . . . . . .160 F5
Maclaren Way 5
  SS12. . . . . .121 E5
Maclennan Rd RM13 . . .155 D2
Macleod CI RM17 . . . . .173 D2
Macmillan Ct 4 CM2 . . . .32 E1
Macmillan Gdns DA1 . . .176 A3
Macmurdo CI SS9 . . . . .146 D7
Macmurdo Rd SS9 . . . .146 D7
Macon Way RM14. . . . . .137 F5
Madden CI DA10. . . . . .177 E1
Maddox CI E4 . . . . .87 D1
Maddox Rd CM20 . . . . . .23 E8
Madeira Ave IG9 . . . . . .146 E2
Madeira Gr IG8. . . . . . .110 C4
Madeleine CI RM6 . . . . .134 C5
Madeleine Flats CM17 . . .23 B7
Madeleine Gdns IG6 . . . .111 E5
Madeline Rd IG1 . . . . . .152 D7
Madeline PI CM1 . . . . . .31 E6
Madells CM16 . . . . .67 F8
Madford Trade Pk
  DA8 . . . . .169 D1
Madison CI 3 RM10 . . .154 B6
Madles La CM4 . . . . . . .75 F1
Madras Rd IG1 . . . . . . .152 B8
Madras Rd IG1 . . . . . . .152 B8
Madrid Ave SS6 . . . . . .123 B7
Mafeking Ave IG2 . . . . .133 D4
Magazine Rd SS3 . . . . .168 C8
Magdalene Gdns E6 . . . .152 A1
Magdalen Gdns CM13 . . .95 E3
MAGDALEN LAVER 25 D5
Magdalen Rd SS1 . . . . .167 F6
Magnalia CI SS15 . . . . .119 C1
Magnet Point RM20. . . . .177 B8
Magnet Rd RM20 . . . . .177 C8
Magnolia CI
  Canvey Island SS8 . . . .164 A2
  Chelmsford CM2 . . . . . .54 D8
  South Ockendon RM15 . .157 E1
Magnolia La SS15 . . . . .119 C1
Magnolia Lo E4 . . . . . . .109 B7
Magnolia PI SS17 . . . . .160 F4
Magnolia Rd SS4 . . . . .125 C5
Magnolias CM1 . . . . . . .119 C6
Magnolia Way
  Pilgrims Hatch CM15. . . . .94 B4
  Rochford SS4. . . . . . . .125 C5
Magnum Ct RM13 . . . . .155 C1
Magpie La CM13 . . . . . .94 C3
Magpies CM16 . . . . . . .45 A7
Magwitch CI CM1 . . . . . .31 F7
Mahonia Dr CM13 . . . . .140 F5
Maida Ave E4 . . . . .109 B8
Maida Rd DA17 . . . . . .169 A3
Maida Way E4 . . . . .87 B2
Maidstone Ave RM5. . . .113 C1

Maidstone Rd RM17 . . . .178 A8
Main Dr CM13 . . . . . . .140 E5
Maine Cres SS6 . . . . . .123 B4
Main Rd
  Bicknacre CM3. . . . . . . .79 A6
  Boreham CM3 . . . . .20 F1
  Broomfield CM1. . . . . . .19 B2
  Chelmsford CM2 . . . . . .55 F7
  Danbury CM3. . . . . .56 A7
  Danbury CM3. . . . . .56 D7
  East Hanningfield CM3 . .78 B8
  East Hanningfield CM3 . .78 C5
  Hawkwell SS5 . . . . . . .124 F4
  Hockley SS5 . . . . .124 D6
  Hullbridge SS5 . . . . . . .101 E4
  Rettendon CM3, SS11 . . .100 B6
  Romford RM1 . . . . . . .136 A8
  St Lawrence CM0 . . . . . .62 D7
  Thundersley SS7 . . . . .145 B6
Maitland PI SS3 . . . . . .149 E1
Maitland Rd SS12. . . . . .121 E5
Maitlands IG10 . . . . . . .88 F6
Maizey Ct CM15 . . . . . .94 A4
Makepeace Rd E11 . . . .132 A7
Makinen Ho IG9 . . . . . . .88 C7
Malan Sq RM12 . . . . . .155 B6
Malby Lo SS0. . . . . . . .166 C8
Malcolm Way E11 . . . . .132 A7
MALDON 37 B3
Maldon Court Sch CM9 . . .36 F3
Maldon District Mus*
  CM9. . . . . .37 B2
Maldon Ho IG9 . . . . .88 C7
Maldon Prim Sch CM9 . . .37 A2
Maldon Rd
  Bradwell on S CM0 . . . . .42 A1
  Bradwell on S, Mill End
  CM0 . . . . .63 C7
  Bradwell Waterside CM0. .41 F1
  Burnham-on-C CM0 . . . .105 E8
  Dagenham RM7. . . . . .135 C4
  Danbury, Gay Bowers
  CM3 . . . . .57 B5
  Danbury, Runsell Green
  CM3 . . . . .57 B5
  Goldhanger CM9 . . . . . .38 E7
  Great Baddow CM2 . . . . .55 C7
  Langford CM9 . . . . .36 D6
  Latchingdon CM3. . . . . .81 F6
  Maldon CM9. . . . . .50 C6
  Margaretting CM4 . . . . . .75 B8
  Mayland CM3, SS12 . . . .61 D1
  Southend-on-S SS2 . . . .148 A1
  Woodham Mortimer CM9 . .57 E6
Maldon Wlk IG8. . . . . . .110 C4
Malford Ct E18 . . . . . . .110 A1
Malford Gr E18 . . . . . . .110 A1
Malgraves SS13 . . . . . .143 B7
Malgraves PI SS13 . . . .143 B7
Malkin Dr CM17 . . . . . . .24 E7
Mallard Cl CM14. . . . . .137 F4
Mallard Ct
  Chingford E4 . . . . .87 D2
  Ilford IG1 . . . . .133 C2
  3 Southend-on-S SS3 . .167 C8
Mallard Rd CM2 . . . . . . .54 A5
Mallards
  Mayland CM3. . . . . . . .83 A8
  Southend-on-S SS3 . . .149 E1
  Wanstead E11 . . . . . . .132 A4
Mallards Rd
  Barking IG11. . . . . . . .153 A1
  Woodford IG8 . . . . . . .110 C4
Mallards Rise CM17. . . . .24 D8
Mallards The SS3 . . . . .150 A4
Mallard Way
  Brentwood CM14 . . . . . .95 B2
  Roydon CM19. . . . . .9 A1
Mallinson CI RM12. . . . .155 C7
Mallow CI CM1 . . . . . . .19 D8
Mallory CM20. . . . . .10 F2
Mallow Ct RM12 . . . . . .97 A1
Mallow Ct RM12 . . . . . .178 E8
Mallow The SS1 . . . . . .167 F6
Mallows Gn CM19. . . . . .23 A3
Mall The RM1. . . . . . . .136 B3
Malmesbury Rd E18 . . . .109 F2
Malmsmead SS3. . . . . .168 C8
Malpas Rd
  Dagenham RM9 . . . . . .153 D6
  Grays RM16. . . . . .174 C3
Malsters Lo 3 SS1 . . . . .167 A7
Malta Rd RM18 . . . . . . .178 F5
Maltese Rd CM1 . . . . . .32 A4
Malthouse PI 6 RM1 . . .135 E6
Malting La EN11 . . . . . .159 A1
Maltings Chase CM4 . . . .74 B3
Maltings Hill CM5 . . . . . .26 E3
Maltings Ind Est The
  SG12 . . . . .8 D4
Maltings La CM16. . . . . .46 A2
Maltings Rd
  Battlesbridge SS11 . . . .100 C3
  Great Baddow CM2 . . . . .55 C7
Maltings The
  1 Gravesend DA11 . . . .179 A1
  Romford RM1 . . . . . . .135 F4
  Southminster CM0 . . . . .84 C4
Malting Villas Rd SS4 . .125 F2
Malvern SS2. . . . . .148 B1
Malvern Ave
  Canvey Island SS8. . . . .163 D3
  Chingford E4 . . . . .109 D3

Malvern Dr
  Ilford IG3 . . . . .152 F8
  Woodford IG8 . . . . . . .110 C6
Malvern Gdns IG10 . . . . .88 F3
Malvern Ho DA11. . . . . .178 D1
Malvern Rd
  Grays RM17. . . . . .173 E2
  Hockley SS5 . . . . .124 F8
  Hornchurch RM11 . . . . .136 A5
Malvina CI SS16 . . . . . .159 F7
Malwood CI SS7. . . . . .144 B5
Malwood Rd SS7 . . . . . .144 B5
Malyon Court CI SS7. . . .145 B4
Malyons SS13 . . . . . . .143 B8
Malyons CI SS13 . . . . . .143 B8
Malyons La SS13 . . . . .143 B8
Malyons La SS5 . . . . . .101 D2
Malyons Mews SS13 . . .143 B8
Malyons PI SS13 . . . . . .143 B8
Malyons The SS7 . . . . .145 B4
Manbrough Ave E6 . . . .152 A2
Manchester Dr SS9 . . . .146 F2
Manchester Way
  CM1 . . . . .110 A8
Mandarin Royal 7
  RM1. . . . . .135 F5
Mandeville CI CM17. . . . .24 C6
Mandeville Prim Sch
  CM21. . . . . .1 D3
Mandeville Way
  Basildon SS15, SS16 . . .141 B5
  Broomfield CM1. . . . . . .19 B3
  South Benfleet SS7 . . . .144 C7
Mandeville Wlk CM13. . . .95 E2
Manford CI IG7 . . . . . . .112 B6
Manford Cross IG7 . . . .112 A5
Manford Ct
  Chigwell IG7 . . . . .111 F5
  1 Redbridge IG7 . . . . .112 A5
Manford Prim Sch
  IG7. . . . . .111 F5
Manford Way
  Chigwell IG7 . . . . .111 F5
  Redbridge IG7 . . . . . . .112 A5
Mangapp Chase CM0 . . .106 A8
Mangapps Rly Mus*
  CM0. . . . . .106 A8
Manilla Ct 5 RM6 . . . . .134 B5
Manilla Rd SS3 . . . . . . .167 C7
Mannering Gdns SS0 . . .147 A3
Manners Cnr SS2. . . . . .147 E5
Manners Gr SS16 . . . . .141 C4
Manning Rd RM10 . . . . .154 A5
Manning St RM15 . . . . .171 C5
Manning Way RM6 . . . . .134 B5
Mannock Dr IG10 . . . . . .89 C7
Mannock Mews E18 . . . .110 B2
Manns Way SS6 . . . . . .123 C5
Manor Ave
  Basildon SS13 . . . . . . .143 C7
  Hornchurch RM11 . . . . .136 C6
Manor CI
  Aveley RM15 . . . . .171 C5
  4 Barking IG11 . . . . . .152 F5
  Chingford E4 . . . . .87 E1
  South Benfleet SS7 . . . .144 D7
  Southend-on-S SS1 . . .167 C7
  Waltham Abbey EN9 . . . .65 D1
Manor Dr CM0 . . . . .54 F7
Manor Farm Dr E4 . . . . .109 E7
Manor Hatch CM18 . . . . .24 A2
Manor Hatch CI CM18. . . .24 A2
Manor Ho CM3 . . . . .57 A5
Manor House Gdns 2
  E11. . . . . .132 B5
Manor Inf Sch IG11. . . . .152 F6
Manor Jun Sch IG11. . . .152 F6
Manor Rd The
  . . . . .135 F6
Manor Rd
  Abridge RM4 . . . . .90 E2
  Barking IG11. . . . . . . .152 F6
  Basildon SS15 . . . . . . .141 B7
  Chelmsford CM2 . . . . . .32 C1
  Chigwell IG7 . . . . .111 D5
  Dagenham RM10 . . . . .154 D6
  Dengie CM0 . . . . .63 D1
  Grays, Little Thurrock
  Marshes RM17 . . . . . .178 D3
  Grays, West Thurrock
  RM20. . . . . .177 C8
  Harlow CM17 . . . . .11 C5
  High Beach IG10 . . . . . .88 B8
  Hockley SS5 . . . . .124 C6
  Hoddesdon EN11 . . . . . .21 A7
  Ilford RM6 . . . . .134 D5
  Loughton IG10. . . . . . . .88 C3
  Maldon CM9 . . . . .36 A4
  Romford RM1 . . . . . . .136 A6
  South Benfleet SS7 . . . .144 D6
  Southend-on-S SS0 . . .166 D7

Manor Rd *continued*
South Woodham Ferrers
  CM3 . . . . 101 C8
Stanford-le-H SS17 . . . . 160 D1
Swanscombe DA10 . . . . 177 D1
Tilbury RM18 . . . . 179 A5
Waltham Abbey EN9 . . . . 65 D6
Woodham Walter CM9 . . . . . . 35 E5
Manor Sq RM8 . . . . 134 C2
Manor The IG8 . . . . 111 A3
Manor Trad Est SS7 . . . . . 144 D7
Manorway IG8 . . . . 110 C5
Manor Way
Brentwood CM14 . . . . 116 A7
Chingford E4 . . . . 109 D6
Corringham SS17 . . . . 161 A1
Northfleet RM17 . . . . 178 A3
Rainham RM13 . . . . 154 E1
Swanscombe DA10 . . . . 177 E3
Manor Way Bsns Ctr
RM13 . . . . 169 D8
Manorway The
Corringham SS17 . . . . 161 D1
Stanford-le-H SS17 . . . . 160 D2
Mansard Cl RM12 . . . . 136 A2
Manse Chase CM9 . . . . 37 A1
Mansel Cl SS9 . . . . 146 E6
Mansel Gr E17 . . . . 109 A2
Manser Ct RM13 . . . . 154 E2
Manser Rd RM13 . . . . 154 E3
Mansfield CM21 . . . . 1 A1
Mansfield Gdns
RM12 . . . . 136 D2
Mansfield Hill E4 . . . . 87 B1
Mansfield Rd
Ilford IG1 . . . . 133 A2
Wanstead E11 . . . . 132 B5
Mansfields CM1 . . . . 30 F1
Manstead Gdns
Dagenham RM6 . . . . 134 C4
Rainham RM13 . . . . 170 B7
Mansted Gdns SS4 . . . . . . 125 D5
Manston Rd CM20 . . . . 23 E8
Manston Way RM12 . . . . . . 155 B6
Manton Rd EN3 . . . . 65 A1
MANWOOD GREEN 13 F5
Maple Ave
Heybridge CM9 . . . . 37 C6
Southend-on-S SS9 . . . . 165 F8
Upminster RM14 . . . . 156 B8
Maple Cl
Brentwood CM13 . . . . 116 F7
Buckhurst Hill IG9 . . . . 110 D7
Hornchurch RM12 . . . . 136 B1
🔟 Redbridge IG6 . . . . 111 E5
Theydon Bois CM16 . . . . 67 D2
Maplecroft La EN9 . . . . 21 E2
Maple Ct
🔟 Dagenham RM8 . . . . . . 134 D4
Southend-on-S SS3 . . . . 168 F8
Stansted Abbotts SG12 . . . . . 8 D3
Mapledene Ave SS5 . . . . . 101 E2
Maple Dr
Chelmsford CM2 . . . . 54 B6
Rayleigh SS6 . . . . 123 C7
South Ockendon RM15 . . . . 157 D1
Mapleford Sweep
SS16 . . . . 142 D4
Maple Gate IG10 . . . . 89 A7
Mapleleaf Cl SS5 . . . . 124 F7
Maple Leaf Cl SG12 . . . . 8 D4
Mapleleafe Gdns IG6 . . . . 133 B8
Mapleleaf Gdns SS12 . . . . 121 B6
Maple Lo IG9 . . . . 88 D1
Maple Mead CM12 . . . . 119 C8
Maple Pk EN11 . . . . 21 C6
Maple Rd RM17 . . . . 178 C8
Maple River Ind Est
CM20 . . . . 11 B6
Maples
Stanford-le-H SS17 . . . . 160 E2
Waltham Abbey EN9 . . . . 66 C4
Maplesfield SS7 . . . . 145 D4
Maple Springs EN9 . . . . 66 A7
Maple Sq SS2 . . . . 148 B2
Maple St RM7 . . . . 135 C7
Maplestead SS14 . . . . 142 D8
Maplestead Rd RM9 . . . . . 153 B4
Maples The
Harlow CM19 . . . . 23 B3
🔟 Wickford SS12 . . . . . . 121 C5
Mapleton Rd E4 . . . . 109 C7
Mapletree La CM4 . . . . 73 E8
Maple Tree La SS16 . . . . . 140 F5
Maple Way
Burnham-on-C CM0 . . . . 106 A6
Canvey Island SS8 . . . . 163 E3
Maplin Cl SS7 . . . . 144 C7
Maplin Ct SS3 . . . . 168 G6
Maplin Gdns SS14 . . . . . . 142 E5
Maplin Mews SS3 . . . . 168 E6
Maplin Way SS1 . . . . 168 C6
Maplin Way N SS1 . . . . . . 149 C1
Mapperley Cl 🔟 E11 . . . . 132 A5
Mapperley Dr IG8 . . . . 109 E3
Marchmant Cl RM12 . . . . . 136 C1
Marconi Gdns CM15 . . . . . . 94 C4
Marconi Rd CM1 . . . . 32 B3
Marcos Rd SS8 . . . . 164 D3
Marcus Ave SS1 . . . . 168 B7
Marcus Ct CM1 . . . . 168 B7
Marcus Gdns SS1 . . . . 168 B7
MARDEN ASH 49 A1
Marden Ash 🔟 SS15 . . . . 141 A6

Marden Cl IG7 . . . . 112 B8
Marden Rd 🔟 RM1 . . . . . 135 E5
Mardyke Cl RM13 . . . . 154 C3
Mardyke Country Pk*
RM15 . . . . 172 F8
Mardyke Ho RM13 . . . . 154 D3
Mardyke Rd CM20 . . . . 11 A2
Maresby Ho E4 . . . . 109 B8
Margaret Ave
Brentwood CM15 . . . . 95 A3
Chingford E4 . . . . 87 B3
Margaret Bondfield Ave
IG11 . . . . 153 A5
Margaret Cl
Epping CM16 . . . . 45 F2
Romford RM2 . . . . 136 B6
Waltham Abbey EN9 . . . . 65 D6
Margaret Dr RM11 . . . . 136 F4
Margaret Rd
Epping CM16 . . . . 46 A2
Romford RM2 . . . . 136 B6
MARGARET RODING 15 D5
MARGARETTING 75 A8
Margaretting CE Prim Sch
CM4 . . . . 74 F8
Margaretting Rd
Chelmsford CM2 . . . . 53 F1
Galleywood CM2 . . . . 54 A2
Wanstead E12 . . . . 132 C3
Writtle CM1 . . . . 53 A6
Margaret Way IG4 . . . . 132 E5
Margarite Way SS12 . . . . . 121 B7
Margaret Rd RM8 . . . . 134 D1
Margeth Rd CM12 . . . . 119 C3
Margherita Pl EN9 . . . . 66 A5
Margherita Rd EN9 . . . . . . 66 A5
Margraten Ave SS8 . . . . . . 164 D2
Marguerite Dr SS9 . . . . . . 146 F1
Mariam Gdns RM12 . . . . . . 136 F2
Marian Cl RM16 . . . . 172 E5
Marian Lawson Ct 🔟
IG7 . . . . 112 A5
Marie Cl SS17 . . . . 161 A7
Marien Ct E4 . . . . 109 D5
Marigold Cl CM1 . . . . 32 F6
Marigold La CM4 . . . . 75 F1
Marigold Pl CM17 . . . . 11 B4
Marina Ave SS6 . . . . 123 C3
Marina Cl SS12 . . . . 147 E4
Marina Gdns RM7 . . . . 135 C6
Marina App SS8 . . . . 164 B2
Marine Ave
Canvey Island SS8 . . . . 164 E2
 SS0 . . . . 166 E7
Southend-on-S SS9, Clifftown
 SS0 . . . . 166 E7
Southend-on-S SS9 . . . . 146 E1
Marine Cl SS9 . . . . 146 A1
Marine Cotts RM13 . . . . . . 170 D6
Marine Ct RM19 . . . . 170 F2
Marine Dr RM13 . . . . 153 B2
Marine Par
Canvey Island SS8 . . . . 164 F2
Mayland CM3 . . . . 60 C1
Southend-on-S, Leigh-on-S
 SS9 . . . . 146 B1
Southend-on-S SS1 . . . . 167 B7
Mariner Rd E12 . . . . 152 A8
Mariners Ct
Great Wakering SS3 . . . . 150 C3
Greenhithe DA9 . . . . 177 B3
Mariners Way CM9 . . . . . . 59 A8
Marine Cl SS9 . . . . 111 D3
Marionette Stps 🔟
SS1 . . . . 167 C7
Marion Gr IG8 . . . . 109 E6
Marisco Cl RM16 . . . . 174 B2
Maritime Ave CM9 . . . . 37 E3
Maritime Cl RM16 . . . . 172 E3
Maritime Gate DA11 . . . . . 178 E1
Marjorams Ave IG10 . . . . . . 89 A7
Mark Ave E4 . . . . 87 B3
Market Ave SS12 . . . . 121 C8
Market Hill CM9 . . . . 37 A3
Market Hill Ct CM9 . . . . 37 A3
Market Ho 🔟 CM20 . . . . . 10 D1
Market Link RM1 . . . . 135 E7
Market Pavement 🔟
SS14 . . . . 142 A5
Market Pl
Abridge RM4 . . . . 90 B6
Ingatestone CM4 . . . . 74 B4
Maldon CM9 . . . . 36 F2
Romford RM1 . . . . 135 E6
Southend-on-S SS3 . . . . 167 A7
Tilbury RM18 . . . . 179 A5
Market Rd
Chelmsford CM1 . . . . 32 B2
Wickford SS12 . . . . 121 C7
Market Sq
Basildon SS14 . . . . 142 A5
🔟 Chelmsford CM2 . . . . . . 32 B2
Rochford SS4 . . . . 125 F2
South Woodham Ferrers
 CM3 . . . . 101 E7
Waltham Abbey EN9 . . . . 65 C6
Market St
Harlow CM17 . . . . 11 C4
Wallend E6 . . . . 152 A3
Markfield Gdns E4 . . . . 87 B2
Mark Hall Cycle Mus &
Gdns* RM20 . . . . 11 B3
Mark Hall Moors CM20 . . . 11 B3
MARK HALL NORTH 11 A3
Mark Hall Sch CM17 . . . . . 11 C3
MARK HALL SOUTH 11 A1

Markham Ho 🔟
RM10 . . . . 135 A1
Markhams SS17 . . . . 160 F3
Markhams Chase
SS15 . . . . 141 D7
Mark La DA12 . . . . 179 E1
Markland Cl CM2 . . . . 54 C3
Markland Dr CM9 . . . . 36 E1
Marklay Dr CM3 . . . . 101 C7
Mark Rd CM0 . . . . 63 F6
Mark's Ave CM5 . . . . 49 A4
Marks Cl
Billericay CM12 . . . . 96 F4
Ingatestone CM4 . . . . 73 F1
Marks Ct SS1 . . . . 167 C7
MARKS GATE 112 E1
Marks Gate Inf Sch
RM6 . . . . 134 E8
Marks Gate Jun Sch
RM6 . . . . 134 E8
Marks Hall CM6 . . . . 15 E3
Marks Hall La CM6 . . . . 15 E3
Marks La CM3 . . . . 99 F8
Marks Rd RM7 . . . . 135 D6
Mark Wade Cl E12 . . . . 132 D2
Markwell Wood CM19 . . . . . 23 B2
Markyate Rd RM8 . . . . 153 B7
Marlands
Redbridge IG5 . . . . 132 E8
Woodford IG5 . . . . 110 F1
Marlborough Ave CM0 . . . . . 63 E3
Marlborough Cl
Grays RM16 . . . . 173 C4
South Benfleet SS7 . . . . 144 D7
Upminster RM14 . . . . 137 E3
Marlborough Ct 🔟
IG9 . . . . 110 C8
Marlborough Dr IG5 . . . . . . 132 E8
Marlborough Gdns
RM14 . . . . 137 E4
Marlborough Ho
CM14 . . . . 116 B6
Marlborough Pl SS1 . . . . . . 166 F7
Marlborough Rd
🔟 Chelmsford CM2 . . . . . . 32 A1
Chingford E4 . . . . 109 B4
Dagenham RM8 . . . . 153 C8
Pilgrims Hatch CM15 . . . . . . 94 A3
Romford RM7 . . . . 135 B7
Southend-on-S SS1 . . . . 167 D8
Wanstead E18 . . . . 132 A8
🔟 Woodford E18 . . . . 110 A1
Marlborough Terr
CM2 . . . . 32 A1
Marlborough Way
CM12 . . . . 97 A5
Marlborough Wlk
SS5 . . . . 124 C6
Marle Gdns EN9 . . . . 65 C7
Marlescroft Way IG10 . . . . . 89 B4
Marlin Cl SS7 . . . . 145 E6
Marlow Ave RM19 . . . . 171 A2
Marlowe Cl
Billericay CM12 . . . . 97 B5
Maldon CM9 . . . . 59 A8
Redbridge IG6 . . . . 111 C2
Marlowe Gdns RM3 . . . . . . 114 C2
Marlowe Ho 🔟 IG8 . . . . . 111 A3
Marlow Gdns SS3 . . . . 147 E4
Marmadue Ave SS6 . . . . . . 123 B5
Marmion App E4 . . . . 109 A6
Marmion Cl E4 . . . . 109 A6
Marmion Ct E4 . . . . 109 A6
Marney Cl CM2 . . . . 54 E8
Marney Dr SS14 . . . . 142 F5
Marquis Ct IG11 . . . . 152 E7
Marquis Dr CM9 . . . . 37 E1
Mar Rd RM15 . . . . 157 C1
Marriotts CM17 . . . . 11 C5
Marsden Ho 🔟 RM3 . . . . 114 F4
Marshall Cl SS9 . . . . 146 A3
Marshalls SS4 . . . . 125 D4
Marshalls Cl SS6 . . . . 123 F2
Marshalls Dr RM1 . . . . 135 E8
Marshalls Park Sch
RM1 . . . . 113 E1
Marshalls Rd RM7 . . . . . . 135 D7
Marsh Farm Ctry Pk*
CM3 . . . . 101 C5
Marsh Farm Rd CM3 . . . . 101 D4
Marshfoot Rd RM16,
RM17 . . . . 173 F1
Marshgate Ctr CM19 . . . . . . 22 D8
Marsh Green Prim Sch
RM10 . . . . 154 A3
Marsh Green Rd
RM10 . . . . 154 A4
Marsh Hill EN9 . . . . 43 E4
Marsh La
Fobbing SS17 . . . . 161 D5
Harlow CM17 . . . . 11 E5
Mountnessing CM13 . . . . 96 A7
Stanstead Abbotts SG12 . . . . 8 D4
Marsh Rd
Burnham-on-C CM0 . . . . 107 B7
Tillingham CM0 . . . . 64 B4
Marsh St
Dartford DA1 . . . . 176 A3
Dartford DA1 . . . . 176 A5
Marsh View Ct SS16 . . . . . 142 E3
Marston Ave RM10 . . . . . . 135 A1
Marston Beck CM2 . . . . 33 A2
Marston Cl RM10 . . . . 135 A1
Marston Ho RM17 . . . . 178 A8

Marston Rd
Hoddesdon EN11 . . . . 21 B7
Woodford IG5 . . . . 110 E1
Marten Rd E17 . . . . 109 A1
Martham Cl IG6 . . . . 112 A8
Martin Terr 🔟 IG6 . . . . . 111 E5
Martindale Ave SS15 . . . . . 119 D2
Martin Dr
Dartford DA2 . . . . 176 C1
Rainham RM13 . . . . 155 B1
Martingale SS7 . . . . 145 B5
Martingale Cl CM11 . . . . 97 D5
Martingale Dr CM1 . . . . 32 F7
Martingale Rd CM11 . . . . . . 97 D5
Martin Gdns RM8 . . . . 153 D8
Martini Dr EN3 . . . . 65 A1
Martin Rd
Aveley RM15 . . . . 171 D5
Dagenham RM8 . . . . 153 D8
Martins Cl SS17 . . . . 160 D3
Martin's Ct SS22 . . . . 148 A1
Martinsfield Cl IG7 . . . . . . 111 E6
Martins Mews SS7 . . . . . . 144 C4
Martinstown Cl RM11 . . . . 137 A5
Martin Wlk SS5 . . . . 124 F4
Martlesham Cl RM12 . . . . . 155 C7
Martley Dr IG2 . . . . 133 B6
Martock Ave SS0 . . . . 147 A5
Martyns Gr SS0 . . . . 147 B2
Marvens CM2 . . . . 54 D3
Marwell Cl RM1 . . . . 136 A6
Marylands Ave SS5 . . . . . . 124 D7
Mary Macarthur Ho
🔟 Belvedere DA17 . . . . . . 169 A3
🔟 Dagenham RM10 . . . . . 135 A1
Mary Rose Cl RM16 . . . . . 172 C2
Mary Slessor Ho 🔟
DA1 . . . . 169 A3
MASCALLS 17 C4
Mascalls Gdns CM14 . . . . 115 F6
Mascalls La
Brentwood CM14 . . . . 115 F6
Great Warley CM14 . . . . 116 A4
Mascalls The CM2 . . . . 54 E8
Mascalls Way CM2 . . . . 54 E8
Masefield Cl RM3 . . . . 114 C2
Masefield Cres RM3 . . . . . 114 C2
Masefield Ct 🔟 CM14 . . . 116 C6
Masefield Dr RM14 . . . . . . 137 C4
Masefield Gdns E6 . . . . . . 152 A1
Masefield Rd
Dartford DA1 . . . . 176 B2
Grays RM16 . . . . 173 E4
Maldon CM9 . . . . 59 A8
MASHBURY 17 C4
Mashbury Rd CM1 . . . . 17 D6
Mashiters Hill RM1 . . . . . . 113 D2
Mashiters Wlk RM1 . . . . . . 135 D8
Mason Dr RM1 . . . . 114 E1
Mason Rd IG8 . . . . 109 E6
Mason Way EN9 . . . . 65 F6
Masters Ct 🔟 RM2 . . . . . 136 B6
Masthead Cl DA2 . . . . 176 C3
MATCHING 13 B4
Matching Field CM15 . . . . . . 71 F2
Matching Gn SS14 . . . . . . 120 D1
MATCHING GREEN 13 D3
Matching Green CE Prim
Sch CM17 . . . . 13 D2
Matching La CM5, CM6 . . . . 14 C6
Matching Rd
Harlow, Harlow Tye
 CM17 . . . . 12 B4
Harlow, Matching CM22 . . . . 13 B8
Hatfield Heath CM22 . . . . 3 B2
MATCHING TYE 12 E3
Matfield Cl CM1 . . . . 32 D7
Mathart Ct E4 . . . . 109 D4
Mathew Ct E4 . . . . 109 D4
Mathews Ho E6 . . . . 152 A4
Mathews Mead CM4 . . . . . . 120 B5
Mathews Villas CM19 . . . . . 22 E6
Mathieson Ho E4 . . . . 87 E2
Matlock Ct E18 . . . . 109 F2
Matlock Gdns RM12 . . . . . 136 E1
Matlock Ho 🔟 RM3 . . . . . 114 D4
Matlock Rd SS8 . . . . 163 F3
Matson Ct IG8 . . . . 109 E3
Matthews Cl RM3 . . . . 114 F2
Maud Gdns IG11 . . . . 152 B5
Maugham Cl SS12 . . . . 121 D5
Maunder Cl RM16 . . . . 172 D2
Maunds Farm CM18 . . . . . . 23 E4
Maunds Hatch CM18 . . . . . 23 E4
Maurice Ct SS8 . . . . 164 D2
Maurice Ho 🔟 CM14 . . . 116 C6
Maurice Lewis Pl 🔟
DA11 . . . . 179 A1
Maurice Rd SS8 . . . . 164 D3
Mavis Gr RM12 . . . . 136 E2
Mawney Cl RM7 . . . . 135 C7
Mawney Rd RM7 . . . . 135 C7
Mawney Sch The
RM7 . . . . 135 D6
Maxey Gdns RM9 . . . . 153 E8
Maxey Rd RM9 . . . . 153 E8
Maximfeldt Rd DA8 . . . . . . 169 E1
Maxim Rd DA8 . . . . 169 E2
Maxwell Ct IG7 . . . . 112 B7
Maya Angelou Ct E4 . . . . . 109 C6
Maya Cl SS3 . . . . 168 E7
Mayall Cl EN3 . . . . 65 A1
May Ave SS8 . . . . 164 D2
Maybank Ave
Hornchurch RM12 . . . . 155 C7
Woodford SS8 . . . . 110 B1
Maybank Lo 🔟 RM12 . . . 155 C7
Maybank Rd E18 . . . . 110 C2

Maybells Commercial
IG11 . . . .
Maybrick Rd RM11 . . . .
Maybrook Ct E11 . . . .
Maybury Cl IG10 . . . .
Maybury Rd IG11 . . . .
Maybush Rd RM11 . . . .
Maycroft Ave RM11 . . . . . .
Maycroft Gdns RM17 . . . . .
May Ct RM17 . . . .
Maydeb Ct RM6 . . . .
Maydells SS13 . . . .
Maydells Ct SS13 . . . .
Maydene CM2 . . . .
Mayer Rd EN9 . . . .
Mayesbrook Rd
Barking IG11 . . . .
Dagenham IG3, RM8 . . . . . .
Mayesford Rd RM6 . . . .
Mayes La
Chelmsford CM2 . . . .
Danbury CM3 . . . .
Mayespark Prim Sch
IG3 . . . .
Mayfair Ave
Basildon SS13 . . . .
Dagenham RM6 . . . .
Ilford IG1 . . . .
Mayfair Gdns IG8 . . . .
Mayfair Ind Area CM3 . . . . .
Mayfield
Swanscombe DA10 . . . .
Waltham Abbey EN9 . . . . . .
Mayfield Ave
Hullbridge SS5 . . . .
Southend-on-S SS9 . . . .
Woodford IG8 . . . .
Mayfield Cl CM17 . . . .
Mayfield Ct CM1 . . . .
Mayfield Gdns CM14 . . . . .
Mayfield Rd
Belvedere DA17 . . . .
Chingford E4 . . . .
Dagenham RM8 . . . .
Writtle CM1 . . . .
Mayfields RM6 . . . .
Mayfield Sch RM8 . . . .
Mayflower Cl
Lower Nazeing EN9 . . . .
Southend-on-S SS2 . . . .
South Ockendon RM15 . . . . .
Mayflower Ct
Canvey Island SS8 . . . .
Chipping Ongar CM5 . . . .
Harlow CM19 . . . .
Mayflower Dr CM9 . . . .
Mayflower High Sch
CM12 . . . .
Mayflower Ho
🔟 Barking IG11 . . . .
Brentwood CM13 . . . .
Mayflower Rd
🔟 Billericay CM11 . . . .
Grays RM16 . . . .
Mayflower Ret Pk
SS14 . . . .
Mayflowers SS7 . . . .
Mayflower Way CM5 . . . . . .
Maygreen Cres RM11 . . . . .
Mayhew Cl E4 . . . .
Mayhill Lo RM3 . . . .
MAYLAND . . . .
Mayland Ave SS8 . . . .
Mayland Cl
Heybridge CM9 . . . .
Mayland CM3 . . . .
Mayland Gn CM3 . . . .
Mayland Hill CM3 . . . .
Mayland Mans 🔟
IG1 . . . .
Mayland Quay CM3 . . . . . .
Maylands Ave RM12 . . . . . .
MAYLANDSEA . . . .
Maylandsea Prim Sch
CM3 . . . .
Maylands Way RM3 . . . . . .
Maylins Dr CM21 . . . .
Maynard Ct
🔟 Holdbrook EN3 . . . .
Waltham Abbey EN9 . . . . . .
Maynards RM11 . . . .
Mayne Crest CM1 . . . .
Maypole Cres IG6 . . . .
Maypole Dr IG7 . . . .
Maypole St CM7 . . . .
May Rd E4 . . . .
Maystocks E18 . . . .
Mayswood Gdns
RM10 . . . .
May Terr IG1 . . . .
Mayrne Prep Sch
CM17 . . . .
Maytree Cl RM13 . . . .
Maytree Wlk SS7 . . . .
May Villa RM2 . . . .
Mayville Rd IG1 . . . .
Maywin Dr RM11 . . . .
May Wlk CM2 . . . .
Maze The SS9 . . . .
Mead Cl
Grays RM16 . . . .
Loughton IG10 . . . .
Romford RM2 . . . .
Mead Cres E4 . . . .
Mead Ct EN9 . . . .
Meade Cl RM8 . . . .

SS13 . . . . 143 C8
Ave
dow CM2 . . . . . 54 D8
IG8 . . . . 110 E5
Prim Sch
le
Rd EN9 . . . . 21 C3
Terr CM2 . . . . . . 54 D8
M6 . . . . 134 D8
3 EN1 . . . . 21 D8
l
ng IG11 . . . . 152 F5
E4 . . . . 87 B1
17 . . . . 175 A3
M3 . . . . 114 C7
ley SS7 . . . . 145 B6
ross EN9 . . . . 65 E5
r
CM11 . . . . 97 C2
and SS8 . . . . . . 163 F6
18 . . . . 23 E4
M13 . . . . 121 E8
r
E16 . . . . 160 B8
on-S SS1 . . . . . . 167 E7
CM4 . . . . 75 F2
a SS11 . . . . 99 E3
nd Rd SS11 . . . 122 A6
nds RM11 . . . . 136 E4
ews CM1 . . . . . . 101 B8
d
1 . . . . 153 A5
RM9 . . . . 153 F6
16 . . . . 45 F2
6 . . . . 173 C5
SS7 . . . . 145 E2
SS5 . . . . 101 E2
G10 . . . . 88 E4
CM3 . . . . 100 C5
CM1 . . . . 135 C3
se
CM11 . . . . 97 C2
CM4 . . . . 72 E8
CI CM13 . . . . . . 117 C4
otts 1
. . . . 74 B3
le
CM2 . . . . 32 C3
6 . . . . 123 D2
eet SS7 . . . . . . 144 B3
CM4 . . . . 32 B3
le Ct CM3 . . . . . 20 E1
le Rd
. . . . 156 C7
The
ford CM2 . . . . . . 32 C2
13 . . . . 117 C4
worth CM21 . . . . 2 A1
ew
S16 . . . . 140 E4
M3 . . . . 56 E1
ich SS15 . . . . . . 94 C3
ew Wlk
. . . . 163 E4
ay
CM0 . . . . 106 A7
7 . . . . 111 C8
3 . . . . 124 E6
RM9 . . . . 153 F6
worth CM21 . . . . 2 A1
RM14 . . . . 137 C1
12 . . . . 121 E3
ay The
. . . . 97 C2
lk
ord CM2 . . . . . . 32 C2
RM9 . . . . 153 F6
Ind Est
. . . . 37 E1
6 . . . . 123 E1
ures CM9 . . . . . 35 D3
M2 . . . . 53 F8
Sch RM3 . . . . 114 B4
. . . . 74 B4
M15 . . . . 116 E8
G3 . . . . 133 F4
r
S16 . . . . 143 A4
CM2 . . . . 32 A1
n CM4 . . . . 74 B4
RM14 . . . . 137 E2
CM13 . . . . 116 C4
r
E 141 B8
EN10 . . . . 21 B2
r
nd SS8 . . . . . . 164 C2
2 . . . . 173 D2
EN11 . . . . 21 A4
CM2 . . . . 152 E8
6 . . . . 37 B1
3 . . . . 123 E1
M2 . . . . 114 A1
eet SS7 . . . . . 144 C3
S8 . . . . 110 C5
t RM8 . . . . . . 134 F2
he
rill IG9 . . . . . . 88 D1
S10 . . . . 88 F3
on-S SS0 . . . . . 166 B8
CM5 . . . . 48 F1
SS9 . . . . 147 A7
3 CM2 . . . . 32 F4
G11 . . . . 133 C1
e Rd
RM16 . . . . . 174 A8
ndon RM16 . . . 158 A1

Medick Ct RM17 . . . . 178 E8
Medina Rd RM17 . . . . . . 173 D2
Medlar Dr RM15 . . . . 157 E1
Medlar Rd RM12 . . . . 178 E8
Medlars Mead CM22 . . . . . 3 F5
Medley Way CM0 . . . . 62 D7
Medoc Cl SS13 . . . . 143 C8
Medora Rd RM7 . . . . 135 D7
Meduza Ct 7 DA12 . . . . . 179 D1
Medway CM0 . . . . 106 A6
Medway Cl
Chelmsford CM1 . . . . 31 D4
Ilford IG1 . . . . 152 C7
Medway Cres SS9 . . . . . . 146 B1
Meeson Bglws CM3 . . . . . 100 C5
Meeson Mdws CM9 . . . . . . 58 E8
Meeson's La RM17 . . . . . . 172 F1
Meesons Mead SS4 . . . . . 125 E3
Meggison Way SS7 . . . . . 144 C3
Meggy Tye CM2 . . . . 33 B5
Meister Ct IG1 . . . . 133 D3
Melanie Ct SS4 . . . . 125 F5
Melba Ct CM1 . . . . 31 C1
Melba Gdns RM18 . . . . . . 179 B7
Melbourne Ave CM1 . . . . . 31 E5
Melbourne Ct
Chelmsford CM1 . . . . 31 E5
Tilbury RM18 . . . . 178 E6
Melbourne Gdns RM6 . . . 134 E6
Melbourne Par CM1 . . . . . 31 E5
Melbourne Park Prim Sch
CM1 . . . . 31 F6
Melbourne Quay 8
. . . . 179 B1
Melbourne Rd
Ilford IG1 . . . . 133 B3
Tilbury RM18 . . . . 178 E6
Melcombe Rd SS7 . . . . . . 144 C3
Meldrum Rd IG3 . . . . 134 A2
Melford Ave IG11 . . . . . . 152 F6
Melford Pl CM14 . . . . 94 F2
Melford Rd IG1 . . . . 133 D2
Melksham Cl RM3 . . . . . . 114 F3
Melksham Dr RM3 . . . . . . 114 F3
Melksham Gdns RM3 . . . . 114 F3
Melksham Rd RM3 . . . . . . 114 F3
Mellish Cl IG11 . . . . 152 F4
Mellish Gdns IG8 . . . . 110 A5
Mellish Way RM11 . . . . . . 136 C6
Mellor Cl CM4 . . . . 74 B4
Mellow Mead SS15 . . . . . 141 B8
Mellow Purgess SS15 . . . 141 C6
Mellow Purgess Cl
SS15 . . . . 141 C6
Mellow Purgess End
SS15 . . . . 141 C6
Mellows Rd IG5 . . . . 132 F8
Melstock Ave RM14 . . . . . 156 C8
Melton Gdns RM1 . . . . . . 135 F4
Melville Ct
Romford RM3 . . . . 114 E3
Southend-on-S SS5 . . . . . 167 D6
Melville Dr SS12 . . . . 121 D4
Melville Heath CM3 . . . . . 101 B8
Melville Rd
Rainham RM13 . . . . 155 B1
Romford RM5 . . . . 113 B2
Memorial Ave E12 . . . . . . 132 E2
Memorial Hts E12 . . . . . . 133 D5
Memory Cl CM9 . . . . 59 A7
Mendip Cl
Rayleigh SS6 . . . . 123 D4
Wickford SS11 . . . . 121 E7
Mendip Cres SS0 . . . . . . 147 A4
Mendip Rd DA11 . . . . 178 D1
Mendip Rd
Chelmsford CM1 . . . . 31 D6
Hornchurch RM11 . . . . . . 136 A4
Ilford IG2 . . . . 133 E6
Southend-on-S SS0 . . . . . 147 A4
Mendips The SS9 . . . . . . 146 F5
Mendoza Cl RM11 . . . . . . 136 E6
Menish Way CM2 . . . . 33 C5
Menthone Pl RM11 . . . . . 136 D4
Mentmore SS16 . . . . 141 B4
Menzies Ave SS15 . . . . . . 140 F6
Meon Cl CM1 . . . . 32 C6
Meppel Ave SS8 . . . . 164 A6
Mercer Ave SS3 . . . . 150 A4
Mercer Rd CM11 . . . . 97 D5
Mercers CM19 . . . . 23 A5
Merchant St CM3 . . . . . . 101 E7
Mercia Cl CM2 . . . . 55 A5
Mercury Cl SS15 . . . . 121 F8
Mercury Ct 8 RM1 . . . . . 135 F5
Mercury Gdns RM1 . . . . . 135 F6
Mercury Rd CM9 . . . . 36 F5
Merdle Sq CM1 . . . . 31 A6
Merebridge Rd RM16 . . . . 172 F6
Meredene SS14 . . . . 142 F5
Meredith Rd RM16 . . . . . . 174 A2
Merefield CM21 . . . . 1 E1
Meresmans RM15 . . . . . . 171 D7
Mereworth Rd CM3 . . . . . 101 C5
Meriadoc Dr CM3 . . . . 74 B4
Meridan Ho EN10 . . . . 21 C2
Meriden Cl IG6 . . . . 111 C2
Meridian Bsns Pk EN9 . . . 65 B4
Meridian Ct RM17 . . . . . . 178 B7
Meridian Way
Stansted Abbotts SG12 . . . 8 B5
Waltham Abbey EN9 . . . . . 65 B4
Meriden RM1 . . . . 135 F4
Meriel Wlk DA9 . . . . 177 B3
Merilies Cl SS0 . . . . 147 B4
Merilies Gdns SS0 . . . . . . 147 B3
Merino Cl E11 . . . . 132 C7

Merlin Cl
Grays RM16 . . . . 172 E3
Redbridge IG6 . . . . 112 C6
Romford RM5 . . . . 113 D4
Waltham Abbey EN9 . . . . . . 66 A5
Merlin Ct SS8 . . . . 164 B3
Merlin Gdns RM5 . . . . 113 D4
Merlin Gr IG6 . . . . 111 C3
Merlin Pl CM1 . . . . 31 F5
Merlin Rd
Romford RM5 . . . . 113 D4
Wanstead E12 . . . . 132 D2
Merlin Way
North Weald Bassett
CM16 . . . . 47 A6
Wickford SS11 . . . . 99 D1
Mermagen Dr RM13 . . . . . 155 B5
Mermaid Way CM9 . . . . . . 59 B8
Merriam Cl E4 . . . . 109 C5
Merricks La SS16 . . . . . . 142 E3
Merrielands Cres
RM9 . . . . 153 F3
Merrielands Ret Pk
RM9 . . . . 153 F3
Merring Way CM19 . . . . . . 22 F7
Merritt Ho RM11 . . . . 135 F4
Merrivale SS7 . . . . 144 C2
Merrivale Ave IG4 . . . . . . 132 D7
Merry Fiddlers RM8 . . . . . 134 F2
Merryfield App SS9 . . . . . 146 E4
Merryfields Ave SS5 . . . . 124 D7
Merryhill Cl E4 . . . . 87 B2
Merrylands SS15 . . . . . . 141 A7
Merrylands Chase
CM13 . . . . 140 D7
Merrylands Prim Sch
SS15 . . . . 141 A6
Merrymeade Chase
CM15 . . . . 94 D1
Mersea Cres SS12 . . . . . . 121 F6
Mersea Ho 4 IG11 . . . . . 152 B6
Mersey Ave RM14 . . . . . . 137 D5
Mersey Way CM1 . . . . 31 C5
Merten Rd RM6 . . . . 134 D4
Merton Ct IG4 . . . . 132 E5
Merton Pl
Grays RM17 . . . . 174 A2
South Woodham Ferrers
CM3 . . . . 101 F6
Merton Rd
Barking IG11 . . . . 152 F5
Hockley SS5 . . . . 124 A8
Ilford IG3 . . . . 133 F4
South Benfleet SS7 . . . . . 144 B6
Messant Cl RM3 . . . . 114 D1
Mess Rd SS3 . . . . 168 F5
Meteor Rd SS0 . . . . 166 D8
Meteor Way E16 . . . . 31 F2
Metford Cres EN3 . . . . 65 A1
Methersgate SS14 . . . . . 142 C7
Methuen Rd DA17 . . . . . . 169 B2
Metsons La CM1 . . . . 51 E2
Metz Ave SS3 . . . . 164 A4
Mews Ct CM2 . . . . 32 B1
Mews Pl IG8 . . . . 110 A6
Mews The
Grays RM17 . . . . 173 C2
Harlow CM18 . . . . 23 E4
Hockley SS5 . . . . 124 C6
Redbridge IG4 . . . . 132 D6
Romford RM1 . . . . 135 E7
Sawbridgeworth CM21 . . . . 1 E3
Meyel Ave SS8 . . . . 164 C5
Meynell Ave SS8 . . . . 164 C2
Meynell Rd RM3 . . . . 114 B3
Mey Wlk SS5 . . . . 124 C6
Mia Ct CM9 . . . . 23 B8
Micawber Way CM1 . . . . . 31 D7
Michael Gdns RM11 . . . . . 136 D7
Michael's Cotts SS3 . . . . 168 C6
Midas Bsns Ctr RM10 . . . 154 B8
Mid Colne SS16 . . . . 142 D4
Middle Boy RM4 . . . . 90 C6
Middle Cloister 3
CM1 . . . . 97 B2
Middle Crockerford
SS16 . . . . 142 C4
Middlefield Ave EN11 . . . . 21 A8
Middlefield Cl EN11 . . . . . 21 A8
Middlefield Rd EN11 . . . . . 21 A8
Middlefield Rd EN11 . . . . . 21 A8
Middle Gn CM15 . . . . 72 C2
Middleham Ct 14 DA2 . . . 176 B1
Middlemead
South Hanningfield
CM3 . . . . 99 C8
West Hanningfield CM2 . . . 77 C3
Middle Mead
Rochford SS4 . . . . 125 F2
Wickford SS11 . . . . 121 E8
Middle Mead Cl CM2 . . . . . 76 F4
Middle Rd
Ingrave CM13 . . . . 117 C6
Waltham Abbey Ho 7 EN9 . 65 B7
Middlesborough Ho 7
RM3 . . . . 114 E3
Middlesburg SS13 . . . . . . 163 E5
Middlesex Ave SS9 . . . . . 146 F3
Middle St EN9 . . . . 44 A8
Middleton Ave E4 . . . . . . 109 A7
Middleton Gdns IG2 . . . . 133 B5
Middleton Hall La
CM15 . . . . 116 E8
Middleton Rd CM15 . . . . . 94 F1
Middleton Row CM15 . . . 101 E6
Midguard Way CM9 . . . . . 58 F8
Midhurst Ave SS0 . . . . . . 147 D4
Midhurst Cl RM12 . . . . . . 155 A8

Midland Ct RM1 . . . . 135 F6
Midsummer Mdw
SS13 . . . . 149 E1
Mighell Ave IG4 . . . . 132 D6
Milbank CM2 . . . . 33 B4
Milbanke Cl SS3 . . . . 149 E1
Milbourn Ct SS4 . . . . 125 F2
Milburn Cres CM1 . . . . . . 31 D1
Mildenhall Ho RM3 . . . . . 113 A5
Mildmay Ct 2 CM2 . . . . . 32 B1
Mildmay Ho CM0 . . . . . . 106 B5
Mildmay Ind Est CM0 . . . 106 B5
Mildmay Jun & Inf Schs
CM2 . . . . 54 B5
Mildmay Rd
Burnham-on-C CM0 . . . . . 106 C5
Chelmsford CM2 . . . . 32 B1
Ilford IG1 . . . . 133 B1
Romford RM7 . . . . 135 C6
Midmays CM3 . . . . 56 C7
Mildred Cl DA1 . . . . 176 A1
Mildred Rd DA8 . . . . 169 E1
Mile Cl EN9 . . . . 65 C6
Miles Cl CM19 . . . . 23 B7
Miles Gray Rd SS14 . . . . 119 F1
Mile Stone Rd DA2 . . . . . 176 B1
Milford Rd RM16 . . . . 173 D5
Milkwell Gdns IG8 . . . . . . 110 B3
Millais Ave E12 . . . . 152 A7
Millais Pl RM18 . . . . 179 B7
Millard Terr RM10 . . . . . . 154 A6
Millars Cl CM1 . . . . 101 E8
Millars The CM1 . . . . 19 A3
Millbank Ave CM5 . . . . 48 F2
Millbrook
Chigwell IG7 . . . . 111 D5
1 Wanstead E18 . . . . . . 132 A8
6 Woodford E18 . . . . 110 A1
Millbrook Bsns Pk EN9 . . . 22 A1
Millbrook Gdns
Dagenham RM6 . . . . 134 E5
Romford RM2 . . . . 113 E2
Mill Cl
Roxwell CM1 . . . . 30 A5
Tillingham CM0 . . . . 63 E4
Mill Cotts
Corringham SS17 . . . . . . 161 D4
Great Baddow CM2 . . . . . . 55 C8
Mill Crn CM19 . . . . 9 A1
Mill Ct CM20 . . . . 10 D3
MILL END 63 E8
Millennium Wlk
CM14 . . . . 116 D8
Miller Ave EN3 . . . . 65 A1
Miller Cl RM5 . . . . 113 A3
Miller Ct RM2 . . . . 136 A8
Millers Croft CM2 . . . . 54 F6
Millersdale CM19 . . . . 23 B4
MILLER'S GREEN 28 C4
Millers Green Rd CM5 . . . . 28 B3
Millers Ho The SG12 . . . . . 8 C4
Miller's La SG12 . . . . 8 C4
Millers Mews 3 CM4 . . . . 74 C4
Millfield
Burnham-on-C CM0 . . . . . 106 B4
High Ongar CM5 . . . . 49 D3
Mill Field CM17 . . . . 11 C4
Millfield Cl SS6 . . . . 123 E3
Millfields
Danbury CM3 . . . . 57 A6
Sawbridgeworth CM21 . . . . 1 F3
Writtle CM1 . . . . 31 A1
Mill Gn
Basildon SS13 . . . . 143 A7
Burnham-on-C CM0 . . . . . 106 B4
Mill Gr CM5 . . . . 49 D3
Mill Grange CM0 . . . . 106 B7
MILL GREEN 73 F7
Mill Green Cl SS13 . . . . . 143 B7
Mill Green Pl SS13 . . . . . 143 B7
Mill Green Rd CM4 . . . . . . 73 F7
Mill Hatch CM20 . . . . 11 A4
Millhaven Cl RM6 . . . . . . 134 B5
Millhead Way SS4 . . . . . . 126 B1
Mill Hill
Chelmsford CM2 . . . . 53 F2
Purleigh CM3 . . . . 58 C1
Shenfield CM15 . . . . 94 F2
South Benfleet SS7 . . . . . 163 E8
Mill Hill Dr CM12 . . . . 97 B5
Mill Ho
7 Rochford SS4 . . . . . . 125 F2
Woodford IG8 . . . . 109 F5
Millhouse Inf Sch
SS15 . . . . 141 C8
Millhouse Jun Sch
SS15 . . . . 141 C8
Millhurst Mews CM17 . . . . 11 E4
Millicent Preston Ho 4
IG11 . . . . 152 D4
Milligans Chase CM2 . . . . 54 B1
Mill La
Broomfield CM1 . . . . 19 C1
Corringham SS17 . . . . . . 161 C7
Dagenham RM6 . . . . 134 E5
Danbury CM3 . . . . 57 A6
Grays RM16 . . . . 172 D1
Harlow CM17 . . . . 11 E4
Harlow CM17 . . . . 11 E4
Hatfield Heath CM22 . . . . . 2 F3
High Ongar CM5 . . . . 49 D2
Hoddesdon EN10 . . . . 21 A2
Horndon on t h SS17 . . . . 159 F3
Ingatestone CM4 . . . . 74 A6

Mill La continued
Kelvedon Hatch CM15 . . . . 71 E2
Little Baddow CM3 . . . . . . 34 E3
Maldon CM9 . . . . 37 A3
Moreton CM5 . . . . 49 E6
Navestock Heath RM4 . . . . 92 B8
Orsett RM16 . . . . 174 A7
Purleigh CM3 . . . . 58 C1
Ramsden Heath CM11 . . . . 98 B5
Rochford SS4 . . . . 126 B2
Sawbridgeworth CM21 . . . . 1 F3
Sewardstone E4 . . . . 87 B6
Stock CM4 . . . . 75 F5
Toot Hill CM5 . . . . 47 E2
Woodford IG8 . . . . 109 F5
Wyatts Green CM15 . . . . . 72 D4
Mill Lo SS2 . . . . 168 E6
Millom Ho 1 RM3 . . . . . . 114 D4
Mill Park Ave RM12 . . . . . 136 E2
Mill Race SG12 . . . . 8 F8
Mill Rd
Aveley RM15 . . . . 171 C6
Billericay CM11 . . . . 119 D6
Burnham-on-C CM0 . . . . . 106 C7
Ilford IG1 . . . . 133 A1
Maldon CM9 . . . . 37 B2
Margaret Roding CM1 . . . . 16 D5
Mayland CM3 . . . . 83 B8
Stock CM4 . . . . 75 F2
Tillingham CM0 . . . . 63 E4
Millsmead Way IG10 . . . . . 88 F7
Millson Bank CM2 . . . . 33 B4
Mill St CM17 . . . . 24 F5
Mills Way CM13 . . . . 95 C1
Mill View CM16 . . . . 173 E7
Mill View Ct CM1 . . . . 30 A5
Millview Mdws SS4 . . . . . 125 F1
Mill Vue Rd CM2 . . . . 32 F2
Milne Ct 4 E18 . . . . 110 A2
Milner Pl CM1 . . . . 96 F5
Milner Rd RM8 . . . . 134 C2
MILTON 179 D1
Milton Ave
Basildon SS16 . . . . 140 F4
Hornchurch RM12 . . . . . . 135 F2
Southend-on-S SS0 . . . . . 166 E7
Milton Cl
Rayleigh SS6 . . . . 124 A2
Southend-on-S SS2 . . . . . 148 A1
Milton Cres
Chipping Ongar CM5 . . . . . 48 F5
Ilford IG2 . . . . 133 C5
Milton Ct
Dagenham RM6 . . . . 134 C4
Southend-on-S SS0 . . . . . 166 E7
Waltham Abbey EN9 . . . . . 65 C5
Milton Hall Gdns SS3 . . . 179 B6
Milton Hall Prim Sch
SS0 . . . . 166 E8
Milton Pl
Chelmsford CM1 . . . . 32 A5
Gravesend DA12 . . . . 179 C1
Southend-on-S SS0 . . . . . 166 F7
Milton Rd
Belvedere DA17 . . . . 169 A2
Brentwood CM14 . . . . 116 C6
Corringham SS17 . . . . . . 160 F6
Gravesend DA12 . . . . 179 C1
Grays RM17 . . . . 173 B1
Maldon CM9 . . . . 59 A8
Romford RM1 . . . . 136 A5
Southend-on-S SS0 . . . . . 166 E8
Swanscombe DA10 . . . . . 177 E1
Milton St
Southend-on-S SS2 . . . . . 148 A1
Swanscombe DA10 . . . . . 177 D1
Waltham Abbey EN9 . . . . . 65 C5
Milwards CM19 . . . . 23 B4
Milwards Prim Sch
CM19 . . . . 23 B4
Mimosa Cl
Basildon SS16 . . . . 140 F4
Chelmsford CM1 . . . . 32 F6
Pilgrims Hatch CM15 . . . . . 94 B4
Romford RM3 . . . . 114 C3
Minchen Rd CM20 . . . . 11 A1
Minehead Ho 6 RM3 . . . . 114 E5
Minerva Rd CM9 . . . . 109 B3
MINNOW END 19 A6
Minster Cl
Basildon SS13 . . . . 143 C4
Minster Ct RM11 . . . . 137 A3
Minster Rd SS15 . . . . 141 C6
Minster Way
Hornchurch RM11 . . . . . . 137 A3
Maldon CM9 . . . . 58 E8
Minton Hts SS4 . . . . 125 C6
Minton La CM17 . . . . 24 F8
Miramar Way CM12 . . . . . 163 E3
Miranda Ho 6 DA17 . . . . 169 A1
Mirosa Dr CM9 . . . . 37 B1
Mirosa Reach CM9 . . . . . . 59 A8
Mirravale Ct 7 IG9 . . . . . 110 C8
Mirravale Trad Est
RM6 . . . . 134 E4
Mirror Stps 1 SS1 . . . . . 167 C2
Misleigh Ct CM15 . . . . 94 F2
Mistley End SS16 . . . . . . 142 C5
Mistley Path SS16 . . . . . . 142 C5
Mistley Rd CM20 . . . . 11 A2
Mistley Side SS16 . . . . . . 142 C5

Mistley Thorn IG1 .... 133 A4
Mistral Ct E4 .... 109 B7
Mitcham Rd IG3 .... 133 F4
Mitchell Cl
  Erith DA17 .... 169 C3
  Rainham RM13 .... 155 C3
Mitchells Ave SS8 ...... 164 D4
Mitchells Wlk SS8 .... 164 D4
Mitchell Way CM1 ...... 101 D8
Mitre Bldgs **3** CM20 ....10 C1
Mitre Ct
  Belvedere DA17 .... 169 A2
  1 Dagenham RM6 ... 134 B4
  9 Woodford E18 ..... 110 A2
Mitre Ho RM7 .... 135 B7
Mitton Vale CM2 .... 32 F2
Moat Cl
  Doddinghurst CM15 ..... 72 C3
  Ramsden Heath CM11 ... 98 C3
Moat Edge Gdns CM12 ..97 A4
Moat End SS1 .... 149 B1
Moat Field SS14 .... 142 C8
Moat Ho CM19 .... 22 E7
Moat Lodge Ho **2**
  SS14 .... 142 C7
Moat Rise SS6 .... 123 D1
Moat The CM5 .... 47 F2
Moby Dick RM6 .... 134 F7
Molesworth EN11 .... 8 A2
Mollands SS16 .... 142 F4
Mollands Ct RM15 ...... 157 E1
Mollands La RM15 ...... 157 D1
Mollison Ave EN3 .... 65 A3
Molrams La CM2 .... 55 B6
Molyneaux Ct CM12 ..... 97 A3
Momples Rd CM20 .... 11 B1
Monarch Cl
  Rainham RM13 .... 155 A3
  Tilbury RM18 .... 179 B5
Monarch Pl IG9 .... 110 C8
Monarch Rd DA17 ...... 169 A3
Monarch Way IG2 ...... 133 D5
Monastery Rd SS15 .... 141 C6
Monkchester Cl IG10 ....89 A8
Monkham's Ave IG8 ... 110 B5
Monkham's Dr IG8 ..... 110 B5
Monkhams Hall EN9 ... 43 C2
Monkham's La IG8 ..... 110 B4
Monksbury CM18 .... 24 A5
Monks Chase CM13 .... 117 C5
Monks Cl EN10 .... 21 A3
Monksford Dr SS5 ...... 101 D1
Monkside SS14 .... 142 D7
Monks Mead CM3 .... 56 F2
Monks Wall DA9 .... 177 C3
Monk's Well **1** DA9 .. 177 C3
Monkswick Rd CM20 .... 10 F1
Monks Wlk CM9 .... 40 E8
Monkswood Ave EN9 ...65 D6
Monkswood Gdns
  IG5 .... 133 A8
Monkwood Cl RM1 ..... 136 A6
Monmouth Ave E18 .... 132 B8
Monmouth Mews
  SS16 .... 140 F5
Monmouth Rd RM9 .... 153 F7
Monnow Gn RM15 ...... 171 C6
Monnow Rd RM15 ...... 171 C6
Monoux Cl CM11 .... 97 D1
Monoux Gr E17 .... 109 A2
Mons Ave CM11 .... 97 D2
Montague Ave SS9 ..... 146 B2
Montague Bldgs **2**
  SS1 .... 167 B8
Montague Ct SS0 ...... 166 D8
Montague Ho **3** IG8 .. 111 A3
Montague Pl SS8 .... 163 E3
Montague Way CM12 ...97 A4
Montagu Gdns CM1 ...... 32 F7
Montalt Ho IG8 .... 109 F6
Montalt Rd IG8 .... 109 F5
Montbazon Ct CM4 ...... 94 B1
Monteagle Ave IG11 ... 152 C6
Monteagle Ct IG11 .... 152 C5
Monteagle Prim Sch
  RM9 .... 153 B4
Montefiore Ave SS6 ... 123 D8
Montfort Ave SS17 ..... 161 A3
Montfort Gdns IG6 ..... 111 C4
Montgomerie Ct E4 ......87 D2
Montgomerie Inf Sch
  SS7 .... 144 B7
Montgomerie Jun Sch
  SS7 .... 144 B7
Montgomery Cl
  Chelmsford CM1 .... 32 E7
  Grays RM16 .... 173 C4
Montgomery Cres
  RM3 .... 114 D5
Montgomery Ct
  2 Dagenham RM10 ... 154 A6
  Southend-on-S SS3 ... 149 E1
Montpelier Cl CM12 .....97 A5
Montpelier Ct **4**
  CM14 .... 116 C7
Montpelier Gdns
  RM6 .... 134 C4
Montpellier Ho IG7 .... 111 C5
Montreal Rd
  Ilford IG1 .... 133 C4
  Tilbury RM18 .... 179 A5
Montrose Ave RM2 ..... 114 C1
Montrose Cl IG8 .... 110 A6

Montrose Ho IG2 .... 133 A5
Montrose Rd CM2 .... 33 A4
Montsale SS13 .... 143 C8
Montserrat Ave IG8 .... 109 D3
Moons Cl SS4 .... 125 D7
Moorcroft SS4 .... 125 D6
Moorcroft Ave SS7 ..... 145 E6
Moore Ave
  Grays RM20 .... 172 E1
  Tilbury RM18 .... 179 B5
Moore Cl CM11 .... 97 D5
Moore Cres RM9 .... 153 B4
Moore Ho RM11 .... 136 A5
Moore Rd DA10 .... 177 E1
Moores Ave SS17 ...... 142 C1
Moorescroft CM15 .... 71 E2
Moore's Pl CM14 .... 116 D8
Moore Twr CM18 .... 23 F7
Moorfields CM18 .... 23 C4
Moor Hall La CM3 .... 56 F2
Moor Hall Rd CM17 ..... 12 A4
Moorhen Ave CM0 .... 62 C8
Moorhen Way CM19 ..... 9 A1
Moor La RM14 .... 137 F4
Moorland Rd RM5 ...... 113 B2
Moorlands Reach CM21 ..2 A1
Moor Park Cl SS9 ...... 146 C5
Moor Park Gdns SS9 .. 146 C5
Mopsies Rd SS14 ...... 142 E6
Moran Ave CM1 .... 32 B7
Morant Gdns RM5 ...... 113 B5
Morant Rd RM16 .... 174 B3
Moray Cl RM1 .... 113 C1
Moray Way RM1 .... 113 E3
Mordaunt Gdns RM9 .. 153 E5
Morden Rd RM6 .... 134 E4
Mordon Rd IG3 .... 133 F4
Morecambe Rd RM12 . 155 B7
Morecambe Ho **5**
  RM3 .... 114 C5
Moreland Ave SS7 ..... 144 C7
Moreland Cl
  Great Wakering SS3 .. 150 A4
  South Benfleet SS7 ... 144 C6
Moreland Rd SS1 .... 99 C2
Morelands Ave RM16 . 173 C4
Moreland Way E4 ..... 109 C7
Moremead EN9 .... 65 D6
Mores La CM14 .... 93 D5
MORETON 26 C2
Moreton Bay Ind Est
  RM2 .... 114 D1
Moreton Bridge CM5 ... 26 D1
Moreton CE Prim Sch
  CM5 .... 26 C3
Moreton Gates CM5 .... 26 C2
Moreton Gdns IG8 .... 110 E5
Moreton Rd
  Chipping Ongar CM5 ... 48 F7
  Fyfield CM5 .... 27 B2
  Moreton CM5 .... 48 B8
Moretons
  Basildon SS13 .... 143 A6
  Galleywood CM2 .... 54 B2
Moretons Cl SS13 ..... 143 A6
Moretons Mews SS13 . 143 A6
Moretons Pl SS13 ..... 143 A6
Morgan Cl RM10 .... 154 A5
Morgan Cres CM16 ..... 67 E3
Morgan Terr RM4 ...... 134 C6
Morgan Way
  Rainham RM13 .... 155 C2
  Woodford IG8 .... 110 E4
Morland Rd
  Dagenham RM10 ...... 154 A5
  Ilford IG1 .... 133 B2
Morley Ave E4 .... 109 D3
Morley Gr CM20 .... 10 C2
Morley Hill SS17 .... 160 F5
Morley Link SS17 ...... 160 F5
Morley Rd
  Barking IG11 .... 152 D4
  Dagenham RM6 ...... 134 E6
  Rochford SS4 .... 125 D3
Mornington Ave
  Ilford IG1 .... 133 A4
  Rochford SS4 .... 126 A2
Mornington Cl IG8 ..... 110 A6
Mornington Cres
  Canvey Island SS8 ... 164 C4
  Hadleigh SS7 .... 145 F3
Mornington Ho SS0 ... 166 C8
Mornington Rd
  Canvey Island SS8 ... 164 C4
  Chingford E4 .... 87 D2
  Loughton IG10 .... 89 C6
  Woodford IG8 .... 109 F6
Morpeth Ho **8** RM1 . 114 D4
Morrab Gdns IG3 ...... 133 F1
Morrells SS16 .... 141 F4
Morrin's Chase SS3 ... 150 D3
Morrins Cl SS13 .... 150 D3
Morris Ave CM11 .... 97 D1
Morris Ct
  Basildon SS15 .... 141 B7
  Chingford E4 .... 109 B7
  Holdbrook EN3 .... 65 A2
  Waltham Abbey EN9 ... 65 F5
Morris Gdns CM1 ...... 176 A2
Morris Ho CM18 .... 23 C5
Morrison Ave E4 .... 109 A4
Morrison Ho RM16 .... 173 D4
Morrison Rd IG11 ...... 153 E3
Morris Rd
  Chelmsford CM2 .... 32 D2
  Dagenham RM8 .... 134 F2
  Romford RM3 .... 114 B3

Mortimer Rd SS6 ...... 123 E5
Mortlake Rd IG1 .... 152 D8
Mosbach Gdns CM13 .. 117 B8
Moseley St SS2 .... 148 D1
Moss Bank RM17 ...... 172 F2
Moss Cl SS16 .... 142 E3
Mossdown Cl DA17 .... 169 A3
Moss Dr SS14 .... 142 E3
Mossford Ct
  Ilford IG6 .... 133 B8
  Redbridge IG6 .... 111 B1
Mossford Gn IG6 ...... 133 C8
Mossford Green Prim Sch
  IG6 .... 111 C1
Mossford La IG6 ...... 111 C1
Moss La
  Hornchurch RM11 .... 136 A5
  Romford RM1 .... 135 F5
Moss Path CM2 .... 54 C3
Moss Rd
  Dagenham RM10 ..... 154 A5
  South Ockendon RM15 172 C8
Moss Wlk CM2 .... 54 B6
Motehill SS16 .... 141 C4
Motherwell Way
  RM20 .... 172 A1
MOTT'S GREEN 2 D6
Mott St
  High Beach IG10 .... 88 A8
  Sewardstone IG10 ..... 87 E8
MOULSHAM 54 A8
Moulsham Chase CM2 .. 54 C8
Moulsham Dr CM2 ..... 54 B8
Moulsham High Sch
  CM2 .... 54 B7
Moulsham Jun & Inf Schs
  CM2 .... 54 B7
Moulsham St
  Chelmsford CM1 .... 32 B2
  Chelmsford, Moulsham
  CM2 .... 32 B1
Moulsham Thrift CM2 .. 54 A6
Moultrie Way RM14 ... 137 E5
Mountain Ash Ave
  CM2 .... 54 A8
Mount Ash Cl SS9 ..... 146 B6
Mount Ave
  Brentwood CM13 ...... 95 B2
  Chingford E4 .... 109 B7
  Hockley SS5 .... 124 E7
  Rayleigh SS6 .... 123 C3
  Romford RM3 .... 115 C4
  Southend-on-S SS0 .. 166 A8
Mountbatten Ct IG9 ... 110 D8
Mountbatten Dr SS3 .. 149 E1
Mountbatten Ho **4**
  RM2 .... 136 C7
Mountbatten Way CM1 ..32 E7
Mount Bovers La SS5 . 124 E3
Mount Cl
  Brentwood CM14 ...... 116 D6
  Hockley SS5 .... 124 D6
  South Benfleet SS7 .. 144 E4
Mountdale Gdns SS9 . 146 F4
Mount Echo Ave E4 .... 87 B1
Mount Echo Dr E4 ..... 87 B1
MOUNT END 68 F7
Mountfield Cl SS17 .... 160 E3
Mountfield Rd E6 ...... 152 A2
Mountfields SS13 ..... 143 C4
Mounthill Ave CM2 ..... 32 D3
Mountier Ct **2** E11 .. 132 A6
MOUNTNESSING 95 D8
Mountnessing CE Prim
  Sch CM15 .... 95 E7
Mountnessing La
  CM15 .... 72 E1
Mountnessing Rd
  Billericay CM12 .... 96 E4
  Blackmore CM4 .... 72 F6
  Mountnessing CM15,
  CM4 .... 73 A4
Mountney Cl CM14 ..... 73 F1
Mount Pleasant
  Ilford IG1 .... 152 C7
  Maldon CM9 .... 36 F2
Mount Pleasant Ave
  CM13 .... 95 A4
Mount Pleasant Cotts
  CM15 .... 95 A4
Mount Pleasant Rd
  Chigwell IG7 .... 111 D6
  Romford RM5 .... 113 D4
  South Woodham Ferrers
  CM3 .... 101 D7
Mount Rd
  Dagenham RM8 .... 134 F1
  Epping CM16 .... 68 C4
  South Benfleet SS7 .. 144 F4
  Wickford SS11 .... 121 E8
Mounts Rd DA9 .... 177 B1
Mount The
  Billericay CM11 .... 97 E3
  Brentwood CM14 ..... 116 C7
  Romford RM3 .... 114 C7
  Stanford-le-H SS17 .. 160 F3
Mount View
  Billericay CM11 .... 97 E2
  Brentwood CM14 ..... 116 C6
Mountview Cl SS16 .... 142 E3
Mountview Cres CM0 .. 62 C8
Mount View Rd E4 ...... 87 D2
Mount Way SS11 ...... 121 E8
Movers La IG11 .... 152 E4

Mowbray Rd CM20 ..... 11 A3
Mowbrays Cl RM5 ..... 113 C1
Mowbrays Rd RM5 .... 113 C1
Mowbray Gdns IG10 ... 89 C8
Mowden Hall La CM3 ... 35 A8
Muckingford Rd RM18,
  SS17 .... 174 E2
Mucking Hall Cotts
  SS3 .... 149 B8
Mucking Hall Rd SS3 . 149 C8
Mucking Wharf Rd
  SS17 .... 175 C7
Mudlands Ind Est
  RM13 .... 154 F2
Muggeridge Rd RM10 . 154 B8
Muirhead Quay IG11 .. 152 C3
Muir Pl SS12 .... 121 D5
Muirway SS7 .... 144 B7
Mulberry Cl
  Chingford E4 .... 109 A8
  Romford RM2 .... 136 C7
Mulberry Ct SS11 ..... 152 F5
Mulberry Dr RM19 .... 170 F2
Mulberry Gn CM17 ..... 11 D4
Mulberry Hill CM15 .... 94 F2
Mulberry Rd SS8 ...... 163 C3
Mulberry The SS12 ... 148 A3
Mulberry Terr CM17 ... 11 B4
Mulberry Way
  Belvedere DA17 ...... 169 C4
  Chelmsford CM1 .... 32 D4
  Ilford IG6 .... 133 C7
  Woodford E18 .... 110 B1
Mulberry Gdns SS16 . 141 B5
Mullein Ct RM17 ...... 178 E8
Mullions The CM12 .... 96 F3
Multon Lea CM1 .... 33 A7
MUNDON 59 E2
Mundon Gdns IG1 .... 133 D3
Mundon Rd IG3 .... 133 D3
Mundon Rd CM9 .... 59 D5
Mungo Park Rd RM13 . 155 A6
Munro Ct **13** SS12 . 121 E5
Munsons Alley CM0 .... 84 D4
Munsterburg Rd SS8 . 164 D5
Munster Ct CM12 .... 96 F5
Murchison Cl CM1 ...... 31 E5
Murchison Rd EN11 ..... 8 B1
Murfitt Way RM14 .... 156 A8
Murray Ho SS1 .... 167 F6
Murray Way SS12 .... 121 D5
Murrell Lock CM2 .... 33 A4
Murrells La SS5 ...... 124 A7
Murthering La
  Navestock Heath RM4 .. 92 B5
  Stapleford Abbotts RM4 91 F3
Murtwell Dr IG7 ...... 111 C4
Musket Gr SS9 .... 146 B7
Muskham Rd CM20 .... 11 B3
Mus of Power * CM9 ... 36 D6
Mutton Row CM5 .... 70 C7
Mygrove Cl RM13 .... 155 D3
Mygrove Gdns RM13 . 155 D3
Mygrove Rd RM13 .... 155 D3
Mylne Ct
  Hoddesdon EN11 .... 8 A1
  Hoddesdon EN11 ..... 21 A8
Myln Mdw CM4 .... 75 F2
Mynards Way CM3 ...... 56 C7
Mynchens SS15 ...... 141 E6
Myrtle Gr RM15 ...... 171 C4
Myrtle Rd
  Brentwood CM14 ..... 116 C6
  Ilford IG1 .... 133 B2
  Romford RM3 .... 114 C4

N

Nabbott Rd CM1 .... 31 E2
Nacton Ct RM4 .... 134 C6
Nadir Ct E11 .... 132 A4
Naffenton Rise IG10 ... 88 D4
Nagle Cl E17 .... 109 D1
Nag's Head La CM14 .. 115 D4
Nairn Ct RM18 .... 178 F5
Nairn Ho CM14 .... 116 C6
Nalla Gdns CM2 .... 54 D6
Namur Rd SS8 .... 164 C5
Nansen Ave SS4 ...... 125 D6
Nantwich Ho **4** RM3 . 114 E5
Napier Ave **9** SS1 .. 167 A8
Napier Cl
  Basildon SS14 .... 142 D6
  Hornchurch RM11 .... 136 B3
Napier Cres SS12 ..... 121 E5
Napier Ct SM1 .... 31 E5
Napier Ct W SS1 ...... 166 F8
Napier Gdns SS7 ..... 145 C6
Napier Ho RM13 ...... 154 F2
Napier Rd
  Rayleigh SS6 .... 123 F3
  Wallend E6 .... 152 A3
Narboro Ct RM1 ...... 136 A5
Nare Rd RM15 .... 171 C6
Narvik Cl CM9 .... 58 E8
Naseby Rd
  Dagenham RM10 ..... 135 A1
  Woodford IG6 .... 133 B8
Nash Dr CM1 .... 19 A3
Nash Rd RM6 .... 134 D7
Natal Rd IG1 .... 152 B8
Natasha Ct RM3 ...... 114 C3
Nathan Cl RM14 ...... 137 E3
Nathan's La CM1 .... 52 E5
National Motor Boat
  Mus * SS16 .... 143 B2
Nation Way E4 .... 87 C1

Naunton Way RM12 ....
Navarre Gdns RM5 ....
Navestock Cl
  Chingford E4 ....
  Rayleigh SS6 ....
Navestock Cres IG8 ...
Navestock Gdns IG8 ..
NAVESTOCK HEATH ...
Navestock Ho **2**
  IG11 ....
NAVESTOCK SIDE ......
Navestock Side CM14 .
Nave The SS15 ....
Navigation Pl CM9 ....
Navigation Rd CM2 ...
Nayland Cl SS12 ......
Nayland Ho SS2 ....
NAZEING ....
Nazeingbury Cl EN9 ..
Nazeingbury Par EN9 .
Nazeing Comm EN9 ...
Nazeing Ho IG9 ....
NAZEING MEAD ....
Nazeing New Rd EN10
Nazeing Prim Sch EN9
Nazeing Rd EN9 ......
Nazeing Rd EN9 ......
Nazeing The SS14 ....
Nazeing Wlk RM13 ....
Neal Ct EN9 ....
Neale Ct
  Dagenham RM8 ....
  Hornchurch RM11 ....
Neasham Rd RM8 .....
Neave Cres RM3 ....
Neave Rose Ct RM7 ..
Nectar Ct **11** EN11 ..
Needham Cl CM11 .....
Neil Armstrong Way
  SS9 ....
Nelmes Cl RM11 ......
Nelmes Cres RM11 ...
Nelmes Dr RM11 .....
Nelmes Prim Sch
  RM11 ....
Nelmes Rd RM11 .....
Nelmes Way RM11 ...
Nelson Cl
  Brentwood CM14 .....
  Rayleigh SS6 ....
  Romford RM7 ....
Nelson Cres CM9 .....
Nelson Ct **2** CM0 ..
Nelson Gdns SS6 .....
Nelson Gr CM1 ....
Nelson Ho
  Greenhithe DA9 ......
  3 Romford RM3 ..
Nelson Mews SS1 ....
Nelson Pl CM3 ....
Nelson Prim Sch E6 ..
Nelson Rd
  Basildon SS14 ....
  Chingford E4 ....
  Orsett RM16 ....
  Rainham RM13 ......
  Rayleigh SS6 ....
  Rochford SS4 ....
  Southend-on-S SS1 ..
  South Ockendon RM15
  Wanstead E11 ....
Nelson St
  Southend-on-S SS1 ..
Nelwyn Ave RM11 ....
Neon Ct IG6 ....
Neptune Bsns Pk
  RM19 ....
Neptune Cl RM13 ....
Neptune Ct
  2 Barking IG11 ...
  Chelmsford CM1 ......
Neptune Wlk DA8 .....
Nesbit Cl SS12 ....
Ness Rd SS3 ....
Nesta Rd IG8 ....
Nestuda Way SS2 ....
Nethan Dr RM15 .....
Netherfield SS7 ....
Netherfield Ct SS12 ..
Netherfield Gdns
  IG11 ....
Netherfield La SG12 ..
Nethergate IG11 ......
Nethrall Rd CM19 ....
Nether Mayne SS16 ..
Nether Priors SS14 ...
NETHER STREET ......
Nethewode Ct DA17 ..
Netley St IG2 ....
NETTESWELL ....
Netteswellbury Farm
  CM18 ....
Netteswell Cross CM2
Netteswell Orch CM20
Netteswell Rd CM20 ..
Netteswell Rectory
  CM20 ....
Netteswell Twr **5**
  CM20 ....
Nevada Rd SS8 ....
Nevell Rd RM16 ......
NEVENDON ....
Nevendon Grange
  SS12 ....

Mews

Mews 121 A2
Rd 121 A2
S12 ..... 121 B4
Trad Est 121 B1
SS6 ..... 145 F8
SS6 ..... 145 E8
rs RM8 ..... 134 D1

RM8 ..... 134 D1
IG6 ..... 111 C2
aw SS14 ..... 142 N6
* IG10 ..... 88 E3
4 ..... 87 B1
M11 ..... 113 E4
SS1 ..... 168 B8
S16 ..... 141 A4
s Way IG7 ..... 111 B7
Side SS15 ..... 141 C5
rs Way CM1 ..... 32 B6
e Sch IG3 ..... 134 B6
Rd RM17 ..... 173 D1
T RM3 ..... 114 C4
Cotts **4** 133 C5
t **4** E11 ..... 132 A7
dns
M3 ..... 114 D4
RM14 ..... 136 F1
Mdw CM22 ..... 3 F5
PARK 133 D5
ark Prim Sch 133 D5
ark Sta 133 D5
E4 ..... 109 C4
.. .. 133 E5
3 ..... 114 D4
lk RM3 ..... 114 D5
Ave IG6 ..... 112 A4
ry Rd SS15 ..... 141 B6

Bsns Pk 23 C4
Rd CM2 ..... 32 D3
s Way CM2 ..... 32 F4
SS3 ..... 168 G8
nd Cl CM3 ..... 56 F1
nd Cres 150 C2

st 152 C3
Dr RM4 ..... 90 C6
RM8 ..... 65 A4
La IG7 ..... 111 A4
ers Science Pk 22 F6
t E4 ..... 109 E7
IG2 ..... 133 D6
EN9 ..... 65 F6
r RM3 ..... 114 E2
a CM9 ..... 59 E4
d SS4 ..... 103 B1
ch CM3 ..... 20 A1
neyard* 58 D2
Eye IG2 ..... 152 A1
n Bsns Ctr 22 F8
Ave 134 D8
IG2 ..... 120 F7
Ave SS2 ..... 148 E2
Ave SS2 ..... 148 F2
Gdns SS2 ..... 148 E2
e Ct **1** 110 A3

Way 155 E8
Cl CM0 ..... 84 E4
Cres CM0 ..... 84 E4
tts Way 32 E7
REEN 30 C2
I IG10 ..... 88 D3
in CM9 ..... 36 E3
Ho IG10 ..... 89 B6
o **1** DA17 ..... 169 A1
*I RM16 ..... 174 A2
Rd IG6 ..... 111 E4

New Park Rd
Rochford SS5 ..... 103 A1
South Benfleet SS7 ..... 144 C5
Newpiece IG10 ..... 89 B6
New Place Gdns
RM14 ..... 137 D2
New Plymouth Ho
RM13 ..... 154 F2
Newport Ave CM3 ..... 81 E5
Newport Cl CM2 ..... 55 B6
Newport Ct SS6 ..... 123 B4
Newports CM21 ..... 1 C1
New Rd
Abridge RM4 ..... 90 D3
Basildon CM12 ..... 119 A3
Brentwood CM14 ..... 116 D8
Broomfield CM1 ..... 19 B1
Burnham-on-C CM0 ..... 106 C5
Canvey Island SS8 ..... 163 E3
Chingford E4 ..... 109 C6
Dagenham RM9, RM10,
RM13 ..... 154 C2
Gravesend DA11 ..... 179 B1
Grays RM17 ..... 178 B8
Great Baddow CM2 ..... 55 A6
Great Wakering SS3 ..... 150 C3
Hadleigh SS7 ..... 145 D3
Harlow CM17 ..... 11 D4
Hoddesdon EN10 ..... 21 A4
Ilford IG3 ..... 133 E2
Ingatestone CM4 ..... 74 C4
Rainham RM13 ..... 155 B2
Southend-on-S SS9 ..... 165 D8
Wanstead E12 ..... 132 E2
New River Ave SG12 ..... 8 B4
New River Cl EN11 ..... 21 B7
New Row
Paglesham Eastend
SS4 ..... 128 A5
Sheering CM22 ..... 12 C8
New Rush Hall Sch The
IG6 ..... 111 C3
New St
Chelmsford CM1 ..... 32 B3
Maldon CM9 ..... 36 F2
Sawbridgeworth CM21 ..... 1 E3
Newstead Ho RM3 ..... 114 D4
Newstead St SS3 ..... 150 B4
Newsum Gdns SS6 ..... 123 A3
New Swan Yd DA11 ..... 179 B1
New Tann Tank Hill Rd RM19,
RM15 ..... 171 A3
New Tavern Fort*
DA12 ..... 179 C1
Newteswell Dr EN9 ..... 65 D7
NEW THUNDERSLEY 144 D7
Newton Cl
Dunmington SS17 ..... 161 A4
Hoddesdon EN11 ..... 8 B2
Newton Dr CM21 ..... 1 D1
Newton Hall Gdns
SS4 ..... 125 C6
Newton Ho DA9 ..... 177 D2
Newton Pk St RM6 ..... 134 D7
Newton Park Rd SS7 ..... 145 B7
Newton Rd
Redbridge IG7 ..... 112 B5
Tilbury RM18 ..... 179 A5
Newton's Ct DA2 ..... 176 D3
Newtons Prim Sch
RM13 ..... 154 D3
New Wanstead E11 ..... 132 A5
New Waverley Rd
SS15 ..... 119 E1
NEW WAY 25 C8
New Way La CM17 ..... 12 D1
New Writtle St CM2 ..... 32 B1
New Zealand Way
RM13 ..... 154 F2
Nicholas Cl
South Ockendon
RM15 ..... 157 C2
Writtle CM1 ..... 31 B1
Nicholas Ln CM1 ..... 31 D6
Nicholas Rd RM8 ..... 134 F1
Nicholl Rd
Basildon SS15 ..... 141 C7
Epping CM16 ..... 67 F8
Nicholls Field CM18 ..... 24 B7
Nichols Ct **1** CM2 ..... 32 A1
Nicholson Cres SS14 ..... 145 C3
Nicholson Ct EN11 ..... 21 B6
Nicholson Gr **12** SS12 ..... 121 C5
Nicholson Ho SS1 ..... 167 B8
Nicholson Pl CM12 ..... 78 B7
Nicholson Rd SS7 ..... 145 B3
Nickleby Rd CM21 ..... 31 D6
Nicola Mews IG6 ..... 111 B4
Nicolas Wlk RM16 ..... 174 B4
Nigel Mews IG2 ..... 152 B8
Nightingale Ave
Chingford E4 ..... 109 E5
Upminster RM14 ..... 137 F3
Nightingale Cl
Chingford E4 ..... 109 E6
Rayleigh SS6 ..... 123 B3
Southend-on-S SS2 ..... 147 E6
Nightingale Cnr 2
CM9 ..... 37 A1
Nightingale Cres
RM3 ..... 114 E1
Nightingale Ct
Grays RM16 ..... 172 C3
4 Wanstead E11 ..... 132 B6
Nightingale Gr RM16 ..... 176 A3
Nightingale La CM11 ..... 132 B6

Nightingale Mews 8
E11 ..... 132 B6
Nightingale Prim Sch
E18 ..... 132 C7
Nightingale Rd SS8 ..... 164 C3
Nightingales
Basildon SS16 ..... 140 F5
Waltham Abbey EN9 ..... 65 E5
NINE ASHES 50 C2
Nine Ashes SG12 ..... 9 D7
Nine Ashes Farm Cotts
CM4 ..... 50 C2
Nine Ashes Rd
Blackmore CM4 ..... 50 D1
Stondon Massey CM15 ..... 72 B6
Ninefields EN9 ..... 65 F6
Nipsells Chase CM3 ..... 61 A1
Nita Rd CM14 ..... 116 C5
Niton Cl SS17 ..... 175 C8
Niven Cl SS12 ..... 121 E5
NOAK BRIDGE 119 F1
Noak Bridge Prim Sch
SS15 ..... 119 F1
Noakes Ave CM2 ..... 54 E6
NOAK HILL 114 E8
Noak Hill CM12 ..... 119 C4
Noak Hill Cl CM12 ..... 119 B4
Noak Hill Rd
Basildon CM12 ..... 119 B4
Romford RM3 ..... 114 D7
Noak Hill Sch RM4 ..... 114 E8
Nobel Sq SS13 ..... 121 C2
Nobel Villas EN9 ..... 65 D5
NOBLESGREEN 146 F7
Nobles Green Cl SS9 ..... 146 E7
Nobles Green Rd SS9 ..... 146 E7
Noel Sq RM8 ..... 153 C8
Nonsuch Cl IG6 ..... 111 B4
Nook The SG12 ..... 8 E3
Norbury Gdns RM6 ..... 134 D6
Norbury Rd E4 ..... 109 A5
Nordenfeldt Rd DA8 ..... 169 D1
Nordic Lo CM9 ..... 58 F8
Nordland Rd SS8 ..... 164 D5
Norland Prim M PM15 ..... 157 D1
Noredale SS3 ..... 168 D5
Nore Rd SS9 ..... 146 C8
Nore View SS16 ..... 140 F4
Norfolk Ave SS16 ..... 146 F3
Norfolk Cl
Basildon SS15 ..... 141 A6
Canvey Island SS8 ..... 164 A5
Dartford DA1 ..... 176 A1
Maldon CM9 ..... 36 E1
Norfolk Ct
4 Ilford RM6 ..... 134 B6
Rochford SS4 ..... 125 D5
Norfolk Dr CM1 ..... 32 A7
Norfolk Ho
5 Gravesend DA12 ..... 179 D1
Romford RM7 ..... 113 A2
Norfolk Pl RM16 ..... 172 C1
Norfolk Rd
Barking IG11 ..... 152 E5
Dagenham RM10 ..... 154 B7
Gravesend DA12 ..... 179 E1
Ilford IG3 ..... 133 E4
Maldon CM9 ..... 36 E1
Romford RM7 ..... 135 C5
Upminster RM14 ..... 137 A2
Wallend E6 ..... 152 A4
Norfolk Way SS8 ..... 163 F5
Norham Ct **16** DA2 ..... 176 B1
Norman Cl
Romford RM5 ..... 113 B1
Waltham Abbey EN9 ..... 65 D6
Norman Cres
Brentwood CM13 ..... 117 A7
Rayleigh SS6 ..... 123 E5
Norman Ct
Ilford IG1 ..... 133 D4
Woodford IG8 ..... 110 B5
Normandy Ave CM0 ..... 106 C5
Normandy Way EN11 ..... 21 D8
Normanhurst CM13 ..... 95 C3
Normanhurst Sch E4 ..... 87 D2
Norman Pl **M** SS9 ..... 165 E8
Norman Rd
Belvedere DA17 ..... 169 B3
Hornchurch RM11 ..... 136 B4
Ilford IG1 ..... 152 B7
Manorshire Dr E4 ..... 109 B6
Normans Rd SS8 ..... 164 D4
Norman Terr SS16 ..... 146 E8
Normanton Pk E4 ..... 109 E8
Norris La EN11 ..... 21 A7
Norris Rd EN11 ..... 21 A6
Norris Rise **4** EN11 ..... 21 A7
Norseman Cl **3** IG3 ..... 134 B3
Norsey Cl CM11 ..... 97 B3
Norsey Dr CM11 ..... 97 D3
Norsey Rd CM11 ..... 97 C4
Norsey View Dr CM12 ..... 97 B6
Norsey Wood Nature
Reserve* CM11 ..... 97 C4
Northallerton Way 15
RM3 ..... 114 D5
Northampton Rd SS16 ..... 140 F4
Northampton Ho 4
RM3 ..... 114 E6
North Ave
Canvey Island SS8 ..... 164 A3
Chelmsford CM1 ..... 31 F5
Southend-on-S SS2 ..... 148 C2
Northbank Rd E17 ..... 109 C1
North Barn EN10 ..... 21 B1
NORTH BENFLEET 143 F8

North Benfleet Hall Rd
Basildon SS12 ..... 122 A1
Basildon SS12 ..... 121 F1
North Boundary Rd
E12 ..... 132 D2
Northbrook Rd IG1 ..... 133 A2
Northbrooks CM19 ..... 23 C7
Northbury Jun d Inf Schs
IG11 ..... 152 C6
North Cl
Dagenham RM10 ..... 154 A4
Redbridge IG7 ..... 112 A5
North Colne SS16 ..... 142 D4
North Cres
Southend-on-S SS2 ..... 147 D5
Wickford SS12 ..... 121 D7
North Crescent Prim Sch
SS12 ..... 121 D7
North Crockerford
SS16 ..... 142 E4
North Cross Rd IG6 ..... 133 C7
North Dell CM1 ..... 32 E7
North Dene CM12 ..... 111 D5
Northdown Gdns IG2 ..... 133 E6
Northdown Rd RM11 ..... 136 B4
North Dr
Brentwood CM13 ..... 96 C2
Great Baddow CM2 ..... 54 F7
Mayland CM3 ..... 60 F1
Romford RM2 ..... 136 C8
NORTHEND 84 E5
Northend CM14 ..... 116 C5
North End
Buckhurst Hill IG9 ..... 88 C2
Romford RM3 ..... 114 C8
Southminster CM0 ..... 84 E5
Northern Ave SS7 ..... 144 C5
Northern Relief Rd
IG11 ..... 152 C5
Northsells Rd SS8 ..... 164 F3
NORTH FAMBRIDGE 103 A8
North Fambridge Sta
CM3 ..... 103 B8
Northfield IG10 ..... 88 D5
Northfield Cl CM11 ..... 97 C2
Northfield Cres RM3 ..... 114 A5
Northfield Gdns RM9 ..... 153 F8
Northfield Path RM9 ..... 153 E8
Northfield Rd
Dagenham RM9 ..... 153 F8
Sawbridgeworth CM21 ..... 1 E4
Northfields RM17 ..... 173 D2
NORTHFLEET 178 C2
Northfleet Ind Est
DA10 ..... 177 F3
Northfleet Sta DA11 ..... 178 B1
North Gate CM20 ..... 10 C1
Northgate Ind Pk
RM5 ..... 112 F1
North Gr CM18 ..... 24 A7
North Hill
Horndon on t H SS17 ..... 160 A3
Little Baddow CM3 ..... 34 D5
North Hill Bsns Pk
SS17 ..... 159 F4
North Hill Dr RM3 ..... 114 D6
North Hill Gn RM3 ..... 114 D6
North Ho CM18 ..... 23 F6
North Kent Ave DA11 ..... 178 C1
Northlands App SS16 ..... 141 C1
Northlands Cl SS17 ..... 160 E5
Northlands Farm Chase
SS17 ..... 160 E7
Northlands Jun d Inf Sch
SS13 ..... 143 B6
Northlands Pavement 3
SS13 ..... 143 B5
NORTH OCKENDON 157 B6
Northolme Cl RM16 ..... 173 C3
Northolt Way RM12 ..... 155 C7
North Pl
Harlow CM20 ..... 11 B5
4 Waltham Abbey EN9 ..... 65 B6
North Rd
Belvedere DA17 ..... 169 B4
Crays Hill CM11 ..... 120 D5
Dagenham RM6 ..... 134 E6
Havering-atte-B RM4 ..... 91 F1
Ilford IG3 ..... 133 E2
Purfleet RM19 ..... 171 C2
Romford RM4 ..... 113 E7
Southend-on-S SS0 ..... 147 E1
South Ockendon RM15 ..... 157 D4
North Residence IG3 ..... 134 B6
North Road Ave
CM14 ..... 116 C8
North Service Rd 6
CM14 ..... 116 C8
NORTH SHOEBURY 149 F1
North Shoebury Rd
SS3 ..... 149 D1
North St
Barking IG11 ..... 152 C5
Great Wakering SS3 ..... 150 B4
Hornchurch RM11 ..... 136 D4
Lower Nazeing EN9 ..... 21 E1
Maldon CM9 ..... 37 B2
Rochford SS4 ..... 125 F2
Romford RM1 ..... 135 D7
Southend-on-S SS0 ..... 165 E8
Southminster CM0 ..... 84 D4

North St continued
Tillingham CM0 ..... 63 E4
North Sta* RM3 ..... 167 A6
NORTH STIFFORD 172 E5
Northumberland Ave
Basildon SS1 ..... 141 C5
Hornchurch RM11 ..... 136 C6
Southend-on-S SS1 ..... 167 D7
Wanstead E12 ..... 132 C3
Northumberland Cres
SS1 ..... 167 D7
Northumberland Ct 1
CM2 ..... 32 F4
Northumberland Ho 11
IG8 ..... 111 A3
Northumberland Rd 175 A4
Northview Ave RM18 ..... 179 A6
North View Cvn Site
IG6 ..... 112 A3
Northview Dr
Southend-on-S SS0 ..... 147 D2
Woodford IG8 ..... 110 D1
Northville Dr SS0 ..... 147 C4
NORTH WEALD BASSETT 47 C5
North Weald Cl
Hornchurch RM11 ..... 155 C5
Wickford SS11 ..... 122 B6
North Weald Sta*
CM16 ..... 47 B4
Northwick Park Prim Sch
SS8 ..... 163 B4
Northwick Rd SS8 ..... 163 B4
Northwick Ret Pk
SS8 ..... 163 B4
Northwood Ho RM6 ..... 174 B4
Northwood Ave RM12 ..... 155 A8
Northwood Dr 2
DA9 ..... 177 A1
Northwood Gdns IG5 ..... 133 A2
Norton Ave SS8 ..... 164 E3
Norton Cl
Chingford E4 ..... 109 C5
Corringham SS17 ..... 161 A3
Norton Ct IG2 ..... 133 E5
NORTON HEATH 50 D5
Norton Heath Rd CM5 ..... 50 E8
Norton La
High Ongar CM5 ..... 49 D5
High Ongar, Norton
Mandeville CM6, SS 50 C6
NORTON MANDEVILLE 49 F6
Norton Pl CM11 ..... 98 C5
Norton Rd
Chelmsford CM1 ..... 32 A3
Dagenham RM10 ..... 154 D6
Ingatestone CM4 ..... 74 B4
Norway Wlk RM13 ..... 155 C1
Norwich Ave SS2 ..... 148 C2
Norwich Cl SS2 ..... 148 C2
Norwich Cres
Ilford RM6 ..... 134 B6
Rayleigh SS6 ..... 123 C5
Norwich Ho SS4 ..... 125 D5
Norwich Mews IG3 ..... 134 A3
Norwich Wlk SS14 ..... 142 F7
Norwood Ave RM7 ..... 135 C4
Norwood Ct DA1 ..... 176 A3
Norwood Dr SS1 ..... 144 E1
NORWOOD END 27 D5
Norwood End
Basildon SS14 ..... 142 D4
Fyfield CM5 ..... 27 D5
Nottage Cl SS17 ..... 160 E4
Nottingham Way
SS16 ..... 140 F5
Nuneaton Rd RM9 ..... 153 E5
Nunns Way RM17 ..... 173 D2
NUPER'S HATCH 91 E2
Nursery Cl
Ilford RM6 ..... 134 D5
Rayleigh SS6 ..... 123 D1
South Ockendon RM15 ..... 157 C1
Woodford IG8 ..... 110 D1
Nursery Fields CM21 ..... 1 D2
Nursery Gdns SS15 ..... 141 D8
Nursery La CM3 ..... 56 F2
Nursery Rd
Chelmsford CM2 ..... 54 B8
Hoddesdon EN11 ..... 8 B1
Hook End CM15 ..... 72 C5
Loughton IG10 ..... 88 D5
Lower Nazeing EN9 ..... 21 D2
Stanford-le-H SS17 ..... 160 E3
Wanstead E12 ..... 132 E2
Nursery Wlk RM7 ..... 135 D5
Nutberry Cl SS13 ..... 173 B4
Nutberry Cl RM16 ..... 173 B4
Nutbrowne Rd RM9 ..... 154 A4
Nutcombe Cres SS4 ..... 125 D4
Nutfield Gdns IG3 ..... 134 A2
Nuthatch Cl CM11 ..... 119 C8
Nutter La E11 ..... 132 C6
Nyall Cl DA17 ..... 169 A1
Nyall Ct RM9 ..... 136 D8
Nyssa Cl IG8 ..... 110 F4
Nyth Cl RM14 ..... 137 D5

O

Oak Ave
Crays Hill CM11 . . . . 120 C4
Upminster RM14 . . . . 156 B8
Wickford SS11 . . . . 122 C7
Oakbank CM13 . . . . 95 E4
Oak Chase SS12 . . . . 121 A7
Oak Cl
Maldon CM9 . . . . 59 B8
Waltham Abbey EN9 . . . . 65 D5
Oak Cnr CM9 . . . . 57 D6
Oak Cotts CM3 . . . . 33 E8
Oak Ct
Chingford E4 . . . . 109 B4
Hadleigh SS7 . . . . 145 E2
South Ockendon RM15 . . . 157 C3
Oakdale Ct E4 . . . . 109 C5
Oakdale Gdns E4 . . . . 109 C5
Oakdale Inf Sch E18 . . . . . 110 B1
Oakdale Jun Sch E18 . . . 110 B1
Oakdale Rd E18 . . . . 110 B1
Oakdene RM3 . . . . 114 F1
Oak Dene Cl RM11 . . . . . . 136 B5
Oakdene Rd SS13 . . . . 143 C8
Oakdown Ho IG7 . . . . 111 F5
Oak Dr CM21 . . . . 11 C8
Oak End CM16 . . . . 23 F6
Oaken Grange Dr SS2 . . 147 E5
Oak Farm Rd CM9 . . . . 35 E1
Oakfield E4 . . . . 109 B5
Oakfield Cl SS7 . . . . 144 C3
Oakfield Ho 2 IG1 . . . . . . 133 B1
Oakfield Lo 5 IG1 . . . . . . 133 B1
Oakfield Prim Sch
SS12 . . . . 121 E5
Oakfield Rd
Ilford IG1 . . . . 133 B1
Rochford SS4 . . . . 103 A1
South Benfleet SS7 . . . . . . 144 C3
Oakfields
Chigwell IG7 . . . . 111 C5
Loughton IG10 . . . . 89 A4
Oak Glade CM16 . . . . 46 D2
Oak Glen RM11 . . . . 136 E8
Oak Gn CM11 . . . . 97 D1
Oakhall Ct E11 . . . . 132 B5
Oak Hall Rd E11 . . . . 132 B5
Oakham Cl SS16 . . . . 140 F5
Oakham Ct SS9 . . . . 146 E2
Oak Hill IG8 . . . . 109 E3
Oak Hill Cl IG8 . . . . 109 D3
Oak Hill Cres IG8 . . . . 109 E3
Oak Hill Ct IG8 . . . . 109 E3
Oak Hill Gdns IG8 . . . . . . 109 F2
Oakhill Prim Sch IG8 . . 109 E4
Oakhill Rd RM19 . . . . 171 B1
Oak Hill Rd RM4 . . . . 91 E1
Oak Ho SS3 . . . . 168 F8
Oakhurst Cl
Redbridge IG6 . . . . 111 C2
Wickford SS12 . . . . 121 C6
Oakhurst Dr SS12 . . . . . . 121 C5
Oakhurst Gdns E4 . . . . 87 F1
Oakhurst Rd
Rayleigh SS6 . . . . 145 F8
Southend-on-S SS2 . . . . . . 148 A2
Oak La
Crays Hill CM11 . . . . 120 C3
Woodford IG8 . . . . 109 F6
Oakland Farm Ind Est
CM4 . . . . 97 F6
Oakland Gdns CM13 . . . . . 95 C4
Oakland Pl IG9 . . . . 110 A8
Oaklands Ave RM1 . . . . . . 135 F7
Oaklands Cres CM2 . . . . . 54 B8
Oaklands Dr
Harlow CM17 . . . . 24 C7
South Ockendon RM15 . . . 172 C8
Oaklands Inf Sch CM2 . . 54 B8
Oaklands Mews SS4 . . . 125 C4
Oaklands Park Ave
IG1 . . . . 133 C2
Oaklands Pk CM15 . . . . 95 B1
Oaklands Sch IG10 . . . . . . 88 D4
Oaklands Way CM4 . . . . . . 34 E2
Oaklea Ave CM2 . . . . 32 E3
Oakleafe Gdns IG6 . . . . . 133 B8
Oakleigh Ave
Hullbridge SS5 . . . . 101 E2
Southend-on-S SS1 . . . . . . 167 D8
Oakleigh Lo IG3 . . . . 134 A1
Oakleigh Park Dr SS6 . . 146 E1
Oakleigh Rise CM16 . . . . . 68 A7
Oakleighs SS7 . . . . 144 C4
Oakley Ave
Barking IG11 . . . . 152 F5
Rayleigh SS6 . . . . 122 F3
Oakley Cl
Chingford E4 . . . . 109 C7
Grays RM20 . . . . 177 C8
Oakley Ct IG10 . . . . 89 A7
Oakley Dr
Billericay CM12 . . . . 96 F5
Romford RM3 . . . . 115 A5
Oak Lo E11 . . . . 132 A4
Oak Lodge Ave IG7 . . . . 111 D5
Oak Lodge Tye CM1 . . . . . 33 A6
Oakmoor Way IG7 . . . . . . 111 E5
Oak Piece CM16 . . . . 47 C6
Oak Rd
Canvey Island SS8 . . . . 164 C3
Crays Hill CM11 . . . . 120 C4

Oak Rd *continued*
Epping CM16 . . . . 45 F1
Grays RM17 . . . . 178 C8
Greenhithe DA9 . . . . 176 E1
Heybridge CM9 . . . . 37 B6
Ramsden Heath CM11 . . . . 98 D5
Rochford SS4 . . . . 125 E2
Romford RM3 . . . . 114 F2
Oak Rd N SS7 . . . . 145 E2
Oak Rd S SS7 . . . . 145 E2
Oak Rise IG9 . . . . 110 D7
Oaks EN9 . . . . 66 C4
Oaks Ave RM5 . . . . 113 C1
Oaks Gr E4 . . . . 109 E8
Oakside Ct
Redbridge IG6 . . . . 111 D1
Wanstead E11 . . . . 132 A7
Oaks La IG2 . . . . 133 E7
Oaks Park High Sch
IG2 . . . . 133 E6
Oaks Ret Pk CM20 . . . . 10 F3
Oak St RM7 . . . . 135 C6
Oaks The
Billericay CM11 . . . . 119 C6
Chingford IG8 . . . . 109 E3
Dartford DA2 . . . . 176 B1
Oaktree Cl CM13 . . . . 116 F7
Oak Tree Cl IG10 . . . . 89 C8
Oaktree Gdns CM17 . . . . . 24 D7
Oaktree Gr IG1 . . . . 152 D7
Oakview Cl SS9 . . . . 146 E3
Oak View Sch IG10 . . . . . . 89 A6
Oakway RM16 . . . . 173 C5
Oak Wlk
Hockley SS5 . . . . 124 E2
South Benfleet SS7 . . . . . . 144 B8
Southend-on-S SS9 . . . . . 146 D4
Oakwood EN9 . . . . 65 C5
Oakwood Ave
Brentwood CM13 . . . . 95 E3
Southend-on-S SS9 . . . . . . 146 E5
Oakwood Chase
RM11 . . . . 136 F4
Oakwood Cl
South Benfleet SS7 . . . . . . 144 B5
Woodford IG8 . . . . 110 E4
Oakwood Ct
Althorne CM3 . . . . 83 A3
Chingford E4 . . . . 87 E2
Romford RM2 . . . . 136 C8
Southend-on-S SS9 . . . . . . 146 E5
Oakwood Dr CM22 . . . . 97 C5
Oakwood Est CM20 . . . . . . 10 F3
Oakwood Gdns IG3 . . . . . 133 F2
Oakwood Gr SS13 . . . . . . 143 B6
Oakwood Hill IG10 . . . . . . 89 B4
Oakwood Hill Ind Est
IG10 . . . . 89 B4
Oakwood Ind Est
DA11 . . . . 178 A2
OakWood Mews 5
CM17 . . . . 11 C4
Oakwood Rd
Corringham SS17 . . . . 161 B3
Rayleigh SS6 . . . . 123 C4
Oakwood Villas SS9 . . . . 146 C7
Oasis Ct CM1 . . . . 32 F5
Oast Ct 3 SS4 . . . . 125 F2
Oast Way SS4 . . . . 125 F2
Oates Rd RM5 . . . . 113 B5
Oban Ct SS11 . . . . 122 B5
Oban Ho 6 IG11 . . . . 152 D3
Oban Rd SS2 . . . . 147 A4
Occasio Ho CM20 . . . . 23 C8
Ockelford Ave CM1 . . . . . . 31 F5
Ockendon Rd RM14 . . . . 157 B7
Ockendon Sch The
RM15 . . . . 172 A8
Ockendon Sta RM15 . . . . 157 B2
Octave Ho CM16 . . . . 67 E3
Odell Cl IG11 . . . . 152 F5
Odeon The SS1 . . . . 152 D5
Odessa Rd SS8 . . . . 164 D3
Odin Lo CM9 . . . . 58 F8
O'Donoghue Ho SS17 . . 160 E2
Ogard Rd EN11 . . . . 21 C8
Ogilvie Ct SS12 . . . . 121 E5
Oglethorpe Rd RM10 . . . 135 A1
Okehampton Rd RM3 . . . 114 C4
Okehampton Sq RM3 . . . 114 C4
Old Barn La CM4 . . . . 77 F2
Old Barns La CM4 . . . . 51 C3
Old Bell La CM3 . . . . 78 B1
Old Brickworks The
RM3 . . . . 115 A3
Oldbury Ave CM2 . . . . 54 F8
Oldbury Cotts SS3 . . . . . . 149 D3
Oldchurch Gdns RM7 . . 135 D4
Old Church Hill SS16 . . . 141 A1
Old Church La CM13 . . . . . 96 B6
Oldchurch Rd RM7 . . . . . 135 E4
Old Church Rd
Basildon SS13 . . . . 143 F5
Chingford E4 . . . . 109 A7
East Hanningfield CM3 . . . . 78 B6
Old Coastguard Cotts
CM0 . . . . 41 C4
Old College Ct CM17 . . . 169 B1
Old Court Rd CM2 . . . . 32 C3
Old Croft Cl CM1 . . . . 16 D5
Old Crown La CM14 . . . . . . 93 D7
Old Ct CM2 . . . . 32 D3
Old Farm Ct CM12 . . . . 97 A4
Old Farm Yd CM22 . . . . 12 C8
Oldfields CM14 . . . . 116 C6
Old Forge Cl CM1 . . . . 16 D5
Old Forge The SS6 . . . . . 123 C3

Old Hall Ct SS3 . . . . 150 A4
Old Hall Rise CM17 . . . . . . 24 E8
OLD HARLOW 11 D4
Old Heath Rd CM3,
CM0 . . . . 84 A2
Old Highway EN11 . . . . 21 C8
Old Hill Ave SS16 . . . . 160 B8
Oldhouse Croft CM20 . . . 10 E2
Old House La
Lower Nazeing EN9 . . . . 43 F8
Roydon CM19 . . . . 22 E6
Old Jenkins Cl SS17 . . . . 160 B1
Old Leigh Rd SS9 . . . . . . 147 A1
Old London Rd
Rawreth SS11 . . . . 122 D6
Woodham Walter CM9 . . . . 35 E1
Old Macdonald's
Educational Farm Pk*
CM14 . . . . 92 F1
Old Maltings Ct The 3
EN11 . . . . 21 A6
Old Market Ret Pk 10
SS13 . . . . 143 B5
Old Market Terr 11
CM14 . . . . 116 C8
Old Mead SS2 . . . . 147 A7
Oldmead Ho 2 RM10 . . . 154 B6
Old Mill Ct E18 . . . . 132 C8
Old Mill La CM22 . . . . 2 B6
Old Mill Par 2 RM1 . . . . . 135 E5
Old Mill Pl RM7 . . . . 135 D5
Old Nazeing Rd EN10 . . . 21 C1
Old Nevendon Rd
SS13 . . . . 121 B3
Old Oaks EN9 . . . . 65 E7
Old Orch CM18 . . . . 23 D6
Old Rd
Harlow CM17 . . . . 11 D5
Navestock Heath RM4 . . . . 92 D5
Old Rectory Ct SS2 . . . . . 148 E1
Old Rectory Rd CM5 . . . . . 70 B5
Old Rectory The CM3 . . . . 78 B7
Old Savill's Cotts IG7 . . 111 C6
Old School Field CM1 . . . . 32 E4
Old School Mews SS3 . . 149 E4
Old Ship La SS4 . . . . 125 F2
Old Shire La EN9 . . . . 66 A5
Old Southend Rd
Southend-on-S SS1 . . . . . . 167 B7
West Hanningfield CM2 . . . . 77 D8
Old Station Rd IG10 . . . . . . 88 E4
Old Street Hill CM22 . . . . . . 3 B1
Old Vicarage Cl CM1 . . . . . 6 C2
Old Wickford Rd CM3 . . 101 B8
Oldwyk SS16 . . . . 142 E4
Oleastor Ct IG5 . . . . 132 E8
Olive Ave SS9 . . . . 146 A2
Oliver Cl
Grays RM20 . . . . 176 F7
Hoddesdon EN11 . . . . 21 B8
Oliver Rd
Brentwood CM15 . . . . 95 A4
Grays RM20 . . . . 177 A7
Rainham RM13 . . . . 154 F4
Olivers RM12 . . . . 136 C2
Olivers Cres SS3 . . . . 150 B4
Oliver Way CM1 . . . . 31 F7
Olive St RM7 . . . . 135 D6
Olivia Dr SS9 . . . . 146 F2
Ollards Ct 1 IG10 . . . . 88 E4
Ollard's Gr IG10 . . . . 88 D5
Olympic Bsns Ctr
SS13 . . . . 120 F2
Olympic Ho 2 IG11 . . . . . 133 B1
Omega Ct 1 RM7 . . . . 135 D5
Omnibus Way E17 . . . . . . 109 A1
One Tree Hill SS16,
SS17 . . . . 141 F1
Ongar Cl RM6 . . . . 134 C6
Ongar Ent Ctr CM5 . . . . . . 49 A5
Ongar Pl CM14 . . . . 116 D8
Ongar Rd
Abridge RM4 . . . . 90 D7
Brentwood CM15 . . . . 94 B2
Fyfield CM5 . . . . 27 C2
Kelvedon Hatch CM15 . . . . 71 D4
Margaret Roding CM6 . . . . 15 D3
Pilgrims Hatch CM15 . . . . . 94 A3
Stondon Massey CM15 . . . . 71 E8
Writtle CM1 . . . . 31 F1
Ongar Sta* CM5 . . . . 49 A4
Ongar War Meml Hospl
CM5 . . . . 49 A5
Ongar Way RM13 . . . . 154 E4
Onslow Cl E4 . . . . 109 D8
Onslow Gdns
Chipping Ongar CM5 . . . . . . 49 A4
Wanstead E18 . . . . 132 C8
Opal Mews 2 IG1 . . . . . . 133 B2
Optima Bsns Pk EN11 . . 21 C7
Orange Gr IG7 . . . . 111 B4
Orange Rd SS8 . . . . 164 D4
Orange Tree Cl CM2 . . . . . 54 C6
Orange Tree Hill RM4 . . 113 E6
Orchard Ave
Billericay CM12 . . . . 97 C5
Brentwood CM13 . . . . 116 F7
Downham CM11 . . . . 99 B8
Hockley SS5 . . . . 124 E7
Rainham RM13 . . . . 155 C1
Rayleigh SS6 . . . . 145 C8
Orchard Cl
Billericay CM12 . . . . 97 C5
Chelmsford CM2 . . . . 54 C6
Chingford E4 . . . . 109 A6
Great Wakering SS3 . . . . . 150 B4
Hockley SS5 . . . . 124 F7

Orchard Cl *continued*
Maldon CM9 . . . . 36 F2
Sheering CM22 . . . . 12 C8
Southminster CM0 . . . . 84 D4
South Ockendon RM15 . . . 157 C1
Stanstead Abbotts SG12 . . . 8 C4
Wanstead E11 . . . . 132 B7
Writtle CM1 . . . . 31 B1
Orchard Croft CM20 . . . . . . 11 A2
Orchard Dr
Grays RM17 . . . . 173 A4
Theydon Bois CM16 . . . . . . 67 E3
Orchard Gdns EN9 . . . . . . 65 C5
Orchard Gr SS9 . . . . 146 F6
Orchard Ho CM4 . . . . 75 E3
Orchard La
Pilgrims Hatch CM15 . . . . . 93 F4
Woodford IG8 . . . . 110 C6
Orchard Lea CM2 . . . . 1 C1
Orchard Mead SS9 . . . . . 146 E5
Orchard Piece CM4 . . . . . . 72 F8
Orchard Rd
Belvedere DA17 . . . . 169 A2
Burnham-on-C CM0 . . . . . 106 C4
Dagenham RM10 . . . . 154 A4
Maldon CM9 . . . . 36 F2
Mayland CM3 . . . . 61 A1
Romford RM7 . . . . 113 B1
South Benfleet SS7 . . . . . . 144 B7
Southminster CM0 . . . . 84 E4
South Ockendon RM15 . . . 172 C8
Swanscombe DA10 . . . . . . 177 E3
Orchard Side SS9 . . . . . . 146 F6
Orchard St CM2 . . . . 32 B1
Orchards The
Epping CM16 . . . . 68 A7
Sawbridgeworth CM21 . . . . . 1 E3
Orchard Terr CM12 . . . . . . 96 F8
Orchard The SS12 . . . . . . 121 B7
Orchard View CM13 . . . . . 140 E5
Orchard Way IG7 . . . . 112 A7
Orchid Rd RM4 . . . . 90 B6
Orchid Pl
Basildon SS15 . . . . 141 D5
South Woodham Ferrers
CM3 . . . . 101 D8
Orchill Dr SS7 . . . . 145 E4
Orchis Gr RM17 . . . . 172 F1
Orchis Way RM3 . . . . 114 F4
Ordnance Rd
Gravesend DA12 . . . . 179 C1
Holdbrook EN3 . . . . 65 A2
Orestes Ct 8 E18 . . . . . . 132 A8
Oreston Rd RM13 . . . . 155 D2
Orford Cres CM1 . . . . 32 D5
Orford Ct 5 DA2 . . . . 176 B1
Orford Rd E18 . . . . 132 B8
Oriel Gdns IG5 . . . . 132 F8
Orion Ho 2 RM7 . . . . 135 D5
Orion Ct SS14 . . . . 121 A1
Orkney Gdns SS12 . . . . . 121 F5
Orlando Dr SS13 . . . . 121 C1
Ormesby Chine CM3 . . . . 101 D5
Ormond Cl RM3 . . . . 114 D1
Ormonde Ave
Rochford SS4 . . . . 125 E3
South Benfleet SS7 . . . . . . 146 A2
Ormonde Ct RM1 . . . . 135 F4
Ormonde Gdns SS9 . . . . 146 A2
Ormonde Rise IG9 . . . . 88 C1
Ormond Ho 2 SS4 . . . . . . 125 F2
Ormonds Cres CM3 . . . . . . 59 E8
Ormsby Rd SS3 . . . . 163 D3
Orplands Cotts CM0 . . . . . 41 F1
Orrmo Rd SS8 . . . . 164 F3
Orsett Ave
Leigh-on-S SS9 . . . . 146 C8
Rayleigh SS6 . . . . 145 C8
Orsett CE Prim Sch
RM16 . . . . 174 A8
Orsett End SS14 . . . . 142 D7
ORSETT HEATH 174 A4
Orsett Heath Cres
RM16 . . . . 174 A3
Orsett Hospl RM16 . . . . . 174 A8
Orsett Ind Pk RM16 . . . . 174 F8
Orsett Rd
Grays RM17 . . . . 173 B1
Horndon on t H SS17 . . . . 159 D2
Orsett Terr IG8 . . . . 110 C3
Orton Cl CM4 . . . . 75 A8
Orton Ct RM7 . . . . 135 D6
Orton Ho 2 RM3 . . . . 114 C3
Orwell RM18 . . . . 179 C3
Orwell Cl SS11 . . . . 169 D8
Orwell Ct SS11 . . . . 122 B5
Orwell Lo 2 E18 . . . . 132 A7
Orwell Way CM0 . . . . 106 A6
Osborne Cl RM11 . . . . 136 B5
Osborne Ho 10 IG6 . . . . . 111 A3
Osborne Hts CM14 . . . . . . 116 B6
Osborne Rd
Basildon, Barstable
SS16 . . . . 142 C5
Basildon, North Benfleet
SS13 . . . . 143 E8
Buckhurst Hill IG9 . . . . 88 B1
Dagenham RM9 . . . . 153 F7
Hoddesdon EN10 . . . . 21 A1
Hornchurch RM11 . . . . 136 C5
Pilgrims Hatch CM15 . . . . . 94 B3
Southend-on-S SS0 . . . . . 147 E1
Osborne Sq RM9 . . . . 153 F8
Osbourne Ave SS5 . . . . . . 124 C6
Osbourne Ho SS0 . . . . . . 147 C1
OSEA ISLAND 39 B1
Osea Rd CM9 . . . . 38 B3
Osea Way CM1 . . . . 32 F5

Osier Dr SS15 . . . . 141 C3
Osprey Cl
Southend-on-S SS3 . . . . . . 168 C7
Wanstead E11 . . . . 132 B6
Osprey Ct
Brentwood CM14 . . . . 94 F8
Waltham Abbey EN9 . . . . . . 65 D6
Osprey Rd EN9 . . . . 65 D6
Ospreys The SS2 . . . . 147 F5
Osprey Way CM2 . . . . 32 E5
Ostell Cres EN3 . . . . 65 A1
OSTEND 85 C4
Osterley Dr SS16 . . . . 142 A2
Osterley Pl CM3 . . . . 59 D6
Otley App IG2 . . . . 133 D6
Otley Dr IG2 . . . . 133 D6
Ottawa Gdns RM10 . . . . . 154 D1
Ottawa Rd RM18 . . . . 179 B5
Otterbourne Rd E4 . . . . . . 109 D6
Ouida Rd SS8 . . . . 163 D5
Oulton Ave SS8 . . . . 164 A2
Oulton Cres SS11 . . . . 122 E6
Oundle Ho 8 RM3 . . . . . . 114 C3
Our Lady Immaculate
Prim Sch CM2 . . . . 54 B8
Our Lady of Lourdes RC
Prim Sch
Southend-on-S SS3 . . . . . . 168 A5
Wanstead E11 . . . . 132 A5
Our Lady of Ransom RC
Prim Sch
Outing Cl SS1 . . . . 167 D7
Outing's La CM15 . . . . 72 E3
Outwood Common Rd
CM11 . . . . 119 E6
Outwood Farm Cl
CM11 . . . . 119 F6
Outwood Farm Rd
CM11 . . . . 119 F6
Oval Gdns RM17 . . . . 178 B8
Oval Rd N RM10 . . . . 154 C1
Oval Rd S RM10 . . . . 154 D1
Overcliff Flats SS0 . . . . . 147 D2
Overcliff Rd RM17 . . . . . . 178 B8
Overmead Dr CM3 . . . . 81 D5
Overstrand Ho RM12 . . . 136 C1
Overton Cl CM2 . . . . 32 F4
Overton Ct E11 . . . . 132 A5
Overton Dr
Dagenham RM6 . . . . 134 A8
South Benfleet SS7 . . . . . . 144 B2
Wanstead E11 . . . . 132 A5
Overton Rd SS7 . . . . 144 B2
Overton Way SS7 . . . . 144 C2
Ovington Gdns CM12 . . . . 96 E2
Owen Cl RM5 . . . . 113 C1
Owen Gdns IG8 . . . . 110 F4
Owen Waters Ho IG5 . . . 110 F1
Owlets Hall Cl RM11 . . . . 136 E8
Owl Pk Cvn Site IG10 . . . 89 D8
Oxcroft Ct SS15 . . . . 141 B5
Oxendon Dr EN11 . . . . 21 A7
Oxford Ave
Grays RM16 . . . . 173 D3
Hornchurch RM11 . . . . 137 A4
Oxford Cl
Basildon SS16 . . . . 142 B1
Romford RM1 . . . . 135 E5
Oxford Ct
Brentwood CM14 . . . . 116 C6
Chelmsford CM2 . . . . 33 A2
Oxford Ho IG6 . . . . 133 A8
Oxford Rd
Canvey Island SS8 . . . . 163 F3
Horndon on t H SS17 . . . . 159 D2
Ilford IG1 . . . . 133 F4
Rochford SS4 . . . . 125 E4
Romford RM3 . . . . 114 D1
Stanford-le-H SS17 . . . . . . 160 E4
Woodford IG8 . . . . 110 B3
Oxley Cl CM13 . . . . 116 F7
Oxley Gdns SS17 . . . . 161 B3
Oxleys Rd EN9 . . . . 65 B3
Oxleys The CM17 . . . . 24 C7
Oxlow La RM10 . . . . 154 A8
Oxney Mead CM1 . . . . 32 A6
Oxted Ho RM13 . . . . 154 F1
Oxwich Cl SS17 . . . . 161 A4
Oyster Catcher Terr 4
IG5 . . . . 110 F1
Oyster Cotts CM22 . . . . 4 A8
Oyster Ct SS8 . . . . 164 D2
Oyster Dr CM2 . . . . 54 A7
Ozonia Ave SS12 . . . . 122 B8
Ozonia Cl SS12 . . . . 122 A8
Ozonia Way SS12 . . . . 122 A8
Ozonia Wlk 3 SS12 . . . . 122 A8

P

Paarl Rd SS8 . . . . 163 C4
Paceheath Cl RM5 . . . . . . 113 C5
Pacific Cl DA10 . . . . 177 E1
Pacific Wharf IG11 . . . . . . 152 D3
Padda Ct SS12 . . . . 121 F7
Paddock Cl
Billericay CM11 . . . . 97 D1
Orsett RM16 . . . . 174 A6
Southend-on-S SS2 . . . . . . 147 E8
Paddock Dr CM1 . . . . 32 A6
Paddock Mead CM18 . . . . 23 C4
Paddocks The
High Roding CM6 . . . . 15 A6
Ingatestone CM4 . . . . 74 F1
Orsett RM16 . . . . 174 A3
Rayleigh SS6 . . . . 123 B1

Pepys Cl
Dartford DA1............21 A6
Tilbury RM18...........179 C6
Pepys Ct
4 Hoddesdon EN11........21 D8
Wickford SS12...........121 C5
Percival Gdns RM6......134 D5
Percival Ho **4** IG8.......110 A6
Percival Rd RM11........136 C5
Percy Cottis Rd SS4.....125 E3
Percy Rd
Ilford IG3................134 A4
Romford RM7............135 C8
Southend-on-S SS9......146 D1
Percy St **2** RM17.......178 C8
Peregrine Cl
Basildon SS16...........142 B4
Southend-on-S SS3.....149 E1
Peregrine Dr
Chelmsford CM2..........54 A4
South Benfleet SS7.....144 C2
Peregrine Gdns SS6....123 B3
Peregrine Rd IG6.......112 C5
Peregrine Wlk 6
RM12....................155 B6
Peregrin Rd EN9.........66 A5
Perkins Cl DA9..........176 F2
Perkins Rd IG2..........133 D6
Perriclose CM1...........32 D7
Perrin Pl CM2.............32 A1
Perry Rd RM13..........154 D3
Perryfield CM17..........13 C2
Perryfield La CM5........27 E5
Perryfields Jun & Inf Sch
CM1......................32 D6
Perry Gn SS14...........142 B8
Perry Gr DA1............176 A3
Perry Hill
Chelmsford CM1..........32 D3
Lower Nazeing EN9.......43 F8
Perry Ho RM13..........154 D3
Perryman Ho IG11......152 C4
Perrymans Farm Rd
IG2.....................133 D6
Perry Rd
Harlow CM18.............23 C4
South Benfleet SS7.....144 B3
Perry Spring
Basildon SS16...........142 D5
Harlow CM17.............24 D6
Perry St CM12............97 B5
Perry Way RM15.........171 C6
Pershore Cl IG2........133 B6
Perth Ho RM18..........179 A5
Perth Rd
Barking IG11............152 D4
Ilford IG1, IG2..........133 B4
Perth Terr IG2...........133 C4
Pertwee Dr
Great Baddow CM2.......54 F6
South Woodham Ferrers
CM3....................101 D7
Petands Ct RM12........136 D1
Peterborough Ave
RM14....................137 F3
Peterborough Gdns
IG1.....................132 C4
Peterborough Way 5
SS14....................142 F8
Peter Bradley Ct RM9..153 F5
Peters Cl RM8...........134 D3
Peters Ct SS15..........141 B6
Petersfield CM1..........32 B7
Petersfield Ave RM3...114 F5
Petersfield Cl RM3.....115 A4
Peter St CM4.............97 F8
Peterswood Inf Sch
CM18....................23 D4
Petrebrook CM2...........33 A3
Petric Cl
Ingatestone CM4.........74 A2
West Horndon CM13....139 C5
Petrel Way CM2...........54 C6
Petresfield Way
CM13....................139 C5
Pett Cl RM11............136 B2
Petticrow Quays CM0...106 C3
Pettits Bvd RM1.........113 E2
Pettits Cl RM1..........113 E1
Pettits La
Doddinghurst CM15......72 C2
Romford RM1............135 F8
Pettits La N RM1.......113 E2
Pettit's Pl RM1.........114 A7
Pettit's Rd RM10........154 A7
Pettley Gdns RM7.......135 D6
Petunia Cres CM1........32 F6
Petworth Gdns SS2.....148 F2
Petworth Way RM12....154 F8
Pevensey Ct **10** E18....110 A2
Pevensey Gdns SS5.....101 F1
Pevensey Way SS15.....143 B6
Peverel Ho **4** RM10....135 A2
Peveril Ct **26** DA2....176 B1
Pewsey Cl E4............109 A5
Phelips Rd CM19.........23 B3
Philan Way RM5.........113 D4
Philbrick Cres CM8.....123 C3
Philbrick Cres W SS6..123 C3
Philip Ave RM7..........135 D3
Philip Cl
Pilgrims Hatch CM15.....94 C3
Romford RM7............135 D3
Philippa Way RM16.....174 B2

Philip Rd RM13........154 E2
Philip Sydney Ct
RM20....................172 D1
Philip Sydney Rd
RM20....................172 D1
Phillida Rd RM3.........115 A1
Phillips Ho RM16.......174 A8
Philmead Rd SS7........144 B2
Philpot Ave SS2........148 E2
Phoenix Bldgs 1
RM13....................155 B1
Phoenix Ct E4...........109 B7
Phoenix Gr CM2..........54 A8
Phoenix Hospl SS0.......1 E2
Phoenix Prim Sch
SS15....................141 C6
Phoenix Way SS7........145 C7
Picador Ho **6** RM10..154 B6
Picardy Manorway
DA17....................169 B4
Picardy Rd DA17........169 A2
Picardy St DA17........169 A3
Picasso Way SS12.......150 A1
Pickering Ave E6.......152 A2
Pickering Ct **15** DA2..176 B1
Pickering Rd IG11.....152 C6
Picketts SS8.............163 D4
Picketts Ave SS5.......146 E4
Picketts Ct SS9........146 E4
Pick Hill EN9............66 A7
Pickwick Ave CM1........31 D6
Pickwick Cl SS15.......141 D7
Picton Cl SS6...........123 E1
Picton Gdns SS6........123 E1
Piercing Hill CM16......67 D4
Piercys SS13............143 B5
Pier Hill SS1...........167 A7
Pier Rd
Gravesend DA11.........178 F1
Greenhithe DA9.........177 B3
Pierrot Stps **5** SS1..167 C7
Pigeon Ct E4...........109 C4
Piggs Corner Complex
RM17....................173 C3
Pigstye Green Rd CM5...51 A8
Pike La RM14...........156 F7
Pike Way CM16...........47 A4
Pilgrims Cl
Billericay CM11..........97 B2
Pilgrims Hatch CM14.....93 F4
Southend-on-S SS2.....148 E1
Pilgrims Ct DA1........176 A2
PILGRIMS HATCH.........94 A4
Pilgrims La RM16.......172 C5
Pilgrim's La
Pilgrims Hatch, Bentley
CM14....................93 D5
Pilgrims Hatch CM14....93 E4
Pilgrims' Rd DA10.....177 E3
Pilgrims View DA9.....177 C1
Pilgrims Way SS7......145 F3
Pilgrims Wlk **8** CM11..97 B2
Pilgrim Way SS15......141 C6
Pilkingtons CM17........24 D8
Pilot Cl SS11..........122 A5
Pilots Pl **6** DA12....179 C1
Pimpernel Way RM3....114 D4
Pinceybrook Rd CM18....23 C4
Pincey Mead SS13.......143 A5
Pindar Rd EN11.........21 C7
Pine Cl
Canvey Island SS8.....163 E3
Ingatestone CM4.........74 C4
Southend-on-S SS9......146 B5
6 Wickford SS12.....121 C5
Pine Cres CM13..........95 D5
Pinecroft
Brentwood CM13.........95 B2
Romford RM2............136 C7
Pine Dr CM4.............74 C4
Pine Lo SS3............168 F8
Pine Rd SS7............145 D2
Pines Rd RM1............31 D5
Pines The
Basildon SS15..........119 C1
Grays RM16............173 B5
Woodford IG8...........110 A4
Pine Tree Pl SS4.......125 E2
Pinetrees SS7..........145 C3
Pineview Ct E4..........87 C1
Pine View Manor
CM16....................46 A1
Pinewood Ave
Rainham RM13...........155 B1
Southend-on-S SS9.....146 D5
Pinewood Cl
Harlow CM17............24 C7
Hullbridge SS5.........101 E2
Stanford-le-H SS17....175 B3
Pinewood Prim Sch
RM5.....................113 B5
Pinewood Rd RM4......113 D6
Pinewood Way CM13.....95 D4
Pinfolds RM15..........171 D7
Pinley Gdns RM9.......153 B4
Pinmill SS14...........142 B6
PINNACLES............23 A8
Pinnacles EN9...........65 E5
Pinnacle The RM6......134 E5
Pinners Ct CM0.........105 F7
Pintail Rd IG6.........112 B1
Pintails **4** SS13.....143 C6
Pintolls CM1...........101 D6
Pioneer Ct
Basildon SS14..........142 C7
Basildon SS14..........142 C8

Pipchin Rd CM1.........31 F6
Piper's Tye CM2..........54 D3
Piper Way IG1...........133 D3
Pippin Cl SS11.........121 F8
Pippins Rd CM0.........106 C6
PIPPS HILL..............119 F1
Pipps Hill Rd N CM11..120 B3
Pishiobury Dr CM21......11 D8
Pitcairn Cl RM7.........135 A7
Pitmans Ct RM1.........167 A8
PITSEA.................143 B5
Pitsea Hall La SS16....143 B3
Pitsea Jun Sch SS13...143 A5
Pitsea Rd SS14.........143 A5
Pitsea Sta SS13........143 B4
Pitsea View Rd CM11...120 D4
Pitseaville Gr SS16....142 E5
Pitt Chase CM2..........54 E5
Pittfields SS16........141 B5
Pittman Cl CM13........117 C5
Pittman Gdns IG1......152 C7
Pittman's Field CM20...10 F1
Place Cotts CM3.........100 C5
Place Farm La CM5......72 A2
Pladda Mews SS12......121 F5
Plains The E4............87 E2
Plain The CM16..........46 B3
Plaistow Cl SS17........160 D2
Plane Tree Cl
Brentwood CM0.........106 B6
Chelmsford CM2.........54 B6
Plantaganet Pl **3** EN9..65 B6
Plantagenet Gdns
RM6.....................134 D4
Plantagenet Pl RM6....134 D4
Plantation Cl DA9.....176 F1
Plantation Rd CM4......20 E1
Plashet Cl SS17........160 D2
Plashet Gdns CM13.....117 A6
Plashets CM22............2 D1
Plashetts SS14.........142 D7
Plas Newydd SS16......167 E6
Plas Newydd Cl SS1....167 E6
Platford Gn RM11.......136 E7
Platinum Ct RM7........135 B8
Playfield Ave RM5......113 C2
Playhouse Sq CM20......23 C8
Plaza Way SS1..........167 D8
Pleasant Cl SS1........167 B7
Pleasant Dr CM12........96 E3
Pleasant Mews SS1.....167 B7
Pleasant Rd SS1........167 B7
Pleasant Terr SS9......165 E8
Pleasant View DA8.....169 E1
PLESHEY...............7 E2
Pleshey Cl
Southend-on-S SS1.....167 F8
6 Wickford SS12.....121 E6
Plomer Ave **2** EN11.....8 A1
Plotlands Mus* SS16...140 E3
Plotters Ct **7** EN11...21 D8
Plough Rise RM14......137 E4
Plover Gdns RM14......137 F3
Plover Ho RM13.........170 A8
Plovers Barron CM15....72 D3
Plovers Mead CM15......72 D3
Plovers The CM0.........62 D7
Plover Wlk CM2..........54 B5
Plowman Way RM8......134 C3
Ployters Rd CM18........23 C4
Plumberow SS15.........141 E6
Plumberow Ave SS5....124 E7
Plumberow Mount Ave
SS5....................124 E8
Plumberow Prim Sch
SS5....................124 E7
Plume Ave CM9..........36 F1
Plume Sch (Lower)
CM9.....................37 A2
Plume Sch (Upper)
CM9.....................36 F2
Plumleys SS13..........143 B7
Plumpton Ave RM12....136 F1
Plumpton Rd EN11.......21 C8
Plumptre La CM3.........56 D5
Plumtree Ave CM2.......54 F6
Plumtree Ct RM10......154 C6
Plumtree Mead IG10....89 A6
Plymouth Ho **10** IG11..153 A5
Plymouth Rd
Chelmsford CM1.........32 E5
Grays RM16............172 C2
Plymtree SS1...........149 C1
Pocklington Cl CM2......33 A3
Poets Cnr RM18.........179 B6
Point Cl SS8...........164 F3
Point Rd SS8...........164 F3
Polegate Cotts RM17...177 E8
Pole Hill Rd E4..........87 C2
Polesworth Rd RM9.....153 D5
Poley Rd SS17..........160 C1
Pollard Cl IG7.........112 A5
Pollard Hatch CM19.....23 B5
Pollards Cl
Loughton IG10..........88 C4
Rochford SS4...........125 F2
Pollard's Gn CM2.........32 F2
Polstead Cl SS16.......123 A3
Polsteads SS16.........142 E3
Polsten Mews CM1.......32 F6
Pomfret Mead SS14.....142 A6
Pompadour Cl CM14....116 C5
Pond Cl SS5............101 E3
Pondfield La CM13......117 A7
Pondfield Rd RM10.....154 B7
Pond La CM22............3 A2

Pond Lees Cl RM10....154 D5
Ponds Rd CM2............54 B1
Pond Wlk RM14.........137 E2
Pontypool Wlk RM3.....114 C4
Poole Ho RM16.........174 C4
Poole Rd RM11.........137 A4
Pooles Ct IG3.........134 A1
Pooles La SS5..........101 E3
Poolhurst Wlk SS5.....101 E4
Pool's La CM1...........51 F4
Poors La SS7...........145 E4
Poors La N SS7.........146 A5
Poors' Piece Nature
Trail* CM3..............34 F1
Popes Cres SS13........143 B5
Popes Wlk SS6.........124 A2
Poplar Cl
Blackmore CM4..........72 E8
Chelmsford CM2.........54 C6
Ingatestone CM4........74 A2
South Woodham RM15...157 D1
South Woodham Ferrers
CM3...................101 C8
Poplar Cotts CM17....24 E5
Poplar Ct
Chingford E4..........109 B4
Hockley SS5...........124 E6
Poplar Dr CM13..........95 C3
Poplar Gr CM0.........106 B5
Poplar Grove Chase
CM9.....................37 B8
Poplar Mount DA17....169 C2
Poplar Rd
Canvey Island SS8.....164 C3
Rayleigh SS6..........145 F8
Wanstead E12..........132 E2
Poplar Row CM16........67 E2
Poplars EN9.............66 C4
Poplars Ave SS5.......124 F4
Poplar Shaw EN9........65 F6
Poplar St RM7.........135 C7
Poppy Cl
Erith DA17............169 B3
Pilgrims Hatch CM15....94 B4
Poppyfield Cl SS9.....146 D6
Poppy Gdns SS15.......141 C5
Poppy Gn CM1...........33 A6
Porchester Cl RM11...136 E5
Porchester Rd CM12.....97 A5
Porlock Ave SS0.......167 A4
Port Ave DA9...........177 B1
Portchester Ct SS9...146 F1
Porter Cl RM20........177 C8
Porters SS13...........143 C8
Porters Ave RM8.......153 C7
Porters Cl CM14.........94 A1
Porters Grange Prim Sch
SS1....................167 B8
PORTERS TOWN........148 B1
Portia Ct **12** IG11....153 A5
Portland Ave SS1.......167 B8
Portland Cl RM6.......134 E6
Portland Commercial Est
IG11...................153 C3
Portland Gdns RM6....134 D6
Portland Pl DA9.......177 C3
Portland Rd DA11......178 D1
Portmadoc Ho **2**
RM3....................114 E6
Portman Dr
Billericay CM12.........97 B5
Woodford IG8..........110 D1
Portmore Gdns RM5....113 A5
Portnoi Cl RM1........113 D1
Portreath Pl CM1........32 A7
Portsea Rd RM18......179 C6
Portway
Chelmsford CM2.........33 B4
Rainham RM13..........155 A4
Poseidon Ct **1** IG11..153 B2
Postman's La CM3.......34 E3
Post Mdw CM1..........119 D6
Post Office Rd
Chelmsford CM2.........32 B8
Harlow CM20............10 D1
Ingatestone CM4........74 B3
Woodham Mortimer CM9...57 E6
Postway Mews 1
IG1....................133 B1
Potash Rd
Billericay CM11.........97 D6
Matching Green CM17...13 D4
Potiphar Pl CM14......116 B6
Potteries The CM0......66 C5
Potters Cl
Danbury CM3............57 A6
Loughton IG10.........88 F7
Potters Field CM17....24 D6
Potter St CM17.........24 C6
POTTER STREET.......24 D6
Potter Street Prim Sch
CM17...................24 C6
Potters Way SS2.......147 F5
Pottery La CM1..........32 A5
Potton Dr SS12........121 B8
Poulton Cl CM9.........59 B8
Pound Cl EN9...........43 E8
Poundfield Rd IG10.....89 A4
Pound Fields CM1........53 B8

Pound La
Basildon, Laindon
SS15...................141 A5
Basildon, North Benfleet
SS12...................142 B8
Orsett RM16............172 C2
Pound La N SS15........141 A5
Pound Lane Central
SS15...................141 A5
Powdermill La EN9......65 B4
Powdermill Mews 2
EN9.....................65 B4
Powdermill Way EN9.....43 B8
Powell Ct SS4..........124 E4
Powell Gdns RM10.......154 B7
Powell Rd
Basildon SS15..........141 A5
Buckhurst Hill IG9......87 C2
Powle Terr IG1..........43 B7
Pownsett Terr IG1......152 D7
Poynder Rd RM18.......179 B5
Poynings Ave SS2......147 F4
Poynings Way RM3......114 C4
Poyntens SS6...........123 E3
Poynters La SS3........162 C4
Pratts Farm La CM3......20 E8
Preaching Cross CM4...56 E1
Precinct The SS4......125 E4
Premier Ave RM16.......172 F2
Prentice Cl SS4.........54 C6
Prentice Hall La CM9....1 E2
Prentice Pl CM17........24 F5
Prescott SS16..........142 E6
Prescott Gn IG10........89 B8
Presidents Ct SS15....141 E6
Preston Ave E4.........109 D8
Preston Dr E11.........132 A5
Preston Gdns
Rayleigh SS6...........123 E3
Redbridge IG1..........133 A3
Preston Ho 3 RM10....97 E1
Preston Rd
Romford RM3............114 A1
Southend-on-S SS0.....147 C3
Prestwood Cl SS7......144 A3
Prestwood Dr
Romford RM5............113 D4
Thundersley SS7.......144 A3
Pretoria Ave SS15......141 D6
Pretoria Cres E4.......109 D8
Pretoria Rd
Chingford E4...........109 D8
Ilford IG1.............133 D4
Romford RM7............134 F4
Priestley Ct RM17.....173 C2
Priestley Gdns RM6...133 A1
Priests Ave RM1........113 E1
Priests Field CM13......32 C6
Priest's La
Brentwood CM15.........95 A1
Shenfield CM15........116 A8
Primley La CM22.........2 D1
Primrose Ave RM6......134 D3
Primrose Cl
Basildon SS16.........142 C4
Canvey Island SS8.....163 E3
Primrose Ct **2** CM14..116 C5
Primrose Field CM18....24 E5
Primrose Glen RM11....136 C7
Primrose Hill
Brentwood CM14.........94 A1
Chelmsford CM1.........32 B4
Primrose Rd E18........110 A2
Primrose Wlk
Maldon CM9.............57 A8
Southminster CM0.......85 C5
Primula Ct SS15........141 C5
Primula Way CM1........33 A6
Prince Ave SS2, SS0....146 D3
Prince Avenue Prim Sch
SS0.....................146 D3
Prince Charles Ave
RM16...................172 F2
Prince Edward Rd
CM11...................97 B5
Prince Philip Ave
RM16...................172 F2
Princes Ave
Corringham SS17.......161 B4
Mayland CM3............59 E7
Southminster CM0......84 C5
Thundersley SS7.......144 B7
Woodford IG8..........110 C3
Princes Cl
Basildon SS15.........141 A5
Billericay CM12........97 B4
North Weald Bassett
CM16...................46 A2
Princes Ct
Billericay CM12........97 B4
Southend-on-S SS2.....148 A1
Princesfield Rd EN9....65 F6
Princes Gate CM20......10 F1
Princes Gdns CM9.......37 A8
Princes Lo SS0..........1 E1
Princes Mews CM12......97 B4
Princes Pk RM13........155 A4
Princes Rd
Buckhurst Hill IG9......87 D8
Burnham-on-C CM0.......85 C5
Canvey Island SS8......163 F2
Chelmsford CM2.........32 A1
Ilford IG6.............133 D6
Maldon CM9.............57 A8
Romford RM1............135 F8

Rd
ck Heath CM14,
.............92 F8
.... Side CM14 ......93 A7
Alexandra Hospl
.............10 C1
Ave RM18 ....175 C2
Ct SS11 ....122 A8
Gdns SS4.......125 D5
Margaret Rd
..............180 D7
Par RM10.......154 A3
Rd SS6........123 F3
st
.d DA11 ....179 B1
on-S SS1 .....166 F8
Way
od CM13.........95 A1
st Hill IG9......110 C8
illiam Ave
............163 F6
Way CM20 .....11 A5
ase RM17 ......172 F2
Cres DA9 .....177 C3
he SS5........101 D1
IG1 ....133 A1
SS14 ....142 C6
eworth CM22 ....2 A2
aster CM0......84 E4
SS14..........142 C6
. RM12.........136 C1
ay CM0........84 E4
e
.J E4 ....109 A7
M17............11 C5
on-S SS2 .....147 F3
ase SS6........123 B6

ird CM1 ....31 E2
J E4 ....109 A7
on EN11........21 A5
natch CM15.....94 A4
J E18 ....110 A2
s SS2 ....147 F4

M18............24 B5
RM6 ....134 B5
RM3 ....114 E3
CM3............56 F1
ead CM15.....72 C3
ws
hurch RM11 ...136 B3
l-on-S SS2 ....148 A3
rk Ind Est
...............148 A4
th RM3........114 E7
im Sch CM3 ....56 F2

G11 ....152 D5
e CM3...........56 E1
IG10...........88 E5
RM3 ....114 E7
le-H SS17 .....160 E3
h SS2 ....147 E3
e
............97 C6
M1............53 B8
ew Rd SS9 ....146 E5
on Cres SS9 ..146 E5
od Dr SS6 ....146 E5
Cl EN3........65 A2
ook Ind Est
..............147 F4
SS7...........145 C5
VELL 147 D3
ll CE Jun & Inf
..............147 F2
ll Chase
..............147 D3
ll Mews SS2....147 F2
ll Priory Mus*
..............147 F3
ll Sq SS1 .....166 F7
ll St SS2 .....148 A1
ll Sta SS2 .....148 A3
nal Pl [2]
..............122 A5
Rd SS9.......146 C6
de CM3........60 F1
de The
on-C CM0 ....106 C4
l-on-S SS3 ...168 C5
Ave SS17 ....160 B1
Bsns Pk
.............89 D5
Cl
e DA17........169 A2
on-S SS1 .....167 C7
Pl
send DA12 ...179 D1
17............178 B8
RM5 ....113 C1
Rd
ch RM11 ......136 F8
Rd IG10 ......110 C5
Way CM13.....95 E5
Ho [7] DA17 ...169 A1
Est SS8.......164 B4
Est SS8.......164 F3
e Pl CM0.....106 C4
e Pl NM5 .....112 F2
e St DA9.....177 A2
l CM13.........97 B1
Ct [15] DA2...176 B1
CM1...........32 A2
CM2 ....54 C2
SS16..........142 C5

Puckleside SS16 ....141 C4
Puckridge Cotts IG7.....111 E7
Pudding La IG7 ....89 F2
Pudsey Hall La SS4 .....104 A2
Puffin Cl
Barking IG11...........153 B2
Wickford SS12.........121 F5
Puffin Dr SS3 ....149 E1
Puffin Terr IG5 ....133 A8
Pugh Pl SS17..........160 D4
Pulborough [1]
RM3 ....114 E3
Pullman Ct SS11........121 D8
Pulpits Cl SS5.........124 F7
Pulteney Gdns [9] E18...132 B8
Pulteney Rd E18.......132 B8
Pump Hill
Great Baddow CM2 ......54 F6
Loughton IG10..........88 F7
Pump La
Chelmsford CM1 ....32 E6
Danbury CM3............56 D5
Epping Green CM16......45 B7
Plesley CM3 ....7 E1
Purleigh CM3...........58 D1
Pump Mead Cl CM0.......84 D4
Pump St SS17 ....160 A2
Punchard Cres EN3 .....65 B1
Punchbowl Cotts SS4....127 D7
Purbeck Ct CM2 ....54 E6
Purbeck Rd RM11.......136 A4
Purcell Cl
Basildon SS15.........141 D8
Stanford-le-H SS17 ....160 C3
Writtle CM1............31 A1
Purcell Way SS17......160 C3
Purdeys Way SS4 ......148 A8
PURFLEET 171 B1
Purfleet By-Pass
RM19 ....171 C1
Purfleet Ind Pk RM15...170 F4
Purfleet Industrial Access
Rd RM15 ....171 A3
Purfleet Prim Sch
RM19 ....171 A2
Purfleet Rd RM15......171 B5
Purford Gn CM18 ....24 A7
Purford Green Jun & Inf
Schs CM18 ....24 A6
Purland Cl RM8.........134 F3
Purleigh Ave IG8.......110 E4
Purleigh Cl SS13 ......121 C1
Purleigh Gr CM3.........81 A5
Purleigh Prim Sch
CM3 ....58 D1
Purleigh Rd SS6........123 B3
Purleigh Wash CM9.....59 B2
Purley Cl IG5..........111 A1
Purley Way SS0 ....147 C5
Purlieu Way CM16.......67 E4
Putney Gdns RM6.......134 B6
Pye Cnr CM20 ....10 D5
Pyenest Rd CM19 ....23 C6
Pym Pl RM17 ....173 A2
Pyms Rd CM2 ....54 B3
Pynchon Mews CM1.....32 D3
Pynchon Paddocks
CM2 ....2 D7
Pyne Gate CM2 ....54 B1
Pynest Green La EN9 ....66 B2
Pypers Hatch CM20......23 F8
Pyrgo Priory Sch
RM3 ....115 A6
Pyrles Gn IG10.........89 B8
Pyrles La IG10..........89 B7
Pytt Field CM17 ....24 B7

Q

Quadrant Arc RM1......135 E6
Quadrant The RM19.....171 C2
Quaker La EN9 ....65 C5
Quale Rd CM2 ....33 B4
Quantock [6] SS1 ......167 A8
Quarles Ct RM5........113 A3
Quarles Park Rd RM6 ...134 B5
Quarry Hill MR17 ......173 A1
Quarry Hill Inf Sch
MR17 ....173 B1
Quarry Hill Jun Sch
RM17 ....173 B1
Quarry Mews RM19 .....171 A2
Quarry Spring CM20 .....24 A8
Quarter Gate CM3 .....101 E5
Quatro Pk SS14........120 F2
Quay La DA9 ....177 B3
Quayside Ind Est CM9 ...37 A4
Quay The CM0...........58 A4
Quebec Ave [4] SS1....167 B8
Quebec Gdns CM3 ......101 D6
Quebec Rd
Ilford IG1 ....133 C4
Tilbury RM18..........178 E5
Queen Anne's Dr SS0....147 C4
Queen Anne's Mews
SS0................147 C4
Queen Anns Gr SS5.....123 D8
Queenborough Gdns
CM0 ....84 D4
Queenborough Rd
RM18 ....175 B2
Queen Elizabeth Ave
SS4.................147 F7
Queen Elizabeth Chase

Queen Elizabeth Ct
EN9 ....65 C3
Queen Elizabeth Dr
SS17................160 F4
Queen Elizabeth II Sq [4]
CM3 ....101 E7
Queen Elizabeth's Hunting
Lo* E4 ....87 F2
Queen Mary Ave
RM18................175 C2
Queen Mary Cl RM1 ....135 F5
Queen Mary RM18 .....175 C2
Queen Mary Sch CM12...65 C4
Queen Mary Villas [14]
E18................110 A2
Queens Ave SS5........101 E4
Queen's Ave
Maldon CM9............37 A1
Southend-on-S SS9 ....146 E1
Woodford IG8 ....110 B5
Queensbridge Ind Pk
RM20 ....177 A8
Queensbury IG9.........88 B1
Queen's Cl CM21 ....1 F4
Queens Ct
Burnham-on-C CM0 .....106 B4
SS9.................165 F8
Southend-on-S SS9 ....146 E1
Queen's Dr E18.........65 A5
Queens Gate IG4.......132 F7
Queensgate Ctr RM17...173 A1
Queensgate Ctr CM20...10 F4
Queen's Gate Mews
CM12................96 F5
Queens Gdns
Rainham RM13 ....154 D3
Upminster RM14 ....137 F5
Queen's Grove Rd E4....87 D1
Queens Hospl RM7 .....135 E4
Queenside Ct RM7......135 C7
Queenside Mews
RM12................136 E2
Queensland Ave SS4....147 F7
Queensland Cres CM1 ...31 E5
Queensland Ct RM18....178 F5
Queens Lo SS7 ....145 C3
Queensmere SS7 ....145 B5
Queens Mews [6] IG9...110 C8
Queens Park Ct CM12...97 B5
Queens Park Cty Prim Sch
CM12................97 B6
Queens Park Rd CM13...115 A2
Queens Rd
Basildon, Steeple View
SS15 ....119 C1
Crays Hill CM11.......120 B4
Loughton IG10..........88 F6
North Weald Bassett
CM16................47 B6
Rayleigh SS6.........123 E2
Southend-on-S, Chalkwell
SS9.................165 F8
Queen's Rd
Barking IG11..........152 C6
Brentwood CM14.......116 D8
Buckhurst Hill IG9.....110 C8
Burnham-on-C CM0 .....106 C4
Chelmsford CM2 ....32 D2
South Benfleet SS7....144 D2
Queen St
Brentwood CM14.......116 C5
Chelmsford CM2 ....32 B4
Fyfield CM5 ....27 E2
Gravesend DA12.......179 B1
Maldon CM9............37 A2
Romford RM7 ....135 D8
Southminster CM0......84 C4
Queensmen Gdns
RM13 ....154 F2
Queensway
Chipping Ongar CM5 ....48 F5
Southend-on-S SS1 ....167 B8
Queensway Ho SS0 ....163 D3
Queensway Lo SS1 .....167 B7
Queens Wlk E4.........87 D1
Queenswood Ave
Brentwood CM13........95 D4
Chingford E4 ....109 C2
Queenswood Gdns
E11.................110 D8
Queenswood Ho
CM14................116 D8
Quendon Ct EN9 ....146 A3
Quendon Rd SS4.......142 E8
Quennell Way CM13 .....95 D2
Quest End SS6 ....123 D5
Quilp Dr CM1...........31 F7
Quilters Cl SS14.......142 D8
Quilters Dr CM12 ....97 B3
Quilters Inf Sch CM12...97 A1
Quilters Straight
SS14................142 E8
Quince Tree Cl RM15...157 C1
Quinion Cl CM1.........31 D7
Quorn Gdns SS9 ....146 E6
Quorn The CM0..........74 A3

R

Rachael Clarke Cl
SS17................160 E4
Rachel Ct [1] CM2......32 B1
Rachel Cl IG6 ....133 D8
Rackenford SS3 ....168 D8
Radbourne Cres E17....109 D1
Radburn Cl CM18 ....24 A4
Radburn Pl DA10 ......177 E2
Radcliffe Rd SS9 ......146 F2
Radford Bsns Ctr CM12..96 F3
Radford Cres CM12 .....97 A3
Radford Ct CM12 ....97 B3
Radford Ho CM12 ....97 B3
Radford Way
Barking IG11..........152 F2
Billericay CM12........97 A3
Radley Ave IG3 ....153 A8
Radley Ct IG7 ....111 E6
RADLEY GREEN 51 D8
Radley Green Rd CM4,
CM5 ....51 C7
Radley's La E18 ....110 A1
Radleys Mead RM10 ....154 B6
Radnor Cres IG4 ....132 F6
Radnor Rd SS4 ....103 C1
Radstock Ho [11] RM3..114 D5
Radwinter Ave SS12 ...121 D6
Rahn Rd CM16..........68 A8
Raider Cl RM7..........113 B2
Radwinter Ave SS12 ...121 D6
Railstore The RM2 .....136 C8
Railway App SS15 .....141 A6
Railway Cotts
Redbridge IG6 ....111 D2
Belvedere DA17.......169 A3
[12] Gravesend DA11...179 B1
Railway Sq
Brentwood CM14.......116 C7
Chelmsford CM1 ....32 A3
Dagenham RM6 ....134 C4
Northfleet DA11........178 A2
Railway Terr
Chingford E17 ....109 C2
Southend-on-S SS2 ....148 A3
Railway St
Chelmsford CM1 ....32 A3
Canvey Island SS8 .....164 B8
Grays RM16...........172 C2
Sheering CM17 ....12 E3
Raine Gdns [4] IG8.....110 A6
RAINHAM 155 A2
Rainham Rd RM10 .....135 B2
Rainham Rd S RM10....155 B3
Rainham St RM13 ......155 A1
Rainham Trad Est
RM13 ....154 F1
Rainham Village Prim Sch
RM13 ....155 A1
Rainsford Ave CM1 .....31 F3
Rainsford La CM1......31 F2
Rainsford Rd CM1 ......31 F3
Rainsford Way RM12 ...136 A3
Raleigh Dr SS15 ....141 C5
Ramblers La [5] CM11...11 D1
Ramblers Way CM0 .....106 B2
Ram Gorse CM20 ....10 B2
Ramparts The SS4......168 G6
Rampart Terr SS3 .....168 G6
Rampton Cl E4 ....109 A6
Ramsay Dr SS16 ....142 E3
Ramsay Rd RM3 ....114 C2
Ramsay Rd E7 ....132 A1
RAMSDEN BELLHOUSE
....................98 D1
Ramsden Hall Sch
CM11................97 F3
RAMSDEN HEATH 98 B1
Ramsden Park Rd
CM11................98 D1
Ramsden View Rd
SS12................120 F6
Ramsey Chase
Latchingdon CM3.......82 A6
Wickford SS12.........121 F6
Ramsey Cl CM9.........37 D4
Ramsey Rd SS4........147 B3
RAMSEY ISLAND 82 D8
Ramsgill App IG2......133 F7
Ramsgill Dr IG2........133 F6
Ramshaw Dr CM2 ....54 D4
Ramuz Dr SS0 ....147 D2
Randall Ct SS14........123 G3
Randalls Dr CM12 ....97 A3
Randall Dr
Hornchurch RM12 .....155 D8
Orsett RM16...........174 A8
Randalls Dr CM12 ....95 A3
Randolph Cl
Maldon CM9............58 F8
Hornchurch RM12 .....155 D8
Randolph Gr RM6......134 C6
Randolph Terr CM1......32 A2
Randway SS6 ....123 D1
Ranelagh Gdns
Ilford IG1 ....133 A3
Redbridge IG1.........132 F3

Ranelagh Gdns continued
Wanstead E11.........132 C6
Ranelagh Rd E6 ....152 A3
Ranger's Rd
Buckhurst Hill E4, IG9,
...................88 A2
Chingford E4 ....87 F2
Ransomes Way CM1 ....32 B4
Rantree Fold SS16.....141 F4
Ranulf Cl CM17 ....11 C6
Ranworth Ave EN11......8 B2
Raphael Ave
Romford RM1 ....135 F8
Tilbury RM18..........179 B7
Raphael Dr
Chelmsford CM1 ....32 F7
Southend-on-S SS3 ....150 A1
Raphael Ind Sch
RM11................136 A5
Raphaels SS15.........141 E6
Raphaels Ct RM1.......135 F7
Rapier Cl RM19........171 A2
Rat La SS6 ....145 C8
Ratsborough Chase
CM0 ....84 C2
Rat's La IG10...........66 B3
Rattwick Dr SS8.......164 F3
Ratty's La EN11.........21 D6
Ravel Gdns RM15......171 C7
Ravel Rd RM15 ....171 D7
Raven Cl CM12 ....96 F4
Raven Cres CM12 ......96 F4
Ravencroft RM16.......174 B4
Ravendale Way SS3....149 D1
Raven Dr SS7 ....144 C2
Ravenings Par IG3.....134 A3
Raven La CM11..........96 F4
Ravenoak Way IG7.....111 E5
Raven Rd E18 ....110 C1
Ravensbourne Cres
RM3 ....136 F8
Ravensbourne Dr CM1...31 E2
Ravensbourne Gdns
IG5.................111 B2
Ravenscourt CM15......94 D1
Ravenscourt Dr
Basildon SS15.........142 E5
Hornchurch RM12 .....136 E1
Ravenscourt Gr RM12..136 E1
Ravens Ct
[6] Gravesend DA12...179 D1
Southend-on-S SS1 ....166 F7
Ravensdale SS16 ....142 B4
Ravensfield SS14 ......142 F6
Ravensfield Cl RM9 ....153 D8
Ravensmere CM16 ......46 A1
Ravenswood Chase
...................147 F7
Ravenswood Cl RM5....113 B5
Rawdon Dr EN11 ....21 A5
Rawlings Farm CM3 ....100 A8
Rawlyn Cl RM16........122 C7
RAWRETH 122 C2
Rawreth Gdns SS11 ....100 E1
Rawreth Ind Est SS6...123 B5
Rawreth La SS11 ....122 C6
Rayburne Ct IG9 ....88 C1
Rayburn Rd RM11......137 A4
Ray Cl
Canvey Island SS8 .....164 A2
Southend-on-S SS9 ....146 B1
Ray Ct IG8 ....110 D4
Raydons Gdns RM9 ....153 E7
Raydons Rd RM9 ......153 E7
Rayfield CM16...........46 A2
Raymond Ave E18 ......109 F1
Raymond Gdns IG8 ....110 E7
Raymond Rd IG2 ....133 D4
Raymonds Cl SS9 ......141 C1
Raymonds Dr SS7 .....144 F6
Raynes Ave E11 ....132 C4
Ray Rd RM5 ....113 B5

Rayside SS14 . . . . 142 C5
Ray The CM1 . . . . 32 E5
Ray Wlk SS9 . . . . 146 B1
Reaburn Ct CM1 . . . . 32 E6
Read Cl SS5 . . . . 125 A4
Reader's Cnr CM2 . . . . 54 E5
Readers Ct CM2 . . . . 54 E5
Reading Cl SS16 . . . . 140 F5
Readings The CM18 . . . . 23 F5
Reads Cl IG1 . . . . 133 B1
Rebels La SS3 . . . . 148 F3
Recreation Ave
  Corringham SS17 . . . . 161 C3
  Romford, Harold Wood
  RM3 . . . . 114 F1
  Romford RM7 . . . . 135 C6
  Southend-on-S SS9 . . . . . . 146 F2
Recreation Ct SS9 . . . . 146 F2
Recreation Wlk CM11 . . . . . . 98 C5
Rectory Ave SS4 . . . . 125 C6
Rectory Chase
  Doddinghurst CM15 . . . . . . 72 C2
  Little Warley CM13 . . . . . . 138 E7
  Southend-on-S SS2 . . . . . . 148 E1
Rectory Cl
  Chingford E4 . . . . 109 A7
  Hadleigh SS7 . . . . 145 E3
  Hunsdonbury SG12 . . . . 9 D8
  Ingatestone CM4 . . . . 74 B4
  Little Waltham CM3 . . . . . . 19 C6
  Stock CM4 . . . . 75 D2
Rectory Cres E11 . . . . 132 C5
Rectory Ct
  Basildon SS13 . . . . 143 C7
  Grays RM17 . . . . 178 D8
  Loughton IG10 . . . . 89 A7
  Woodford E18 . . . . 109 F2
Rectory Field CM19 . . . . 23 B6
Rectory Garth SS6 . . . . 123 D3
Rectory Gdns
  Basildon SS13 . . . . 143 C6
  Upminster RM14 . . . . 137 E2
Rectory Gr
  Southend-on-S SS9 . . . . . . 165 D8
  Wickford SS11 . . . . 121 F7
Rectory Ho **7** CM12 . . . . . . 97 B2
Rectory La
  Chelmsford CM1 . . . . 32 B4
  Harlow CM19 . . . . 23 B6
  Ingrave CM13 . . . . 117 E3
  Latchingdon CM3 . . . . 82 B3
  Loughton IG10 . . . . 89 B6
  Rettendon SS11 . . . . 124 B2
  Woodham Mortimer CM9 . . . . 57 F6
Rectory Park Dr SS13 . . . . . 143 B5
Rectory Rd
  Basildon SS13 . . . . 143 C6
  Dagenham RM10 . . . . 154 B5
  Grays RM17 . . . . 173 D2
  Hadleigh SS7 . . . . 145 E3
  Hockley SS5 . . . . 125 B4
  Little Burstead CM12 . . . . . 119 A2
  Little Ilford E12 . . . . 152 A7
  North Fambridge CM3 . . . . . 103 A8
  Orsett RM16 . . . . 174 B7
  Stanford-le-H SS17 . . . . . . 160 C1
  West Tilbury RM18 . . . . . . 179 D8
  Woodham Walter CM9 . . . . . 35 D3
  Writtle CM1 . . . . 53 B8
Rectory Terr
  Hockley SS5 . . . . 125 B4
  Stanford-le-H SS17 . . . . . . 160 C1
Rectory Wood CM20 . . . . . . 10 C1
Redbrick Row CM22 . . . . 2 B8
REDBRIDGE 132 C6
Redbridge Coll RM6 . . . . . . 134 B6
Redbridge Ct IG4 . . . . 132 D5
Redbridge Ent Ctr
  IG1 . . . . 133 C2
Redbridge Foyer IG1 . . . . . . 133 C2
Redbridge Ho IG4 . . . . 132 D6
Redbridge La E IG4 . . . . . . 132 E6
Redbridge La W E11 . . . . . . 132 C5
Redbridge Mus IG1 . . . . . . 133 B1
Redbridge Prim Sch
  IG4 . . . . 132 D5
Redbridge Sta IG4 . . . . 132 D5
Redbrook Cl SS17 . . . . 175 A3
Redbury Cl RM13 . . . . 155 B1
Redcar Rd RM3 . . . . 114 F5
Redcliff Dr SS9 . . . . 165 F8
Redden Court Rd
  RM3 . . . . 136 F8
Redden Court Sch
  RM3 . . . . 136 F8
Reddings La CM0 . . . . 63 C3
Redfern Gdns RM2 . . . . 114 D1
Redgate Cl SS11 . . . . 122 A8
Redgates Pl CM2 . . . . 32 D4
Redgrave Ct **13** CM14 . . . . . 116 C7
Redgrave Rd IG6 . . . . 142 E4
Redgrove Ho CM16 . . . . 46 A2
Redhills Rd CM3 . . . . 101 E8
Red Ho The RM3 . . . . 114 D6
Redif Ho RM10 . . . . 154 B8
Redinge The CM11 . . . . 119 D7
Redlie Cl SS17 . . . . 160 D4
Red Lion Cres CM17 . . . . . . 24 C6
Red Lion La CM17 . . . . 24 D6

Redmans Ind Est
  RM18 . . . . 180 A8
Redmayne Dr CM2 . . . . 53 F8
Red Oaks Mead CM16 . . . . . 67 D2
Redo Ho **2** E12 . . . . 152 A7
Red Rd CM14 . . . . 116 B6
Redricks La CM21 . . . . 11 A6
Redriff Rd RM7 . . . . 113 B1
Redrose La CM4 . . . . 50 E1
Redruth Cl CM1 . . . . 32 E5
Redruth Gdns RM3 . . . . 114 F5
Redruth Rd RM3 . . . . 114 F5
Redruth Wlk RM3 . . . . 114 F5
Redshank Cres CM3 . . . . . . 79 D1
Redshank Dr RM9 . . . . 37 C5
Red Shank Ho RM13 . . . . . . 170 A8
Redstart Mans 8
  E12 . . . . 133 A1
Redstock Rd SS2 . . . . 148 A2
Red Willow CM18 . . . . 22 F5
Redwing Ct RM3 . . . . 114 D3
Redwing Dr CM11 . . . . 119 E8
Redwood Chase
  RM15 . . . . 157 D1
Redwood Cl IG9 . . . . 110 B8
Redwood Cl DA1 . . . . 176 A1
Redwood Dr
  Basildon SS15 . . . . 119 D1
  Writtle CM1 . . . . 30 F1
Redwood Gdns
  Chingford E4 . . . . 87 B3
  Redbridge IG7 . . . . 112 A5
Redwoods The SS8 . . . . . . 163 E3
Reed Ct DA9 . . . . 177 C3
Reede Gdns RM10 . . . . 154 B7
Reede Rd RM10 . . . . 154 B6
Reede Way RM10 . . . . 154 B6
Reedings Jun Sch CM21 . . . . 1 E3
Reedings Way CM21 . . . . 1 F4
Reed Mans **7** E11 . . . . 132 A5
Reed Pond Wlk
  Basildon SS15 . . . . 141 B4
  Romford RM2 . . . . 113 F1
Reeds Farm CM1 . . . . 30 F3
Reeds Way SS12 . . . . 121 C8
Ree Lane Cotts IG10 . . . . . . 89 A7
Reesland Cl E12 . . . . 152 A6
Reeves Cl
  Basildon SS16 . . . . 140 F4
  Stondon Massey CM15 . . . . 72 B5
Reeves La CM19 . . . . 22 D5
Reeves Way CM3 . . . . 101 E7
Regal Cl CM2 . . . . 54 D8
Regal Ho IG2 . . . . 133 D5
Regan Cl SS17 . . . . 160 E4
Regarder Rd IG7 . . . . 112 B5
Regarth Ave RM1 . . . . 135 E5
Regatta Ct SS9 . . . . 165 F8
Regency Cl
  Chelmsford CM2 . . . . 32 D3
  Chigwell IG7 . . . . 111 C5
  Rochford SS4 . . . . 125 E2
  Wickford SS11 . . . . 99 D2
Regency Ct
  Brentwood CM14 . . . . 116 C8
  Harlow CM18 . . . . 24 A5
  Heybridge CM9 . . . . 37 A5
  Hockley SS5 . . . . 124 E6
  2 Woodford E18 . . . . . . 110 A1
Regency Gdns RM11 . . . . . . 136 C4
Regency Gns SS12 . . . . . . 147 F3
Regency Lo **1** IG9 . . . . . . 110 D8
Regent Cl
  Grays RM17 . . . . 173 C4
  Rayleigh SS6 . . . . 123 B4
Regent Ct
  Basildon SS15 . . . . 141 E8
  Romford RM2 . . . . 136 B8
Regent Dr CM12 . . . . 96 F5
Regent Gdns IG3 . . . . 134 A5
Regent Rd CM16 . . . . 45 F1
Regents Cl CM0 . . . . 84 D4
Regents Ct
  Burnham-on-C CM0 . . . . . . 106 B4
  2 Gravesend DA11 . . . . . 179 B1
  Southend-on-S SS1 . . . . . . 166 F7
Regents Dr IG8 . . . . 111 A3
Regents Pl IG10 . . . . 88 D2
Regent Sq DA17 . . . . 169 B2
Reginald Mews 4
  CM17 . . . . 11 C1
Reginald Rd RM3 . . . . 115 A2
Regina Rd CM1 . . . . 32 C3
Reigate Rd IG3 . . . . 133 F2
Rembrandt Cl
  5 Canvey Island
  SS8 . . . . 164 A3
  Southend-on-S SS3 . . . . . . 168 G8
Rembrandt Gr CM1 . . . . 32 E6
Remembrance Ave
  CM0 . . . . 106 B4
Renacres SS16 . . . . 141 F4
Rennie Ct **5** EN3 . . . . 65 A1
Rennie Pl CM2 . . . . 33 B3
Renoir Pl CM1 . . . . 32 F7
Renown Cl RM7 . . . . 113 B2
Renown The SS3 . . . . 168 F8
Renwick Ind Est IG11 . . . . . 153 B3
Renwick Rd IG11 . . . . 153 B2
Repton Ave RM2 . . . . 136 A8
Repton Cl SS13 . . . . 121 A1
Repton Ct SS13 . . . . 121 A1
Repton Ct IG5 . . . . 110 F2
Repton Dr RM2 . . . . 136 A7
Repton Gdns RM2 . . . . . . 136 A7
Repton Gr
  Southend-on-S SS2 . . . . . . 147 A7
  Woodford IG5 . . . . 110 F2

Repulse Cl RM5 . . . . 113 B2
Reservoir CI DA9 . . . . 177 C1
Rest Cotts SS4 . . . . 104 E1
Retford Cl RM3 . . . . 115 A4
Retford Path RM3 . . . . 115 A4
Retford Rd RM3 . . . . 115 A4
Retingham Way E4 . . . . . . 109 B8
Retort Cl SS11 . . . . 167 D6
Retreat Cvn Site The
  IG9 . . . . 110 A8
Retreat Rd
  Hockley SS5 . . . . 124 E6
  Southend-on-S SS0 . . . . . 166 E7
Retreat The
  Brentwood CM14 . . . . 94 B1
  Grays RM17 . . . . 178 B8
  Shenfield CM13 . . . . 95 B3
Retreat Way IG7 . . . . 112 B7
RETTENDON 78 B1
Rettendon Cl SS6 . . . . 123 A3
Rettendon Gdns SS11 . . . . . 99 E1
Rettendon Prim Sch
  CM3 . . . . 100 C5
Rettendon Turnpike
  SS11 . . . . 100 C3
Rettendon View SS11 . . . . . 121 F8
Reubens Rd CM13 . . . . 95 B3
Review Lo RM10 . . . . 154 B3
Review Rd RM10 . . . . 154 B4
Rex Par **3** IG8 . . . . 110 C4
Reydon Ave E11 . . . . 132 C5
Reynard Ct CM2 . . . . 54 F6
Reynolds Ave
  Dagenham RM6 . . . . 134 C4
  Little Ilford E12 . . . . 152 A7
Reynolds Ct RM6 . . . . 134 D8
Reynolds Gate SS4 . . . . . . 101 E6
Reynolds Gdns SS4 . . . . . . 125 D5
Reynolds Ho SS2 . . . . 147 F2
Rhapsody Cres CM14 . . . . . 116 B5
Rhoda Rd SS7 . . . . 144 E4
Rhoda Rd N SS7 . . . . 144 E5
RHS Garden Hyde Hall*
  SS3 . . . . 78 E4
Rhum Mews SS16 . . . . . . 122 A5
Ribble Cl IG8 . . . . 110 C4
Richard Alibon Prim Sch
  RM10 . . . . 154 A7
Richard Blackburn Ho
  RM7 . . . . 135 E2
Richard Burton Ct 5
  IG9 . . . . 110 C8
Richard Fell Ho 3
  E12 . . . . 152 A8
Richards Ave RM7 . . . . 135 C5
Richardson Cl DA9 . . . . 176 F2
Richardson Gdns 17
  RM10 . . . . 154 B6
Richardson Pl CM1 . . . . 31 F4
Riches Rd IG1 . . . . 133 C2
Richmond Ave
  Chingford E4 . . . . 109 D5
  South Benfleet SS7 . . . . . . 144 C2
  Southend-on-S, Cambridge
  Town SS3 . . . . 168 D6
  Southend-on-S SS0 . . . . . 167 A7
  Southend-on-S, Westcliff-on-S
  SS0 . . . . 166 E8
Richmond Ave Prim Sch
  SS3 . . . . 168 D6
Richmond Cres E4 . . . . 109 D5
Richmond Ct
  2 Loughton IG10 . . . . . . 88 D4
  4 Romford RM1 . . . . . . 135 F5
  Southend-on-S, Chalkwell
  SS9 . . . . 166 A6
  Southend-on-S SS0 . . . . . 168 D6
Richmond Dr
  Rayleigh SS6 . . . . 145 D8
  4 Redbridge IG8 . . . . . 111 A3
  Southend-on-S SS0 . . . . . 147 C4
Richmond Pk IG10 . . . . 88 D2
Richmond Rd
  Chelmsford CM2 . . . . 33 A4
  Chingford E4 . . . . 87 D1
  Grays RM17 . . . . 173 C1
  Ilford IG1 . . . . 133 C1
  Romford RM1 . . . . 135 F5
  Wickford SS11 . . . . 99 C2
Richmond St SS2 . . . . 148 D1
Richmond Way E11 . . . . . . 132 A2
Ricketts Dr CM12 . . . . 96 F3
Rickling SS16 . . . . 142 F4
Riddiford Dr CM2 . . . . 31 E4
Riddings La CM18 . . . . 24 A4
Ridgemount SS7 . . . . 144 E4
Ridges The E4 . . . . 109 A8
Ridge The CM3 . . . . 34 E2
Ridgeway
  Billericay CM12 . . . . 119 A8
  Brentwood CM13 . . . . 95 B1
  Grays RM17 . . . . 173 E2
  Ingatestone CM4 . . . . 74 A2
  Maldon CM9 . . . . 59 A8
  Rayleigh SS6 . . . . 123 C1
  Southend-on-S SS9 . . . . . 146 B1
Ridge Way SS5 . . . . 101 E4
Ridgeway Gdns
  Redbridge IG4 . . . . 132 C6
  Southend-on-S SS0 . . . . . 166 B8
Ridgeways CM17 . . . . 24 E8
Ridgeway The
  Chingford E4 . . . . 87 C1
  Romford, Harold Wood
  RM3 . . . . 114 F2
  Romford RM2 . . . . 114 B8
  Southend-on-S SS0 . . . . . 166 B8
Ridgewell Ave CM1 . . . . 31 F4

Ridgewell Cl RM10 . . . . . . 154 B4
Ridgewell Gr RM12 . . . . . . 155 C5
Ridgmont Pl RM11 . . . . . . 136 D5
Ridgwell Ave RM16 . . . . . . 159 A1
Ridings The
  Canvey Island SS8 . . . . . 164 A5
  Great Baddow CM2 . . . . . 54 D7
  1 Redbridge IG7 . . . . . 112 B6
  Rochford SS4 . . . . 125 F1
Ridley Cl
  Barking IG11 . . . . 152 F5
  Romford RM3 . . . . 114 B2
Ridley Cotts CM3 . . . . 80 C3
Ridley Rd
  Basildon SS13 . . . . 121 C1
  Chelmsford CM1 . . . . 32 B8
Riffams Ct SS13 . . . . 143 C8
Riffams Dr SS13 . . . . 143 C8
Riffams CM13 . . . . 117 B7
Riffhams Chase CM3 . . . . . 34 D2
Riffhams Dr CM2 . . . . 55 A7
Riffhams La
  Danbury CM3 . . . . 56 C8
  Little Baddow CM3 . . . . . . 34 C1
Rigby Gdns RM16 . . . . . . 174 B2
Rigby Mews IG1 . . . . 133 A2
Rigby Pl EN3 . . . . 65 A2
Rignal's La CM2 . . . . 54 D3
Rill Ct **4** IG11 . . . . 152 C3
Ringwood Ave RM12 . . . . . 136 D2
Ringwood Cl CM9 . . . . 36 C7
Ringwood Ho **9** RM3 . . . . 114 D4
Ripley Rd
  Belvedere DA17 . . . . 169 A2
  Ilford IG3 . . . . 133 F2
Ripley View IG10 . . . . 67 B1
Ripon Gdns IG1 . . . . 132 E4
Ripon Ho **6** RM3 . . . . . . 114 D4
Ripple Ct **6** IG11 . . . . . . 152 D4
Ripple Inf Sch IG11 . . . . . . 152 E5
Ripple Jun Sch IG11 . . . . . 152 E4
Ripple Rd
  Barking IG11 . . . . 152 C5
  Barking IG11 . . . . 152 E4
  Dagenham IG11 . . . . 152 F6
Rippleside Commercial
  Est IG11 . . . . 153 C4
Risdens CM18 . . . . 23 D5
Risebridge Chase
  RM1 . . . . 113 F3
Risebridge Rd RM2 . . . . . . 114 A2
RISE PARK 113 F2
Rise Park Bvd RM1 . . . . . . 113 F2
Rise Park Jun & Inf Sch
  RM1 . . . . 113 D2
Rise Park Par RM1 . . . . . . 113 E1
Rise Pk SS15 . . . . 141 F6
Rise The
  Buckhurst Hill IG9 . . . . . . 88 D1
  Chingford E4 . . . . 87 E1
  Greenhithe DA9 . . . . 177 A1
  Wanstead E11 . . . . 132 A6
Riseway CM1 . . . . 116 E7
Risings Terr RM11 . . . . . . 136 F8
Rising The CM11 . . . . 97 D1
Rivendell Vale CM3 . . . . . . 101 C6
Rivenhall
  Thundersley SS7 . . . . 145 B8
  Wickford SS11 . . . . 122 A6
River Ho RM11 . . . . 21 B7
River Blackwater Chalet
  Site CM9 . . . . 37 C3
River Cl
  Holdbrook EN8 . . . . 65 A5
  Rainham RM13 . . . . 170 B8
  Wanstead E11 . . . . 132 C5
River Cotts CM3 . . . . 33 F8
River Ct
  Purfleet RM19 . . . . 170 F2
  Sawbridgeworth CM21 . . . . 1 F3
  Wanstead E11 . . . . 132 C5
Riverdale SS9 . . . . 146 D7
Riverdale Cl IG11 . . . . 153 B7
Riverdale Rd DA8 . . . . 169 C1
Riverdene Rd IG1 . . . . 133 B1
River Dr RM14 . . . . 137 B3
Riverfield La CM21 . . . . 1 E3
River Lee Ctry Pk*
  EN9 . . . . 43 B1
Rivermead Gate CM1 . . . . . 32 B4
Rivermead Ind Est
  CM1 . . . . 32 B4
River Meads SG12 . . . . . . 8 C4
Rivermill CM20 . . . . 10 C2
River Rd
  Barking IG11 . . . . 152 E2
  Barking IG11 . . . . 153 B1
  Brentwood CM14 . . . . 115 F6
  Buckhurst Hill IG9 . . . . . . 88 E1
River Road Bsns Pk
  IG11 . . . . 153 B3
Riversdale Rd RM5 . . . . . . 113 B3
Rivers Hospl (private) The
  CM21 . . . . 1 C1
Riverside CM1 . . . . 32 C3
Riverside Ave EN10 . . . . . . 21 A1
Riverside Cotts
  North Fambridge
  CM3 . . . . 103 A6
  Stanstead Abbotts SG12 . . . 8 C4
Riverside Ct
  Chingford E4 . . . . 87 B3
  Harlow CM20 . . . . 11 C6
  Wickford SS11 . . . . 120 D8
Riverside Ho SS11 . . . . . . 121 D8
Riverside Ind Est
  Barking IG11 . . . . 153 A2

Riverside Ind Est contin...
  Rochford SS4 . . . .
Riverside Jun & Inf Sch...
  Riverton SS5 . . . .
Riverside Pk CM1 . . . .
Riverside Rd CM1 . . . .
Riverside Wlk SS12 . . . .
Riverside Works IG11 . . . . . .
Riversmead EN11 . . . .
Riverton Dr CM0 . . . .
Rivertons SS16 . . . .
Riverview
  Basildon SS16 . . . .
  Dartford DA1 . . . .
River View CM1 . . . .
River View Cl SS15 . . . .
Riverview Ct
  Basildon SS16 . . . .
  10 Belvedere DA17 . . . . .
  Greenhithe DA9 . . . .
Riverview Flats 13
  RM19 . . . .
Riverview Gdns SS5 . . . . . .
River View Rd SS7 . . . .
Riverview Terr 1
  RM19 . . . .
River View Terr CM3 . . . . . .
River Way
  Harlow CM20 . . . .
  Loughton IG10 . . . .
Riviera Dr SS1 . . . .
Rivington Ave IG8 . . . .
Rivington Ct **5** RM12 . . . . .
RJ Mitchell Prim Sch 1
  RM12 . . . .
RO24 CM19 . . . .
Roach Ave SS6 . . . .
Roach Vale SS9 . . . .
Roach View Bsns Pk
  SS4 . . . .
Robert Cl
  8 Barking IG11 . . . .
  Billericay CM12 . . . .
  Chelmsford CM2 . . . .
  Chigwell IG7 . . . .
Robert Clack Lower Sc...
  RM8 . . . .
Robert Clack Upper Sc...
  RM8 . . . .
Robert Daniells Ct
  CM16 . . . .
Robert Drake Prim Sc...
  The SS7 . . . .
Robert Leonard Ind Es...
  SS2 . . . .
Roberts Cl RM3 . . . .
Roberts Ct CM2 . . . .
Roberts Ho RM10 . . . .
Robertson Ct RM17 . . . . . .
Robertson Dr SS12 . . . . . .
Roberts Pl RM10 . . . .
Roberts Rd
  Basildon SS15 . . . .
  Belvedere DA17 . . . .
  Chingford E17 . . . .
  North Fambridge CM3 . . . . .
Robert Way SS11 . . . .
Robin Cl
  Billericay CM12 . . . .
  Romford RM5 . . . .
  Stanstead Abbotts SG12 . . .
Robin Hood Rd CM15 . . . . . .
Robinia Cl
  Basildon SS15 . . . .
  Redbridge IG6 . . . .
Robin's La CM16 . . . .
Robinson Cl RM12 . . . .
Robinson Rd
  Dagenham RM10 . . . .
  Horndon on t H SS17 . . . . .
Robinsons Cl CM0 . . . .
Robinson Way DA11 . . . . . .
Robins The CM15 . . . .
Robin Way CM2 . . . .
Robjohns Rd CM1 . . . .
Roborough Wlk
  RM12 . . . .
Roca Ct E11 . . . .
Roche Ave SS4 . . . .
Roche Cl SS4 . . . .
Rochefort Dr SS4 . . . .
Rochehall Way SS4 . . . . . .
Rochester Dr SS0 . . . .
Rochester Gdns IG1 . . . . . .
Rochester Mews SS0 . . . . .
Rochester Rd SS4 . . . .
Rochester Way
  Basildon SS14 . . . .
  6 Basildon SS16 . . . . . .
Rocheway SS4 . . . .
ROCHFORD . . . .
Rochford Ave
  Brentwood CM15 . . . .
  Ilford RM6 . . . .
  Loughton IG10 . . . .
  Southend-on-S SS0 . . . . . .
  Waltham Abbey EN9 . . . . . .
Rochford Cl
  Hornchurch RM12 . . . .
  Wickford SS11 . . . .
Rochford Garden Way...
  SS4 . . . .
Rochford Gn CM18 . . . .
Rochford Hall Cl SS4 . . . . .

Hall Cotts
125 D1
Ho EN9 65 D6
Prim Sch
125 E2
Rd
and SS8 164 D3
d CM2 32 C1
on-S SS2 147 E5
Sta SS4 125 E1
Cl SS4 125 F2
2 147 A7
Gdns
136 E5
RM10 154 B7
m Ave
136 B4
Ct RM17 173 C1
Ave SS9 147 A1
Ct CM15 95 A2
Rd RM10 154 B7
Gdns IG10 89 C6
Dr SS1 167 F8
M17 11 F4
G1 133 A1
CM5 15 A1
14 94 B1
IG8 110 E4
5 27 D2
ering SS3 150 B4
CM15 71 F2
ns IG10 88 E3
l RM4 90 B6
spl (BUPA)
132 D8
Hill IG9, IG7 88 E1
7 89 A1
N IG8 110 E2
S IG4 132 D7
gh CM3 101 E7
IG1 132 D5
m Sch
8 153 C7
G8 110 E3
IG10 88 F3
e SS17 160 D4
E4 109 D5
im Sch CM6 15 C8
e
n-S SS9 146 D7
RM14 137 D5
rd IG8 110 C4
ey High Sch
88 E4
ey Sta
110 D6
w
Hill IG9 88 D1
ngar CM5 49 B4
M13 155 D3
S12 121 E7
s EN11 21 A8
ngar CM5 48 F2
11 132 B7
y
CM1 53 E7
M7 113 B2
S3 149 E4
E4 109 C3
ts IG9 88 C2
IG9 88 C1
IG6 112 B4
ad Est
112 B4
SS2 148 F1
RM1 135 E7
dns SS2 148 F2
le's
es RM1 135 E7
s RM10 154 A7
9 RM10 135 A1
RM10 154 A7
173 C2
SS8 164 D2
S6 101 D6
IG4 132 F6
ns IG8 110 A2
142 A7
SS13 143 A5
SS8 164 B4
CM1 32 B7
16 134 E7
ay CM14 116 C7
CM1 52 F8
G2 133 A6
E4 109 C5
Ave E4 109 B5
Rd E4 109 B5
SS17 159 F3
Way SS8 163 C3
8 175 C2
36 F4
ng CM15 95 E8
13 154 D3
SS11 122 A5
ord CM2 32 B1
13 154 D3
G9 88 C1
vs 7 EN11 21 A7
152 B6

Roman Rd *continued*
Ingatestone CM4 73 F1
Little Waltham CM3 19 B5
Mountnessing CM15 95 E8
Roman Rise CM21 1 D2
Romans Farm Chase
CM0 106 C7
Romanshurst CM9 37 A4
Romans Pl CM1 31 B1
Roman St 8 EN11 21 A7
Romans Way CM1 31 B1
Roman Vale CM17 11 C5
Roman Way
Billericay CM12 119 A8
Burnham-on-C CM0 106 B8
Waltham Abbey EN9 65 B4
Romany Stps 17 SS1 167 C7
Rom Cres RM7 135 F4
Romeland EN9 65 C6
ROMFORD 135 D7
Romford Rd
Aveley RM15 171 C7
Chipping Ongar CM5 70 F7
Ilford E12 133 A1
Redbridge IG6 112 C5
Upminster RM15 156 C1
Romford Sta RM1 135 E5
Romney Chase RM11 137 A5
Romney Ho SS4 125 F2
Romney Rd CM12 96 F1
Romsey Cl
Hockley SS5 124 D6
South Benfleet SS7 144 B5
Stanford-le-H SS17 160 B1
Romsey Cres SS7 144 B5
Romsey Dr SS7 144 B5
Romsey Gdns RM9 153 D4
Romsey Rd
Dagenham RM9 153 D4
South Benfleet SS7 144 A5
Romsey Way SS7 144 B5
Romside Pl 4 RM7 135 D7
Rom Valley Way RM7 135 E4
Ronald Dr SS6 123 A4
Ronald Hill Gr SS9 146 D1
Ronald Park Ave SS0 147 C2
Ronald Rd RM3 115 A2
Roneo Cnr RM12 135 F3
Roneo Link RM12 135 F3
Ronnie La E12 152 A8
Ron Todd Cl RM10 154 A4
Ronver Lo E4 109 E7
Roodegate SS14 142 A6
Rook Cl RM13 155 A5
Rookery Cl
Rayleigh SS6 123 C2
Stanford-le-H SS17 160 B1
Rookery Cres RM10 154 B5
Rookery Ct RM20 177 A8
Rookery Hill SS17 161 C2
Rookery La CM3 80 E1
Rookery Rd CM4 50 D3
Rookery The RM20 177 A8
Rookery View RM17 173 D1
Rookes Cres CM1 53 F8
Rookley Ct 15 RM19 171 B1
Rook Lo IG1 132 D5
Rookwood Ave IG10 89 C6
Rookwood Cl RM17 173 B2
Rookwood Gdns E4 109 F8
Rookwood Ho 2
IG11 152 D3
Rookyards SS16 142 E5
Roosevel Ave SS8 164 A4
Roosevelt Rd 1 SS15 141 A6
Roosevelt Way RM10 154 D6
Roothings The CM9 37 B5
Roots Hall Ave SS2 147 F2
Roots Hall Dr SS2 147 E2
Roots Hall (Southend
United FC) SS2 147 E2
Ropers Ave E4 109 C5
Roper's Chase CM1 53 A7
Ropers Yd 12 CM14 116 C8
Rope Wlk CM9 37 A1
Rosalind Ct 6 IG11 153 A5
Rosary Ct CM15 116 E8
Rosary Gdns SS0 147 B4
Rosbach Rd SS8 164 D3
Rosberg Rd SS8 164 E3
Roscommon Way
SS8 163 C4
Rose Acre SS14 142 F6
Roseacre Cl RM11 136 F4
Roseacres CM21 1 D3
Rose Ave E18 110 B1
Rosebank EN9 65 E6
Rose Bank CM14 116 D7
Rosebank Ave RM12 155 C7
Rosebay Ave CM12 96 F5
Roseberry Ave
Basildon SS16 141 B4
South Benfleet SS7 144 C7
Roseberry Cl RM14 137 F5
Roseberry Ct SS7 144 C7
Roseberry Gdns
RM14 137 F5
Roseberry Wlk SS7 144 C7
Rosebery Rd
Chelmsford CM2 54 B8
Grays RM17 177 E8
Rosebury Ct CM13 95 D3
Rosebury Sq 2 IG8 111 A3
Rose Cl 10 SS12 121 E5
Rose Cotts
Harlow CM17 24 F5
Willingale CM5 28 D3
Rosecroft Cl SS16 141 A4

Rose & Crown Mews
CM0 84 D4
Rose Ct IG1 152 B6
Rosedale Dr RM9 153 B5
Rosedale Gdns RM9 153 B5
Rosedale Rd
Dagenham RM9 153 B5
Grays RM17 173 D1
Romford RM1 135 C8
Rosedene Gdns IG2 133 A7
Rose Dr CM0 84 D3
Rose Glen
Chelmsford CM2 54 C7
Romford RM7 135 E3
Rosehatch Ave RM6 134 D8
Rose La
Billericay CM12 97 A2
Dagenham RM6 134 E7
Roselaine SS14 142 B7
Roselands Ave EN11 8 A1
Roselawn Fields CM1 32 B8
Roseley Cotts CM20 10 B4
Rosemary Ave RM1 135 F8
Rosemary Cl
1 Harlow CM17 11 C4
South Ockendon RM15 157 C2
Rosemary Cotts CM3 20 E1
Rosemary Dr IG4 132 D6
Rosemary Gdns RM8 134 F3
Rosemary Lo SS2 147 F1
Rosemead SS7 144 C7
Rosemead Gdns CM13 95 D5
Rosemount CM19 23 A5
Rosemount Cl IG8 110 F4
Rose Park Ct IG5 110 F1
Rose Rd SS8 164 A3
Roserna Rd SS8 164 D3
Rose St DA11 178 B1
Roses The IG8 109 F3
Rose Tree Mews IG8 110 E4
Rosetti Terr 4 RM8 153 B8
Rose Vale EN11 21 A6
Rose Valley CM14 116 D7
Rose Valley Cres
SS17 160 E4
Rose Way SS4 148 A8
Rosewood Ave RM12 155 A7
Rosewood Cl RM15 157 E2
Rosewood Ct RM6 134 C6
Rosewood Ho 8
CM14 116 C7
Rosewood La SS3 168 F7
Rosher Ho DA11 178 F1
ROSHERVILLE 178 E1
Rosherville CE Prim Sch
DA11 178 E1
Rosherville Way
DA11 178 E1
Rosilian Dr SS5 102 C1
Roslings Cl CM1 31 D5
Roslyn Gdns RM2 113 F1
Rossall Cl RM11 136 A5
Ross Ave RM8 134 F3
Rossdene Gdns CM6 15 D7
Rossendale CM1 31 E1
Rosshill Ind Pk SS2 148 A4
Rossiter Rd SS3 168 H8
Rosslyn Ave
Chingford E4 109 F8
Dagenham RM8 135 A4
Romford RM3 114 F1
Rosslyn Cl SS5 124 E7
Rosslyn Ct SS17 160 C1
Rosslyn Rd
Barking IG11 152 D5
Billericay CM12 96 F2
Hockley SS5 124 E7
Ross Way SS16 141 B3
Rothbury Ave RM13 170 B8
Rothbury Ho 5 RM3 114 D4
Rothbury Rd CM1 31 D1
Roth Dr CM13 117 B8
Rothesay Ave CM2 54 A8
Rothmans Ave CM2 54 E6
Rothwell Cl SS9 146 C6
Rothwell Gdns RM9 153 C4
Rothwell Rd RM9 153 C4
Rotunda The 1 RM7 135 D6
Rough Hill Farm Cotts
CM3 78 C7
Roughtallys CM16 46 F4
Roughtons CM2 54 C3
Roundacre SS14 142 A6
Roundaway Rd IG5 110 F1
ROUNDBUSH 81 B8
Roundbush Bglws CM9 81 C8
ROUNDBUSH GREEN 5 C2
Roundbush Rd CM9 81 A8
Rounders Ct 12 RM10 154 B6
Round Hill Rd SS7 145 A2
Roundhills EN9 65 E4
Roundmead Ave IG10 89 A6
Roundmead Cl IG10 89 A7
Roundwood Ave CM13 95 B2
Roundwood Gr CM13 95 B2
Roundwood Lake
CM13 95 B2
Rounton Rd EN9 65 E6
Rous Chase CM2 54 B1
Rous Rd IG9 88 E1
Rover Ave IG6 111 F4
Rowallen Par RM8 134 C3
Rowan Cl
Ilford IG1 152 D7
Rayleigh SS6 123 B6
Rowan Dr CM9 37 C5
Rowan Gr RM15 171 C6
Rowan Green E CM13 116 F7

Rowan Green W
CM13 116 F7
Rowan Ho
4 Basildon SS13 143 B8
Ilford IG1 152 D7
Rowans EN9 66 C4
Rowans The
Aveley RM15 171 C5
Billericay CM11 119 D8
Rayleigh SS9 146 B6
Rowans Way
Loughton IG10 88 F5
Wickford SS11 121 E8
Rowan Way
Canewdon SS4 104 E1
Ilford RM6 134 C8
South Ockendon RM15 157 C1
Rowan Wlk
Hornchurch RM11 136 D7
Sawbridgeworth CM21 1 E2
Southend-on-S SS9 146 D6
Rowden Par E4 109 A4
Rowden Park Gdns
E4 109 A4
Rowden Rd E4 109 B4
Rowdowns Rd RM9 153 F5
Rowe Gdns IG11 153 A3
Rowenhall SS15 140 F6
Rowhedge CM13 117 B7
Rowhedge Cl SS13 121 D2
Rowland Cres IG7 111 E6
Rowlands Rd RM8 134 F2
Rowlands The SS7 144 E3
Rowland Wlk RM4 113 E7
Rowley Mead CM16 46 C6
Rowley Rd RM16 174 A8
Rowney Gdns
Dagenham RM9 153 C6
Sawbridgeworth CM21 11 C8
Rowney Rd RM9 153 B6
Rowney Wood CM21 1 C1
Rows The 1 CM20 10 D1
Roxburgh Ave RM14 137 C1
ROXWELL 30 B6
Roxwell Ave CM1 31 D3
Roxwell CE Prim Sch
CM1 30 A6
Roxwell Cres SS12 121 E6
Roxwell Gdns CM13 95 C4
Roxwell Ho IG10 88 E2
Roxwell Rd
Barking IG11 153 A3
Chelmsford CM1 31 C4
Roxwell CM1 30 E5
Writtle CM1 31 A4
Roxwell Way IG8 110 C3
Roxy Ave RM6 134 C4
Royal Artillery Way
SS2 148 F2
Royal Cl
Ilford IG3 134 A4
Rochford SS4 125 D5
Royal Cres IG2 133 D5
Royal Ct
Basildon SS15 141 B7
3 Brentwood CM14 116 C7
Maldon CM9 37 A1
Rayleigh SS9 146 B8
Southend-on-S SS2 148 A1
Royal Docks Rd E6 152 B1
Royal Gunpowder Mills*
EN9 65 B7
Royal Jubilee Ct RM2 136 A8
Royal Liberty Sch The
RM2 136 C8
Royal Mews SS1 167 A7
Royal Oak Chase
SS15 141 E8
Royal Oak Ct RM8 134 C2
Royal Oak Dr SS11 122 A8
Royal Par 16 RM10 154 B6
Royal Pier Mews 9
DA11 179 B1
Royal Pier Rd DA12 179 C1
Royals The SS1 167 A7
Royal Terr SS1 167 A7
Roycraft Ave IG11 152 F3
Roycroft Cl E18 110 B2
ROYDON 9 B1
Roydon Bridge SS14 142 D8
Roydonbury Ind Est
CM19 22 E8
Roydon Cl IG10 88 E2
ROYDON HAMLET 22 C4
Roydon Lodge Chalet Est
CM19 9 C1
Roydon Mill Leisure Pk
CM19 9 A1
Roydon Prim Sch
CM19 22 B8
Roydon Rd
Harlow CM19 9 E1
Stanstead Abbotts SG12 8 E4
Roydon Sta CM19 9 B2
Royer Cl SS5 125 A4
Roy Gdns IG2 133 F6
Royle Cl RM2 136 B6
Royston Ave
Basildon SS15 119 D1
Chingford E4 109 B5
Southend-on-S SS2 148 B3
Royston Ct IG1 132 D5
Royston Gdns IG1 132 D5
Royston Par IG1 132 D5
Royston Rd RM3 115 A3
Rubens Cl SS3 168 G8
Rubens Gate CM1 32 F7
Rubicon Ave SS11 121 F8

Rubin Pl EN3 65 A2
Ruby Ct
5 Rainham RM13 155 A1
Southend-on-S SS9 146 E5
RUDLEY GREEN 58 C2
Rudyard Ct CM14 116 B5
Rue De St Lawrence
EN9 65 C5
Ruffles Cl SS6 123 E3
Rugby Gdns RM9 153 C6
Rugby Rd RM9 153 C6
Rumbold Rd EN11 21 C8
Rumbullion Dr CM12 96 F3
Rumford Sh Hall The
RM1 135 E7
Rumsey Fields CM3 56 F7
Rumsey Row CM1 31 B1
Runcorn Ho 5 RM3 114 E4
Rundells CM18 24 A4
Rundells Wlk SS14 142 E7
Rundels Cotts SS7 145 A6
Rundels The SS7 145 A6
Runnel Ct 7 IG11 152 C3
Running Mare La CM2 54 A3
Running Waters
CM13 117 A6
Runnymede Chase
SS7 145 A5
Runnymede Ct SS17 160 C1
Runnymede Rd
Canvey Island SS8 164 B3
Stanford-le-H SS17 160 C1
Runsell Cl CM3 56 F7
RUNSELL GREEN 57 B7
Runsell La CM3 56 F8
Runsell View CM3 57 A7
RUNWELL 99 E1
Runwell Chase SS11 100 A3
Runwell Gdns SS11 99 D2
Runwell Hospl SS11 100 A5
Runwell Prim Sch
SS11 99 D2
Runwell Rd SS11 100 B3
Runwell Terr SS1 166 F7
Runwood Rd SS8 163 C3
Rupert Rd CM0 84 C4
Rural Cl RM11 136 B3
Rural Vale DA11 178 E1
Rurik Ct CM9 58 F8
Rushbottom La SS7 144 B7
Rush Cl
South Benfleet SS7 144 B6
Stanstead Abbotts SG12 8 C4
Rushcroft Rd E4 109 B3
Rush Croft Sports Coll
E4 109 B3
Rushdene Ct CM15 94 C2
Rushdene Rd
Billericay CM12 96 F1
Brentwood CM15 94 C2
Rushden Gdns
Ilford IG5 133 A8
Redbridge IG5 111 A1
Rushdon Cl
Grays RM17 173 A3
Romford RM1 136 A6
Rushdon Ct RM1 136 A6
Rush Dr EN9 65 C3
Rushes La CM0 63 A1
Rushes Mead CM18 23 E6
Rushfield CM21 1 E2
Rush Green Gdns
RM7 135 C3
Rush Green Inf Sch
RM7 135 D3
Rush Green Jun Sch
RM7 135 D3
Rush Green Rd RM7 135 D3
Rushley SS13 121 D1
Rushley Cl
Grays RM16 173 D5
Great Wakering SS3 150 A4
Rushleydale CM1 32 E5
Rushmere Ave RM14 137 C1
Rusholme Ave RM10 135 A1
Rushton Gr CM17 24 E8
Ruskin Ave
Southend-on-S SS2 148 B2
Upminster RM14 137 C4
Waltham Abbey EN9 65 E5
Ruskin Dene CM12 97 A3
Ruskin Gdns RM3 114 B3
Ruskin Gr DA1 176 A2
Ruskin Path 2 SS12 121 D5
Ruskin Rd
Belvedere DA17 169 A2
Chelmsford CM2 32 E2
Grays RM16 174 A2
Stanford-le-H SS17 160 C1
Ruskoi Rd SS8 163 F5
Rusper Rd RM9 153 C6
Russell Cl
Basildon SS15 141 B6
Brentwood CM15 94 B2
Russell Ct SS11 121 F7
Russell Gdns
Chelmsford CM2 54 A4
Ilford IG1 133 D4
Wickford SS11 121 F7
Russell Gr SS4 126 A2
RUSSELL GREEN 20 D6
Russell Lo 5 E4 109 C8
Russell Quay DA11 179 A1
Russell Rd
Buckhurst Hill IG9 88 C1

222 Rus–St N

Russell Rd *continued*
Gravesend DA12 179 D1
Grays RM17 173 A2
North Fambridge CM3 81 B1
Tilbury RM18 178 F5
Tilbury RM18 178 F6
Russell Way CM1 53 E7
Russell Wilson Ct
RM3 115 A2
Russet Cl SS17 160 D3
Russet Ho RM17 178 C7
Russets CM2 54 D3
Russets Cl E4 109 D6
Russets The SS4 125 D5
Russetts
Basildon SS16 141 A5
Hornchurch RM11 136 E7
Russet Way
Burnham-on-C CM0 106 C6
Hockley SS5 124 F8
Rustic Cl RM14 137 E3
Rutherford Cl
Billericay CM12 97 A5
Southend-on-S SS9 146 C6
Rutherfords CM1 19 B1
Ruthven Cl SS12 121 D6
Rutland App RM11 137 A6
Rutland Ave SS1 167 E7
Rutland Cl SS15 141 A6
Rutland Dr
Hornchurch RM11 137 A6
Rayleigh SS6 123 C7
Rutland Gate DA17 169 B1
Rutland Gdns
Dagenham RM8 153 C7
Rochford SS4 125 C5
Rutland Ho RM7 113 A1
Rutland Rd
Chelmsford CM1 32 A7
Ilford IG1 133 B1
North Fambridge CM3 103 A7
Wanstead E11 132 B6
Rutley Cl RM3 114 D1
Ryan Ct RM7 135 C5
Rydal Cl
Hullbridge SS5 101 D3
Rayleigh SS6 123 E2
Rydal Dr CM9 59 B8
Ryde Cl SS9 146 B5
Ryde Dr SS17 175 C8
Ryder Gdns RM13 154 F6
Ryder Way SS13 121 D2
Ryde The SS9 146 B5
Rye Cl RM12 155 C7
Ryecroft CM19 23 B8
Ryecroft Ave IG5 111 B1
Ryedene SS16 142 F3
Ryedene Cl SS16 142 E3
Ryedene Com Prim Sch
SS16 142 F3
Ryedene Pl SS16 142 F3
Ryefeld Cl EN11 8 B2
Rye Field The CM3 34 D3
RYE HILL 23 E1
Rye Hill Rd CM18 23 E2
Rye House Gatehouse*
EN11 21 D8
Rye House Sta EN11 21 C8
Rye Mead SS16 141 C4
Rye Mead Cotts EN11 21 C8
RYE PARK 21 B7
Rye Park Ind Est EN11 21 D7
Rye Rd EN11 21 C8
Ryes La CM22 3 B7
Rye Wlk CM4 74 A2
Rykhill RM16 174 B3
Rylands Rd SS2 148 D2
Ryle The CM1 53 A8
Rysley CM3 34 D4

S

Sabina Rd RM16 174 C2
SABINE'S GREEN 92 F6
Sabines Rd RM4 92 E6
Sable Way SS15 140 F7
Sachfield Dr RM16 172 E3
Sackville Cl CM1 31 E3
Sackville Cres RM3 114 E2
Sackville Gdns IG1 132 F3
Sackville Rd SS2 148 E1
Sacred Heart of Mary
Girls' Sch RM14 137 B2
Sacred Heart RC Prim Sch
SS1 167 C8
Saddle Rise CM1 32 E8
Saddleworth Rd RM3 114 C4
Saddleworth Sq RM3 114 C4
Sadlers SS7 144 B6
Sadlers Cl CM11 97 D5
Sadlers Mead CM18 24 A7
Saffory Cl SS9 146 C7
Saffron Cl
Horndon on t H SS17 160 A3
West Horndon CM13 139 D5
Saffron Croft CM9 36 E2
Saffron Ct SS15 140 F6
Saffron Dr SS14 142 D7
Saffron Gdns SS17 159 F1
Saffron Rd
Grays RM16 172 C2
Romford RM5 113 D1
Saffron Wlk CM11 97 B2
Sage Mews SS17 160 E3
St Agnes Dr SS8 163 D4
St Agnes Rd CM12 119 C3
St Aidans Ct 4 IG11 153 B3
St Aidan's RC Prim Sch
IG1 133 D3
St Albans Ave RM14 137 E2
St Alban's Ave E6 152 A2
St Alban's Cres IG8 110 A2
St Albans RC Prim Sch
CM20 10 F2
St Alban's RC Prim Sch
RM12 155 B5
St Albans Rd IG3 133 F4
St Alban's Rd
Coopersale CM16 46 D2
Woodford IG8 110 A3
St Andrews Ave
Hornchurch RM12 155 A8
Rainham RM12 154 F7
St Andrews CE Prim Sch
CM16 47 C6
St Andrew's CE Prim Sch
SG12 8 D4
St Andrews Cl
Canvey Island SS8 163 D4
North Weald Bassett
CM16 47 D7
St Andrews Ct 15
DA11 179 B1
St Andrews Dr CM11 97 B3
St Andrew's Ho CM20 10 F2
St Andrews La 2
SS15 141 C7
St Andrew's Mdw
CM18 23 F7
St Andrews Pl CM15 116 F8
St Andrews Rd
Boreham CM3 20 F1
Romford RM7 135 D5
Southend-on-S SS3 168 D6
St Andrew's Rd
Redbridge IG1 132 F4
Rochford SS4 125 E2
Tilbury RM18 178 E5
St Anne Line RC Jun & Inf
Schs SS15 141 F6
St Annes RM16 173 B5
St Annes Cl RM16 173 B5
St Annes Ct CM1 32 C3
St Anne's Pk EN10 21 A4
St Annes Rd SS8 164 E3
St Anne's Rd CM15 95 C8
St Anne's Sch CM2 32 A1
St Annes Terr 6 IG6 111 E5
St Ann's IG11 152 C4
St Anns Cl 3 SS15 141 C7
St Ann's Rd
2 Barking IG11 152 C4
Southend-on-S SS2 148 A1
St Anselm's RC Prim Sch
DA1 176 A2
St Anthony's Ave IG8 110 C3
St Anthony's Dr CM2 54 C7
St Antony's RC Prim Sch
IG8 110 A6
St Aubyn's Sch IG8 109 F3
St Audrey's SS1 168 B7
St Augustine Rd
RM16 174 B2
St Augustine's Ave
SS1 168 B7
St Augustine's RC Prim
Sch
Hoddesdon EN11 21 B6
Ilford IG2 133 B6
St Awdry's Rd IG11 152 D5
St Barnabas Rd IG8 110 C3
St Bede's RC Prim Sch
RM6 134 C6
St Benet's Rd SS2 147 F3
St Bernard's High Sch &
Art Coll SS0 166 E8
St Catharine's Rd EN10 21 A4
St Catherines Cl SS11 121 F8
St Catherine's Hoddesdon
CE Prim Sch EN11 21 B6
St Catherine's Rd
Chelmsford CM1 31 E2
Chingford E4 109 A8
St Cecilia Rd RM16 174 B2
St Cedd's CE Prim Sch
CM0 42 B2
St Cedds Ct RM16 173 B5
St Cedd's Sch CM1 32 A4
St Chads Cl 4 SS15 141 C7
St Chad's Gdns RM6 134 E4
St Chad's Rd
Dagenham RM6 134 E4
Tilbury RM16, RM18 179 A7
St Charles Dr SS11 121 E7
St Charles Rd CM14 94 B1
St Christopher Sch The
SS9 146 F4
St Christophers Cl
SS8 163 D4
St Clair Cl IG5 110 F1
St Clare Mdw SS4 125 F3
St Clement's Ave
Grays RM20 177 B8
Southend-on-S SS9 146 E2
St Clements Cl SS5 125 A4
St Clement's Cl SS7 144 D5
St Clement's Cres
SS7 144 D5
St Clements Ct
3 Grays RM17 177 F8
Purfleet RM19 171 A2
Waltham Abbey EN9 65 C6
St Clement's Ct SS9 165 D8
St Clement's Dr SS9 146 E3
St Clements Rd DA9 177 C3
St Clement's Rd
Grays RM20 177 C7
South Benfleet SS7 144 D5
St Clement's Way
RM20 176 F8
St Cleres Cres SS11 121 F7
St Clere's Sch SS17 175 C8
St Cleres Way CM3 56 D7
St Cross Ct EN11 21 A4
St Cross RC Prim Sch
EN11 21 A4
St Cuthberts Rd EN11 8 C1
St Davids Ct
Basildon SS16 142 E3
5 Wanstead E11 132 B6
St David's Ct RM1 135 F4
St Davids Dr SS9 146 A3
St David's Rd SS16 141 B4
St Davids Terr SS9 146 A3
St David's Way SS11 121 E7
St Davids Wlk SS8 163 D4
St Dionis Rd E12 132 E1
St Dunstan's Rd SG12 9 D8
St Edith's Ct CM12 97 A1
St Ediths La CM12 97 A1
St Edmund's Cl SS2 148 C3
St Edmunds Rd DA1 176 A3
St Edmund's Rd IG1 132 F5
St Edmund's Way
CM17 11 C4
St Edward's CE Comp Sch
RM7 135 A5
St Edward's CE Prim Sch
RM1 135 E8
St Edwards Way RM1,
RM7 135 D6
St Egberts Way E4 87 C1
SS Peter & Paul's Prim
Sch IG1 133 D1
St Erkenwald Mews
IG11 152 D4
St Erkenwald Rd
IG11 152 D4
St Erkenwalds Cl SS1 167 C8
St Ethelburga Ct RM3 115 A1
St Fabian's Dr CM1 31 E4
St Fidelis' Rd DA8 169 D1
St Francis Ct SS2 148 C1
St Francis RC Prim Sch
CM9 36 F3
St Francis' Rd DA8 169 D2
St Francis Way
Grays RM16 174 C3
Ilford IG1 152 D8
St Gabriel's Cl E11 132 B3
St Gabriels Ct SS13 143 B5
St George's Ave
Grays RM17 173 C2
Hornchurch RM11 136 F4
St Georges Cl
Heybridge Basin CM9 37 E3
Hook End CM15 72 B4
St Georges Ct
Brentwood CM13 95 C2
Romford RM7 135 C7
St George's Ct CM14 94 B2
St George's Ctr DA11 179 B1
St George's Dr SS0 147 E3
St George's Hospl
RM12 155 D7
St George's La SS3 168 F6
St George's Park Ave
SS0 147 B2
St George's RC Prim Sch
SS3 168 E8
St Georges Rd RM9 153 E8
St George's Rd IG1 132 F4
St Georges Wlk
Canvey Island SS8 163 D4
South Benfleet SS7 144 B6
St Giles Ave RM10 154 B5
St Giles Cl
Dagenham RM10 154 B5
Maldon CM9 36 E2
Orsett RM16 174 A8
St Giles Cres CM9 36 E2
St Gregorys Ho CM16 68 A8
St Guiberts Rd SS8 163 E5
St Helens Ct RM13 155 A1
St Helen's Ct CM16 46 A1
St Helen's RC Inf Sch
CM14 116 D8
St Helen's RC Prim Sch
SS0 166 F8
St Helen's Rd
Redbridge IG1 132 F5
Southend-on-S SS0 166 E8
St Helens Wlk CM12 96 F4
St Hildas Sch SS0 147 C1
St Ives Cl RM3 114 F3
St Ivians Dr RM2 136 A8
St James Ave SS1 168 B7
St James' Ave CM5 49 A1
St James Ave E SS17 160 E3
St James Ave W SS17 160 E3
St James CE Prim Sch
CM18 23 D4
St James Cl
Canvey Island SS8 163 D4
Southend-on-S SS0 147 A3
St James Ct
Canvey Island SS8 164 B1
Greenhithe DA9 176 F1
Romford RM1 135 F7
Wanstead E12 132 C2
St James Ctr CM20 11 A4
St James Gate IG9 88 B1
St James Gdns
Ilford RM6 134 B7
Southend-on-S SS0 147 A3
St Jame's Ho 9 RM1 135 F6
St James La DA9 176 E1
St James Mews CM12 97 A2
St James Pk CM1 31 D4
St James Rd SS16 142 D5
St James's Ave DA11 179 A1
St James's Rd
Brentwood CM14 116 C7
Gravesend DA11 179 A1
St James's St DA11 179 A1
St James's Wlk SS5 124 C6
St John Fisher RC Jun Sch
IG10 89 C7
St John Payne RC Comp
Sch CM1 31 F6
St John's Ave
Brentwood CM14 116 D6
Chelmsford CM2 54 B8
Harlow CM17 11 C4
St John's CE Prim Sch
IG9 88 B1
St John's CE Sch CM16 45 E1
St Johns Cl
1 Basildon SS15 141 C7
Great Wakering SS3 150 B3
St John's Cl RM13 155 A5
St Johns Cres SS8 163 D3
St Johns Ct
Erith DA8 169 D1
Mayland CM3 83 A8
Southend-on-S SS1 166 F7
St John's Ct IG9 88 B1
St John's Danbury CE
Prim Sch CM3 56 E7
St Johns Dr SS6 122 F4
St John's Gn CM1 31 B1
St John's Hospl CM2 53 F6
St Johns La SG12 8 A6
St John's Lo IG10 88 F7
St Johns Mews SS17 160 F4
St Johns Pl CM11 98 B4
St Johns RC Sch IG8 111 A5
St Johns Rd
Grays RM16 174 B1
Ilford IG2 133 E4
Romford RM5 113 C5
St John's Rd
Barking IG11 152 E4
Billericay CM11 97 B3
Chelmsford CM2 54 B8
Chingford E4 109 B6
Chingford, Highams Park
E17 109 C1
Epping CM16 45 F1
Erith DA8 169 D1
Great Wakering SS3 150 B3
Hadleigh SS7 145 C3
Loughton IG10 88 F7
Southend-on-S SS0 166 E8
Writtle CM1 31 B1
St John's Sch CM12 97 B3
St John's Way SS17 160 F4
St Johns Wlk CM17 11 C4
St John The Baptist CE
Prim Sch SG12 8 A5
St Joseph's Convent Sch
E11 132 A5
St Joseph's Ct E4 87 D2
St Josephs RC Prim Sch
IG11 152 C4
St Joseph's RC Prim Sch
Canvey Island SS8 164 B4
Dagenham RM9 153 F8
South Woodham Ferrers
CM3 101 E7
Stanford-le-H SS17 160 D2
Upminster RM14 137 B2
St Joseph The Worker RC
Prim Sch CM13 95 C3
St Judes Ct IG8 110 E3
St Katherine's CE Prim
Sch SS8 164 A5
St Katherines Ct SS8 163 E3
St Kathryns Pl RM14 137 C2
St Kilda's Rd CM15 94 C2
ST LAWRENCE 62 B8
St Lawrence Ct SS9 146 E6
St Lawrence Dr
Steeple CM0 62 B8
St Lawrence CM0 40 B1
St Lawrence Gdns
Blackmore CM4 72 E8
Southend-on-S SS9 146 E6
St Lawrence Hill CM0 62 E5
St Lawrence Rd
Tillingham CM0 63 D5
Upminster RM14 137 C2
St Leonard's Ave E4 109 D4
St Leonards Cl RM17 177 F8
St Leonards Gdns
IG1 152 C7
St Leonards Rd EN9 43 D6
St Leonard's Rd SS1 167 B7
St Leonards Way
RM11 136 B2
St Luke's Ave IG1 152 B7
St Lukes Cl
8 Basildon SS15 141 C7
Canvey Island SS8 163 D4
St Luke's Path 1 IG1 152 B7
St Lukes Pl SS4 125 E2
St Luke's RC Prim Sch
CM19 23 C6
St Luke's Rd SS2
ST MARGARETS
St Margarets IG11
St Margaret's Ave
SS17
St Margarets CE Prim
IG11
St Margaret's CE Prim
SS13
St Margaret's Hospl
CM16
St Margaret's Rd
Chelmsford CM2
Hoddesdon SG12
Wanstead E12
St Margarets Sta SG12
St Mark's Ave DA11
St Mark's Field SS4
St Marks Pl RM10
St Marks Rd SS8
St Mark's Rd SS7
St Mark's West Essex
Sch CM18
St Martins Cl
South Benfleet SS7
White Roothing or White
Roding CM6
St Martin's Cl SS6
St Martin's Mews CM5
St Martins Rd EN11
St Martin's Sch CM13
St Martins Sq SS14
St Marys IG11
St Mary's Ave
Billericay CM12
Brentwood CM15
Wanstead E11
St Mary's Bglws CM1
St Mary's Cath* CM1
St Mary's CE Prim Sc
Burnham-on-C CM0
Hatfield Broad Oak CM2
Shenfield CM15
Woodham Ferrers CM3
St Marys Cl
South Benfleet SS7
Southend-on-S SS3
St Mary's Cl
Grays RM17
Great Baddow CM2
St Mary's Cres SS13
St Mary's Ct CM9
St Mary's Ct SS2
St Mary's Dr SS7
St Mary's Hare Park S
RM2
St Mary's Ho 6 CM0
St Mary's La
Maldon CM9
Upminster RM14
West Horndon CM13
St Mary's Lo E11
St Marys Mead CM1
St Mary's Path SS13
St Mary's Prittlewell
Prim Sch SS2
St Mary's RC Prim Sc
Chingford E4
Hornchurch RM12
Tilbury RM18
St Marys Rd
Ilford IG1
Wickford SS12
St Mary's Rd
Burnham-on-C CM0
Grays RM16
Greenhithe DA9
South Benfleet SS7
Southend-on-S SS2
St Marys Way IG7
St Matthew's Cl RM13
St Michaels Ave SS13
St Michaels CE Prep
SS9
St Michaels Cl
Aveley RM15
Harlow CM20
Latchingdon CM3
St Michael's Dr CM1
St Michael's Mews
CM6
St Michaels Rd
Canvey Island SS8
Grays RM16
St Michael's Rd
Chelmsford CM2
Hadleigh SS7
Hoddesdon EN10
St Michaels Wlk CM2
St Mildreds Rd CM2
St Nazaire Rd CM1
St Neot's Rd RM3
St Nicholas Ave
RM12
St Nicholas CE Prim
CM0
St Nicholas CE Sch
SS6
St Nicholas Ct E4
St Nicholas Gn 1
CM17
St Nicholas Gr CM13
St Nicholas La SS15
St Nicholas Pl IG10
St Nicholas Rd CM0
St Nicholas Sch
Harlow CM17
Southend-on-S SS2

s Rd E6 . . . . 152 A4
CI SS12 . . . . 121 E6
's Ct E3 . . . . 109 E3
's PI RM16 . . . . 174 C2
t's RC Prim Sch 113 B2
CI RM15 . . . . . . 171 C6
Ct SS0 . . . . 166 E8
idns CM12 . . . . 97 A4
PI RM15 . . . . . . 171 C6
Rd
s11 . . . . 152 C4
land SS8 . . . . . . 163 D4
Vay EN9 . . . . . . .65 D6
Ave
Ongar CM5 . . . . . 49 A5
M9 . . . . .36 F2
CE Prim Sch 76 F4
CE Prim Sch 115 E8
Chapel* 182 A5
CI
er CM9 . . . . .38 E6
. . . . 133 F7
Ct SS3 . . . . 168 G7
CM0 . . . . .63 E8
Field CM0 . . . . 106 A7
High Sch 106 B6
Hospl CM9 . . . . .36 F2
Pavement 120 F1
RC Prim Sch 119 E6
RC Prim Sch
RM9 . . . . 153 F4
M1 . . . . 135 E8
Rd
and SS8 . . . . . . 163 D4
. . . . .174 B2
S5 . . . . .124 B7
Rd
I CM14 . . . . 116 B6
d CM1 . . . . .31 E2
Terr SS12 . . . . 121 C7
Wlk CM12 . . . . . .96 F4
Priory Sch 54 A8
RC Prim Sch 31 F6
s PI CM14 . . . . . 116 B5
Cres IG8 . . . . . . 110 A3
ns Cres 117 A6
ns Ct CM3 . . . . .83 A8
ns Rd CM3 . . . . . .81 A4
s Cotts CM2 . . . 55 C3
k RM16 . . . . 174 C2
RC Prim Sch 153 C8
CI SS14 . . . . . 142 F5
RC Prim Sch
S14 . . . . 142 F6
S4 . . . . 125 E3
Wlk RM16 . . . . . 174 B3
Ct E4 . . . . .87 D2
' Ct CM14 . . . . . 116 D8
Gdns IG1 . . . . . 152 C6
More High Sch . . . 147 A3
of Canterbury
h CM15 . . . . .94 D2
of Canterbury
ch CM15 . . . . . . .94 D2
of Canterbury
Sch RM17 . . . . 173 B2
Rd
0A17 . . . . 169 C4
CM14 . . . . 116 D8
S4 . . . . 103 B4
's CI CM9 . . . . . .66 B6
's PI ▲ 178 C8
's Row CM0 . . . . .42 B2
RC Jun & Inf 114 B4
s Ave DA11 . . . . 176 A2
T'S HAMLET 93 B1
s RC Prim Sch . . . 134 C2
Rd
d CM2 . . . . .54 B8
A1 . . . . 176 A1
s Rd SS0 . . . . . . 166 E7
's CI IG7 . . . . . . 111 C5
SS9 . . . . 146 D7
ns SS9 . . . . 146 D7
ft CM18 . . . . .23 F5
RM19 . . . . 171 A2
Way RM13 . . . . . 169 E7
Dr RM6 . . . . 134 E5
Pk IG10 . . . . .88 D4
ss SS12 . . . . . . 121 F6
ws SS12 . . . . . . 121 F6
SS6 . . . . 123 B4
ay CM1 . . . . .31 E6
Dr CM11 . . . . . . .97 D2
CM3 . . . . .78 B1
SS15 . . . . 119 F2
ave
t1 . . . . 152 E5
SS0 . . . . 147 E1
-H SS17 . . . . . . 160 D1
t
t6 . . . . 123 C5

Salisbury CI continued
Upminster RM14 . . . . 137 F2
Salisbury Ct SS9 . . . . . . 146 D2
Salisbury Gdns ▲
IG9 . . . . 110 D8
Salisbury Hall Gdns
E4 . . . . 109 A4
Salisbury Rd
Chingford E4 . . . . 109 A7
Dagenham RM10 . . . . . . 154 B6
Grays RM17 . . . . 173 C1
Hoddesdon EN11 . . . . .21 C8
Ilford IG3 . . . . 133 E2
Romford RM2 . . . . 136 B6
Southend-on-S SS9 . . . . . 146 D1
Salix Rd RM17 . . . . 178 E8
Sally Murray CI E12 . . . . . 152 A8
Salmond's Gr CM13 . . . . . 117 C5
Salmon Par CM1 . . . . .32 B3
Salmon Rd DA17 . . . . 169 A1
Saltash Rd IG6 . . . . 111 D3
Saltcoats CM3 . . . . 101 D8
Saltcoats Pk & Compass
Gdns * CM3 . . . . 101 F7
Saltcote Maltings CM9 . . . . .37 E4
Saltern Ct ▲ IG11 . . . . . . 153 B2
Salter PI CM2 . . . . .32 F2
Saltford Ct DA8 . . . . 169 E1
Saltings The
Greenhithe DA9 . . . . 177 C3
Hadleigh SS7 . . . . 145 D3
Salt's Gn CM1 . . . . .16 D2
Salway CI IG8 . . . . 110 A3
Samantha Mews RM4 . . . . . 113 E7
Samian Ct CM9 . . . . .36 F5
Samphire Ct RM17 . . . . . . 178 E8
Samson Ct ▲ DA17 . . . . . . 169 A2
Samson Ho SS15 . . . . 119 B1
Samuel Manor CM2 . . . . . . .32 F3
Samuel Rd SM16 . . . . 141 B4
Samuel's Cnr SS3 . . . . . . 150 D3
Samuels Dr SS1 . . . . 168 B8
Sanctuary Gdn SS17 . . . . 160 E2
Sanctuary Rd SS1 . . . . . . 146 A3
Sandbanks SS7 . . . . 145 D2
Sandcliff Rd DA8 . . . . 169 D1
Sandering Gdns CM9 . . . . . .37 C5
Sanderlings SS7 . . . . 146 C4
Sanderling Way DA9 . . . . . 177 A1
Sanders Draper Sch &
Specialist Science Coll
The RM12 . . . . 155 B8
Sanderson CM13 . . . . 139 C5
Sanderson Ct SS14 . . . . . 142 C5
Sanders Rd SS8 . . . . 164 A6
Sandford Ave IG10 . . . . . . .89 C6
Sandford Mill Rd
Chelmsford CM2 . . . . .32 F2
Chelmsford CM2 . . . . .33 B2
Great Baddow CM2 . . . . . . .55 C8
Sandford Rd CM2 . . . . .32 E3
Sandgate Rd RM7 . . . . . . 135 C4
Sandhill Rd SS9 . . . . 146 C8
Sandhurst SS8 . . . . 163 C3
Sandhurst CI SS9 . . . . 146 F4
Sandhurst Ct SS9 . . . . 146 F4
Sandhurst Dr IG3 . . . . 152 F8
Sandhurst Rd RM18 . . . . . 179 C5
Sand Island Ctr CM0 . . . . . 106 A5
Sandleigh Rd SS9 . . . . . . 147 A1
SANDON 55 D6
Sandon Brook PI CM2 . . . . .55 E8
Sandon CI
Basildon SS14 . . . . 142 F5
Rochford SS4 . . . . 125 D3
Sandon Ct
Basildon SS14 . . . . 142 F5
Ilford IG3 . . . . 134 A1
SANDON GREEN 55 C6
Sandon Hall Bridleway
CM2 . . . . .55 D4
Sandon Rd SS14 . . . . 142 F5
Sandon Sch The CM2 . . . . .55 B6
Sandown Ave
Dagenham RM10 . . . . 154 C6
Hornchurch RM12 . . . . 136 D2
Southend-on-S SS0 . . . . . 147 B2
Sandown Ct CM1 . . . . .49 A1
Sandown Rd SS14 . . . . . . 142 F5
Sandown Sch CM10 . . . . . 146 C6
Sandpiper CI
Greenhithe DA9 . . . . 177 A1
Heybridge CM9 . . . . .37 C5
Southend-on-S SS3 . . . . . 168 E8
Sandpipers SS3 . . . . 168 G6
Sandpiper Terr IG5 . . . . . 133 B8
Sandpiper Wlk CM2 . . . . . . .54 C6
Sandpit La
Burnham-on-C CM0 . . . . . 106 C5
Pilgrims Hatch CM14 . . . . . .93 F2
Sandpit Rd SS3 . . . . 168 H8
Sandringham Ave
Harlow CM19 . . . . .22 E8
Hockley SS5 . . . . 124 D6
Sandringham CI
Ilford IG6 . . . . 133 C8
Stanford-le-H SS17 . . . . . 160 E3
Sandringham Ct SS12 . . . . 145 E2
Sandringham Gdns
IG6 . . . . 133 C8
Sandringham Lo ▲
EN11 . . . . .21 A6
Sandringham PI CM2 . . . . . .32 C2

Sandringham Rd
Barking IG11 . . . . 152 F6
Basildon SS15 . . . . 141 E8
Pilgrims Hatch CM15 . . . . . .94 B3
Southend-on-S SS1 . . . . . 167 D7
Sands Way IG8 . . . . 110 F4
Sandyhill Rd IG1 . . . . 152 B8
Sandy La
Aveley RM15 . . . . 171 A6
Grays, Chadwell St M
RM16 . . . . 174 C1
Grays, West Thurrock
RM20 . . . . 177 B8
Sangster Ct SS4 . . . . 123 F2
San Juan Dr RM16 . . . . . . 172 C2
San Luis Dr RM16 . . . . 172 C2
San Marcos Dr RM16 . . . . 172 C2
San Remo Mans SS0 . . . . 166 E7
San Remo Par SS0 . . . . . . 166 E7
San Remo Rd SS8 . . . . . . 164 D3
Sans Souci SS9 . . . . 165 D8
Santiago Way RM16 . . . . . 172 D1
Sappers Ct CM21 . . . . .1 F2
Sapphire Ct RM8 . . . . 134 C3
Sapphire CI SS1 . . . . 167 D6
Sapphire Ho ▲ RM13 . . . . 155 A1
Sara Cres DA9 . . . . 177 B3
Sarbir Ind Pk CM17 . . . . . .11 C5
Sark Gr SS12 . . . . 121 F5
Sarre Ave RM12 . . . . 155 C6
Sassoon Way ▲ CM9 . . . . . .37 A1
Satanita Rd SS1 . . . . 166 D8
Saunders CI IG1 . . . . 133 D3
Saunton Rd RM12 . . . . 136 A2
Savannah Hts SS9 . . . . . . 147 A1
Savernake Rd CM1 . . . . . . .31 E1
Savill Ct IG8 . . . . 109 F4
Saville Rd RM6 . . . . 134 F4
Savill Row IG8 . . . . 109 F4
Savoy CI SS16 . . . . 141 A5
Savoy Wood CM19 . . . . . . .23 B2
SAWBRIDGEWORTH 1 C5
Sawbridgeworth Rd
Hatfield Heath CM22 . . . . . .2 D3
Little Hallingbury CM22 . . . . .2 B6
Sawbridgeworth Sta
CM21 . . . . .2 A3
Sawkins Ave CM2 . . . . .54 D6
Sawkins CI CM2 . . . . .54 D6
Sawkins Gdns CM2 . . . . . . .54 D6
Sawney Brook CM1 . . . . . . .31 A1
Sawston Ct ▲ RM19 . . . . . 171 B1
Sawyer's Chase RM4 . . . . . .90 B6
Sawyers Ct CM15 . . . . .94 F3
Sawyers Ct SS1 . . . . .94 D1
Sawyers Hall Coll of
Science & Tech
CM15 . . . . .94 C2
Sawyer's Hall La CM15 . . . . .94 C2
Saxham Rd E4 . . . . 109 D7
Saxon CI
Brentwood CM13 . . . . 117 A7
Rayleigh SS6 . . . . 123 E5
Romford RM3 . . . . 114 F1
Wickford SS11 . . . . .99 E1
Saxon Ct
Maldon CM9 . . . . .37 A3
South Benfleet SS7 . . . . . . 144 C5
Saxon Gdns SS3 . . . . 168 D7
Saxon Ho RM14 . . . . 138 D4
Saxon PI SS4 . . . . 125 F2
Saxon Rd IG1 . . . . 152 B7
Saxonville SS7 . . . . 144 B4
Saxon Way
Chelmsford CM1 . . . . .32 B7
Maldon CM9 . . . . .37 B1
South Benfleet SS7 . . . . . . 144 C2
Waltham Abbey EN9 . . . . . .65 C6
Sayer CI DA9 . . . . 177 A2
Sayers SS7 . . . . 145 A7
Sayesbury Ave CM21 . . . . . .1 E3
Sayesbury Rd CM21 . . . . . . .1 E3
Sayes Gdns CM21 . . . . .1 F2
Saywell Brook CM2 . . . . . . .33 A2
Scalby Rd CM0 . . . . .84 A3
Scaldhurst SS13 . . . . 143 C8
Scarborough Dr SS9 . . . . . 146 E2
Scarborough Rd CM0 . . . . . .84 A3
Scargill Jun & Inf Sch
RM13 . . . . 155 A6
Scarlets Croft CM3 . . . . . . .78 C7
Scarletts SS14 . . . . 142 C8
Scholars Ho ▲ E4 . . . . .87 D1
Scholars Rd E4 . . . . .87 D1
Scholars Way ▲ RM2 . . . . . 136 B6
School Bglws CM1 . . . . .30 A5
Schoolfield Rd RM20 . . . . . 177 A8
School Green La CM16 . . . . .47 C6
Schoolhouse Gdns
IG10 . . . . .89 B5
School La
Abbess Roding CM5 . . . . . .14 F3
Basildon SS12 . . . . 122 A2
Beauchamp Roding CM5 . . . .28 A7
Broomfield CM1 . . . . .19 B1
Chelmsford CM1 . . . . .31 F8
Chigwell IG7 . . . . 111 F6
Harlow CM20 . . . . .10 E2
High Easter CM1 . . . . .6 B3
Ingrave CM13 . . . . 117 C4
Orsett RM16 . . . . 174 A8
South Benfleet SS7 . . . . . . 163 D8
Stock CM4 . . . . .78 C2
Tilgate Green CM5 . . . . . . .25 D6
School Rd
Billericay CM12 . . . . 119 A8

School Rd continued
Dagenham RM10 . . . . 154 B4
Downham CM11 . . . . .98 F5
Kelvedon Hatch CM15 . . . . .71 F2
Margaret Roding CM1 . . . . . .16 C5
Stanford Rivers CM5 . . . . . .70 B7
School View Rd CM1 . . . . . .31 F3
School Villas CM6 . . . . .5 E7
School Way
Dagenham RM8 . . . . 134 C1
Southend-on-S SS9 . . . . . 146 F3
Schooner CI IG11 . . . . 153 B2
Schooner Ct DA2 . . . . 176 C3
Schooner Ho DA8 . . . . 169 E1
Scilla Ct RM17 . . . . 178 D8
Scimitar Park Ind Est
SS13 . . . . 121 D2
Scimitar Pk SS13 . . . . 121 D2
Scimitar Pk CM19 . . . . .9 F1
Scoter CI IG8 . . . . 110 B3
Scotland Rd IG9 . . . . .88 C1
Scotney Wlk RM12 . . . . . . 155 C7
SCOT'S GREEN 31 F8
Scott Ave SG12 . . . . .8 B4
Scott CI EN11 . . . . .21 C6
Scott Ct SS2 . . . . 121 E5
Scottes La ▲ RM8 . . . . . . 134 D3
Scott Ho
Grays RM16 . . . . 172 C1
Romford RM11 . . . . 136 A5
Southend-on-S SS9 . . . . . 147 A7
Scott Rd RM16 . . . . 174 A2
Scotts CI RM12 . . . . 155 C7
Scotts Hall Cotts SS4 . . . . 126 D8
Scotts Hall Rd SS4 . . . . . . 126 D7
Scotts Hill CM0 . . . . .84 B4
Scotts Prim Sch
RM12 . . . . 155 C7
Scotts Wlk
Chelmsford CM1 . . . . .31 D5
Rayleigh SS6 . . . . 124 A2
Scraley Rd CM9 . . . . .37 E6
Scratton Rd
Southend-on-S SS1 . . . . . 166 F7
Stanford-le-H SS17 . . . . . 160 D2
Scrattons Terr IG11 . . . . . 153 D4
Scrub La SS2 . . . . 145 F3
Scrub Rise CM12 . . . . 118 E8
Scurvy Hall La CM3 . . . . . . .19 B8
Scylla CI CM9 . . . . .37 C6
Seaborough Rd RM16 . . . . 174 C3
Seabrink SS9 . . . . 166 A8
Seabrooke Rise RM17 . . . . 178 B8
Seabrook Gdns
Boreham CM3 . . . . .20 F1
Romford RM7 . . . . 135 A4
Seabrook Rd
Dagenham RM8 . . . . 134 D1
Great Baddow CM2 . . . . . . .55 A6
Seaburn Ct RM13 . . . . 154 E3
Sea-End Cvn Site
CM0 . . . . 106 D3
Seaforth Ave SS2 . . . . 148 C2
Seaforth CI RM1 . . . . 113 E3
Seaforth Ct RM11 . . . . .21 B4
Seaforth Gdns IG8 . . . . . . 110 C5
Seaforth Gr SS2 . . . . 148 D2
Seaforth Rd SS0 . . . . 166 D7
Seagard Ct SS3 . . . . 144 C5
Seagry Rd E11 . . . . 132 B8
Seagull CI IG11 . . . . 153 A2
Seagull Rd RM7 . . . . 173 A1
Seamans La CM4 . . . . .76 C2
Seamer Rd CM0 . . . . .84 A3
Seamore Ave SS7 . . . . 144 C6
Seamore CI SS7 . . . . 144 C6
Seamore Wlk SS7 . . . . . . 144 C6
Sea Reach SS9 . . . . 165 E8
Seaton Ave IG3 . . . . 152 F7
Seaview Ave SS16 . . . . . . 142 D3
Seaview Dr SS0 . . . . 150 C3
Sea View Par
Mayland CM3 . . . . .60 F2
St Lawrence CM0 . . . . .40 C1
Sea View Prom CM0 . . . . . .40 C1
Seaview Rd
Canvey Island SS8 . . . . . . 164 C2
Southend-on-S, Leigh-on-S
SS9 . . . . 165 E8
Southend-on-S, Shoeburyness
SS3 . . . . 168 E6
Seaview Terr SS7 . . . . 145 F3
Seawall Ho ▲ IG11 . . . . . . 152 C3
Sea Watch SS1 . . . . 167 B7
Seaway
Canvey Island SS8 . . . . . . 164 B2
St Lawrence CM0 . . . . .62 C8
Seax Ct SS15 . . . . 140 F7
Seax Way SS15 . . . . 140 F7
Sebastian Ave CM15 . . . . . .93 A3
Sebastian Ct ▲ IG11 . . . . . 152 F5
Sebert CI RM11 . . . . 119 C7
Second Ave
Basildon SS16 . . . . 140 E4
Basildon SS12 . . . . 118 F7
Canvey Island SS8 . . . . . . 163 E4
Chelmsford CM1 . . . . .32 B5
Dagenham RM10 . . . . 154 B3
Grays RM20 . . . . 177 A8
Harlow CM20 . . . . .23 F8
Hook End CM15 . . . . .72 C5
Hullbridge SS5 . . . . 124 E2
Ilford IG2 . . . . 133 D6
Ilford RM6 . . . . 134 C6
Southend-on-S SS0 . . . . . 166 B7
Stanford-le-H SS17 . . . . . 160 D3
Thundersley SS7 . . . . 145 A6
Wickford SS11 . . . . 122 A6
Seddon Ct ▲ RM7 . . . . . . 135 D7

Seddons Wlk SS5 . . . . 124 E6
Sedge Ct RM17 . . . . 178 E7
Sedgefield CI RM3 . . . . . . 114 F6
Sedgefield Cres RM3 . . . . 114 F6
Sedge Gn EN9 . . . . .21 E3
Sedgemoor SS3 . . . . 149 D1
Sedgemoor Dr RM10 . . . . 154 A8
Sedley Rise IG10 . . . . .88 F7
Seedbed Ctr SS3 . . . . 168 F7
Seedbed Ctr The
RM7 . . . . 135 E4
Seeleys CM17 . . . . .11 C4
Seetha Ho IG1 . . . . 133 D2
Sejant Ho RM17 . . . . 178 B8
Selborne Ave E12 . . . . 152 A8
Selborne Rd IG1 . . . . 133 A2
Selbourne Rd
Hockley SS5 . . . . 124 E6
South Benfleet SS7 . . . . . . 144 D6
Southend-on-S SS2 . . . . . 148 C3
Seldon CI SS0 . . . . 147 B3
Seldon Ct SS3 . . . . 168 H8
Selinas La RM8 . . . . 134 F4
Selsdon CI RM5 . . . . 113 C2
Selsdon Rd E11 . . . . 132 A4
Selwood Rd CM14 . . . . . . 115 F7
Selworthy CI
Billericay CM11 . . . . 119 C7
Wanstead IG1 . . . . 132 A6
Selwyn Ave
Chingford E4 . . . . 109 C4
Ilford IG3 . . . . 133 F5
Southend-on-S SS2 . . . . . 148 G2
Selwyn Rd
Southend-on-S SS2 . . . . . 148 C3
Tilbury RM18 . . . . 178 F5
Semper Rd RM16 . . . . 174 C4
Semples SS17 . . . . 160 F2
Serena Ct RM12 . . . . 136 C2
Sergeants Green La
EN9 . . . . .66 C6
Service Industry Bays
CM20 . . . . .10 F2
Seton Gdns RM9 . . . . 153 C5
Settle Rd RM3 . . . . 115 A6
Seven Acres SS11 . . . . 121 F8
Seven Arches Rd
CM14 . . . . 116 E7
Seven Ash Gn CM1 . . . . . . .32 C5
SEVEN KINGS 133 F3
Seven Kings High Sch
IG1 . . . . 133 D4
Seven Kings Rd IG3 . . . . . 133 F2
Seven Kings Sta IG3 . . . . . 133 E3
Sevenoaks Ct RM3 . . . . . . 114 C6
Seventh Ave
Canvey Island SS8 . . . . . . 163 E4
Chelmsford CM1 . . . . .32 B6
Seven Ways Par IG2 . . . . . 133 A6
Severn Ave RM18 . . . . 175 B3
Severn Dr CM1 . . . . 136 B8
Severn Dr RM14 . . . . 137 D5
Severn Rd RM15 . . . . 171 C7
Severns Field CM16 . . . . . .46 A2
Sewards End SS12 . . . . . . 121 E6
SEWARDSTONE 87 C8
SEWARDSTONEBURY 87 E4
Sewardstone Gdns E4 . . . . .87 B4
Sewardstone Rd
Chingford E4 . . . . .87 B5
Epping CM16 . . . . .65 D3
Waltham Abbey EN9 . . . . . .65 C3
Sewardstone St EN9 . . . . . .65 C5
Sewell Harris CI CM20 . . . . .11 C1
Sewell Ho SS13 . . . . 143 C5
Sexton CI RM13 . . . . 154 F4
Sexton Rd RM18 . . . . 178 F6
Seymer Rd RM1 . . . . 135 D8
Seymour CI
Basildon SS15 . . . . 141 D6
Loughton IG10 . . . . .88 E3
Seymour Ct E4 . . . . 109 F8
Seymour Dr CM2 . . . . 132 F3
Seymour Mews CM21 . . . . .11 E7
Seymour PI RM11 . . . . 136 D4
Seymour Rd
Chingford E4 . . . . .87 B1
Hadleigh SS7 . . . . 145 F3
Southend-on-S SS7 . . . . . 147 C1
Tilbury RM18 . . . . 178 F6
Seymours
Harlow CM19 . . . . .22 F5
Harlow CM19 . . . . .23 A5
Seymour's IG10 . . . . .89 A8
Seymour Wy SS12 . . . . . . 121 E6
Shafter Rd RM10 . . . . 154 C6
Shaftesbury IG10 . . . . .88 D6
Shaftesbury Ave SS1 . . . . 167 E6
Shaftesbury Ct RM14 . . . . 134 C4
Shaftesbury La DA1 . . . . . 176 B3
Shaftesbury Rd
Chingford E4 . . . . .87 D1
Epping CM16 . . . . .65 F7
Romford RM1 . . . . 135 F5
Shaftesburys The
IG11 . . . . 152 C3
Shaftsbury Ct SS13 . . . . . 143 B7
Shakespeare Ave
Basildon SS16 . . . . 141 A5
Billericay CM11 . . . . .97 D2
Rayleigh SS6 . . . . 124 A2
Southend-on-S SS0 . . . . . 147 E2
Tilbury RM18 . . . . 179 B6
Shakespeare Ct EN11 . . . . . .8 A2
Shakespeare Dr
Maldon CM9 . . . . .59 A8

Shakespeare Dr continued
Southend-on-S SS0 . . . . . **147** E2
Shakespeare Rd
Dartford DA1 . . . . **176** B3
8 Romford RM1 . . . . **135** F5
Shakespeare Sq IG6 . . . . . **111** C4
Shakeston Cl CM1 . . . . **53** B8
Shakletons CM5 . . . . **49** A3
Shalford **4** IG8 . . . . **110** C4
Shalford Lo CM1 . . . . **32** B8
Shalford Rd CM11 . . . . **97** D2
Shanklin Ave CM12 . . . . . . **97** A2
Shanklin Dr SS0 . . . . **147** B2
Shannon Ave SS6 . . . . **123** D1
Shannon Cl SS9 . . . . **146** E4
Shannon Way
Aveley RM15 . . . . **171** C6
Canvey Island SS8 . . . . . . **163** D3
Shardelow Ave CM1 . . . . . . **33** A8
Sharlands Cl SS11 . . . . . . **121** F8
Sharnbrook SS3 . . . . **149** D2
Sharpecroft CM19 . . . . **23** C8
Sharpington Cl CM2 . . . . . . **54** C3
Shaw Ave IG11 . . . . **153** E3
Shawbridge CM19 . . . . **23** C5
Shaw Cl
Hornchurch RM11 . . . . . . **136** B3
Wickford SS12 . . . . **121** D5
Shaw Cres
Brentwood CM13 . . . . **95** D5
Tilbury RM18 . . . . **179** C6
Shaw Gdns IG11 . . . . **153** E3
Shaw Prim Sch RM15 . . . . . **72** B7
Shaw The CM22 . . . . **3** A3
Shearers Way CM3 . . . . **20** F1
Shearwater Cl RM11 . . . . . **153** A2
Sheepcotes CM2 . . . . **33** B5
Sheepcotes La
Little Waltham CM3 . . . . . . **19** C7
Southminster CM0 . . . . **84** D5
Sheepcotes Rd RM6 . . . . . **134** E7
SHEERING **12** D8
Sheering CE Prim Sch
CM22 . . . . **12** D8
Sheering Ct SS6 . . . . **123** A3
Sheering Dr CM17 . . . . **11** E4
Sheering Lower Rd
CM21 . . . . **2** A2
Sheering Mill La CM21 . . . . . **1** F2
Sheering Rd CM17 . . . . . . **11** F4
Sheerwater Cl CM0 . . . . . **106** B5
Sheffield Dr RM3 . . . . **115** A5
Sheffield Gdns RM3 . . . . . **115** A5
Sheila Cl RM5 . . . . **113** B3
Sheila Rd RM5 . . . . **113** B3
Sheilings The RM11 . . . . . **136** F6
Sheldon Ave IG5 . . . . **111** B1
Sheldon Cl
Corringham SS17 . . . . **161** B4
Harlow CM17 . . . . **24** D8
Sheldon Ct CM13 . . . . **95** B3
Sheldon Ho E4 . . . . **109** E4
Sheldon Rd
Canvey Island SS8 . . . . . . **164** E3
Dagenham RM9 . . . . **153** E5
Sheldrick Link CM2 . . . . . . **33** B4
Shelford Cl RM16 . . . . **174** A8
Shellbeach Rd SS8 . . . . . **164** D2
SHELLEY **48** F5
Shelley Ave RM12 . . . . . . **135** F2
Shelley Cl
Chipping Ongar CM5 . . . . . **48** F5
Maldon CM9 . . . . **59** A8
Shelley Ct
Waltham Abbey EN9 . . . . . . **65** F6
8 Wanstead E11 . . . . . **132** A7
Shelley Gr IG10 . . . . **88** F5
Shelley Pl
Rayleigh SS6 . . . . **123** A3
Tilbury RM18 . . . . **179** B6
Shelley Prim Sch CM5 . . . . **48** F5
Shelley Rd
Brentwood CM13 . . . . **95** D2
Chelmsford CM2 . . . . **32** D2
Shelley Sq SS2 . . . . **148** B2
SHELLOW BOWELLS **28** F4
Shellow Rd CM5 . . . . **28** D4
Shelly Ave SS16 . . . . **141** A5
Shelsley Dr SS16 . . . . **141** C3
SHENFIELD **94** E2
Shenfield Cres CM15 . . . . **116** E7
Shenfield Ct CM18 . . . . **23** C5
Shenfield Gdns CM13 . . . . . **95** B3
Shenfield Gn CM15 . . . . **95** A2
Shenfield High Sch
CM15 . . . . **95** A4
Shenfield Pl CM15 . . . . **94** E2
Shenfield Rd
Brentwood CM15 . . . . **94** E1
Woodford IG8 . . . . **110** B3
Shenfield Sta CM15 . . . . . . **95** A2
Shenley Rd DA1 . . . . **176** A1
Shen Place Almshouses
CM15 . . . . **94** D1
Shenstone Gdns
Ilford IG2 . . . . **133** F6
Romford RM3 . . . . **114** C2
Shenval Ho CM20 . . . . **11** A4
Shenval Ind Est CM20 . . . . **11** A4
Shepard Cl SS9 . . . . **147** A6
Shepeshall SS15 . . . . **141** E5
Shephards Ct SS5 . . . . . . **124** E5
Shepherds Cl
Hadleigh SS7 . . . . **145** E4
Ilford RM6 . . . . **134** D7

Shepherds Hill RM3 . . . . . **115** B1
Shepherds Wlk SS7 . . . . . **145** E4
Shepley Mews EN3 . . . . **65** A2
Sheppard Dr CM2 . . . . **33** A4
Sheppards CM19 . . . . **22** F5
Sheppey Gdns RM9 . . . . . **153** C5
Sheppey Rd RM9 . . . . **153** C5
Sherards Ho CM19 . . . . **23** B6
Sherards Orch CM19 . . . . . **23** B6
Sherborne Gdns RM5 . . . . **113** A5
Sherborne Rd CM1 . . . . **32** D5
Sherborne St SS2 . . . . . . **147** E6
Sherbourne Dr SS13 . . . . . **121** A1
Sherbourne Gdns
SS2 . . . . **147** F6
Sheredan Rd E4 . . . . **109** E5
Sheree Rd IG2 . . . . **133** A6
Sherfield Rd RM17 . . . . . . **178** B8
Sheridan Ave SS7 . . . . . . **145** B3
Sheridan Cl
Rayleigh SS6 . . . . **123** F2
Romford RM3 . . . . **114** C3
Sheridan Ct DA1 . . . . **176** A3
Sheridan Mews **8**
E11 . . . . **132** B5
Sheridan Rd DA17 . . . . . . **169** A2
Sheringham Ave
Little Ilford E12 . . . . **152** A7
Romford RM7 . . . . **135** C5
Sheringham Cl SS17 . . . . . **160** E3
Sheringham Dr IG11 . . . . . **153** A7
Sheriton Sq SS3 . . . . **123** D4
Sherman Gdns RM6 . . . . . **134** C5
Shernbroke Rd EN9 . . . . . . **65** F5
Sherwood Ho **1**
E18 . . . . **132** A7
Sherry Hill SS11 . . . . **152** D5
Sherry Way SS7 . . . . **145** E6
Sherwood RM16 . . . . **172** E5
Sherwood Ave E18 . . . . . . **132** B8
Sherwood Cl SS16 . . . . . . **141** A4
Sherwood Cres SS7 . . . . . **145** E4
Sherwood Dr CM1 . . . . **31** D1
Sherwood Gdns IG11 . . . . **152** D5
Sherwood Ho CM18 . . . . . . **23** F6
Sherwood Rd IG6 . . . . **133** D7
Sherwood Way SS2 . . . . . **148** E2
Shevon Way CM14 . . . . . . **115** F6
Shilliber Wlk IG7 . . . . **111** F7
Shillingstone SS3 . . . . . . **149** D1
Shingle Ct EN9 . . . . **66** A6
Ship Cotts CM2 . . . . **76** B6
Ship La RM15 . . . . **171** E4
Ship Rd
Burnham-on-C CM0 . . . . . **106** C4
West Hanningfield CM2 . . . **76** C5
Shipton Cl RM8 . . . . **134** D1
Shipwrights Cl SS7 . . . . . **145** B1
Shipwrights Dr SS7 . . . . . **145** B3
Shirebourn Vale CM3 . . . . **101** D6
Shire Cl
Billericay CM11 . . . . **97** D5
Chelmsford CM1 . . . . **32** F7
Shirley Ct
Ilford IG2 . . . . **133** D1
Loughton IG10 . . . . **88** F7
Shirley Gdns
Barking IG11 . . . . **152** E6
Basildon SS13 . . . . **143** C8
Hornchurch RM12 . . . . . . **136** C2
Shirley Lo SS9 . . . . **146** E5
Shirley Rd SS9 . . . . **146** E5
Shoebury Ave SS3 . . . . . . **168** F7
Shoebury Common Rd
SS3 . . . . **168** C5
SHOEBURYNESS **168** E5
Shoeburyness High Sch
SS3 . . . . **168** D7
Shoeburyness Sta
SS3 . . . . **168** F7
Shoebury Rd
Great Wakering SS3 . . . . . **150** C3
Southend-on-S SS1 . . . . . **149** B1
Shoe La SS0 . . . . **147** D1
Shonks Mill Rd RM4 . . . . . . **70** C1
Shooters Dr EN9 . . . . **21** E1
Shopland Hall Rd
SS4 . . . . **148** D6
Shopland Rd SS4 . . . . . . **148** C7
Shop Row CM5 . . . . **128** A5
Shorefield SS7 . . . . **144** B3
Shorefield Gdns SS0 . . . . **166** E7
Shorefield Rd SS0 . . . . . . **166** D7
Shore Point IG9 . . . . **110** B8
Shore Rd CM0 . . . . **106** C4
Shore The DA11 . . . . **178** C2
Short Acre SS14 . . . . **142** B6
Shortcroft CM15 . . . . **71** F2
Shortcrofts Rd RM9 . . . . . **153** F6
Shorter Ave CM15 . . . . **94** F2
Short La CM11 . . . . **98** C4
Shortlands SS14 . . . . **142** B6
Shortlands Ave CM5 . . . . . . **48** F5
Short Rd
Canvey Island SS8 . . . . . . **164** B4
Hadleigh SS7 . . . . **145** D2
Short St SS2 . . . . **148** A1
Shorwell Ct **18** RM19 . . . . **171** B1
SHOTGATE **122** B6
Shrewsbury Cl SS16 . . . . . **140** F5
Shrewsbury Dr SS7 . . . . . **144** D7
Shropshire Ct CM2 . . . . **54** F5
Shrubberies The
Chigwell IG7 . . . . **111** C5
Ilford IG2 . . . . **133** F6
Woodford E18 . . . . **110** A1
Writtle CM1 . . . . **52** F8
Shrubbery Cl SS15 . . . . . . **141** D8

Shrubbery The
Upminster RM14 . . . . **137** C1
7 Wanstead E11 . . . . . **132** B6
Shrublands Cl
Chelmsford CM2 . . . . **32** C2
Chigwell IG7 . . . . **111** C4
Sibley Row EN9 . . . . **22** E2
Sibneys Gn CM18 . . . . **23** A4
Siddons Cl SS17 . . . . **175** A3
Sidings The IG10 . . . . **88** E3
Sidmouth Ave SS0 . . . . . . **147** D5
Sidmouth Rd CM1 . . . . **32** E6
Sidney Elson Way E6 . . . . **152** A3
Sidney Pl CM11 . . . . **33** A7
Sidney Rd
Theydon Bois CM16 . . . . . . **67** D3
Wanstead E7 . . . . **132** A1
Sidwell Ave SS7 . . . . **144** E1
Sidwell Chase SS7 . . . . . **144** E1
Sidwell La SS7 . . . . **144** E1
Sidwell Pk SS7 . . . . **144** E1
Sierra Dr RM10 . . . . **154** B3
Silchester Cnr SS3 . . . . . **149** B3
Silva Island Way SS12 . . . **121** F5
Silver Birch Ave CM16 . . . . **46** E4
Silver Birches CM13 . . . . . . **95** A1
Silver Birch Lo SS4 . . . . . **125** E2
Silver Birch Mews
SS6 . . . . **111** C4
Silverdale
Rayleigh SS6 . . . . **145** E8
Stanford-le-H SS17 . . . . . **160** D4
Thundersley SS7 . . . . **144** F7
Silverdale Ave
Ilford IG3 . . . . **133** F6
Southend-on-S SS0 . . . . . **147** E2
Silverdale Dr RM12 . . . . . **155** B7
Silverdale E SS17 . . . . . . **160** D4
Silverdale Par IG3 . . . . . . **133** F6
Silverdale Rd E4 . . . . **109** D4
Silver La CM5 . . . . **29** A2
Silverlink Ct SS6 . . . . **123** D4
Silverlocke Rd RM17 . . . . **178** D8
Silvermead **7** E18 . . . . . **110** A2
Silvermere Ave RM5 . . . . . **113** B4
Silverpoint Marine
SS8 . . . . **165** A3
Silver Rd CM0 . . . . **106** C4
Silvers IG9 . . . . **88** C1
Silversea Dr SS0 . . . . **147** B2
Silver Spring Cl DA8 . . . . . **169** B1
Silver St
Abridge RM4 . . . . **90** B6
Maldon CM9 . . . . **36** F3
Waltham Abbey EN9 . . . . . . **65** C6
Silverthorn Cl SS4 . . . . . . **125** D4
Silverthorne SS8 . . . . **163** F3
Silverthorn Gdns E4 . . . . **109** A8
Silvertown Ave SS17 . . . . **160** D2
Silvertree Cl SS5 . . . . . . **124** B6
Silver Way
Romford RM7 . . . . **135** B8
1 Wickford SS11 . . . . **121** C4
Silverwood Cl
Grays RM16 . . . . **173** A6
Harlow CM16 . . . . **22** E3
Silvester Way CM2 . . . . . . **54** C4
Simmonds La CM7 . . . . **59** A1
Simmonds Way CM3 . . . . . **56** F8
Simmons Dr RM8 . . . . **134** E1
Simmons La E4 . . . . **109** D8
Simmons Rd RM15 . . . . . . **173** A5
Simon Campion Ct
CM16 . . . . **46** A1
Simplicity La **6** CM17 . . . . **11** D1
Simpson Rd RM13 . . . . . . **154** F6
Sims Cl RM1 . . . . **135** F7
Sinclair Rd E4 . . . . **109** A5
Sinclair Wlk SS12 . . . . . . **121** D5
Singleton Cl RM12 . . . . . . **154** F8
Singleton Rd RM9 . . . . . . **153** F7
Sippetts Cr IG1 . . . . **133** D3
Sirdar Rd SS5 . . . . **145** D8
Sir Francis Way CM14 . . . **116** B8
Sir George Monoux Sixth
Form Coll E17 . . . . **109** B1
Sir Walter Raleigh Dr
CM4 . . . . **74** B3
Sir W Petre Almshouses
CM4 . . . . **74** B3
Sisley Rd IG11 . . . . **152** F4
Siviter Way RM10 . . . . . . **154** B5
Sixpenny Ct **6** IG11 . . . . **152** C6
Sixth Ave
Canvey Island SS8 . . . . . . **163** E4
Chelmsford CM1 . . . . **32** B6
Thundersley SS7 . . . . **145** A5
Skarnings Ct EN9 . . . . **66** A6
Skeale's Ct RM12 . . . . . . **136** C1
Skelter Stps **9** SS1 . . . . **167** C2
Skerry Rise CM1 . . . . **32** B7
Skinner's La CM7 . . . . **54** B3
Skipper Ct **6** IG11 . . . . . **152** C6
Skippers Ct **4** DA9 . . . . **177** B2
Skipsey Ave E6 . . . . **152** A1
Skreens Ct CM11 . . . . **31** D4
Skylark Cl CM11 . . . . **97** C1
Skylark Wlk SS7 . . . . **54** B5
Sky Peals Rd IG8 . . . . . . **109** D3
Slacksbury Hatch
CM19 . . . . **23** B8
Slade End IG8 . . . . **67** F3
Slade's La CM2 . . . . **54** A3
Slades The SS16 . . . . **142** E3
Slaney Rd RM1 . . . . **135** E6
Sleepers Farm Rd
RM16 . . . . **174** B4

Slewins Cl RM11 . . . . **136** C6
Slewins La RM11 . . . . **136** C6
Slipe La EN10 . . . . **43** A7
Sloane Mews SS12 . . . . **96** F5
Sloan Ho RM10 . . . . **154** B5
Slough La CM3 . . . . **57** D3
Slough Rd
Danbury CM3 . . . . **57** C3
High Easter CM1 . . . . **6** B2
Smallgains Ave SS8 . . . . . **164** E4
Small Gains La CM4 . . . . . . **97** E8
Smallholdings SS2 . . . . . . **147** D6
Smarden Cl DA17 . . . . **169** A1
Smart Cl RM3 . . . . **114** B2
Smart's La IG10 . . . . **88** E5
Smartt Ave SS8 . . . . **164** E4
Smeaton Cl EN9 . . . . **65** E7
Smeaton Rd
Chigwell IG8 . . . . **110** F5
Holdbrook EN3 . . . . **65** A2
Smither's Chase SS2 . . . . **148** B5
Smithers Dr CM2 . . . . **55** A6
Smith's Ave CM3 . . . . **83** A8
Smiths Ct CM16 . . . . **46** C6
Smith St SS3 . . . . **168** F6
Smithy The CM21 . . . . **1** E3
Smollett Pl SS12 . . . . **121** D4
Smugglers Wlk **3**
DA9 . . . . **177** B2
Smyatts Cl CM0 . . . . **84** D3
Smythe Cl CM11 . . . . **97** D5
Smythe Rd CM11 . . . . **97** D5
Smythe Row CM3 . . . . **80** C4
Snakes Hill CM14 . . . . **93** C6
Snakes La SS2 . . . . **147** A6
Snakes La E IG8 . . . . **110** C4
Snakes La W IG8 . . . . **110** B4
SNARESBROOK **132** A7
Snaresbrook Hall **12**
E18 . . . . **132** A8
Snaresbrook Prim Sch
E18 . . . . **132** A7
Snaresbrook Sta E11 . . . . **132** A6
Snelling Gr CM2 . . . . **54** F6
Snoreham Gdns CM3 . . . . . **82** B5
Snowden Hill DA11 . . . . . **178** A2
Snowdon Ct **5** RM4 . . . . . **21** A2
Snovdonia Cl SS13 . . . . . **143** C8
Snowdrop Cl CM1 . . . . **32** E7
Snowdrop Path RM3 . . . . **114** D3
Soames Mead CM15 . . . . . . **72** A6
Soane St SS13 . . . . **121** B1
Softwater La SS7 . . . . **145** E3
Solar Ct RM12 . . . . **136** C2
Solid La CM15 . . . . **93** F8
Solway RM18 . . . . **175** C3
Somerby Cl EN10 . . . . **21** A2
Somerby Rd IG11 . . . . **152** D5
Somercotes SS15 . . . . . . **141** C5
Somercotes Ct SS15 . . . . **141** C5
Somerdean **2** SS13 . . . . **143** C6
Somersby Gdns IG4 . . . . . **132** F6
Somerset Ave
Rochford SS4 . . . . **125** C3
Southend-on-S SS0 . . . . . **147** B4
Somerset Cl IG8 . . . . **110** A2
Somerset Cres SS3 . . . . . **147** B4
Somerset Ct **9** IG9 . . . . **110** C8
Somerset Gdns
Basildon SS13 . . . . **143** B6
Hornchurch RM11 . . . . . . **137** A3
Somerset Pl CM1 . . . . **32** A7
Somerset Rd
Basildon SS16 . . . . **141** B6
Hornchurch RM11 . . . . . . **136** E1
Linford SS17 . . . . **175** A4
Somers Heath Prim Sch
RM15 . . . . **172** A6
Somerton Ave SS0 . . . . . . **147** B5
Somerville Gdns SS9 . . . . **165** F8
Somerville Rd RM6 . . . . . **134** C6
Somnes Ave SS8 . . . . **163** D4
Sonning Way SS3 . . . . . . **149** D1
Sonters Down CM3 . . . . . **100** C5
Soper Mews **8** EN3 . . . . . **65** A1
Soper Sq **2** CM17 . . . . . . **11** C1
Sopwith Cres SS11 . . . . . **122** B5
Sorrel Ct RM17 . . . . **178** D8
Sorrell Cl
Goldhanger CM9 . . . . **38** E7
Little Waltham CM3 . . . . . . **19** B6
Sorrells The SS17 . . . . . . **160** F3
Sorrels The SS7 . . . . **144** D7
Sorrel Wlk RM1 . . . . **135** F8
Southall Ho **4** RM3 . . . . . **114** A4
Southall Way CM14 . . . . . **115** F6
South Ave
Basildon SS16 . . . . **160** B7
Chingford E4 . . . . **87** C2
Hullbridge SS5 . . . . **101** E1
Southend-on-S SS3 . . . . . **148** C1
South Beech Ave
SS4 . . . . **121** D7
SOUTH BENFLEET **144** E3
South Benfleet
Foundation Prim Sch
SS7 . . . . **144** D2
South Block CM21 . . . . **1** F2
Southborough Dr
SS0 . . . . **147** B2
Southborough Rd CM2 . . . . **54** A8
South Boundary Rd
E12 . . . . **132** F1
Southbourne Gdns
Ilford IG1 . . . . **152** C2
Southend-on-S SS0 . . . . . **147** B4
Southbourne Gr
Hockley SS5 . . . . **125** A6

Southbourne Gr continue
Southend-on-S SS0 . . . . .
Wickford SS12 . . . .
Southbrook CM21 . . . .
Southbury Cl RM12 . . . . . .
Southbury Ct **8** RM1 . . . .
South Charlton Mead
EN11 . . . .
SOUTHCHURCH
Southchurch Ave
Southend-on-S,
Shoeburyness SS3 . . . .
Southend-on-S SS1 . . . . .
Southchurch Bvd SS2 . . . .
Southchurch Hall Cl
SS1 . . . .
Southchurch Hall Mus
SS1 . . . .
Southchurch Rd SS1. .
South Cl RM10 . . . .
Southcliff SS7 . . . .
South Colne SS16 . . . .
Southcote Cres SS14. .
Southcote Row **2**
SS14. . . . .
Southcote Sq SS14 . . . . . .
South Cres CM2 . . . .
South Crockerford
SS16. . . . .
South Cross Rd IG6. .
Southdale IG7 . . . .
Southdown Cres IG2. .
Southdown Rd RM11. .
South Dr
Brentwood CM14 . . . . . .
Romford RM2 . . . .
Wanstead E12 . . . .
South East Essex Coll
Arts & Tech
Southend-on-S SS1 . . . .
Southend-on-S SS2 . . . .
South East Essex Sixtl
Form Coll SS7 . . . .
Southend Arterial Rd
Basildon SS12, SS6,
SS7 . . . .
Basildon, Steeple View **6**
SS7 . . . .
Great Warley CM13,
RM14 . . . .
Rayleigh SS6 . . . .
Romford RM2 . . . .
Upminster RM14,
RM11 . . . .
West Horndon CM13 . . . .
Southend Central Sta
SS1 . . . .
Southend East
(Southchurch Village
Boys SS0 . . . .
Southend High Sch fc
Girls SS2 . . . .
Southend High Sch fc
Boys SS0 . . . .
Southend Ho SS17. .
Southend La EN9 . . . .
SOUTHEND-ON-S
Southend-on-Sea Ce
Mus & Planetarium
SS2 . . . .
Southend-on-Sea Sea
Ctr* SS1 . . . .
Southend-on-Sea
(Victoria) Sta SS2 . .
Southend Pier Mus*
SS1 . . . .
Southend Pier Rlwy*
SS1 . . . .
Southend Rd
Billericay CM11 . . . .
Grays RM17. . . . .
Great Baddow CM2 . . . .
Great Wakering SS3 . . . .
Hockley SS5. . . . .
Howe Green CM2 . . . . . .
Rochford SS4. . . . .
Stanford-le-H SS17 . . . .
Wallend E12 . . . .
Wickford SS11 . . . .
Woodford IG8 . . . .
Woodham Mortimer
CM9 . . . .
South End Rd RM12,
RM13 . . . .
Southend Rd (North
Circular Rd) E17,
E18 . . . .
Souther Cross CM1 . .
Souther Cross Cotts
CM1 . . . .
Souther Cross Rd CM1
Southern Dr
Loughton IG10. . . . .
South Woodham Ferrers
CM3 . . . .
Southernhay
Basildon SS14 . . . .
Loughton IG10. . . . .
Southern La RM19 . . . .
Southern Terr **2** EN11
Southern Way
Harlow CM19. . . . .
Romford RM7 . . . .
Southey Cl CM9 . . . .
Southey Wlk RM18 . . . .
Southfalls Rd SS8 . . . .

FAMBRIDGE 103 B4
ld Chase
.................118 E1
ld Cl SS7......145 E5
ld Dr SS7 .....145 E5
ld Rd EN11......21 A7
IELDS
...............140 F7
l St Mary 174 D7
ld Way CM0 .....84 C4
et Rd DA10......177 F1
ate
CM20...........23 D8
RM19 ....171 C2
e Ho 🏛
.............142 A6
e Mews SS3 ...150 B3
te Rd E12 .....132 E1
REEN 119 D7
een Jun & Inf
M11.............119 C7
nnels 🏛
..............142 B6
all Dr RM13....170 B8
ANNINGFIELD
................99 C8
nningfield Rd
1, CM1.........99 C8
nningfield Way
...............99 D3
l
SS16, SS17 ....160 A7
on t H SS17....160 A3
I Cl CM3 ......56 D6
l Cres SS17 ....160 A3
ORNCHURCH
...............154 F3
use Chase
..............59 C7
nt Ave DA11 ...178 C1
ds Chase CM2 ...55 E2
ds Rd CM11....120 E6
d Terr 🏛
................171 B1
yne SS14 .....143 A5
ws SS2 ......148 C1
NSTER
.............84 E4
ster CE Prim Sch
................84 D4
ster Rd
CM3...........83 C4
on CM0.........85 A7
on-C CM0.....106 B8
ce CM0 ....62 F3
ster Sta CM0 ...84 E4
CKENDON 172 C7
nance Rd
...............65 A2

land SS8.......164 E2
endon RM15 ...172 C8
k Bsns Ctr
................133 E2
k Cres IG1....133 E1
k Dr
s11............152 E8
k Prim Sch
................133 E1
M20............11 A4
abbey EN9 .....65 C6
nt SS0 ....147 C4
nrose Hill
................31 F3

/ange SS17 ...142 C1
CM11..........120 D5
RM6...........134 E5
M20............11 A4
..............134 C6
endon RM15 ...172 C7
idence IG3 ...134 B6
ge CM1.........97 C2
ng SS14........142 E6
Ave SS9 .....146 D1
Ho 🏛 RM43...114 D5

on S CM0 ....42 A2
CM14...........116 C8
ham CM3 ......18 E7
M13 ....154 D3
S4............135 C5
M1............135 E6
M1............135 F5
Abbotts SG12 ....8 C4
CM0............63 E3
I' SS1 ....167 B3
FFORD 172 E1
I' RM16.......174 D8
Ave RM18......179 A6
Cl CM3 ....101 D8
I' Cl SS6 .....145 F8
I' Cres IG2...133 B5
Dr
on-S SS0 ......147 C2
C18...........132 B8
ham RM14 .....137 B1
Hts RM20 .....177 C8
Rd
S16 ....142 E5
3..............56 D6
5..............124 F7
Rd
..............177 C8

South View Rd *continued*
Loughton IG10..........88 F3
Rettendon CM3 ....100 C5
South Benfleet SS7 ... 144 C3
Southview Terr CM3 .....56 D6
Southwalters SS8.......163 F4
Southview Path SS14...142 F7
South Wash Rd SS15....119 E1
Southway SS16.........141 D2
South Way RM19 ....171 E3
SOUTH WEALD 115 E8
South Weald Dr EN9 ....65 D6
South Weald Rd
CM14 ....116 A7
Southwell Cl RM16 ....172 C1
Southwell Link SS15 ...141 D5
Southwell Rd SS7 .....144 E4
Southwick Gdns SS8....163 F3
Southwick Rd SS8......163 F3
South Wlk SS14 ....142 B5
Southwold Cres SS7....144 C5
Southwold Dr IG11 ....153 A7
Southwood Chase
CM3...............57 A4
Southwood Ct
Basildon SS14 ......142 D8
Billericay CM11 ......119 C7
South Woodford Sta
E18................110 B1
Southwood Gdns
Ilford IG2 ....133 B7
Rayleigh SS9 ....146 B8
SOUTH WOODHAM
FERRERS 101 E8
South Woodham Ferrers
Sta CM3 ....101 C8
Southwood Prim Sch
RM9 ....153 E8
Sovereign Cl SS4 .....125 E2
Sovereign Ct
🏛 Brentwood CM14 ...116 C7
Harlow CM19..........23 B5
Southend-on-S, Leigh-on-S
SS9................146 E2
Southend-on-S, Shoeburyness
SS3...............168 E7
Sovereign Ho RM13....155 B2
Sovereign Mews SS0...166 E8
Sovereign Pk SS14....120 E1
Sovereign Rd IG11....153 C2
Sovereign Terr 🏛 CM1...31 F7
Sowrey Ave RM13......155 A6
Spa Cl SS5 ....124 E6
Spa Dr SS5 ....124 E6
Spacelreaze Hill IG10..88 F5
Sparkbridge 🏛 SS15...141 A6
Sparks Cl RM8........134 D2
Spar La CM3 ....58 C3
Sparrow Ct E4........109 C4
Sparrow Gn RM10 .....135 B1
Sparrows CI CM1.......52 A5
Sparrows Herne SS16...142 B4
Sparrow's La
Hatfield Heath CM22........3 F1
White Roothing or White
Roding CM17, CM22.......13 E6
Spearhead Ho IG11....152 E4
Spearpoint Gdns IG2...133 F7
Spectrum Twr 🏛 IG1...133 C2
Speedwell Ct RM17 ....178 E7
SPELLBROOK 1 F8
Spellbrook Cl SG12 ....121 F6
Spellbrook La E CM22.....1 F8
Spellbrook La W SM21....1 F7
Spellbrook Prim Sch
SG13..................1 F7
Spells Ct CM0..........84 D4
Spencer Cl
Billericay CM12 ....96 F5
Epping CM16 ....46 B2
Maldon CM9...........59 A8
Woodford IG8 ....110 C5
Spencer Ct
Hornchurch RM12 .....136 A1
South Woodham Ferrers
CM3 ....101 E7
Spencer Gdns SS4.....125 E5
Spencer Ho SS0 ....147 A1
Spencer Rd
Chingford E17 ....109 C1
Ilford IG3 ....133 F3
Rainham RM13 ....154 D3
South Benfleet SS7....144 D6
Spencers SS5 ....124 F4
Spencers Croft SS12...121 C7
Spencer Wlk RM18 ....179 B6
Spenders Cl SS14.....142 D8
Spendow Gn CM1........31 D7
Spenser Cres RM14 ...137 C4
Speyside Wlk 🏛 SS12..121 E5
Spey Way RM1 ....113 E3
Spilsby Rd RM3........114 E3
Spindle Beams SS4...125 F1

Spindles RM18 ....179 A7
Spingate Cl RM12.....155 D7
Spinnaker Cl IG11 ....153 B2
Spinnaker Dr CM9 ......37 E3
Spinnakers The SS7....144 B4
Spinnaker The CM3 ....101 E5
Spinney Cl
Rainham RM13 ....154 E3
Wickford SS11.......121 F7
Spinney Ct CM21 ....1 E2
Spinney Gdns RM9......153 E7
Spinney Jun & Inf Schs
CM20...............11 A1
Spinneys The
Hockley SS5.........124 D5
Rayleigh SS6 ....124 A1
Southend-on-S SS9 ...146 F7
Spinney The
Billericay CM12 ......97 B4
Brentwood CM13......95 C3
Chipping Ongar CM5 ...48 F1
🏛 Harlow CM20........11 A1
Loughton IG10........89 B5
Orsett RM16 ....159 A1
Spinneywood SS15 ....141 A8
Spinning Wheel Mead
CM18................24 A5
Spire Green Ctr CM19...22 E7
Spire Rd SS15........141 C7
Spires The
Brentwood CM14 .....116 D8
Great Baddow CM2 .....54 F6
SPITALBROOK 21 B4
Spital La CM14 ....115 F6
Spital Rd
Maldon CM9..........36 F2
Maldon CM9..........58 D7
Sporehams La
Danbury CM3.........56 C4
Howe Green CM2, CM3...55 F4
Sporhams SS16.......141 F4
Sports Wlk CM2 ....63 E4
Spratt Hall Rd E11....132 A5
Spread Eagle Pl 🏛
CM4...............74 C4
Spriggs Ct CM16.......46 A2
Spriggs La CM4.......51 A2
Spriggs Oak CM16 .....46 A2
Springbank Ave
RM12 ....155 C7
Springbok Ho CM2 .....54 F5
Spring Cl
Dagenham RM8 ......134 D3
Little Baddow CM3 ....34 D5
Spring Ct
Southend-on-S SS0 ...147 D2
🏛 Wanstead E18 ......132 B8
Spring Elms La CM3....34 F3
Springfarm Cl RM13 ...155 C2
SPRINGFIELD 32 E6
Springfield
Brentwood CM15......94 C1
Epping CM16 ....67 F7
Hadleigh SS7 ....145 D4
Springfield Ave CM13...95 E2
Springfield Cl CM5 ....48 F5
Springfield Cotts CM9...37 B3
Springfield Dr
🏛 Ilford IG2 ....152 B7
Rayleigh SS6 ....123 A4
Upminster RM14 .....137 B1
Springfield Gn CM1.....32 E4
Springfield Ind Est
CM0 ....106 A5
Springfield Lyons App
CM0 ....106 A6
Springfield Nursery Sch
CM0 ....106 A6
Springfield Park Ave
CM2 ....32 E2
Springfield Park Hill
CM2 ....32 D2
Springfield Park La
CM2 ....32 D2
Springfield Park Rd
CM2 ....32 E2
Springfield Pl CM1.....32 E2
Springfield Rd
Billericay CM12 ......97 B5
Canvey Island SS8...164 F3
Chelmsford CM2......32 E4
Chingford E4..........87 E2
Grays RM16........173 E4
Wickford SS11.......121 F6
Stambridge Hme Farm
SS4 ....101 C5
Stambridge Rd
RM7 ....135 C5
Stamford Ave
Horchurch RM12 .....136 A1
Rayleigh SS6 ....123 C2
Romford RM7 ....135 C5

Springhead Rd DA11... 178 D1
Spring Hills CM20 ......10 B1
Spring Hills Twr CM20....10 A1
Springhouse La SS12 ...161 A2
Springhouse Rd SS17 ...160 F4
Spring La CM9 ....37 B4
Springleigh Pl SS0 ...147 D2
Spring Mews CM21........1 E2
Spring Pl 🏛 IG11.....152 C3
Spring Pond Cl CM2.....54 E8
Spring Pond Mdw
CM15 ....72 C4
Springpond Rd RM9 ...153 E7
Spring Rise CM2........54 C2
Spring Vale DA9 ......177 C1
Springway SS9 ....59 C4
Springwater Gr SS9 ...146 C7
Springwater Gr SS9 ...146 C7
Springwater Rd SS9 ...146 C8
Springwell Cl SG12 ......8 C3
Springwood Way
RM1 ....136 A6
Spruce Cl SS15 ....119 C1
Spruce Dr CM18........23 E3
Spruce Hills Rd E17 ...109 C1
Sprundel Ave SS8 .....164 D2
Spur Cl RM4...........90 B6
Spurgate CM13 ....95 B1
Spurgeon Cl 🏛 RM17 ...178 C8
Spurgeon Rd RM9 .....153 F6
Spurling Wks EN11 .....21 C7
Spur Rd IG11.........152 C2
Spurway Par 🏛 IG2...132 F6
Squadrons App RM12 ...155 D6
Square St 🏛 CM17......11 C1
Square The
🏛 Brentwood CM14 ...116 C8
Heybridge CM9 ....37 A5
Horndon on t H SS17...159 F3
Ilford IG1 ....133 A4
Sawbridgeworth CM21 ...1 E2
Stock CM4 ....75 E2
Tillingham CM0 ....63 E4
Woodford IG8 ....110 A5
Squires Ct EN11 ....21 A5
Squire St SS3 ....168 D7
Squirrels Cl SS16 .....31 F5
Squirrels Ct SS16.....141 B3
Squirrel's Chase
RM16 ....174 A4
Squirrels Ct CM2 .....136 C7
Squirrel's Heath Ave
RM6 ....136 B8
Squirrels Heath Jun Sch
RM2 ....136 B8
Squirrels Heath La RM11,
RM2 ....136 D7
Squirrels Heath Rd
RM11 ....114 F1
Squirrel's La IG10 ....110 D7
Stablecroft CM1 ....32 E8
Stable Mews SS2 .....147 F2
Stables The
Buckhurst Hill IG9 .....88 C2
Sawbridgeworth CM21 ...2 B1
Stacey Dr SS16........141 C2
Stacey's Mount CM11...120 C5
Stackfield CM20 ....11 A4
Staddies CM22 ....2 B8
Stadium Rd SS2 ......148 A1
Stadium Trad Est
SS7...............145 C7
Stadium Way
Harlow CM19..........9 F1
Thunderlsley SS7 ....145 C4
Staffa Cl SS12.......121 F5
Stafford Ave RM11 ....156 D8
Stafford Cl
Grays RM16........172 C2
Greenhithe DA9 .....176 F2
Linford SS17 ....175 A3
Stafford Cl EN10......21 A3
Stafford Dr SS16 .....140 F4
Stafford Ho RM10 .....21 A3
Stafford Rd
RM11 ....136 D8
Stafford WIk SS3 ....164 A5
Stagden Cross SS14...142 D8
Stagden Cross Villas
CM1 ....6 E2
Staggart Gn CM2......110 F4
Stag Hts IG9 ....110 B8
Stains Hall Rd CM0....58 B4
Stainforth Rd IG2 ....133 D5
Stairs Rd SS3 ....150 F4
Stalham Way 🏛 RM13...111 B2
Stambridge St CM0 .....28 A7
Standard Ave CM17......11 E4
Standard Rd DA17......169 A1
Standen
Horndon RM12 ....155 B8
Stanhope Rd
Rayleigh SS6 ....123 C2
Romford RM7 ....135 C5

Staneway SS16 ....141 D3
Stanfield Rd SS2 .....148 A1
Stanfields Ct CM20 .....10 E1
Stanford Cl
Romford RM7 ....135 B5
Woodford IG8 ....110 E5
Stanford Gdns
...................66 A6
Stanford Gdns RM15...171 E5
Stanford Hall 🏛 SS17...160 F3
Stanford Ho
🏛 Barking IG11 .....153 B3
East Tilbury RM18 ....175 B2
STANFORD-LE-H 160 E1
Stanford-Le-Hope By-
Pass
Basildon SS16, SS17 ...142 B1
Orsett RM16 ....174 D8
Stanford-le-H SS17 ...160 D4
Stanford-le-Hope Prim
Sch SS17 ....160 D1
Stanford-le-Hope Sta
...................160 C1
Stanford Marshes Nature
Reserve* SS17......175 C7
Stanford Rd
Canvey Island SS8....164 A3
Harlow CM19.........21 C7
Orsett SS17, RM16 ...174 E8
Stanford-le-H SS17 ...160 B1
STANFORD RIVERS 70 C6
Stanford Rivers Rd
CM5 ....71 A8
Stanhope Gdns
🏛 Dagenham RM8 ....134 F1
Redbridge IG1 ....132 F3
Stanhope Rd
Dagenham RM8 ......134 F1
Rainham RM13 ......155 A3
Swanscombe DA10 ....177 F1
Stanhope Rd SS11 ....167 C8
Stanley Ave
Barking IG11 ....152 F3
Dagenham RM8 ......134 F3
Dagenham RM6 ......136 A7
Stanley Cl
Greenhithe DA9......176 E2
Hornchurch RM12 .....136 C2
Stanley Pl CM5 ....49 A2
Stanley Rd
Bulphan RM14 ....158 F8
Canvey Island SS8....164 D4
Chingford E4 ....87 D1
Grays RM17.........178 B6
Ilford IG1 ....133 D2
Rochford SS4 ....125 C7
South Benfleet SS7 ...144 D6
Southend-on-S SS1 ...167 B7
Stanley Rd N RM13 ...154 E4
Stanley Rd S RM13...154 F3
Stanley Rise 32 F3
Stanley Terr CM1......97 A1
Stanmore Rd
Belvedere DA17 ......169 C2
Wickford SS11.......122 B6
Stanmore Way IG10 .....89 A8
Stannetts SS15 ......141 B8
Stansfield Ct SS7....144 B7
Stansfield Rd SS7....144 B7
Stansgate Rd
Dagenham RM10 .....135 A1
Steeple CM0 ....61 F5
STANSTEAD ABBOTTS 8 E4
Stanstead Dr EN11.....21 B8
Stanstead Rd
Hoddesdon EN11........8 B1
Stansted CM24 ......132 B6
Stansted Cl
Billericay CM11 ......97 D2
Chelmsford CM1 ......31 E1
Stanton Ct 🏛 RM10...154 A6
Stanton Gate RM7 ....135 D6
Stantons CM20 ....10 B1
Stanway Cl 🏛 IG7....111 E5
Stanway Rd
Southend-on-S SS7 ...144 C5
Waltham Abbey EN9 ...66 A6
Stanwyck Dr IG7......161 C6
Stanwyck Gdns RM3...114 B5
Staples Road Jun & Inf
Sch IG10 ....88 E6
Staple Tye CM18........23 D4
Staple Tye Sh Mews
CM18 ....23 C5

Stapley Rd DA17. . . . . . . 169 A1
Starboard Ave DA9 . . . . . .177 B1
Starboard View CM3 . . . .101 E6
Star Bsns Ctr RM13 . . . . .169 D8
Starch House La IG6. . . . .111 D1
Star La
  Epping CM16 . . . . .46 A1
  Great Wakering SS3 . . . . .149 E3
  Ingatestone CM4. . . . . . . .74 C4
Star Lane Ind Est SS3. . . .149 E3
Starling Cl
  Buckhurst Hill IG9 . . . . . . .88 A1
  Thundersley SS7 . . . . .144 B6
Starmans Cl RM9 . . . . . .153 E4
State Mans IG6. . . . . .111 C1
State Par IG6 . . . . .111 C1
Station App
  Basildon, Laindon
    SS15 . . . . .141 C5
  Basildon, Pitsea SS16 . . . .143 B4
  Buckhurst Hill IG9 . . . . . .110 D6
  Burnham-on-C CM0. . . . .106 B5
  Canvey Island SS8. . . . . .163 F6
  Grays RM17. . . . . .178 A8
  Harlow CM20. . . . . .11 C5
  Hockley SS5. . . . . .124 E6
  North Fambridge CM3 . . .103 B8
  Southend-on-S, Prittlewell
    SS2 . . . . .147 F2
  Southend-on-S SS1 . . . . .167 A8
  South Woodham Ferrers
    CM3 . . . . .101 C8
  Theydon Bois CM16. . . . . .67 D3
  Upminster RM14 . . . . . . .137 C2
  Wanstead E11 . . . . .132 A6
  Wickford SS11 . . . . .121 D8
  Woodford IG8 . . . . .110 B4
  2 Woodford, Snaresbrook
    E18 . . . . .110 B1
Station Ave
  Rayleigh SS6 . . . . .123 C3
  Southend-on-S SS2 . . . . .148 A3
  Wickford SS11 . . . . .121 D8
Station Cres
  Cold Norton CM3 . . . . .80 F5
  Rayleigh SS6 . . . . .123 D3
Station Ct
  Chipping Ongar CM5 . . . . .49 A3
  Wickford SS11 . . . . .121 D8
Station Est **1** E18 . . . . . . .110 B1
Station Gate SS15 . . . . .141 C5
Station Ind Est CM0. . . . .106 B5
Station La
  Basildon SS13 . . . . .143 B5
  Hornchurch RM12 . . . . . .136 E2
  Ingatestone CM4. . . . . . . .74 B3
Station Par
  Barking IG11 . . . . .152 C5
  Dagenham RM10 . . . . . . .154 A6
  Hornchurch RM12 . . . . . .155 B8
  3 Romford RM1 . . . . . . .135 E5
  2 Wanstead E11 . . . . . . .132 A6
  Woodford IG8 . . . . .110 D6
Station Pas E18 . . . . .110 B1
Station Rd
  Althorne CM3 . . . . .82 F1
  Belhedere DA17. . . . . . . .169 A3
  Billericay CM12 . . . . .96 F2
  Burnham-on-C CM0 . . . . .106 B5
  Canvey Island SS8. . . . . .164 E2
  Chigwell IG7 . . . . .111 B7
  Chingford E4 . . . . .87 D1
  Cold Norton CM3 . . . . .81 A5
  East Tilbury RM18 . . . . . .180 B7
  Epping CM16 . . . . .68 A8
  Greenhithe DA9. . . . . . . .177 A2
  Greenhithe DA9 . . . . .177 A3
  Harlow CM17. . . . . .11 C4
  Hockley SS5. . . . . .124 E6
  Hoddesdon EN10. . . . . . . .21 A3
  Holdbrook EN9. . . . . .90 A5
  Ilford, Barkingside IG6 . . .133 D8
  Ilford IG1 . . . . .133 B1
  Loughton IG10. . . . . .88 E4
  Maldon CM9. . . . . .37 A3
  Northfleet DA11. . . . . . . .178 B1
  North Weald Bassett
    CM16 . . . . .47 B4
  Rayleigh SS6 . . . . .123 C3
  Romford, Chadwell Heath RM6,
    RM8 . . . . .134 D4
  Romford, Harold Wood
    RM3 . . . . .114 F2
  Romford RM2 . . . . .136 C7
  Sawbridgeworth CM21 . . . .1 F3
  South Benfleet SS7 . . . . .163 D8
  Southend-on-S, Eastwood
    SS9 . . . . .146 A3
  Southend-on-S, Leigh-on-S
    SS9 . . . . .146 E1
  Southend-on-S, Thorpe Bay
    SS1 . . . . .168 B8
  Southend-on-S, Westcliff-on-S
    SS0 . . . . .166 D7
  Southminster CM0. . . . . . .84 E4
  Stanstead Abbotts SG12 . . .8 C4
  Upminster RM14 . . . . . . .137 C2
  West Horndon CM13 . . . . .139 D5
  Wickford SS11 . . . . .121 C6
Station Rd N DA17. . . . . .169 B3
Station Sq RM2. . . . . . . .136 B7
Station Way
  Basildon SS14, SS16 . . . . .142 A5
  Buckhurst Hill IG9 . . . . . .110 D6
Staveley Ct **4** E11. . . . . .132 A6

Staverton Rd RM11 . . . . .136 D5
Stays La SS5. . . . . .29 A3
Steadman Ho 4
  RM10 . . . . .135 A1
Steamer Terr **2** CM1. . . . .32 A3
Stebbings SS16. . . . . .141 C4
Stebbings Ct **5** CM0. . . . .106 C4
Stebbing Way SS11 . . . . .153 A3
Steed Cl RM11. . . . . .136 B2
Steeds Way SS10 . . . . .88 E6
Steel App IG11 . . . . .153 B3
Steele Ave CM4 . . . . .177 A2
Steen Cl CM4. . . . . .74 B4
STEEPLE 61 E3
Steeple Cl
  Heybridge CM9 . . . . .37 D5
  Rochford SS4. . . . . .125 D3
Steeplefield SS9 . . . . .146 E6
Steeple Gate SS7 . . . . . . .145 E2
Steeplehall SS13 . . . . . . .143 A5
Steeple Hts SS7 . . . . .144 B6
Steeple Mdws CM0 . . . . . . .84 B4
Steeple Rd
  Latchingdon CM3. . . . . . . .82 D7
  Steeple CM0 . . . . .62 C4
  Steeple CM0 . . . . .84 A1
STEEPLE VIEW 119 B1
Steeple View RM17 . . . . .173 A1
Steeple Way CM15. . . . . . .72 B2
Steerforth Cl CM1. . . . . . . .31 D7
Steli Ave SS8 . . . . .163 F5
Stella Maris Cl SS8 . . . . .164 F3
Sten Cl EN3 . . . . .65 A2
Stenning Ave SS17. . . . . .175 B2
Stephen Ave RM13. . . . . .155 A6
Stephens Cl RM3 . . . . . . .114 C5
Stephens Cres SS17 . . . . .159 F3
Stephenson Ave
  RM18 . . . . .179 A6
Stephenson Cl
  Hoddesdon EN11. . . . . . . .21 C6
  Hoddesdon EN11. . . . . . . .21 D6
Stephenson Rd
  North Fambridge
    CM3 . . . . .103 A8
  Southend-on-S SS9 . . . . .146 C6
Sterling Ind Est RM10. . . .154 B8
Stern Cl IG11. . . . . .153 C3
Sterry Cres RM10 . . . . . . .154 A7
Sterry Gdns RM10 . . . . . .154 A6
Sterry Ho RM13. . . . . .155 B2
Sterry Rd
  Barking IG11. . . . . .152 F4
  Dagenham RM10 . . . . . . .154 A7
Stevanne Ct **1** DA17. . . . .169 A1
Stevenage Rd E6 . . . . . . .152 A6
Stevens Cl SS8 . . . . .164 D4
Stevenson Way SS12. . . . .121 C5
Stevens Rd RM8 . . . . .134 C1
Stevens Way IG7 . . . . . . .111 E6
STEWARDS 23 E3
Stewards Cl CM16 . . . . . . .68 A6
Stewards Elm Farm La
  SS4. . . . . .126 D4
STEWARD'S GREEN 68 B7
Stewards Green Rd
  CM16 . . . . .68 B6
Stewards Sch CM18. . . . . . .23 D4
Stewards Wlk RM1 . . . . . .135 E6
Stewart Ave RM14 . . . . . .137 B1
Stewart Pl SS12 . . . . .121 F5
Stewart Rainbird Ho 1
  E12. . . . . .152 A7
Stewart Rd CM2 . . . . .54 A6
Steyning Ave SS12 . . . . . .148 E1
Stickland Rd DA17. . . . . .169 A2
Stifford Clays Jun Sch
  RM16 . . . . .173 B5
Stifford Clays Jun Sch
  RM16 . . . . .173 B5
Stifford Clays Rd
  Grays RM16. . . . . .173 B6
  Orsett RM16. . . . . .173 B7
Stifford Hill RM16 . . . . . .172 C5
Stifford Prim Sch
  RM17. . . . . .172 F1
Stifford Rd
  Aveley RM15 . . . . .171 E5
  South Ockendon RM15 . . .172 B6
Stile Croft CM18 . . . . .24 A6
Stile La SS6 . . . . .123 D2
Stilemans SS11. . . . . .121 D8
Stiles Cl DA8 . . . . .169 B1
Stiles The CM9 . . . . .37 E3
Stillwells SS4 . . . . .126 A2
Stirling Ave SS9 . . . . .146 B2
Stirling Ct
  Rainham RM13 . . . . .155 B2
  Rayleigh SS6 . . . . .123 B5
Stirling Pl SS13. . . . . .143 B8
Stirrup Cl CM1 . . . . .32 C7
Stivvy's Rd CM9 . . . . .35 C3
STOCK 75 F3
Stock CE Prim Sch
  CM4. . . . . .75 D3
Stock Chase CM9 . . . . .37 B5
Stock Cl SS2 . . . . .147 F4
Stockdale Rd RM8 . . . . . .134 F2
Stocker Gdns RM9. . . . . . .153 C5
Stockfield Ave EN11 . . . . . .21 B8
Stock Ind Pk SS2 . . . . . . .148 A4
Stock La SS4 . . . . .74 D3
Stockland Rd RM7 . . . . . .135 D5
Stock Park Ct SS2 . . . . . .146 E6
Stock Rd
  Billericay CM12 . . . . .97 C5
  Gallywood CM2 . . . . .54 B2
  Southend-on-S SS2 . . . . .147 F4

Stock Rd continued
  Stock CM4 . . . . .75 D1
  Stock CM4 . . . . .76 B6
Stocksfield CM15 . . . . .71 F2
Stocks La CM15 . . . . .71 F1
Stock Terr CM9 . . . . .37 B5
Stockwell Cl CM11 . . . . . .119 D7
Stockwood SS7 . . . . .145 B7
Stoke Ave IG6 . . . . .112 A4
Stokefelde SS13 . . . . .143 B7
Stoke Rd RM13 . . . . .155 D2
Stokesay Ct **11** DA2 . . . . .176 B1
Stokes Cotts IG6 . . . . .111 C2
Stokes Ct SS2 . . . . .148 E2
Stonard Rd RM8 . . . . .153 B8
Stonards Hill
  Epping CM16 . . . . .68 C8
  Loughton IG10. . . . . .88 F4
STONDON MASSEY 72 A6
Stondon Rd CM0. . . . . .49 B1
STONE 177 D1
STONEBRIDGE 149 A6
Stonebridge Rd DA11 . . . .178 B2
STONE CASTLE 177 A1
Stone Castle Dr DA9. . . . .177 A1
Stonechat Rd CM11. . . . . .119 C8
Stone Cl RM8. . . . . .134 C2
Stone Cross 3 CM20 . . . .10 D1
Stone Crossing Halt
  DA9 . . . . .176 E2
Stone Ct DA8. . . . . .169 F1
Stonegate CM4 . . . . .74 C3
Stonehall Ave IG1 . . . . . . .132 E5
Stonehall Bsns Pk
  CM17 . . . . .13 B5
Stonehill Cl SS9 . . . . .146 F4
Stonehill Ct E4. . . . . .87 B2
Stonehill Rd
  Roxwell CM1 . . . . .29 F3
  Southend-on-S SS9 . . . . .146 F5
Stone Ho RM12. . . . . .136 D1
Stonehouse Cnr
  RM19 . . . . .176 E8
Stoneleigh CM21. . . . . .1 D3
Stoneleigh Dr IG5. . . . . . .132 E8
Stoneleigh Dr EN11. . . . . . .8 B1
Stoneleigh IG5. . . . . .132 F8
Stoneleigh SS7 . . . . .144 F6
Stonely Cres CM9 . . . . .37 A4
Stoneness Rd RM20 . . . . .177 C7
Stone Place Rd DA9 . . . . .176 E2
Stone St DA11. . . . . .179 B1
Stonewood Rd DA8. . . . . .169 E1
Stoney Bridge Dr EN9 . . . .66 A5
Stoneycroft Rd IG8 . . . . . .110 E4
Stone Yd **2** CM11 . . . . . .116 C8
STONEYHILLS 106 C8
Stoney Hills
  Burnham-on-C CM0 . . . . .106 C8
  Ramsden Heath CM11. . . . .98 B5
Stony La CM5 . . . . .48 C8
Stony Path IG10 . . . . .88 F8
Stonyshotts EN9. . . . . .65 E6
Stony Way CM11. . . . . .98 A5
Stony Wood CM18 . . . . .23 E7
Storas Ct **9** RM19 . . . . . .171 B1
Stormonts Way SS16. . . . .141 D2
Storms Way CM2 . . . . .33 B2
Stornoway Rd SS2 . . . . . .148 D1
Storr Gdns CM13 . . . . .95 D4
Stortford Rd
  Hatfield Heath CM22. . . . . .2 E4
  Hoddesdon EN11. . . . . . . .21 C7
  Leaden Roding CM6. . . . . .15 B7
Stort Mill CM20. . . . . .11 B6
Stour Cl SS3 . . . . .168 E6
Stour Rd
  Dagenham RM10 . . . . . . .135 A2
  Grays RM16. . . . . .174 A1
Stour Wk RM14 . . . . .137 E5
Stowe Ct SS0. . . . . .147 E1
Stowe Pl SS2 . . . . .148 C2
Stowe's La CM0 . . . . .63 D4
Stowe Villas SS2 . . . . . . .147 C3
STOW MARIES 80 C4
Stow Rd CM3 . . . . .80 D5
Stow The CM20 . . . . .10 F2
Stow Villas CM3 . . . . .80 C4
Stradbroke Dr IG7. . . . . . .111 B4
Stradbroke Gr
  Buckhurst Hill IG9 . . . . . . .88 D1
  Ilford IG5 . . . . .133 A8
  Redbridge IG5 . . . . .132 F8
  Woodford IG5 . . . . .110 E1
Stradbroke Pk IG7. . . . . . .111 B4
Strafford Ave IG5. . . . . . . .111 A1
Straight Rd RM3. . . . . . . .114 C3
Straits The EN9. . . . . .65 B7
Strangman Ave SS7 . . . . .145 B4
Strasbourg Rd SS8 . . . . . .164 D5
Stratford Cl
  Barking IG11 . . . . .153 A5
  Dagenham RM10 . . . . . . .154 C5
Stratford Gdns SS17 . . . . .160 D3
Stratford Ho
  Rayleigh SS6 . . . . .123 D2
  6 Romford RM3 . . . . . . .114 D4
Strathfield Gdns
  IG11. . . . . .152 D6
Strathmore RM18. . . . . . . .175 C2
Strathmore Gdns
  RM12 . . . . .135 F3
Strathmore Rd DA1. . . . . .103 B8
Stratton Dr IG11. . . . . . . .152 F6
Stratton Ho IG11. . . . . . . .166 F7
Stratton Rd RM3 . . . . .115 A5
Stratton Wlk RM3 . . . . . . .115 A5
Street The
  Gallywood CM2 . . . . .54 B2

Street The continued
  High Ongar CM5 . . . . .49 D4
  High Roding CM6. . . . . .5 E7
  Latchingdon CM3. . . . . . . .82 A5
  Little Waltham CM3 . . . . . .19 B6
  Mashbury CM1. . . . . .17 B8
  Pleshey CM3 . . . . .7 F2
  Purleigh CM3, CM9 . . . . . .58 F1
  Roxwell CM1 . . . . .30 B6
  Sheering CM27 . . . . .12 C8
  Steeple CM0 . . . . .61 F2
  Stow Maries CM3 . . . . . . .80 C4
  Willingale CM5 . . . . .28 D3
  Woodham Ferrers CM3 . . . .79 B4
  Woodham Walter CM9 . . . .35 D2
Stroma Ave SS8 . . . . .163 F6
Stroma Gdns SS3. . . . . . . .168 D6
Stromburg Rd SS8. . . . . . .163 F5
Stromness Pl **8** SS2. . . . .167 C8
Stromness Rd SS2 . . . . . .148 C1
Strood Ave RM7 . . . . .135 D3
STROUD GREEN 125 B2
Stroud Rd **12** RM3 . . . . . .114 D5
Strouds Cl RM6. . . . . .134 B6
Struan Ave SS17. . . . . . . .160 E5
Struan Ho **15** E11 . . . . . .132 A6
Stuart Cl
  Canvey Island SS8. . . . . .164 B4
  Great Baddow CM2 . . . . . .55 B6
  Great Wakering SS3 . . . . .149 F4
Stuart Ho
  Pilgrims Hatch CM15. . . . . .94 B4
  Southend-on-S SS2 . . . . .148 A2
Stuart Ct E4 . . . . .109 F8
Stuart Ho EN9. . . . . .65 F6
Stuart Rd
  Barking IG11 . . . . .152 F4
  Gravesend DA11 . . . . . . .179 A1
  Grays RM17. . . . . .173 B1
  Southend-on-S SS2 . . . . .148 B2
Stuarts RM11. . . . . .136 E3
Stuart St SS2. . . . . .148 A3
Stuart Way CM11. . . . . .97 E1
Stubbers La RM14 . . . . . .156 E5
Stubbs Mews **5** RM8 . . . .153 B8
Stublands SS13 . . . . .143 B6
Studland Ave SS12. . . . . . .120 F8
Studley Ave E4 . . . . .109 D3
Studley Ct IG4 . . . . .132 D5
Studley Dr IG4 . . . . .132 D5
Studley Rd RM9 . . . . .153 D5
Stump La CM1. . . . . .32 D4
Sturge Ave E17 . . . . .109 B2
Sturrocks SS16 . . . . .142 E3
Sudbrook Cl SS12 . . . . . . .121 D6
Sudbury Cl SS15. . . . . . . .124 F4
Sudbury Ct **1** RM6 . . . . . .134 B6
Sudbury Rd
  Barking IG11 . . . . .152 F7
  Canvey Island SS8. . . . . .163 F5
  Downham CM11. . . . . .99 A5
Sudburys Farm Rd
  CM12 . . . . .118 C6
Sudeley Gdns SS8 . . . . . . .124 D6
Sudicamps Ct EN9. . . . . . . .66 A6
Suffield Rd E4 . . . . .109 B6
Suffolk Ave SS9 . . . . .146 F3
Suffolk Cres CM9 . . . . .36 E1
Suffolk Ct
  Maldon CM9. . . . . .36 E1
  2 Ilford, Little Heath
    RM6. . . . . .134 C5
  Rochford SS4. . . . . .125 E2
Suffolk Dr
  Basildon SS15 . . . . .141 B6
  Chelmsford CM2 . . . . .33 A4
Suffolk Ho RM7. . . . . .113 A2
Suffolk Rd
  Barking IG11 . . . . .152 D5
  Dagenham RM10 . . . . . . .154 C7
  Gravesend DA12 . . . . . . .179 D1
  Ilford IG3 . . . . .133 E5
Suffolk Wlk SS8 . . . . .124 D6
Sugden Ave SS12 . . . . . . .121 A7
Sugden Way IG11 . . . . . . .152 F3
Sullivan Rd RM18 . . . . . . .179 A6
Sullivan Way SS15 . . . . . .141 A5
Sultan Rd E11 . . . . .132 B7
Summercourt Rd SS0 . . . .166 E8
Summerdale
  Althorne CM3 . . . . .83 A3
  Billericay CM12 . . . . .97 A2
Summerfield Ho RM9 . . . .153 D8
Summerfield Rd IG10 . . . . .88 D3
Summerfields CM4 . . . . . . .74 C3
Summerhill CM3. . . . . .83 A3
Summerlands SS8 . . . . . . .163 F5
Summerwood Cl SS7 . . . . .145 C3
Summit Dr IG8 . . . . .110 D1
Summit The IG10 . . . . .88 F8
SUMNERS 23 A4
Sumners Farm Ct
  CM19 . . . . .23 A3
Sumners Link SS15 . . . . . .140 E6
Sumpters Way SS2 . . . . . .147 F5
Sunbury Cl SS3 . . . . .149 E2
Sunbury Way CM9 . . . . . . .58 F8
Sunderland Way E12. . . . .132 D2
Sundew Ct RM17. . . . . . . .178 D8
Sundridge Cl DA1 . . . . . . .176 A1
Sunflower Cl **5** CM1. . . . . .32 F6
Sunflower Way RM3 . . . . .114 D2
SUNKEN MARSH 164 D5
Sunnedon SS16. . . . . .142 D5
Sunningdale SS8 . . . . .164 C4

Sunningdale Ave
  Barking IG11. . . . . .152 F6
  Rainham RM13 . . . . .155 A5
  Southend-on-S SS9 . . . . .146 C1
Sunningdale Ct SS1 . . . . .147 E6
Sunningdale Rd
  Althorne CM3 . . . . .83 A2
  Chelmsford CM1 . . . . .31 D3
  Rainham RM13 . . . . .155 A5
Sunninghill Gdns IG2. . . . .133 D6
Sunnings La RM14 . . . . . .156 C7
Sunnybank Cl SS9 . . . . . .146 B6
Sunny Croft CM18 . . . . . . .24 A7
Sunnycroft Gdns
  RM14 . . . . .137 E8
Sunnydene Ave E4. . . . . . .109 F3
Sunnydene Cl RM3 . . . . . .114 E2
Sunnyfield Gdns SS5. . . . .124 B6
Sunnymead Flats 10
  CM0 . . . . .106 C4
SUNNYMEDE 96 E2
Sunnymede IG7 . . . . .111 A7
Sunnymede Cl SS7 . . . . . .144 C3
Sunnymede Dr IG6 . . . . . .133 A6
Sunnymede Inf Sch
  CM11. . . . . .96 F2
Sunnymede Jun Sch
  CM11. . . . . .96 F2
Sunny Mews RM5. . . . . . . .113 D2
Sunny Rd SS5 . . . . .29 A3
Sunnyside
  Basildon SS15 . . . . .141 B6
  Lower Nazeing EN9 . . . . . .66 D6
Sunnyside Dr E4 . . . . . . .109 B3
Sunnyside Gdns
  RM14 . . . . .137 E8
Sunnyside Rd
  Epping CM16 . . . . .68 A6
  Ilford IG1 . . . . .133 E5
Sunny Way CM0 . . . . .106 B5
Sunnyway Cotts CM3 . . . . .80 D6
Sun Ray Ave CM3 . . . . .82 C6
Sunray Ho SS0 . . . . .166 D8
Sun Rd DA10 . . . . .177 A4
Sunrise Ave
  Chelmsford CM1 . . . . .32 C6
  Hornchurch RM12 . . . . . .155 A8
Sunrise Lo RM17 . . . . .173 A1
Sunset Ave
  Chingford E4 . . . . .87 B1
  Woodford IG8 . . . . .109 F3
Sunset Ct **4** IG8 . . . . . . .109 F3
Sunset Dr RM3 . . . . .113 D8
Sunset Mews RM5. . . . . . .113 D2
Sunshine Cl SS5 . . . . .124 A6
Sun St
  Billericay CM12 . . . . .96 E2
  Sawbridgeworth CM21 . . . .1 E3
  Waltham Abbey EN9 . . . . .65 E4
Surbiton Ave SS1 . . . . . . .168 C8
Surbiton Rd SS2. . . . . . . .147 E6
Surig Rd SS8 . . . . .164 A2
Surman Cres CM13 . . . . . . .95 B3
Surmans Cl RM9. . . . . . . .154 A7
Surman Terr RM1 . . . . . . .135 E6
Surrey Ave SS9 . . . . .146 D5
Surrey Dr RM11 . . . . .137 A3
Surrey Ho RM7 . . . . .113 B2
Surrey Rd
  Barking IG11. . . . . .152 F7
  Dagenham RM10 . . . . . . .135 B1
Surrey Way SS15 . . . . . . .141 A5
Surridge Cl RM13. . . . . . .155 A4
Susan Cl RM7. . . . . .135 C7
Susan Fielder Cotts **8**
  SS8. . . . . .164 A3
Susan Lawrence Ho 8
  E12. . . . . .152 B7
Sussex Ave RM3 . . . . .114 C3
Sussex Cl
  Basildon SS15 . . . . .141 A5
  Boreham CM3 . . . . .20 F1
  Canvey Island SS8. . . . . .164 A2
  Hoddesdon EN11. . . . . . . .21 A4
  Redbridge IG4 . . . . .132 E6
Sussex Ct CM12 . . . . .96 F1
Sussex Ho RM7 . . . . .113 B2
Sussex Rd
  Brentwood CM14. . . . . . . .94 A1
  Wallend E6. . . . . .152 C3
Sussex Terr **2** RM11 . . . . .137 A4
Sussex Way
  Billericay CM12 . . . . .97 A2
  Canvey Island SS8. . . . . .164 A2
Sutcliffe Cl SS12. . . . . . . .121 E6
Sutherland Bvd SS9 . . . . .146 B4
Sutherland Ct RM3. . . . . .114 E2
Sutherland Ho
  Chelmsford CM1 . . . . .32 C6
  5 Redbridge IG8 . . . . . .110 B1
Sutherland Pl SS12 . . . . . .121 D7
Sutherland Rd DA17. . . . .169 A2
Sutton Acres CM22 . . . . . . .2 B1
Sutton Cl IG10 . . . . .89 A7
Sutton Court Dr SS4. . . . .125 F2
Sutton Ct SS2 . . . . .147 F2
Sutton Ford Cotts
  SS4. . . . . .125 F2
Sutton Gdns IG11. . . . . . .153 A5
Sutton Gn Sch IG11. . . . . .153 A4
Sutton Mead CM2 . . . . . . .33 C4
Sutton Rd
  Barking IG11. . . . . .153 A4
  Rochford SS3, SS4,
    SS2 . . . . .147 E6
SUTTONS 156 A5
Suttons Ave RM12 . . . . . .155 C6

Bsns Pk
. . . . .154 E2
Gdns RM12 . . . . . . 136 D1
La RM12 . . . . 155 D7
Prim Sch
. . . . .155 D8
Rd SS3 . . . . 168 H8
m Ct **1** RM6 . . . . 134 C5
Ind Est SS4 . . . . . 125 D3
d RM15 . . . . 171 C7
d SS7 . . . . .145 B5
Cl
M16 . . . . 172 C2
he DA9 . . . . 176 F2
SS6 . . . . 123 B3
cliffe SS3 . . . . . . 149 D1
Ct
twood CM14 . . . . . 116 C7
d IG8 . . . . 109 D3
2 . . . . .133 B6
Dale SS16 . . . . . . 142 C4
Dr SS7 . . . . 144 C2
Path CM2 . . . . .54 B5
Rd SS11 . . . . .99 C2
s CM17 . . . . .11 C4
WS CROSS 73 A2
s The CM11 . . . . . 119 C8
Wlk **1** RM12. . . .155 B8
Rd
d E4 . . . . 109 C3
l-on-S SS2 . . . . . . 148 B1
e RM14 . . . . 137 F3
rne Dr
. . . . 155 D8
SS15 . . . . .141 E6
Ct
M9 . . . . .37 B4
nfleet SS7 . . . . . . 144 B5
SS11 . . . . 121 D8
Hatch CM15 . . . . . .71 E2
8 . . . . .88 C2
4 . . . . .75 C5
Ct **1** 99 D1
d SS16 . . . . 142 D4
y CM19 . . . . .9 A1
Jdock **5**
. . . . 116 C8
Pike Rd EN3. . . . . .65 A1
OMBE 177 D1
mbe Bsns Ctr
. . . . .177 E2
mbe Cross
. . . . 177 D2
nbe St DA10. . . . .177 F1
mbe Sta
. . . . .177 F1
een Cl SS7 . . . . . 145 A6
be IG10 . . . . .89 B7
sture CM1. . . . . . . .32 D6
d SS16 . . . . 142 E4
Hatch CM15 . . . . . .71 E2
RM1 . . . . 135 E6
ays SS11 . . . . 167 D6
ar Ave SS7 . . . . . 144 D2
ar Dr SS15 . . . . . 119 D1
Rd SS13 . . . . .163 E4
estnut Mews
. . . . .97 A2
ve
SS. 125 A4
-on-S SS2 . . . . . . .147 F1
l SS6 . . . . 123 B4
t SS2 . . . . .147 F1
ark Sch The
. . . . 123 C4
d DA10 . . . . .177 E1
M17 . . . . .24 C6
l Abbotts SG12 . . .8 C3
- RM14 . . . . 137 E3
Rd E18 . . . . 132 B8
Rd RM16 . . . . 172 C2
e Ct SS13 . . . . . . 121 B2
e Rd SS13 . . . . . . 121 C1
e Gdns
. . . . .179 B6
Cl
. . . . 133 E3
Gdns RM3. . . . . . . 114 F5
La RM3 . . . . 114 F5
t Terr **3**
. . . . 167 C7
CM1 . . . . .32 A4
ar Ave RM14 . . . . 156 A8
Cl
and SS8. . . . . 163 F3
IG10 . . . . .89 B7
SS6 . . . . 123 B6
18 . . . . 179 A5
Ct
. . . . 169 D1
M12 . . . . 135 F3
on-S SS3 . . . . 168 F7
SS11 . . . . 121 D8
Dr CM14 . . . . .99 C2
Field CM19 . . . . . . .23 A5
Gr
M2 . . . . 114 A1
on-S SS2 . . . . 148 B2
Ho
rst Hill IG9 . . . . . 110 D8
SS11 . . . . 121 E7
Mews SS8 . . . . . . 169 D1
Rd EN9. . . . . .37 C6
. . . . .66 C4

Sycamores The
Aveley RM15 . . . . . . 171 D5
14 Basildon SS13 . . . 143 C6
Sycamore Way
Canewdon SS4. . . . . . 104 D1
Chelmsford CM2 . . . . . .54 C6
South Ockendon RM15 . . 157 D1
Sycamore Wlk IG6 . . . 136 C7
Sydenham Cl RM1. . . . . 135 F7
Sydervelt Rd SS8 . . . . 164 A4
Sydner Cl CM2 . . . . . . .55 A5
Sydney Rd
Redbridge IG6 . . . . . . 111 C1
South Benfleet SS7 . . . 144 C4
Southend-on-S SS9 . . . . 146 B2
Tilbury RM18. . . . . 179 A5
Wanstead E11 . . . . . . .132 B5
Woodford IG8 . . . . 110 A6
Sydney Russell Sch The
RM9 . . . . 153 D7
Sykes Mead SS6 . . . . . 123 D1
Sylvan Ave
Dagenham RM6 . . . . . .134 F5
Hornchurch RM11 . . . . 136 F5
Sylvan Cl
Basildon SS15 . . . . . . .141 B6
Canvey Island SS8. . . . .164 B2
Chelmsford CM2 . . . . . .54 B6
Grays RM16. . . . . .172 E3
Sylvan Ct SS15 . . . . . .140 F7
Sylvan Mews DA9 . . . . .177 B3
Sylvan Rd
Ilford IG1 . . . . 133 C2
Wanstead E11 . . . . . . .132 A6
Sylvan Tryst CM12. . . . .97 B4
Sylvan Way
Basildon SS15 . . . . . . .140 F7
Chigwell IG7 . . . . .112 B7
Dagenham RM8 . . . . . .134 B1
Southend-on-S SS9 . . . . 146 A4
Sylvester Gdns IG6 . . . .112 B5
Sylvesters CM7 . . . . . . .22 F6
Sylvia Ave CM13 . . . . . 117 C8
Sylvia Pankhurst Ho **10**
RM10 . . . . 135 A1
Symons Ave SS9 . . . . . 146 E7
Syracuse Ave RM13 . . . .155 E2
Syringa Ct RM17. . . . . . 178 D8

T

Tabora Ave SS8. . . . . . .163 F5
Tabors Ave CM2 . . . . . .54 F8
Tabors Ct CM15. . . . . . .94 F2
Tabor's Hill CM2 . . . . . .54 F7
Tabrum's La SS11. . . . . 101 A6
Tabrums Ct CM3. . . . . . .79 C1
Tabrums Way RM14 . . . .137 E4
Tadlows Cl RM14 . . . . . 155 B8
Tadworth Par RM12 . . . 155 B8
Taffrail Gdns CM3 . . . . 101 E5
Tailors Ct SS2 . . . . . . .147 F5
Tait Mews CM9 . . . . . . .37 A2
Taits SS17 . . . . 160 F2
Takeley Cl
Romford RM5 . . . . 113 D1
Waltham Abbey EN9 . . . .65 D6
Takely End SS16 . . . . . 142 A5
Takely Ride SS16 . . . . . 142 A5
Talbot Ave SS6 . . . . . . 123 C3
Talbot Gdns IG3 . . . . . .134 A2
Talbot Rd
Dagenham RM9 . . . . . .153 F5
Wallend E6. . . . . 152 A3
Talbrook CM14. . . . . . . 115 F7
Talgarth Ho **3** RM3. . . . 114 E4
Talisman Cl **2** IG2 . . . 133 B3
Talisman Wlk CM11 . . . .97 D6
Tallis Cl SS17. . . . . . . 160 C3
Tallis Ct RM2 . . . . 136 C8
Tallis Rd SS15 . . . . . . 141 D8
Tallis Way CM14 . . . . . 115 D1
Tallon Rd CM13 . . . . . . .95 E4
Tallow Cl RM9 . . . . 153 E6
Tallow Gate CM3 . . . . . 101 E6
Tall Trees Cl RM11 . . . .136 E5
Tally-Ho Dr CM13. . . . . .96 C1
Talus Cl RM19 . . . . 171 D2
Tama Cotts RM14 . . . . .137 F2
Tamar Cl RM14 . . . . . . 137 E5
Tamar Dr RM15 . . . . . . 171 C7
Tamarisk SS7 . . . . 144 C4
Tamarisk Rd RM15 . . . . 157 C1
Tamar Rise CM1 . . . . . .32 C6
Tamar Sq IG8 . . . . 110 B4
Tamworth Ave IG8 . . . . 109 E4
Tanfield Dr CM12 . . . . . .97 A2
Tanfield Tye Cotts
CM2 . . . . .76 E7
Tangent Link RM3 . . . . 114 D2
Tangham Wlk SS14 . . . .142 C7
Tangmere Cl SS11 . . . . 122 B6
Tanners Cres RM12 . . . 155 B6
Tan House La
Navestock Heath CM14 . . 92 F5
Navestock Side CM14. . . .93 A6
Tankerville Dr SS9 . . . . 146 D3
Tank Hill Rd
Purfleet RM15 . . . . 171 A3
Purfleet RM19 . . . . 171 A2
Tank La RM19 . . . . 171 B2
Tanners La IG6 . . . . . . 133 C8
Tanner St IG11 . . . . . . 152 C6
Tanners Way
Hunsdonbury SG12 . . . . . .9 D8
South Woodham Ferrers
CM3 . . . . 101 C8

Tannery Cl RM10 . . . . .135 B1
Tanswell Ave SS13 . . . . . .143 B6
Tanswell Ct SS13 . . . . . . 143 B6
Tanswell Ct SS13 . . . . . . .143 B7
Tansy Cl RM3 . . . . .114 E4
Tantelen Rd SS8 . . . . . . .163 F5
Tantony Gr RM6 . . . . 134 D8
Tanys Ct CM20 . . . . .10 F3
Tany's Dell CM20 . . . . 11 A3
Tany's Dell Com Prim Sch
CM20 . . . . .11 A3
Tapley Rd CM20 . . . . .31 F7
Taranto Rd SS8 . . . . 164 D3
Tarlings CM20 . . . . .10 F3
Tarnworth Rd RM3 . . . . . .115 A4
TARPOTS 144 C4
Tarragon Ct IG1, IG3 . . . .133 E2
Tasker Ho **3** IG11 . . . . . 152 D3
Tasker Rd RM16 . . . . 174 B3
Tasman Cl SS17 . . . . . . .160 F4
Tasman Ct CM1 . . . . .31 E5
Tasmania Ho RM14 . . . . . 179 A6
Tatsfield Ave EN9. . . . . . . .43 E8
Tatsford Villas EN9. . . . . . .21 C1
Tattenham Rd SS15 . . . . . 141 B7
Tattersall Gdns SS9 . . . . . 146 A4
Tattersalls Chase CM0 . . . .84 E4
Tattersall Way CM1 . . . . . .53 E7
Tattershall Ct **3** DA2 . . . .176 B1
Tatton St **6** CM17 . . . . . .11 C1
Taunton Cl IG6 . . . . 111 F4
Taunton Dr SS0 . . . . 147 B4
Taunton Ho RM3. . . . . . . 114 F5
Taunton Rd
Chelmsford CM1 . . . . .32 E5
Northfleet DA11. . . . . . . 178 A2
Romford RM3 . . . . 114 C6
Taverners Green Cl
SS12 . . . . 121 E6
TAVERNERS GREEN 4 C8
Taverners Way
Chingford E4 . . . . .87 E1
Hoddesdon EN11 . . . . . . .21 A6
Tavistock Cl RM3 . . . . . . 114 D2
Tavistock Gdns IG3 . . . . . 152 E8
Tavistock Ho **1** IG8 . . . . 110 A4
Tavistock Rd
Basildon SS15 . . . . 141 C8
Chelmsford CM1 . . . . .32 E5
Wanstead E18 . . . . 132 A8
Tawney Comm CM16 . . . . .69 F7
Tawney La RM4. . . . . .69 D4
Tawneys Rd CM18 . . . . . . .23 F6
Tawny Ave RM14 . . . . . . .156 F7
Taylifers CM19. . . . . .23 A3
Taylor Cl CM1 . . . . .31 E4
Taylor Gdns RM3 . . . . . . 114 D2
Taylors IG7. . . . . .90 A2
Taylors Ave RM11 . . . . . . .21 A5
Tayside Wlk **6** SS12 . . . 121 E5
Tay Way RM1 . . . . 113 F2
Tebbys SS15 . . . . 141 E6
Teal Ave CM3. . . . . .83 A8
Teal Ct CM3 . . . . .83 A8
Teazle Mead CM16 . . . . . .46 B6
Ted Hennem Ho
RM10 . . . . .135 B1
Tees Cl RM14 . . . . .137 D5
Tees Ct CM1. . . . . .32 C5
Tees Rd CM1 . . . . .32 C6
Teigngrace SS1. . . . . 168 D8
Teignmouth Dr SS6 . . . . . 123 D5
Telegraph Mews
Ilford, Goodmayes
IG3 . . . . 134 A3
Ilford, Seven Kings IG3. . . 133 F3
Telese Ave SS6 . . . . 164 D3
Telford Ho **2** DA17 . . . . 169 A3
Telford Pl CM1 . . . . .32 D4
Telham Rd E6 . . . . .152 A3
Tempest Mead CM16 . . . . .47 B4
Tempest Way RM11 . . . . . 155 A6
Templar Cl CM17 . . . . .11 D1
Templar Ho RM11 . . . . . . 155 A6
Temple Ave SS9 . . . . 146 A6
Temple Bank CM20 . . . . . 11 B5
Temple Cl
Basildon SS15 . . . . 141 C7
Billericay CM12 . . . . .96 F5
Hadleigh SS7 . . . . 164 A3
Temple Ct SS2 . . . . 148 C3
Temple Farm Ind Est
CM2 . . . . .76 B6
Temple Farm Trad Est
CM2 . . . . .76 C6
TEMPLE FIELDS 11 A4
Templefields Ent Ctr
CM20 . . . . .11 A3
Temple Gate Cotts
CM20 . . . . .11 A3
Temple Gdns RM8 . . . . . . 134 D1
Temple Hall Ct E4 . . . . . . 109 D8
TEMPLE HILL 176 A2
Temple Hill Com Prim Sch
DA1 . . . . 176 A2
Temple Mead CM19 . . . . . .22 F5
Temple Mews RM16 . . . . . 174 A2
Temple Rd SS9 . . . . 146 A6
Temple Sutton Prim Sch
SS2 . . . . 148 C3
Temple Way
Maldon CM9. . . . . .36 F5
Rayleigh SS6 . . . . 123 B5
Templewood Ct SS7 . . . . 145 D3

Temple Wood Est CM2 . . . .76 B6
Templewood Rd SS7 . . . . 145 D3
Tempton Ave SS8 . . . . . . 164 E4
Tempus Ct E18 . . . . 110 A2
Ten Acre App CM9 . . . . . . .36 F5
Tenby Cl RM6 . . . . 134 C5
Tenby Rd RM6 . . . . 134 E5
Tendring Ave SS6 . . . . . . 123 A3
Tendring Cl CM13 . . . . . . .95 D4
Tendring Mews CM18 . . . . .23 E7
Tendring Rd CM18 . . . . . . .23 E6
Tendring Way RM6 . . . . . 134 C6
Tenney Ho RM17 . . . . 178 C7
Tennyson Ave
Grays RM17. . . . . 173 C3
Southend-on-S SS2 . . . . 148 B2
Waltham Abbey EN9 . . . . .65 E5
Wanstead E11 . . . . 132 A4
Tennyson Ct SS3 . . . . 149 A2
Tennyson Dr **9** SS13. . . .143 B5
Tennyson Ho CM16 . . . . . .68 A8
Tennyson Rd
Brentwood CM13 . . . . . . .95 D2
Chelmsford CM1 . . . . . . .31 F5
Dartford DA1 . . . . 176 A2
Maldon CM9. . . . . .59 A8
Romford RM3 . . . . 114 C3
Tensing Gdns CM12. . . . . .97 A1
Tenterden Rd RM8 . . . . . 134 F2
Tenterfield Rd CM9 . . . . . .37 A2
Teramo Rd SS8 . . . . 164 D3
Tercel Path IG7 . . . . 112 B6
Terence Webster Rd
SS12. . . . . 121 E6
Terling Cl SS16. . . . . 142 B5
Terling Rd RM8 . . . . 135 A2
Terlings Pk CM20 . . . . . . .10 D4
Terlings The CM14 . . . . . 116 A7
Terminus Dr SS7 . . . . . . 168 F7
Terminus Dr SS16 . . . . . 143 B4
Terminus St CM20 . . . . . . 10 D1
Terms Ave SS8 . . . . 164 A5
Tern Cl CM3 . . . . .83 A8
Tern Ct CM14 . . . . 115 F6
Tern Gdns RM14 . . . . . . 137 E3
Terni Rd SS8. . . . . 164 A5
Tern Way CM14 . . . . 115 E6
Terrace St DA12 . . . . 179 B1
Terrace The
Chingford E4 . . . . 109 E7
2 Gravesend DA12 . . . 179 C1
Rayleigh SS6 . . . . 123 C7
Southend-on-S, Chalkwell
SS9 . . . . 165 E8
1 Woodford IG8 . . . . . 110 A4
Terrace Wlk RM9 . . . . . . 153 F7
Terr The SS7 . . . . 163 D8
Terront Rd N15 . . . . 121 C1
Tewkesbury Cl RM10 . . . . .88 E3
Tewkes Rd SS8 . . . . 164 D3
Thackeray Ave RM18 . . . 179 B6
Thackeray Dr RM6. . . . . . 134 B5
Thackeray Row **1**
SS12. . . . . 121 C5
Thamassing Cl CM13 . . . . 117 B8
Thames Ave
Chelmsford CM1 . . . . . . .31 D4
Dagenham RM9 . . . . 154 C2
Thames Cl
Corringham SS17. . . . . . 161 A2
Rainham RM13 . . . . 170 B7
Rayleigh SS6 . . . . 123 C7
Southend-on-S SS9 . . . . 146 B1
Thames Cres SS17 . . . . . 161 C4
Thames Ct SS13 . . . . . . 164 B1
Thames Dr
Grays RM16 . . . . 174 A1
Southend-on-S SS9 . . . . 146 A1
Thames Gate DA1 . . . . . . 176 A2
Thamesgate Sh Ctr **12**
DA11 . . . . 179 B1
Thames Gateway Pk
RM9 . . . . 153 F2
Thameshill Ave RM5 . . . . 113 C1
Thameside Cres **8**
SS8 . . . . 164 A3
Thameside Inf Sch
RM17 . . . . 178 C8
Thameside Jun Sch
RM17 . . . . 178 C8
Thames Rd
Basildon SS16 . . . . 141 C5
Canvey Island SS8. . . . . 163 F4
Ilford IG11 . . . . 152 D3
Thames View Bsns Ctr
IG11 . . . . 152 E2
Thames View Inf Sch
IG11 . . . . 153 A3
Thames View Lo IG11 . . . 152 E2
Thameside Cl CM13 . . . . 116 D4
Canvey Island SS8. . . . . 163 F3

Thamley RM19. . . . . 171 A2
Thanet Grange SS0 . . . . 147 C5
Thatchers Cl IG10 . . . . . . .89 C7
Thatchers Croft CM3. . . . .81 F6
Thatches Gr RM6 . . . . . . 134 E7
Thaxted Bold CM13 . . . . . .95 D4
Thaxted Cl CM13 . . . . . . .95 C4
Thaxted Ho RM10 . . . . . . 154 B5
Thaxted Lo **3** E18 . . . . . 132 B8
Thaxted Rd IG9 . . . . .88 E2
Thaxted Way RM9 . . . . . . .65 D6
Thaxted Wlk RM13 . . . . . 154 E5
Thear Cl SS0 . . . . 147 C4
Thele Ave SG12. . . . . .8 D4
Thele Est SG12 . . . . .8 E4
Theleway Cl EN11 . . . . . . .8 B1
Thelma Ave SS6 . . . . 164 A4
Theobalds Ave RM17 . . . . 173 C1
Theobalds Ct SS15 . . . . . 146 C1
Theobalds Rd SS9 . . . . . 146 C1
Thetford Cl CM1 . . . . .31 E1
Thetford Gdns RM9 . . . . . 153 E4
Thetford Pl SS15 . . . . . . 119 D1
Thetford Rd RM9 . . . . . . 153 D5
THEYDON BOIS 67 D3
Theydon Bois Prim Sch
CM16 . . . . .67 E3
Theydon Bois Sta
CM16 . . . . .67 D3
Theydon Bower CM13 . . . . .95 D4
Theydon Bower 68 A8
Theydon Cl
Brentwood CM13 . . . . . . .95 D4
Southend-on-S SS11 . . . 121 B8
THEYDON GARNON 68 C3
Theydon Gr
Epping CM16 . . . . .46 A1
Woodford IG8 . . . . 110 C4
THEYDON MOUNT 69 A3
Theydon Park Rd
CM16 . . . . .67 E1
Theydon Pl CM16 . . . . . . .67 D6
Theydon Rd CM16 . . . . . . .67 D6
Thicket Gr RM9 . . . . 153 C6
Thielen Rd SS8 . . . . 164 A4
Thieves' Cnr CM1 . . . . . . .31 A4
Third Ave
Basildon SS16 . . . . 140 E3
Canvey Island SS8. . . . . 163 E4
Chelmsford CM1 . . . . . . .32 D5
Grays RM20. . . . . 177 A8
Halstead CM19 . . . . .23 C7
Ilford RM6 . . . . 134 C5
Stanford-le-H SS17 . . . . 160 E4
Thundersley SS7 . . . . . . 145 A6
Wickford SS11 . . . . 122 A4
Third Wlk SS8 . . . . 163 E4
Thirlmere Rd SS7. . . . . . 144 E7
Thirlmere Rd CM16 . . . . . .46 D6
Thissell Rd SS8 . . . . 164 B4
Thistle Cl SS15 . . . . 119 F1
Thistledene Ave RM5 . . . . 113 B5
Thistledown SS14 . . . . . . 142 C6
Thistle Mead IG10 . . . . . . .89 A6
Thistley Cl
Goldhanger CM9 . . . . . . .38 E6
Southend-on-S SS9 . . . . 146 F4
Thoby La SS11 . . . . .73 C1
Thomas Arnold Prim Sch
RM9 . . . . 153 F5
Thomas Bata Ave
IG11 . . . . 175 B2
Thomas Cl
Brentwood CM15 . . . . . . 116 F7
Chelmsford CM2 . . . . . . .32 F3
Thomas Ct RM8 . . . . 134 C2
Thomas Dr SS8 . . . . 163 F4
Thomas England Ho **3**
RM7 . . . . 135 D5
Thomas Rd SS13 . . . . . . 121 C1
Thomas Rd SS13 . . . . . . 143 E7
Thomas Sims Ct
RM12 . . . . 155 B7
Thomas Willingale Sch
IG10 . . . . .89 C6
Thompson Ave SS6 . . . . . 164 F3
Thompson Cl IG1 . . . . . . 133 C2
Thompson Rd RM9 . . . . . 153 E7
Thorington Ave SS6 . . . . 124 A1
Thorington Rd SS6 . . . . . 101 C6
Thornberry Ave 101 F7
Thornborough Ave
SS3 . . . . 144 B4
Thornbrook CM16 . . . . . . .46 D6
Thornbury Cl EN11 . . . . . .8 B2
Thornbury Ho **3**
RM3 . . . . 114 D5
Thorndale SS7 . . . . 145 B7
Thorndales CM14 . . . . . . 116 D6
Thorndon App CM13 . . . . 117 D3
Thorndon Cl IG10 . . . . . . .89 C6
Thorndon Countryside
Ctr* CM13 . . . . 116 C4
Thorndon Ct CM13 . . . . . 116 C4
Thorndon Ctry Pk*
CM13 . . . . 117 D1
Little Warley CM13 . . . . . 116 F3
Thorndon Gate CM13 . . . . 117 B4
Thorndon Hall CM13 . . . . 117 B4

Thorndon Lo CM13 .... 117 C4
Thorndon Park Cl
  SS9 .... 146 C5
Thorndon Park Cres
  SS9 .... 146 B5
Thorndon Park Dr
  SS9 .... 146 C5
Thorney Bay Rd SS8 .... 164 A2
Thorneycroft Dr EN3 .... 65 A2
Thornford Gdns SS2 .... 147 F5
Thornhill
  North Weald Bassett
  CM16 .... 47 C5
  Purleigh CM3 .... 58 D1
  Southend-on-S SS9 .... 146 E4
Thornhill Gdns IG11 .... 152 E5
Thorn La RM13 .... 155 D3
Thornridge CM14 .... 94 B1
Thorns The CM15 .... 93 E8
Thornton Ho **5** E11 ... 132 A5
Thornton Pl CM4 .... 75 E2
Thornton Rd
  Belvedere DA17 .... 169 B2
  Ilford IG1 .... 152 B8
Thorntons CM13 .... 117 D4
Thorntons Farm Ave
  RM7 .... 135 D2
Thornton Way SS15 .... 141 A6
THORNWOOD 46 C7
Thornwood Cl E18 ..... 110 B1
Thornwood Ct SS9 ..... 146 D6
Thornwood Ho IG9 ..... 88 E2
Thornwood Rd CM16 ... 46 B3
Thorogood Way
  RM13 .... 154 E4
Thorold Rd IG1 .... 133 C3
Thorolds SS16 .... 142 E3
THORPE BAY 168 B7
Thorpe Bay Gdns SS1 .. 168 B6
Thorpe Bay Sta SS1 ... 168 B8
Thorpe Bold CM13 ..... 95 C4
Thorpe Cl
  Hockley SS5 .... 124 F4
  Wickford SS12 .... 121 F6
Thorpedale Gdns IG1,
  IG6 .... 133 B7
Thorpedene Ave SS5 ... 101 E2
Thorpedene Gdns
  SS3 .... 168 D6
Thorpedene Inf Sch
  SS3 .... 168 C7
Thorpedene Jun Sch
  SS3 .... 168 C7
Thorpe Espl SS1 ...... 168 B6
Thorpe Gdns SS5 ...... 124 F4
Thorpe Greenways Inf Sch
  SS1 .... 167 E7
Thorpe Greenways Jun
  Sch SS1 .... 167 E7
Thorpe Hall Ave SS1 ... 168 A7
Thorpe Hall Cl SS1 .... 168 A8
Thorpe Hall Prim Sch
  E17 .... 109 C2
Thorpe Hall Rd E17 ... 109 C2
Thorpe Hall SS1 ...... 149 A2
Thorpe Lo
  Romford RM11 .... 136 D5
  Southend-on-S SS3 .... 167 D6
Thorpe Rd
  Barking IG11 .... 152 D5
  Chingford E17 .... 109 C2
  Hockley SS5 .... 124 F3
  Hockley SS5 .... 124 F4
  Wanstead E7 .... 132 A1
Thorp Leas SS8 .... 164 B2
Thorrington Bold
  CM13 .... 95 D4
Thorrington Cross
  SS14 .... 142 C6
Thors Oak SS17 .... 160 E2
Thrapston Ho **10** RM3 . 114 E5
Threadneedle St **2**
  CM1 .... 32 B2
Three Horseshoes Rd
  CM19 .... 23 B6
Three Mile Hill CM4 ... 53 C2
Threshelford SS16 ..... 141 F4
THRESHERS BUSH 25 B7
Thrift Gn CM13 .... 117 A7
Thrifts Mead CM16 .... 67 E2
Thrift Wood CM3 ...... 56 F1
Thriftwood Sch CM2 ... 54 B3
Throwley Cl SS13 ..... 143 C5
Thunderer Rd RM9 .... 153 E1
THUNDERSLEY 144 E6
Thundersley Church Rd
  SS7 .... 144 D6
Thundersley Gr SS7 ... 144 F5
Thundersley Park Rd
  SS7 .... 144 E3
Thundersley Prim Sch
  SS7 .... 145 A6
Thurgood Rd EN11 .... 21 A8
Thurlby Cl IG8 .... 110 F5
Thurlby Ho IG8 .... 110 F5
Thurlestone Ave IG3 .. 152 F8
Thurloe Gdns RM11 ... 135 F5
Thurloe Wlk RM17 .... 173 A3
Thurlow Cl E4 .... 109 B4
Thurlow Cl SS11 **3** .. 132 A6
Thurlow Dr SS1 ...... 167 F8
Thurlow Gdns IG6 .... 111 D4
Thurlstone SS7 ...... 145 C5

Thurrock & Basildon Coll
  (Nethermayne Campus)
  SS16 .... 141 F4
Thurrock & Basildon Coll
  (Woodview Campus)
  RM16 .... 173 F2
Thurrock Bsns Ctr
  RM20 .... 176 F8
Thurrock Com Hospl
  RM16 .... 173 C5
Thurrock Commercial Ctr
  RM15 .... 170 F4
Thurrock Commercial Pk
  RM15 .... 170 F5
Thurrock Ent Ctr
  RM17 .... 178 A8
Thurrock Local History
  Mus* RM17 .... 173 B1
Thurrock Park Way
  RM18 .... 178 D7
Thurso Cl RM18 ...... 115 B4
Thurstans CM19 ...... 23 C3
Thurston Ave SS2 ..... 148 E1
Thynne Rd CM11 ...... 97 C2
Tickenhall Dr CM17 ... 24 D7
Tickfield Ave SS2 ..... 147 F2
Tideway
  Maldon CM9 .... 59 B8
  Southend-on-S SS1 .... 167 D6
Tidworth Ave IG2 ..... 99 E2
Tidy's La CM16 .... 46 B2
Tighfield Wlk CM3 .... 101 C5
Tilburg Rd SS8 .... 164 A4
TILBURY 179 B4
Tilbury Fort* RM18 ... 179 C3
Tilbury Manor Inf Sch
  RM18 .... 179 B7
Tilbury Manor Jun Sch
  RM18 .... 179 B7
Tilbury Mead CM18 ... 24 A6
Tilbury Rd CM13 ..... 139 E5
Tilbury Town Sta
  RM18 .... 178 F5
Tilegate Ho CM18 .... 23 F6
Tilegate Rd
  Harlow CM18 .... 23 F6
  Tilgate Green CM5 .... 25 D5
TILGATE GREEN 25 D5
Tilia Ct RM11 .... 136 D4
TILLINGHAM 63 F4
Tillingham Bold CM13 . 95 D4
Tillingham Ct EN9 .... 66 A6
Tillingham Gn **6**
  SS15 .... 141 A6
Tillingham Hall CM0 .. 63 E4
Tillingham Rd
  Southminster CM0 ..... 84 F6
  Tillingham CM0 .... 63 B2
Tillingham Way SS6 ... 123 A3
Tillotson Rd IG1 ..... 133 A4
Tillwicks Rd CM18 .... 24 A6
Tilney Cl IG9 .... 110 A8
Tilney Dr IG9 .... 110 A8
Tilney Rd
  Buckhurst Hill IG9 .... 110 B8
  Dagenham RM9 .... 153 F6
Tilney Turn SS16 ..... 142 F4
Timber Ct RM17 ...... 178 A8
Timberdene Ave IG6 .. 111 C2
Timberlog Cl SS14 .... 142 E6
Timberlog La SS14,
  SS16 .... 142 E6
Timbermans View
  SS16 .... 142 F4
Timber Wharf Cotts
  SS11 .... 100 E2
Time Sq SS14 .... 142 A5
Timsons La CM2 ...... 32 E4
Tindall Cl RM3 .... 114 F1
Tindall Mews RM12 ... 136 C1
Tindal Sq **3** CM1 ... 32 B2
Tindal St CM1 .... 32 B2
Tine Rd
  1 Chigwell IG7 ..... 111 E5
  Chigwell IG7 .... 111 F5
Tinker's La SS4 ...... 125 F1
Tinkler Side SS14 .... 142 B6
Tinnocks La CM0 ..... 40 B1
Tintagel Ct RM11 .... 136 A4
Tintagel Way CM9 .... 58 E8
Tintern Ave SS2 ...... 147 C2
Tintern Mews SS0 .... 147 C1
Tiplers Bridge CM11 .. 98 B5
Tippersfield SS7 ..... 144 E4
Tipps Cross CM15 .... 72 B5
Tipps Cross La CM15 .. 72 B4
Tipps Cross Mead CM15 72 B4
Tiptree
  Chingford E4 .... 109 C2
  Hornchurch RM11 ..... 137 A3
  Southend-on-S SS9 .... 146 F4
Tiptree Cres
  Ilford IG5 .... 133 A8
  Redbridge IG5 .... 111 A1
Tiptree Gr SS12 ...... 95 D4
Tiptree Gr SS12 ...... 121 D7
Tiree Chase SS12 .... 121 F5
Titan Rd RM17 .... 173 A1
Tithe Barn Agricultural &
  Folk Mus The*
  RM14 .... 137 D4
Tithelands CM19 ..... 23 A5
Tithe The SS12 ...... 121 B6
Titley Cl E4 .... 109 A5
Tiverton Ave IG5 .... 133 A8
Tiverton Gr RM3 ..... 115 A5
Tobruk Rd CM1 ...... 31 F6
Toddbrook CM19 ..... 23 B7

Todd Cl RM13 .... 155 D1
Toft Ave RM17 .... 173 D2
Tofts Chase CM3 ..... 34 E5
Tolbut Ct **5** RM1 ... 135 F5
Tolcairn Ct **2** DA17 . 169 A1
Toledo Cl SS1 .... 167 B8
Toledo Rd SS1 .... 167 B8
TOLLESBURY 40 E8
Tollesbury Cl **1** SS12 . 121 E6
Tollesbury Ct CM1 ... 32 C8
Tollesbury Gdns IG6 .. 133 D8
Tollgate SS7 .... 145 C6
Tollgate Rd DA2 ..... 176 D1
Tolworth Gdns RM6 .. 134 D6
Tolworth Par RM6 .... 134 E6
Tomkins Cl SS17 ..... 160 C3
Tomkyns La
  Romford RM14 .... 115 D1
  Upminster RM14 ...... 137 D7
Tomlinson Ho **19**
  CM14 .... 116 C7
Tomlins Orch IG11 ... 152 C4
Tomlyns Cl CM13 .... 95 E3
Tom Mann Cl IG11 ... 152 E4
Tomswood Ct IG6 ... 111 C2
Tomswood Hill IG6 .. 111 C3
Tomswood Rd IG7 .... 111 A4
Tom Tit La CM9 ...... 57 E7
Tonbridge Rd
  Hockley SS5 .... 124 F8
  Romford RM3 .... 114 D3
Tongres Rd SS8 ...... 164 A4
Took Dr CM3 .... 101 C6
TOOT HILL 47 F2
Toot Hill Rd CM5 .... 47 F1
Topaz Ct **3** RM13 ... 155 A1
Top House Rise E4 ... 87 C2
Toplands Ave RM15 .. 171 C5
Toppesfield Ave SS12 . 121 C5
Top Rd CM9 .... 35 D2
Tora Ct **12** IG9 ..... 110 C8
Torbitt Way IG2 ..... 133 F6
Tor Bryan CM4 ...... 74 B2
Torfell **5** E18 ...... 109 F1
Torney Ct SS16 ...... 140 F4
Toronto Rd
  Ilford IG1 .... 133 C3
  Tilbury RM18 .... 179 A6
Torquay Cl SS6 ...... 123 D5
Torquay Dr SS9 ...... 146 E1
Torquay Gdns IG4 ... 132 D7
Torquay Rd CM1 ..... 32 D5
Torrance Ct RM11 ... 136 C3
Torrell's Hall Cotts
  CM5 .... 28 E5
Torridge Rd RM18 ... 175 C2
Torrington SS3 ...... 168 D8
Torrington Cl CM1 ... 32 E5
Torrington Dr IG10 .. 89 C5
Torrington Gdns IG10. 89 C5
Torrington Rd
  Dagenham RM8 .... 134 F3
  Wanstead E18 .... 132 A8
Torsi Rd SS8 .... 164 D3
Torvill Ct **17** CM14 .. 116 C7
Totman Cl SS6 ...... 145 D8
Totman Cres SS6 .... 145 D8
Totnes Wlk CM1 ..... 32 D6
Toucan Cl SS3 ...... 149 E1
Toucan Way SS16 .... 142 A3
Tovey Ave EN11 ..... 21 A8
Tovey Cl EN9 .... 43 E8
Tower Ave
  Basildon SS15 .... 141 C7
Tower Cl CM14 ...... 31 F4
Tower Ct
  North Weald Bassett
  CM16 .... 47 D7
  Redbridge IG6 .... 111 B4
Tower Court Mews
  SS0 .... 166 E7
Tower Ct
  Brentwood CM14 ..... 116 C8
  Chipping Ongar CM5 .. 49 A2
  Southend-on-S SS0 ... 166 E7
Tower Ctr **1** EN11 ... 21 A6
Towerfield Cl SS3 .... 168 E7
Towerfield Rd SS3 ... 168 E7
Tower Hill CM14 ..... 116 C8
Tower Ho CM13 ...... 95 D2
Tower Hts **10** EN11 .. 21 A7
TOWER PARK 101 E4
Tower Rd
  Belvedere DA17 ...... 169 C2
  Epping CM16 .... 45 F1
  Writtle CM1 .... 31 B7
Tower Side SS5 ...... 101 E4
Towers Inf Sch RM11 . 136 C4
Towers Jun Sch
  RM11 .... 136 C4
Towers Rd
  Grays RM17 .... 173 C1
  Heybridge CM9 .... 37 C5
Town Croft CM1 ..... 32 A5
Towneley Cotts RM4 .. 91 E1
Townfield Rd SS4 .... 125 F2
Townfields SS2 ...... 148 A2
Townfield St CM1 .... 32 B3
Townfield Wlk SS3 ... 149 E4
Towngate Bsns Pk
  IG11 .... 153 A2
Town Mead Rd EN9 .. 65 C5
TOWN PARK 10 E2
Town Pier Sq DA11 .. 179 B1
Town Quay IG11 ..... 152 B4
Town Quay Wharf
  IG11 .... 152 B4
Townsend CM2 ...... 33 B5

Town Sq SS14 .... 142 A6
Tracyes Rd CM18 .... 24 B6
Traddles Ct CM1 .... 31 F6
Trade City RM3 ...... 114 D2
Trafalgar Bsns Ctr
  IG11 .... 152 F1
Trafalgar Ct E4 ..... 152 A4
Trafalgar Ho IG11 ... 153 B2
Trafalgar Pl E11 .... 132 A7
Trafalgar Rd
  Rainham RM13 .... 154 F3
  Southend-on-S SS3 ... 168 D7
Trafalgar Way CM12 .. 97 B3
Trafford Cl IG6 ...... 111 F4
Tramway Ho DA8 .... 169 E1
Tranquil Rise CM8 ... 169 E1
Trap's Hill IG10 ..... 88 F5
Trasa Ct **9** RM17 ... 178 C8
Travers Way SS13 ... 143 D7
Trayford Ct **8** RM19 . 171 B1
Treacle Mine Rdbt
  RM16 .... 173 F4
Treble Rd DA10 ..... 177 E1
Treebeard Copse
  CM3 .... 101 C6
Treeby Ct E4 .... 65 A2
Treecot Dr SS9 ...... 147 A4
Treelawn Dr SS9 .... 146 F4
Treelawn Dr SS9 .... 147 A4
Treelawn Gdns SS9 .. 146 F4
Tree Top Mews RM10 . 154 D6
Tree Tops
  Brentwood CM15 ..... 94 C1
  1 Woodford IG8 .... 110 A6
Treetops Sch RM17 .. 173 B2
Treetops View IG10 .. 88 D2
Trefgarne Rd RM10 .. 135 A2
Trefoil Ho RM17 ..... 178 B7
Tregaron Ho **3** RM3 . 114 D4
Treherm Rd IG6 ..... 111 D3
Trelawn CM1 .... 33 E8
Trelawn Ho RM16 ... 172 C3
Trelawney Rd IG6 ... 111 D3
Trenance Gdns IG3 .. 134 A1
Trenchard Cres CM1 . 32 D8
Trenchard Lo CM1 ... 32 C7
Trenders Ave SS6 ... 123 B7
Trenham Ave SS13 ... 143 D7
Trent Ct EN11 .... 21 A7
Trent Rd IG6 .... 175 C2
Trent Ave RM14 ..... 137 D5
Trentbridge Cl IG6 .. 111 F4
Trent Cl
  Burnham-on-C CM0 ... 106 A6
  Wickford SS12 .... 121 D6
Trent Ho E11 .... 132 A6
Trent Rd
  Buckhurst Hill IG9 ... 88 B1
  Chelmsford CM1 ..... 31 D5
Trescoe Gdns RM5 ... 113 C5
Tresco Gdns IG3 .... 134 A2
Tresco Way SS12 .... 121 F5
Tresham Rd IG11 .... 152 F5
Tresswell Rd RM9 ... 153 E4
Trevera Ct EN11 .... 21 A7
Trevor Cl CM12 ..... 118 F7
Trevor Rd IG8 .... 110 A3
Trevose Rd E17 ..... 109 D2
Trewithen Ct SS6 ... 146 A8
Triangle Garage CM9 . 37 B5
Triangle The
  Barking IG11 .... 152 C6
  Basildon SS16 .... 141 B4
Trianon Ct **10** SS13 . 143 C6
Trident Ind Est EN11 . 21 C7
Trienna Ct CM1 ..... 117 B7
Trilby Cl IG1 .... 133 E4
Trimble Cl CM4 ..... 74 B4
Trimley Cl SS14 ..... 142 C7
Trindehay SS15 ..... 141 E5
Trinder Way SS12 ... 121 B6
Tring Cl
  Ilford IG2 .... 133 D6
  Romford RM3 .... 114 F6
Tring Gdns RM3 .... 114 F6
Tring Gn RM3 .... 114 F6
Tring Wlk RM3 ...... 114 F6
Trinidad Gdns RM10 . 154 D5
Trinity Ave SS0 ..... 166 E7
Trinity Cl
  Basildon SS15 .... 141 C6
  Billericay CM11 ...... 119 C6
  Chelmsford CM2 ..... 32 D3
  Ilford IG6 .... 133 C8
  Rayleigh SS6 .... 123 C1
  Southend-on-S SS2 .. 148 D1
Trinity Ct E4 .... 109 C8
Trinity Gdns **11** E18 . 132 B8
Trinity Ho RM17 .... 178 B7
Trinity Lo SS2 ...... 148 D1
Trinity RC High Sch
  (Lower) IG8 .... 110 A6
Trinity RC High Sch
  (Upper) IG8 .... 110 A6
Trinity RC High Sch
  (Upper Sch) IG8 .... 109 F6
Trinity Rd
  Billericay CM11 ...... 119 C6
  Chelmsford CM2 ..... 32 D2
  Ilford IG6 .... 133 C8
  Rayleigh SS6 .... 123 C1
  Southend-on-S SS2 .. 148 D1
Trinity Road Prim Sch
  CM2 .... 32 D2
Trinity Row **8** SS4 ... 101 E7
Trinity St Mary's CE Prim
  Sch CM3 .... 101 E7
Trinity Sch
  Belvedere DA17 ..... 169 C2
  Dagenham RM10 ..... 154 A8
Trinity Sq SS3 ...... 101 E7
Trinity Terr IG9 ..... 88 B2

Trinity Wood Rd SS5 .
Tripat Cl SS17 ......
Tripton Rd CM18 ....
Triton Cl IG9 ....
Triton Lo DA8 ......
Triton Way CM3 ....
Triumph Cl RM16 ...
Triumph Ho IG11 ...
Trivett Cl DA9 ......
Trojan Terr CM21 ...
Troopers Dr RM3 ...
Tropical Wings World &
  Wildlife* CM3 ....
Trotter's Gap SS12 ..
Trotters Rd CM18 ...
Trotwood IG7 ....
Trotwood Cl
  Brentwood CM15 ....
  Chelmsford CM1 ....
Troubridge Cl CM3 ..
Trowbridge Rd RM3 .
Truelove Cl CM4 ....
Truman Cl **2** SS15 ...
Trumpeter Cl CM12 ..
Trunnions The SS4 ..
Truro Cres IG1 ......
Truro Gdns IG1 .....
Truro Wlk RM3 .....
Trusses Rd
  Bradwell on S CM0 ..
  Bradwell Waterside CM0.
Trustons Gdns CM3 ..
Trust The RM12 .....
Tryfan Cl IG2 ....
Tuck Rd RM13 ......
Tudor Ave
  Romford RM2 ....
  Stanford-le-H SS17 ...
Tudor Cl
  Brentwood CM15 ....
  Chigwell IG7 ....
  Hunsdonbury SG12 ..
  Ingatestone CM4 ....
  Rayleigh SS6 ....
  Southend-on-S SS9 ..
  Thundersley SS7 ....
  Woodford IG8 ....
Tudor Court Prim Sch
  RM16 ....
Tudor Cres IG6 .....
Tudor Ct
  Basildon SS15 ......
  Romford RM3 ....
  Sawbridgeworth CM21 .
Tudor Dr RM2 ......
Tudor Gdns
  Romford RM2 ....
  Southend-on-S SS9,
  Upminster RM14 .....
Tudor Mews
  Romford RM1 ....
  Southend-on-S SS9 ..
Tudor Par RM6 .....
Tudor Pl
  Buckhurst Hill IG9 ...
  Mayland CM3 ....
Tudor Rd
  Barking IG11 ....
  Canvey Island SS8 ...
  Chingford E4 ....
  Southend-on-S, Noblesgr
  SS7 ....
Tudor Way
  Hockley SS5 ....
  Waltham Abbey EN9 ..
  Wickford SS12 ......
Tudor Wlk SS12 ....
Tufnell Rd IG7 .....
Tufton Rd E4 ....
Tugby Pl CM1 ......
Tulip Cl
  Chelmsford CM1 ....
  Pilgrims Hatch CM15..
  Romford RM3 ....
Tulip Gdns
  Chingford E4 ....
  Ilford IG1 ....
Tumbler Rd CM18 ...
Tunbridge Rd SS2 ...
Tunfield Rd EN11 ...
Tunnel Cotts RM20 ..
Tunnmeade CM20 ...
Tunstall Ave IG6 ....
Tunstall Cl SS13 ....
Tupman Cl CM1 .....
Turkey Oaks CM1 ...
Turnage Rd RM8 ...
Turner Cl
  Basildon SS15 ......
  Southend-on-S SS3 ..
Turner Rd RM12 ....
Turners Ct CM15 ....
Turners Ct RM4 .....
Turnors CM20 ......
Turnpike La RM18 ..
Turnpike Rd CM12 ..
Turpin Ave RM5 ....
Turpin Cl CM21 ....
Turpin Rd RM16 ....
Turpin's La IG8 .....
Turpins The SS14 ...
Turret Ct CM1 ......
Tusser Ct CM1 .....
Tutors Way CM3 ....

ebee La IG9 ...... 110 A8
eby Cotts RM4 ...... 90 E2
n Terr 2 SS12 ...... 121 C5
d RM18 ...... 175 C2
d Glen RM1 ...... 113 D3
d Gn RM1 ...... 113 D3
d Way RM1 ...... 113 D3
ee Acre Ho 5

.... 133 A1
tyman CI IG8 ...... 110 A5
e CI IG11 ...... 153 B2
Oaks CM2 ......33 A4
tead SS12 ...... 121 F6
en La CM2 ......54 B2
e Fee CM3 ......57 A8
ree Island Nature
erve * SS9 ...... 165 B7
rd Ave SS3 ...... 150 A4
rd Rd IG1 ...... 152 C7
d Rd SS8 ...... 164 C5
ns The CM13 ...... 117 D8
urst Hill IG10 ......88 F5
OMMON 118 F8
mmon Rd

.... 118 E7
REEN 23 E6
een Village

.... 23 F5
ds CM12 ...... 118 F8
e CM3 ......78 C7
n RM11 ...... 136 F7
rst Gdns IG1 ...... 152 C7
CROSS

d SS9 ...... 115 A6
Ct 9 CM14 ...... 116 C6
S GREEN 47 D7
d CM19 ......22 D3
Ride CM3 ...... 101 E7
ay CM14 ......94 B1
d SS7 ...... 145 C3
low SS4 ...... 125 E3
CI IG7 ...... 111 F6
Croft CM19 ......23 B6
ay SS6 ...... 123 E4
CI SS5 ...... 101 D3
Ho SS5 ...... 101 D3
La CM3 ......57 B5
18 ...... 175 C2
RM14 ...... 137 D5
ns RM15 ...... 171 C6
se CM14 ...... 116 C5
d SS5 ...... 124 D5
ord CM2 ......32 E4
e RM14 ...... 137 B2
he SS17 ...... 161 A2
Way CM2 ......54 F7
I CM11 ...... 119 C6
d

y CM11 ...... 119 C6
eon-S SS1 ...... 168 A7
SS1 ...... 167 B8
6 SS13 ...... 143 C6
d SS2 ...... 101 D3
Mews CM11 ...... 119 D6
d CM11 ...... 119 D6
ch The CM1 ......32 E5
CM18 ......23 F5
I RM4 ......91 F2
ead CM3 ......33 E8
RM15 ...... 157 C2
n Way CM1 ...... 101 C2
CM1 ......32 E4

s RM5 ...... 113 A4
Ct 8 E18 ...... 110 A1
Rd SS7 ...... 144 E7
Way RM12 ...... 155 A7
e SS3 ...... 168 D6
.... 35 C6
I Rd CM9 ......35 E7
CM9 ......35 E6
CM9 ......35 C8
y SS11 ...... 122 A8
RM19 ...... 119 E6
Ho 1 RM3 ...... 114 E4
st London

.... 153 A8
ex (Southend
SS1 ...... 167 A8
M4 ......75 E2
n Sch IG1 ...... 152 B7

Uphall Rd IG1 ...... 152 B7
Uphavering Ho RM12 ...... 136 C2
Upland CI CM12 ......96 F4
Upland Court Rd RM3 ...... 114 F1
Upland Dr CM12 ......96 F4
Upland Rd
  Billericay CM12 ......96 F4
  Southend-on-S SS9 ...... 166 A8
  Thornwood CM16 ......45 F6
Uplands CI
  Hockley SS5 ...... 124 F5
  South Benfleet SS7 ...... 144 B3
Uplands Dr CM1 ......32 D7
Uplands Park Ct SS6 ...... 123 E3
Uplands Park Rd SS6 ...... 123 D3
Uplands Rd
  Brentwood CM14 ...... 116 E6
  Hockley SS5 ...... 124 F5
  Ilford RM6 ...... 134 D8
  South Benfleet SS7 ...... 144 B3
  Woodford IG8 ...... 110 E3
Uplands The IG10 ......88 F6
UPMINSTER 137 C2
Upminster Bridge Sta
  RM12 ...... 136 F2
Upminster Inf Sch
  RM14 ...... 137 C2
Upminster Jun Sch
  RM14 ...... 137 C2
Upminster Mill *
  RM14 ...... 137 B2
Upminster Rd RM11 ...... 136 F2
Upminster Rd N
  RM13 ...... 155 D2
Upminster Rd S RM13 ...... 155 B1
Upminster Sta RM14 ...... 137 C2
Upminster Trad Pk
  RM14 ...... 138 D4
Upney CI RM7 ...... 113 B1
Upney Ct 2 IG11 ...... 152 F5
Upney La IG11 ...... 152 F5
Upney Sta IG11 ...... 152 F5
Uppark Dr IG2 ...... 133 C5
Upper Abbey Rd
  DA17 ...... 169 A2
Upper Ave SS13 ...... 143 E8
Upper Brentwood Rd
  RM2 ...... 136 C3
Upper Bridge Rd CM2 ......32 A1
Upper Chase
  Althorne SS8 ......82 F3
  2 Chelmsford CM2 ......54 A8
Upper Church Hill
  DA9 ...... 176 E2
Upper Cornsland
  CM14 ...... 116 D7
Upper Holly Hill Rd
  DA17 ...... 169 B1
Upper Hook CM18 ......23 F6
Upper Lambricks SS6 ...... 123 E4
Upper Market Rd 3
  SS12 ...... 121 C8
Upper Marsh La EN11 ......21 A5
Upper Mayne SS14,
  SS15 ...... 141 F7
Upper Mealines CM18 ......24 A5
Upper Moors CM3 ......18 F7
Upper Park Rd
  Harlow CM20 ......10 B1
  Loughton IG10 ......88 D4
Upper Rainham Rd
  Hornchurch RM12 ...... 135 F2
  Rainham RM12 ...... 154 F8
Upper Roman Rd CM2 ......32 B1
Upper Ryle CM14 ......94 B2
Upper Sheridan Rd 3
  DA17 ...... 169 A2
Upper Stonyfield CM19 ......23 B8
Upper Swaines CM16 ......45 F1
UPSHIRE 66 D7
Upshire Mews EN9 ......66 A6
Upshire Prim Foundation
  Sch EN9 ......66 B6
Upshire Rd EN9 ......66 A6
Upton CI SS17 ...... 160 D2
Upton Ho RM3 ...... 114 D5
Upway SS6 ...... 123 D3
Upway The SS14 ...... 142 C8
Upwood Ct CM1 ...... 135 F7
Urban Ave RM12 ...... 136 C1
Urmond Rd SS8 ...... 164 A4
Urswick Gdns RM9 ...... 153 E5
Urswick Rd RM9 ...... 153 E5
Uttons Ave SS9 ...... 165 D8
Uvedale Rd RM10 ...... 135 A1
Uxbridge CI SS11 ...... 121 F6

V

Vaagen Rd SS8 ...... 164 B4
Vadsoe Rd SS8 ...... 164 B5
Valance Ave E4 ......87 F1
Valance Way SS16 ...... 141 C4
Vale Ave SS2 ...... 148 A2
Valebrook IG1 ...... 133 A2
Vale CI CM15 ......93 F4
Vale CI CM4 ......97 D6
Vale End CM2 ......32 E7
Valence Ave RM8 ...... 134 D2
Valence Cir RM8 ...... 134 D1
Valence House Mus *
  RM8 ...... 134 D2
Valence Inf Sch RM8 ...... 134 D1

Valence Jun Sch
  RM8 ...... 134 D2
Valence Wood Rd
  RM8 ...... 134 E1
Valentines
  Stock CM4 ......75 F2
  6 Wickford SS12 ...... 121 D6
Valentines High Sch
  (Upper) IG2 ...... 133 A5
Valentines Rd IG1 ...... 133 B3
Valentines Way RM7 ...... 135 E2
Valentine The IG2 ...... 133 A5
Valerie Ho SS9 ...... 146 E2
Vale The
  Basildon SS16 ...... 142 D3
  Brentwood CM14 ......94 C1
  Stock CM4 ......97 D7
  Woodford IG8 ...... 110 A3
Valiant CI RM7 ...... 113 B1
Valkyrie Rd SS2 ...... 166 D8
Vallance CI SS2 ...... 148 E3
Valletta CI CM1 ......32 A3
Valley Bridge CM1 ......32 B6
Valley CI
  Loughton IG10 ......88 F3
  Waltham Abbey EN9 ......65 C7
Valley CI IG8 ...... 110 B3
Valley Gdns DA9 ...... 177 B1
Valley Hill IG10 ......88 E3
Valley Lo IG10 ......88 F3
Valmar Ave SS17 ...... 160 B1
Vanbrugh Ave SS6 ...... 123 C8
Vanderwalt Ave SS8 ...... 164 D3
Van Dieman's La CM2 ......54 C8
Van Diemans Pass

Vanessa CI DA17 ...... 169 A1
VANGE 142 A5
Vange Corner Dr
  SS16 ...... 142 B1
Vange Hill Ct SS16 ...... 142 E4
Vange Hill Dr SS16 ...... 142 E4
Vange Park Rd SS16 ...... 142 E2
Vange Prim Sch SS17 ...... 142 D2
Vange Riverview Ctr
  SS16 ...... 142 A1
Vanguard CI RM7 ...... 113 B1
Vanguards The SS3 ...... 168 F7
Vanguard Way SS3 ...... 168 F7
Varangian Ho IG10 ......88 E6
Vantorts CI CM21 ......1 E2
Vantorts Rd CM21 ......1 E2
Varden CI CM1 ......31 F6
Vardon Dr SS9 ...... 146 B3
Vaughan CI
  Hornchurch RM12 ...... 155 E8
  Redbridge IG1 ...... 132 F4
Vaughan Ct SS4 ...... 125 E5
Vaughan Gdns
  Ilford IG1 ...... 133 A4
  Redbridge IG1 ...... 132 F4
Vaughan Williams Rd
  SS15 ...... 141 C8
Vaughan Williams Way
  CM14 ...... 116 B6
Vaulx Rd SS8 ...... 164 B4
Velizy Ave CM20 ......10 D1
Vellacotts CM1 ......32 B7
Venables CI
  Canvey Island SS8 ...... 164 C4
  Dagenham RM10 ...... 154 B8
Venette CI RM13 ...... 170 B8
Venlo Rd SS8 ...... 164 B5
Venmead CI 7 DA17 ...... 169 A2
Venta Way CM9 ......59 B8
Ventnor Gdns IG11 ...... 152 E6
Ventnor Mans IG11 ...... 152 E6
Verey Cres RM12 ...... 155 D7
Vera Rd CM1 ......99 A2
Verbena CI RM15 ...... 172 C7
Verderers Rd IG7 ...... 112 A6
Vere Rd IG10 ......89 C5
Vermeer Cres SS3 ...... 168 G8
Vermeer Ride CM1 ......32 F7
Vernal CI SS17 ...... 143 C8
Verney Gdns RM9 ...... 153 E6
Verney Rd RM9 ...... 153 E6
Vernon Ave
  Rayleigh SS6 ...... 123 B4
  Woodford IG8 ...... 110 D1
Vernon Cnr CM4 ......75 C2
Vernon Cres CM13 ...... 117 A7
Vernon Ct SS9 ...... 146 C1
Vernon Rd
  Ilford IG1 ...... 133 F3
  North Fambridge CM3 ......81 A3
  Romford RM5 ...... 113 C5
  Southend-on-S SS9 ...... 146 C1
  Swanscombe DA10 ...... 177 F1
Vernons Wlk 8 SS13 ...... 121 A1
Veronica CI CM1 ......32 B7
Veronique Gdns IG6 ...... 133 C6
Verons Wlk 10 SS14 ...... 142 F8
Vert Ho RM17 ...... 178 C7
Vestry CI SS15 ...... 141 C7
Vexil CI RM19 ...... 171 D2
Voysey Gdns RM10 ...... 135 A1
Viaduct Rd CM1 ......32 C6
Viaduct The E18 ...... 110 B1
Viborg Gdns CM9 ......58 E8
Vica Cotts CM3 ......34 D5

Vicarage CI
  Basildon SS15 ...... 141 C6
  Brentwood CM14 ...... 115 E6
  Canvey Island SS8 ...... 163 D3
  Roxwell CM1 ......30 B5
Vicarage Ct
  8 Billericay CM12 ......97 B2
  Southminster CM0 ......84 D2
  Waltham Abbey EN9 ......66 A5
  Woodford IG8 ...... 110 E3
Vicarage Dr
  Barking IG11 ...... 152 C5
  Northfleet DA11 ...... 178 C1
Vicarage Field Sh Ctr The
  IG11 ...... 152 C5
Vicarage Hill SS7 ...... 144 E2
Vicarage Hts SS7 ...... 144 E1
Vicarage La
  Chigwell IG7 ...... 111 D7
  Great Baddow CM2 ......54 F5
  Ilford IG1 ...... 133 D3
  Mundon CM9 ......59 E2
  North Weald Bassett

  Green CM16 ......47 B7
  North Weald Bassett, Tyler's
  Green CM16 ......47 D7
  Tillingham CM0 ......63 E4
  Wallend E6 ...... 152 A2
Vicarage Mdw CM0 ......84 D3
Vicarage Mews CM4 ......54 F6
Vicarage Rd
  Chelmsford CM2 ......54 B8
  Coopersale CM16 ......46 C2
  Dagenham RM10 ...... 154 B5
  Hornchurch RM12 ...... 136 A3
  Pleshey CM3 ......29 A2
  Roxwell CM1 ......30 D5
  Woodford IG8 ...... 110 E3
Vicarage Sq RM17 ...... 178 A8
Vicarage Wood CM20 ......11 A1
Vicar's Wlk RM4 ...... 134 B1
Viceroy CI
  Horndon on t H SS17 ...... 159 F3
  Southend-on-S SS0 ...... 166 B7
Vickers Rd
  Erith DA8 ...... 169 C1
  Southend-on-S SS7 ...... 147 D6
Victor App RM12 ...... 136 C2
Victor Ave SS13 ...... 143 D6
Victor CI RM12 ...... 136 C2
Victor Ct
  Hornchurch RM12 ...... 136 D3
  Rainham RM13 ...... 154 D3
Victor Dr SS9 ...... 165 F8
Victor Gdns
  Hockley SS5 ...... 124 F5
  Hornchurch RM12 ...... 136 D3
Victoria Ave
  Basildon SS16 ...... 141 C3
  Grays RM16 ...... 173 C4
  Rayleigh SS6 ...... 123 B4
  Romford RM5 ...... 113 B4
  Wickford SS12 ...... 121 C7
  Southend-on-S SS2 ...... 147 F2
Victoria Bsns Pk SS2 ...... 148 A2
Victoria Cotts
  Heybridge CM9 ......37 A5
  Ilford IG1 ...... 133 C6
Victoria Cres
  Basildon SS15 ...... 141 B8
  Chelmsford CM1 ......32 A3
  Wickford SS12 ...... 121 B7
Victoria Ct
  1 Brentwood CM14 ...... 116 C6
  Harlow CM20 ......10 B1
  Romford RM1 ...... 136 A6
  4 Southend-on-S, Westcliff-on-S
  SS0 ...... 166 F1
  1 Wanstead E18 ...... 132 B8
  Wickford SS11 ...... 122 A5
Victoria Dr
  Great Wakering SS3 ...... 150 C2
  Southend-on-S SS9 ...... 146 E1
Victoria Ho
  2 Romford, Ardleigh Green
  RM2 ...... 136 C7
  2 Romford RM1 ...... 135 F5
Victoria Lanes Sh Ctr
  SS1 ...... 167 A7
Victoria Plaza 4 SS1 ...... 167 A8
Victoria Plaza SS1 1
  SS1 ...... 167 A8
Victoria Rd
  Barking IG11 ...... 152 B6
  Basildon, Laindon SS15 ...... 141 A7
  Basildon, Vange SS16 ...... 142 D2
  Brentwood CM14 ...... 116 C6
  Buckhurst Hill IG9 ...... 110 D8
  Bulphan RM14 ...... 158 F8
  Chelmsford CM1 ......32 B3
  Chingford E4 ......88 A2
  Chingford, Highams Park
  E17 ...... 109 C1
  Cold Norton CM3 ......80 F6
  Dagenham RM10 ...... 154 C7
  Horndon on t H SS17 ...... 159 F3
  Maldon CM9 ......37 A2
  Rayleigh SS6 ...... 123 E3
  Romford RM1 ...... 135 F5
  Southend-on-S, Chalkwell
  SS0 ...... 165 E8
  Southend-on-S SS1 ...... 167 D7
  South Woodham Ferrers
  CM3 ...... 101 D6

Tut–Wag 229

Victoria Rd continued
  Stanford-le-H SS17 ...... 160 C2
  Waltham Abbey EN9 ......65 C5
  Wanstead E18 ...... 132 B8
  Writtle CM1 ......30 F1
Victoria Rd S CM1 ......32 B2
Victoria's Way RM15 ...... 172 C8
Victor Mew CI SS12 ...... 121 D5
Victor's Cres CM13 ...... 117 B8
Victor Wlk RM12 ...... 136 D3
Victory CI
  Grays RM16 ...... 172 D2
  Wickford SS11 ...... 122 A5
Victory Ct 4 IG11 ...... 153 B2
Victory La 125 D6
Victory Lo DA8 ...... 169 E1
Victory Rd
  Rainham RM13 ...... 155 A3
  Wickford SS11 ...... 132 B7
Victory Way
  Dartford DA2 ...... 176 C3
  Romford RM7 ...... 113 B1
Vienna CI IG5 ...... 110 D3
View CI IG7 ...... 111 D5
Viewpoint RM17 ...... 178 A8
Vigerons Way RM16 ...... 174 B2
Vignoles Rd RM7 ...... 135 A4
Vi & John Rubens Ho
  IG2 ...... 133 A5
Viking Bsns Ctr RM7 ...... 135 C4
Viking CI SS13 ...... 168 C7
Viking Rd CM9 ......36 E1
Vikings Way SS8 ...... 163 D3
Viking Way
  Belvedere DA8 ...... 169 C3
  Pilgrims Hatch CM15 ......94 B3
  Rainham RM13 ...... 155 A1
  Wickford SS11 ......99 E2
Village Arc The 2 E4 ......87 E1
Village CI
  Chingford E4 ...... 109 C5
  Hoddesdon EN11 ......21 D8
Village Dr SS13 ...... 163 E3
Village Gn SS4 ......33 A2
Village Gn SS4 ...... 104 D1
Village Hall CI SS8 ...... 163 D3
Village Home The
  IG6 ...... 133 C8
Village Hts IG8 ...... 110 F5
Village Inf Sch RM10 ...... 154 A8
Village Sq CM2 ......33 A3
Village Way IG6 ...... 133 C8
Villa Rd SS7 ...... 144 C4
Villiers Ct E4 ......33 E8
Villiers Way SS14 ...... 144 F5
Vincent Ave SS13 ...... 159 F3
Vincent CI
  Corringham SS17 ...... 161 B2
  Redbridge IG6 ...... 111 C4
  Southend-on-S SS3 ...... 168 A7
Vincent Ct CM14 ...... 116 B8
Vincent Lo CM3 ...... 101 B4
Vincent Mews SS12 ...... 168 E7
Vincent Rd
  Dagenham RM13 ...... 153 E5
  Rainham RM13 ...... 155 C1
  Rochford SS4 ...... 103 B1
Vincent Way CM12 ......97 A5
Vine CI SS13 ...... 142 E6
Vine CI 10 DA11 ...... 179 B1
Vine Gdns IG1 ...... 152 C7
Vine Gr CM20 ......10 D1
Vineries CI RM9 ...... 153 F6
Vine St RM17 ...... 135 C7
Vine Way CM14 ......94 C1
Vineyards The CM7 ...... 137 F2
Vintage Mews E4 ...... 109 A6
Vinters The SS2 ...... 147 F5
Viola CI
  Basildon SS15 ...... 141 C5
  South Ockendon RM15 ...... 157 C2
Violet CI CM1 ......32 E7
Violet Rd E18 ...... 110 B1
Virginia CI
  South Benfleet SS7 ...... 144 B7
Virginia Gdns IG6 ...... 111 D1
Virley CI CM9 ......37 D4
Vista Dr IG4 ...... 132 D6
Vista St SS1 ...... 121 F7
Voluntary PI E11 ...... 132 A5
Volvnycke Ave CM9 ......58 F8
Voorburg Rd SS8 ...... 164 C4
Vowler Rd SS16 ...... 141 B4
Voysey Gdns SS13 ...... 121 B1

W

Waalwyk Dr SS8 ...... 164 C4
Waarden Rd SS8 ...... 164 B4
Waarem Ave SS8 ...... 164 B4
Wadeville Ave RM6 ...... 134 F4
Wadeville CI DA17 ...... 169 A1
Wadham CM20 ...... 109 B3
Wadham CI CM4 ......74 B4
Wadham Park Ave
  SS5 ...... 102 A1
Wadham Rd E17 ...... 109 B2
Wadhurst Ct E6 ...... 152 A3
Wagon Mead CM22 ......3 A3
Wagstaff Gdns RM9 ...... 153 C5
Wagtail Dr CM9 ......37 C5

Waikato Lo IG9.......... 88 C1
Wainfleet Ave RM5 ..... 113 C1
Wainwright Ave CM13... 95 D3
Wake Arms Rdbt IG10 ... 66 F3
Wakefield Ave CM12 ..... 97 A2
Wakefield Gdns IG1 ... 132 E5
Wakefield Rd DA9 ...... 177 C2
Wakelin Chase CM6...... 74 A3
Wakerfield Cl RM11....136 F6
Wakering Ave SS3 ...... 168 G7
Wakering Rd
  Barking IG11 .... 152 C5
  Great Wakering SS3 ....150 B1
  Southend-on-S SS1,
  SS3 .... 149 A2
Wakescoline SS11 ...... 122 A6
Walace Ct EN3 .... 65 A2
Walbrook **10** E18 ..... 132 A8
Waldeck Rd DA1...... 176 A1
Waldegrave SS16 ......142 B4
Waldegrave Ct
  11 Barking IG11 .... 152 D4
  Upminster RM14 ....137 B3
Waldegrave Gdns
  RM14 .... 137 B2
Waldegrave Rd RM8 ... 134 C2
Walden Ave RM13 ..... 154 D3
Walden Rd RM11 ..... 136 D5
Walden Way
  Hornchurch RM11 ..... 136 D5
  Redbridge IG6 .... 111 E3
Waldon RM18.......... 175 C3
Waldringfield SS14 .... 142 B7
Walford Pl CM2........ 32 F2
Walfords Cl CM17....... 11 C3
Walfrey Gdns RM9 ..... 153 E5
Walker Ave CM5 .... 27 D2
Walker Dr SS9.......... 146 A2
Walkers Cl CM1 .... 32 D7
Walkers Sq SS17....... 160 D1
Walkey Way SS3...... 168 H7
Walk The
  Billericay CM12........ 97 A1
  Hornchurch RM11 ..... 136 F2
  Hullbridge SS5 .... 101 D3
Walkways SS8 .... 163 F5
Wallace Binder Cl CM9 ..36 F1
Wallace Ct SS5 .... 101 D3
Wallace Cres CM2 .... 54 D8
Wallace Dr SS12........ 121 E5
Wallace Gdns DA10 ... 177 E1
Wallace Rd RM17 ..... 173 A2
Wallace's La CM3....... 20 F4
Wallace St SS3 .... 168 F7
Wallasea Gdns CM1.... 32 F5
WALLASEA ISLAND 105 F2
Wall Chase CM6 .... 7 F7
WALLEND 152 A4
Wall End Ct E6 .... 152 A4
Wall End Rd E6........ 152 A5
Wallenger Ave RM2...136 B8
Wallers Cl
  Dagenham RM9........153 E4
  Woodford IG8 ....110 F4
Waller's Hoppet IG10 ... 88 F7
Wallers Way EN11 .... 8 B1
Wallflower Ct **11** CM1...32 F6
Wallingford Ho **2**
  RM3 .... 114 C4
Wallington Rd IG3....133 F4
Wallis Ave SS2 .... 147 F2
Wallis Cl RM11 .... 136 B3
Wallis Ct EN9.......... 65 B4
Wallis Pk DA11 .... 178 B2
Wall Rd SS8 .... 164 F3
WALL'S GREEN 29 B2
Walmer Cl
  Enfield EN9 .... 109 B8
  Romford RM7 ....113 B1
Walnut Cl
  Basildon SS15 .... 119 C1
  Ilford IG6 .... 133 C7
Walnut Ct SS5 ....124 E7
Walnut Gr
  Harlow CM20.......... 10 B1
  Hornchurch RM12 .... 136 D3
Walnut Tree Ave CM21 ... 1 E4
Walnut Tree Cl EN11 ....21 A6
Walnut Tree Cotts
  CM3 .... 18 E5
Walnut Tree Cres CM21 ...1 E2
Walnut Tree Rd
  Dagenham RM8........134 E2
  Erith DA8 ....169 E1
Walnut Way IG9....... 110 D7
Walpole Cl RM17 ..... 173 C2
Walpole Rd E18 .... 109 F2
Walpole Wlk SS6 .... 124 A2
Walsham Ent Ctr
  RM17................ 173 C1
Walsingham Cl **7**
  SS15 .... 141 C7
Walsingham Ho E4 .... 87 D2
Walsingham Rd SS2 ...148 B2
Walsingham Way
  CM12................. 97 B5
Walter Hurford Par **5**
  E12.................. 152 A8
Walter Mead Cl CM5....49 A4
Walters Cl
  Galleywood CM2 .... 54 C3
  Southend-on-S SS9 ...146 E6
WALTHAM ABBEY 65 D7

Waltham Abbey* EN9....65 C6
Waltham Cl **11** CM13....95 C3
Waltham Cres SS2......148 B3
Waltham Ct E17 .... 109 C2
Waltham Forest Coll
  E17.................109 B1
Waltham Glen CM2 ..... 54 C7
Waltham Holy Cross Inf
  Sch EN9 .... 65 D6
Waltham Holy Cross Jun
  Sch EN9 .... 65 D6
Waltham Park Way
  E17.................. 109 A3
Waltham Pk E17....... 109 A2
Waltham Rd
  Lower Nazeing EN9..... 44 A6
  Rayleigh SS6 ....123 B3
  Woodford IG8 ....110 E4
Walthams SS13 .... 143 B7
Walthams Pl SS13 .... 143 B7
Walthamstow Acad
  E17.................. 109 A2
Walthamstow Ave E4 .. 109 A3
Walthamstow Ave (North
  Circular Rd) E4 ...... 109 A3
Walthamstow Bsns Ctr
  E17.................. 109 C1
Waltham Way E4 .... 87 A1
Walton Ct
  Basildon SS15 .... 141 C8
  Hoddesdon EN11....... 21 C8
Walton Gdns
  Brentwood CM13....... 95 C4
  Waltham Abbey EN9 ... 65 B6
Walton Hall Farm Mus*
  SS17 .... 175 B5
Walton Hall La CM3..... 58 B1
Walton Rd
  Hoddesdon EN11....... 21 C8
  Little Ilford E12 .... 152 A8
  Romford RM5 .... 112 F3
  Southend-on-S SS1 ...167 F6
Walton's Hall Rd
  SS17................ 175 B5
Wambrook SS3 .... 149 D1
Wambrook Cl CM13.... 95 C1
Wamburg Rd SS8 ..... 164 E4
Wanderer Dr IG11..... 153 C2
Wangey Rd RM6......134 D4
Wannock Gdns IG6 .... 111 B3
Wansfell Coll CM16 .... 67 D4
Wansfell Gdns SS1 ...167 F8
Wansford Cl CM14..... 115 F7
Wansford Rd IG8 ..... 110 C2
WANSTEAD 132 C5
Wanstead Church Sch
  E11................ 132 A6
Wanstead High Sch
  E11................ 132 C5
Wanstead Hospl E11 ...132 B7
Wanstead Pl E11 .... 132 A6
Wanstead La IG1...... 132 E5
Wanstead Park Ave
  E12................ 132 D2
Wanstead Park Rd
  Ilford IG1 .... 133 A2
  Redbridge IG1....... 133 A2
Wanstead Pl E11 ..... 132 A6
Wanstead Sta E11 ... 132 B5
Wantage Ho **10** RM3 ... 114 D4
Wantfield Cotts CM4....74 F8
Wantz Chase CM9 ...... 37 A2
Wantz Cnr CM2......... 76 E5
Wantz Haven CM9 ..... 37 A2
Wantz La RM13....... 155 B1
Wantz Rd
  Dagenham RM10....... 154 B7
  Maldon CM9........... 37 A2
  Margaretting CM4..... 75 A8
Warboys Cres E4 ..... 109 C5
Warburtons SS17 .... 161 A2
Warburton Terr E17 ...109 B1
Ward Ave RM17....... 173 B2
Ward Cl SS15......... 141 D5
Warden Ave RM5 ..... 113 C5
Ward Gdns RM3 ...... 114 E1
Ward Hatch CM20 ..... 11 A3
Wardle Way CM1...... 31 E7
Wardona Ct
  Northfleet DA11....... 178 B2
  Swanscombe DA10 .... 177 F1
Wardour Ct **9** DA2 ... 176 B1
Ward Path CM4......... 33 B4
Wards Rd IG2........ 133 D4
Waremead Rd IG2.... 133 B6
Ware Rd EN11.......... 8 A1
Warescot Cl CM15..... 94 B2
Warescot Rd CM15.... 94 B2
Wares Rd
  Margaret Roding CM1... 16 C5
  Mashbury CM1........ 17 A4
WARLEY 116 D5
Warley Ave RM6...... 134 F4
Warley Gap CM13 .... 116 C3
Warley Hall La CM14...138 F4
Warley Hill CM13,
  CM14 .... 116 C5
Warley Hill Bsns Pk The
  CM13 .... 116 C4
Warley Hospl CM14 ...116 B5
Warley Mount CM14 ..116 C6
Warley Prim Sch
  CM14 .... 116 C5
Warley Rd
  Great Warley CM13 ....116 B3
  Redbridge IG5........ 111 A2
  Romford CM13......... 115 E1
  Woodford IG8 ....110 B3

Warley St CM13, RM14 ...138 C5
Warleywoods Cres
  CM14 .... 116 B6
Warlow Cl EN3 .... 65 A2
Warminster Ho RM3 ...114 F5
Warner Cl CM11 .... 97 D1
Warners Bridge Chase
  SS4................ 147 F6
Warners Cl IG8........ 110 A5
Warners Gdns SS4.... 147 E6
Warren Chase SS7 .... 145 A4
Warren Cl
  Broomfield CM1........ 19 B3
  Rayleigh SS6 .... 145 C8
  Southend-on-S SS17 ...160 D1
Warren Comp Sch The
  RM6................ 134 F6
Warren Ct IG7........ 111 D6
Warren Dr
  Basildon SS14 .... 142 E6
  Hornchurch RM12 .... 136 B1
  Wickford SS11........ 122 A8
Warren Dr The E11 ... 132 C4
Warren Farm Cotts
  RM6................ 134 F7
Warren Field CM16 .... 68 A7
Warren Hastings Ct
  DA11 .... 178 F1
Warren Hill IG10 ...... 88 C4
Warren Hts
  Grays RM16.......... 172 E2
  Loughton IG10....... 88 C4
Warren Jun Sch RM6 ...134 F6
Warren La
  Doddinghurst CM15..... 94 A8
  Grays RM16.......... 172 D2
Warren Pond Rd E4 .... 87 F2
Warren Prim Sch
  RM16 .... 172 C3
Warren Rd
  Chingford E4 .... 109 C8
  Ilford IG6 .... 133 D6
  Southend-on-S SS9 ... 146 A3
  South Hanningfield CM3 ...99 D7
  Wanstead E11........ 132 C4
Warren Terr
  Grays RM16.......... 172 D4
  Ilford RM6.......... 134 D7
Warren The CM12....... 96 E4
Warriner Ave RM12 ... 136 D2
Warrington Gdns
  RM11 .... 136 D5
Warrington Rd RM8....134 E2
Warrington
  Billericay CM12....... 96 F3
  Dagenham RM8........ 134 D2
Warrior Ho **7** SS1 ... 167 A8
Warrior Sq
  Little Ilford E12 .... 152 A8
  Southend-on-S SS1 ...167 A8
  Southend-on-S SS1 ...167 A8
Warrior Sq N SS1.... 167 A8
Warrior Sq Square Rd
  SS3................ 168 F5
Warwick Cl
  Canvey Island SS8.... 164 A5
  Hornchurch RM11 .... 136 F7
  Maldon CM9.......... 37 A1
  Rayleigh SS6 .... 123 F1
  South Benfleet SS7 ...144 D7
Warwick Cres CM9.... 37 A1
Warwick Ct
  Brentwood CM13....... 117 B7
  Burnham-on-C CM0 ... 106 B4
Warwick Dr
  Maldon CM9.......... 37 A1
  Rochford SS4........ 147 F7
Warwick Gdns
  Ilford IG1 .... 133 B3
  Rayleigh SS6 .... 123 F1
  Romford RM2 .... 136 C8
Warwick Gn SS6....... 124 A1
Warwick La RM13,
  RM14 .... 156 B3
Warwick Par CM3 .... 101 D8
Warwick Pl
  Northfleet DA11....... 178 B2
  Pilgrims Hatch CM14....93 C5
Warwick Rd
  Chingford E4 .... 109 A5
  Rainham RM13 ...... 155 D2
  Rayleigh SS6 .... 123 F1
  Rayleigh SS6 .... 146 B8
  Southend-on-S SS1 ...167 F6
  Southend-on-S SS1 ...167 C1
Warwick Sq CM1....... 31 F4
Washington Ave
  SS15............... 141 A6
Washington Cl CM9....36 E1
Washington Cl CM9....36 E1
Washington Rd
  Maldon CM9.......... 36 F1
  2 Woodford E18 ....109 F1
Wash La CM9.......... 38 B7
Wash Rd
  Basildon SS15 .... 119 E2
  Brentwood CM13....... 95 E4
Watchfield La SS6..... 124 C3
Watchbeach Rd RM9 ...153 C6
Waterdene SS8....... 163 F5
Waterfall **20** SS1 .... 167 C7
Waterfalls Rd SS16 ... 141 B3
Waterford Cl DA17 ... 169 A3
Waterford Rd SS3 .... 168 D5
Waterfront Wlk SS14...120 B1

Watergardens The
  IG8................ 110 A5
Waterglade Ind Pk
  RM20 .... 176 F8
Waterhale SS1 .... 149 A1
Waterhall Ave E4...... 109 E6
Waterhouse La CM1 .... 31 F1
Waterhouse Moor
  CM18 .... 23 F7
Waterhouse St CM1.... 31 F1
Water La
  Harlow CM19.......... 23 A5
  Ilford IG3 .... 133 F1
  Purfleet RM19....... 171 A2
  Roydon CM19......... 22 E4
Water Lane Prim Sch
  CM19 .... 23 A6
Waterloo Gdns RM7 ...135 E5
Waterloo La CM11 ..... 32 C2
Waterloo Rd
  Brentwood CM14...... 94 C1
  Redbridge IG6........ 111 C1
  Romford RM7 .... 135 E5
  Southend-on-S SS3 ...168 D7
Watermans RM1...... 135 F6
Watermans Way
  Greenhithe DA9....... 177 B3
  North Weald Bassett
  CM16 .... 47 A4
Watermark Ct **4**
  RM6................ 134 B5
Water Mdws
  Basildon SS13 .... 143 A4
  Chelmsford CM1...... 31 F4
Waters Edge SS0 ..... 166 D7
Waters Edge Ct DA8 ...169 F1
Waterside RM10...... 154 A7
Waterside SS16 .... 167 D6
Waterside Cl
  Barking IG11 .... 153 A8
  Romford RM3 .... 115 A3
Waterside Ind Est
  EN11 .... 21 D5
Waterside Mead SS8...163 F6
Waterside Pl CM22 ..... 2 E2
Waterside Rd
  Bradwell Waterside
  CM0 .... 41 F3
  Paglesham Eastend
  SS4................ 128 A5
Waters Mead SS1..... 168 A6
Watersmeet CM19 ..... 23 B4
Waterson Rd RM16 ... 174 C2
Waterson Vale CM2.... 54 C8
Waters Villas CM22 ..... 4 A6
Waterville Dr SS16.... 143 A4
Waterways Bsns Ctr **11**
  EN3................ 65 A1
Waterworks La SS17 ...161 D5
Watery La
  Battlesbridge SS11 ... 101 C1
  Matching Green CM17....26 D8
Wates Way CM15 .... 94 D1
Watford Ho RM3....... 114 F5
Watkin Mews EN3...... 65 A2
Watkins Cl SS13 ..... 121 D1
Watkins Way SS3.... 149 F1
Watlington Rd
  Harlow CM17........ 11 D4
  South Benfleet SS7 ...144 B2
Watson Ave E6 .... 152 A5
Watson Cl
  Grays RM20......... 177 A6
  Southend-on-S SS3 ...168 D7
Watson Ct **8** CM14 ... 116 C7
Watson Gdns RM3 ... 114 D1
Watsons Lo **9** RM10 ...154 B6
WATTON'S GREEN 92 B3
Watts Cres RM19 .... 171 C2
Watt's La SS14 .... 125 F1
Wat Tyler Ctry Pk*
  SS16 .... 143 B2
Wat Tyler Way SS16 ...162 B8
Wavell Cl CM1........ 32 D8
Waveney Dr CM1...... 32 C6
Waverley Bridge Ct
  CM9................. 37 B5
Waverley Cl E18 ...... 110 C1
Waverley Cres
  Romford RM3 .... 114 C3
  Wickford SS11........ 99 C3
Waverley Gdns
  Barking IG11 .... 152 E3
  Grays RM16......... 173 A4
  Ilford IG6 .... 111 C1
  Ilford IG6 .... 111 C1
Waverley Rd
  Basildon SS15 .... 119 E1
  Rainham RM13 ...... 155 B2
  South Benfleet SS7 ...144 C6
  Woodford E18 .... 110 C2
Wavertree Rd
  South Benfleet SS7 ...144 B4
  Woodford IG8 .... 110 A1
Waxwell Rd SS5 ..... 101 E2
Waycross Rd RM4 .... 137 C5
Wayfarer Gdns CM0... 106 A5
Wayfaring Gn RM17 ...172 F1
Waylands Cl SS12 .... 122 D8
Waylands
  Basildon SS15 .... 141 A8
  Southend-on-S SS9 ...146 B6
Waymans RM15...... 171 D7
Wayre St CM17 .... 11 C4
Wayre The CM17...... 11 C4
Wayside CM3......... 56 E8
Wayside Ave RM12....136 D2
Wayside Cl RM1..... 135 F8

Wayside Commercial Est
  IG11................
Wayside Gdns RM10 .....
Wayside Mews IG2 .....
Weald Bridge Rd CM16 ...
Weald Cl CM14 ....
Weald Ctry Pk* CM14.....
Weald Ctry Pk Visitor
  Ctr* CM14 ....
Wealden Ho CM15 ......
Weald Hall La CM16 ....
Weald Hall La Ind Est
  CM14 ....
Weald Park Way
  CM14 ....
Weald Pl CM14 ....
Weald Rd
  South Weald CM14 ....
  South Weald CM14 ....
Weald The SS8 ....
Weald Way RM7 ....
Weale Rd E4 ....
Wear Dr CM1 ....
Weare Gifford SS3 ....
Weaverdale SS3 ......
Weavers Cl **2** E11 ....
Weavers Ct **5** E11 ....
Weavers Ho **5** E11 ...
Webb Cl CM0 ....
Webber Ho **6** IG11 ...
Webb Ho **7** RM13 ...
Webbscroft Rd RM10....
Webley Ct EN3 ....
Webster Cl
  Hornchurch RM12 .....
  Waltham Abbey EN9 ...
Webster St SS6 ....
Webster Pl CM4 ......
Webster St SS13 .....
Websters Way SS6 ....
Wedderburn Rd IG11...
Wedds Way SS3 ......
Wedgewood Cl E11 ....
Wedgewood Dr CM17...
Wedgwood Ct SS4 ....
Wedgwood Way SS4....
Wedhey CM19 ....
Wedlake Cl CM11 .....
Wedmore Ave IG5 ....
Wednesbury Gdns
  RM3 ....
Wednesbury Gn RM3...
Wednesbury Rd RM3...
Weekes Cl SS17 .....
Weel Rd SS8 ....
Weight Rd CM2 .....
Weind The CM16......
WEIR
Weirbrook SS7 ....
Weir Farm Rd SS6....
Weir Gdns SS6 ....
Weir Pond Rd SS4 ....
Weir Wynd CM12 .....
Welbeck Cl SS3.......
Welbeck Dr SS16 .....
Welbeck Rd SS8 ......
Welbeck Rise SS16 ....
Welch Cl SS2 ....
Welland Mnth ....
Welland Ave CM1 .....
Welland Rd CM1 .....
Well Cottage Cl E11 ...
Weller Gr CM1.......
Wellesley CM19 ......
Wellesley Hospl SS2 ...
Wellesley Rd
  Brentwood CM14......
  Ilford IG1 ....
  Wanstead E11........
Wellfields IG10 ......
Wellingborough Ho
  RM3 ....
Wellingbury SS7 .....
Welling Rd RM16 ....
Wellington Ave
  Chingford E4 ....
  Hullbridge SS5.......
  Southend-on-S SS0 ...
Wellington Cl
  Chelmsford CM1 .....
  Dagenham RM10......
Wellington Ct RM16....
Wellington Dr RM10 ...
Wellington Hill IG10...
Wellington Ho **2**
  RM4 ....
Wellingtonia Ave
  CM12...............
Wellington Mews
  CM12...............
Wellington Pas **7**
  E11................
Wellington Pl CM14....
Wellington Prim Sch
  E4..................
Wellington Rd
  Hockley SS5.........
  Maldon CM9.........
  North Weald Bassett
  CM16 ....
  Rayleigh SS6 ....
  Tilbury RM18........
  Wanstead E11........
Wellingtons The CM0
Well La
  Danbury CM3 ....
  Galleywood CM2 .....
  Harlow CM19.........

continued
CM20. . . . . .23 A8
s Hatch CM15. . . . .93 F6
ckendon RM16 . . .172 E5
M4 . . . . .75 E1
d IG3 . . . . .134 A4
ad CM12. . . . . . . .119 C7
ads CM2 . . . . .54 B8
re SS2 . . . . .147 D6

ord CM1 . . . . .32 D5
ford RM1 . . . . . . .135 E5
d SS6 . . . . .123 E4
Ins
don SS14 . . . . . . .142 F8
am RM10 . . . . . . .154 B7
d RM13 . . . . .154 F6
ge IG1. . . . . .132 E4
d IG11 . . . . .153 A5
rk Sch IG7 . . . . . .111 F6
im Sch IG8. . . . . .110 A6
d CM1. . . . . .32 A3
d Gdns SS0 . . . .147 B3
d Rd E6. . . . . . . .152 A3
Gn SS14 . . . . . . .142 E8
r CM9 . . . . .37 B5
d Rd IG3 . . . . . . .134 A4
Way SS4 . . . . . . .126 A1
y Ave CM3 . . . . . .83 A8
e SS16 . . . . .142 F4
CI SS4 . . . . .125 C4
er Ct SS17 . . . . . .160 D1
er Gdns

. . . . .117 B7
r Way CM12 . . . .155 C7
Dr SS0 . . . . .147 E2
Gdns CM13 . . . . .95 C3
s La CM4. . . . . . . .72 E6
STON 170 E6
ton Rd RM13 . . . .170 C7
Ave IG8 . . . . .110 A3
CI RM5 . . . . .113 A5
ale Ave IG5 . . . . .112 E1
Rd SS7 . . . . .145 B5
th Ct E4 . . . . . . .109 D5
th Ho

. . . . .111 A3
th Mdws CM9. . . .36 F2
th PI RM16. . . . . .173 D3
th Prim Sch

. . . . .36 F1
th Rd SS2. . . . . .148 B3
th Way

. . . . .155 B2
Hall Rd

. . . . .133 A8
e IG5. . . . . .132 F8
SS3. . . . . .167 B8
ns CM12. . . . . . . .96 F5
SS1 . . . . .167 B7
Rd SS8 . . . . .164 B5
IG3. . . . . .133 E5
CI CM0 . . . . .63 E4
d IG10 . . . . .89 C6

CM3 . . . . .82 E2
SS16 . . . . .140 E4
rd CM1 . . . . .31 F5
e SS5. . . . . .101 C3
CM3. . . . . .60 E1
k IG11 . . . . .152 B4
ch Ave SS11 . . . .121 E7
ch Ct SS11 . . . . .121 E7
ch Mews

. . . . .121 D7
redere CM3. . . . . .56 F7
ugh Prim Sch

. . . . .147 E2
ugh Rd SS0 . . . . .147 D2
ne CI

SS7. . . . . .145 D5
S5. . . . . .125 A7
ne Ct SS0 . . . . . . .147 D2
ne Dr CM14 . . . . .115 F6
ne Gdns

. . . . .97 B5

ne Gr
rd CM2 . . . . .54 D7
-on-S SS0 . . . . . .147 B3
ers Rd CM9 . . . . .35 C4
SS4 . . . . .125 D4
Ct

g IG11 . . . . .152 D4
rst Hill IG9 . . . . .110 C8
Dr CM14 . . . . . . .116 C8
Ho SS2 . . . . .148 C2
La IG9. . . . . .110 C8
Rd

11 . . . . .152 D4
d CM14 . . . . .116 C8
Hill IG9 . . . . .88 C1
. . . . .133 A2
g11 . . . . .133 A2
n SS2 . . . . .148 C2
Rise CM17 . . . . . .24 D7
Terr RM14 . . . . . .137 E2
se

g 36 F3
M9 . . . . .59 E1

n En11 . . . . .21 A8
M13 . . . . .155 B1
ve SS0. . . . . .166 E7
Dr SS9. . . . . .146 D1
e SS3. . . . . .164 E2
High Sch for

. . . . .147 A3

Westcliff High Sch for
Girls SS0 . . . . .147 A3
WESTCLIFF-ON-SEA

. . . . .166 D8
Westcliff Par SS0. . .166 E7
Westcliff Park Dr

SS0. . . . . .147 D2
Westcliff Prep Day Sch

SS0. . . . . .166 C8
Westcliff Sta SS0 . .166 D8
West Cloister CM11 . . . .97 B2
West Cres SS8. . . . . .163 F4
West Crescent Rd **1**

DA12 . . . . .179 C1
West Croft CM11. . . . .97 B1
Westcroft Ct EN10 . . .21 A4
West Ct CM21 . . . . .1 E3
West Dene Dr RM3 . .114 D5
Westerdale CM1. . . . . .32 D7
Westerings
Bicknacre CM3. . . . . .56 F2
Purleigh CM3. . . . . . .58 D1
Westerings Prim Sch The

SS5. . . . . .124 E4
Westerings The
Great Baddow CM2. . .54 F5
Hockley SS5. . . . . . .124 E4
Westerland Ave SS8 . .164 D3
Western Ave
Brentwood CM14. . . . .94 C1
Dagenham RM10 . . .154 D6
Epping CM16 . . . . . . .67 F7
Romford RM2 . . . . . .114 C1
Western Cross CI

. . . . .177 C1
Western Ct **10** RM1 . . .135 E6
Western Espl
Canvey Island SS8. . .164 B1
Southend-on-S SS0,

SS1 . . . . .166 E7
Western Mews **9**

CM14 . . . . .116 C8
Western Mews CM12. . . .97 A2
Western Rd
Billericay CM12 . . . . . .97 A2
Brentwood CM14. . . .116 C8
Burnham-on-C CM0 . .106 C4
Hadleigh SS7 . . . . . .145 E6
Lower Nazeing EN9 . . .21 E1
Rayleigh SS6 . . . . . .123 B1
Romford RM1 . . . . . .135 F6
Southend-on-S SS9 . .146 B1
Western Terr **1** EN11 . . . .8 B1
Westernville Gdns

. . . . .133 C4
Westfield
Basildon SS15 . . . . .141 A8
Harlow CM18. . . . . . .23 E7
Loughton IG10. . . . . .88 C4
Westfield Ave CM1. . . . .32 A4
Westfield Bglws CM9 . . .59 E1
Westfield CI
Rayleigh SS6 . . . . . .123 B5
Wickford SS11. . . . . .121 F8
Westfield Gdns RM6 . .134 C5
Westfield Park Dr

IG8. . . . . .110 E4
Westfield Rd
Dagenham RM9 . . . .153 F8
Hoddesdon EN11 . . . .21 A7
WestHest Trad Est

SS11. . . . . .121 F6
Westgate
Basildon SS14 . . . . .142 A6
Southend-on-S SS3 . .168 E6
West Gate

Harlow CM20 . . . . . . .10 C1
Harlow CM20 . . . . . . .23 C8
Westgate Ho **6** SS4 . .125 F2
Westgate Pk SS14 . . .142 A5
West Gn SS7 . . . . . . .144 B5
West Gr IG8 . . . . .110 C5
WEST HANNINGFIELD

. . . . .77 B4
West Hanningfield Rd
Great Baddow CM2. . . .55 A3
West Hanningfield CM2. .76 E7
West Hatch High Sch

IG7. . . . . .110 F5
West Hayes CM22 . . . . .3 A3
West Ho IG11 . . . . . .152 B6
West Hook SS16 . . . .140 F4
WEST HORNDON

CM13 . . . . .139 D5
West Horndon Prim Sch

CM13 . . . . .139 C5
West Horndon Sta

CM13 . . . . .139 C5
West House Est CM0 . .84 D4
West Kent Ave CM21 . . .178 C1
Westlake Ave SS13. . .143 E6
Westland Ave RM11. . .136 E3
Westlands Com Prim Sch

CM1 . . . . .31 E2
Westland View RM16 . .173 A6
West Lawn CM2 . . . . .54 C2
Westleigh Ave SS9. . .146 D1
Westleigh Ct
Southend-on-S SS9 . .146 D1
16 Wanstead E11 . . .132 A6
West Ley CM0 . . . . . .106 C5
WESTLEY HEIGHTS

. . . . .141 D2
Westley Rd SS16. . . . .141 C2
West Lo RM17 . . . . . .173 B2

Westlyn CI RM13. . . . . .155 C1
West Malling Way

RM12 . . . . .155 C7
Westman Rd SS8 . . . .164 E3
Westmarch CM3 . . . . .101 C6
West Mayne SS15. . . . .140 E6
Westmayne Ind Pk

SS15. . . . . .140 E6
Westmede
Basildon SS16 . . . . . .141 C5
Chigwell IG7 . . . . . . .111 C4
West Mill RM11. . . . . .178 F1
Westminster Ct **4**

E11. . . . . .132 B5
Westminster Dr
Hockley SS5. . . . . . .124 D6
Southend-on-S SS0 . .147 B2
Westminster Gdns
Barking IG11 . . . . . .152 E3
Chingford E4 . . . . . . .87 E1
Redbridge IG6. . . . . .111 D1
Westminster Mans

SS0. . . . . .147 B2
Westmoreland Ave

RM11 . . . . .136 C6
Westmorland CI CM12 . .132 D2
Weston Ave RM20. . . .171 F1
Weston CI CM13 . . . . . .95 C2
Westone Mans **6**

IG11 . . . . .152 F5
Weston Gn RM9 . . . . .153 F8
Weston Rd
Dagenham RM9 . . . .153 E8
Southend-on-S SS1 . .167 A7
West Park Ave CM12. . . .97 A3
West Park CI RM6 . . . .134 E6
West Park Cres CM12 . .97 A2
West Park Dr CM12 . . . .97 A2
West Park Hill CM14 . .116 A7
West PI CM20 . . . . .11 A3
West Point PI SS8 . . . .163 C3
Westray Wlk SS12 . . .122 A5
West Rd
Dagenham RM6 . . . .134 E5
Halstead CM2 . . . . . .11 A4
Romford RM7 . . . . . .135 D4
Sawbridgeworth CM21 . . .1 C3
Southend-on-S, Cambridge

Town SS3 . . . . .168 D6
Southend-on-S SS0 . .147 E1
South Ockendon RM15 . .157 B2
West Ridge CM2 . . . . .119 A8
Westrow Dr IG11 . . . .153 A7
Westrow Gdns IG3. . . .133 F1
West Sq

Harlow CM20. . . . . . .10 C1
Maldon CM9. . . . . . . .36 F3
West St
Erith DA8 . . . . .169 E1
Gravesend DA11 . . . .179 B1
Grays RM17 . . . . . . .178 A8
Harwich CM23. . . . . .22 E7
Southend-on-S, Chalkwell

SS9 . . . . .165 E8
Southend-on-S SS0,

SS2 . . . . .147 E2
West Station Ind Est

CM9. . . . . .36 E1
West Station Rd SS9 . .36 E1
West Thorpe SS14 . . .142 B6
WEST THURROCK 177 D8
West Thurrock Prim Sch

RM20. . . . . .177 A8
West Thurrock Way

Grays RM20. . . . . . .172 B2
Purfleet RM20 . . . . .171 F2
WEST TILBURY 179 E8
West View
Ilford RM6. . . . . . . .134 C6
Loughton IG10. . . . . .88 F6
Westview Dr IG8 . . . . .110 D1
Westview CI SS14 . . . .155 C2
West View Dr SS6. . . .123 B1
Westward Ho SS1. . . . .166 F7
Westward Rd E4 . . . . .109 A5
Westwater SS7 . . . . . .144 B4
Westway
Chelmsford CM1 . . . . .53 D8
South Woodham Ferrers

CM3 . . . . .101 C7
West Wlk CM14 . . . . .116 C8
West Wlk CM20 . . . . . .23 C8
Westwood Ave CM14. . .116 A6
Westwood Gdns SS7 . .145 C4
Westwood Gdns SS7 . .145 D5
West Wood Prim Sch

SS7. . . . . .145 D4
Westwood Rd
Canvey Island SS8. . .164 B3
Ilford IG3. . . . . .134 A4
Wetherland SS15 . . . .141 C2
Wetherly CI CM17. . . . .11 F4
Wethersfield CI SS6 . .123 A3
Wethersfield Way

SS11. . . . . .122 B5
Weybourne CI CM3 . . . .58 E6
Weybourne Gdns SS3 . .168 B3
Weybridge Wlk SS3 . .149 E1
Weydale CM1 . . . . . . .32 E6
Weyland Rd RM8 . . . . .134 F1
Weymarks SS3 . . . . . .141 D7
Weymouth Dr RM20. . .172 D1
Weymouth Rd CM1 . . . .32 E6

Whadden Chase CM4. . .74 A3
Whalebone Ave RM6. . .134 F5
Whalebone Gr RM6 . . .134 F5
Whalebone La N RM6. .134 E8
Whalebone La S RM6,

RM8 . . . . .134 F4
Wharf CI SS17 . . . . . .160 D1
Wharf Ho DA8. . . . . . .169 E1
Wharf Rd
Brentwood CM14 . . . .116 C7
Chelmsford CM2 . . . . .32 C2
Fobbing SS17 . . . . . .161 D3
Gravesend DA12 . . . .179 E1
Grays RM17. . . . . . .177 F8
Heybridge Basin CM9 . .37 F4
Hoddesdon EN10 . . . . .43 A7
Stanford-le-H SS17 . .175 E7
Wharf Rd S RM17. . . . .177 F8
Wharfside CI DA8. . . . .169 F1
Wharley Hook CM18 . . .24 A5
Wharnecliffe Ho **3**

DA9 . . . . .177 B1
Wharton Dr CM1 . . . . . .33 A7
Wheatear PI CM11. . . . .97 C1
Wheatfields
3 Brentwood CM14 . .116 C6
Harlow CM17. . . . . . .11 D6
Rochford SS4. . . . . .126 D4
Wheatfield Way
Basildon SS14 . . . . .141 A4
Chelmsford CM1 . . . . .31 F3
Wheatley CI
Greenhithe DA9. . . . .177 A2
Hornchurch RM11 . . .136 D6
Rochford SS4. . . . . .125 D4
Sawbridgeworth CM21 . . .1 C1
Wheatley Mans **8**

IG11 . . . . .153 A5
Wheatley Rd SS17 . . . .161 B8
Wheatshead Rd RM1 . .135 F5
Wheatstone Rd DA8 . .169 D1
Wheeler CI IG8. . . . . .110 F5
Wheelers CM16. . . . . . .46 A2
Wheelers CI EN9 . . . . . .21 F1
Wheelers Cross IG11 . .152 D3
Wheelers Farm Gdns

CM16 . . . . .47 B5
Wheeler's Hill CM3 . . . .19 C6
Wheelers La
Fobbing SS17 . . . . . .161 D4
Pilgrims Hatch CM14. . .93 B6
West Farm Dr RM10 . .135 C1
Wheelwrights The

SS2. . . . . .148 A5
Whernside Ave SS4 . . .164 C5
Whieldon Grange

CM17. . . . . .24 E7
Whinhams Way CM12 . .96 F3
Whistler Mews **1**

RM8. . . . . .153 B7
Whistler Rise SS3 . . . .168 G8
Whitakers Way IG10 . . .88 B7
Whitbread PI **11**

CM14 . . . . .116 C7
Whitby Ave CM13 . . . .117 D4
Whitby CI DA9. . . . . . .177 A2
Whitby Rd CM0 . . . . . .106 C5
Whitchurch Rd RM3 . .114 E6
Whitcroft SS16 . . . . . .141 C3
Whitebarn La RM10. . .154 A4
Whitebeam CI CM2 . . . .53 F7
Whitebeam Dr RM15 . .157 C2
White Bridge Jun & Inf

Schs The IG10 . . . . .88 F2
White Elm Rd CM3. . . . .57 A2
Whitefield Ct CM3. . . . .83 A8
Whitefield Schs E17 . .109 D1
Whitefriars Cres SS9 . .166 C8
Whitegate Rd SS1. . . .167 A8
White Gates RM12 . . . .136 C3
White Gdns RM10. . . . .154 A6
White Hall RM4. . . . . . .90 B6
Whitehall CI
Chigwell IG7 . . . . . . .112 A7
Lower Nazeing EN9 . . .21 E1
Whitehall Cotts SS12 . . .9 D8
Whitehall Est CM19. . . .23 C7
Whitehall La
Corringham SS17. . . .161 C6
Grays RM17 . . . . . . .173 C1
Woodford IG9 . . . . . .110 A8
Whitehall Lo IG8 . . . . .110 A7
Whitehall Rd

E4. . . . . .109 C8
Whitehall Rd
Chingford E4 . . . . . . .109 C8
Grays RM17 . . . . . . .173 C2
Woodford IG8 . . . . . .110 A7
White Hall Rd DA8 . . . .150 B4
White Hart CI SS3. . . .168 C5
White Hart Cotts CM2. .33 A6
White Hart La
Brentwood CM14 . . . .116 C8
Chelmsford CM1 . . . . .32 F4
Hockley SS5. . . . . . .124 F5
Romford RM7 . . . . . .113 A1
White Hart Yd DA11. . .179 B1
Whitehead CI CM1. . . . .32 A4
Whitehills Rd IG10 . . . .89 A6
White Horse La CM9 . . .36 F2
White Ho The IG3 . . . .134 A3
White House Chase **1**

SS6. . . . . .123 E1
White House Cres CM2 . .54 D8
White House Ct **3**

SS6. . . . . .123 E1

Whitehouse Mdws

SS9. . . . . .147 A6
Whitehouse Mews **2**

SS6. . . . . .123 E1
Whitehouse Rd
Southend-on-S SS9 . .147 A6
South Woodham Ferrers

CM3 . . . . .101 D8
Whitelands CM15. . . . . .72 D4
Whitelands CI SS11. . . .99 E1
Whitelands Way RM3 . .114 E8
White Lyons Rd CM14. .116 C7
White Mead CM1 . . . . . .19 B2
White Post Field CM21. . .1 D2
White Rd SS8 . . . . . . .163 C3
WHITE ROOTHING OR
WHITE RODING 14 C8
Whites Ave IG2 . . . . . .133 E5
Whitesbridge La CM4. . .53 D1
Whites CI DA9 . . . . . . .177 C1
White's Hill CM4. . . . . . .75 F1
Whiteshott SS16 . . . . .142 A4
Whitesmith Dr CM2 . . . .96 E3
Whitethorn Gdns
Chelmsford CM2 . . . . .54 C7
Hornchurch RM11 . . .136 C5
White Tree CM3 . . . . .101 B6
Whitewaits CM20 . . . . .10 E1
Whiteways
Billericay CM11. . . . . .97 E3
Canvey Island SS8. . .164 D2
Southend-on-S SS9 . .146 F6
Whitfield CI IG1. . . . . .132 F4
Whitfield Link CM3. . . . .54 D7
Whitfield SS17. . . . . . .160 F2
Whiting Ave IG11 . . . .152 B5
Whiting The IG2. . . . . .133 E6
Whitley Ct EN11 . . . . . .21 B8
Whitley Rd EN11. . . . . .21 B8
Whitmore Ave
Grays RM16 . . . . . . .173 B6
Romford RM3 . . . . . .114 E1
Whitmore Ct CM16. . . .174 E7
Whitmore Cres CM2 . . .33 B4
Whitmore Ct SS14 . . . .142 E8
Whitmore Jun & Inf Sch

SS14. . . . . .120 E1
Whitmore Way SS14 . .142 D8
Whitnell Ct SS14 . . . . .142 D8
Whittingham Ave SS12 . .148 E2
Whittingstall Rd EN11 . .21 C8
Whittington Rd CM13 . . .95 D4
Whitwell Ct SS17 . . . .175 D4
Whitworth Cres EN3 . . .65 A2
Whybrews SS12. . . . . .160 F2
Whybridge CI RM13. . .154 F6
Whybridge Inf Sch

RM13 . . . . .155 A4
Whybridge Jun Sch

RM13 . . . . .154 F4
Whytewaters SS16 . . .142 F4
Whyverne CI CM1. . . . . .32 E6
Wick Beech Ave SS11. .121 E7
Wick Chase SS1 . . . . .167 F7
Wick Cres SS12 . . . . .121 E5
Wick Dr
Wickford, Nevendon

SS12. . . . . .121 E5
Wickford SS12. . . . . .121 D7
Wickets Way IG6. . . . .111 F4
Wick Farm Rd CM0 . . . .62 C8
Wickfield Ash CM1. . . . .31 F6
Wickfields IG7 . . . . . .111 D4
WICKFORD 121 A5
Wickford Ave SS13. . . .143 B5
Wickford Bsns Pk **3**

SS11. . . . . .122 A5
Wickford CE Inf Sch

SS11. . . . . .121 E8
Wickford CI RM3 . . . . .114 F5
Wickford Dr RM3 . . . . .114 F5
Wickford Hall SS11. . . .121 F8
Wickford Inf Sch The

SS12. . . . . .121 C7
Wickford Mews **7**

SS13. . . . . .143 A6
Wickford PI **8** SS13 . .143 A6
Wickford Rd
Southend-on-S SS0 . .166 E7
South Woodham Ferrers

CM3 . . . . .101 B8
Wickford Sta SS12 . . .121 C8
Wick Glen CM11 . . . . . .96 F4
Wickham Bsns Pk

SS14. . . . . .120 F2
Wickham Cres SS13 . . .31 F6
Wickham Cres SS12 . .142 C5
Wickham Rd
Chingford E4 . . . . . . .109 C3
Grays RM16. . . . . . .174 C4
Wickham's Chase CM3. .57 C2
Wickhay SS15 . . . . . . .141 F5
Wickhay Cotts CM3. . . .34 D5
Wick La SS11 . . . . . . .121 E7
Wicklands Rd SS12. . . . .9 D8
Wicklow Ave CM1. . . . . .31 B5
Wicklow Way SS3. . . . .168 C7
Wickmead CI SS2. . . . .148 E2
Wick Place Farm

RM14 . . . . .159 A8
Wick Rd Ho. 106 D4
Widbrook CM15. . . . . . .72 C3

Wid Cl CM13 . . . . .95 D4
Widecombe Cl RM3 . . . . 114 D2
Widecombe Gdns
  IG4 .132 E7
WIDFORD 53 E6
Widford Chase CM2 . . . . .53 F7
Widford Cl CM2 . . . . .53 F7
Widford Gr CM2 . . . . .53 F7
Widford Ind Est CM1 . . . . .53 E8
Widford Lodge Sch
  CM2 .53 F7
Widford Park Pl CM2 . . . . .53 F7
Widford Rd CM2 . . . . .53 F7
Widgeons SS13 . . . . 143 C6
Wid Terr CM15 . . . . .72 C3
Widworthy Hayes
  CM13 . . . . .95 B1
Wiggins La CM12 . . . . 118 E6
Wiggin's La CM12 . . . . 118 E7
Wiggins View CM2 . . . . . . .33 B4
Wigham Ho IG11 . . . . 152 C5
Wigley Bush La CM14 . . . 115 E7
Wigram Rd E11 . . . . 132 C5
Wigton Rd RM3 . . . . 114 E6
Wilde Cl RM18 . . . . 179 C5
Wilfred Ave RM13 . . . . . . 170 A8
Wilfred St 15 DA11 . . . . . 179 B1
Wilkes Rd CM13 . . . . .95 D4
Wilkin Ct SS9 . . . . 146 D2
Wilkinson Cl DA1 . . . . 176 A3
Wilkinson Drop SS7 . . . . 145 E2
Wilkinsons Mead CM2 . . .33 A4
Willetts Mews EN11 . . . . . .21 A7
William Ash Cl RM9 . . . . 153 B6
William Bellamy Inf Sch
  RM10 . . . . 135 A2
William Bellamy Jun Sch
  RM10 . . . . 135 A2
William Cl RM5 . . . . 113 D2
William Ct
  4 Belvedere DA17 . . . . 169 A2
  Ilford IG6 . . . . 133 D7
William de Ferrers Sch
  CM3 . . . . 101 E7
William Edwards Sch &
  Sports Coll RM16 . . . . . 173 B6
William Ford CE Jun Sch
  RM10 . . . . 154 A5
William Hunter Way
  CM14 . . . . 116 C8
William Martin CE Jun &
  Inf Schs CM18 . . . . .23 F6
William Pike Ho 4
  RM7 . . . . 135 D5
William Rd SS13 . . . . 143 F6
William Read Prim Sch
  SS8 . . . . 163 F3
Williams Gn SS5 . . . . 101 E3
William Smith Ho 10
  DA17 . . . . 169 A3
Williamsons Way
  SS7 . . . . 160 F5
Williams Rd CM1 . . . . .19 B1
William St
  Barking IG11 . . . . 152 C5
  Grays RM17 . . . . 178 C8
William Tansley Smith Ho
  RM12 . . . . 136 F2
William Torbitt Prim Sch
  IG2 . . . . 133 F6
WILLINGALE 28 D3
Willingale Ave SS6 . . . . . 123 A3
Willingale Cl
  Brentwood CM13 . . . . . .95 E3
  Loughton IG10 . . . . .89 C7
  Woodford IG8 . . . . 110 C4
Willingale Ct CM16 . . . . . .67 E3
Willingale Rd
  Fyfield CM5 . . . . .27 F2
  Loughton IG10 . . . . .89 D7
  Willingale CM4, CM5 . . .50 E6
Willingales The 9
  SS15 . . . . 141 A6
Willingale Way SS1 . . . . . 149 A1
Willinghall CE Prim
  IG10 . . . . .65 D7
Willis Ho 2 E12 . . . . 133 A1
Willis Rd DA8 . . . . 169 D2
Willmott Rd SS2 . . . . 147 D6
Willoughby Dr
  Chelmsford CM2 . . . . . . .32 F2
  Rainham RM13 . . . . 154 E5
Willowbank CM2 . . . . .54 B3
Willowbrook Prim Sch
  CM13 . . . . .95 D3
Willow Cl
  8 Dagenham RM8 . . . . 134 D4
  Ilford IG6 . . . . 152 C7
Willowdale Ctr SS12 . . . . 121 D8
Willowdene SS15 . . . . .93 F4
Willowdene Ct CM14 . . . . 116 C6
Willow Dr SS6 . . . . 123 C4

Willowfield
  Basildon SS15 . . . . 119 C1
  Harlow CM18 . . . . .23 D6
Willow Gn CM4 . . . . .74 B4
Willow Gr CM3 . . . . .79 A1
Willowherb Wlk RM3 . . . 114 C3
Willowhill SS17 . . . . 160 E5
Willow Ho 1 SS13 . . . . . . 143 B8
Willow Lo
  South Benfleet SS7 . . . . 144 F6
  Southend-on-S SS3 . . . . 168 F8
Willowmead IG7 . . . . 112 A7
Willow Mead CM21 . . . . . . .1 E2
Willowmeade CM11 . . . . . .98 C5
Willow Par RM14 . . . . 137 E3
Willow Path EN9 . . . . .65 E5
Willow Pk CM4 . . . . .74 D4
Willow Pl CM17 . . . . .25 A4
Willow Rd RM6 . . . . 134 C5
Willows Prim Sch
  CM14 . . . . 142 C8
Willow St
  Chingford E4 . . . . .87 D2
  Romford RM7 . . . . 135 C7
Willows The
  13 Basildon SS13 . . . . . 143 C6
  Billericay CM11 . . . . 119 D7
  Boreham CM3 . . . . .33 F8
  Chelmsford CM1 . . . . . . .32 A2
  Grays RM17 . . . . 178 E8
  1 Loughton IG10 . . . . . . .88 D4
  South Benfleet SS7 . . . . 144 B4
  Southend-on-S SS1 . . . . 149 A1
  Wallend E12 . . . . 152 A5
Willow Tree Cl RM4 . . . . . .90 B6
Willow Way RM3 . . . . 115 B4
Willow Wlk
  Canewdon SS4 . . . . 104 D1
  Hadleigh SS7 . . . . 145 D3
  Heybridge CM9 . . . . .37 C6
  Hockley SS5 . . . . 124 F6
  Upminster RM14 . . . . . . 137 E3
Will Perrin Ct RM13 . . . . 155 A4
Wills Hill SS17 . . . . 160 D3
Wilmington Gdns
  IG11 . . . . 152 E5
Wilmot Gn CM13 . . . . 116 C4
Wilmot Ho CM13 . . . . 116 C4
Wilmslowe SS8 . . . . 164 E5
Wilmslow Ho 3 RM3 . . . 114 E6
Wilnett Ct 4 RM6 . . . . . . 134 B4
Wilnett Villas 5 RM6 . . . 134 B4
Wilrich Ave SS8 . . . . 164 D3
Wilshire Ave CM2 . . . . . . .32 F3
Wilsman Rd RM15 . . . . . . 157 C3
Wilsner SS13 . . . . 143 C7
Wilson Cl SS17 . . . . 175 C8
Wilson Ct SS12 . . . . 121 C6
Wilson Rd
  Redbridge IG1 . . . . 132 F4
  Southend-on-S SS1 . . . . 166 F7
Wilson's Cnr CM14,
  CM15 . . . . 116 D8
Wilson's Ct CM9 . . . . .37 B2
Wilthorne Gdns RM10 . . . 154 B5
Wilton Ct 8 IG8 . . . . 110 A4
Wilton Dr RM5 . . . . 113 D3
Wiltshire Ave RM11 . . . . 136 F7
Wiltshire Cl IG1 . . . . 152 C6
Wimarc Cres SS4 . . . . . . 123 B4
Wimbish Ct SS13 . . . . . . 143 B6
Wimbish End SS13 . . . . . 143 B6
Wimbish Mews SS13 . . . 143 B6
Wimborne Cl
  Buckhurst Hill IG9 . . . . 110 C8
  Sawbridgeworth CM21 . . .1 D2
Wimborne Rd SS12 . . . . 121 B8
Wimborne SS15 . . . . 141 A7
Wimhurst Cl SS5 . . . . . . 124 E7
Wimbrook Cl SS6 . . . . . . 145 E8
Wimbrook Rd SS6 . . . . . 145 E8
Wincanton Gdns
  Ilford IG6 . . . . 133 B8
  Redbridge IG6 . . . . 111 B1
Wincanton Rd RM3 . . . . 114 D7
Winchcombe Cl SS9 . . . 146 E3
Winchelsea Dr CM2 . . . . .54 E7
Winchester Ave RM14 . . . 137 F2
Winchester Cl
  Southend-on-S SS9 . . . . 146 F7
  8 Waltham Abbey EN9 . .65 B6
Winchester Ct 9
  DA17 . . . . 169 A1
Winchester Dr SS6 . . . . . 123 B6
Winchester Gdns
  SS15 . . . . 119 C1
Winchester Ho 8
  IG11 . . . . 153 A5
Winchester Rd
  Chingford E4 . . . . 109 C3
  Ilford IG1 . . . . 133 D1
Wickford Cl CM3 . . . . .19 B6
Wincoat Cl SS7 . . . . 144 C3
Wincoat Dr SS7 . . . . 144 C3
Windermere Ave
  Hornchurch RM12 . . . . . 155 A8
  Hullbridge SS5 . . . . 101 D2
Windermere Gdns
  IG4 . . . . 132 E6
Windermere Rd
  South Benfleet SS7 . . . . 144 E2
  Southend-on-S SS1 . . . . 167 C8
Wind Hill CM5 . . . . .26 A4
Winding Way RM8 . . . . . . 134 C1
Windley Tye CM1 . . . . . . .31 E3
Windmill
  Upminster RM14 . . . . . . 137 A2
  Waltham Abbey EN9 . . . . .65 E5

Windmill Fields CM17 . . . . .11 F4
Windmill Hts CM12 . . . . . 119 B8
Windmill Mdws CM6 . . . . . .5 C2
Windmill St DA12 . . . . 179 B1
Windmills The CM1 . . . . . .19 B3
Windmill Stps 8 SS1 . . . . 167 C7
Windmill Way CM1 . . . . . .71 E2
Windrush Ct SS8 . . . . 164 E1
Windrush Dr CM1 . . . . . . .32 C6
Windsor Ave
  Corringham SS17 . . . . . . 161 A4
  Grays RM16 . . . . 173 B4
Windsor Cl
  Canvey Island SS8 . . . . . 164 B3
  Southend-on-S SS9 . . . . 146 E3
Windsor Gdns
  Hadleigh SS7 . . . . 145 C4
  Hockley SS5 . . . . 125 B4
  Wickford SS11 . . . . .99 D1
Windsor Mews SS6 . . . . . 123 C1
Windsor Rd
  Basildon SS13, CM11 . . . 143 E8
  Chingford E4 . . . . 109 B6
  Dagenham RM8 . . . . 134 E1
  Hornchurch RM11 . . . . . 136 C4
  Ilford IG1 . . . . 152 C8
  Pilgrims Hatch CM15 . . . .94 B3
  Ramsden Heath CM11 . . .98 D4
  Southend-on-S SS0 . . . . 147 E1
  Wanstead E11 . . . . 132 A2
Windsors The IG9 . . . . . . 110 E8
Windsor Trad Est
  SS1 . . . . .98 D4
Windsor Way
  Chelmsford CM1 . . . . . . .31 E1
  Rayleigh SS6 . . . . 123 E1
Windsor Wood EN9 . . . . . .65 E6
Windward Way CM3 . . . . . 101 F6
Windy Hill CM13 . . . . .95 C1
Winfields SS13 . . . . 143 C7
Winford Dr RM10 . . . . . . .21 A1
Wingate Rd IG1 . . . . 152 B7
Wingfield CM17 . . . . 172 F1
Wingfield Cl CM13 . . . . . . 117 A7
Wingfield Dr RM16 . . . . . 174 A8
Wingfield Gdns RM14 . . . 137 F5
Wingletye La RM11 . . . . . 137 A5
Wingrave Cres CM14 . . . . 115 E6
Wingrave Ct CM14 . . . . . . 115 E6
Wingrove Ct CM1 . . . . . . .32 A6
Wingrove Dr 6 RM19 . . . 171 B1
Wing Rd IG11 . . . . .42 A8
Wingway CM14 . . . . .94 C1
Winifred Ave RM12 . . . . . 155 E8
Winifred Rd
  Basildon SS13 . . . . 143 B6
  Dagenham RM8 . . . . 134 E3
  Erith DA8 . . . . 169 E1
Winmill Rd RM8 . . . . 134 F1
Winn Bridge Cl IG8 . . . . . 110 D2
Winningales Ct IG5 . . . . . 132 B8
Winnowers Ct 1 SS4 . . . . 125 F1
Winns Ave E17 . . . . 109 A1
Winns Terr E17 . . . . 109 A1
Winsbeach E17 . . . . 109 D1
Winsford Gdns SS0 . . . . . 147 A4
Winsford Way CM2 . . . . . .33 C6
Winslow Gr E4 . . . . 109 E8
Winstanley Way SS14 . . . 142 A8
Winstead Gdns RM10 . . . 154 C7
Winston Cl
  Greenhithe DA9 . . . . 176 F1
  Romford RM7 . . . . 135 B7
Winston Way IG1 . . . . 133 B1
Winstree SS13 . . . . 143 B8
Winstree Rd CM0 . . . . 106 B5
Winterbourne Rd
  RM8 . . . . 134 C2
Winter Folly SS15 . . . . 141 E5
Winter Gdns CM1 . . . . .32 B6
WINTER GARDENS 163 E8
Winter Gardens Jun & Inf
  Schs SS8 . . . . 164 A5
Winter Gardens Path
  SS8 . . . . 163 E7
Winterscroft Rd 5
  EN11 . . . . .21 A7
Winters Cl E4 . . . . 109 B7
Winters Way EN9 . . . . . . .66 A6
Winterswyk Ave SS4 . . . . 164 E3
Winton Ave
  Southend-on-S SS0 . . . . 166 E7
  Wickford SS12 . . . . 121 A8
Winton Lo SS0 . . . . 147 C1
Wiscombe Hill SS16 . . . . 141 C3
Wisdons Cl RM10 . . . . 135 B3
Wisemans Gdns CM21 . . . .1 C1
Wissants CM19 . . . . .23 C4
Wistaria Cl CM15 . . . . .94 B4
Wisteria Cl SS12 . . . . 121 D6
Wisteria Lo 7 CM1 . . . . . . .32 F6
Witchards SS16 . . . . 142 B5
Witham Cl IG10 . . . . .88 E3
Witham Gdns CM13 . . . . . 139 D5
Witham Rd
  Dagenham RM10 . . . . . . 154 A7
  Langford CM9 . . . . .36 D7
  Romford RM2 . . . . 136 B6
Witherings The RM11 . . . 136 F6
Withy Mead E4 . . . . 109 D7
Withypool SS3 . . . . 149 D1
Withywindle The
  CM3 . . . . 101 C6
Witney Rd CM0 . . . . 106 C4
Wittem Rd SS8 . . . . 164 B5
Witterings The SS8 . . . . . 164 A5
Wittering Wlk RM12 . . . . 155 C6

Wix Rd RM9 . . . . 153 D4
Woburn Ave
  Hornchurch RM12 . . . . . 155 A8
  Theydon Bois CM16 . . . . .67 E2
Woburn Ct
  Chelmsford CM2 . . . . .32 A1
  Hornchurch RM12 . . . . . 155 A8
  8 Woodford E18 . . . . . . 110 A1
Woburn Ho CM16 . . . . .67 E2
Woburn Pl CM12 . . . . .96 F5
Wodehouse Rd DA1 . . . . . 176 A3
Woking Rd RM16 . . . . 174 B3
Wollaston Cres SS13 . . . . 121 D2
Wollaston Way SS13 . . . . 121 D2
Wolmers Hey CM3 . . . . . . .18 F7
Wolseley Rd
  Chelmsford CM2 . . . . .32 A1
  Romford RM7 . . . . 135 C6
Wolsey Ave E6 . . . . 152 A2
Wolsey Gdns RM16 . . . . . 173 C6
Wolverton Ho 1 RM3 . . . 114 E5
Wonston Rd CM0 . . . . .84 C4
Wood Ave
  Hockley SS5 . . . . 124 E8
  Purfleet RM19 . . . . 171 C2
Woodberry Cl
  Canvey Island SS8 . . . . . 164 A6
  Southend-on-S SS9 . . . . 146 C5
Woodberry Down
  CM16 .46 A3
Woodberry Rd SS11 . . . . . 122 A6
Woodberry Way E4 . . . . . . .87 C2
Woodbine Cl CM19 . . . . . . .23 C6
Woodbine Close Pk
  EN9 . . . . .66 C4
Woodbine Pl E11 . . . . 132 A5
Woodbridge Ct RM3 . . . . 114 D6
Woodbridge Ct IG8 . . . . . 110 E3
Woodbridge High Sch
  IG8 . . . . 110 B3
Woodbridge La RM3 . . . . 114 D7
Woodbridge Rd IG11 . . . . 152 F7
Woodbrook Cres CM12 . . .96 F3
Woodbrooke Way
  SS13 . . . . 161 B4
Woodbrook Gdns EN9 . . . .65 E6
Woodburn Cl SS7 . . . . 145 B4
Woodbury Cl E11 . . . . 132 B7
Woodbury Hill IG10 . . . . . .88 E7
Wood Cdr CM9 . . . . .36 B2
Woodcote App SS2 . . . . . 144 B7
Woodcote Ave RM12 . . . . 155 A8
Woodcote Cres 7
  SS13 . . . . 143 C6
Woodcote Mews IG10 . . . .88 D2
Woodcote Rd
  Southend-on-S SS9 . . . . 147 A2
  Wanstead E11 . . . . 132 A4
Woodcotes SS7 . . . . 149 E1
Woodcote Way SS7 . . . . . 144 B7
Woodcroft CM18 . . . . .23 D6
Woodcroft Ave SG12 . . . . .8 E4
Woodcroft Cl SS7 . . . . 145 C4
Woodcutters 106 B8
Woodcutters Ave
  Grays RM16 . . . . 173 C4
  Southend-on-S SS9 . . . . 146 D5
Woodcutters Cl
  RM11 . . . . 136 D7
Wood Dale CM2 . . . . .54 E6
Woodedge Cl E4 . . . . .87 F1
WOODEND 14 D1
Wood End SS5 . . . . 124 D5
Woodend Cl SS7 . . . . 145 C4
Woodend Rd E17 . . . . 109 C1
Wood Farm Cl SS9 . . . . . . 146 D4
Woodfield 5 SS12 . . . . . . 121 D6
Woodfield Cotts
  Heybridge CM9 . . . . .37 C6
  Ingatestone CM4 . . . . . . .74 D5
Woodfield Dr RM2 . . . . . . 136 A7
Woodfield Gdns SS9 . . . . 165 F8
Woodfield Park Dr
  SS9 . . . . 147 A1
Woodfield Rd
  Hadleigh SS7 . . . . 146 A3
  Basildon SS13 . . . . 166 A8
Woodfield Terr CM16 . . . . .46 C6
Woodfield Way RM12 . . . 136 D3
Woodfines The RM11 . . . . 136 E3
WOODFORD 110 D5
Woodford Ave
  Ilford IG2 . . . . 133 A6
  Redbridge IG4 . . . . 132 E7
WOODFORD BRIDGE . . . 110 E3
Woodford Bridge Rd
  IG4 . . . . 132 E7
Woodford Ct IG8 . . . . .66 A6
Woodford Cty High Sch
  for Girls IG8 . . . . 110 F4
Woodford Green Prep Sch
  IG8 . . . . 110 B3
Woodford Green Prim Sch
  IG8 . . . . 110 A5
Woodford Ho 5 E18 . . . . 132 A7
Woodford New Rd
  Chingford E17 . . . . 109 E1
  Woodford IG8, E17 . . . . 109 F3
  Woodford IG8, E18 . . . . 132 A8
Woodford Sta E18 . . . . . . 110 B4
Woodford Trad Est
  Redbridge IG8 . . . . 132 D8
Woodford Wlk IG8 . . . . . . 110 D1
WOODFORD WELLS 110 B7
Wood Gn SS13 . . . . 121 B1
Woodgrange Cl SS1 . . . . . 167 E8

Woodgrange Ct EN11 . . . . .11 F4
Woodgrange Dr SS1
WOOD GREEN
Woodgrange Rd EN9
Woodhall Cres RM11
Woodhall Hill CM1
Woodhall Par CM1
Woodhall Rd CM1
Woodham Ct 2 CM3
WOODHAM FERRERS
Woodham Halt CM3
Woodham Ley Prim Sch
  SS7
WOODHAM MORTIMER
Woodham Mortimer Rd
  CM9
Woodham Park Dr
  CM3
Woodham Rd
  Battlesbridge SS11
  South Benfleet SS7
  South Woodham Ferrers
  CM3
  Stow Maries CM3
WOODHAM WALTER
Woodham Walter CE Pri
  Sch CM9
Woodham Way SG12
Woodhaven Gdns
  IG6
Woodhays 1 SS13
WOODHILL
Woodhill CM18
Woodhill Common Rd
  CM3
Woodhill Rd
  Chelmsford CM2
  Danbury CM3
Woodhouse La CM3
Woodhurst Rd SS8
Wooding Gr CM19
Wood La
  Dagenham RM8, RM9,
  Heybridge CM9
  Hockley SS5
  Hornchurch RM12
  Mundon CM9
  Willingale CM5
  Woodford IG8
Woodland Ave
  Brentwood CM13
  Little Ilford E12
  Wanstead E11
Woodland Cl
  Brentwood CM13
  Ingatestone CM4
  South Benfleet SS7
  Woodford IG8
Woodland Ct 13 E11
Woodland Gr CM16
Woodland Park Chase
  CM3
Woodland Rd
  Chelmsford CM1
  Chingford E4
  Loughton IG10
Woodlands
  Althorne CM3
  Broomfield CM1
  Epping CM16
  Great Waltham CM1
Woodlands Ave
  Dagenham RM6
  Hornchurch RM11
  Rayleigh SS6
  Wanstead E11
Woodlands Cl
  Basildon SS16
  Grays RM16
  Hockley SS5
  Hoddesdon EN11
  Rayleigh SS6
Woodlands Dr
  Basildon SS17
  Hoddesdon EN11
Woodlands Inf Sch
  IG1
Woodlands Jun Sch
  IG1
Woodlands Par SS5
Woodlands Pk SS9
Woodlands Rd
  Hockley SS5
  Ilford IG1
  Romford, Harold Wood
  RM3
  Romford RM1
  Wickford SS12
Woodlands Sch
  Basildon SS16
  Chelmsford CM1
  Great Warley CM13
Woodlands The SS3
Woodland Way
  Chipping Ongar CM5
  Greenhithe DA9
  Theydon Bois CM16
  Woodford IG8
Woodleigh 3 E18
Woodleigh Ave SS9
Woodleys CM20
Woodley Wlk SS3
Woodman SS7
Woodmanhurst Rd
  SS17
Woodman La E4

nan Path IG6.....111 E4
nan Rd
wood CM14.......116 D5
idge IG7.......111 F5
Meads CM16 .....46 B2
nill Mews EN11...21 B8
ond Ave SS5....124 E5
Rd CM9...........37 B6
edon Cl CM19 .....22 B7
edon Farm La
...................66 D4

...................66 E3
offe Cl CM2......33 A3
ose Lo **6** CM1 ...32 F6
ush Way RM6.... 134 D7
hire Rd RM10....135 B1
ide
urst Hill IG9.......110 C8
addow CM3 .....34 F1
n CM9............59 E2
nster CM0.......84 C4
ose CM16 ......46 D5
ide Ave SS7.....144 C8
ide Chase SS5...124 E4
t
wood CM13.......95 D4
m RM13 ....155 C1
nd-on-S SS9 ....146 B6
de Cotts
Common CM1 ....52 C5
stone CM4........73 F7
n CM9...........59 E2
de Ct
nd-on-S SS9 ....146 B5
ad E12..........132 C3
de Gdns E4 .....109 B4
de Gn CM2 ....3 A8
de Ind Est
..................46 D5
de Prim Sch
..................173 F3
de Rd
y, South Fambridge
...................102 F1
SS5...........124 B5
rd IG8 ....110 A6
de Sch DA17 ....169 B2
de View SS7.....144 D8
t
ford CM2........54 A7
M17.............178 C8
he SS7..........145 F3
ock Ave RM3 ...115 B4
ock Cres
SS15..........140 F6
SS5...........124 D6
ock Gdns
SS15..........140 F6
S3............134 A2
ock Pl CM2.....54 F5
ock Rd E17 ....109 D1
ew SS15 ......140 E4

Wood View RM16,
RM17 ....173 E2
Woodview Ave E4 ...... 109 C6
Woodville Cl SS4 ......125 D3
Woodville Gdns IG6 ....133 B7
Woodville Prim Sch The
CM3 ....79 D1
Woodville Rd
Canvey Island SS8.......164 D3
Woodford E18 ....110 B1
Woodward Cl RM17.....173 B2
Woodward Gdns RM9...153 C5
Woodward Hts RM17....173 B2
Woodward Rd RM9 .....153 C5
Woodwards CM19........23 C6
Woodward Terr DA9 ....176 E1
Woodville CM13..........95 A1
Woodyards
Bradwell on S CM0 ....42 A3
Bradwell Waterside CM0....41 F3
Woodyard The CM16 .....46 C3
Wool CM3 ....7 F2
Woolards Way CM3 .....101 D7
Woolden Ho E4 ....87 E2
Woolf Wlk RM18.......179 C5
Woolhampton Way
IG7.....................112 B7
Woolifers Ave SS17....161 B3
Woollard St EN9.......65 C5
Woollard Way CM4 .....72 A8
Woolmer Gn SS15 .....141 E7
Woolmonger's La CM4...72 A8
Woolpack SS3...........168 D7
Woolshotts Rd SS12 ....120 F7
Woolwich Ct **10** EN3 ....65 A1
Woolwich Manor Way
E6......................152 A1
Woolwich Rd DA17 .....169 A1
Woolwich Rd RM11.....136 D6
Worcester Ave RM14....137 F2
Worcester Cl
Basildon SS16 ....140 F5
Greenhithe DA9..........177 B3
Mayland CM3.............61 A1
Stanford-le-H SS17 ......160 D3
Worcester Cres IG8.....110 C6
Worcester Dr CM2 ......55 A5
Worcester Dr SS6 ......123 F1
Worcester Gdns IG1....132 E4
Worcester Rd CM0 ......106 C6
Wordsworth Ave
Maldon CM9.............59 A8
F1 **Wordsworth Cl**
Romford RM3 ....114 C2
Southend-on-S SS2 ......148 B2
Tilbury RM18 ....179 C5
Wordsworth Ct CM1 .....32 A5
Wordsworth Way
CM1 ....176 A3
Workhouse La CM3.......79 B2
Wormley Ct EN9.........66 A6
Wormyngford Ct EN9....66 A6
Worrin Cl CM15.........94 F1

Worrin Rd CM15........94 F1
Worthing Cl RM17......177 E8
Worthing Rd SS15 .....141 B6
Wouldham Rd RM17 ....177 E8
Wrackhall Ct SS8......164 E2
Wrangley Ct EN9 ....66 A6
Wray Ave IG5 ....133 A8
Wray Cl RM11 ....136 D4
Wraysbury Dr SS15 ....119 D1
Wren Ave SS9 ....146 D7
Wren Cl
Billericay CM11.........97 C1
South Benfleet SS7 .....144 B6
Southend-on-S SS9 .....146 D7
Wren Dr EN9...........66 A5
Wren Gdns
Dagenham RM9 ....153 D7
Hornchurch RM12 ....135 F3
Wren Pl CM14 ....116 D7
Wren Rd RM9 ....153 D7
Wrens The CM19........23 B8
Wren Terr
Ilford IG5 ....133 A8
Loughton IG10..........89 B8
Wren Wlk RM18 ....179 B7
Wrexham Rd
Basildon SS15 ....141 B5
Romford RM3 ....114 D7
Wright Cl DA10........177 D1
Wright Mead CM2......33 B4
Wrightsbridge Rd
Brentwood CM14........92 F1
South Weald CM14 ......93 A1
Wrights Cl RM10......154 B8
Wrights Ct
Brentwood CM13.........95 D3
Harlow CM17............24 C6
WRIGHT'S GREEN 2 D7
Wrights Green La CM22...2 D7
Wrights La CM15 ....72 D3
Wrigley Cl E4 ....109 D5
Wrington Ho RM3 .....114 F5
WRITTLE 31 A2
Writtle Coll CM1.......31 B3
Writtle Coll (Cow
Watering Campus)
CM1 ....30 E2
Writtle Jun & Inf Schs
CM1 ....53 A8
Writtle Park Cotts CM1 ..52 B4
Writtle Rd
Chelmsford CM1 ....53 E8
Margaretting CM4.......52 F2
Writtle Wlk
Basildon SS14 ....142 E7
Rainham RM13 ....154 E4
Wroths Path IG10 ......88 F8
Wroxall Cl CM9........153 C6
Wroxham Cl SS9.......146 B6
Wroxham Way IG6......111 B2
Wr Twr Rd CM14.......116 C5
Wr Twr Site CM5.......14 B2
Wyatts Dr SS1.........167 F8

WYATTS GREEN 72 D4
Wyatts Green La CM15 ...72 D3
Wyatt's Green Rd
CM15....................72 E2
Wyburn Rd SS7........145 E6
Wyburns Ave SS6......145 E8
Wyburns Ave E SS6......145 E8
Wyburns Prim Sch
SS6.....................145 F8
Wych Elm CM20..........10 C1
Wych Elm Cl RM11......137 A4
Wych Elm Rd RM11.....137 A5
Wychford Dr CM21.......1 C1
Wych Mews SS15......119 D1
Wychwood Gdns
Ilford IG5 ....133 A7
Redbridge IG5..........132 F7
Wycke Hill CM9..........58 D8
Wycke Hill Bsns Pk
CM9.....................58 E8
Wycke La CM9..........40 E8
Wycombe Ave SS7.....144 B6
Wycombe Rd IG2.......132 F6
Wyemead Cres E4 .....109 E8
Wyfields IG5 ....111 B2
Wyhill Wlk RM10 ......154 C6
Wykeham Ave
Dagenham RM9 ....153 C6
Hornchurch RM11 ......136 D5
Wykeham Gn RM9 .....153 C6
Wykeham Prim Sch
RM12...................136 A3
Wykeham Rd CM1.......31 B1
Wykes Gn SS14........142 D7
Wyldwood Cl CM17......11 C6
Wymark Cl RM11 ......155 A3
Wynndale Rd E18......110 B2
Wynters SS16 ....142 B4
Wyse's Rd
Edney Common CM1......52 A6
Roxwell CM1 ....51 F7
Wythams SS13..........143 C7
Wythefield SS13 143
A6 Wythenshawe Rd
RM10...................135 A1
Wyvern Ho RM17......178 B8

Y
Yale Way RM12 ....155 A8
Yamburg Rd SS8.......164 D3
Yantlet SS15 ....146 E2
Yardeley SS15 ....141 E6
Yardley Cl E4..........87 B4
Yardley La E4...........87 B4
Yardley Prim Sch E4....87 C3
Yarnacott SS3.........168 D8
Yarnton Way DA17 .....169 A3
Yarwood Rd CM2 ....32 E2
Yeldham Lock CM2 .....33 A2
Yellowpine Way IG7....112 B6
Yelverton Cl RM3 .....114 D2

Yeoman Way IG6 ......111 C4
Yeovil Chase SS0 .....147 B4
Yeovil Ct SS2.........148 D2
Yevele Way RM11 .....136 E4
Yew Cl
Basildon SS15 ....119 D1
Buckhurst Hill IG9......110 D8
Yewlands
Hoddesdon EN11.........21 A5
Sawbridgeworth CM21.....1 E1
Yewlands Dr EN11 .....21 A5
Yew Tree Cl CM13......95 B3
Yew Tree Gdns
Chelmsford CM2 ....54 C6
Dagenham RM6.........134 E6
4 Romford RM7.........135 D6
Yew Wlk EN11..........21 A5
Yonge Cl CM3..........20 E1
York Ave SS17 ....161 A4
York Cl
Rayleigh SS6 ....146 A8
Southend-on-S SS1 .....94 F2
York Cres IG10 ....88 E6
Yorkes CM18 ....23 F5
York Hill IG10 ....88 E6
York Ho
Chingford E4 ....109 A6
1 Ilford IG1...........133 B2
Loughton IG10..........89 D5
York Mews IG1 ....133 A1
York Pl IG1 ....133 A2
York Rd
Billericay CM12.........97 A5
Burnham-on-C CM0.......106 C4
Chelmsford CM2 ....54 A8
Chingford E4 ....109 A6
Horndon on t H SS17....159 F4
Ilford IG1 ....133 A1
North Weald Bassett
CM16..................47 A4
Rainham RM13 ....154 D5
Rayleigh SS1 ....146 A8
Rochford SS4 ....125 C7
Shenfield CM15..........94 F7
Southend-on-S SS1 .....167 B7
York Rise SS6 ....146 A8
Young Cl SS9..........147 A7
Youngs Rd IG2 ....133 D6
Yoxford Ct **6** RM6.....134 B6
Yoxley App IG2.........133 C5
Yoxley Dr IG2 ....133 C5

Z
Zandi Rd SS8..........164 D2
Zealand Dr SS8.......164 E3
Zelham Dr SS8........164 D3
Zenith SS14 ....120 E2
Zider Pass SS8 ....164 F3

Addresses

Name and Address	Telephone	Page	Grid reference

Addresses

ame and Address	Telephone	Page	Grid reference

Addresses

Name and Address	Telephone	Page	Grid reference

NH	NJ	NK		
NN	NO	NP		
NS	NT	NU		
NX	NY	NZ		
SC	SD	SE	TA	
SH	SJ	SK	TF	TG
SN	SO	SP	TL	TM
SS	ST	SU	TQ	TR
SX	SY	SZ	TV	

Using the Ordnance Survey National Grid

Any feature in this atlas can be given a unique reference to help you find the same feature on other Ordnance Survey maps of the area, or to help someone else locate you if they do not have a Street Atlas.

The grid squares in this atlas match the Ordnance Survey National Grid and are at 500 metre intervals. The small figures at the bottom and sides of every other grid line are the National Grid kilometre values (**00** to **99** km) and are repeated across the country every 100 km (see left).

To give a unique National Grid reference you need to locate where in the country you are. The country is divided into 100 km squares with each square given a unique two-letter reference. Use the administrative map to determine in which 100 km square a particular page of this atlas falls.

The bold letters and numbers between each grid line (**A** to **F**, **1** to **8**) are for use within a specific Street Atlas only, and when used with the page number, are a convenient way of referencing these grid squares.

Example *The railway bridge over DARLEY GREEN RD in grid square B1*

Step 1: Identify the two-letter reference, in this example the page is in **SP**

Step 2: Identify the 1 km square in which the railway bridge falls. Use the figures in the southwest corner of this square: Eastings **17**, Northings **74**. This gives a unique reference: **SP 17 74**, accurate to 1 km.

Step 3: To give a more precise reference accurate to 100 m you need to estimate how many tenths along and how many tenths up this 1 km square the feature is (to help with this the 1 km square is divided into four 500 m squares). This makes the bridge about **8** tenths along and about **1** tenth up from the southwest corner.

This gives a unique reference: **SP 178 741**, accurate to 100 m.

Eastings (read from left to right along the bottom) come before Northings (read from bottom to top). If you have trouble remembering say to yourself "Along the hall, THEN up the stairs"!

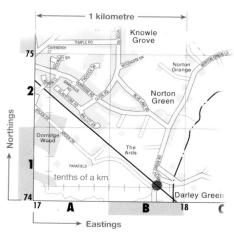

PHILIP'S MAPS
the Gold Standard for drivers

◆ **Philip's street atlases cover every county in England, Wales, Northern Ireland and much of Scotland**

◆ Every named street is shown, including alleys, lanes and walkways

◆ Thousands of additional features marked: stations, public buildings, car parks, places of interest

◆ Route-planning maps to get you close to your destination

◆ Postcodes on the maps and in the index

◆ Widely used by the emergency services, transport companies and local authorities

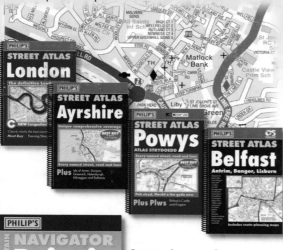

For national mapping, choose
Philip's Navigator Britain
the most detailed road atlas available of England, Wales and Scotland. Hailed by Auto Express as 'the ultimate road atlas', the atlas shows every road and lane in Britain.

Street atlases currently available

England

Bedfordshire and Luton	Surrey
Berkshire	East Sussex
Birmingham and West Midlands	West Sussex
Bristol and Bath	Tyne and Wear
Buckinghamshire and Milton Keynes	Warwickshire and Coventry
Cambridgeshire and Peterborough	Wiltshire and Sw
	Worcestershire
Cheshire	East Yorkshire Northern Lincoln
Cornwall	North Yorkshire
Cumbria	South Yorkshire
Derbyshire	West Yorkshire
Devon	
Dorset	**Wales**
County Durham and Teesside	Anglesey, Conw and Gwynedd
Essex	Cardiff, Swanse and The Valleys
North Essex	Carmarthenshire Pembrokeshire
South Essex	Swansea
Gloucestershire and Bristol	Ceredigion and South Gwynedd
Hampshire	
North Hampshire	Denbighshire, Flintshire, Wrex
South Hampshire	
Herefordshire Monmouthshire	Herefordshire Monmouthshire
Hertfordshire	Powys
Isle of Wight	
Kent	**Scotland**
East Kent	Aberdeenshire
West Kent	Ayrshire
Lancashire	Dumfries and G
Leicestershire and Rutland	Edinburgh and I Central Scotland
Lincolnshire	Fife and Tayside
Liverpool and Merseyside	Glasgow and V Central Scotland
London	Inverness and M
Greater Manchester	Lanarkshire
Norfolk	Scottish Borders
Northamptonshire	
Northumberland	**Northern Ire**
Nottinghamshire	County Antrim County Londonc
Oxfordshire	County Armagh County Down
Shropshire	
Somerset	Belfast
Staffordshire	County Tyrone
Suffolk	County Fermana

How to order
Philip's maps and atlases are available from boo
motorway services and petrol stations. You can
from the publisher by phoning **0207 531 8**
online at **www.philips-maps.co.uk**
For bulk orders only, e-mail philips@philips-map